Believers Church
Bible Commentary

Douglas B. Miller and Loren L. Johns, Editors

"Swartley traces the implications of John not only for history and theology but for ethics, discipleship, worship, preaching, mission, and peacemaking. He connects John with the difficulties of believing and following Jesus in a world where disciples may not find welcome, and where Christians must engage respectfully in dialogue with others." —*David Rensberger, author of* Johannine Faith and Liberating Community

"This commentary is notable for its hermeneutical responsibility, elucidating the Gospel's bearing on many a vital issue in the life of the church today and firmly grasping such nettles as the Gospel's vituperative attacks on 'the Jews.'" —*Richard Bauckham, professor emeritus of New Testament studies, University of St. Andrews, Scotland*

"Willard Swartley offers a balanced and highly readable study of John's Gospel, drawing on a range of interpretive traditions and methods. While the focus is pastoral, there is sufficient discussion of the text, and bibliographic notes, to alert readers to alternative views and the complexities of the text." —*Mary L. Coloe, associate professor of New Testament, Australian Catholic University*

"Addressing thoughtfully the Johannine riddles, this commentary makes John's text come alive for expert and novice readers alike—a feature that distinguishes the Believers Church Bible Commentary series among other fine works available today." —*Paul N. Anderson, professor of biblical and Quaker studies, George Fox University*

BELIEVERS CHURCH BIBLE COMMENTARY

Old Testament
Genesis, by Eugene F. Roop, 1987
Exodus, by Waldemar Janzen, 2000
Joshua, by Gordon H. Matties, 2012
Judges, by Terry L. Brensinger, 1999
Ruth, Jonah, Esther, by Eugene F. Roop, 2002
Psalms, by James H. Waltner, 2006
Proverbs, by John W. Miller, 2004
Ecclesiastes, by Douglas B. Miller, 2010
Isaiah, by Ivan D. Friesen, 2009
Jeremiah, by Elmer A. Martens, 1986
Ezekiel, by Millard C. Lind, 1996
Daniel, by Paul M. Lederach, 1994
Hosea, Amos, by Allen R. Guenther, 1998

New Testament
Matthew, by Richard B. Gardner, 1991
Mark, by Timothy J. Geddert, 2001
John, by Willard Swartley, 2013
Acts, by Chalmer E. Faw, 1993
Romans, by John E. Toews, 2004
2 Corinthians, by V. George Shillington, 1998
Ephesians, by Thomas R. Yoder Neufeld, 2002
Colossians, Philemon, by Ernest D. Martin, 1993
1-2 Thessalonians, by Jacob W. Elias, 1995
1-2 Timothy, Titus, by Paul M. Zehr, 2010
1-2 Peter, Jude, by Erland Waltner and J. Daryl Charles, 1999
1, 2, 3 John, by J. E. McDermond, 2011
Revelation, by John R. Yeatts, 2003

Old Testament Editors
Elmer A. Martens, Mennonite Brethren Biblical Seminary, Fresno, California
Douglas B. Miller, Tabor College, Hillsboro, Kansas

New Testament Editors
Willard M. Swartley, Anabaptist Mennonite Biblical Seminary, Elkhart,
Indiana
Loren L. Johns, Anabaptist Mennonite Biblical Seminary, Elkhart, Indiana

Editorial Council
David W. Baker, Brethren Church
W. Derek Suderman, Mennonite Church Canada
Christina A. Bucher, Church of the Brethren
John Yeatts, Brethren in Christ Church
Gordon H. Matties, Mennonite Brethren Church
Paul M. Zehr (chair), Mennonite Church USA

Believers Church
Bible Commentary

John

Willard M. Swartley

HERALD PRESS
Harrisonburg, Virginia
Waterloo, Ontario

Library of Congress Cataloging-in-Publication Data
Swartley, Willard M., 1936-
    John / Willard M. Swartley
        p. cm. — (Believers church Bible commentary)
    Includes bibliographical references and index.
    ISBN: 978-0-8361-9667-2 (pbk. : alk. paper)
    1. Bible. N.T. John—Commentaries. I. Title.
    BS2615.53.S94 2013   226.5'07   2012039123

Except as otherwise indicated, Bible text is from the *New Revised Standard Version Bible*, copyright 1989 by the Division of Christian Education of the National Council of the Churches of Christ in the USA, and used by permission. Quotations marked TNIV are from *The Holy Bible, Today's New International Version*™, copyright © 2001 by International Bible Society®, all rights reserved, used by permission of The Zondervan Corporation. Other versions briefly compared are listed with Abbreviations.

BELIEVERS CHURCH BIBLE COMMENTARY: JOHN
Copyright © 2013 by Herald Press, Harrisonburg, VA 22802
        Released simultaneously in Canada by Herald Press,
        Waterloo, ON N2L 6H7. All rights reserved
Library of Congress Control Number: 2012039123
International Standard Book Number: 978-0-8361-9667-2
Printed in the United States of America
Cover by Merrill R. Miller

20 19 18 17 16 15 14 13   10 9 8 7 6 5 4 3 2 1

To order or request information please call 1-800-245-7894 in the U.S. or 1-800-631-6535 in Canada. Or visit www.heraldpress.com.

To my spouse, Mary;
my children, Louisa and Kenton;
my grandchildren, John and Michael; Kristen, Jeremy, Libby, and Michelle;
and to all who are becoming "children of God,"
especially my Gospel of John students

Abbreviations

*	*see* TBC
+	*see* TLC
//	parallel reference
=	parallel to, equal
ANE	Ancient Near East
Ant.	*Jewish Antiquities*, by Josephus
[Chiasm]	Sample reference to essay in the back of the commentary
b.	Babylonian Talmud, with its tractates
ca.	circa, around
CD	*Damascus Document*
cf.	compare
ch./chs.	chapter(s)
DSS	Dead Sea Scrolls
ed(s).	editor(s), edition
e.g.	for example
Ep.	epistle
esp.	especially
ET	English translation
FC	Fathers of the Church [series]. Washington, DC, 1947–
Gk.	Greek
Heb.	Hebrew
Hist. eccl.	*Ecclesiastical History*, by Eusebius
i.e.	*id est*, that is
LXX	Septuagint (Greek translation of the Hebrew Bible)
m.	*Mishnah*, with its tractates
MM	*Martyrs Mirror. See* Braght in the bibliography.
MS(S)	manuscript(s)
MT	Masoretic Text (Heb.) of the Old Testament
n	note
NT	New Testament
OT	Old Testament
p^{75}	sample reference to a papyrus
par.	parallel(s)
pl.	plural
1QH	*Thanksgiving Hymns*, DSS
1QS	*Rule of the Community*, DSS
sg.	singular
Sir	Sirach (Latin: Ecclesiasticus), the Wisdom of Jesus Son of Sirach
TBC	Text in Biblical Context, after comments on a unit
TLC	Text in the Life of the Church, after comments on a unit
trans.	translation, translator/s, translated by
v./vv.	verse/verses
Wis	Wisdom of Solomon
w1, 2, 3	Markers (in the Essays only) pointing to further discussion online at: www.heraldpress.com/bcbc/john

| y. | Jerusalem Talmud (tractates) |
| x | times, such as a term appearing 2x (2 times) |

English Bible Versions

AT	author's translation or paraphrase
CEB	Common English Bible
CEV	Contemporary English Version
JB	Jerusalem Bible
KJV	King James Version (= Authorized Version)
LB	Living Bible
NAB	New American Bible
NASB	New American Standard Bible
NEB	New English Bible
NIRV	New International Reader's Version
NIV	New International Version (1984)
NJB	New Jerusalem Bible
NKJV	New King James Version
NLT	New Living Translation
NRSV	New Revised Standard Version
REB	Revised English Bible
RSV	Revised Standard Version
TEV	Today's English Version (= Good News Bible)
TNIV	Today's New International Version

Contents

Series Foreword

The Believers Church Bible Commentary Series makes available a new tool for basic Bible study. It is published for all who seek to more fully understand the original message of Scripture and its meaning for today—Sunday school teachers, members of Bible study groups, students, pastors, and others. The series is based on the conviction that God is still speaking to all who will listen, and that the Holy Spirit makes the Word a living and authoritative guide for all who want to know and do God's will.

The desire to help as wide a range of readers as possible has determined the approach of the writers. Since no blocks of biblical text are provided, readers may continue to use the translation with which they are most familiar. The writers of the series use the New Revised Standard Version and the New International Version on a comparative basis. They indicate which text they follow most closely and where they make their own translations. The writers have not worked alone, but in consultation with select counselors, the series' editors, and the Editorial Council.

Every volume illuminates the Scriptures; provides necessary theological, sociological, and ethical meanings; and in general makes "the rough places plain." Critical issues are not avoided, but neither are they moved into the foreground as debates among scholars. Each section offers Explanatory Notes, followed by focused articles, "The Text in Biblical Context" and "The Text in the Life of the Church." This commentary aids the interpretive process but does not try to supersede the authority of the Word and Spirit as discerned in the gathered church.

The term *believers church* has often been used in the history of the church. Since the sixteenth century, it has frequently been applied to the Anabaptists and later the Mennonites, as well as to the Church of the Brethren and similar groups. As a descriptive term, it includes more than Mennonites and Brethren. *Believers church* now represents specific theological understandings, such as believers baptism, commitment to the Rule of Christ in Matthew 18:15-20 as crucial for church membership, belief in the power of love in all relationships, and willingness to follow Christ in the way of the cross. The writers chosen for the series stand in this tradition.

Believers church people have always been known for their emphasis on obedience to the simple meaning of Scripture. Because of this, they do not have a long history of deep historical-critical biblical scholarship. This series attempts to be faithful to the Scriptures while also taking archaeology and current biblical studies seriously. Doing this means that at many points the writers will not differ greatly from interpretations that can be found in many other good commentaries. Yet these writers share basic convictions about Christ, the church and its mission, God and history, human nature, the Christian life, and other doctrines. These presuppositions do shape a writer's interpretation of Scripture. Thus this series, like all other commentaries, stands within a specific historical church tradition.

Many in this stream of the church have expressed a need for help in Bible study. This is justification enough to produce the Believers Church Bible Commentary. Nevertheless, the Holy Spirit is not bound to any tradition. May this series be an instrument in breaking down walls between Christians in North America and around the world, bringing new joy in obedience through a fuller understanding of the Word.

—The Editorial Council

Author's Preface

My journey with John began with an eight-credit-hour elementary Greek course with Dorothy Kemrer at Eastern Mennonite College. This was enriched later by an inductive study with Professor Howard Charles on John (chs. 1–12) at Associated (now Anabaptist) Mennonite Biblical Seminary. Then a decade later I took a challenging PhD course on John's Gospel at Princeton Theological Seminary with Professor Bertil Gärtner. The Gospel's richness, riddles, and enigmas fascinated me.

Through teaching John at Conrad Grebel College in 1975–76, I learned more, using Marsh as the primary text. In 1992 I began teaching John at AMBS, with the privilege of teaching the Gospel one term with Marlin Miller, who had some interest in writing the Believers Church Bible Commentary on John. The six times I taught John at AMBS expanded my interest and appreciation for John's rich themes, artful composition, and irresolvable problems. Hence, when the BCBC Editorial Council invited me to write the commentary on John, I agreed. The Gospel shines with rich resources for teaching and preaching.

Writing this commentary would have been impossible without the help of a hermeneutical community. Five persons read all or parts of the manuscript, giving valued assistance. Sue Steiner, a pastor with literary acumen, read all of it and gave helpful response. Wes Howard-Brook and Jerry Truex, peer readers who have written on John's Gospel (commentary and dissertation respectively), made good suggestions on sources, with critical and affirming comments on selected portions. Phil Yoder (Elkhart, Indiana) gave helpful pastoral insights. Nekeisha Alexis-Baker improved style in the early part with ethnic sensitivity and valued suggestions.

Students in the Gospel of John course at AMBS (in 2004 and 2006) were strategic to my hermeneutical community. Each chose a por-

19

tion of John for a research paper, following the BCBC format. These papers and "Text Studies," some also from earlier classes, inspired this writing from 2006 to 2012. Here I honor these contributions:

Prologue	Leonard Beechy, Pam Short
John 3	"Eternal Life": Jewel Gingerich Longenecker; Marlin Miller's notes on John
John 4	Juanita Laverty, Lois Siemens; Adam Tice (music lyrics)
John 5	Pam Short
John 6	Margaret Shaw
John 7	Jim Longley
7:53–8:11	Betty Lou Green, Jim Longley, Paula Snyder Belousek
8:31-59	Rachel Siemens
John 9	Gunnar Carlson
John 10	Homare Miyazaki (see bibliography); Marlin Miller, from his notes on John
John 11	Lois Siemens; Adam Tice (with music lyrics)
John 12	Rachel Epp Miller
John 13	Anne Mitchell
John 14	Marlin Miller's notes and manuscript text on John
John 15	Margaret Shaw, Lane Miller
John 17	Leonard Beechy, Amy Kratzer, Lois Siemens, Pam Short
18:28–19:16a	Wanda Stopher
John 20	Jim Longley, Rachel Ringenberg, Wanda Stopher
John 21	Leonard Beechy, Gunnar Carlson, Wanda Stopher

Susan Kennel Harrison, for an early synopsis of John's structure and themes

Those who contributed also to several Essays (e.g., Pam Short on [Glory, p. 516])

Homare Miyazaki, for his significant MA thesis on John's feast structure, blended with a chiastic analysis of the Gospel

Other helpers were Gene Herr, John A. Lapp, Wilbert Shenk, and Willard Roth. Gerald Stover suggested rich resources for Jesus' prayer that they may all be one (John 17:21, 23). The bibliography extends the hermeneutical community to worldwide perspectives over three generations of scholarship on John. Literature on John's Gospel is endless; numerous sources worthy of consideration had to be passed up.

With her perceptive eye, Mary Swartley (my wife) caught many mistakes and spotted problems in clarity and consistency, helping me much on the whole manuscript. Chris Benda assisted also in catching mistakes; thanks to him for reading much of the manuscript and Web supplement. In its final stages, the NT Editor Loren Johns and the BCBC Editorial Council provided much help, as well as the Herald Press editors, Amy Gingerich, David Garber, and Byron Rempel-Burkholder. Thanking all who contributed to this "labor of love," a key motif in John's Gospel, I am indebted to this hermeneutical community and now invite readers into this "community" as well.

The Editorial Council judged the first submitted manuscript too long and requested a reduction of almost one-third, although they did not want to lose what could not fit into a shorter volume. Following their proposal, a good portion of the original manuscript is now in a separate file, accessible as a Web supplement. Often this supplement engages diverse scholarly views and provides further discussion of difficult issues that arise in interpreting John's Gospel. Readers will see a superscript code (w) after some subheadings in the commentary. These refer the reader to the Web supplement. In the essays a superscript w plus a number 1, 2, 3, etc., code appears within a given essay entry when additional relevant discussion is to be found in the Web supplement. This online resource is accessible at www.heraldpress.com/bcbc/john.

Parts of the original commentary now appear in a separate book titled *Living Gift: John's Jesus in Meditation and Poetry, Art and Song*. It contains meditations and poetic contributions from AMBS students in the 2004 and 2006 Gospel of John courses and additional sources on the topics of the book's title. This volume, copiously indexed, aids spiritual formation and provides resources for worship leaders, song leaders, pastors, and all who appreciate truth and beauty in poetry, song, and art. It is available from Evangel Press: www.evangelpublishing.com.

Introduction

No other book in the New Testament is both more and less transparent than John. On one level, all is clear and easy to understand; on another, the reader is mystified by double meanings and symbolic depth, together with long discourses and fast-moving dialogues with quick topical turns on deep subjects.

Kaleidoscopic, scintillating, and puzzling is John's Gospel. Filled with light and life in the first half, the Gospel breathes lavish love and costly discipleship in its second half. So distinctive, so refreshing! Yet it also offends on some crucial points. It is like a delicious cake with some eggshells that crunch between the teeth. John's voice differs regularly from Mark's, Matthew's, and Luke's. Hearing John is a journey into new Gospel terrain. Any commentary on this Gospel pales alongside the literary excellence and dramatic power of the Gospel text [*Drama in John, p. 510*]. Therefore, I encourage users of this commentary to read aloud each unit of Scripture before reading the commentary on that text (e.g., the units in the Prologue, John 6:35-40; 15:1-11; each unit in ch. 17). Commentary needs the Scripture more than Scripture needs commentary.

John's Gospel begins with creation, evoking Genesis 1:1–2:4a, and tells the story of new creation in its major themes. An "ontology of peace" pervades both narratives (Neville: 176, 180; cf., however, Ollenburger, 2013). After a stunning prologue, John presents John the Witness and Jesus in a one-week frame of "Seven Days of New Creation" (1:19–2:11). The narrative plot, controlled by *the hour*, moves inexorably toward Jesus being lifted up on the cross for glorification, culminating in resurrection, implied ascension, and Pentecost, choreographed with peace, mission, and authority to forgive or retain sins. Two related characters, Peter and the beloved disciple, dot the narrative landscape and personalize Jesus' teaching: love—what it costs and knows. The Gospel ends with these two characters in the limelight.

John's Gospel is the high point of NT theology, for it is rooted in the space and time of Jesus' history while also extending Paul's "theology of the cross" to a new level. In full unity with God, the Son with the Father, Jesus participates in divine mutual glorification through the cross, in sovereignty, love, and freedom. In John, Jesus is not only God's agent, the instrument of creation and salvation, but also the essential and full manifestation of God in their love-unity who reveals the gift of salvation for whosoever will (see Schnelle 2009: 660, 749–50).

Themes and Purpose[w]

John's major themes and the Gospel's purpose are inseparable. John states the Gospel's purpose in 20:31: *These signs are written so that you may believe that Jesus is the Messiah, the Son of God, and that through believing you may have life in his name* (AT). John's Christology presents Jesus as Revealer in bold portrait, with the intent of bringing people to faith and/or, more likely, to encourage believers to continue in their faith in Jesus the Messiah, Son of God. The intimacy between the Son and the Father and between Jesus and his followers strengthens believers' assurance of eternal life (17:3).

In the introduction of *Greater than Caesar*, Thatcher rightly claims that the essential thematic heart of John's Gospel is Christology: "John, the Evangelist, was driven by a desire to lead the reader to a proper understanding of who Jesus was and of why we must have 'life in his name' or not at all" (Thatcher 2009: 4–5). Indeed, "the Gospel's portrayal of Jesus is simultaneously an exploration and an exposition of the dynamics of what causes people both to miss and discover their true nature in God—in other words, the respective dynamics of being 'from the world' and 'from God'" (Moberly: 248).

Many themes tumble over each other throughout the Gospel, often in pairs or triplets. Christology and revelation are inseparably linked key themes. God reveals Godself through the Son. In the prologue the Logos becomes flesh to reveal God to humanity; in the Gospel narrative Jesus claims an "I AM" identity. Jesus' self-revelation comes through many christological titles. Among the Gospels, John alone emphasizes Jesus' preexistence *[Christology, p. 507]*.

---

w   Where the superscript w occurs after headings, please see the commentary's online Web Supplement for additional material. Go to: www.heraldpress.com/bcbc/john.

Primary Themes of John's Gospel

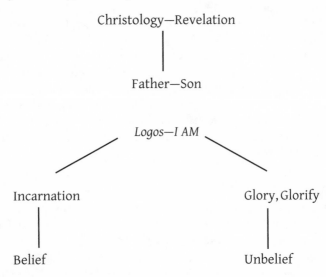

The *Father-Son* relationship is the heartbeat of the Gospel. "The confession that Jesus and the Father are one is John's christological abbreviation" (Appold: 280). The Son desires to *glorify* the Father, and the Father desires to *glorify* the Son *[Glory, p. 516]*. A companion motif to *glorify* is *my hour*, which dots the plot for the timing of the Son's *glorification* of the Father (2:4; 12:20-23, 27-28; 13:1, 31; 17:1). Jesus *lifted up* on the cross culminates the mutual glorification (17:1-2). By so doing, Jesus the Son draws all people to himself and to God the Father (12:32).

An emphasis on *belief* and *unbelief* also pervades the Gospel, especially in its first half (chs. 2–12). John 12 culminates Jesus' public ministry with sustained attention to the dilemma of unbelief, rooting it prophetically in Isaiah. Unbelief appears to win over belief at times in the narrative. Yet just as the darkness does not overcome the light (1:5), so unbelief does not overcome belief. Belief promises eternal life, while unbelief promises judgment—judgment by the word Jesus has spoken (12:47-49; 3:18-21). Crucifixion is trumped by resurrection and Pentecost. Two other terms, *seeing* and *knowing*, are both also used frequently and are closely related to *believing*. The crucial relation between seeing and believing is stated succinctly in 20:29, a capstone verse in the Gospel.

Flowing out of these themes is a moral/ethical emphasis on *light, life,* and *love*. Light versus darkness appears in the prologue

(1:4b-5, 9) and is prominent in Jesus' discourses in chapters 7–10 at the two great light festivals (Tabernacles and Dedication). Jesus declares, *I am the light of the world* (8:12). In chapter 9, light continues as a central metaphor (v. 5): *seeing* is contrasted to *blindness*. Jesus' final plea to the crowd that hears the voice from heaven calls people to "walk in the light" (12:29, 34-36).

The word *life* or *live* (noun and verb) and the compound (*give life*) occur fifty-four times in the Gospel, mostly in the first half of the narrative (e.g., 1:3-4; 3:15, 16, 36; often in chs. 5–6, 10–11). In 17:3; 20:31; and 6:40, Jesus' gift of life is the purpose of his coming into the world. Jesus gives himself for *the life of the world* (6:51) *[Eternal Life, p. 513]*.

The term *love* occasionally occurs in the first half of the Gospel (notably 3:16, contrasting to its use in 5:42). But *love* occurs frequently in the second half of the Gospel. *Love* (both noun and verb) appear fifty-seven times in the Gospel. It is the identity mark of Jesus' disciples (13:14-35; 14:23-24). *Love one another* is John's default ethical command. Love is the litmus test for discipleship. It even restores Peter after his three denials (21:15-17). Love binds together the Son and Father in their mutual self-donation to the world (15:9-10, 12-13) and in their relationship to each other, existing *before the foundation of the world* (17:24d, 26). Love, too, is the unique characteristic of the enigmatic figure known as the beloved disciple *[Beloved Disciple, p. 505]*.

Other paired themes in John are prominent:

- *truth* linked with *testify/witness*;
- *send/sent* with mission and both with *unity: that they may all be one* (17:21, 23);
- the *Paraclete/Holy Spirit* with *peace/peacemaking*; and
- *disciples* or *discipleship* with *following* Jesus.

Each of these pairs or triplets provides a lens to perceive distinctive emphases in the Gospel. John 5–12 and 18–19 might be viewed as "truth on trial" (Lincoln 2000). Since the narrative presents Jesus and/or his adversaries on trial, the role of witnesses who testify is central in the narrative cast, culminating in Pilate's query to Jesus: *What is truth?* (18:38). Bauckham's work on *witness* and *testify* (2006: 358–411, 472–508; 2007: 82–91) is essential to understand the role of eyewitness in the Gospel and the thematic emphases on *witness* and *testify* *[Witness, p. 534]*.

In John 1–10, John the *Witness* ("Baptist" in the Synoptics) appears first in 1:6-8 and is last referred to in 10:40-41 as bookends witnessing to Jesus' public ministry. In the Gospel this *Witness* is named simply "John." Immediately after 10:40-41, we meet Lazarus, the one whom Jesus loved (11:3-5). In the rest of the Gospel *the disciple whom Jesus loved* plays a major role as eyewitness to Jesus' Jerusalem ministry (19:35; 21:24). He is never named "John." Hence the issues of authorship and the identity of the beloved disciple are perplexing *[Beloved Disciple, p. 505]*.

Mission is widely espoused as an important theme related to *sent* or *send* (Oyer: 446). John's great commission links peace and mission, though John's *peace* theme is often slighted in commentaries and monographs (Swartley 2006a: 304–23; TLC for John 20).

Disciple(ship) and *following* appear in a distinctive manner in John. Most of the disciples come to Jesus, with John's initial help and through friendship connections. Jesus explicitly calls only two disciples with *Follow me*: Philip at the outset (1:43) and Peter at the end (21:19, 22). *Disciple* occurs thirty-eight times. In 21:1-2 seven disciples gather, though only three are named. Much of Jesus' teaching focuses indirectly on what it means to follow Jesus. The most explicit, significant text on discipleship is John 13:34-35, where love for one another is the identity marker of Jesus' disciples *[Disciples and Discipleship, p. 509]*.

One more frequent motif in John is *world*. It has different connotations in differing contexts. See the comments on 1:10-11 and the essay *[World, p. 538]*. Other topics in John of special interest are the following:

- The God of the Gospel of John (Thompson 2001a).

- Christology: Jesus is identified with many titles *[Christology, p. 507]*.

- Jews in John. John's frequent reference to *the Jews* appears seventy-one times, with thirty-eight of those uses negative *["The Jews," p. 520]*. Not all Jews appear in a negative light. The "puzzle" is to discover who "the Jews" are who seek to kill Jesus, fully aware that almost all the main characters are Jews, including Jesus.

- Politics in and political dimensions of John. See Ethics of the Gospel, page 38.

- Women in John. The positive role of women is a striking feature of the Gospel *[Women, p. 536]*.

- John's extensive use of the Old Testament (OT), and John's many references to Jewish festivals, structuring the Gospel around them *[Feasts, p. 516]*.

- Jesus as bridegroom and/or new temple. See comments on John 2–4; 14:1-3.

- John's cosmology. Here the Gospel's extensive duality between "above" and "below" is striking [Duality, p. 511].

- Jesus' plea for unity among all believers: "that they may all be one" (17:21, 23). See comments on John 17 and the essay [Ecumenical Relations, p. 511].

Setting and Occasion of John's Gospel: Date and Authorship[w]

Earlier hypotheses (prominent from 1840 to 1920) held the Gospel reflects mid-second century theology. Tübingen scholar F. C. Baur proposed John was written around AD 150–70, long after the other canonical Gospels and at a time when numerous gnostic gospels were being written. At the other extreme, British scholar J. A. T. Robinson proposed a date in the sixties, before the fall of Jerusalem (1976, 1985). His case is compelling and has never been adequately rebutted [Authorship, p. 502].

External evidence has now disproved the late dating. Papias (ca. 130) locates John's Gospel origin in Ephesus. The discovery of p^{52} (contains MS fragments of John 18:31-33 and 37-38) in 1920 and rediscovery in 1934 (Metzger 1992: 38) is carbon-dated ca. 125. Basilides (ca. 130–135), cited in Hippolytus of Rome, quotes John 1:9 (Refutation of All Heresies 7.10). Most scholars now date John around AD 90.

Papias mentions two Johns: the apostle and the elder. Given the internal testimony of 2 and 3 John (v. 1 in each), John the elder and/or the Johannine community he represents is most likely their author. Evidence from Polycrates in 170 suggests that the disciple-witness for John's Gospel is from Jerusalem, with priestly affiliation (cf. John 18:15).

From the third century onward, tradition has regarded the author of the Gospel to be John the apostle. Some scholars argue from internal evidence that the beloved disciple, the Gospel's certifying witness (19:34-35; 21:24), is Lazarus, since John 11:3-5 indicates he was the disciple whom Jesus loved [Beloved Disciple, p. 505]. The determination of the religious leaders to kill Lazarus after he was raised (12:13-18) and the enigma about the beloved disciple's death at the end of the Gospel (21:19-21) make Lazarus a candidate, at least for the Jerusalem-oriented tradition. The affirmation in 21:24b links the author to the beloved disciple, the key testifier for the Gospel. Other proposals for authorship, not widely held, are Thomas (Charlesworth 1995) or Mary Magdalene (Schneiders 2003; Maccini) because of their prominent roles in John 20.

So the main contestants are these: a Jerusalem-based disciple (maybe Lazarus) with priestly affiliation; John the elder; John the apostle; or simply the Johannine community, which many scholars advocate. Barclay (xxxv–xl) wrestles with this issue, noting that it would be presumptuous for John to call himself the beloved disciple. He considers Lazarus but concludes that John the elder is the writer [Authorship, p. 502]. Whenever the eyewitness or beloved disciple is regarded also as author, the same arrogant presumption applies, unless the designation itself was added later. This argues for distinguishing between the two so that the final author or editor is the voice of the Johannine community, testifying to the veracity of the eyewitness/beloved disciple. Perhaps we should not try to name an author for the Gospel, for as J. Ramsey Michaels says, "Whoever the author is—which we cannot know—he tells his story freely . . . [yet] retains his privacy, a privacy that even the most inquisitive commentator will do well to respect" (24).

John's references to "synagogue exclusion" (9:22; 12:42; 16:2) indicate a date later than that of the Synoptic Gospels. The view has been reinforced by J. Louis Martyn (1978: 90–121; see also his 1st [1968] and 2nd editions [1979] cited in the 2003 entry), who has constructed a likely setting for such exclusion. He links this emphasis to the addition of the twelfth benediction to the Eighteen Benedictions, which he theorized occurred at Yavneh (Jamnia) several years after Jerusalem's fall. This benediction speaks of excluding heretics from the synagogue: "For the apostates let there be no hope. . . . Let the Nazarenes [Christians] and the Minim [heretics] . . . be blotted out of the Book of Life" (Martyn 1979: 58; 2003: 62). Martyn thus proposes a "two-level reading" of John: one level reflects Jesus' time; the second reflects the time of synagogue exclusion—when the Gospel was written. Martyn's theory was popular for a quarter century (1968 to early 1990s) and continues to be valued for its reconstruction of the socioreligious context of John (Smith 2003), even though the causal attribution of Jewish persecution of messianic believers to the twelfth benediction has been severely challenged.

Other proposals regarding the Gospel's origin have emerged. Köstenberger (2005: 205–12) regards the fall of Jerusalem and the loss of the temple as consequential to the Gospel's dating and theological emphases. The Gospel presents new understandings of Jewish-Christian faith vis-à-vis the loss of the temple (Köstenberger 2005; Hill; Suderman; cf. Kerr 2002 and Coloe 2001, who develop the new temple theme). Köstenberger considers it probable that the Synoptic Gospels were written while Jerusalem was still standing in

light of the warnings in Jesus' apocalyptic discourses. John, however, written in the aftermath of the loss, sets forth acute theological ramifications for messianic believers (2005: 207, 216). In light of
these considerations, the most viable date for the final form of
John's Gospel is in the AD 90s.

This understanding of the origins of John's Gospel explains why
John shifted the temple cleansing to the beginning of Jesus' ministry: the destruction of the temple provides the lens through which
to read the Gospel. The Gospel transforms the meaning of Israel's
faith traditions. Jesus' discourses on Israel's festivals provide the
structure of the Gospel's first half. Chapters 12–19 are oriented to
Passover.

Because the temple is no more, the Shekinah glory dwells among
us. *Destroy this temple . . .* (2:19) signals Jesus' death. True worship is
neither in the Jerusalem temple nor on Mount Gerizim (4:20-24).
Jesus' farewell discourse focuses on the *place* that Jesus prepares for
us (14:1-3) and on *abiding* or *remaining* in Jesus and praying in Jesus'
name. Jesus' promise of the coming Paraclete replaces the apocalyptic discourses of the Synoptics. Jesus' resurrection is the raised
temple, and Thomas's climactic confession is true worship: *My Lord
and my God!* (20:28). God's dwelling among God's people punctuates
the narrative (see TBC "Temple" after comments on 4:3).

O'Day reminds us that "one of the distinctive traits of the Fourth
Gospel is the indissoluble union of story and theological interpretation in its telling of the story of Jesus" (1995: 661). She suggests that
rather than shaping our reading only by Martyn's two historical
levels in the Gospel (Jesus' time and the Johannine community's
time of synagogue exclusion)—or even the impact of the fall of the
temple—we should look at "two levels" from the perspective of
preaching: the discourses in the Gospel were preached as homilies
of Jesus to, by, and in the Johannine community—and indeed to all
Christian believers, as Bauckham (1998b) and Klink have argued.
These preaching discourses reenact the two levels of Jesus and later
believers, "inviting the readers to see their experience in the drama
enacted before their eyes" (O'Day 1995: 662).

Relation of John's Gospel to the Epistles and Revelation

Most scholars hold that the Gospel was written first and the
Epistles later. The Epistles address issues in churches where a
schism has occurred. Talbert, however, argues for the priority of
the epistles (3–4, 56–57), contending that the Gospel was written
to address issues raised in the Epistles. His rationale does not

persuade. He also grants that the Epistles may have been written alongside the Gospel. Von Wahlde's view that the Epistles were written between his reconstructed second and third editions has some merit (2010: 1.376–85; 3.12). In teaching the Gospel and the Epistles, I treated the Epistles alongside John 13–17 because of their common emphases on love for one another and obeying what Jesus taught as the test of the true believer's identity.

In his outstanding treatment of "Johannine Theology," Schnelle (2009: 661, 732–33) weds the Gospel and the Epistles, showing inherent unity on a variety of topics: their common use of "(little) children (*tekna/teknia*) of God" or being "born (begotten) of God" (John 1:12, 13; 3:3, 7; 11:52; 13:33; 1 John 2:1, 12, 28, 29; 3:1, 2, 7, 9, 10, 18; 4:4, 7; 5:21; 2 John 1, 4, 13; 3 John 4) and the permeating emphasis on *love* and *love for one another* as the theological heart of both (passim in John 13–17; 21:15-17; and 1 John). First John interweaves the Gospel's themes of light and love and applies the ethic of love to concrete conduct: how one responds to brothers and sisters in need (733). Love for one another assures one of salvation and manifests those born of God.

The Gospel and Epistles likely emerged around the same time: for von Wahlde (2010: 1.52–53), the Epistles were written between the second and third editions of the Gospel (65–70?). He gives eight reasons why the final Gospel edition is to be dated after 1 John (1.376–85). Von Wahlde concludes that the third [final] edition of the Gospel was "completed perhaps by AD 85-90, and certainly before AD 100" (1.390).

Striking differences are also notable. While both speak of *the world* as that which opposes those born of God and which even hates believers (John 15:18-25), *the Jews*, prominent in the Gospel, never occurs in the Epistles. The opponents in the Epistles separate theology from ethics. They claim to be believers and to know God but do not show it in life (McDermond: passim). Furthermore, they depreciate Jesus' humanity, denying Christ has come in the flesh (1 John 4:1-6; 2 John 7). This defective belief is "the spirit of the antichrist" (1 John 4:3; cf. 2:18, 22). Most likely, a group with these beliefs seceded from the Johannine community and tried to win younger believers to their side (2:18-29; 2–3 John; see McDermond, on these texts).

Whether Revelation emanates from the same Johannine author or theological "circle" of believers is debatable. The dominant view, reflecting early church skepticism (Culpepper 2000: 14–15), disconnects Revelation from the Gospel's authorship. Some striking similarities, however, suggest theological connection. John is named in

Revelation 1:1, 4, 9, and then "I" recurs thereafter in chapter 1. The appearance of the "Son of Man" (1:13) echoes the *Son of Man* Christology in the Gospel. In 19:13 (cf. Yeatts: 357–58) the name of the rider on the white horse is "The Word of God" (*ho Logos tou Theou*), matching John 1:1. John's Gospel theology reflects Jewish Christianity with "no temple," as also does Revelation's vision of the future (21:22). The Lamb is the light in both. The Spirit teaches and advocates for believers in John's Gospel (chs. 14–16; Smalley 1998: 289–300) and in Revelation inspires prophecy (1:10; 19:10). Seeing is a motif common to both, but with different connotations. The christological imagery in the frames of Revelation (chs. 1 and 22, as in 1:13 and 22:17) echo imagery from the Gospel, even *bridal* (John 2:1-12; 3:29; 4:4-26). Revelation 21:6 and 22:17 match the Gospel's *water of life* in 7:37-39. A similar ethos pervades the entire Johannine corpus (Swartley 2006a: 276–89; cf. Culpepper 2000: 9–27): a conflictive moral, ecclesial, and political stance of believers in the hostile world.

But differences are also significant. The genre of Revelation is different—thoroughly apocalyptic—and Revelation's extended visions have no Gospel parallel. Johns notes the Lamb in Revelation (28x) is *arnion*, which fits the martyr tradition; it is not the *amnos* of John 1:29, 36, which echoes deliverance (and sacrificial) themes. Their cosmological dualities differ: in the Gospel *from above* and *from below* are oppositional; in Revelation the alternating heavenly and earthly scenes are complementary. The verb *believe* (*pisteuō*) occurs in the Gospel one hundred times, but never in Revelation. Further, the adjective/noun (*pistos*) appears only once in the Gospel, the last word in 20:27, but occurs eight times in Revelation to denote the "faithful" who follow the Lamb.

These observations inform but do not resolve the issue of authorship. Culpepper does not believe Revelation stems from the Gospel's author, but from the Johannine "school" of thought. He notes that Revelation and 2-3 John gained canonical acceptance late, due to doubt about authorship and apostolic connections (2000: 15–16).

Relation to the Synoptic Gospels (Audience of the Gospel)[w]

John's Gospel differs in its content from that of the Synoptic Gospels about 90 percent. Jesus' parables, exorcisms, and nativity stories (Matthew and Luke) chronicled in the Synoptics are not in John; nor does John report Jesus' wilderness temptations. John has no Gethsemane agony narrative per se, but he does narrate Jesus' threefold agony-turmoil [*tarrassō*] experience in 11:33; 12:27; 13:21. Numerous John/Synoptic parallel events seem similar but are not the same in the details:

- Jesus' cleansing of the temple is located at the beginning of Jesus' ministry in John.

- Jesus feeds the five thousand (6:1-14) and then follows a storm on the sea, with Jesus walking on the water (6:16-21), but details vary; 6:15 is unique to John.

- Jesus heals a blind man, but John's account (ch. 9) is located in Jerusalem, not in Galilee; it is a different episode.

- Mary anoints Jesus for his burial (12:1-8) and Jesus triumphantly enters Jerusalem (12:12-15), but again details vary.

- John 18-19 is similar to the Synoptics' passion narrative, but John's emphases differ.

John elaborates on some of Jesus' key pithy sayings in the Synoptics. This relationship may be understood as John's metatext in relation to Jesus' Synoptic sayings. For example, Jesus' *new wine* sign in John (2:1-10) is metatext on Jesus' saying in Mark on "new wine" (2:22). In lively style Kysar (1976: 3-21) presents more fully the differences and similarities between John and the Synoptics.

At the root of John's distinctiveness (cf. Dunn 1991, "Let John Be John") are the many events of Jesus' ministry located in Jerusalem that are not mentioned in the Synoptics. The first two-thirds of the Synoptic Gospels report events in Galilee. John and the Synoptics thus represent traditions from two different locations of Jesus' ministry. Numerous scholars believe John's three-year span, not present in the Synoptics, is more historically reliable.

Seeking to resolve the problem of differences, second century Papias proposed that John's Gospel reports many events in the first two years of Jesus' ministry, whereas the Synoptics treat only the last year, *after* John the Baptist is arrested (Eusebius, *Hist. eccl.* 2.24). Though John indeed presents Jesus' ministry in a three-year span instead of the Synoptics' one-year span, Papias's and Eusebius's solution hardly satisfies. Much of John's distinctive content occurs in his last fifteen chapters (7-21), which recount Jesus' last half year of ministry! Mark (source for Matt and Luke—thus, the Synoptics) and John are better viewed as bi-optic Gospel accounts (Anderson 2007: 127-84; 2011: 125-29).

Clement of Alexandria (writing ca. 188-210) describes John as the "spiritual" Gospel (so reported by Eusebius, *Hist. eccl.* 6.14.6), but this says too little and too much. It is too little because *spiritual* in today's Western world often means a quick vitamin boost for thought and nurture. John goes deeper, beckoning readers to contemplation and worship. It is too much because for some *spiritual* means that it downplays the moral and political. John's spirituality is both political and ethical: it invites believers to risk life amid persecution while also feasting on Christ for life-sustaining strength and empowerment.

The canonical order of the four Gospels varies in Greek, Latin, and Syriac manuscripts. In some, John is first; in others, second; and in a few, third. Eusebius, in his Canon Tables, and Jerome popularized the order we know (Metzger 1987: 296–97).

History and Theology (or Philosophy) in John[w]

Each of the Synoptic Gospels presents theological interpretations of the Jesus traditions that include a radical transformation of Israel's faith traditions (Swartley 1994). John likewise takes historical traditions of Jesus plus independent traditions together with Israel's faith traditions in the OT and sets forth a scintillating Gospel of Jesus Christ, with content largely different from the Synoptics. John is indeed historical at its core, as the work of the "Jesus, John, and History" group of the SBL has demonstrated over the past nine years (see the articles in Anderson, Just, and Thatcher 2008, 2009, in the multivolume work *John, Jesus, and History*). Robinson's case for *The Priority of John* (1985) and Wenham's "Historical View of John's Gospel" (1998) argue for an early date for John (before 70), which in turn bears on its historicity. John's scope of place names indicates historical reliability. While fifteen are shared with the Synoptics,

> a surprising number are peculiar to John: Cana, Tiberias, Sychar, Joseph's field, Jacob's well, Mount Gerizim, Aenon near Salim, Bethany beyond Jordan, the house of Mary, Martha, and Lazarus, the place of Jesus' meeting with Martha, the tomb of Lazarus, Ephraim, the Pool of Bethesda, the Pool of Siloam, Solomon's Portico, the Wadi Kidron, the garden where Jesus was arrested, the door of the High Priest's court, the Pavement/Gabbatha, the garden in which Jesus' tomb was located. (Robinson 1985: 52, citing Scobie: 84)

The fourth Gospel is also toned with certain polemical interests and purposes, evident in three dimensions. First, the Gospel reflects polemic against followers of John the Witness (most sharply in 3:22-36), who regard him as the Messiah or continue to look for the

Messiah. The main portion of Jesus' public ministry is framed by John's personage and role (1:19–10:42). In this polemic, accent falls on Jesus' messianic significance within the array of first-century Judaisms: not John the Witness, but Jesus!

Second, the Gospel is toned with a polemic against *the Jews*, however that term is defined *["The Jews," p. 520]*.

A third more subtle polemic arises from the beloved disciple's relation to Peter. This may be understood as a challenge to hierarchical power in church leadership, since Peter elsewhere in Gospel literature is viewed as an institutional leader. The threefold question Jesus puts to Peter, *Do you love me?* makes the love charism foundational for leadership in the Johannine community of believers (13:31-35; 21:15-19—where *love* not *office* [Kragerud's thesis] is the basis of Peter's authority).

As we seek to understand John's Gospel, five time-levels beckon our attention, often simultaneously. First, we encounter Jesus in the text-history: Jesus in his day, teaching and doing signs and works. Second, the contemporary time of John the Evangelist shines through the text as history also, in which the Jesus-history interacts prophetically with issues in John's faith community. Third, the earlier text-history of Israel's faith traditions plays into John's narrative as well, for early Christians understood Jesus in light of the OT, their Scripture. Fourth, the time of the reader's life situation and knowledge interacts with the text and its history from then until their own time. The Gospel is read afresh in every generation, with fresh meaning. This for John is *krisis* (decision/judgment) time, the moment of decision when confronted with the penetration of light into the soul-world of the reader. This *krisis*-time leads to salvation or judgment. Fifth, there is eternal time, both the preexistence of the Word/Jesus/Son and also time into eternity, to enjoy the blissful union with the *perichōrēsis* (a technical term referring to how the three persons of the Trinity—Father, Son, and Holy Spirit—"coinhere" in each other). This fifth time is linked to *krisis* time by *eternal life*, occurring often in John *[Eternal Life, p. 513]*.

History, theology, and spirituality are interwoven in John's Gospel. As Dorothy Lee (2010) points out, John's Gospel is highly sensory. More than any of the other Gospels, *seeing* and *hearing* richly punctuate the narrative. *Touch*, *taste*, and *smell* are also significantly present (cf. the stench of Lazarus's tomb with the aroma of Mary's lavish loving anointing of Jesus' feet—back-to-back stories in chs. 11–12). This sensory dimension attests to Jesus' humanity, which is valued in the Gospel.

OT Scripture and John[w]

No other NT Scripture is so permeated with OT thought, imagery, and festival traditions. Beasley-Murray says it well: "[John] is the product of a mind soaked in the Old Testament, to a degree to which no other work in the New Testament approximates" (1999: lxix). While the Synoptics are shaped by the key events or epochs of Israel's faith story (exodus, land-gift, temple, and kingship; cf. Swartley 1994), John's Gospel is shaped by Israel's major festivals. In both cases the genius of the Gospel tradition is both to honor its faith heritage and to transform it. Jesus deepens and consummates OT faith, both theologically and ethically (see "Ethics of the Gospel" p. 38). Identifying the eighteen OT quotations in John (and there are many more allusions), some with two OT text connections and one with three such connections (Culpepper 2000: 19–20; cf. von Wahlde 2010: 3.295–323), is only one dimension of John's OT dependence. Some texts are adapted and employed for christological themes, underwriting John's literary purpose. John's OT citations swell at the end of Jesus' public ministry (ch. 12) and near the end of the passion narrative (19:24-37). Of the fifteen OT texts that C. H. Dodd identified as influential in shaping NT theological understandings (1952: 31–62), six appear in John and one in 1 John:

Psalm 2:7	John 1:49
Isaiah 6:9-10	John 12:40
Isaiah 53:1	John 12:38
Isaiah 40:3-5	John 1:23
Zechariah 9:9	John 12:15
Deuteronomy 18:15, 19	John 1:21, 45; 5:46; 6:14; 7:40
[Jeremiah 31:31-34	1 John 2:27]

In the Gospel's six, the expected prophet of Deuteronomy 18 plays a key role, as Meeks's landmark study documents (1967). But John's OT debt is much greater than quoted texts, for the Gospel's thought world draws on OT theological tropes such as wisdom traditions lying behind or within his *Logos* theology and Christology, joined also to the *Memra* gospel of synagogue worship (Boyarin 2001); *Memra* is Aramaic for *Word* and often used as a substitute for "the Lord"; see comments on 1:1-2, p. 47).

The Genesis 1 creation account is the foretext for John 1:1-5 and the Gospel's many new-creation features. Jesus' absolute uses of *I AM* and his *I Am* declarations with predicate adjectives utilizing metaphoric imagery build upon OT motifs as well: *bread of life* (John 6) draws on the Moses manna tradition; John 10 to its "true shepherd" teaching connects with Ezekiel 34 and 37 and a stream of other OT shepherd texts (see comments on John 6 and 10). The key *Son of Man* Christology in John is deeply rooted in Israel's faith traditions (Daniel, *1 Enoch*, and perhaps Ezekiel). John's emphasis on the Paraclete draws also on OT faith traditions, as Johnston's work demonstrates.[w]

Festival Structure[w]

Another stream of evidence for the OT canopy over John is the Gospel's focus on Israel's feasts for its narrative's structure. This raises the question of the relation of history and theology in John. Since the festival structure is the framework of Jesus' ministry, John's Gospel contributes distinctive historical perspective to Jesus' ministry—or is it a *theological* perspective? Second-century church leaders favored John's chronology and geography, since John's geography is correlated with festivals, mostly in Jerusalem (6:4, however, refers to the Passover Festival set in Galilee).

With its many meals and festivals and rich literary features, John's Gospel is a rich feast, delicious in narrative art.

Composition History and Literary Features[w]

Much has been written on possible sources behind the present text or dislocations within the text. Various theories of earlier sources behind the Gospel's final form have been proposed, most notably Fortna's signs' source (1970) and Raymond Brown's multistage development of the Gospel's tradition (1979: 166-69). Most recently von Wahlde's three-volume tome of 2,156 pages (2010), including the Johannine Epistles, proposes and sets forth the content of two editions of John that preceded the Gospel's third and final edition. In this magnum opus, von Wahlde outlines the conceptual-historical development of the Gospel's composition within the Johannine community. He identifies criteria for deciding which portions belong in the first edition (in 55–65? see 1.50), the second (in 60–65? see 1.51–52), and the third (389 to 390; see 1.385–89). His detailed analysis explains apparent dislocations, its many aporias (puzzling difficulties), and why Jesus' opponents are one time "Pharisees, chief priests, and rulers" (first edition), other times the hostile Jews (second edition), yet never including all Jews. His work has numerous commending features but nonetheless remains hypothetical (for a review, see Swartley 2012b).

During the last two decades, however, the dominant method for study of John is narrative analysis of the Gospel's present form. This commentary utilizes the narrative method, seeking to understand the Gospel in its canonical form. The Gospel is best appreciated by seeking to understand it as an integrated whole, rather than by dissecting it piecemeal into multiple sources, relocating parts to "correct" assumed dislocations, or searching out one or several editorial streams of emphasis—all part of the dicey history of scholarly interpretations of the fourth Gospel. Ruth Edwards, viewing John as a literary whole, puts it nicely:

> It was Alfred Loisy who once described John's Gospel as a "seamless robe." It is indeed the most integrated of all the Gospels: historical narrative, imaginative reconstruction, christology, theology and ethics are woven together into a continuous story which carries the reader along from its mysterious opening in the *logos* "hymn" to its glorious conclusion in Jesus' resurrection and commissioning of the disciples. (1997: 101)

This commentary values the literary artistry of the Gospel's final form. John's Gospel is replete with irony, metaphors, symbolism, misunderstandings, and double meanings. Basic definitions of these features are the following:

Irony: What is spoken or acted on one level of meaning (often sarcastic) in its setting has another meaning for the reader who perceives Jesus' royal identity and affirms it (e.g., mocking Jesus by putting the purple robe on him).

Metaphors: Perception of one reality through the lens of another (Webster: 7). The reader seeks to understand the connection between the levels of meaning (e.g., *the good shepherd*). As Moody Smith puts it, "The text is a consistent metaphor, or arrangement of related metaphors" (1999: 282). Metaphors elicit multiple meanings.

Misunderstandings: A saying or event is understood one way by Jesus' disciples or opponents. The narrator, however, clues the reader to understand it in a different way.

Double entendre: A given word or phrase has two or more meanings, such as *anōthen* in John 3: born *from above*, born *again*, or born *anew*.

Symbolism: A word, image, or story carries a deeper level of meaning. John's Gospel is highly symbolic, as in John 2 (wedding and temple) and 4 (Samaritan woman).

John's literary style "interweaves narrative, dialogue, and discourse to create lengthy drama-like scenes (e.g., 4:4-42; 6:1-69; 9:1-10:21; 11:1-44). . . . Story and theological interpretation are inseparably intertwined in John" (O'Day 1995: 494).

John artistically uses chiasm *[Chiasms, p. 507]* and has a penchant for numbers: seven signs, seven *I AM* absolute texts; seven *I am* declarations with predicate nominatives, seven witnesses, a seven-day structure to present the beginning of John's and Jesus' ministries, seven scenes in the Jesus-Pilate trial narrative, and seven scenes of the beloved disciple—each to be elaborated in due course, often in the essays *[Numbers, p. 528]*.

John the Evangelist creates a new symbolic world, with disciples and characters that often differ from those we know from the Synoptic Gospels. Through the cacophony of all these riddles, Jesus speaks truth: Be born from above, believe, or perish.

Plot and Characters[w]

Plot and characters intertwine in John's artistry. Jesus is God's chosen agent to reveal God's glory by doing God's works, speaking God's words, and fulfilling God's purpose in exposing the human need for salvation through God's faithful Son, lifted on the cross. Jesus promises the Paraclete (chs. 14–16) and bestows the Holy Spirit on the disciples (20:19-23) to continue Jesus' words and works through the Gospel's testimony.

The disciples (Andrew, Nathanael, Peter, Philip, and Thomas) and the Jerusalem temple authorities who seek to kill Jesus are key characters in the execution of the plot *["The Jews," p. 520]*. John the Witness and the man born blind play significant roles. Women characters play major roles in the disclosure of Jesus' identity: Jesus' mother, Mary; the Samaritan woman; Martha and Mary of Bethany; and Mary Magdalene. Judas and Pilate also play prominent roles.

Ethics of the Gospel[w]

In John's Gospel ethics has been marginalized or absent in the last century's literature on John, as citations by Kanagaraj (2005) and van der Watt (2006) indicate. Schrage in *The Ethics of the New Testament* notably says, "We may ask whether a chapter on the Johannine writings even belongs in a book on the ethics of the New Testament" (297). Meeks marginalizes ethics in John: "The only rule is 'love for another' and that is both vague in application and narrowly circumscribed" (1996: 318). He dismisses the example set by

Jesus in washing his disciples' feet, even though Jesus' command to "do likewise" calls for similar humble service (319), an *ethical* injunction. The ethos of the Gospel, he says—with its love/hate emphases, withdrawal from the world, and stigmatization of the Jews—cannot be normative for Christian ethics (317). He reiterates, "This Gospel does not provide moral instruction, . . . nor does its narrative directly model character to be emulated" (322).

Six years later Moody Smith (2002: 112) takes up the topic, first summarizing Meek's contribution. But he identifies other points that have explicit or implicit ethical import. In neither the Gospel nor the Epistles does John anywhere advocate violence against enemies. One's obedience to Jesus' commands (pl.) proves one's love for Jesus (14:15, 23), a point Segovia made clear years earlier (1981: 263). Segovia observes that love for Jesus occurs seven times (always using the verb *agapaō*), and is connected to keeping (*tēreō* or *echō*) Jesus' commands (*entolai*) or word(s) (*logos/logoi*). He focuses on 13:31–14:31, with its four occurrences of *agapaō* in 14:15, 21a, 23a, 24a (262). Von Wahlde (1990) also observes John's use of both *commandments* (pl.) and *commandment* (sg.).

Indian scholar Kanagaraj turns a fresh furrow in expanding the field of ethical considerations in John. Noting the regrettable marginalization of the topic, he speaks of the "implied ethics" in the Gospel and makes a persuasive case that each of the Ten Commandments (Decalogue) is assumed as binding or explicitly reinforced in the Gospel (2005). Van der Watt (2006: 153–55) affirms the same, though he demurs on whether John reflects, even as implied ethic, the tenth commandment, "Do not covet" (154).

Van der Watt distinguishes between the ethos and ethics of the Gospel. Ethos includes how the Johannine characters conduct themselves, giving "insight into how the commandments are interpreted and understood" (153). The ethos includes shared social behavior and a shared value system. When the Pharisees charge Jesus with blasphemy (10:33), they appeal to commandments one and three of the Decalogue (cf. 4:23-24; 17:3). Jesus counters those charges, claiming that he works with and by God. "The Jews" seek human glory, rather than God's, jeopardizing their obedience to these commandments. The controversies on the law hinge on proper understanding of the commandments (156–57).

Jesus' repeated claim to be doing the works of God elicits obedience that leads to belief, or disobedience that leads to judgment (157–59). The new command (sg.) to love one another entails the practice of reciprocity; it is a "poignant cry for solidarity" (quoting

Hays 1996: 147). This love is visible in actions, which footwashing illustrates; it entails responsibility to others in the community (1 John 3:14-18). Furthermore, this love command is networked into a Father-Son-disciple relationship, and the love of believers is "networked into the love of the family. They love Jesus—by *obeying* his commandments" (Van der Watt 2006: 162–63). Van der Watt (166–71) returns to social practices as expressions of this love: sharing meals, footwashing, and continuing Jesus' mission.

Kanagaraj and van der Watt contribute new insights. The relation between mission and peacemaking in John adds another dimension (see summary in TBC for ch. 20). Jesus' sending forth his disciples to carry on his mission is linked to his *Peace be with you*. It turns commission into ethical command, a neglected topic in Johannine studies. Smith's point—and Hays's emphasis for the entire NT—that John nowhere condones violence can be extended: Jesus commands Peter, representing all the disciples, *Put your sword back into its sheath* (18:11). In 18:36 he cites the rationale for the command: *My kingdom is not from this world. If my kingdom were from this world, my followers would be fighting to keep me from being handed over to the Jews.*

This foray into the ethics of John's Gospel must be juxtaposed with emphases that ethically offend, as Culpepper (1996) and P. Bruce note in their treatments of John's ethical contribution. Thus these topics are discussed in this commentary:

- The Gospel and the Jews
- The Gospel and exclusivism

Political Perspective

Another dimension of ethics in John is the Gospel's political perspective, as emphasized in numerous recent studies of John. Thatcher highlights the political dimension as one significant component of John's Christology: "John's Christology is his response to Rome" (2009: 5). In John's presentation of Jesus, this theme permeates the narrative, from the roles of the Jews, to Judas, to the high priest Caiaphas, and to Pilate, Caesar's Palestinian deputy. Rome, with its culture and politics—its need to keep the Jews, their temple, and the Jesus-believers subservient to the empire—provides the macrolandscape of the narrative. Jesus finally lands in Rome's hand as *King of the Jews!* This angle into the Gospel must be assessed together with the spiritual quality and the evangelistic bent of the narrative. John's Gospel has many hues in its rainbow. This commentary seeks to let each hue shine, blending with others.

Titles ascribed to Jesus in John are titles that Roman emperors claimed for themselves, often with divine status. In the confession of the Samaritans, Jesus is *the Savior of the world* is a description implying emperor status and function. While Julius Caesar was the first leader to acclaim himself as "savior," emperors later claimed the same or were hailed with additional "adulatory modifiers . . . : Augustus, Tiberius, Claudius, Nero, Vespasian, Titus, Trajan, and Hadrian" (Cassidy 1992: 13; fuller discussion occurs in Carter 2008: 176–203). In eastern parts of the empire, Nero was revered with this title.

Similarly, the title *lord* was employed by some emperors, notably Nero. Egyptian papyri provide evidence for use of *lord* already in Augustus's time, in speaking of offering sacrifices to "the god and lord emperor" Augustus. Pottery fragments attest the use of *lord* for Vespasian and Domitian, and evidence shows its use for Trajan and Hadrian (Cassidy: 1–14). The third title, "Lord and God" in that order, is not as prevalent, but "narrows to the rule of just one emperor, Domitian," who apparently demanded that people so address him (Cassidy: 14). Thomas's climactic christological confession, *My Lord and my God*, makes Jesus, not Domitian, the true Lord and God. Note that John likely was written during his reign.

Loyalty to and worship of Jesus counters the worship of the emperor. The chief priests' confession, *We have no king but the emperor* (19:15), contrasts with Thomas's confession, *My Lord and my God* (20:28). With this angle into John's Christology, belief in Jesus as Messiah and Son of God—political titles—means more than personal salvation. It puts personal faith into the dynamics of corporate loyalty: standing in solidarity with the Jesus community rather than conforming to emperor loyalty and worship. In this respect John's Gospel theologically accords with Revelation.

Jesus' sovereignty in the trial narrative of John 18–19 and in the whole Gospel takes on political significance as well. Käsemann's caricature that the divine Jesus never quite touches the earth is exposed for its failure to interpret Jesus' sovereignty as a political stance against emperor power and self-deification or deification by popular acclaim. It does not force a choice between the "Lord of glory" and the incarnate man whose obedience to do the works of God leads even to his death on a cross—Rome's way of disposing with troublemakers. Jesus' death and resurrection are put into a new and relevant light, for John's first readers and for Jesus' followers through time. Rensberger's two chapters "The Trial of Jesus and the Politics of John" and "The Gospel of John and Liberation" perceptively demonstrate how politics and ethics are intrinsic to the Gospel's moral vision (1988; cf. his 1984 article). Carter's contribution extends earlier discussion of John's political perspective, especially his chapters on "Eternal Rome and Eternal Life" (2008: 204–34) *[Eternal Life, p. 513]* and "John's Father and the Emperor as Father of the Fatherland" (235–55). Putting John on ethical discount domesticates Jesus' call for his followers to be an alternative community of light, life, love, and peace. Throughout John, *witnesses testify* to Jesus. Is Jesus or his opponents on trial? Or is it really the Gospel readers *[Witness, p. 534]*?

Symbolism and Spirituality in John[w]

John is rich in symbolism, and this does not negate its historical value. Webster proposes that John's eight "eating and drinking" symbolic narratives enhance the Gospel's soteriology: "An important metaphor for 'believing' is that of ingesting Jesus," evident in the parallelism between 6:40 and 6:54, which harks back to the powerful 1:14 declaration that *the Word became flesh [sarx]* (v. 3). When my three-year-old son was asked, "What does your father do for a living," he thought a while and said, "He eats." *Ingesting Jesus* reminds us that we live by believing and eating, for eternal life.

The Gospel has power to form people. Adela Yarbro Collins reminds us that "the symbols we use have a powerful effect." This power is useful not only for personal spiritual reflection, but also for the church corporately. "Wherever that vision is allowed to have an effect, the tendency will be away from a structured institution which emphasizes roles, status, and hierarchy, and toward a gathering of people working together in an egalitarian way characteristic of mutuality" (1982: 51).

Jey Kanagaraj compares John's distinctive spirituality with Indian religious thought and culture, especially Hindu and Sikh beliefs. In discussing John's *Logos*, Kanagaraj suggests that *Om*, the means to attain Brahman, is a preaching/teaching connection. *Om*, first uttered by God, enables humans to know each other and themselves (40). John uses a well-known concept, Logos, and makes it serve the Gospel's purpose. Hence *Om* can be used to refer to the one true God and "to proclaim the self-revelation of that one God by incarnation" (40). In today's pluralistic world, Kanagaraj offers a gift in showing how John's theology, spirituality, and moral vision connect with and differ from foundational understandings in Indian religion and culture. Enlightenment (John 1:5, 9) is central to Buddhist thought. With its eightfold path of training in virtuous conduct, it enables "a change in one's consciousness" (48). John's Gospel, rich in symbolism, seeks also through its *signs* and rich *I AM* metaphors to create a new symbolic world, uniting us to Jesus and to God *["I AM," p. 518]*. This is mysticism of a special sort (Dumm; Sanford), gained not by our efforts, but through God's incarnation in his only Son, so that we may receive eternal life *[Eternal Life, p. 513]*. John's spiritual ethos consists of rebirth, confession of Jesus' identity, and the command to *love one another* as *I have loved you*. This ethos blends with a politics that serves God alone.

John's spirituality and Christology contribute distinctive emphases to atonement. The Father's lavish love and the Son's generous gift *to* and *for* (*hyper*) the life of the world (6:51), for his sheep (10:11, 15; cf. 11:51-52), was and is not an act of divine violence, but an unfathomable gift. The violence of the cross is inevitable because of human sin: "When God comes into the world in his Son, there are only two possibilities: either the world will die, or God will die in his Son" (Ellul: 62). The latter occurs: the Father's/Son's atoning gift is described in varied metaphors—"Lamb of God" (John 1:29, 36) and a shepherd's laying down his life (John 10:17-18). This divine generosity creates humans anew to reflect the divine image (Eph 4:24; 2 Pet 1:4). Jesus' life, death, and resurrection reveal the means and ends of God's salvation, inviting believers into abundant life (John 10:10b), to *abide in* Jesus (John 15), and into the intimacy of the Father-Son union (John 17:21, 23; cf. Paul's "in Christ"), to live the light, life, and love of the eternal *I AM*.

Prologue

John 1:1-18

Overture to the Gospel

The glory of the Lord shall be revealed,
and all people shall see it together,
for the mouth of the Lord has spoken.
—Isaiah 40:5 (also Handel's *Messiah*)

The voice of the mystical eagle
sounds in . . . [our] ears.
Let our exterior sense
catch the sound that passes;
let our mind within
penetrate the meaning that abides.
—Eriugena, introducing John's prologue, around 860 (trans. O'Meara,
via Brodie: 133)

PREVIEW[w]

Darkness? Yes darkness! Thirty-three students are going through
Hezekiah's tunnel with water coming up to some shoulders and
candles burning out due to lack of oxygen. Would the group make it
out alive? The leader decides it is not safe to move through the
"stopper" point (two-thirds of the way through), where the ceiling

w   Where the superscript w occurs after headings, please see the commentary's online Web
Supplement for additional material. Go to: www.heraldpress.com/bcbc/john.

drops a foot, leaving only six inches of space between the water and stone. He orders the group to turn around and exit from the entrance. With full bodies now blocking the water flow, the water keeps rising. Candles flicker out, one by one, then . . . darkness.

One wise student passes along a saving word: walk sideways to let the water pass. With that counsel the group barely makes it to safety, emerging into the light.

In God's creation through the Word, light overcomes darkness. As this group stands in the glow of the bright sun, drying off, a ray of God's glory shines, with the sun analogous to the Son, whose glory explodes our imagination. This is a tiny window into the creation, salvation, and glory that marks John's prologue. The Son tells the story of God's salvation. "In John 1:1-18 the Fourth Evangelist gives the Gospel reader the theological road map of God's self-revelation in Jesus. John 1:1-18 does not allow readers to distance themselves from that revelation, but instead draws the reader into the theological claims of the text" (O'Day 1995: 524).

The majestic soaring eagle symbolizes John's Gospel in the early church. John's prologue begins its flight beyond time and history and descends to earth so that the Word can live among us. *The Word-Logos* tones the prologue, but acts as subject only in verses 1 and 14.

The prologue is a work of art! It begins with the preexistence of the Word, a coparticipating agent in creation, bringing forth life and light, to whom John witnesses. The Word shines as a light in the darkness, enlightening human beings coming into the world. The Word coming into the world elicits both negative and positive responses. The Word makes its abode with humans through incarnation. The incarnate Word's brilliant *glory* credentials the "one and only" Son of the Father. He is full of grace and truth. His fullness of glory, enhanced by John's *witness* to the light, extends God's former gift of grace in the law given by Moses—thus, *grace upon grace* (1:16). The epiphany of the only God-Son as Word-Speech tells "God's Story" (Moloney 1998: 47). The "story of Jesus is not ultimately a story about Jesus; it is, in fact, a story of God" (O'Day 1995: 524).

OUTLINE

A The Preexistent Word, Agent of Creation, 1:1-5
   B John: Witness to the Light, 1:6-8
      C The True Light, 1:9-11
         D God's Gift to Those Who Receive the Logos, 1:12-13
      C´ Word Made Flesh, Resplendent in Glory, 1:14
   B´ Witness to the Word Made Flesh, 1:15-17

John's Witness, 1:15
Fullness, Grace upon Grace, 1:16-17
A´ The Incarnate Word, Revealing God, 1:18

EXPLANATORY NOTES

Even though the John portions in the prologue provide a coherent separate introduction and the didactic hymnic portions are also a coherent unit, they may indeed have been composed as side-by-side components, integrated by the Gospel author (see "Authorship" in the introduction and essays).

Unity of the Prologue with the Gospel Narrative[w]

The prologue functions as an unfolding drama of the *Logos's* preexistence with God onward to the incarnate God-Son, who reveals God. It is an overture to the main topics of the Gospel's narrative. This commentary regards the prologue as essential to the Gospel.

Key themes are in both the prologue and the entire Gospel:

- The divinity of the *Logos* in the prologue and numerous "divine" christological titles (cf. the absolute *I AMs*)
- Jesus as source of (eternal) life (cf. chs. 3; 5–6; 11)
- Jesus, bringing light into the world (cf. 8:12–9:41)
- Faith and unbelief (passim)
- Glory and glorification (passim)
- Grace and truth, mostly on truth (cf. chs. 8; 14; 19)
- Jewish law subservient to Jesus as revealer of God
- Polemic re John's role, always only a witness (cf. chs. 1; 3; 5)
- Many witnesses to Jesus' claims dotting the Gospel landscape
- Jesus' coming into the world (*kosmos*) and the world rejecting him

(For listing themes in John, cf. Valentine 293–303; Barrett 1978: 126.)

The prologue introduces three important themes of the Gospel's narrative. First, Christology and discipleship are intertwined. The opening verses emphasize Jesus' essential unity with the Father as agent of creation. The Word's oneness with God embraces both *being* and *action* (*works* and *signs* in the Gospel's narrative). This distinctive Christology is reiterated throughout the Gospel. At the same time, the center of the chiastic structure (D in the outline for this chapter) describes those who believe as receiving the *power* (or authority) *to become children of God.* This is the new identity of disciples who respond positively to the Word. Their belief says yes to the distinctive Christology of the Gospel (see John's purpose statement in 20:30-31).

Second, while salvation is offered, it is also refused: *His own . . . did not receive him* (1:11). This anticipates the Gospel's prominent theme of unbelief. Summary responses throughout the narrative emphasize unbelief—just as sharply or even more sharply as belief. The concluding chapter of Jesus' public ministry focuses on unbelief as an issue requiring special explanation (12:37-50).

Third, virtually all commentators emphasize that the Word (Son/God in v. 18) is Jesus, the *incarnate Revealer* of God, in the Gospel's narrative. The Son is the *exegete* of the Father (1:18 AT). Commentators differ on whether this revelation is supremely disclosed through Jesus' being lifted up on the cross or through Jesus' glory, by which Jesus reveals a victorious God. Larsson (84) rhetorically queries, "Does the uplifted Revealer sail above the earth as a kind of radiant hovercraft or is he uplifted because he is executed? And is he glorified *in spite of* or *because* of dying on the cross?" Larsson (84–88) documents these two streams of emphasis appearing through the early church fathers, the Reformers, and current expositors of John's Gospel.

A motif that recurs throughout the Gospel and that interacts with these themes is *witness* or *testify.* In verses 6-8 and 15, John, known in the Synoptic Gospels as "the Baptist," is introduced as *witness* to Jesus. This—and this alone—is his role in John's Gospel. Hence this commentary identifies him as John the Witness. He *testifies* to Jesus. In the Gospel's recurring mention of John, he is always witness. Other witnesses punctuate the Gospel narrative also, advancing the main themes that permeate the Gospel.

The Preexistent Word, Agent of Creation 1:1-5

1:1-2 Eternal Preexistence

Each of the four Gospels has its own distinctive opening. Mark begins with Jesus' fulfilling OT prophetic texts pregnant with messianic expectation; Matthew, with a genealogy linking Jesus to the Abrahamic and Davidic covenant promises; and Luke, certifying the historical witnesses of the narrative he writes about Jesus. John begins by locating the One of whom he writes with God as the eternal Word, cocreator, and life-giver and light-giver. Only John begins with Jesus' preexistence.

The opening verse locates the Word temporally, spatially, and ontologically. The Word was in the *beginning*, was *with* God, and *was* God. John's prologue has greatly influenced the historical development of Christian theology, and 1:1 together with 1:14 and 18 have played significant roles in that influence.

The prologue never mentions Jesus; the accent falls rather on the *Logos*-Word coming into the world that God-*Logos* created. The term *Word* has multifaceted meaning. In Greek thought *Word/Logos* is a philosophical term denoting the rationality and structure of the cosmos and of the systems that order the cosmos, such as the interrelation of the galactic bodies, gravity, the seasons, space and time, and the species. John's prologue leads the reflective reader to soar to the metaphysical, universal, cosmological realm, with *Logos/Word* the subject! John's prologue connects to both the Greek philosophical and Hebrew prophetic traditions.

The significance of the Hebrew tradition cannot be overestimated. The opening phrase, *in the beginning* (*en archē*), echoes precisely the first words of Genesis 1:1 (LXX). John shapes his Logos-creation story to reflect Genesis 1, both in this opening phrase and in choosing *Logos/Dabar* to designate the Agent of creation who *was in the beginning, was with God*, and *was God*.

The Gospel begins when, where, and how God begins. To know more would deny God's Godness. The same holds for *Word/Logos*. Humans cannot fathom the profundity of this opening claim. *Word/ Logos* connects to the key Hebrew word *dabar* (speak/speech). The *word* (*dabar*) brings events, deeds, and the visible world into being. *Logos* denotes the dynamic, creative power of the *word*, spoken by God as in Genesis 1:1–2:3 (LXX) to create the world and all that is in it. Genesis 1, liturgically arranged, portrays creation as coming into being by *word/command*, the *word* of God. God *said*, "Let there be light," and light came into being. So goes the seven-day drama of God's creating power and action. Further, at the end of Day 6, "God saw all that he had made, and . . . it was *very good*" (Gen 1:31a). Genesis 1 narrates creation as fulfillment of the *word*, the *word* of God. This is also the view of the psalmist, "By the *word* of the Lord the heavens were made, and all their host by the *breath* of his *mouth*" (Ps 33:6, emphasis added). In these Word-speech/*Logos* narratives, God creates a peaceable home for humans in which light shatters and overcomes darkness. John is a Gospel of life, light, and love!

Second, God *calls* forth a covenant people and discloses to Moses the divine *name* YHWH (Exod 3:13-15). *Speech/word* brings a people into existence by God's calling Abraham and Moses. God's special name (Exod 6:2-3) releases power to deliver the people from bondage, thus fulfilling God's promises to Abraham. This same *word/power* continues in the prophetic tradition, where prophets in the tradition of Moses are God's mouthpiece. Similarly, Isaiah 55:10-11 declares that God's *word* goes forth to accomplish that for which it is sent. In the prophetic literature "the word of the Lord" initiates the prophet's call and mission (Jer 1:4; Isa 9:8; Ezek 1:3; Hos 1:1; Amos 3:1; see the last part of "Gathering Disciples" in the TBC after 2:12). God's spoken word creates; the prophet is God's mouthpiece.

A third arena for understanding *Logos* within the Hebraic tradition is God's gift of the Torah. Torah was/is the *word* of God that directs, sustains, and empowers the life of God's people, as Exodus 24 and 34 disclose. Many psalms extol the Torah as word of God. Virtually every verse of Psalm 119 (176 of them structured as an acrostic of the Hebrew alphabet) owns and celebrates God's Torah, statutes, commandments, law, precepts, judgments, or word. "The Lord exists forever; your word is firmly fixed in heaven" (v. 89).

A fourth and fifth context for understanding *Logos* in the Hebraic tradition are two companions of *word* in God's self-disclosure: *glory* and *wisdom* (cf. these five themes with Lee's three; 2002: 30-32). These are companions to the *dabar*-speech tradition. See comments on 1:14 for *Glory [Glory, p. 516]*. One apocryphal text, Wisdom 9:1-2, puts *word* and *wisdom* in synonymous parallelism:

> [You] have made all things by your *word*,
>   and by your *wisdom* have formed humankind. (1b-2a, emphasis added)

Much said of the *Word* in John's prologue is analogous to that said of *wisdom* in the OT (including Sirach and Wisdom). In Sirach 24:1-3, *wisdom speaks* of her *glory*. Later rabbinic literature associated word, wisdom, and glory as well (cf. *Gen Rab.* 1:1, where God consults Torah and creates wisdom). John's Gospel often speaks of *glory* but never mentions *wisdom* (*sophia*)—one of the puzzles of the Gospel. The manifestation of God's *glory* is dramatically linked with *Word* in John 1:14:

> *The Word became flesh,...*
>   *and we have beheld his glory.* (RSV)

Some OT texts in which God's *name*-word and *glory* are interconnected are Exodus 33:17-23 (note the YHWH name in v. 19) and Isaiah 6:1-8 in Isaiah's call. *Lord of hosts* (YHWH Ṣebaot) is in synonymous parallel with *glory*:

Holy, holy, holy is the Lord of hosts;
    the whole earth is full of his glory. (Isa 6:3)

In addition to the Greek and Hebrew contexts, another linguistic-theological dimension must be considered to understand John's use of *Logos/Word*. Aramaic, the common language of Palestine in the first century, was the language of the synagogue. The synagogue Scriptures were the Targums, the OT text in Aramaic, the cultural language of the Jews in the time of Ezra. The Aramaic for *Logos/Word* is *Memra*. Boyarin (2001) has persuasively argued that John's *Logos* theology is derived directly from the Jewish synagogue *Memra* theology. He cites over a dozen Aramaic Torah texts that use *Memra* for YHWH, thus denoting the divine One, who in numerous texts is actor in creation. When Moses pleads with God for divine certification of his mission to confront Pharaoh in Exodus 3:13-15, the *Targum Neofiti 1* reads, "I, My *Memra*, will be with you." Other Targums identify *Memra* as support: "And he said: Because my *Memra* will be your support" (Boyarin 2001: 258). The performing role of *Memra* in *creation* and *revealing* occurs in numerous texts (Gen 1:3; 18:1; 19:24; Exod 17:5-6; Deut 32:39). Boyarin concludes, "The *Memra* performs many, if not all, of the functions of Christian Logos theology" (256–57). *Memra/Logos/Word* designates divine being, with YHWH affiliation. Boyarin thus says John's "high Logos Christology" is not problematic to Jewish and early Christian solidarity. Schnackenburg (1.486–87), however, rejects the significance of the *Memra* association, emphasizing instead the differences between Philo's *Logos* and *Logos* in John's Gospel—yet a difference that does not negate Boyarin's point.

Boyarin contends that John's departure from the Jewish *Memra* theology comes with verse 14, where the *Logos* becomes flesh: "When the text announces in v. 14 that 'the Word became flesh,' that announcement is an iconic representation of the moment that the Christian narrative begins to diverge from the Jewish Koine [i.e., common Jewish theology] and form its own nascent Christian kerygma" (2001: 261). Boyarin contends that the *Logos* as true God (Nicaea, in 325) is fully Jewish; the parting with Judaism arises from the *Logos* as true human!

Commentators diverge on the degree to which John's prologue connects with the rational Hellenistic mind or the Hebrew understanding of God's *word* as the creative, upholding power of the universe. Philo, a Jewish philosopher-theologian contemporary to

Jesus, synthesized Jewish and Greek thought by integrating the OT *word/dabar* tradition with the *logos* in Stoicism. He espoused a Jewish-Greek philosophy that regarded *Logos* as the rational, ordering principle of the universe, both in its origins and ongoing governance. In light of Philo's synthesis, William Temple (1939: 8) says nothing could be more misleading than to pit the Hebraic and Hellenic against each other. Boyarin (2001) concurs, citing several texts from Philo to make the point. He concludes, "The Logos is both a part of God and also a separate being, the Word that God created in the beginning in order to create everything else: the Word that both is God, therefore, and is with God" (2001: 250). Boyarin acknowledges that "if Philo is not on the road to Damascus here, he is surely on a way that leads to Nicea [Nicaea] and the controversies over the second person of the Trinity" (251).

Another angle to the Hebraic/Hellenic context for the Gospel recognizes that the Gospel is steeped in Jewish Scripture and structured by Jewish festivals, and all the main characters are Jews. Yet non-Jews are part of the plot as well: two key figures in John 4, a possible reference to Gentiles in 11:52, and the crucial role of the Greeks who *wish to see Jesus* in 12:21-22. Two of Jesus' disciples, Andrew and Philip, have Greek names. That Jesus' hour auspiciously comes when the Greeks inquire about Jesus indicates that Gentile Christians and potential Gentile Christians are a significant audience of this Gospel. Logos is John's first play on double entendre.

Whereas Mark's narrative plot is paced by the messianic secret, John's plot bursts with shock of divine claims. John 1:1 jolts the reader with *Logos*, the One with God from the beginning, who indeed was and is God. John 1:14 declares, This divine One *became flesh* and dwelt among humans—another shock, incomprehensible! Moloney gets it right in translating 1:1c as "What God was, the Word was" (1998: 42, as in NEB).

Verse 2 seals this point: *From the very beginning the Word was with God.* This declares the Word's (Son's) preexistence and closes off speculation concerning when the Word began. The Word was, always! This distinctive contribution of John's prologue asserts the eternity of the Word and sets forth the continuity of the Word's incarnation with its prior activity in creation. As creative power and incarnational humility, *Logos* is John's unique way of introducing Jesus.

1:3-4a Present in Creation, Giving Life

In verses 1-2 one verb, *was* (*ēn*), is used four times. In verse 3 the Greek verb for *was* or *became* (*ginomai*) occurs three times. These verbs alternate throughout the prologue. The verb *ginomai* has a multifaceted meaning. It can be translated *became*, *create*, *come into being*, or *generate*. Forms of *ginomai* recur in verses 6, 10, 12, 13, 14a, 15, and 17. It heads verse 6 and recurs in the first line in verse 14. In several of its ten uses in the prologue, it is translated *became* or *become* and has the sense of *come into being*. In verse 3, however, *ginomai* is translated as *create* (i.e., *cause* to come into being). In the past tense (aorist) infinitive, it describes those who receive the Logos as *becoming children of God* (v. 12). Clearly, *ginomai* has a range of meaning, with most uses denoting the emergence of the new. Schoneveld translates it as *emerge*, to designate the new *coming forth* into time and space.

Verse 3 presents us with a profound mystery: how the world and all that is in it came into being through the *Word-Logos*. It presents us also with a textual problem: do the last two words in Greek (*ho gegonen*) belong to the thought unit of verse 3, or do they belong to verse 4? Put with 3, we translate 3b *and without him not anything was made that was made. In him was life . . .* (RSV, also KJV, NIV, NKJV, and most church fathers). If put with verse 4, we translate it *and without him not anything was made. What has come into being in him was life . . .* (NRSV, NEB). Metzger (1994: 167–68) and numerous commentators argue for the NRSV punctuation on the basis of its "staircase" poetic parallelism: the ending of one line matches the beginning of the next line.

What does it mean to affirm that the *Word-Logos* was the agent, coparticipant with God in the creation of *all things*? Is this creation ex nihilo? Yes and no. Yes, in that God's creation through or by the Logos brought into existence that which before did not exist (cf. Rom 4:17; Heb 11:3). Yes also, in the sense that if compared to creation myths of that time—both in the OT and NT—creation in the Genesis account is not the result of warfare among the gods or of an inferior gods constructing the world as evil matter (*hylē* in Gnosticism), from which humans must escape through special *gnōsis*, knowledge. Yes, further, in the sense that the world God created was and is good—the material nature of the world is good, in both the ethical and aesthetic senses.

Many OT scriptures stress God's sovereignty in and through creation. The creation language is not so much about "existence and nonexistence, but the revelation of an absolute power and the absence of such power." Scripture employs such "contrasts to exhibit God's omnipotence (Is. 40:17 and Jer. 23–26)" (Dyrness: 66).

Creation ex nihilo means that the creature is from God and no other source: "It exists through God and not otherwise. Hence it is not itself God, or an emanation of God. Nor is it self-engendered and therefore independent of God" (Barth: 155). With John's Logos emphasis, the same is to be said: the Logos is the source of creation.

But the *no* to this question must also be heard. There is no creationism-versus-evolution debate in the prologue. Those ideas and concepts are not in the minds of the biblical writers. John uses the verb *ginomai*, meaning "coming into existence." It is both a point action and a process concept—hence the suggestion above of *emergence* as a possible translation, in the various uses of *ginomai*. Creation did occur at the dawn of time, marking "the absolute beginning of the created world" (Eichrodt: 72). But it should also be recognized, as Ellis points out, that a creating process is built into the creation event, as the language of Genesis 1 indicates: God said,

- Let the *earth bring forth* vegetation.
- Let the *waters bring forth* swarms of living creatures.
- Let the *earth bring forth* living creatures.

God is the Creator-Enabler who blesses and enables humanity to procreate and care for the earth. "The creation story is an enabling story prompted by the divine word" (Ellis: 80). At the same time, "nothing but the autonomous decree of the transcendent God determined the form of creation. That the *creation ex nihilo* thereby enters the picture is incontestable" (Eichrodt: 72). This means that whatever scientific theory we may hold, big bang (with or without a quantum bounce), evolutionary stages, or intelligent design, we must own God's initiating role as creator in the event, process, or design of laws and species, unless we divorce Scripture from science or vice versa.

God's creative activity continues through time and nature. The OT celebrates the diversity and wonder of God's creation. Numerous Psalm texts view God's creative actions as having a beginning and continuous action (Pss 8; 19:1-6; 89:5-14; 104; 105:1-5; 136:1-9; 147; 148:1-10). Changing forms of species, with some dying away and others beginning through the mechanisms of evolving forms of life—not life itself, which begins with creation—may be seen as God's pattern "to bring biological diversity into being." Neither Genesis nor John describes these mechanisms. Rather, they affirm "God's immanent ongoing creative relationship with the whole universe, including its biological diversity" (Alexander and White: 98). The intent of Scripture is not to answer *how* in any scientific manner, but to stress the power of God's *word*, and to reveal that this *Logos*-Word became incarnate. This occurs with purpose: to shine God's glory into the world *[World, p. 538]* and lead to belief in Jesus as Messiah and Son of God.

John's Gospel is rightly called *The Gospel of Life*, the title of Beasley-Murray's book (1991). In the first part of John, Jesus' public ministry (John 1–12), the word *life* (*zōē*) occurs fifty times.

1:4b-5 *The Life Is Light for All, Shining in the Darkness*

The instrumentality of the *Logos* in creation continues in linking both life and light to the *Word's* creative work, echoing the Genesis narrative. When God speaks, "there was light" (1:3), and life came into being. God's *word* commands the earth to bring forth the vegetation (vv. 11-12). All sorts of *living* creatures in the heavens and on earth (1:20, 24) are created. The fourth evangelist speaks of life first, and the life then becomes the light of humankind. This light shines into the darkness (an echo perhaps of the "void and darkness" of Gen 1:2). However, in John both light and darkness not only describe the cosmological reality; they also comprise the moral dimension, human responses to the *Logos*-Creator (3:18-21; ch. 9).

Translations differ for the verb in the final clause of verse 5: *the darkness has not overcome it* [the light] (RSV, NRSV, NIV 2011), or *the darkness has not understood it* (NASB 1999; NIV 1984). The KJV also took the latter meaning: and *the darkness comprehended it not* (cf. NASB online revision). The Greek verb (*katelaben*) can mean either. The same verb occurs in 12:35, where both the RSV and NRSV translate it *overtake*. If the cosmological milieu is foremost, then *overcome* or *overtake* is better; if the moral-belief dimension is in view, then *understand* or *comprehend* is better. At this point in the unfolding narrative of the Gospel, the cosmological realm takes priority. But if we look back on the prologue from the Gospel narrative as a whole, with belief/unbelief as a major theme, then *understand* or *comprehend* fits the situation (cf. ch. 9 as a classic example).

So far in the prologue, however, we have not yet come to the historical plane, the incarnation of the Logos. Hence the portrait we gaze upon at this juncture is the *Logos*-Creator bringing forth life and shining light into the cosmological darkness. The darkness does not overcome or overtake the light, but the light keeps shining, always. The Word-*Logos* continuously pierces and dispels the darkness: *shine* appears surprisingly in the present tense—the first present tense in the book, expressing continuing action; *overcome* is a point action in past tense, yet it may also connote durative and culminating effect, which here applies. The light shines, eternally *[Light, p. 527]*.

John: Witness to the Light 1:6-8

The prologue now links the transcendent, metaphysical reality to the historical, bringing onto the narrative stage a witness to the light (Hooker: 357–58). John *appears* (*egeneto*, a form of the verb *ginomai*) de novo as witness to the light, with cosmological and moral connotation. The narrative has one noun and two verbs for *witness* (*martyria/martyreō*) [*Witness, p. 534*]. John is a *witness* and only a witness to the light. In this Gospel John is never called "the Baptist," even though his baptizing function is described in 1:28, 31; 3:23; 10:40 (cf. Mark 1:4; 6:14; Matt 3:11). Because this Gospel is known as John's Gospel and this witness is called John, we must distinguish the two. In this commentary "John the Witness" designates this John. Other than denoting John as witness, no word here from him or description about his diet or clothing is stated—quite different from the reports in the Synoptics (cf. the parallel portrait of John the Baptist in Mark 1:4-8!). The purpose of John's witness is stated: *so that all might believe through him.* This is the first hearing of the Gospel's purpose (20:30-31).

The True Light 1:9-11

1:9 Coming into the World[w]

The TNIV (contra NRSV) rightly puts verse 9 with 10-11. This is the first use of the term *world* in John, with three more occurrences in verse 10. It occurs next in verse 29: John the Witness identifies Jesus as *the Lamb of God who takes away the sins of the world!* [*World, p. 538*].

Verse 9 is difficult because it is not clear how three important assertions fit together. Following the Greek word order, it would read: *He was the true light, the one who enlightens all people, coming into the world.* Does *coming into the world* modify *light* or *people*? Grammatically it can be either. Most translations link it to *true light*, thus, *The true light was coming into the world.* Or does *coming into the world* modify *all people*? The KJV and Augustine (Beasley-Murray 1999: 6, 12) opt for *enlightening all people who come into the world.* This is good Quaker theology and may be correct. Beasley-Murray (12) bolsters this point by stating, "The expression 'all who come into the world' was common among Jews to denote everyone."

The *light coming* option expands the thought of verses 4b-5, which makes good sense. The light continues to shine, always, everywhere. It may thus anticipate verse 14, but it remains on the cosmological plane, a point Need passionately argues, dismayed at the tendency to move these poetic portions of the narrative into history before verse

14, when the *Logos* becomes flesh, entering into history. Drawing on Borgen's essays on the "true light" (1983), Boyarin (2001: 267) proposes that John 1:1-5 is a midrash, a "targumic" paraphrase on Genesis 1:1-5, and "the rest of the prologue is a tripartite expansion of this paraphrase, making clear that the midrash of the Logos is to be applied to the appearance of Jesus Christ." Written before Need's article, Boyarin (2001) would concur that the prologue remains on the cosmological, universal level until verse 14.

Opting for the *Logos enlightening all* [people] *who come into the world* does not mean that all people are saved, as the Gospel makes clear (3:19-21; 8:12; 9:1-4; 11:10; 12:36), though universal salvation is available for all (Volf 2008) *[Duality, p. 511]*. Some respond positively to the light, and some negatively (12:36-46) *[Belief, p. 504]*.

1:10-11 Two Rejections: The World and His Own[w]

Forms of *ginomai* (*become, bring into being*) occur three times in verse 3; *witness* (*martyria*) occurs three times in verses 7-8; and *world* (*kosmos*) occurs three times in verse 10. *World* occurs seventy-eight times in John's Gospel, but with different connotations: positive (3:16), neutral (8:26), and hostile—the greatest number of uses (cf. Burge 2000: 57). This verse contains all three connotations, determined by what is said or implied about the world: first, neutral—*He was in the world*; second, positive—*the world came into being through him*; and third, negative—*the world did not know him*. In the negative use the world opposes Jesus *[World, p. 538]*.

When verse 10 speaks of the cosmological, created world, with tacit reference to its people, does *the world did not know him* refer to all people not knowing God, similar to Paul's declaration in Romans 1:18-20? Or is it more specific, clarified in John 1:11: *He came unto his own, and his own did not receive him* (AT)? The NRSV and most modern translations supply the word *people*, tilting the meaning toward Israel, God's chosen people. O'Day says verse 10 refers to "the fate of the Word in the world" and verse 11 to the fate of the Word as it comes to "'his own people'—either Israel and the Jewish people or more broadly the very humanity who came into being through the Word but nonetheless 'did not receive him'" (1995: 521).

Some commentators blend *his own people* with humanity more broadly (e.g., O'Day 1995 and Burge 2000: 58). *His own* in verse 11 could mean *his own home* or *his own people*. Need argues for *his own home*, which in context is the creation he has made. He saves the pivotal turn of the Word's entry into history for the incarnation in verse 14: "Although there may be an element of ambiguity here, it seems that vv. 10 and 11 cannot yet refer to Jesus himself coming to Israel" (402). In John's later narrative, however, *his own* becomes specific: God's chosen people. The OT quotations in 12:38-40, summing up the people's response to Jesus' ministry, verify this view, which conforms to wider NT emphases, including Paul (cf. Rom 9–11).

God's Gift to Those Who Receive the Logos 1:12-13

1:12 Become Children of God

The eternal God-Logos, Creator, light shining in the darkness, waits to be received by *his own*. This is God's hospitality—God gives, but God also waits for us to receive the divine gift: *to all who received him, who believed in his name.* We believe in a person and receive a name. *We become children of God.* Culpepper observes the OT context of God's making Israel a loved son/child (e.g., Hos 11:1):

> The relationship is conceived of in legal and moral, rather than primarily physical, terms and carries with it the obligations and promises of the covenants with Abraham, Moses, and David. Israel, like a natural child, was subject to God to receive his teaching, and to enjoy his loving-kindness. By claiming the designation *tekna theou*, the Johannine community was identifying itself . . . [as standing within this tradition]. (2001: 78, transliteration supplied)

This new identity arises from God-Logos, who *gives* the *power* or *authority* to *become children of God. Becoming children of God* summarizes the Gospel's call to discipleship, a *communal* discipleship, since the *authority* to become God's children is given to *them* (cf. Howard-Brook 1994: 55–56). In the context of its original audience, this is the identity-gift of the Johannine community, a clear sense of being and living as children of God. Permeating 1 John as well, the theme denotes the believers' identity (3:1-2; 5:2) and contrasts that identity to *children of the devil* (3:10).

When this phrase is seen in the perspective of discipleship as explicated in 1 John, it becomes clear why this power and authority is needed: to live in the *world* as a new creation, desiring not the things of the flesh or darkness, but those things that mark the life of the Spirit (cf. John 3:18-21).

1:13 Born Not of the Human Will, but of God

Verse 13 presents a sharp contrast for the origin of this new identity: born not of blood or of the will of the flesh or of the will of man, but of God.

Blood (*haimatōn*), here in the genitive plural, echoes the founding and recurring bloodshed of humankind (R. Brown 1966: 12; Howard-Brook 1994: 56; see, e.g., Isa 5:7d; Mic 3:10; Hab 2:12; Hos 4:2; 1 Kings 2:5, 33; 2 Kings 9:7, 26), rooted in selfishness, jealousy, and greed. Cain's killing Abel is the founding murder of which Jesus speaks in Luke 11:49-51//Matt 23:34-35 (contra Girard; cf. Swartley 2000).

The *flesh*, as elsewhere in John, describes the earthly condition in contrast to the heavenly and the life-giving power of the Spirit (3:8-12; 6:63) *[Flesh, p. 516]*. *Will of man* (*anēr* used here instead of *anthrōpos*) may allude to virginal conception (cf. 8:41). But since the subject noun is *Word* in the prologue and not *Jesus*, it more likely denotes the human sphere and meshes with John's frequent contrast between seeking human glory or divine glory. *Born of God* means they are born "in co-filiation with the only begotten Son of God" (Eriugena, via Bamford: 108). The gift and reception of this inheritance is by God's grace and love, through *believing* in him whom God sent. This gift transforms Jesus' disciples from fleshly desires to Spirit-desires through heeding Jesus' word (cf. 6:63).

Word Made Flesh, Resplendent in Glory 1:14

1:14a Word Became Flesh

Verse 14 is pivotal in the Gospel's theological affirmation: *The Word became flesh and lived among us.* "Flesh here . . . [indicates] the full humanity which the divine Logos assumes, a humanity that is embodied and spirited" (Lee 2002: 34). The Word-*Logos* becoming (*ginomai*) *flesh* in verse 14 subtly contrasts to *flesh* in verse 13. While both uses refer to the human sphere, the first use excludes flesh as a generating power *to become children of God*. The second use in verse 14 includes flesh to denote the fully human condition into which Jesus descends. The term *dwell among us* (*skēnoō*) reflects the OT experience of God as dwelling among the people, with divine presence in the tent/tabernacle (*skēnē*).

> "And the word became flesh." God "pitched his tent." The consonants of the Greek word are those of the Hebrew word (*shekinah*) which denotes the presence and glory of God. The "tent of meeting" was where God dwelt with his people and where his glory was seen (Ex. 40:34-38). The same glory had filled the Temple of Solomon (I Kings 8:10f.). (Newbigin 1982: 8)

(Compare Ezek 11:22-23; Zech 2:10; Matt 17:4; and Luke 9:33.)

14b Glory, Full of Grace and Truth[w]

In her study of temple symbolism, Coloe (2001: 135–36) notes that God's glory-cloud filled the temple (1 Kings 8:4-11). But the *Logos* who is creation's life and light for all is now the "tabernacling" presence, God's Shekinah among the people (John 1:14).

Just as God's glory signified God's real presence in the tabernacle, so the *Logos*-become-flesh reveals God's glory, God's real presence among us (D. M. Smith 2002: 121). God's glory in Christ is the Revealer of God's own self. But the jolting claim is that this divine glory (*doxa*) is revealed in the flesh (*sarx*). The text does not say that *Logos* became a human (*anthrōpos*), nor a man (*anēr*), but *flesh*. Lee quotes Augustine to grasp the paradox: "Born, yet not born, carnal yet spiritual, weak yet strong, dying yet living" (2002: 34). God's glory is revealed in and dwells in the flesh—what a paradox! C. K. Barrett asserts, "The paradox . . . runs through the whole gospel: the *doxa* is not to be seen alongside the *sarx*, nor through the *sarx* as through a window; it is to be seen in the *sarx* and nowhere else" (1978: 165; cf. Gen 1:26-27; Dan 7:13-14). This is a radical claim for the full humanity of Jesus (Thompson 1988). In his homily on the prologue, Eriugena writes that *fullness of grace* "refers to the fullness of deification and of his sanctification as a human being." In *truth* Jesus fulfills the truth of the law and symbols of OT Scripture, so that the NT with Jesus at its center reveals fully that truth (in Bamford: 113).

The entire Gospel narrative reveals God's *glory* (17:22): "Jesus' life, teaching, and signs have been the revelation of the *doxa* of God. . . . The *doxa*, which is the love bestowed upon the Son by the Father, . . . is present in the human story in the *doxa* that Jesus has given to the believers" (Moloney 1998: 474). God's glory is fully unveiled "in his hour" at the cross, as 13:1-3 and 17:1-5 make clear. It is the *glory* of the cross, vindicated by the resurrection (cf. Motyer 2001: 92).

The verb that links the reader to glory is one of John's five *seeing* words (*theaomai*). The dramatic and symbolic elements are present in *theaomai*, which prepares for what is seen, *glory/doxa*. *We have beheld his glory* presupposes the narrative of Moses' request, "Show me your glory" (*kabod*, Exod 33:18).

The phrase, *the glory as of a father's only son*, introduces the term *monogenēs*, translated in the KJV as *only begotten son* (also in 3:16), or *the only Son from the Father* (RSV; *a father's only son*, NRSV). Here for the first time God-*Word* becomes Father-Son, the dominant designation throughout the Gospel. The *only Son* echoes the Isaac story (Gen 22) and points in anticipation to Jesus' manifesting glory in his death (cf. 17:1-5). In 1:1 *the Word was God*; in Father and Son a distinction is maintained, as well as by the word *as* (*hōs*), indicating that we do not behold the glory of the Father directly, but the Father's glory in the Son (Moloney 1998: 39) *[Glory, p. 516]*.

The final phrase, *full of grace and truth*, is certainly an echo of Exodus 34:6, referring to God's steadfast love (*ḥesed*, usually translated *charis/truth* in the LXX) and faithfulness (*'emet*, which may be translated *truth*). This coupling of *steadfast love* (*ḥesed*) and *faithfulness* (*'emet/'emunah*) occurs often in the OT (e.g., Pss 85:10; 89:14). Many interpreters regard Exodus 34:6 as the origin of this phrase in John 1:14 (Evans 1993a: 81n2). God's loving-kindness and faithfulness assure that God remains true to God's covenant promises, and sustains the covenant people now and forever. The *glory* of the *Logos* become flesh now incarnates these foundational attributes of God. In the only Son do we know God's unfailing love (*ḥesed*-grace) and faithful truth (*'emunah*).

Witness to the Word Made Flesh 1:15-17[w]

1:15 John's Witness

John enters the narrative, extending his role as witness, specified three times earlier in verses 7-8, and now again in verse 15. In addition he solemnly declares or cries out (*krazō*), *This was he of whom I said, "He who comes after me ranks ahead of me because he was before me."* The fourth evangelist's portrait of John lacks not only the designation *the Baptist*, but also the Baptist's eschatological judgment that we see in Matthew 3 and Luke 3. Rather, John's Gospel accentuates John's role as *witness*. *Witnessing* consists of drawing people to faith to *confess* Jesus' identity (1:20) and certifying Jesus' claims regarding his person and mission. Harris (39–48) amplifies the meaning of *witness* in John's usage by showing the scope of its voices:

- John (1:7-8, 15, 19, 32-34; 3:26, 32-33; 5:32, 36)
- the Samaritan woman (4:39)
- the Scriptures (5:29)
- the works of Jesus (10:25)
- the crowd (12:17)
- Jesus himself (3:11; 4:44; 7:7; 8:14, 18; 13:21; 18:37)
- God, concerning Jesus (5:36-37; 8:18)
- the Paraclete, concerning Jesus (15:26)

- disciples (15:27)
- the beloved disciple (19:35; 21:24)

Witness as verb occurs thirty-three times; as noun, fourteen times (Harris: 39; in the Epistles, ten and seven). The term signifies a *courtroom* ethos in John (Lincoln 2000).

Witness(ing) goes beyond *confessing identity* and *certifying identity*. It functions similar to *sign* (*sēmeion*), pointing beyond the *earthly* to the *heavenly*: John intends "the reader to understand by 'witnessing' any activity by and through which the heavenly character and origin of Jesus, his actions and his words, are communicated" (Harris: 48).

1:16-17 *Fullness: Grace upon Grace*

These two verses explicitly introduce Moses into the *Word-salvation* drama. The *fullness* is the fullness of God's grace and truth in the incarnate Son. The phrase *grace upon grace* (*charin anti charitos*) most likely refers to God's grace manifest in the Word-Son layered over God's grace given in the Torah, which means that the two clauses of verse 17 are not antithetical but in staircase parallelism. The word *upon*, *anti* in Greek, has a root meaning of "face-to-face," one layer facing another. It also means *instead of* in numerous NT uses. In atonement language *anti* never loses the relatedness of the two parties, that of the Redeemer with the redeemed (Mark 10:45). The law given through Moses is one layer of divine gift; the *grace and truth* that *came through Jesus Christ* is the layer over the earlier revelation. If we view the two clauses antithetically, we undermine Jesus' appeal to Moses as witness to himself (5:46).

The Incarnate Word, Revealing God 1:18[w]

Capping 1:1 and 14, John 1:18 declares John's bold and scintillating Christology and the Gospel as divine revelation. This grand declaration confronts us with a textual challenge in the Greek because manuscripts vary. In the second phrase, what goes with the adjective *only* (*monogenēs*)? Here are some versions:

- *the only begotten Son* (KJV)
- *the only Son* (RSV, NRSV margin)
- *the only God* (RSV margin, from some reliable early MSS)
- *God the only Son* (NRSV)
- *an only Son, God* (NRSV margin)

- *God the one and only* (NIV 1984)

- *the one and only Son, who is himself God* (TNIV, NIV 2011)

The manuscript evidence leans strongly toward *the only* (the pre-ferred translation for *monogenēs*) and *God* (*theos*) for the variant *[Textual Variants, p. 532]*. Both Talbert (77) and Burge (2000: 60–61) accept *God/theos* as the likely original "because the revealer is *theos/* divine (vv. 1, 18), he can make the Father known" (Talbert). The "explicit affirmation of Christ's divinity is likely original" (Burge 2000). Combining the two is a compromise.

The first declaration of the verse *No one has ever seen God* surely echoes Exodus 33:20 (cf. v. 23), "You cannot see my face, for a human cannot see my face and live" (trans. by Evans 1993a: 80). Evans (81) also notes that John's positioning Jesus in the Father's bosom (God's "front") and existing with God in eternity (1:1) contrasts to "Moses' fleeting glimpse of God's 'back.'" The greater *grace and truth* (echo-ing Exod 34:6) flow from the God-Son who uniquely can and does reveal God to humanity. No one, except this God-Son, "can see God and thus know him in his innermost life" (cf. 5:37; 6:46; Rossé: 37). Only this one is able to reveal God in God's divine fullness.

The *only God* (Word-Son), metaphorically located in *the bosom of the Father* (RSV), is rendered *close to the Father's heart* (NRSV) or *in clos-est relationship with the Father* (TNIV). The term *bosom* (*kolpos*) occurs only one other time in John, to denote the beloved disciple's reclining on Jesus' bosom (*kolpos*) at the Last Supper (13:23). Since the preposi-tion before *bosom* is the Greek *eis*, which indicates "motion toward," rather than *en* (connoting place or location), the phrase may be translated *The Son, turned toward the bosom of the Father*. Thus the Word eternally moves toward the Father (Rossé: 12n2). This emphasis pre-pares for Jesus' frequent claim in John that what he does and says accords with what the Father does and says. Further, this nuance prepares for Jesus' farewell discourse, where he speaks of going to his Father (14:1-2), culminating in his prayer, where he moves in spirit into the presence of his Father. The prologue and prayer may be viewed as bookends to the Son's intimacy with his Father.

The subject of the final clause is *that one*, followed by only one word, a verb meaning *declared, revealed,* or *exegeted* (the Greek is *exēgeomai*, from which we get the English word *exegesis*). The verb has no object, except perhaps by inference: *the story to follow*. By *being* the God-Son, Jesus reveals the Father by who he is and what he does. "By being himself, Jesus reveals the Father" (Rossé: 25). Jesus exegetes or reveals God. Moloney (1998: 47) renders it, "He has told God's story."

THE TEXT IN BIBLICAL CONTEXT

Genesis 1 and the Prologue[w]

The explanatory section for this chapter noted several connections between Genesis 1 and the prologue. Craig Evans (1993: 78) puts the numerous parallels, based upon the Septuagint version of Genesis, side by side in tabular format.

The parallels between these two texts are striking. Clearly the fourth evangelist intends to tell how the new creation story begins: by God's sending the Word into the world. Paul too speaks of Jesus Christ's work as "a new creation" (2 Cor 5:17). Ed Miller, in *Salvation History*, sees a fundamental theological link between the larger OT salvation story and John 1:3-4. The *Logos* as Life and Light permeates both (E. Miller: 8–11, 17–22, 84, 96, 109).

The Word, Jesus Christ, Agent of Creation[w]

John 1:3-4 is not the only NT text that speaks of Jesus Christ as the agent of creation. Other texts (Col 1:15-17; Heb 1:2-3a) declare the same. The first stanza of the Colossian hymn affirms Christ's supremacy over all creation in rank and time, for he is the "first-born of all creation" (v. 15) and "before all things" (v. 17). Furthermore, in Christ all things hold together. Using language from scientific physics to make the theological point, Christ is the ultimate "field of force" that holds all things together.

The text in Hebrews makes three arresting points. First, Christ who as God's agent "created the worlds" is the reflection of God's "glory," corresponding with John 1:14, *We have beheld his glory* (RSV). Second, the phrase "exact imprint of God's very being," is similar to John 1:1, *The Word was God*. Third, the Son-Creator "sustains all things by his powerful word." The *word* is the creative power, both *in the beginning* at the dawn of creation and in the continuing action of creation and redemption.

Furthermore, this inclusion of Jesus Christ in the divine identity as Creator implicitly affirms the preexistence of the Word, identified as God-Son in John 1:18. Three more NT texts make a similar claim as John 1, in addition to the two cited texts above: 1 Corinthians 8:6; Hebrews 1:10-12; Revelation 3:14 (here "the faithful and true witness" is the *origin* of creation). First Corinthians 8:6, the only text explicitly naming Jesus Christ, is especially striking since it shows a carefully formulated parallelism between God as creator and Jesus as creator:

> But to us there is but one God, the Father,
> of whom are all things, and we in him;
> and one Lord Jesus Christ,
> by whom are all things, and we by him. (KJV)

(Compare Rom 11:36, "For from him and through him and to him are all things.")

This text echoes Israel's Shema (*šemaʿ*): "Hear, O Israel: The Lord our God (*is*) one Lord" (Deut 6:4). Bauckham holds that Paul has arranged these words in synonymous parallelism to affirm that God the Father and the Lord Jesus Christ are/is one. Paul profoundly grasps Jesus Christ's identification with YHWH (Lord), the one God from the beginning, before the world was created (1998a: 37–38). Paul, a Jew (as was Jesus), repeated the Shema at least twice a day.

This interlocking of the Shema and its monotheism with the identity of Jesus Christ as included in God's identity shows that Jesus is one with God and God-Jesus is one. The divine identity of Jesus does not compete in any way with a robust monotheism. By linking Jesus to God's identity as Creator, Jesus is included within the divine cosmic sovereignty as creator and sustainer of the universe. This inclusion of Jesus Christ in the divine identity of Creator implicitly affirms the preexistence of Jesus Christ.

The Glory Drama of Scripture

Isaiah 40:5 expresses Israel's eschatological hope for God's glory to be revealed: "Then the glory of the Lord shall be revealed, and all people shall see it together, for the mouth of the Lord has spoken." The glory of the Lord is now revealed through the Logos, the only Son of the Father, Jesus Christ. This motif appears elsewhere as well: "But the earth will be filled with the knowledge of the glory of the Lord, as the waters cover the sea" (Hab 2:14; cf. Isa 11:9). The well-known text of Isaiah 6:1-8 hinges on the manifestation of God's glory, prompting Isaiah's confession of his unworthiness in the face of God's holiness and glory. This numinous encounter with God's Godness calls, sends, and empowers him for his ministry to a rejecting and obstinate people (6:9-11). Both Exodus and Isaiah often speak of God's glory, as do the Psalms. Glory appears prominently in OT Scripture in relation to three types of experience:

- God's saving deliverance of Israel from bondage (Exod 14:4; 16:6-12; 24:15-18; 33:17-23; 29:42-43; 40:34-38);

- In prophetic texts, in the call of the prophet (Isa 6:1-8; Ezek 1–3) and in oracles of eschatological hope (Isa 40:5; 42:8, 12; 60:1, 19; Ezek 43:2; Dan 7:14);

- In psalms of praise for God's sovereign majesty in creation power and rule as king (Pss 8; 24; 29; 72 [end of second Psalms book]; 96 [worship]; 104:31; 148:13).

With these psalms is the majestic exultation that is my favorite: "Be exalted, O God, above the heavens. Let your glory be over all the earth" (in Ps 57:5, 11). Psalm 108:4-5 adds: "Your steadfast love is higher than the heavens, and your faithfulness reaches to the clouds." God's steadfast love (*ḥesed*) and faithfulness (*'emet*), motifs in John 1:14, prompt the exclamation: "Be exalted, O God. . . . Let your glory be over all the earth."

Glory (*doxa*) is a visible manifestation of God's majesty, holiness, and power. Raymond Brown shows *glory's* frequency in various biblical books (1966: 503) [*Glory, p. 516*]. Second Corinthians 3:7-13 connects *glory* and *ministry*; 3:8, when put alongside John 1:14, describes the model of Jesus' ministry in the flesh: "How much more will the ministry of the Spirit come in glory?" The correlation of the two emphases comes with 1:14c, *We beheld his glory*, precisely in his fleshly, yet Spirit-empowered ministry. This strikes a pattern for us in our ministry: the two poles of *flesh* and *glory* dwell together! The last verse in 2 Corinthians 3 sets forth our goal of spiritual growth with *glory* imagery: "And all of us, with unveiled faces, seeing the glory of the Lord as though reflected in a mirror, are being transformed into the same image from one degree of glory to another; for this comes from the Lord, the Spirit" (3:18).

The Pauline benediction in Ephesians 3:21-22 views the church as the voice of "praise of [God's] glory," culminating in that recurring phrase in 1:12 and 14: "Now to him who by the power at work within us is able to accomplish abundantly far more than all we can ask or imagine, to him be glory in the church and in Christ Jesus to all generations, forever and ever. Amen." The choirs of Revelation continue the praise (5:11-13; 7:9-12; cf. 19:1-2, 6-7). The "slaughtered Lamb" who receives the glory is the Word-become-flesh in John's Gospel, lifted up to draw/save all people through belief in Jesus the Christ, Son of God.

THE TEXT IN THE LIFE OF THE CHURCH

Creation: Life and Light[w]

Much discussion of John's prologue focuses on *the Word*, and rightly so. But the theme of creation with its generation of life and light is also important. "Light and life are the keys John uses in this great song of faith; they are the primary colors in this stunning portrait" (Card: 4). *Glory and fullness* parallel *creation, life,* and *light*. Where the glory of the Lord shines, life abounds. "The eschatological goal, the essence of salvation, according to the Fourth Gospel, is . . . eternal life" (D. M. Smith 1995: 149). Glory complements God's creation light. Light proceeds from God, and it is *good* (Gen 1:3-4). Indeed the prologue leans toward the Trinity (discussed in the Web supplement).

Source of Spirituality in Symbol, Song, and Art

Hope always draws the soul from the beauty which is seen to what is beyond,
always kindles the desire for the hidden through what is constantly perceived.
Therefore, the ardent lover of beauty,
although receiving what is always visible as an image of what he desires,
yet longs to be filled with the very stamp of the archetype.
—Gregory of Nyssa (Nes: inside cover)

"To inquire about John's theology is like asking about the meaning of a symphony. The meaning, Beethoven would say, is not in talking about it but in listening to it. In the case of the gospel, the meaning lies in living it" and experiencing *restful union* with God through Jesus Christ (Brodie: 55). The mystery of the prologue, with its images of light and darkness, flesh and glory, stirs the imagination, leading into the meditative and contemplative. Its symbolism connects with people of all ages, in personal development and throughout time. It provides a resource for women and men to reflect on their spiritual journeys. It invites all people to participate in the life of the *Word*, who tents among us.

Light plays a major role in art, and in some depictions the path to God is through Christ as Light. The iconography of the Eastern Orthodox Church features light with great intention in the halos that surround the head of Jesus, on whom God's favor rests. Often this is true in the illuminations of crèches. In one such scene there is written along the side of the crib, "And the Word became flesh and lived among us" (Nes: 31). In Jaroslav Pelikan's collection, *The Illustrated Jesus Through the Centuries*, one is hard pressed to find an art piece that does not reflect light. If not directly surrounding Jesus' head, light sometimes seems to come from his very face, or in more subtle exposures, it beams through a window (130). Rembrandt's dramatic use of light and darkness (chiaroscuro) has Jesus shine in darkness, the only subject matter of the canvas.

Through its symbolism, its high Christology, and its hope for humanity, the prologue has been a rich source for worship music. *Hymnal: A Worship Book* lists thirteen hymns based on this text. The author of "O Come, All Ye Faithful" apparently sees this text as a "birth narrative" as he combines Bethlehem with "True God of true God, Light of light eternal, . . . Word of the Father . . . ." Martin Luther offers us "Savior of the Nations, Come!" an advent hymn declaring that Jesus "was the Word of God made flesh, woman's offspring, pure and fresh" (*HWB*: 212, 173, 882 [index]).

Since the prologue is intertextually related to Genesis 1, the moving narration "Creation" by James Weldon Johnson, evokes the God-Logos-Word power of both creation and new creation in John's Gospel prologue.

The Prologue as Doxological Theology[w]

John's prologue has inspired art, poetry, and music. Naturally so, for it is poetic, laced with rich metaphors. Even the John the Witness sections contribute to the genre, for he functions as witness, testifying doxologically to the Word as coming and come into the world. Witness, from beholding his *glory* (*doxa*), is an act of contemplation (Lindars 1957: 26). The *fullness of grace and truth* is the gift of contemplative *seeing* (*theaomai*, 1:14). In trying to enter the mind of John, Lindars (1957: 23) says, "I had the overwhelming impression that the figure of Christ was always there in his imagination, static and yet full of life, containing in himself the whole Gospel." John *sees* the rich symbolism, whether *Logos*, the *I AM* self-claims, living water, bread of life, the door, the vine, the beloved disciple. The language of the Gospel is metaphorical. The prologue does not give us a scientific description of how the Word created all things. Rather, it invites us to contemplate the Word as Creator in much the same way that the psalmist contemplates the place of the human in the vastness of the universe: "What are human beings that you are mindful of them, mortals that you care for them? Yet you have made them a little lower than God [or "angels"], and crowned them with glory and honor" (Ps 8:4-5).

Creation, as wonderful as it is, is not the object of worship; rather, the Creator, the Word, is the Person worthy of worship. In contemplating that the *Word was God*, became *flesh*, and uniquely *reveals God*, we glimpse the glory, grace, and truth of John's world of contemplative seeing. This *seeing* is knowledge of God that sets humans in right relationship to the created order, as caring stewards of the earth and all that is in it. It leads us to appreciate its beauty, to value the land and not exploit it, and to treasure all living creatures in their infinite varieties of species, sizes, shapes, sounds, and role in the ecological web of life.

It sets the stage also for comprehending the significance of scientific knowledge, the two hundred billion stars in our Milky Way galaxy, and the more than one hundred billion galaxies flung in space beyond our own (Gingerich: 27). The human being is also a wonder of wonders, with DNA codes and brains with unbelievable complexity: "The number of synaptic interconnections in a single human brain vastly exceeds the number of stars in our Milky Way: 10^{15} synapses versus about 10^{11} stars" (Gingerich: 30).

Wonder of all wonders is that the *Word*, God's agent to create all things, became incarnate to *reveal* God, whom no one has ever seen (1:18), and restore soul communion of believers with the Father's-Son's "mutual indwelling" (John 17:20-24). The prologue leaps the great gap between Creator and creature. It beckons us to hear the Gospel in wonder and worship, akin to Revelation with its liturgical choirs of praise. In John's Gospel the Son is coeternal with, and ever turns toward the Father, the twenty-twenty lens for the Gospel's story. *Believers* become *children of God*, born of the Spirit to be in union with the Son and the Father. Thus *knowing* Jesus' identity is exultation of Jesus, by faith *seeing* God in Jesus' words and signs.

Part 1

Acceptance and Rejection: The First Passover

You are my *witnesses*, says the Lord,
and my servant whom I have chosen,
so that you may *know* and *believe* me
and understand that *I am he* ["I AM"].
—Isaiah 43:10, emphasis added

John 1:19–2:12

A Week of New Creation

PREVIEW

How do people come to faith? My brother Henry, who began four church plants—long before that term was used—had his unique way. After a first casual meeting with someone, he would call on them in their homes, carrying along board games to play. Soon into the conversation he would suggest playing a game, if they had time. Often they became friends and continued their friendship by becoming part of the church. John's account of disciples gathering around Jesus largely through friends' witnessing to their friends is so unlike the Synoptic Gospels' portrait of Jesus calling disciples, "Follow me."

John 1:19-51 focuses on Jesus' gathering of disciples. Why include the wedding at Cana? The wedding at Cana appears to be a new topic, part of a new unit. But the time structure of this portion of the Gospel argues for treating it as one whole. The narrative is punctuated by three uses of *the next day* and then a *third day* structure that adds up to a seven-day, one-week structure. The wedding culminates the first week of Jesus' ministry, as did the Sabbath in the creation story (Gen 1:1–2:4). John 1:19-28 is Day 1; *the next day* is introduced in verse 29, another in 35, then one in 43, making Days 2-4. The wedding thus occurs on *the third day* (2:1) *after* the four days in chapter 1. Thus I title this unit "A Week of New Creation."

The subthemes of this new creation are these:

- John is *witness* to Jesus.

- Jesus is hailed with an astounding range of christological titles.

- Jesus gathers disciples—the formation of a new community.

- Jesus is the "new dwelling" or "meeting place" that "shows forth" (cf. *exēgeomai* in 1:18) God's glory, grace, and truth among humans.
- Jesus becomes the wedding host who changes water into tasty wine.

This first section discloses Jesus' rich christological identity, both messianic and divine. It also portrays what it means to encounter Jesus or to be encountered by him. The first disciples come to *know* and *see* who he is, then follow him. The climax of this unit is the wedding wine, the first *sign* (2:11) that *reveals* Jesus' *glory,* and his disciples' *believing* in him.

OUTLINE

John's Role in Relation to Jesus (Day 1), 1:19-28
John's Witness to Jesus' Identity and Work (Day 2), 1:29-34
John's Disciples Follow Jesus, the Lamb of God (Day 3), 1:35-42
Jesus Finds More Disciples (Day 4), 1:43-51
Jesus Turns Water into Wine in Cana (Day 7), 2:1-12

EXPLANATORY NOTES

The Structure and Christology of This Section[w]

Here I combine Jesus' gathering of disciples with their christological confessions:

A The Baptist *witnesses* to Jesus (1:19-39): *Behold, the Lamb of God.*
    B Andrew *finds* Simon (1:40-41): *We have found the Messiah.*
        C Jesus *changes* Simon's name to Peter (1:42).
    B´ Philip *finds* Nathanael (1:43-45): fulfills Moses and the
        Prophets; son of Joseph.
A´ Nathanael *witnesses* to Jesus (1:46-51): *You are the Son of God, . . .*
King of Israel!
        C´ Jesus *changes* water into wine: wedding (Day 7).

The center of this chiasm and the *sign* in Cana announce that *change* comes with Jesus. The unit refocuses Jesus as God's agent in creation: Jesus creates a disciple band and changes water into wine. *New, new, new* marks John's Gospel beginnings—and much of the

---

w   Where the superscript w occurs after headings, please see the commentary's online Web Supplement for additional material. Go to: http://www.heraldpress.com/bcbc/john.

Gospel. Jesus' changing Simon's name to Peter (Rock) and his changing of water into wine occur through his spoken word, so that his
work as Word-*Logos* continues. The Genesis theme of creation continues in this first week of Jesus' activity as the Incarnate One, come
in flesh to live among humans and bring new life.

The chapter 1 portion combines discipleship and Christology.
The christological disclosures of Jesus are as prominent as the discipleship emphases. Here lies the key to this unit: Jesus' unfolding
identity is inextricably intertwined with discipleship. It is important to see in this unit the revealing of Jesus' identity through confessional responses of Jesus' first followers (cf. Brodie: 146–47). The
connection of christological *confession* to *seeing, knowing,* and *following* Jesus is also important. Christology and discipleship are one
whole in gospel revelation, as elsewhere emphasized (Swartley
1981/1999: 137–57; 2006a: 100–112).

The range of christological titles in this unit is unsurpassed by
any other one chapter in the entire NT, as Burge 2000 also notes
(80). These are *Messiah* (vv. 20, 41), *the prophet* (v. 21), *Lamb of God* (v.
29, 36), *chosen* (*Son*) *of God* (v. 34), *Rabbi/Teacher* (vv. 38, 49), *Christ/
Anointed one* (v. 41), *Nazarene* (v. 45), *Son of God* (v. 49), *King of Israel* (v.
49), and *Son of Man* (v. 51) [*Christology, p. 507*].

With such an array of titles from those encountering Jesus, witness is strategic to this section. The *sign* at Cana extends that witness. Even his mother functions in the narrative as witness to his
miracle-working power. Viewing the narrative as onstage, we see
witnesses again and again—in people, speech, works, and signs! The
entire narrative witnesses to Jesus' glory and christological identity.

Numerous scholars see other structural patterns in early John.
Some include in this unit the cleansing of the temple. Another
extends it to include John 3, and another through John 4. In light of
these varied perceptions, all cogent in at least one respect or more,
one must conclude that John's Gospel shows great literary skill in
weaving together motifs and literary strands that produce an artful
narrative of many delights.

John's Role in Relation to Jesus (Day 1) 1:19-28

1:19-23 John's Identity

Three emphases appear in 1:19 that riddle the entire Gospel: *witness* (*martyria*); the Jews in Jerusalem; and *Who are you?* In the next
paragraph John testifies to Jesus as the Gospel's first witness. This
paragraph focuses on the other two motifs. *The Jews,* who send

priests and Levites to inquire about Jesus' identity, want to know how John understands himself *["The Jews," p. 520]*. The angle of questioning represents messianic curiosity, perhaps for fear that the awesome *kairos* (time fulfillment) of history is now come. John simply says, *I am not the Messiah.* Then follows a question about the expected messianic forerunner: *Are you Elijah?* Again John says *No.* They then ask, *Are you the prophet?* the expected figure coming to announce the Messiah's coming. John's response? A third *No!* Then they ask, *Who are you?*

After three negative responses, John defines his role as *the voice of one crying in the wilderness* with the message *Make straight the way of the Lord.* Two points are important: John diminishes his role and magnifies the One his *voice* announces. He calls the leaders to come to terms with this coming One. Second, when John's Gospel was written, a significant group of the followers of John the Witness regarded *him* as Messiah. John's Gospel refutes those claims, here and every time John the Witness reappears.

John's denial that he is either Elijah (Mal 4:5) or *the prophet* (cf. Deut 18:15-19)—figures expected in the end-time sequence of events before the Messiah comes—appears to conflict with the Synoptic Gospels. In Matthew 11:14 Jesus says that John *is the Elijah who is to come.* In Luke 7:26 Jesus identifies John as *a prophet* and even *more than a prophet,* though *a* prophet is not necessarily *the* prophet. Commentators resolve this dilemma various ways:

- Jesus knew John's actual role better than John himself did, or the Gospels' authors simply had differing points of view regarding John's role (Marsh: 122). Neither of these fully satisfies.

- The discrepancy is best explained by understanding "that John was fulfilling the forerunner's *role* of Elijah" (cf. "with the spirit and power of Elijah," Luke 1:17) but "denies that he is Elijah who has returned to earth" (Burge 2000: 72).

- The precision of John's testimony is important: *He confessed and did not deny it,* but *confessed* "is an indication that the right confession of messiahship will be important to the right understanding of the identity of both the Baptist and Jesus" (Moloney 1998: 52). Further, his vigorous denial that he is not one of the expected precursor figures, *I am not* (*ouk eimi,* v. 21), prepares the way for Jesus' later—and only Jesus' rightful—claim, *I AM* (4:26, et al.; Moloney 1998: 52; Freed 1979: 288–89) *["I AM," p. 518].*

Burge's view resolves the contradiction, whereas Moloney explains *why* a contradiction appears to exist, as the fourth evangelist's effort to delegitimize John's disciples. They should leave John and follow Jesus, as 1:35-40 testifies. Marsh does not take into account the problem of John's disciples.

John's positive statement of self-identification fully concurs with the Synoptic Gospels: *I am the voice of one crying out in the wilderness, make straight the way of the Lord* (cf. Mark 1:3; Matt 3:3; Luke 3:4). John thus sees himself as fulfilling prophet Isaiah's eschatological call, to prepare *the way of the Lord*! Having diminished his own self in the end-time scheme, he accentuates the work of the coming One by linking the messianic hope to the *way of the Lord*. This is a significant messianic disclosure. (Isaiah's "way" prophecy informed Qumran's messianic end-time hope also, in 1QS 8.14.) In John the phrase also identifies Jesus with the title *the Lord* or designates God's own coming as Lord in Jesus the Messiah, or both!

1:24-28 John's Baptizing and Why

The text now says the *Pharisees* sent the inquiring delegation, but in verse 19 it was *the Jews*. Pharisees are interchanged later also with *the Jews* (7:32, 35, 40 [*they* refers back to *the Jews* of v. 35 and likely also to the Pharisees of v. 32], 45; 9:13-18) [*"The Jews," p. 520*]. Since the Witness refuses identity with any of the expected end-time messianic precursors, the *priests and Levites* (1:19) press the question *Why are you baptizing?* John's answer contrasts his status with that of *the one standing among you whom you do not know* (AT)—a verb with a double meaning. In John *knowing* functions parallel to *believing*, and thus here represents more than simply cognitive awareness. It points to knowledge that leads to belief. John says he baptizes with water, and he is unworthy even to untie this coming One's sandals, intimating his lower-than-slave position.

The Gospel locates John's baptismal activity at Bethany beyond (east of) the Jordan (v. 28; cf. 3:26; 10:40). This detail is not in the other three Gospels. While the location of this Bethany is not certain, it has been traditionally identified as about five miles northeast of the Dead Sea (cf. von Wahlde 2010: 2.39).

John's Witness to Jesus' Identity and Work (Day 2) 1:29-34

1:29 Lamb of God Taking Away the Sin of the World[w]

On this second day we hear and see only John and Jesus. John's identification of Jesus is mind-boggling. John's distinctive description of Jesus' person and work casts the Gospel's main character into sharp relief. John first introduces *Jesus* in verse 29 (the name *Jesus* does not occur in the prologue). John introduces Jesus by acclaiming him *Lamb of God*.

To identify Jesus as *Lamb of God* could situate Jesus within any one of three traditions (Talbert: 81): the Exodus paschal lamb (12:1-11); the slain Lamb of Revelation, who conquers evil in the world (5:9; 7:17; 17:14); or the sacrificial lamb (Isa 53:7-12; cf. Gen 22:8). But John's identification is more precise: *the Lamb of God who takes away the sin of the world!* To identify John's acclaim of Jesus as echoing the paschal lamb involves a mismatch of terms: John's *amnos* for Lamb does not match the traditional *pascha* for the Passover lamb (cf. 1 Cor 5:7). The Lamb (*arnion*) in Revelation signifies the martyr tradition (Johns: 140–204).

John's acclaim, however, may refer to the Passover Lamb (Exod 12:1-3), not as sacrifice for sins but as a symbol of deliverance and liberation (e.g., O'Day and Hylen: 30). *Sin* in verse 29 is singular, not plural, as it is in later Christian eucharistic liturgies. The singular denotes "the world's collective alienation from God" (30). Sacrifices for human sins (pl.) required a goat, sheep, or bull (Lev 4–5), not a lamb. The *lamb* commemorated Israel's deliverance from slavery in Egypt. Jesus thus comes as light and life to reclaim the world from its alienation, its sin. This means that John the Witness identifies Jesus as the Savior and Deliverer of the world, who has come from God to restore the world to God.

If one seeks connection between *amnos* in John 1:29, 36 and antecedents in the Greek Septuagint, the most likely text is Isaiah 53, which uses *amnos* in Isaiah 53:7b for *lamb* in parallel to *sheep*: "like a lamb that is led to the slaughter, and like a sheep that before its shearers is silent, so he opened not his mouth" (the LXX reverses *lamb* and *sheep*, but NRSV follows the Hebrew). Further, in the larger text, Isaiah 53:4-12, *sins* (pl., *hamartias*) occurs seven times (vv. 4, 5, 6, 10, 11, 12 [2x]). In this Isaiah 53 portrait of the lamb, the emphasis clearly falls on God's accepting the lamb as a sacrificial atonement for sin (cf. 1 John 2:2; 4:10). Jesus is the Lamb (*amnos*) that gives his life for sinners, thus pouring "out himself to death" and bearing "the sins of many" (Isa 53:12). In so doing Jesus *is the Lamb of God who takes away the sin of the world.* John likely draws upon both traditions, Isaiah 53 and Exodus 12, since John 19:14, 31 connects Jesus' death to that of the Passover lamb (Lincoln 2005: 113; John 19:33, 36 also speaks of Jesus' legs not broken, thus echoing the stipulations of the Passover lamb in Exod 12:46). This early identification of Jesus anticipates the well-known salvation offer of John 3:16-17. Jesus is God's salvation gift to the world (cf. John 6:51c).

1:30-33 John's Witness: I Saw the Spirit Light on Him; He Will Baptize in the Holy Spirit

John's witness to Jesus as the Lamb who saves from sin is now expanded to connect with the prologue's preexistent Word: [He] *ranks ahead of me because he was before me* (30b). Further, John does not know him except by revelation. In a repeated statement *I did not know him* (31, 33), John points to the Spirit's descent upon Jesus as God's signal to him: thus John did not have *special* knowledge to recognize Jesus. Rather, the Spirit's descent points out to him that this is the One who will baptize with the Holy Spirit.

The point is twofold. John baptizes with water for repentance of sin; Jesus baptizes with the Holy Spirit. This baptism will put within humans a new heart and a new spirit, in the language of Ezekiel's eschatological hope for the coming messianic gift (36:26-27; 37:14; and 34:26 in the figurative "showers of blessing"). Similar messianic anticipations are voiced elsewhere also (Isa 32:15 and renewal in a general sense in Ps 104:30). First then, is the categorical distinction between John's and Jesus' baptisms. Second, John gives a reason for baptizing Jesus, *that he might be revealed to Israel* (1:31c). This reason is different from that in Matthew, which is to *fulfill all righteousness* (Matt 3:15c). Each purpose identifies an aspect of what Jesus' baptism signifies, carrying forward each author's Gospel's emphasis: John, Jesus as divine revealer; Matthew, Jesus as *fulfillment* of God's righteousness (Matt 5:17).

In 1:32 John witnesses to seeing the Spirit descend from heaven and remain on him (Jesus): *I saw the Spirit descending from heaven like a dove, and it remained on him. I myself did not know him, but the one who sent me to baptize with water said to me, "He on whom you see the Spirit descend and remain is the one who baptizes with the Holy Spirit."* This is John's witness to the Spirit's anointing of Jesus. It contrasts to the Synoptic accounts where John baptizes Jesus. John's Gospel says no such thing and thus undermines the Witness's followers' belief that John is superior to Jesus. Instead, John witnesses to Jesus' anointing by God as the Holy Spirit descends upon and remains on Jesus. The word for remain is *menō*, which occurs in chapter 15, translated there as *abide*. Verse 33 repeats the descending and abiding (*menō*) of verse 32, making this the crucial point in identifying the one who baptizes with the Holy Spirit and who is the Son of God (1:34). This early use of *remain* or *abide* strikes a key motif of John's Gospel, anticipating the unique "mutual indwelling" of Father and Son (Coloe 2001; cf. Thompson 2001: 230–40).

John's account of the Spirit's descent upon Jesus differs from that of the Synoptics. John the Witness does not baptize Jesus, since that would conflict with the subordinate role into which the fourth evangelist puts John. Rather, John's Gospel narrates the Spirit's descent on Jesus as a report of a past event, to which he now bears witness. In Mark, the event of the Spirit's descent upon Jesus is narrated as it happens, as part of a baptism scene, with Jesus (and the readers) hearing the voice from heaven declaring Jesus to be Son of God, in whom God is well pleased. In Mark, baptism calls Jesus to his mission of declared Son. In John's Gospel, the voice of John witnesses to God's anointing of Jesus with the Holy Spirit.

1:34 Son of God

In the fourth Gospel John speaks from the witness stand, *I have seen and have borne witness* (RSV). John declares a theological truth to which history bows: Jesus *is the Son of God*. In Mark 1:11 God's voice declares this truth, and no human in the narrative declares it until 15:39, when the centurion confesses, "Truly, this man was the Son of God" (KJV; *the* connotes *very* here since the text is anarthous, which while it could mean "*a* Son of God," rather denotes essence, as in John 1:1, *was* [*very* or *truly*; not *a*] *God*). Christologically, John begins where Mark ends. Jesus begins his mission in the world fully disclosed not only as God's Son, but even as the Word coexistent with God from the beginning (John 1:1-5).

If the purpose of the Gospel's Day 1 presentation of John is to set the record straight regarding his preparatory role in relation to Jesus, Day 2 makes it clear that John's role is eclipsed by Jesus who, empowered by God's Spirit and declared God's Son, will now carry forward God's mission in the world. This mission will be revelation and salvation, grounded in the Spirit's power and the Son's authority. Baptizing with the Spirit will open the new messianic era in which the old becomes new—in people and practices.

John's Disciples Follow Jesus, the Lamb of God (Day 3) 1:35-42

1:35-37 John Points His Disciples to Jesus[w]

The opening scene of this day presents John as standing (tense is of past completed durative action) with two disciples onstage, waiting for the action. It happens: Jesus walks by, and John exclaims,

Look, here is the Lamb of God! As if programmed, the disciples, upon hearing this, switch from following John to following Jesus. While John's primary role is to *witness* to Jesus, he also functions in this Gospel to authorize his disciples to follow Jesus, a point of import in the first century since John's (the Witness's) disciples continued as a group, with some living even today in southern Iraq, Iran, Syria, and Jordan.

The *standing* with John now ends when the two disciples follow Jesus after they hear John's declarative *the Lamb of God*. Here is the Gospel's first catechism in discipleship. Standing ends, motion begins. With the motion of following, learning also begins. Typical in John's Gospel, believing and doing are linked. Once following begins, believing shortly follows, as it does in these opening scenes.

1:38-40 The Two Disciples Follow and Remain with Jesus

Jesus' direction also changes. Sensing, or even *knowing*—a key motif in John—those behind him, he turns and sees the two disciples following. So Jesus asks them, in his first spoken word in John, *What are you looking for?* The disciples address Jesus as *Rabbi*, meaning honored religious teacher, and query, *Where are you staying?* or literally, *Where do you dwell* or *abide [menō]?* Jesus answers, *Come and see.* They are delighted and do just that, for here potentially could begin—and actually does, as it turns out—the customary rabbi-discipleship relationship, in which "living with" and "learning from" is the model of spiritual formation. They *saw where he was staying, and they remained with him that day.* The word *remained (menō)* matches the last word of verse 38, *Where do you live [stay or abide]?* This is the second double use of this word in this unit (see vv. 32, 33). It alerts us to one of John's spiritual motifs and connects to 1:14, where the divine Word comes to dwell among us.

The time, tenth hour of the day in Greek (4:00 p.m.), perplexes. Since a new day begins at sundown in Jewish reckoning, it may be, as Talbert takes it (82), that the two inquirers stay with Jesus for Day 4, and that 1:43 begins Day 5. This would put the Cana miracle on Day 8 instead of 7 (a Syriac textual variant reflects this view by inserting *early in the morning* at the beginning of v. 41). My outline follows the seven-day structure.

Since the Greek word for *remain (menō)* is used also in John 15 for branches *abiding* in the vine, much is packed into these terse sentences. From the first glimpse of discipleship in John, *following* takes on the distinctive Johannine *union* with the disciple-believers linked to Jesus, as vine to branch.

Of these two disciples who leave John and join Jesus, Andrew is named and the other is unnamed. Andrew is introduced as Simon Peter's brother. The unnamed disciple *may* or may *not* be *the other disciple* we meet later in John (18:15; 20:2; cf. 21:2d) and who in 20:2 is identified as the disciple Jesus loved, linking him to the beloved disciple.

1:41-42 Simon Peter Follows; Jesus Renames Him

In the next scene, John is no longer in the narrative. Andrew finds his brother Simon to declare to him an astounding discovery: *We have found the Messiah.* Andrew and his partner ask Jesus, *Where do you dwell* Given John's theology on *dwelling* (1:14; 14:2), this is important. Similarly, *remaining* with Jesus to *see* and *know him* is also a key motif of the Gospel.

The newly declared followers of Jesus dialogue with Jesus. The narrator portrays Andrew as a witness to Jesus. Andrew is the Gospel's first missionary. Here he does what he will later also do: bring people to Jesus (6:8-9; 12:22). *We have found* is a fervent testimony to what Andrew discovered by *abiding* with Jesus for some time. Now is the awesome moment: the long-awaited Messiah, the One anointed by God, has come to us and now may be seen with our eyes and touched with our hands (cf. 1 John 1:1).

Andrew brings his brother to Jesus. Jesus looks intently at this new inquirer and immediately enlists him with a new identification. Although *You are Simon Son of John*, you are now called *Cephas*, the Aramaic word (*kepha*) for the Greek *petra*, meaning rock. In his Gospel paraphrase, Clarence Jordan identifies Peter as *Rock Johnson!* A certain irony regarding Peter's role emerges in John's Gospel, for it differs from that in the Synoptic Gospels. John's Gospel is the most explicit in narrating Jesus' changing Simon's name to Peter, which signals for him a leading role in Jesus' mission. While Peter is a leading disciple throughout John's Gospel, he is subordinated to the beloved disciple, who never receives a proper name but is the model disciple in chapters 13–21. And although Simon is now *Peter*, a rock, will he be a rock in his following Jesus? Will Peter be truly Peter? With the exception of *Simon Peter's* confession in 6:68, Peter's narrative role as *Rock* is compromised. The significance of his new name is suspended until 21:15-17, when Jesus again addresses him as Simon, looping back to this, the moment of their first encounter. Only as he is restored in 21:18-19 does it become clear that Peter will truly be a *Rock*.

Naming or renaming someone carries great significance in Scripture, as OT stories often illustrate: God changes Jacob (meaning "he clutches" his brother's heel; Burge 2000: 76) to Israel (Gen 32:28). Hosea and Isaiah name their children to signify the prophets' message to Israel (Hos 1:4-6; Isa 8:3; cf. 7:3). The children's names disclose the meaning of impending events. Jesus renames Simon to Peter to signify his role in Jesus' mission, despite his failings.

On this third day, a new community emerges with Jesus as magnet. While Andrew plays a significant role in bringing his brother Simon to Jesus, and Peter is renamed *Rock*, we learn nothing about the unnamed disciple. The Gospel shrouds his identity and role in mystery. Why does the narrator tease us with this unknown figure? Is this disciple unnamed because he plays an insignificant role in the story, or is this a deliberate gap to arouse suspense for what unfolds later in the Gospel? Is this John's technique, analogous to Mark's secrecy: concealing and revealing simultaneously? We may think we know the answer, but the answer may not be exactly what we think! Here begins one of the Gospel's puzzles.

Jesus Finds More Disciples (Day 4) 1:43-51

1:43-45 Jesus Calls Philip to Follow; He Finds Nathanael

While Days 2 and 3 are not located geographically, Day 4 is. Jesus decides to go to Galilee, the location for the rest of this unit. Jesus takes the initiative to look for more disciples. He finds Philip, who is from Bethsaida (v. 44a), Andrew's and Peter's hometown. But it is Jesus, not Andrew, who finds Philip and then tersely calls him, *Follow me*. Jesus calls only Philip with the standard master-disciple call, "Follow me." Philip follows and immediately finds another person, Nathanael, to whom Philip dares to say, *We have found him about whom Moses in the law and the prophets wrote, Jesus son of Joseph from Nazareth*. Swiftly the narrative moves from three to five followers, with Philip the only one whom Jesus himself calls. The other four are the fruit of John's, Andrew's, and Philip's witness. Little wonder that this portion of Scripture is often used, and rightly so, to motivate people to invite friends and neighbors to follow Jesus!

In 1:45 Philip describes Jesus' most complete earthly credentials in the Gospel. We learn that Jesus comes from Nazareth. And we learn that Jesus is the son of Joseph. This information prepares the reader for narrative comments in 7:27 and 41. Philip's declaration attests to Jesus' earthly abode, a key point in assessing this Gospel's portrait of Jesus, both divine and human (Thompson 1988; contra Käsemann: 44–45). However, the information about Jesus' paternal father, hometown, and ministry in Galilee is meager compared to that in Matthew and Luke. Rather, to understand that Jesus' origin is *from above*—a contested issue in Jesus' debates with the Jews—is to *know* Jesus in John. Philip reappears in crucial roles later in the Gospel: expressing concern regarding enough food to feed the multitude of five thousand (6:5-7); receiving the Greeks who want to see Jesus (12:21-22); and saying during Jesus' farewell, *Lord, show us the Father, and we will be satisfied* (14:8-9).

1:46-48 Jesus and Nathanael Spar to Know One Another

Nathanael's response to Philip is low key, with a dubious inference, *Can anything good come out of Nazareth?* Philip's response repeats what Jesus said to the first inquirers from John's followers, *Come and see.* The personal encounter, the relational dimension, is all-important in the rabbi-disciple bonding. Jesus' word about Nathanael, spoken declaratively for all to hear as Nathanael approaches him, totally disarms Nathanael's skepticism. Jesus' word astounds: *Here is truly an Israelite in whom there is no deceit [guile, KJV]!* The character description takes on depth and punch as the encounter unfolds and climaxes with an unambiguous allusion to the Jacob story in the OT (v. 51). If Jacob typified cunning guile and deception in relation to his father, brother, and uncle, Nathanael's character contrasts sharply.

Stunned, Nathanael queries, *Where did you get to know me?* Jesus replies, *I saw you under the fig tree before Philip called you.* "So what?" our modern mind asks. *Under the fig tree* may be descriptive of Nathanael's character, true to the meaning of his name, "gift of God." The fig tree image in Judaism connotes shalom, meditating on and keeping the law, eschewing evil and doing good (1 Kings 4:25; Mic 4:4; Zech 3:10). Hence Jesus' *seeing* Nathanael under the fig tree connotes quality of religious character, exemplary of a true Israelite, one who seeks to *see* God and do God's will.

1:49 Nathanael Comes to Know Jesus (Rabbi, Son of God, King of Israel)

Nathanael rises to the challenge, confessing Jesus to be not only *Rabbi*, but also *Son of God, King of Israel [Christology, p. 507]*. One can contend, as Moloney (1998: 56) does, that this is no more than standard Jewish messianic expectation falling far short of John's christological claims for Jesus, but this judgment is ill-founded. One cannot expect these disciples to confess the Christology of the prologue or John's acclaim of Jesus as Lamb of God. Such would render the account dreadfully artificial, lacking historical credibility.

1:50-51 Jesus Grants Nathanael to See Heaven Opened on the Son of Man[w]

Nathanael's confession is authentic, opening the way for Jesus to disclose further his divine identity. If you *believe because I told you that I saw you under the fig tree,* be assured that you *will see greater things than these.* Jesus then reveals an *above* perspective to his identity, beginning his declaration with authenticating words, *Truly* [RSV], *truly [Amēn, amēn], . . . you will see heaven opened and the angels of God ascending and descending upon the Son of Man.*

See is an important connective in the transition between verses 47-48 and 50-51. This is John's form of the sixth beatitude, "Blessed are the pure in heart, for they will see God" (Matt 5:8). Nathanael is without guile or deceit; he is pure in heart. He is a true Israelite. Rabbinic writers took the word *Israel* to mean "Man seeing God" (*'iš ra'eh'el*) (O'Neill: 374n1). Thus Nathanael, the *true* Israelite, sees God (1:18), the very God whom Jesus reveals. Also important, the verb for *see* (*horaō*) requires a plural subject. Thus, though addressed to Nathanael, the saying in its full import transcends the immediate dialogue. It is, as it were, opening the door of heaven to all who emulate Nathanael in belief and behavior. The ladder, with angels ascending and descending upon the Son of Man, marks Jesus as the way to heaven, to God.

To understand the ladder imagery and its significance, read the story of Jacob in Genesis 28:12, 16-19a. Jesus' word to Nathanael builds upon the imagery of Jacob's encounter with God as he leaves home and goes off to Ur, the land from which Abraham came. In this context, with his head on a stone for a pillow, Jacob dreams and sees a ladder stretching from earth to heaven, with angels of God ascending and descending on *it*. In John 1:51, however, Nathanael, representing believers, will *see the angels of God ascending and descending upon the Son of Man.* What does *it* refer to in Genesis 28:12? The ladder? If so, Barrett is right in saying, "For the ladder John substitutes Son of man" (1978: 187). But rabbinic reflection on Genesis 28:12 (in Heb.) took the masculine pronoun ending to refer to Jacob (though the LXX *ep' autēs* is feminine) so that the angels went up and down upon him, Jacob. John's use of the text infers that this Son of Man, indeed Jesus, shuttles between heaven and earth (cf. the Shekinah glory of 1:14; R. Brown 1966: 90).

Numerous other traditions came to be associated with this ladder linking earth and heaven, most notably that the *ascending* angels take the prayers of the saints to God. The *descending* angels bring down heavenly manna, as food for Israel in the wilderness and for Jesus to sustain him during his temptations in the wilderness (Mark 1:13;

Matt 4:11)—possibly also when an angel *strengthens* Jesus in the garden before his arrest (Luke 22:43). Building on the image of the ladder going from the stone (later, altar) to heaven, O'Neill says it well:

> John 1:51 has preserved for us an ancient Jewish tradition that taught that the Son of Man would be seen as the altar and the sacrificial victim [but John would not say *victim*; see later discussion for John 17] on the altar to which the people would come and, as participating in that sacrifice, see the angels taking their prayers to heaven and coming back with gracious answers to their petitions. (379)

Jesus Turns Water into Wine in Cana (Day 7) 2:1-12

2:1-2 *Time and Place of the Wedding*

This story begins with a time locator: *on the third day*. Presumably this means three days after the events narrated in chapter 1. However, it could be understood as a literary-theological motif, similar to its recurrence in the Synoptic Gospels to anticipate Jesus' resurrection. The seven accumulated days in John's narrative echo the creation story of Genesis. The wedding on the seventh day thus corresponds to God's Sabbath, when God finished and rested from the work (Gen 2:1-3). Both the seventh day and the eighth day (if that chronology is preferred) represent the new order of life in the early church's theological reflection. Jesus' new wine announces new life come now!

The place-locator is *Cana*, nine miles north of Nazareth. Moloney (1998: v–vi, 63–65) holds that *Cana* is a structural marker, so that the narrative section runs *From Cana to Cana* (chs. 2–4), since the last episode of chapter 4 is *He came again to Cana in Galilee* (4:46). It is debatable whether John counts Galilee as the "land of reception," as in the Synoptic Gospels (Swartley 1994: 39–43), since in Galilee the Jews head up a murmuring response (John 6:41, 52) [*"The Jews," p. 520*].

The text indicates that both Jesus' mother and his disciples were invited and went to the wedding. No indication is given of family or community connections. They appear, though, as significant guests at the wedding event.

2:3-5 *Problem: No Wine; Mother's Initiative and Son's Response*

These verses consist of dialogue between Jesus' mother and her son Jesus. The significant feature about this wedding is that *the wine gave out*. Strikingly, Jesus' mother takes charge. She speaks at both the beginning and end of the unit, as this chiasm shows:

A Mother says, *They have no wine.*
>B Jesus says, *Woman, what concern is that to me and to you?* (AT).
>B′ *My hour has not yet come.*
A′ Mother says to the servants, *Do whatever he tells you.*

Why does Jesus address his mother in this impersonal way? Matand Bulembat (67, 69) points out that Jesus' address, *Woman*, is respectful from a Congolese perspective; he suggests a translation for Western readers: "Madam" or "Lady." Jesus again addresses his mother as *Woman* in 19:26c. The vocative for *woman* (*gynai*) is used elsewhere in John (4:21; 8:10; 20:13, 15) and by Jesus elsewhere in the NT (Matt 15:28; Luke 22:57). It is not demeaning but is a tender sympathetic response to one distressed, feeling abandoned, or needing consolation and moral support. Viewing 2:4 together with 4:21 and 20:15 suggests that Jesus' vocative address, *Woman*, signals dramatic self-disclosure of his identity (Reinhartz 2003: 19).

What does Jesus' first response mean? Literally it is *What to me and to you?* Raymond Brown (1966: 99) proposes two potential meanings in light of this phrase's use elsewhere:

1. When one party is unjustly bothering another, the injured party may ask, "What have I done to you that you should do this to me?" (Judg 11:12; 2 Chron 35:21; 1 Kings 17:18).

2. When someone is asked to get involved in a matter and feels it is not their business, the one asked may say to the petitioner, "That is *your* business; how am *I* involved?" (2 Kings 3:13; Hos 14:8).

Brown says meaning 1 implies hostility (cf. Mark 1:24; 5:7 with par. Matt 8:29; Luke 8:28), while meaning 2 represents simple disengagement.

Jesus' response could thus mean "Why are you publicly treating me this way? Get off my back," or, "This is none of my business. Don't bother me." The question has the import, How does what you are telling me to do fit with my God-given life purpose (cf. Talbert: 85)? Literarily, it is a backhanded way of shining God's glory on this event, memorializing it theologically and missionally. Highlighted in this manner, Jesus solves the problem with the wine, doing more than his mother could imagine. His miracle is denoted as a *sign*, a key term in this Gospel [*Signs, p. 529*]. Jesus' last *sign* in his public ministry is his raising of Lazarus. Thus wedding (2:1-11) and raising (ch. 11) bookend Jesus' mission! Like the parables in the Synoptics, the *signs* in John either elicit faith or provoke unbelief.

However, Jesus' second statement, *My hour has not yet come*, introduces a tension. Why? Because his mission cannot be fully revealed at this point in time, he announces a not-yet motif. *My hour has not yet come* is a recurring trope in John that creates narrative suspense. Its meaning cannot now be disclosed but must wait until later in the narrative's artful presentation of Jesus' self-revelation. This narrative suspense is similar to Mark's prominent secrecy theme (Swartley 1981/1999: 60–73, 112–30, 198–99).

Though Jesus' response is puzzling, it is clear that his mother takes charge of the situation and is confident her son will solve the problem. Jesus accommodates, after his perplexing answer in B´. In this scenario, the wedding and its "players" take on symbolic significance. We are not told whose wedding this is, but the lack of wine alarms. So mother and son now take charge in order to make this wedding a good one, with plenty of good wine. The headwaiter, normally in charge of such things, tastes the new wine but remains clueless about what has happened. In his chiastic analysis, Matand Bulembat (63) contrasts the mother's role to that of the headwaiter, who would normally be in charge of such matters. Jesus' mother takes charge, and the servants do what she tells them: "They obey only Jesus' mother and Jesus himself." Matand Bulembat (68) concludes, "The synonymous and antithetical parallelism existing between the mother of Jesus and the head-waiter on the one hand, and between Jesus and the bridegroom on the other, discloses that the behaviour of Jesus' mother was that of a competent head-waiter, and the conduct of Jesus, that of a genuine bridegroom" (cf. 3:29).

Jesus' mother does not speak again in John's narrative, though 2:12 indicates that Jesus went with his mother and brothers and disciples down to Capernaum, *and they remained there a few days*. In a fascinating essay Gench (10–12) points out that Jesus' mother appears in scenes in John's Gospel that have no parallels in the Synoptic Gospels. These are "entrance" (2:1-12) and "exit" points (19:26-30). In neither is she identified by name, which may indicate that, like other anonymous figures, she functions in some model role, which is awe, confidence, and familial love. Nonetheless, her role is shrouded in mystery: taking charge at a wedding and hearing Jesus' word to her at the foot of the cross. Jesus asks his mother to care for the disciple Jesus loved and the beloved disciple to care for Jesus' mother, thus assuming Jesus' role as son. After this bond between mother and beloved disciple is sealed, the narrative moves quickly to Jesus' final word, *It is finished*. Tucked between these two points is Jesus' word *I am thirsty*. Further, in John a sponge full of *wine* (from a jar of sour wine!) is offered to him on a branch of hyssop. *When Jesus had received the wine, he said, "It is finished."* Jesus makes *good* wedding wine; at the cross he drinks *sour* wine.

A kaleidoscope of images and meanings floods one's mind in reflecting upon these entrance and exit scenes where Jesus' mother figures into Jesus' ministry. If one perceives Jesus' response to his mother as irritation in this entrance scene, the Gospel's portrait of her in the exit scene presents a different view. When Jesus dies, we see and hear him expressing deep love for his mother. In the symbolism of this pair—mother and beloved disciple—the love-community of believers has its future in what weddings signify: a new historical reality based in love relationships. At the cross a new Jesus-family is born, symbolically birthed by the beloved disciple and Jesus' mother, giving her son to be *the Savior of the world* (4:42). Jesus' earthly ministry is framed by these two scenes of Jesus and his mother. The wine of the wedding is refracted through the prism of the wine of memorial.

2:6-10 Jesus Turns Water into Wine—Really Good Wine

We don't know if the six stone water jars holding around 150 gallons each had been filled with wine already consumed or not. If so, it must have been a huge wedding party. Emphasis falls rather on the use of these jars for water: *for the Jewish rites of purification*. This function of the jars signals what almost all commentators recognize: what is about to happen has symbolic meaning. Jesus commands the servants to fill the jars with water up to the brim. Next Jesus tells them to draw some wine out and take it to the chief steward. The *steward taste[s] the water that had become wine.*

Puzzled, since he didn't know where it came from, though the servants did, the steward calls the bridegroom and says to him, *Everyone serves the good wine first, and then the inferior wine after the guests have become drunk. But you have kept the good wine until now.* The text reports no word of response from the bridegroom, which mystifies the reader. Who is the bridegroom? Why no word of response?

Coloe's (2007: 53–66) perception that John 3 thematically continues John 2 throws light on this mystery. The crucial verses appear in the next appearance of John the Witness in the narrative (3:22-30), in which two themes hook to the wedding miracle: *a discussion about purification* (3:25, echoing 2:6) and John the Witness's further disclosure about his role in relation to the Messiah (3:28-30). John the Witness says,

I said,
"I am not the Messiah, but I have been sent ahead of him."
He who has the bride is the bridegroom.
The friend of the bridegroom, who stands and hears him,
rejoices greatly at the bridegroom's voice.
For this reason my joy has been fulfilled.
He must increase, but I must decrease.

While exposition of this riddle must wait for the next unit, John the Witness's identification of himself as *friend of the bridegroom* illumines the query: who is the bridegroom in 2:9d? The story functions on several levels: a historical level reporting a wedding event to which Jesus and his mother were invited as guests *and* a symbolic level where the shape of the narrative—what is said and what is not said—teases the reader toward a *spiritual* symbolic meaning. On the historical level the bridegroom, of course, is not Jesus. But symbolically, in relation to 3:29, Jesus is the bridegroom (Matand Bulembat: 68–71; Marsh: 142; Schneiders 1999: 35, 135; McWhirter: 56, 79) who, after the first wine runs out, makes *the better wine* for the feast, enabling the wedding guests to celebrate—lots of wine for lots of people!

Nor should one miss in both these texts that Jewish *rites of purification* (2:6; 3:25) have been eclipsed by a new reality for God's peoplehood, a point extended in the signs of John 5 and 9. The water becomes the wine of Jesus' new covenant (cf. Chennattu).

2:11 Jesus' First Sign Reveals His Glory; His Disciples Believe in Him

Jesus' first sign, the first action of his public ministry, announces a new reality. His ministry begins with a wedding; he makes wine for that wedding. And this is a sign. A sign of what? Verse 11 answers: the sign *revealed his glory* (echo of 1:14, *We have seen his glory*). Further, his disciples *believed* in him. They wager their future on him.

Some earlier scholars regarded signs as ambiguous, even negative, in birthing faith. But with more recent narrative analysis, a shift has occurred: signs function positively in John. The term for *sign* (*sēmeion*) occurs seventeen times. The oft-recurring complementary term *work* (*ergon*) is broader in meaning. Both play a positive role; they witness to Jesus' claims about himself and God. A sign in John does not indicate failed faith or perverse desire (as in Mark 8:11-13). In John, signs play positively and crucially on the *witness* stage of the Gospel. Their function is to persuade and lead to faith, as the purpose statement in 20:30-31 indicates.

The literature on *signs* in John's Gospel is vast. Johns and Miller (1994) show the weaknesses of previously held positions:

- that an earlier "signs source" viewed signs positively, but the Gospel's final redactor viewed signs negatively (this is von Wahlde's view [2010]—a key difference between the Gospel's first and second editions), or
- that the narrator both affirms and critiques signs as part of the literary plot; the tension is not resolved.

A third view, argued persuasively by Johns and Miller, regards *signs* in John as playing a consistently positive role (521, 533). Signs witness to Jesus' mission and identity, and they corroborate other witnesses in the Gospel, eliciting faith in Jesus as Messiah and Son of God *[Signs, p. 529]*.

Jesus' disciples believe in him. With this astounding wedding start for Jesus' public ministry, the drama of the Gospel captures not only our attention, but also our imagination and heart. Will we join the emerging community around Jesus, one that, according to Jesus' word to Nathanael, *"will see greater things than these: . . . heaven opened and the angels of God ascending and descending upon the Son of Man"*? Will we welcome the new creation, signified by a wedding, God's new work in Jesus among us?

2:12 Rest Time in Capernaum

The dramatic week of events ends with rest. This suggests Sabbath retreat: Jesus spends several days in Capernaum, a small but thriving fishing town by the Sea of Galilee. Jesus' companions consist of *his mother, his brothers, and his disciples*—possibly ten to twelve people. Where do they stay? Tradition tells us it may have been at Peter's home (cf. Mark 1:29-31).

This unit ends in Galilee. The next unit is located in Jerusalem. Between 2:12 and chapter 7, three shifts occur between Galilee and Jerusalem. These are strategic to the Gospel's structural design.

THE TEXT IN BIBLICAL CONTEXT

Gathering Disciples

Jesus' call to Philip, *Follow me* (1:43), sounds much like Jesus' call of the first four disciples in Mark (1:16-20) and Matthew (4:18-22; Luke differs: see 5:1-10 for Peter's call, with others then following Jesus also, 5:11). Philip is not among those first four called. John's account of Jesus' gathering of his first disciples reveals a dialogical encounter whereby the disciples are linked to Jesus step-by-step. The transfer of John the Witness's followers to Jesus is distinctive to John's Gospel. John locates Jesus across the Jordan River at Bethany for Jesus' gathering of his first disciples.

The inclusion of Nathanael among the first disciples is another distinctive feature. Nathanael does not appear in any of the Synoptic lists of the disciples (Mark 3:16-17; Matt 10:2-4; Luke 6:12-16) or in Acts 1:13. Some solve this puzzle by identifying Nathanael with Bartholomew, but evidence for this is meager. Even so, Bartholomew plays no specific role in the Synoptic narratives, whereas Nathanael does—here, and again in John 21:2. He is named with Simon Peter and Thomas, both of whom play key roles in John's Gospel. With these differences it seems clear that John utilized different sources of Gospel tradition. In the Synoptic Gospels, Jesus' pre-Caesarea Philippi public ministry occurs mostly in Galilee, except for Matthew's and Luke's birth narratives. But Jesus' ministry in John is located mostly in Jerusalem. John is known as the Jerusalem Gospel.

Though the four Gospels present Jesus' gathering of disciples with somewhat different emphases, all conform to two main patterns common in the Greco-Roman world, where religious or philosophical leaders gathered disciples (Talbert: 83–84). These two patterns are summons and response (dominant in the Synoptics) and coming to or gathering around a teacher through the testimony of another (the model dominant in John). In the OT great leaders are introduced through call narratives (i.e., Abraham and Sarah, Moses, Isaiah, and Jeremiah). Martens (1986: 36) has tabulated numerous key features of these various calls: divine meeting, word of identification, commission, objection, reassurance, and sign. The issue of authority looms large in the prophet's acceptance of the call (Lind: 38–39). Lind (39–40) also documents the continuance of God's calling key leaders through the history of the church.

The Gospels conform only partially to the OT patterns of call. But in all four Gospels, the essential heart of the event is encounter with God or Jesus. In Acts, Luke narrates Paul's call as a dramatic encounter with Jesus Christ (chs. 9; 22; 26). In this call Paul's view of Jesus changes completely: Paul recognizes Jesus as Messiah and Savior and receives his commission to take the gospel to the Gentiles (cf. Eph 3:1-13).

God's New Age Has Come

In reflecting on the Cana miracle of abundant wine, the symbolic level of the story's meaning evokes fulfillment of messianic hopes:

> What was it about this particular sign that revealed for them the presence of God—"of glory"—in Jesus? Though the story does not spell it out for us, those who carried Old Testament promises in their hearts would have found its meaning quite clear: abundance of wine was one of the consistent Old Testament images for the joy of the messianic "last days" and the arrival of God's new age (see Amos 9:13-14; Joel 3:18; Jer 31:12; Isa 25:6-10). John affirms that, in the one who provided lavish wine at Cana, the promised day has arrived and God's abundant blessings are poured out upon believers. (Gench: 12)

The Isaiah text with its anticipated "feast of fat things" (RSV) evokes abundance, and this is surely the intent of the Cana wedding with its surfeit of wine. Another OT text, Hosea 2:14-21, envisions a wedding in the wilderness, when God renews his covenant with Israel. In the Synoptic Gospels, especially Luke, Jesus often eats with people—all sorts of people—and hosts banquets, welcoming outsiders to the feast. These emphases are central to the proclamation of the gospel of the kingdom (Moessner: 3–4, 174–76, 211, 273; Swartley 1994: 133–34). John begins Jesus' ministry with a wedding meal, setting the stage for John's trope of "Ingesting Jesus" (Webster).

Summing up Jesus' gathering disciples and fulfilling God's covenant promises, Kelly and Moloney (70) put it succinctly, "A new family of Jesus is being brought into existence in the light of the hour that is about to strike. In the power of the Word, the purifying water of the OT (2:6) will be changed into the wine of the New Covenant." It appears that John's Gospel frequently exposits in signs or discourses statements in the synoptic Gospels. For example, the wedding echoes Mark 2:22: "No one puts new wine into old wineskins; otherwise, the wine will burst the skins, and the wine is lost, and so are the skins; but one puts new wine into fresh wineskins."

THE TEXT IN THE LIFE OF THE CHURCH

The Lamb, Our Sin, and the Bridegroom

The effort to locate OT origins for Jesus' identity and work as Lamb of God marks the commentaries through the ages. But the distinctions we seek as to what *Lamb* signifies are modern. Early church commentators contribute numerous insights; they do not separate one set of meanings from the other, but genially blend them. One emphasizes the "spotless sacrifice" whose way John prepared (Cyril of Alexandria). Another contrasts the lamb to a ram, sheep, or any animal used for sacrifices, but does so to stress that a lamb is in its prime of life and is thus preferred for the perpetual holocausts for the people's sin (Origen). Eusebius identifies Jesus as Lamb with the lamb of Isaiah 53, and Bede speaks of the lamb slaying "the lion of sin and death." Augustine links Jesus as Lamb with the ram caught in the bush—thus complete with a crown of thorns—as Abraham was about to sacrifice Isaac. Melito of Sardis associates the image with "the paschal lamb prefigured in God's leading his people out of the bondage of Egypt through the shedding of his own blood." Ambrose links Jesus the Lamb to the first lamb in Genesis, Abel's acceptable offering. Romanus Melodus views Jesus the Lamb as taking the place of the scapegoat (Elowsky: 67, 70–71), as also does *Epistle of Barnabas 7*.

The distinction between *sins* and *sin* may not seem important in our modern view: *sins* is simply the plural of *sin*. In biblical thought, however, *sins* denote actions whereas *sin* describes the human nature or propensity. In Paul, sin is a *power* that holds humans in its sway (see Toews on Sin as a personified *Power*: 409–11, 387–413). Early Christian liturgies began using "sins of the world" not to assign another meaning to sin, but to stress and include the vastness of human sin(s). The *sin* offering in Leviticus is for all the sins of the people. Likewise, Jesus as the Lamb who takes away the sin of the world bears "our sins in his body on the tree, that we might die to sin" (1 Pet 2:24a, RSV; NRSV has *cross* for *tree*, and *free from sins* for *die to sin* [Gr. is pl., *hamartias*]).

Fluidity between *sin* and *sins* is present in Anabaptist writings, with rich images where John 1:29 or 36 is specified as a textual reference, often with other references. Dirk Philips illustrates this as follows: "Christ Jesus is the garment of righteousness, yes, the innocent and unblemished Lamb of God with which every believing and baptized Christian is clothed" (76–77); "who by his death has taken away the sins of the whole world" (91). Philips says more: Jesus is Mediator, Reconciler, Peacemaker. "He is the Lamb of God who takes away the sins of the world" (102). "With his body he bore the sins of the world upon the wood of the cross" (335). In a hymn text Philips declares, "He has delivered us, out of pure love" (643). Correlating the Lamb with death and sin recurs a dozen times, citing either John 1:29 or 36 (664).

Compiler van Braght in his introduction to *Martyrs Mirror* references John 1:29 eight times: "He by His coming, would redeem, liberate, and raise the fallen race of man from their sin, guilt, and unrighteousness" (39). Seven more times John 1:29 is cited or referenced in a catalog of martyr witnesses (70, 380, 458, 685, 787, 829, 1041). One text unites "Lamb of God" with "the Bridegroom of the church" (70)—the bookends of this unit! In another, 1:29 is cited to support deliverance from destruction and restoring to eternal salvation (458). It is also cited to back up a citation of Romans 5:18 (685). In all cases where the Lamb text is cited, *sin* occurs, except in one where *sins* occur (829). John Michael Talbot's musical *Light Eternal* contains a marvelous piece on the Lamb of God who takes away the sins of the world, most useful for worship and meditation focused on this text.

The allusions proposed above in the wedding event were certainly perceived by early church commentators. Cyril of Alexandria sees Jesus as "the bridegroom from heaven" (*Commentary on John* 2.1), and Augustine says, "Is it any wonder that he who came to that house for a wedding came to this world for a wedding" (*Tractates on the Gospel of John* 8.4.1–3; Elowsky: 88–89). "For Bede the third day signifies the dawning age of grace, which supersedes the ages of the patriarchs and the Law" (M. Edwards: 36).

The symbolic richness of John's narrative has been valued through the ages for its spiritual meaning, edifying the soul as well as the mind. Early church leaders highly valued John's Gospel, though its standing was tenuous among some groups. It was valued also by gnostics (Pagels 1989). In later centuries mystical writers treasured it, seeing its symbols as lighted pathways to God (Eriugena, in Bamford). Symbolized by the soaring eagle, the Gospel lifts the gaze of the reader upward, with angels attending.

"Come and See," and Abide

In John the dominant pattern is that people become disciples by another's witness to Jesus, who has magnetic attraction: *Come and see* (1:39, 46; cf. 4:29). This invitation, after Jesus' first words, *What are you looking for?* (1:38), is a model for our gospel witness. Making these two words of Jesus central to our thinking will energize our sense of witness. What would it mean to name your congregation "Come and See" church?

Distinctive to John's Gospel is gathering disciples in tandem with disclosure of Jesus' identity. A wide array of christological titles appears in 1:19-51 [*Christology, p. 507*]. In John, Philip is the lone case illustrating the call-and-response pattern. These features invite us to reflect on how people come to be followers of Jesus today. Both patterns (witness and call) are evident today as well. Sometimes people come to Jesus because they hear a call, a deep inner sense of God or Jesus as calling them. Both Augustine and John Wesley illustrate this. When one receives Christ in response to the preaching of the gospel, the dominant missions' pattern—summons and response—occurs.

In both patterns it is important to ask how people say "yes" to following Jesus. How do people learn who he is and how relationship (*abiding* in Jesus) begins and flourishes? Traditionally churches have used a catechism manual to impart cognitive knowledge, but more is needed: growth in experiential knowledge. The mentoring model can develop this experiential side—a Christian more mature in faith intentionally relates to a beginner in the faith. This may be an extension of "Come and See," leading a young believer to *remain* with Jesus.

Different people come to the gospel and the church in different ways. Jesus invites Andrew and "the other disciple" to *come*, Philip to *follow*, Nathanael to *see*, and Simon to *become*. This illustrates variety in approach and response. Jesus is a master teacher. From Jesus we gain wisdom to know how to connect, invite, and foster growth.

Various patterns of initiation and catechism may be considered as "seekers" come to Jesus. The early church considered it essential that people coming from paganism have an extended initiation or catechetical period to prepare for baptism (Webber: 35–37, 82; Kreider 2006: 17–20; E. Ferguson: 229–68). Christian formation is a process in Christian growth (Shenk 2007).

This unit of Scripture is punctuated with *abiding* or *remaining* in three different events: Jesus' baptism, where the Spirit *remains* or *abides* on Jesus (1:32, 33), the disciples *abiding* with Jesus for a day (1:38-39), and Jesus' and his inner group staying or *abiding* in Capernaum (2:12). In contrast, our social networking culture connects one quickly to people all around the world in code language. Television ads shift images every several seconds, and films construct stories that take us everywhere in and beyond the universe, but never with an "abiding" place. In contrast, John's Gospel stresses *abiding*. These texts anticipate chapter 15: *Abide in me as I abide in you*. *Abiding* is essential to discipleship. It grounds the church's peace witness and guides us when and how to respond to situations and needs. Let us *remain, dwell,* or *abide* with Jesus, *see* the ascending and descending angels, and *taste* the new wine! *Abiding* in Jesus in our peacemaking efforts tempers, complements, and critiques our peace activism.

SERMON STARTERS

"What are you looking for?" catches people's attention and evokes their desires. This connects to the Gospel's emphasis on discipleship: do we really want to know Jesus? What must we give up to follow or remain with him long enough to learn to know who Jesus is? What would it mean for us today to consciously develop a "Come and see" and "abiding" ethos? Would we visit more and "text" less? Would we discover anew that eating together and remaining longer strengthens our church's body life?

If the wedding in Cana is the focus of the sermon, one might preach on "What if Jesus shows up at your party (or wedding)?" Or, the angle might shift to whether you would invite Jesus to your wedding party! With this angle the sermon could also connect to discipleship.

Another focus might be on "Excessive Joy and Generosity: Wine, Wine, and More Wine." In the *Christian Century* Lectionary commentary on this wedding, we read:

> Jesus takes an important vehicle for the law and fills it with wine—gallons of it. People often say this story is not about Jesus offending anyone. It is about joy, generosity, abundance. Even so, maybe these things are occasionally offensive. Excess: excessive generosity, excessive abundance, excessive *anything* often offends. Something bursts out of the bounds of the expected—something delicious: excessive life and love. (Blue: 18)

John 2:13–4:3

From Old to New: Temple, Birth, Baptism; Communities in Conflict

PREVIEW

Jesus' nonviolent protest in the temple is shocking—turning over the tables of the money changers and driving out the merchants. Why? He was angered at the money exchange, which robbed the poor pilgrims. Ted and Company presented a wonderful sketch on money, "You Can't Take It with You," and used this incident to show how ridiculous the money exchange was. Roman coins, which the pilgrims brought with them, had to be changed into Jewish coins in order to buy sacrificial animals. The process becomes hilarious as each exchange robs the pilgrims by levying "exchange fees," which must be paid with Jewish money, which then becomes another exchange with an additional fee—a process that never ends! Soon the would-be worshipers are cheated out of all their money, with barely enough left to buy a pigeon. Little wonder that Jesus is incensed with the money changers! Well done, Ted and Company! We now understand Jesus' anger; he flips over the table, with coins rolling everywhere, to stop the oppression of the poor. Jesus' word judges severely!

Jesus' cleansing of the temple is often paired with the wedding in Cana, since both symbolically inaugurate a new order. Both critique Judaism's purification rituals and temple practices. The unity of the two events may be perceived at the eucharistic level: the wine of Jesus' blood (2:1-11) and the destroyed temple-body (2:19, 21). Jesus speaks of *the temple of his body* (his death) and the disciples remember this after *he was raised from the dead* (2:22-23), the two events the eucharist celebrates. This helps explain why John relocates the cleansing of the temple so early in Jesus' ministry. The wedding wine and temple-body are John's theological keynotes.

The new coordinates, Jerusalem and Passover (2:13), signal a turn in the narrative, with 2:23-25 segueing into Nicodemus's encounter with Jesus and the discourse that follows. In 3:14-16 Jesus says he will give his life to save those who believe in him, and they will receive eternal life. In Nicodemus's dialogue with Jesus, we learn the necessity of new birth through baptism with water and the Spirit. Nicodemus comes by night, not in the light that Jesus brings into the world. The dialogue proceeds on two levels: Jesus speaks on one level, Nicodemus hears (and speaks) on another. It indeed is *night*! We meet both unbelieving Jews (2:14-22) and many believing Jews (2:23), in whom, however, Jesus did not believe (*pisteuō* is used for both verbs).

Since baptism is mentioned in the dialogue with Nicodemus, John's reentry into the narrative is predictable. John's earlier witness focused on the comparative differences between his baptism and that of the One coming. This comparison and contrast continues. John reiterates his subordinate role to Jesus. The specific references to Jesus and John both baptizing define the two movements in relation to one another.

The text reflects rivalry between the Jesus and the John communities. The evangelist elevates John the Witness but also intimates that his followers refused to acknowledge Jesus and his superior claims, to which John witnesses. Such refusal brings severe judgment (the wrath of God, 3:36).

The unit sets up a drama that invites readers to locate themselves in relation to Jesus' claims about himself: the new temple of his body; new birth; salvation through belief in him; the one to whom John witnesses; and source of eternal life. Jesus invites all into the kingdom of God through baptism by both water and Spirit, to be born again (or born from above), to move from the darkness, forsake evil deeds, and come into the light, *so that it may be clearly seen that their deeds have been done in God* (3:21b). *Whoever* [*thus*] *believes in the Son has eternal life* (v. 36a).

OUTLINE

Jesus Cleanses the Temple, 2:13-22
Jesus Does Not Trust Himself to Human Response, 2:23-25
Nicodemus's Encounter with Jesus, 3:1-12
Jesus Extends the Significance of the Dialogue, 3:13-21
John the Witness Reenters the Narrative: John's and Jesus'
Baptisms, 3:22–4:3

EXPLANATORY NOTES

This section describes Jesus' first cycle of ministry in Jerusalem, with Passover near.

Jesus Cleanses the Temple 2:13-22

Compared to Jesus' early activity in the Synoptic Gospels, four differences are striking:

- Jesus goes to Jerusalem early in his ministry.
- Jesus' ministry stretches over three Passovers (2:13; 6:4; 11:55).
- Jesus' demonstration in the temple occurs early in the narrative.
- Jesus' action in the temple is interpreted differently than in the Synoptic Gospels.

John may have placed Jesus' prophetic confrontation in the temple so early in his narrative because the fall of the temple motivated the composition of John's Gospel. If so, the Gospel's theology accentuates how believers understand Jewish religious practices in light of Jesus' becoming the new temple (Kerr; Coloe 2001; Hill; Draper). John responds to the catastrophic consequences of the fall of the temple, Israel's central religious institution (Köstenberger 2005: 207, 216). John's Gospel spells out the theological implications of this loss from a Christian perspective. Jesus' word *Destroy this temple* provides a lens through which to read the Gospel. The imperative may be a command to the Jews or Romans, but is more likely a prophetic declaration, that segues into his *body* prophecy (2:19c, 21). The Gospel has a "fulfillment-transformational" theology: Jesus fulfills and transforms both the temple's and the festivals' functions in Israel. Thus we notice:

- The festivals provide the structure of the Gospel; God's Shekinah glory dwells among us.

- True worship occurs in neither the temple of Jerusalem nor that of Gerizim (4:20-24).

- Jesus' farewell discourse and prayer (chs. 14–17) replace the apocalyptic discourse.

- God's dwelling among his people through Jesus punctuates the narrative.

- Jesus' resurrection is the raised temple (2:19-22).

- Thomas's climactic confession, *My Lord and my God!* is true worship (20:28).

2:13 *The Passover Is at Hand*[w]

Passovers shape the chronology of Jesus' ministry in John. Only from John do we derive the chronology that Jesus' ministry extends over three years, since he goes to Jerusalem for three Passovers (2:13; cf. 5:1 [an unnamed feast—Passover?]; 6:4; 11:55). Numerous scholars develop the significance of the festivals (Daise; Miyazaki; Suderman; Yee). Jesus claims for himself what they signify.

The Passover originates from and celebrates Israel's deliverance from Egypt, as narrated in Exodus 12. Israel's deliverance from bondage manifests God's enduring steadfast love for Israel, God's elect people. God dwells with them in a portable tent over which God's Shekinah glory hovered, with a cloud by day and fire by night. These direct the journeying of God's covenant people, bonded to God by both covenant and Torah. In David's and Solomon's time, the tabernacle becomes a *temple*. Passover, with annual sacrifices prescribed for each family clan, commemorates Israel's deliverance and God's presence among them in tent and temple.

In Jesus' time Jerusalem's population was around 50,000, but at Passover it swelled to 180,000 (Jeremias: 75–84). One can hardly imagine the congestion and pressure put upon the festival rituals: purification rites, the exchange of money, the purchase of animals, and all the sacrificial bloodletting.

---

w   Where the superscript w occurs after headings, please see the commentary's online Web Supplement for additional material. Go to: http://www.heraldpress.com/bcbc/john.

2:14-17 Jesus' Action in the Temple[w]

This episode is likely the same event as reported in the other Gospels on the day after Palm Sunday (Matt 21:12-13; Mark 11:15-17; Luke 19:45-46). Some scholars argue for two cleansings (Morris: 166–69, who in his notes cites Plummer, Bailey, Murray, and Tasker in support). It is difficult, however, to imagine how such an event could have occurred so early in Jesus' ministry, since it would have precipitated his arrest, as it does in the Synoptics. John most likely shifted it to the beginning for theological reasons in support of his narrative purpose (cf. Burge 2000: 94–95). Together with the wedding in Cana, these two events present Jesus as transforming Jewish practices. A seismic shift is taking place with Jesus. These events parallel the Synoptics' keynote proclamations of the kingdom (Mark 1:14-15; Matt 4:12-17; Luke 4:16-21). Immediately after these events, John explains how to *enter the kingdom of God* (3:3, 5).

In John, Jesus drives out the animals and overturns the tables of the money changers. The wrong he protests is the use of the temple court for money changing, necessary for Passover pilgrims because only Jewish coins could be used to purchase the animals. With prophetic passion he protests "traders in the house of the Lord of hosts" (Zech 14:21). Coin exchange, from Roman to Jewish money to purchase an animal for sacrifice, became a gross extortion of the poor. Jesus' action is a nonviolent protest against the economic desecration of the temple. The money changers and the sellers of sacrificial animals became oppressive. Even if their profit was modest, the poor could not afford it; Jesus identifies with the poor people (cf. Bredin 2003: 49-50).

John differs from the Synoptics on four points: (1) naming the animals, oxen and sheep, along with the doves; (2) Jesus makes a whip of cords to drive out the animals; (3) Jesus speaks to those who are selling the doves; and (4) Jesus makes a concluding comment that the disciples (later) remember. In the Synoptics Jesus quotes Isaiah 56:7 and Jeremiah 7:11 (for exposition see Geddert: 266–68; Gardner: 313–15). But in John 2:17 Jesus quotes Psalm 69:9: "It is zeal for your house that has consumed me" (68:10 LXX). Verse 16 likely alludes to Zechariah 14:21: "And there shall no longer be traders in the house of the Lord of hosts on that day." Jesus' *zeal* drives out mercenary *traders*. Jesus' *word* strikes hard: the temple will be destroyed! Indeed, Jesus' confrontation of the misuse of the temple is a prophetic action symbolically announcing the imminent end of the temple (cf. Meier 2001: 3.501; E. P. Sanders 1985: 69–76).

The oxen and sheep were used in the sacrifices prescribed in Leviticus 1 and 3 for holocausts atoning for sin and for the peace offerings (reaffirming the covenant). The fact that Jesus speaks to the sellers of the doves means he did not drive the doves out by a whip—a comical sight indeed, had he tried—since the doves were the sacrifice of the poor. Rather, he commands the sellers to move this exchange system out of the courts of the Lord. Was Jesus violent in this dramatic action? Did Jesus use the whip on the people? The text says, *Making a whip of cords, he drove all [pantas exebalen] of them out of the temple, both the sheep and the cattle.* Who or what does *pantas* (all) refer to? *Pantas* is a plural masculine. The masculine does not correspond to the neuter *probata* (sheep), but it does agree in number, case, and gender with the masculine *boas* (oxen/cattle). More important, the particular *both-and* construction in Greek shows that Jesus used the whip on both the sheep and the cattle and not on the people (so specified in NRSV, NIV, GNB). This exegesis and translation takes the phrase *both the sheep and oxen* to be explanatory of the *all* (pantas) that Jesus drove out with a whip. Verse 16 supports this interpretation in saying that Jesus, after driving *all* out, speaks to those selling the doves. Macgregor (1954: 17–18) and J. Ferguson (28–30) make the further point that if Jesus had used the whip on people, he would most certainly have been in immediate trouble. We thus conclude that John portrays Jesus as using the whip on the sheep and oxen only, not on the people. This was a prophetic act, not an incident of violence against people. The text does not justify war or violence against others.

Early church interpreters of the first three centuries regarded this as a nonviolent act. With Augustine this began to shift, and the text was used to authorize use of violence. This view of the text prevailed in medieval commentaries and was used to justify violence against heretics and national defense against enemies. Current scholarship is divided on this issue. Many commentators regard Jesus' action as violent and others as nonviolent. For an extensive description of how this text has been interpreted through the centuries and proper exegesis of the text, see Alexis-Baker's well-researched, perceptive article.

John draws on Zechariah to depict Jesus as a suffering figure who will be pierced by his own people (Zech 12:10b). This suffering awakens the oppressors to what they have done. Jesus' death exposes the violence of the world, which God loves, and to which God sent Jesus to save (John 3:14-17). Jesus' body, the temple to be raised (vv. 21-22), proclaims salvation. Jesus gives himself *for the life*

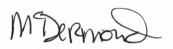

of the world (6:35-51); he opens the way to overcome the violence that crucified him. Jesus' commission in John (20:19-23), delegating to his disciples authority to forgive sins, will render obsolete the temple's sacrificial functions.

In all four Gospels the verb used for *drive out* is *ekballō* (as in John 2:15), the term used of exorcism in the Gospels (cf. John 12:31). Does this action fall into this category, as Howard-Brook contends (1994: 83)? Elements of exorcism are present: Jesus *throws out* the corrupting practices. With the "cleansing" of the temple, Jesus' death as a sacrifice once and for all (see Heb 9:23–10:10) will end animal sacrifice and the oppressive taxation that sustained it. In Jewish rabbinic tradition, the temple was built on the place where Abraham bound Isaac. In judging the sacrificial system, Jesus transforms the Isaac tradition by becoming the new Isaac (Bredin: 46). Jesus' death is intrinsically linked to the temple cleansing (2:19, 21). Later Jesus, like Isaac, carries his wood for his own sacrifice (John 19:17; cf. R. Brown 1966: 226).

With Jesus' death in view, the episode harks back to 1:29, 36, where Jesus is introduced as *the Lamb of God who takes away the sin of the world*. The Lamb, echoing the suffering servant in Isaiah 52:13–53:12, lays down his life of his own accord (10:18; Bredin: 45–46). In John, as well as Mark (Swartley 1981/1999: 187–89), Jesus through his death and resurrection is the new temple, made not of wood and stone but a temple "not made with hands" (Mark 14:58, truth spoken ironically by a false witness). Jesus is the new divine dwelling place that renders the temple's sacrificial system useless. Without need for sacrifice anymore, the need for the temple also ends. Jesus' chasing the sacrificial animals out of the temple "at the very least symbolized an attack, and note that 'attack' is not far from 'destruction'" (E. P. Sanders: 70–71). Nowhere in John or Mark is there any intimation that the temple is to be rebuilt. Rather, Jesus is the new temple (cf. Hoskins: 202). Regaining the land or rebuilding the temple is not the Gospels' gospel.

The distinctive heart of this Johannine account is Jesus' command in verse 16, spoken to those who sold the doves, *Take these things out of here! Stop making my Father's house a marketplace!* In this authoritative word two key points emerge: first, this commerce of sacrificial offerings must end. Second, Jesus claims the temple as his *Father's house* (cf. Luke 2:49, an event not found in John, however). This warrants Jesus' ending this abominable trafficking of buying and selling (purchasing animals for sacrifice and exchanging idolatrous Roman coins into acceptable coins). The claim is also intrinsically christological, for Jesus here discloses his special relationship to the holy, forgiving God of Israel. Coloe rightly proposes that *my Father's house* is the chiastic center of John 1:19–4:54 (2007: 36). Jesus' reclaiming the temple for his Father is vintage Johannine Christology, in sync with the dominant Father-Son portrait of the Gospel. Jesus' temple claim causes collision between Jesus and *the Jews*, recurring often hereafter in John *["The Jews," p. 520]*.

Another feature distinctive to John's account is the narrative structure of a double panel, a diptych, by ending each part with *his disciples remembered*. In this first panel (v. 17), they remember *that it was written, "Zeal for your house will consume me."* What does this mean? Psalm 119 says, "My zeal consumes me because my foes forget your words." The psalmist is despised yet still loves God's word (vv. 139, 141). Jesus, as God's messenger (Mal 3:1), enters the temple with uplifted hand (cf. Isa 26:11). This zeal explains the intensity of Jesus' prophetic word and action and alludes also to his death—he will be *consumed* by virtue of this *zeal* (Coloe 2001: 74).

The disciples' *remembering* also points to a later time, his death and departure, after which the Spirit will bring to remembrance those things Jesus said (14:26). *Remembering* elsewhere in the Gospel refers also to Jesus' death (2:22; 12:16; 15:20; 16:4, 21; Coloe 2001: 75). Kerr (ch. 3) interprets this sign as two-sided; as salvation and judgment temple-cleansing fulfills the eschatological prophecy: "And there shall no longer be traders in the house of the Lord of hosts on that day" (Zech 14:21). It also sheds light on Jesus' instruction on *temple* and *dwelling* later in the Gospel. It prepares for John's Gospel's ultimate contribution: the mutual indwelling of God and Jesus to which believers are incorporated—thus becoming the new body and temple of Jesus (2:21; cf. 4:24; 14:1-3, texts where the temple theme in John is developed further; Coloe 2001, 2007). The prologue's overture, the Word tabernacles among us (1:14), now plays forte.

The resurrection prompts memory of Jesus' word. When therefore (*hote oun*, v. 22a) Jesus is raised from the dead, his disciples *remember* what he said, with recall of the prophecy. Then it says, *They believed the scripture and the word Jesus said*. Hays (2003: 221) hears this as "an authorial voice-over directed to the reader. . . . [John] is teaching his readers how to read. Look beyond the literal sense, he whispers, and read for figuration." Jesus' figurative word on the temple's future is fulfilled in his resurrection. Other similar texts Jesus cited are illumined for the disciples after the resurrection (Mark 12:18-27; Luke 24:13-35) and in light of "eschatological hope" (Hays 2003: 224-34).

2:18-22 Jesus Interprets His Action[w]

This portion begins with a question from *the Jews, What sign can you show us for doing this?* Jesus' answer astounds: *Destroy this temple, and in three days I will raise it up.* The Jews glare and declare: How silly! It took *forty-six years* to build this *temple* under Herod's great building program, and you will rebuild it *in three days?!* The Jews *misunderstand* Jesus (as often in John). Jesus means one thing, and the Jews understand another. Indeed Herod (and his successors) have already spent forty-six years in building the temple (begun in 20 BC, not completed until AD 64, then in 70 destroyed; 18,000 men worked full time; Burge: 96). Jesus does not mean he will rebuild the physical temple structure. By using the Greek term *naos* for temple, Jesus refers to the sanctuary, the place where the divine and human meet. But the Jews think of the physical temple, the building with its courtyard, *hieron* (2:14, 15; 5:14; 7:14, 28; 8:2, 20, 59; 10:23; 11:56; 18:20; cf. the play on these terms in Mark: Swartley 1981/1999: 188–89).

Jesus' word against the temple later leads to the charge of blasphemy (Truex: 227–50). At Jesus' trial the term *have spoken badly* (18:23 AT) scores the OT's blasphemy charge of "speaking evil against" or cursing someone or thing (Truex: 240). This charge in Jewish law is the basis for one to be cut off from the people, "put out of the synagogue," and/or put to death. The event also anticipates and interprets in part later Gospel emphases: Jesus is the "new temple" (Coloe 2001; Hoskins: 108–81). The theme reappears in Jesus' word on worship in 4:19-24 and 14:1-2, where Jesus is God's dwelling for believers.

The new temple that Jesus builds through his death and resurrection (2:21-22a) consists of believers in Jesus, who gives life (4:46-54; 5:26; 11:1-44) and an eternal dwelling (14:2). As Coloe (2007: 56) cogently says, "From the cross the Nazarene Temple-builder raises up the Father's house in the formation of the household of disciples/children of God." Pointing to the irony of Nathanael's question, *Can anything good come out of Nazareth?* in 1:46, she asserts that for John, "*everything* comes from the Nazarene." "Jesus, the Nazarene is the ultimate gift of God (Nathana-el), for the salvation of the world (3:16)." Beautiful and precious! Praise the Lord!

Again, this panel ends with *remembering*. Verse 22 capsulizes this portion by a double *remembering*: that Jesus had said this about the temple and that they believed the Scripture Jesus had spoken (the *zeal consuming* text of Ps 69:9). In this way the skilled narrator rounds off this important story, an event that forecasts the ramifications of Jesus' ministry. The new will *transform* the old (cf. Coloe 2001, 2007; Hoskins: 147–93; Köstenberger 2005: 228–42; Suderman: 82–90).

Jesus Does Not Trust Himself to Human Response 2:23-25

Surprisingly, *many believed in his name because they saw the signs that he was doing!* The temple episode is not specifically called a *sign*, but this statement infers that it, along with other deeds done in Jerusalem during the festival, is a sign. But Jesus sees deeper. Jesus knows *all people*; he *knew what was in everyone.* He did *not entrust himself to them*; he needed no one *to testify about anyone*, for he knew them. The same Greek word (*pisteuō*) describes both the many who *believed* and Jesus not *believing* their response.

This is a puzzling paragraph and makes sense only in relation to the later story. Though many believe, their belief cannot be fully trusted *[Belief, p. 504] [Signs, p. 529]*. Why? The paragraph introduces the following story of Nicodemus, a Pharisee who comes by night.

Nicodemus's Encounter with Jesus 3:1-12

It is difficult to know where Jesus' dialogue with Nicodemus ends. Since verse 12 is the last direct speech, marked by *I tell you*, some take it as the ending of the dialogue. Here, *you* is plural, but it is already plural in the second half of verse 7: *You must be born again* (NIV). This alternation between the singular and plural *you* suggests that Nicodemus represents a group. Since the rationale for understanding *born anew/from above* continues through verse 15, the dialogue may end there. This illustrates John's literary technique of moving from an encounter or a sign into a discourse, sometimes without a clear marker where one ends and the other begins.

Abstracting Jesus' well-known call to be *born again* (v. 3 NIV) from its context of dialogue with Nicodemus leads to misuse of this text. This narrative, with three or four terms of double meaning, readily fogs comprehension (cf. O'Day 2002: 16–28).

Nicodemus's religious standing in the Jewish community is highlighted: *he is a man of the Pharisees, . . . a ruler of the Jews* (RSV). What follows, however, casts a shadow. Nicodemus comes to Jesus *by night.* This suggests stealth, harking back to 2:25: not all is *light* here. Why does he come to Jesus in a clandestine manner? This narrative detail may introduce a degree of tension between Nicodemus and the Pharisees he represents or possibly between Nicodemus and Jesus (O'Day 2002: 19). Nicodemus's motive is ambiguous. Does he really want to know and understand Jesus, or is he psyching out Jesus, to report back to his critical colleagues?

Nicodemus does not ask a question but appears to affirm (or flatter?) Jesus, recognizing that if he were not a rabbi sent from God, he would not be able to do these signs. But even this inquiring statement has an edge to it. Jesus' answer neither affirms nor denies his source of authority. Rather, as the voice of God, Jesus calls Nicodemus to decision: *Truly* [RSV], *truly I tell you, no one can see the kingdom of God without being born from above.* What sort of an answer is this to Nicodemus's query? Jesus pitches a curveball: "You wonder about my authority—whether it comes from God—let me assure you that unless you are ready to think about being born *anōthen*, you won't see God's kingdom." Nicodemus, fanning at Jesus' words, trying to make sense of them, bites the wrong angle of the double hook, the physical *again* side of *anōthen*, and rightly says, "That's impossible—to enter my mother's womb and come out again!"

Jesus proceeds on the spiritual level of *anōthen*, being born from *above*—that, too is being born *again*, but of a different type. *Anōthen* can have any of three meanings: *again* (KJV, NIV), *anew* (RSV), or *from above* (NRSV). Jesus follows by luring Nicodemus into new categories of thought: being born of *water and Spirit*, contrasting birth in *the flesh* with birth of *the Spirit*, and pointing to the *Spirit-wind*: it blows where it chooses (vv. 5-8). Punctuating this, Jesus again declares, *You must be born from above, anew, again* (v. 7b). This is as mysterious as the wind, which blows where it will. *We do not know where it comes from or where it goes* [v. 8c]. *So it is with everyone who is born of the Spirit* [v. 8d]. As *anōthen* has double meaning, so also *pneuma* may mean *wind* or *spirit/Spirit*.

Is it any wonder that Nicodemus is befuddled, "out of his league" even though credentialed as Pharisee and ruler? Taken aback, he says, *How can these things be?* (v. 9). Indeed, "Jesus' world seems quite opaque to him" (Meeks 1972: 54). Jesus' answer is not sympathetic to him in his confusion: *Are you a teacher of Israel, and yet you do not understand these things?* Though schooled well in Jewish law (note Nicodemus's use of *our law*—not Moses's law—in 7:51), he represents the earthbound mind, unable to grasp the meaning of birth from above, the realm of Spirit in contrast to that of the flesh.

In this story Nicodemus is typecast. He represents those who have standing in the Jewish community but remain "outside the light" (Meeks 1972: 54–55; Rensberger 1988: 38–41). Or Nicodemus may represent "secret believers" within Judaism, as Louis Martyn (2003: 88) and Raymond Brown (1979: 71–73) have proposed. This is not clear. The historical question of his believer status cannot be answered definitely. Once Jesus is crucified, *perhaps* then he is fully transformed (see 19:38-39). The fifth-century *Gospel of Nicodemus*, drawing however on second-century sources, views him this way.

On a different level, that of the Gospel readers, the narrative penetrates through and beyond Nicodemus, directly to the reader. In the context of the drama of chapter 2, we can no longer be spectators. We are drawn in to encounter Jesus: Am I with Nicodemus? Or am I with Jesus in my comprehension and willingness to enter a different world, the realm of Spirit and risk—birth from above? Do I say yes to birth from above by the Spirit—to enter the kingdom and receive Jesus as the One come from above, descending to earth to make the only true God known to humankind?

Nicodemus speaks no more, though 3:11-15 appear as Jesus' continued speech to him, while also moving from the dialogue genre to discourse. In verse 11 Jesus also appears to represent a community—the community that believes—for he says, *Truly, truly, . . . we speak of what we know and testify to what we have seen; yet you* [pl.] *do not receive our testimony.* This *we know* forms a bookend to Nicodemus's *we know* in verse 2; Jesus and Nicodemus represent *differing* personal and communal stances in their knowledge of God, in response to Jesus' exegesis of God (1:18).

Jesus now delves deeper into the differing mind-sets. Verse 12 contrasts the earthly with the heavenly. If Nicodemus cannot understand *earthly* things, how could he ever hope to understand the *heavenly* things? Now Jesus directly addresses the issue of his identity, which Nicodemus probed at the beginning. But Jesus' answer is no more transparent than his earlier riddles.

Jesus Extends the Significance of the Dialogue 3:13-21[w]

Both verses 13 and 14 contain the title *Son of Man*, echoing Jesus' word to Nathanael in 1:51, and with similar mystery, for in both cases it is combined with *ascent* and *descent* imagery. The accent falls on the descent of the Son of Man, inferring his heavenly status with God—though ascent is the precondition of descent (v. 13). In his descent the Son of Man fulfills a salvation typology from Moses's action to save God's people. *Just as Moses lifted up the serpent in the wilderness, so* [*also*] *must* [the Greek is *dei*, as in the Synoptic passion-and-resurrection predictions (e.g., Mark 8:31)] *the Son of Man be lifted up* [*hypsoō*]. This is at least the third double entendre of this interchange. *Hypsoō* in John means both the lifting up of Jesus on the cross, analogous to the serpent on the tree, and the lifting up of Jesus into glory. Sharply put, *to be lifted up* is *to be glorified* (cf. 8:28; 12:23, 28, 32, 34). In one word, *hypsoō*, John describes the two-stage christological hymn in Philippians 2:6-11: humiliation and exaltation.

Then Jesus speaks the climactic word: *that whoever believes [this] may have eternal life in him* (AT). What a stretch! The usual reading is to make the phrase *in him* the predicative complement of *believe*, as *eis auton* is in verse 16. Indeed, John often speaks of *believing in him* [Jesus], but then he regularly uses *eis auton*. But here in 3:15, and only here, he uses *en autō*, which is best translated as a locative dative: *whoever believes might have eternal life in him*. The many textual variants witness to the attempts of scribes to solve this matter. The harder (more difficult) reading, usually to be preferred, does not conform to John's customary use of *believe in*[to] *him*. This locative meaning and translation, which numerous commentators commend, solves the problem. Eternal life *in him* (v. 15) is made possible through *believing in*[to] *him* (v. 16). *Eternal life* is a major theme in John. It denotes life both in the age to come and its dawning even *now* in Jesus (cf. 17:3): God's gift of eternal life is for us now in Jesus and in the future. Eternal life is thus both ethical (cf. Luke 10:25-37) and eschatological *[Eternal Life, p. 513]*.

3:16-21 Jesus Extends the Significance of the Dialogue

Jesus further explicates the dialogue, continuing to reveal God. John 3:16 has been rightly called the "golden text" of the Bible. It is a gem summarizing essential gospel elements. Four foundational theological affirmations flow from this text. First, God loves the world. This love drives the divine revelation of incarnation, the content of the gospel, and the Gospels themselves as part of God's gift. Casting the net further, God's love motivates the entire biblical revelation, including creation and covenant (see the recurring refrain in Ps 136). God enters relationship with humans because of love. Israel's special standing with God is not because of their number or importance, but because God loves *them* (Deut 7:7-9), and *us*!

Second, God gives his only Son to lead humans to salvation. This giving is radical, unreserved, risky, and painful. It's the story we know so well, but we often fail to be moved by its sublime and simple truth: God loves so much that he gave what he cherished most, his only Son. Paul's great hymn in Philippians 2:5-11 complements this truth by telling the story from the Son's side. The Son willingly gives himself, even unto death, unto death on a cross for our salvation. For this, God highly exalts him through (in John) the Father's glorification and exaltation of the Son. Salvation is a gift, the point of verse 17. Further, it is for *all*: the term *whoever* denotes potential universal response.

Third, all people who hear this gospel and receive the gift of salvation will *not perish*, but live now within the new relationship between God and humans formed through and by Jesus. The invitation is for people to *believe into [eis] Jesus* (AT), which means staking our life on his gift of salvation, saying yes to Jesus, and becoming bathed in the divine love of the Father and the Son (see John 17 for the mutuality of love). Through faith in God's Son, they and we receive the greatest gift possible.

Fourth, the gift received by faith is eternal life. It is a gift available to all: everyone. The gift of eternal life begins now and continues eternally *[Eternal Life, p. 513]*. Through the Word-Son coming into the world, God saves all those who receive his gift.

Verse 17 reiterates and restates God's purpose in sending his only Son, not to condemn (*krinō*) the world but to save (*sōzō*) the world (*kosmos*). The accent falls on God's initiative and love for the world. We find no hint of the Son's reluctance nor the idea that the Father punishes the Son for the sins of the world. Rather, Father and Son are always one in John, and the salvation gift is the self-donation of God-Jesus.

Beasley-Murray has aptly titled one of his books on John as *Gospel of Life* (1991). *Life* occurs forty-seven times in chapters 1–12, then six times in 13–17, and only once in 18–21 (20:31). In contrast, *love* occurs only six times in chapters 1–12, then thirty-one times in 13–17, and twenty times in 20–21. John is the Gospel of *life* and *love*, with sequential emphases in that order: the first half offers *life* to whomsoever. The concentration on love occurs in Jesus' discourse to his disciples. *Light* also occurs frequently in the first half of the Gospel, especially prominent in the prologue. Hence *light, life, and love* mark God's processional, coming into the world as the Word, the Son. The call to believe into Jesus, the Son, is also the call to believe into God, the Father. In John we find no "separation time." God and the Word, the Father and the Son, are always one: in Jesus' life and death, glorification and resurrection. This is God's gift of salvation.

Conversely, *judgment* and *condemnation* are for those who refuse to believe into Jesus, who refuse to come to the light that proceeds from the Father and the Son. The Son does nothing on his own. The *word* that proceeds from the Father and through the Son judges and condemns, just as it saves and generates new birth (*from above, again*). God's love and light bring crisis, a decisive moment, into the world (cf. Billy Graham's "Hour of Decision").

This "world of darkness" explains the judgment of 3:19: *The light has come into the world, and people loved darkness rather than light because their deeds were evil.* The next verses extend the logic. Those who love their habitat of darkness will not come to the light lest their deeds be exposed. They rather hate the light, while those *who do what is true come to the light* (v. 21a). Further, this shows that those who come to the light do their deeds in the God-light habitat (v. 21b). The opposition of light and darkness appears in Jewish literature before Jesus (in Qumran, the contrast between "the sons of light and the sons of darkness" [1QS 1.9–11, 16–24]) and in the Christian community before John's Gospel was written (e.g., on Rom 13:11-14, see Toews: 327–31; on Eph 5:3-14, see Yoder Neufeld 2002: 228–36, 245–46). First John 2:9-11 also speaks of light and darkness; here love for the brother and sister is evidence of living in the light, while hatred for one's brother or sister is evidence of living in darkness (cf. 1 John 1:5-7) [Light, p. 527].

John the Witness Reenters the Narrative: John's and Jesus' Baptisms 3:22–4:3

Jesus and his disciples retreat to the Judean countryside, the setting for what follows.

3:22-26 Alarm over Many Being Baptized by John and Jesus

Jesus spends some time *in the Judean countryside* and is baptizing (but see 4:2). The text gives no clue about the length of time. Is it weeks or months? Nor does it describe anything about how or why this baptizing ministry occurs. Does it signify the "new birth"—a likely conclusion in light of the narrative context? Is it water baptism that includes the Holy Spirit baptism (cf. Titus 3:5-6)? Any additional comment about Jesus (and/or his disciples) baptizing does not occur until 4:1-2, marking the bookend of this unit.

The evangelist's interest lies elsewhere, as the text shifts to John *baptizing at Aenon near Salim* (strikingly, it appears that John still has his own disciples [3:25], even though he has earlier directed some of them to Jesus!). That people keep coming to John for baptism indicates that his special ministry continues (which continues to today in the Mandean John the Baptist followers in Iraq), which could be seen as an anomaly since "the greater one" is now come (cf. 1:29-30; Acts 19:1-7 shows that John's following continued after Jesus' death and resurrection). Verse 24 is strange, in referring to John's imprisonment, an event we otherwise know about from the Synoptics

(Mark 6:14-29//Matt 14:1-12//Luke 9:7-9). Does this indicate that John the Evangelist knew the Synoptics and was purposefully correlating his time scheme with theirs? Perhaps so.

John is quizzed by *a Jew* (p[75], Codex Vaticanus) or *Jews* (p[66], Codex Sinaiticus, et al.) on purification—perhaps with the implication: Does this baptism nullify and replace the law's rituals regarding washings and ablutions? On the variant readings, the singular is likely correct since it is the harder reading. Also, *a Jew* is less likely to be a scribal change or accidental error in copying, since the plural, *the Jews*, is common in John.

The inquirer drops out of the narrative, and John's disciples now quiz John. However, purification is not the issue. Rather, we want you to know that the one to whom you earlier testified is also now baptizing—*and all are going to him*. Did the Jew in his inquiry tell them this? The bookend comment in 4:1 may imply that he did. This new information about Jesus' and his disciples' (4:2) baptizing many people has two functions: it may, by implication, suggest that John is querying whether they should stop baptizing, since the "real one" has now come and is taking over. Second, it serves clearly as the narrator's emcee function to have John make an important speech—his last major speech in the Gospel. This speech has no analogies in the Synoptic Gospels, though some lines of it are found in John's earlier speech in all four Gospels. The purpose of this speech is to underscore once again, unequivocally, John's subordinate role to Jesus, or put conversely, Jesus' superior role to John and his ministry.

3:27-30 John's Subordinate Role to Jesus: Friend of the Bridegroom

Jesus' and his disciples' greater success in baptism leads to four considerations in John's speech (Talbert: 106). The first appeals to God's gift from heaven: We receive what God gives (v. 27). In this case God endows Jesus with the superior calling and mission; hence, the greater success for his mission in baptism. But is the point really "greater success" or the "greater position" of Jesus in God's salvation economy?

Second, John's bearing witness is rehearsed (cf. 1:15, 27, 30) and reaffirmed: *You yourselves are my witnesses that I said, "I am not the Messiah, but I have been sent ahead of him"* (v. 28). The evangelist recapitulates and underscores his purpose, to show that John's role is only to prepare for the Messiah. This negatively critiques those still following John—presumably at the time the evangelist writes.

Third, John's role as *friend of the bridegroom* is the key new point. That John describes his role with this image is most significant.

Echoing the wedding of 2:1-10, it identifies Jesus as the bride-groom, a claim Jesus himself also makes in Mark's Gospel (2:19-20//Matt 9:15-16//Luke 5:34-35). The metaphor builds upon a long history of nuptial imagery of God's relation to God's covenant people. Compared to all other descriptions of John's relation to Jesus, this is theologically profound. It testifies to Jesus' superiority in God's salvation drama and purpose. That the query of John's disciples triggers this acclaim intensifies the call to John's disciples to stop following John and follow Jesus, who now heads the people of God. Identifying John as *friend* of the bridegroom, the Gospel squelches any competition between John and Jesus.

In Jewish custom the bridegroom's friend brought the bride to the bridegroom. He then stood guard over the bridal chamber but would never interfere with the joyful love of the bridegroom and bride consummating their union (Talbert: 106). Further, when John turned two of his disciples over to Jesus (1:36-38), he was, as friend of the bridegroom, bringing the bride to the betrothal and marriage (Coloe 2007: 33). Talbert's emphasis on "joyful love" has its textual basis in the last two phrases of verse 29: *The friend of the bridegroom, who stands and hears him, rejoices greatly at the bridegroom's voice. For this reason my joy has been fulfilled.*

When we think of John the Witness, we usually visualize a hair-shirted wilderness ascetic calling people to repent, intoning judg-ment and doom. But John's Gospel offers a delightful contrast: John is Jesus' *friend* who stands by the bridegroom at Jesus' wedding, and he (John) is filled with joy! If one may, for homiletic purposes, com-bine Luke's testimony with John's Gospel on this point, the bookend life-portrait of John the Witness portrays him as a joyful character! Luke 1:44b says the babe in Elizabeth's womb "leaped for joy" upon hearing pregnant Mary's greeting. John the Witness is filled with joy over Jesus—before he is born and in his last speech in John! He is delighted when we sing, "Joy to the world, the Lord is come!"

Fourth, *He must increase, but I must decrease.* Indeed, this is so if Jesus is the bridegroom and John is the friend of the bridegroom. The superiority of Jesus' position in God's salvation advent is clear. Hence, this concluding directive, to John's followers and to all, is a trumpet proclamation: in Jesus you find the way to God, who journeyed with his people for centuries, wooing them as a bride, with undying love.

3:31-36 The One Who Has Come from Above: Life-and-Death Significance[w]

The intent of this unit is to reiterate the key emphases and con-sequences of Jesus' dialogue with Nicodemus. Thus it begins, *He who comes from above is above all.* The evangelist is positioning Jesus above all other humans (Meeks 1972: 56). Verse 32 is exactly parallel to verse 11, but in the third-person singular. Further, verses 33-36 make verses 11-21 plainer and more incisive: upon hearing the message, does one receive it and does one accept the messenger? Later in the Gospel, *believing* the testimony of Jesus becomes the all-important issue (5:31-41; 8:12-20; 18:37). These verses and Jesus' words to Nicodemus press the decision (*krisis*) of faith: Will hearers acknowledge Jesus as the One whom God sent, the *beloved* Son (Meeks 1972: 56–57)?

Verses 33-34 make three significant claims. First, Jesus speaks the words of God because he has been sent by God. His words are the words of his Father. Second, Jesus the Son has received from his Father *the Spirit without measure.* His words will thus be testimony of the highest order, higher than that of the prophets. His words are *Spirit and life* (6:63 NIV 2011), and they give life (cf. 5:26). Third, because *the Father loves the Son,* he *has placed all things in his hands.* The RSV reads, *has given all things into his hand.* This point anticipates the narrative to follow, especially 5:27-30. *Love* is the prime mover in Jesus' authority. By this love God seeks to save the world—through believing on the Son and receiving the gift of *eternal life* (v. 36).

It is open to debate whether verses 31-36 are the evangelist's summary of the preceding discourse or a continuation of John the Witness's speech. Those who regard 3:31-36 as John's continued speaking may be correct (Wilson; Rensberger 1988: 54–61). For what John says reinforces what Jesus has said about himself in 3:13-21. Stylistic features of both sections support this view, as Wilson shows (37). John, the faithful witness, contrasts to Nicodemus, who appears not to have comprehended Jesus' word.

4:1-2 Pharisees Stirred Up: Clarifying Who Is Doing the Baptism

It is not clear from whom Jesus learns what the Pharisees have heard: *Jesus is making and baptizing more disciples than John.* Perhaps he was informed by his disciples, who in turn were informed by John's disciples, who were told this by *a Jew* (3:25). But the baptizing activities of the two disciple groups are apparently at different locations (3:22-23). Nonetheless, the evangelist informs the reader that the spotlight is on Jesus and his growing movement. For Jesus' safety and to accomplish fully his mission, it is time to relocate—hence 4:3.

But an important clarification must also be made. Jesus himself did not baptize (though 3:22b says he did). Rather, his disciples are doing the baptizing. For some reason, which we do not fully know, this is an important distinction. Apparently the reference is to baptism with water only, but Jesus' mission, as foretold by John, is to baptize with the Holy Spirit (1:33c). Is the qualification against Jesus' baptizing a narrative arrest in order to save the punch for the Holy Spirit baptism later in the narrative (see the discussions of 7:37-39 and 20:19-23)? Lincoln proposes that this way of speaking about Jesus in relation to John's baptizing ministry has a twofold function for the Johannine believers who sought clarity on the relation of John's baptism to baptism in the name of Jesus: "As it stands, the parenthetical comment in 4:2 still maintains the claim that Christian baptism went back to the same time as John's baptism, but through its distinction between Jesus and his disciples, Jesus himself is shielded from being viewed simply as taking up John's practice" (2005: 166). In short, Christian baptism differs qualitatively from John's baptism even though in some respects it is continuous with John's baptism, for in Jesus' baptism water signifies rebirth (John 3:4-7). John 7:37-39 and 20:22-23 clarify this distinction: *Jesus* bestows the Spirit upon the disciples. Yet the text nowhere disparages John but rather portrays him as a faithful witness to Jesus (Rensberger 1988: 57, 61).

4:3 Time for Jesus to Head Back to Galilee

Are the Galilean retreats (here and in 2:1-12) a type of relief from the intensity of Jesus' work in Judea? It would seem so, though the tide turns in Galilee also, at least to some extent, in chapter 6 with the feeding of the five thousand. But as the journey unfolds, another priority arises on the horizon—the mission to Samaria!

THE TEXT IN BIBLICAL CONTEXT

The Temple as Jesus' Father's House[w]

In both Luke 2:49 and John 2:16 Jesus claims the temple as *my Father's house*. This is striking for several reasons. The likely historical setting of John, after the loss of the Jerusalem temple, contributes to this enigma of John's relocating the temple's cleansing in the narrative. The impact of the temple's destruction on the faith practices of Jewish Christians makes Jesus' prophetic reclaiming of the temple a logical *first* action as Jesus enters Jerusalem. Luke's account of Jesus' temple cleansing is quite short (19:45-46). If John knew only Luke, such treatment would have played into his decision to put the "cleansing" first and to magnify its theological significance, which he certainly does. Further, Luke's account of Jesus' word in the temple at age twelve might also have prompted Jesus' reclaiming of the temple as his Father's house (cf. Luke 2:49), where Jesus says, "'Did you not know that I must be in my Father's house?'"

Jesus' pronouncement *my Father's house* (John 2:16c) has far-reaching implications for Christology and eschatology. It is a strong claim that Jesus as Messiah marks the turn of the ages. The coming of the Messiah and the restoration of the temple were twin features of the messianic hope. Some prophetic strands emphasize that the Messiah's coming will inaugurate the era of Gentile inclusion into God's peoplehood (Isa 2:1-4; 56:6-7; Mic 4:1-7; Ezek 40–48; Zech 6:15; *Psalms of Solomon* 17; McKelvey: 9–24). Both Luke's and John's distinctive ways of portraying Gentile inclusion logically follow: twice Luke refers to the Gentiles in chapter 4 after Jesus' Nazareth sermon (vv. 25-30), and John 4 highlights the receptivity of the Samaritans and a Roman official.

For Luke, "my Father's house" contributes to his strong emphasis on Jesus as *Son of God* and on Jesus' two prayers on the cross, in which he addresses God as "Father" (Luke 23:34, 46). For John it sets the stage for a mutual indwelling relationship between Father and Son that culminates in Jesus' prayer in chapter 17: the *Father* (17:1), *Holy Father* (v. 11), *Righteous Father* (v. 25), and Jesus' last commission, *As the Father has sent me, so I send you* (20:21).

My Father's house harks back to God's promise to David that not he but his son will build the temple. But the Lord promises David, "I will be a father to him and he shall be a son to me" (2 Sam 7:14). Every Jew, upon hearing "my Father's house" in Luke or John, would know that the ancient promise was taking on new resonance and residence *here and now*! God's royalty promise to David's lineage *forever* is now focused in Jesus. Jesus fulfills the royal messianic hope of all righteous and devout Jews, as was Zechariah, struck dumb in Luke. This Gospel begins in the temple, which Jesus later calls *my Father's house*.

In John, *temple* and *divine dwelling* permeate the narrative, as Mary Coloe has masterfully shown in two of her books (2001, 2007; also Kerr; Hoskins). The temple theme, begun in 1:14, 51, grows in John: in chapters 2, 3, 4, 7, 10, 14, 18–19. Temple imagery appears elsewhere in the NT (1 Cor 3:16-17; 6:19; Eph 2:19-22). Each use differs slightly. In the first Corinthian text, believers are God's temple, with the Holy Spirit dwelling in the corporate community. In the second, where Paul proscribes prostitution for believers, the physical body of the believer is God's temple, with the Holy Spirit dwelling therein. In the third text the believers, Jews and Gentiles as formerly alienated but now united by Christ's peace, are "joined together . . . into a holy temple in the Lord" (2:21). "The temple of God, the dwelling of God, is made up of erstwhile enemies now at peace with each other and with God *in Christ*" (Yoder Neufeld 2002: 124–33, esp. 128).

Eternal Life in John[w]

Eternal life is a major Johannine motif, though *life* permeates both OT and NT, and *eternal life* occurs elsewhere in the NT (Mark 10:29-30; Matt 25:46; Rom 2:7-8; Gal 6:8; Titus 1:2; 3:7; Jude 21). In Luke 10:25, the lawyer asks Jesus, "What must I do to inherit eternal life?" Jesus answers through the good Samaritan story. He says that if you show mercy as the Samaritan did, you will "live." The term occurs also in late OT books and other Jewish literature. *Eternal life* carries forward the Hebrew term *leḥayyey 'olam* (Dan 12:2) and is connected with the hope for the "coming age." This age begins with Jesus' coming and will continue, for eternal life is both a present and future promise (John 5:24-25, 29) *[Eternal Life, p. 513]*.

Compared to the Synoptics and Paul, it appears that *eternal life* in John denotes one of the Gospel's core salvation motifs. It is analogous to "kingdom of God" in the Synoptics and to the "righteousness of God" in Paul. John uses *kingdom of God* several times in Jesus' encounter with Nicodemus. As in the Synoptics, Jesus in John speaks about how one *can see/enter the kingdom of God* (3:3, 5). But it is not a recurring motif compared to *eternal life* (3:15, 16, 36; 4:14; 5:24; 6:40, 47, 54, 68; et al.). John 10:10 introduces having *life . . . abundantly.* Jesus comes to bring life. This indeed is one of John's Gospel's major motifs.

Jesus, the Bridegroom

The evangelist's designation of John as friend of the bridegroom and Mark's riddle that "wedding guests cannot fast while the bridegroom is with them, can they?" (2:19a) is an arresting parallel. Mark uses "bridegroom" in each of the next two declarations: "As long as they have the bridegroom with them, they cannot fast. The days will come when the bridegroom is taken away from them, and then they will fast on that day" (2:19b-20). The similarities between Mark (with parallel in Matt 9:15; Luke 5:34-35) and John are striking. In both, the bridegroom sayings are prompted by actions of John's disciples! But a striking difference is the speaker. In Matthew, Jesus responds to John's disciples' question about fasting; in Mark and Luke it is "people" or "they" who ask. In the fourth Gospel, John the Witness responds to his own disciples' alarm about Jesus' baptizing. John's disciples prompt the discussion on the meaning of Jesus as Messiah-elect. They are searching for the clues, the "markers" of the One hoped for. In this light, John's phrase *he who has the bride* alludes to Jesus' baptizing—gathering his bride in that manner. He, John the Witness, is friend of the bridegroom!

Nuptial imagery laces both testaments in describing God's relation to Israel, his elect peoplehood (see Hos 2:19-21; Jer 2:2-3; Isa 54:5-6; 62:4-5; Ezek 16:1-14). In the NT, God's relation to the church is described also in nuptial imagery (2 Cor 11:2; Eph 5:25-27; Rev 21:2). God indicts Israel for unfaithfulness in this nuptial relationship through their recurring addiction to idolatry—worshiping Baal and other gods. The Lord God indicts Israel for idolatry on the one hand and dependence on war power and wealth on the other (Isa 2:5-8, 18-20). Israel's unfaithfulness is harlotry (Ezek 23; Lind: 193-98). Hosea (chs. 1–3; 6:4-6) depicts God's pathos, hurt, and anger over Israel's flirting with other gods, courting other partners. But God cannot forsake God's covenant love and promise. God will take Israel back into the wilderness and allure her again (2:14). The people's heart will change, and they will put away the Baals (2:16). "I take you for my wife forever: I will take you in righteousness and in justice, in steadfast love, and in mercy" (2:19; Guenther: 38–73). In Ephesians 5:25-27, Christ is wedded to the church as his bride. Here Christ is *cleansing her with the washing of the water by the word*, most likely a reference to baptism (Yoder Neufeld 2002: 262). Given this imagery from Ephesians, it is striking that the fourth evangelist locates the bridegroom imagery for Jesus right after the Witness's disciples' query about Jesus' baptizing many (with a qualifying later notation in 4:2). Baptism and bride go together, steady-like!

THE TEXT IN THE LIFE OF THE CHURCH

The New Birth[w]

Early church writers frequently speak of the new birth. Cyprian (third century), in *Epistle 1* to *Donatus 3-4*, writes of his conversion in "born-again" language, as commentary on John 3:3, 5: "While I was still lying in darkness, . . . remote from truth and light, I used to regard it as a difficult matter . . . that a man should be capable of being born again . . . and . . . be able to put off what he had previously been" (Talbert: 99).

The issue of whether and how one is "born again" continued in Christian history. "Maximus the Confessor (580–662) said there are two ways of being born of God, one by which a person becomes a child of God, but still in potency, with the ability to sin; the other by which a person is actually transformed totally by complete submission to the Holy Spirit" (Malatesta: 249). This reflects Roman Catholic theology with two levels of Christian ethics: the first level, that of laity; and the second, that achieved by only monks and nuns.

Menno Simons wrote a treatise on *The New Birth* around 1537 (enlarged and corrected in the Wenger edition of Menno's writings). Menno (92) emphasizes repentance as the first step to new birth. Even that repentance originates in "the Word of the Lord, rightly taught and rightly understood and received in the heart by faith through the Holy Ghost." Menno's instruction on the new birth exhorts those born again to show the new birth in moral living (an emphasis permeating 1 John). If they do not live in obedience to Christ, he strongly denounces their new-birth claims. Baptized as infants, they do deeds of wickedness. His descriptions are long and vivid. He enumerates the sinful pleasures of "rulers and potentates." Next he names more perverse sins of "the regents and judges," including accepting bribes, even "gifts to shed innocent blood." Then he lambasts the sins of the "divines, preachers, priests, or monks": carnality, false interpretation of Scripture, hatred, lying, and so forth. Finally Menno lists the more sordid sins of the common people: "lying, cheating, cursing, gambling, drinking, and fighting" (98–99). Such living does not manifest the new birth, whose recipients know nothing of hatred and vengeance, but rather demonstrate love toward those who hate them.

Menno identifies at length the marks of those born again—how their lives reflect the teachings of Christ. He then devotes several pages to chastising the dominant society, accusing them of every sort of sin and wickedness. Menno reiterates that repentance must precede new birth. But if those who claim new birth go on sinning, change is not manifest. His final appeal negates the validity of infant baptism because it does not lead to regenerate living, but rather to degenerate living (96–97).

In the late twentieth century, a rather peculiar phenomenon hit the American media. Politicians and Hollywood celebrities testified to being "born again." "To be born again" garnered support for personal fame. On occasion it produced a radical change of lifestyle, evidence that the testimony possessed integrity. Christians who for years took their Christian confession and living seriously were reticent to cheer those new instant "born-againers." Mennonites, learning from Menno, expect a changed and holy life to testify to such a claim.

The popular view too often reduces being born again to an individualistic experience with God that guarantees a one-way ticket to heaven, but produces no good moral character. Thus hedonistic lifestyles continue.

In John's Gospel vision, being *born again* means living in the light, being obedient to God and God's word. It also promises eternal life that begins even now. It means quitting sinful behaviors (1 John 3:9). In presenting eight different confessional understandings of baptism, ranging from exorcism to ecstasy, Russell Haitch uses John Howard Yoder's writings to describe believers baptism, under the chapter subtitle "Baptism into the New Humanity" (23–45). Baptism means entering into new creation and community where a person's particular history, ethnic identity, and special gifts are not quashed but honored, while also relativized by the primacy of the corporate life of the new community. All who repent of their alienated life from God and are baptized are "invited to be united and equal with fellow believers." Baptism is not just a new start for the person, or that plus a new society. Instead, it commences living in the new regime of Jesus Christ: Jesus is "the bearer of a new possibility of human, social, and therefore political relationships. His baptism is the inauguration and his cross is the culmination of that new regime in which his disciples are called to share" (Haitch: 37; J. H. Yoder 1994: 52).

John 3:16 in Evangelism (and Philosophy[w])

John 3:16 has often been used in evangelism. Its evangelistic power, the Gospel's Magna Carta, prompted by Max Lucado's reflection, is exemplified here with my modifications:

> God loves.
> God will not let you go; God claims you.
> God gave [cf. 1 Cor 15:3; Gal 1:4; 3:13].
> We believe [John 14:6; Acts 4:12].
> Believing, we receive eternal life.
> We live [1 Peter 1:3; 2 Timothy 1:10; Romans 14:8b].
> "Whether we live or . . . die, we are the Lord's."

John 4:4-54

Jesus' Peace Mission: Savior of the World

PREVIEW

Palestinians ride buses into Jewish neighborhoods to oppose the current apartheid Israel imposes upon the Palestinians. Rosa Parks remains seated in the front seat to protest racial segregation, even when she is told to sit in the back. White Americans drive into a "township" in South Africa in 1982 to visit "colored" friends when they know it violates prevailing social boundaries. Jesus risks going through Samaria, knowing he could be stoned to death.

John 4 marks an important turn in Jesus' ministry. Jesus is under "divine necessity" (*dei* in v. 4) to pass through Samaria on the way to Galilee. Jesus' encounter with the Samaritan woman is Jesus' intentional mission, significant for both mission and peacemaking. What are the ramifications of passing through enemy land?

The Samaritan woman, a marginalized person, contrasts with Nicodemus, a religious leader of repute. In moving from John 3 to John 4, the narrative shifts from the failure of a leading Pharisee to openly believe in Jesus to this engaging dialogue with a Samaritan *woman* who believes, despite the enmity between Jews and Samaritans. If Nicodemus cannot comprehend Jesus, how can this Samaritan woman? Strikingly, the imagery of water and the theme of *belief* connect the two stories. On this score, while Nicodemus's response is at best secret belief, the Samaritan woman's is public testimony. She is the Gospel's first and only believer whose witness wins the conversion of many hometown people. Both figures

119

encounter Jesus personally: in the first, Nicodemus takes the initiative, seeking out Jesus. In the second, Jesus seeks out the Samaritan woman. Both figures function as representatives of a people's response to Jesus as Revealer and Savior.

The story of Jesus and the Samaritan woman begs to be read on multiple levels of meaning: literal, historical, and figural levels. Is this narrative to be understood in terms of ancient hospitality customs (Alterbury) or with the overtones of betrothal, reflecting OT archetypal stories (Gen 24; 29)? If the latter, what does 3:29 mean, where John the Witness identifies Jesus as bridegroom?

What does Jesus' mission mean in its historical racial context? This nonkosher encounter becomes the occasion for Jesus to reveal his divine identity—to this *woman . . . in public!* The necessary emphatic inclusion of Samaritans as the first and only people in the Gospel who accept and affirm Jesus as *the Savior of the world* (4:42) compels historical reflection on what role Samaritans had in the community out of which and to which the Gospel was written, without excluding the churchwide, first-century audience. The story exudes theological-ethical meaning in which mission and peacemaking blend beautifully, a point of no small significance for the story's relevance to the life of the church today.

In this narrative the role of the disciples is intriguing. Their presence with Jesus frames the woman's presence: the disciples had gone away to buy food (v. 8); thus Jesus and the woman are the only characters onstage for the encounter. When the disciples return (v. 27), they marvel that Jesus is talking to a woman. When they come, the woman leaves her jar at the well and heads home with an urgent message to her people. At that same time, Jesus gives his disciples a mission charge. While Jesus initiates mission and the Samaritan woman consummates mission, the disciples receive a commission for mission (4:35-38).

Another mission story occurs next. At the request of a Roman official, another "enemy type," Jesus heals his dying boy. The Gentile official is also a prototype of faith in Jesus. Not only does he go home believing Jesus' words *Your son will live*, but also when he discovers that his son was healed of his infirmity at the very time Jesus spoke those words, *he himself believed, and all his household* (RSV). This is Jesus' second sign in Galilee.

These two stories, twinned together in mission and peacemaking, with unlikely heroes, unveil the Gospel's theological intentions.

OUTLINE

Jesus and the Samaritan Woman, 4:4-26
Triune Mission, 4:27-42
Geographical Transition: Return to Cana in Galilee, 4:43-45
Jesus Heals the Roman Official's Son, 4:46-54

EXPLANATORY NOTES

Jesus and the Samaritan Woman 4:4-26[w]

Commentators often present John 4:4-42 as a chiasm, with verses 19-24 on worship at the center. Most, however, neglect Jesus' *I AM* self-revelation to the Samaritan woman in verses 25-26. This chiasm portrays in C and C′ the interconnection between true worship and Jesus' true identity, *I AM*:

A Meeting of Jesus and the *Samaritan* woman at the well (4:5-9)
    B Dialogue with woman on *living water* (4:10-15)
        C Dialogue on *true worship* (4:16-24)
        C′ Jesus reveals his *I AM identity* (4:25-26)
    B′ Dialogue with disciples on *true food* (4:27-38)
A′ Meeting of *Samaritans* and Jesus (4:39-42)

This chiasm presents the varied topics as a seamless whole. *Well* and *living water*, both symbolic of betrothal, lead to *husbands*, then to true worship that includes Jesus' christological disclosure, and finally to the food of mission and *increase* (4:35-38). The Samaritan woman functions representatively. Lee (1993: 38–39; 2002: 72) presents three scenes, each centered on an image: living water (*hydōr zōn*, 4:10), *sacred place* (*topos*, 4:20), and food/harvest (*brōsis/brōma/therismos*, 4:32/34/35). These material images disclose spiritual reality, which some perceive to be sacramental: water/wine and bread (M. Collins: 3–4).

4:4-6 *The Setting: Sychar in Samaria*

That Jesus *must* go through Samaria is most significant. The term translated "it is necessary" (*dei*) occurs here as the climax to four previous uses (also later in 4:20 and 24):

- *It is necessary* to be born from above (3:7).
- *It is necessary* that the Son of Man be lifted up (3:14).
- *It is necessary* for Jesus to increase (3:30).
- *It is necessary* for Jesus to go through Samaria (4:4).

The latter is both geographical and theological necessity. These four uses respectively speak of salvation, suffering and glory, Christology, and mission. All serve the Gospel's purpose, stated in 20:31: *that you may believe that Jesus is the Messiah, the Son of God, and that through believing you may have life in his name* (AT). Raymond Collins, in assessing the *typecast* features of characters in John, suggests that Nicodemus, the Samaritan woman, and others *build* faith in the believers as these stories are proclaimed in homilies and sermons (7–8). They also *lead* to faith. These encounters are *necessary* for Jesus to accomplish his mission and the Gospel to fulfill its purpose.

Jesus meets the Samaritan woman at the historic Jacob's well at Sychar. Although many commentators identify Sychar as modern Askar, two ancient Syrian manuscripts read *Shechem*, the city destroyed under John Hyrcanus. Jacob's well is closer to where Shechem was than to modern Askar (D. M. Smith 1999: 110–11).

Jesus is tired and thirsty, arriving at the well at noon, in the heat of the day. The woman comes to draw water at noon instead of early morning, when most women come. Perhaps she comes then because she is vulnerable to verbal abuse from other women. But it may also allude to an earlier betrothal story at a well: Jacob's meeting Rachel (Gen 29:7), thus clueing the reader how to read this narrative.

Jesus' need to go through Samaria means the Gospel is inherently both missional and peacemaking. The enmity between Jews and Samaritans was long and deep. This enmity developed and spiraled over centuries. Originating at the time of the exile of the Northern Kingdom (721 BC), the hostility increased in the postexilic period of Ezra and Nehemiah (ca. 464–438 BC). The returned Babylonian Jewry regarded itself as the "holy seed" (Ezra 9:2) or faithful "remnant" (9:15), in contrast to those who had stayed in Israel and intermarried with the locals who practiced pagan worship. They thus became "unclean with the pollutions of the peoples of the lands, with their abominations" (Ezra 9:11).

The Samaritans under Sanballat, their Persian governor, first volunteered to help the returned exiles rebuild the temple, but the "true Israelites"—as they regarded themselves—sent them packing (Ezra 4:1-3). Hence the Samaritans obstructed Nehemiah's rebuilding the wall around the city (Neh 6:1-14). Postexilic Jewry vigorously sought to protect itself from this "pollution" by forbidding marriage to foreigners. The wall built around Jerusalem protected not only physically but also religiously and ethnically, symbolizing hostility toward Samaritans. During the postexilic decades and centuries, two contesting ideologies prevailed in Jewry: one, more self-protective against outsiders (cf. Deut 23:1-8; Nahum), and another more inclusive of outsiders (Isa 40–55; 56:1-8; Jonah; Ruth).

Alexander the Great's conquest and the rule of the Ptolemies exacerbated the tension between the two peoples. According to Josephus (*Ant.* 18.4.1–2, §§ 85–89) the final schism occurred when Alexander gave the Samaritans permission to build their own temple on Mount Gerizim—though no archaeological remains have been found. Josephus narrates that the temple was burned under the rule of Hasmonean leader John Hyrcanus (Donahue: 154n21; Mor: 16). A text from Sirach (ca. 120 BC) shows the depth of Jewish antipathy toward the Samaritans, whom they considered semipagan: "Two nations my soul detests, and the third is not even a people: Those who live in Seir, and the Philistines, and the foolish people that live in Shechem" (50:25-26). The Septuagint renders the last part: "those dwelling on the mountain of Samaria."

4:7-18 Living Water: Jesus Dialogues with a Woman at the Well[w]

This dialogue between Jesus and the Samaritan woman is longer than any other recorded in the Gospels. Jesus talks longer with her than anyone else, including any of his disciples, accusers, family, or petitioners for healing.

The woman, confounded to see a *Jewish* man at the well, is *incredulous* that this anonymous Jew speaks to her, asking her to give him a drink of water. She becomes curious when he promises living water that would never end. Then she is *intrigued*—perhaps *dismayed*, when Jesus makes a disarming personal request that she fetch her husband. Finally she is *open* to revelation about God through this Jew, Jesus, and she is *astonished* when she learns who Jesus is.

In light of the long-standing enmity between Jews and Samaritans, readers are shocked by this intimately personal and deeply theological dialogue on issues that divided the communities. It becomes christological, and the woman becomes the Gospel's ideal missioner. Her people confess Jesus' messianic identity, *the Savior of the world!*

The encounter violates other cultural prohibitions also. In Jewish and Samaritan society, women were not to converse with

men in public. If a woman did so, it reflected negatively on her character, classifying her with loose, immoral women. Talbert (112) cites
two rabbinic texts (m. 'Abot 1:5; b. Qiddušim 70a) that forbid a man to
publicly converse with a woman or even to greet a woman: "It is
forbidden to give a woman any greeting." Verse 9 explains the
double social offense of Jesus' initiative:

> WOMAN: *How is it that you, a [man] Jew, ask a drink of me, a woman of
> Samaria?*
> NARRATOR: *For Jews have no dealings with Samaritans.* (RSV)

The shock of this encounter is intensified by the narrator's skill. The
disciples have left Jesus; these two are *alone* in this encounter and
ensuing dialogue. The breaches of religious and social boundaries,
so culturally deep, are virtually unimaginable.

The key motif in the dialogue is *water*. Jesus is thirsty and asks
for a drink. The woman is shocked, not only at his speaking to her
but also with the prospect of this man's sipping water from her
bucket. The Greek verb in verse 9b (*synchraomai*) means "to use in
common," like using the same utensils. Sharing the bucket violated
Jewish law. Though Jesus requests water to quench his thirst, the
text does not say that the woman ever gave it to him. Rather, Jesus
redirects the dialogue by offering her *living water*, promising she
will never thirst again.

In this exchange the water of Jacob's *well* (*phrear*, vv. 11, 12),
accessed via a deep shaft, contrasts to the *living water* (v. 10d), which
is a *spring* [*pēgē*] *of water gushing up to eternal life* (v. 14). The woman
eagerly asks for this water so she will not need to come to this well
(*phrear*) to draw water. Jesus speaks of *living water* (*hydōr zōn*), a
phrase that could mean "running water," a double entendre that
plays into her misunderstanding. But Jesus means the water of life,
not natural running water. The woman does not yet know this (D.
M. Smith 1999: 113).

When Jesus offers the Samaritan woman *living water*—puzzling
but intriguing to her—she modifies her stance and addresses Jesus
as *Lord/Sir* (*kyrie*), not as a confessional title, though the narrator
may intend a double meaning here as well, but as respectful address:
"This sudden usage is in stark contrast with their first exchange
where she did not show any form of respect" (Botha: 124). The
woman adopts a more cautious tone in verse 9. The vocative address
(*Sir*) occurs again in verse 15, when she eagerly requests this gift of
living water welling up to eternal life (v. 14 RSV). It disappears in verse
17, when the woman is threatened by Jesus' spiritual probe; but it

reappears in verse 19, as she comes to perceive Jesus to be a *prophet*. Despite the jarring initiatives of this Jewish man, the woman now shows Jesus more respect than she normally would to Jews.

Four features or motifs link this narrative to John 3, even to 2:1-10. First, in offering *living water*, Jesus speaks on one level of meaning, and the woman hears on another, analogous to Nicodemus's misunderstanding of *anōthen*: born *again* or *anew* or *from above*. Second, the literary context to Jesus' offer of *living water* is water baptism (3:23–4:2). Third, John the Witness identifies Jesus as bridegroom and himself as friend of the bridegroom (3:29), and this story in John 4 has betrothal overtones. Fourth, the water and bridegroom motifs—as well as women, wells, and waterpots—link the text to the wedding in Cana in 2:1-11. The conjoining of this imagery in the narrative flow beckons one to see a deeper, figural level, indeed a work of art (Trudinger: 10).

The bridegroom imagery is important, echoing OT texts where God is portrayed in nuptial relation to the covenant people. McWhirter (1–78) discusses numerous OT backgrounds (Jer 33:10-11; Gen 29:1-20; Song of Sol 1:12; 3:1-4; Ps 45). Not only is the nuptial imagery significant, but this imagery also carries messianic import crucial to understanding the encounter between Jesus and the Samaritan woman. The necessity (*dei*) for Jesus to go through Samaria to meet a woman at a well, the open conversation, and then her return home—all carry betrothal overtones: see the OT stories of Abraham's servant meeting Rebekah at the well when seeking a wife for Isaac (Gen 24:10-27), Jacob's meeting Rachel at the well (Gen 29:4-12), and Moses' meeting Zipporah at a well (Exod 2:15-22).

As with John 3, Jesus' dialogue partners struggle to perceive *spirit* reality. The Samaritan woman leaps the gap; Nicodemus does not. Jesus' gift of *eternal life* unites both narratives (cf. 3:15-16). Jesus' promise of *eternal life* in 4:14, upon receiving this *living water*, anticipates *eternal life* in 4:36, in Jesus' mission commission to his disciples. Many Samaritans believe and receive this gift (v. 42). Lee (1993: 38; cf. 2002: 71) cites five unifying motifs: water, baptism, Spirit, world, and witness (see 3:5-8, 16, 22-30). A sixth motif is *life/living*.

It is difficult to capture the tone and inflection of both Jesus' and the Samaritan woman's voices. Was Jesus' request for water spoken as a demand, as Pazdan (1987: 146) suggests? Or was it a request put gently, which I think is more realistic, given the dicey situation? Was the woman's voice that of a superior teacher, since she was on her own turf, knew about the well, and could draw water—when

Jesus did not even have a bucket? She knew the importance of Jacob, who gave a special land portion (Heb. *šekem*, a play on the name of the town, *Shechem*) to Joseph's son, Ephraim (Gen 48:22). And she knew of Mount Gerizim, another pillar in her own faith history and identity (Pazdan: 147). I expect an edge of superiority in her voice, especially in her question, *Where [pothen] do you get that living water?* (v. 11). She knew the wells available: "Certainly this guy can't outwit us natives to the region!" she infers. O'Day (1986b: 66) suggests that *pothen* is ironic: readers know what the woman does not know. She is ignorant of Jesus' gifts and identity.

Jesus then shocks the woman, shifting the topic (not, however, if read at the figural level) of the dialogue. When asked to call her husband (v. 16), she says, *I have no husband*, an ironic understatement (v. 17), as the ensuing dialogue reveals. Her tone changes, since now she learns that Jesus has insight into her life. He must be a *prophet*!

In his prophetic perception, Jesus declares otherwise: *You are right in saying, "I have no husband," for you have had five husbands, and the one you have now is not your husband. What you have said is true!* What is the significance of Jesus' encasing his response in a double affirmation of this woman's veracity? Is it irony? O'Day believes so: "The emphasis . . . Jesus places on the veracity of the woman's statements is such overt irony that it borders on biting sarcasm" (1986b: 67). The woman, rightly declaring Jesus to be a prophet, shifts the dialogue to another topic (but which is again the same topic at the figural level), the long-standing dispute between Jews and Samaritans about the proper place to worship. "A prophet, if he really is one, should have an answer!"

Though in a literal reading this woman carries a moral stigma, the text does not dwell on that point—not even on the man with whom she is currently living, who is not her husband. In Jewish culture—and likely Samaritan as well—only men could initiate divorce, except for exceptional cases of abuse (E. de Boer: 113). The rabbis approved up to three divorces, though legally more were admissible (Barrett 1978: 235). Yet this woman may not have been divorced, but rather a levirate spouse five times (cf. Mark 12:18-23; Deut 24:1-4). For Jesus does not dwell on her behavior as immoral. Jesus engages her theologically about the proper place of worship, a key point in the racial enmity. Jesus continues the "salvation" conversation with her—in public—to welcome her to the living water. He persists in order that she and her fellow Samaritans, though rejected by Jews, might come to know him as *the Savior of the world* (v. 42).

Jesus' mission in Samaria shatters boundaries of religion and politics, gender codes, and marital practices. Present-day Muslim cultural practices are more at home in first-century Palestine than are our Western notions on gender, divorce, and remarriage. Jesus' going into Samaria is culturally subversive. The textual flow is from exposing the boundaries, onward to shattering and transcending them by extending the living water of salvation to a marginalized and oppressed woman, and eventually to welcoming the alienated Samaritans—not just the woman—into the solidarity of messianic salvation. The story *performs*; its narration *shows* and *effects* transformation. It heals the rivalry of alienated peoples (H. Boers: 200).

This narrative has been interpreted various ways, ranging from a literal-historical appropriation of the text to several levels of symbolic significance. Numerous commentators regard the Samaritan woman figurally, representing Samaritan infidelity in worship since Samaritans are said to have had five idolatries (2 Kings 17:29-31; Josephus, *Ant.* 9.14.3). Some commentators contend against the figural (allegorical?) interpretations (Beasley-Murray 1999: 61; Bultmann: 188; Michaels: 247; Morris: 235), pointing out that the 2 Kings text mentions seven, not five, gods or goddesses. In the figural interpretations, however, the dialogue topics are not disjointed but logically proceed from water to husbands to worship. Some elements of the figural are persuasive. If one preaches or teaches the text at a figural level, a sermon might address how Christians connect with those of other faiths and witness to Hindus and other polytheists, who honor numerous gods and goddesses. Verse 24's instruction to *worship the Father in spirit and truth* then carries new depth and relevance in our religiously pluralistic society.

Interpreting this narrative as fulfillment of *He must increase* (3:30), McWhirter (58-59) says, "In a scene reminiscent of biblical betrothal narratives, the bridegroom-Messiah adds to his increase with a host of Samaritan believers." This narrative becomes a Magna Carta for the early church's mission to the Samaritans (cf. Acts 1:8; 8:4-24).

The notion that one must choose between the historical and the symbolic must be rejected (Léon-Dufour). Jesus' self-disclosure as *I AM* related to worship *in spirit and truth* is the intended narrator's emphasis. The interpretive perspectives that highlight this point should receive priority in our use of the story (see comments on vv. 25-26, p. 129).

Whatever the situation of her many husbands, the narrative portrays the woman not as a victim crushed by her experiences, but as a laudable witness to Jesus' identity as prophet and Messiah. In Jesus' encounter with her, she is first and finally a human being whose dignity Jesus values, a trusted hearer, and a bearer of Jesus' salvation news. She receives the *living water* and in turn shares it with her townsfolk. She says, *Come and see a man who told me . . .* (v. 29, an echo of Jesus' *Come and see* in 1:39 and Philip's in 1:46c). To the first and successive readers—even to us—Jesus offers the gift of living water, release from our religious provincialism that blinds us to God's grace for our lives, and beckons us to open our eyes to see God's revelation in Jesus.

With all its richness this narrative demonstrates that in John, Jesus not only mediates revelation but also *is* revelation. The narrative not only reports Jesus as revealer, but also "allows the reader to *experience* Jesus' revelation for himself or herself" (Gail O'Day 1986a: 668; cf. 1986b: 92). The *revelation* and *transformation* it effects is Jesus' salvation, crumbling structures and prejudices of partitioning, alienation, and enmity.

4:19-24 True Worship

This paragraph has been rightly understood as the pivotal center of the entire dialogue. The verb *worship* occurs eight times, thus stressing its importance in the story (Cahill: 44). Here the woman-turned-theologian initiates and directs the conversation. She presses it on to its climax in verse 26. Speaking with a Jewish man whom she now perceives to be *a prophet* (v. 19), she launches into the most sensitive issue dividing Samaritans and Jews: rival claims to the right place for worship, Jerusalem or Mount Gerizim.

When this paragraph is viewed by itself, the rival claims appear petulant, with Jesus judging against Samaritan worship—not its location but its integrity—when he says, *You worship what you do not know; we worship what we know, for salvation is from the Jews* (v. 22). The *we* of Jesus' statement identifies Jesus with the Jews, as does the final salvation claim. Jesus speaks as a Jew and for the Jews. When Jesus' word, however, is put within the context of Jesus' self-disclosure, any latent triumphalism is judged and transcended. Verse 24 defines God as *spirit*, undermining *place* claims. The important point is that we *worship [God] in spirit and truth.* True worship, whether Samaritan or Jewish, is not defined or limited by place, but by integrity of heart and spirit, echoing OT prophetic critiques of sacrifice (Pss 40:6-8; 50:7-23; 51:16-17; Mic 6:1-8).

Jesus' word on worship begins with *The hour is coming and now is* (v. 23). This term signals eschatological consummation. Future hope enters human experience *now.* Though Jesus' dialogue partner does not know it, the readers know that this *hour* is also the hour of Jesus' death and glorification (2:4; 12:23; 13:1; 17:1). For Gospel readers, this phrase signals *Stop, listen, and understand!* While the disciples are off buying food, "you, a Samaritan woman, now perceive what they do not yet understand." Verse 24 redefines everything: the need for temples and holy places, space and place, spirit and truth. Jesus leads the woman and readers into a "thin space" between earth and heaven, where usual stabilizing categories give way to surprises of grace. The *holy* comes to humans; worship in spirit and truth renders rivalry and enmity out of order. The *holy* amid the human radiates the larger Gospel paradox: the God-Word become *flesh*; humans beholding the divine *glory* (Lee 2002; Evans 1993a).

4:25-26 Jesus' Messianic Self-Disclosure

In John 4:25, the woman sounds more Jewish than Samaritan: *I know that the Messiah is coming (he who is called Christ); when he comes, he will show us all things* (RSV). Jesus in turn says, *I am he, the one who is speaking to you.* The usual interpretation is that Jesus here reveals himself as the Messiah. But Samaritans expected the *Taheb* (Restorer; based esp. on Deut 18:18), not a messiah. This dissonance may indicate that at the time of the writing of the fourth Gospel, Samaritans were already incorporated into the Jewish Christian community and had accepted the messianic hopes of the Jews. Jesus' voice is clear: *Salvation is from the Jews* (v. 22c).

Jesus' response transcends the Taheb / Messiah distinction. The Greek *egō eimi* (*I am*) begins John's frequent *I AM* claims of Jesus. *The one speaking to you* reiterates verse 10c and establishes the connection between Jesus and his *I AM* identity (Moloney: 130) [*"I AM," p. 518*]. Such disclosure transcends the Samaritan Taheb/Jewish Messiah polarity and harks back to God's self-disclosure to Moses (Exod 3:14-15) as God's eternal *I AM*. For both Samaritans (who regarded only the Torah as Scripture) and Jews, this knowledge of God was foundational. In this perspective, Jesus' self-disclosure, in keeping with John 1:1, 18, critiques both expectations—for the Taheb (based on Deut 18:15, 18) and for the Messiah (based on the Prophets). Jesus is greater than both. "Nothing in her tradition could have prepared her for the radical power of Jesus' self-revelation" (O'Day 2002: 53). For that reason, true worship cannot be confined to either Jerusalem or Gerizim. It will eternally transcend both, springing forth like living water, in spirit and truth. "The worshipful interrelationship of God and believers is more fundamental than the claims of any tradition to have an exclusive hold on God's presence" (O'Day 2002: 51).

Jesus' *I AM* disclosure climaxes this discussion about husbands and worship and judges the five idolatries that the Samaritans blended with their worship. As the lens for his identity, Jesus' appeal to God's revelation to Moses, "I AM WHO I AM" (Exod 3:14), makes the figural interpretation the most persuasive. In addition to the seamless flow from husbands to worship to christological revelation, Jesus' self-revelation anchors his identity in monotheism: the Lord God revealed to Moses is alone to be worshiped.

Triune Mission 4:27-42

4:27-30 The Disciples Return; The Woman Leaves to Proclaim

This paragraph and the next display split-screen actions. On one screen we see the disciples returning with food. On the other screen we see the Samaritan woman leaving her water jar, running back to the city, and testifying to her townsfolk. Meanwhile we see and hear the disciples urging Jesus to eat; and then Jesus teaching the disciples about food from above, which blends into fields ripe for harvest—mission food.

As the disciples return, they see Jesus talking to this Samaritan woman in public. They ask no questions of her or him—possibly because they are dumbstruck at such a sunlight episode defying cultural norms. The woman, too, is uncharacteristically mute. She simply "up and leaves," driven to tell what she has discovered. She is on a mission back home! Her water has become wine! She is intoxicated with Jesus!

Her evangelistic manner is laudable. She invites her townsfolk to *come and see* for themselves, introducing her newfound friend as one *who told me everything I have ever done.* Then she asks an open question with an implied negative trailing off into a positive: *He cannot be the Messiah, can he?* The negative *mē* in the question expects a negative response, here implying: "It's a long shot, I know." But whatever her reputation in the community, she says enough to open the door to the crowd's inquiry. The people leave the city, go out to meet Jesus, to see him for themselves.

The woman is doing what Jesus now teaches his disciples to do.

4:31-38 True Food; Jesus Commissions His Disciples[w]

Meanwhile, the disciples engage Jesus, urging him to eat the food they have brought. Yet Jesus astounds them by not eating but discoursing, *I have food to eat that you do not know about.* While the disciples wonder at this, Jesus explains, *My food is to do the will of him who sent me and to complete his work.* Jesus' saying echoes a biblical motif (Deut 8:3, quoted by Jesus in Matt 4:4 and Luke 4:4 when tempted by Satan). Two Johannine special emphases emerge: Jesus does *the will of him who sent him* (cf. 5:36; 10:37-38; 17:4), and Jesus' clear sense of having been *sent* (here a form of *pempō*, but elsewhere in John also *apostellō*). Linda Oyer (1997: 446) tabulates the sixty times these verb(al)s occur in John.

Harvest normally comes four months after sowing (v. 35a), with firstfruits in spring, shortly after Passover (2:13); yet in his mission charge to the disciples, Jesus declares that *the fields are already ripe for harvesting*, allowing for no interval at all (v. 35c; Barrett 1978: 241). While in the Synoptics, Jesus' teachings with the image of *harvest* often point to an eschatological future, here the *harvest* is at hand, reflecting Johannine realized eschatology (without denying future eschatology, as in 5:25-29) *[Eschatology, p. 512]*. Here the connection to what is happening on the other screen should not be missed. Even now, as Jesus speaks, Samaritans are hearing the good news of Jesus as God's *I AM* coming afresh into the world to give *living water* and *eternal life: The reaper is already receiving wages and is gathering fruit for eternal life, so that the sower and the reaper may rejoice together* (v. 36). Is this an allusion to Jesus, the *sower,* and the Samaritan woman, the *reaper? Reaping* likely refers to what Jesus soon says to the disciples. Quoting a proverb, Jesus reiterates: *One sows and another reaps* (v. 37). Jesus then addresses the disciples directly: *I sent you [apesteila] to reap that for which you did not labor.* The disciples enter into others' labors (v. 38). Does this suggest an earlier mission to the Samaritans prior to John's Gospel (cf. Acts 6:5; 8:14-15)? If so, the timing in this verse reflects the Gospel's time rather than Jesus' time.

4:39-42 Samaritans Believe: Jesus Is the Savior of the World

The climax to this astonishing story presents two layers of faith response from the Samaritan townspeople. First, some believed *because of the woman's testimony* (v. 39). Second, *many more believed because of his word* (v. 41)—what Jesus taught during the *two days* he stayed (*abode/menō* of ch. 15) with the Samaritans (v. 40c). The confession of their belief, *the Savior of the world* (v. 42), transcends both the Taheb and Messiah traditions. The particular gives way to the universal: *I AM* (v. 26) is the *Savior of the world.* Here is the Gospel's profoundest christological claim and missional vision. No fudging, no christological reductionism, no pluralist confessional stew. This woman emerges in the narrative as the vehicle of the grandest revelation to her neighbors and all Gospel readers: *Jesus reveals God* to and for all people!

This particular confession of the Samaritan community has political significance, as does 11:47-52 and the trial narrative especially. In varied forms "Savior of the world" was a title of Roman rulers from Julius Caesar to Hadrian. This precise form was used (*sōtēr tou kosmou*) for Augustus and Hadrian. Craig Koester (1990: 667, 680) contends that the text intends to evoke in the reader imperial associations and show that the Samaritan confession places them beyond "a form of worship tainted by charges of idolatry to true worship of God, and beyond national identity defined by colonial powers to become true people of God." Richard Cassidy (1992: 84–85) affirms the political interpretation yet stresses another point, the theme of persecution in John, prominent in Jesus' farewell discourse. Through this Samaritan confession and Jesus' teaching throughout the Gospel, John seeks "to encourage his readers not ever to be swayed or intimidated by the aggrandizing claims of the Roman emperors who styled themselves as saviors."

Geographical Transition: Return to Cana in Galilee 4:43-45

These verses give a rationale for Jesus' return to Galilee: Jesus' own testimony (cf. Mark 6:4; Luke 4:23) *that a prophet has no honor in the prophet's own country*. The inference is that in John's Gospel *Jerusalem* is Jesus' country. In John, indeed, Jesus does most of his public ministry in Jerusalem, in connection with festivals, mostly Passovers. Coming to terms with this portrait, so different from that of the Synoptics, raises the difficult question of how John is related to the Synoptics. Do Mark and John preserve two different streams of eyewitness testimony to Jesus' ministry—with Matthew and Luke building upon Mark? Bauckham (2007: 36–67) answers yes. The key eyewitness is the Beloved disciple in John—not John the apostle but John, a Jerusalem disciple. Some commentators, with good reason, call John the "Jerusalem Gospel."

The Galileans honor Jesus on the basis of what they saw and heard Jesus do in Jerusalem. News about Jesus undoubtedly traveled ahead of him to Galilee. The comment in 4:45 that the Galileans welcomed him seems to indicate a polarity in types of faith response between Jerusalem and Galilee, including Samaria, not unlike that in the Synoptic Gospels (Freyne: 271–72; Swartley 1994: 39–43, 269–77).

This typology may shed light on the vexing issue of why John's Gospel types the Jews as negative to Jesus, even though Jesus himself, his disciples, and his special friends (ch. 11) are Jews—and throughout the narrative many Jews believe. However, one must be cautious and critical of this typology, for John 6 is located in Galilee.

The Jews are there also, testing and opposing Jesus. So what works for the Synoptic Gospels may not work for John [*"The Jews," p. 520*].

Jesus Heals the Roman Official's Son 4:46-54

This miracle occurs in Cana, when Jesus arrives there from Samaria/Judea (v. 54). This Cana miracle evokes memory of the earlier one done there when Jesus changes water into wine. This point together with the ending phrase, *the second sign that Jesus did after coming from Judea to Galilee*, means that the two Cana signs form bookends to these three chapters. For this reason some scholars (Coloe 2007: 36; Moloney 1998: 63) have argued that John 2–4 is one unit: from Cana (2:1) to Cana (4:46).

The official's son who is healed is in Capernaum, however. Thus this story is similar to one in the Synoptics (Matt 8:5-13; Luke 7:1-10). Indeed, it may be John's version of the same event. Matthew and Luke put this story in a lead position for Jesus' public healing ministry, attesting the faith of a Gentile. In John this is Jesus' only healing story in Galilee. It also attests to the remarkable faith of a Gentile (yet the text is not explicit on ethnic identity). The *royal official* (*Gr. basilikos*) is likely a Roman who served in the court of Herod Antipas, tetrarch of Galilee (D. M. Smith 1999: 125).

The official seeks out Jesus and begs him to come to his home to heal his son, who is *at the point of death* (v. 47c). Jesus responds, *Unless you see signs and wonders you will not believe*. Many read Jesus' response as off-putting, an expression of exasperation. Such a reading would be truer to Mark's Gospel (8:11-12) than to John's, for in John signs serve a positive function (2:11; 20:30-31; Johns and Miller 1994; Motyer 1997: 64–67) [*Signs, p. 529*]. As Johns and Miller read it, this is not an expression of exasperation but a solemn affirmation of the positive role that signs play—for this official as well as for all who are called to believe in Jesus. At the end of this story, the sign indeed leads the father and *his whole household* to believe (vv. 53b-54). If one applies to Jesus' statement a negative nuance to the word *signs*, this result would be difficult to explain.

When the official persists in his petition, Jesus speaks the word, *Go; your son will live*. The official believes and goes home. But as he is going, his servants meet him on the road and tell him that his son has recovered. He is alive! When the official asks when this occurred, they say, *Yesterday at one in the afternoon the fever left him*. The *father*—an interesting change in designation from *official*—knows it was the very time when Jesus spoke the healing word. As a result, he believes in Jesus, together with his household.

Unlike the preceding story, the official makes no christological confession. His *belief* is the climax of the story. The healing is a *sign*; it has led to faith in Jesus.

THE TEXT IN BIBLICAL CONTEXT

Jesus and the Ancestors[w]

As Westerners we will not likely think this story is significant to the topic of *ancestors* (4:20). But an extensive study involving multicultural readers worldwide suggests otherwise. A Nigerian group observes that "the Samaritan woman minced no words in presenting to Jesus the Samaritans' belief in their ancestors whose deeds and benevolence are worthy of remembrance: 'Are you greater than our father Jacob, who gave us this well?'" Later her statement, *Our fathers worshiped on this mountain*, builds the case for ancestral respect. The women in the study group saw this Samaritan woman as "an apostle of ancestorhood" (Jonker: 323, 324 in de Wit).

Jesus and the Samaritans

This story has significant implications for understanding this Gospel's ethical contribution. It is commonly held that John differs from other dominant NT voices (Matthew, Luke, and Paul) in that it nowhere commands love for the enemy and instead only commands in-group love for one another. This has played into the notion that John is sectarian, concerned only about internal group relations, how believers are to relate to one another, and has a negative stance toward the world. The community's love stops at its boundaries, according to this evaluation, which is applied to the Johannine Epistles as well.

John 4 explodes this notion and requires a rethinking of this dominant Johannine stereotype. A fair reading of the Gospel must consider the impact of this story and the one that follows it on the nature of the Johannine ethic. Though Luke has three stories that depict Jesus as challenging Jewish hatred of Samaritans (9:51-55; 10:29-37; 17:11-19), none is as christologically crucial as "Jesus and the Samaritan woman." This story makes it unequivocally clear that Jesus desired to include Samaritans in his mission and that Samaritans perceive and confess Jesus' christological identity. An entire Samaritan village confesses Jesus to be *the Savior of the world*. The barriers break, and God's love, Jesus' love, embraces the hated enemy. The enemy people have a cardinal place in the kingdom, which Nicodemus, a devout Jew, could not *see* or *understand*.

With this story as focal lens, Luke's Samaritan stories gain strength and significance. In the first (Luke 9:51-56), Samaritan villagers refuse to welcome Jesus as he heads south toward Jerusalem. The venom between the two groups lies in the word *because* (9:53b): *because* he is going to Jerusalem, Samaritans want nothing to do with Jesus and his itinerant band. For all the villagers know, they might be a band of terrorists, invading their country. So they kick Jesus out. Jesus' disciples understandably want to retaliate. James and John, the "Sons of Thunder" (Mark 3:17), ask Jesus, in his mighty power, to authorize them to call down fire from heaven and consume them. Can this "John of Thunder," bent on retribution against the Samaritans, be the John who promulgates the Johannine Gospel tradition, with love as hallmark of true disciple identity (13:35)? If so, what a change! Jesus rebukes (a strong word in Greek) the "thunderbirds" and says, "Let's go on to the next village." Surely, the disciples are snorting as they feel the reprimand and try to snuff out their psychic fire. In this first encounter with Samaritans in Luke, Jesus confronts the ethnic hatred.

What a context for Jesus' good Samaritan story (Luke 10:25-37)! In this story Jesus dares to make a Samaritan the model for moral emulation. This well-known story is framed by the motif of eternal life in the question posed to Jesus by a lawyer, "What must I do to inherit eternal life?" (10:25). The lawyer knows the commandments and sums them up brilliantly with the double love command: Love God and love your neighbor. Jesus says, "You have given the right answer; do this, and you will live." Case closed!

But no, the lawyer knows that "the devil is in the details," so he wants to know the exclusion policies. Certainly not everyone is my neighbor! This legal haggling opens the door for Jesus' dynamite. Jesus tells a story of an injured man by the road and the responses of three passersby: a priest, a Levite, and a Samaritan. Only the Samaritan stops to help, and then Jesus turns the screw: "Which of these three, do you think, was a neighbor to the man who fell into the hands of the robbers?" The lawyer answers rightly, "The one who showed him mercy," to which Jesus replies, "Go and do likewise." This seals the case: this is the way to eternal life!

Back-to-back, these two stories exemplify love of enemy. The first illustrates nonretaliation, a consistent NT teaching (Swartley, ed. 1992), and the second, a subversion of enemy ideology: the Samaritan's moral response surpasses that of the religious Jew. In the third Lukan incident, a Samaritan again becomes a moral model to emulate (17:11-19). Jesus heals ten lepers, but only one—a

Samaritan—returns to give thanks. In Luke's long "journey" narrative (9:51–19:44), Jesus encounters or speaks of Samaritans three times; this fact indicates that Jesus may have made it a practice to go through Samaria on trips between Judea and Galilee, likely to the chagrin of his disciples. All these Samaritan stories subvert the enemy myth. Like John 4, they have profound implications for both peacemaking and mission. While in Luke these journeys appear in the later period of Jesus' ministry, in John the Samaritan trip is early in the Gospel's chronology, between the first Passover (2:13) and an unnamed feast in 5:1.

In contrast to Luke and John, Mark makes no mention of Samaritans. In Matthew, Jesus restricts his disciples from entering Samaria as he sends them out on a gospel mission: "Go nowhere among the Gentiles, and enter no town of the Samaritans" (10:5b). But this is a command that the narrative later breaches and supersedes, first by profusely citing OT texts to authorize Gentiles as gospel recipients (12:17-21), demonstrated then in 15:21-31 (cf. 8:5-13), and finally by giving the great commission, in which Jesus commands his followers to "make disciples of all nations, baptizing . . . and teaching them" all he taught them (28:19-20). Clearly this includes Samaritans (for fuller discussion, see Swartley 2006a: 62 and 62n34).

Nonetheless, Luke and John are unique in their portrayal of fulfilling Matthew's great commission in regard to Samaritans (contra Matt 10:5), subverting the enemy feud. In John, Jesus first discloses his identity, *I AM*, to a Samaritan woman. Peacemaking, mission, worship, and precious Christology blend on Samaritan soil—to a woman, in public! What a bold ethic of enemy love, making of this Samaritan woman an apostolic witness to her own people!

Living Water[w]

John 3 and 4 are linked by *water*. In John 3, Nicodemus fails to understand birth from above—a baptism *by water and Spirit*. Since he is a teacher of Israel, Jesus laments his inability to comprehend. In John 4, the Samaritan woman, an unlikely candidate for understanding spiritual matters, ends up believing Jesus' word about *living water, . . . gushing up to eternal life*. Here is a paradox: the insider becomes outsider, and the outsider becomes insider. *Water*, a symbol of life—like the Archimedean lever that turns the world—occasions both stumbling and salvation. In 2 Kings 5, dipping seven times in the water brought sight and healing to Naaman (cf. the blind man's washing in Siloam in John 9). At the end of John 3 and beginning of

John 4, the water motif is present also in discussion of baptism and precisely in the differentiation between John and Jesus on baptism. While the text first says that Jesus was baptizing in 3:22b, 3:26, and 4:1b, the narrator intentionally corrects this: No, Jesus didn't baptize, but his disciples did (4:2). Perhaps this point, important to the Gospel, reserves Jesus for another more stellar role: Jesus gives living water to the Samaritan woman. Jesus promises and gives more than baptism with water; he gives *living water* that generates new birth and eternal life.

Water, flowing or running, frequently occurs in Scripture as a symbol of life (Isa 55:1; Ezek 47:1-8; Zech 14:8). Hear Jeremiah's prophetic word: "My people have committed two sins: they have rejected me, a source of living water, and they have hewn out for themselves cisterns, cracked cisterns which hold no water" (2:13 REB). Carmichael cites a wider range of OT *water* references to provide scriptural foregrounding for an inherent connection between water, marriage, and birthing, so that the story of the Samaritan woman is not only a betrothal that births descendants—the Samaritans who believe—but is also linked to John 3 by the *water-birth* imagery. In John 7:37, Jesus cries out on the last day of the festival, *Let anyone who is thirsty come to me, and let the one who believes in me drink.* The narrator links this word with a quotation from an unknown source, *Out of the believer's heart shall flow rivers of living water* (v. 38). But then comes a caveat: Not yet! *Now he said this about the Spirit, which believers in him were to receive, for as yet there was no Spirit, because Jesus was not yet glorified.* In 19:34 the one who testifies as eyewitness says he saw *blood and water* coming out of Jesus' side. Moore links these latter two texts together: the first foreshadows the second (1994: 57–59). The water of life comes from the side of the Crucified, after which the Spirit pours out on the believers (the bride) the gift of life that revitalizes the disheartened disciples. The *living water* that Jesus offers (4:10) represents the Spirit (cf. 1:32-33), who glorifies Jesus (16:14) and testifies on behalf of him (15:26).

The biblical drama of salvation culminates with a new city, from which flows a river with the tree of life on either side, the leaves of which are "for the healing of the nations" (Rev 22:1-2). The final call to salvation in Revelation, echoing Isaiah 55:1a, is "Let everyone who is thirsty come. Let anyone who wishes take the water of life as a gift" (Rev 22:17c-d). The "Spirit and the bride" (including believing Samaritans) speak the Bridegroom's invitation to the woman at the well, to receive *living water, . . . gushing up to eternal life.*

THE TEXT IN THE LIFE OF THE CHURCH

Ancient and Modern Eyes on This Text[w]

Both the early church leaders and modern commentators differ over whether Jesus' encounter with the Samaritan woman should be understood figurally (symbolically) or more literally. Origen (ca. 185–254, the first to write extended commentary on this passage) links the story to OT bridal narratives in Genesis 24 and 29 and says, "There, one comes to the wells and waters that brides may be found; and the church is united to Christ in the bath of water" (*Homilies on Genesis* 10.5, cited by McWhirter: 1). Origen regards the five husbands as the five senses, with the sixth signifying spiritual perception, which was still deficient, threatened by unsound teaching (Day: 11–12). Augustine interpreted the sixth relationship as illicit cohabitation with a man, but allegorically connected the five husbands with five bodily senses, similar to Origen (Day: 13). "Augustine thinks that the purpose of the exchange is to reveal Christ as the true spouse of the soul" (*Homily* 15.19, cited by M. Edwards: 56). Medieval commentators compare this woman's leaving her water jar to the male disciples leaving their fishing nets. Thomas Aquinas "credits her with 'taking on the role of an apostle' . . . [for] she left her work (the water jar) to proclaim the good news just as the apostles left their work . . . when called to follow Christ" (Day: 17).

In the Eastern church the Samaritan woman emerged as a model of conversion and salvation. Gregory of Nazianzus says of her, "Blessed is he from whom Jesus asks drink, as He did from that Samaritan woman, and gives a well of water springing up to eternal life" (Day: 12). The Eastern Orthodox church bestowed sainthood upon her, naming her Saint Photeine, and composed a beautiful prayer to pray to Saint Photeine, to have her appeal to Christ for salvation on the supplicant's behalf. The legacy of the mother churches (Western and Eastern) bestows praise and honor upon this woman (Day: 17–18).

Reformers Luther and Calvin continue with praise for her, but also speak of her shady character being transformed through encounter with Christ. Calvin has harsh words about her, blaming her for driving away five husbands. Jesus' rebuke brings her to submission and new character. After making this point in his commentary, Calvin has kinder words for her: an example of discipleship in giving up her water pot to follow Jesus and in her teaching mission to her home people (Day: 19–23). From the early church through the Middle Ages to the Reformation, commentators regard "the

Samaritan woman as a model for the conversion of a pagan to Christianity" (Day: 23). Menno Simons most often appeals to John 4:24 to stress that God is Spirit, and true worship is in spirit and truth (254, 340, 491, 862).

After a unique and masterful portrayal of the Samaritan woman in history, art, and literature, Day devotes a comparatively short chapter to her own understanding of the narrative. She does not side with the early church's allegorical or the modern figural interpretations, but sees the woman as one oppressed by life's circumstances. She may have outlived some of her husbands, and others may have divorced her for no fault of her own:

> Her life had been especially difficult, and [this series of marriages] probably meant that she was an object of either pity or ridicule, perhaps both. Certainly in a culture oriented toward honor and shame values, honor was not attributed to her. The fact that she is now living with a man who is not her husband may not be a matter of her choice, but a matter of necessity in order to have the protection of a man and a place to live. (170)

Day's view resembles Schottroff's, but she does not restrict the woman's oppression to the law of levirate marriage. Her situation was likely worse, since the levirate practice was socially acceptable, even though hard for the woman to bear. Day widens the window of historical reality: "A woman five times rejected through divorce or abandoned through death has experienced one of human life's most poignant sufferings many times. If we consider this possibility, a whole new light is shed on this entire narrative" (172). Day also does not read the Samaritan woman's first questions as mocking or arrogant in tone. Later (in vv. 16-18) she makes no effort to defend herself. Day sees her "as a faithful child of God, within the limits of her ability and understanding, even before her encounter with Jesus" (174). She is "an example as a faithful convert and apostolic witness," and she is a woman of religious devotion and good character as well. God rewarded her piety "by sending her a unique revelation. Just as promised in John's prologue, God sent her spiritual light so that she might become an enlightened child of God through her belief in Jesus Christ" (175).

Mission and Peacemaking[w]

The literature on mission in John is extensive, as Martin Erdmann (207-8), Teresa Okure's monograph on John 4:1-42, and Linda Oyer's dissertation on John's mission-sending text exemplify. This story is a model for cross-cultural communication. The meeting place is a well, a point of common human need, providing a natural opportunity for encounter and, in this case, discovery. The woman discovers who Jesus is; Jesus finds Samaritan receptivity. Witherington (1995: 124) writes eloquently on linking mission with crossing cultural boundaries, criticizing the "target-audience" strategy in the church growth movement for failing to cross "socioeconomic, ethnic, and racial barriers and for exhorting Christians to get on with doing so." But Witherington does not discuss the degree of enmity—historical and racial—between the Samaritans and Jews.

Judith Gundry-Volf, however, has noted the peacemaking/reconciling dimension. She pairs the narrative about the Samaritan woman in John 4 with that of the Syrophoenician Woman in Mark 7:24-30, and then identifies them as paradigmatic for Christian mission and peacemaking:

> The Gospel stories of Jesus' encounters with the Samaritan woman (John 4:1-42) and the Syrophoenician woman (Mark 7:24-30; Matt 15:21-28) can both be read as tales about the inclusion of the "other," about crossing the boundaries caused by ethnic, religious, social, and gender otherness and bringing about a new, inclusive community of salvation. Exclusion is overcome in two radically different, but complementary models for dealing with a problem both urgent and complex in our own world. In John 4, the divine gift of the Spirit breaks down barriers between peoples and leads to reconciliation and fellowship. In Mark 7 and Matthew 15, human insistence on divine mercy, which is blind mercy, dramatically reverses a pattern of exclusion. (1995: 508)

Gundry-Volf thus emphasizes the socioethical dimensions of the Gospel. In John 4 mission and peacemaking are integrally linked. What we often conceive here as a dual entity is ontologically one in Scripture, as other texts (Luke 2; Acts 10; Eph 2) explicitly show. Paul's calling, rooted in his conversion, is to announce Jesus Christ's peace to the Gentiles, making peace with the enemy.

SERMON STARTERS

Today many people move from church to church, searching for the "right place" to worship. Jesus shifts the woman's assumption that *place* is important to a point of more critical importance: the right *way* of worship, from the heart, *in spirit and truth*.

Another focus might be the *surprise* of finding God and/or Jesus in unlikely places such as Samaria, with its connotations, and not in designated places such as Gerizim or Jerusalem. What does it mean to encounter God in spirit and truth? What role does Jesus hold in that encounter? You may wish to present the text as readers theater (see Swartley, 2013 for such an arrangement of the text).

A third approach would begin with and cycle back to the *necessity* of Jesus' going through Samaria. This would focus the sermon on the integral relation of mission and peacemaking, the core of the chapter's contribution.

Part 2

Rejection and Acceptance: The Second Passover

I am God, and also henceforth *I am He*;
there is no one who can deliver [snatch] *from my hand*;
I *work* and who can hinder it?
—Isaiah 43:13, emphasis added

John 5

Jesus Does God's Work; "Trial" Begins

PREVIEW

One ordinary early fall morning a fascinating story appeared in our local newspaper. It reported the mysterious, miraculous healing of a quadriplegic person in a nearby town, Bristol, Indiana. Laura Nauman, who suffered for five years from a degenerative disorder of the nervous system, diagnosed in 1991 as spinal muscular atrophy, woke up September 2, 1995, able to walk. The *Elkhart Truth* (Oct. 1) reported Laura's unprecedented healing, quoting words of amazement from her doctor, Bristol physician Alan H. Bierlein, and the First Baptist Church pastor John Blodgett. Both went to her home on Saturday, the morning of the new Laura, and during the next nine hours watched her walk, drive a four-wheeler, and ride in a convertible. A related *Truth* article narrated her church's response when on the next Sunday morning her pastor mentioned her name. One person thought, "Oh, she must have died," but instead Laura got up out of her familiar wheelchair and bounded across the platform—to the congregation's amazement, clapping, and praising the Lord. The healing is inexplicable. Whether Laura or church people were praying for miraculous healing was not reported. The miracle was a gift of God's lavish love and generous grace, as are Jesus' Gospel miracles.

In John 5 the mood of the Gospel changes. Until now the narrative pulsed with hope. Even with hints of impending conflict (1:10-11; 2:24; 3:12, 20, 36), hope resounds:

144

- The prologue exhibits overall a positive tone.

- John the Witness strongly affirms the One who is to come.

- Disciples (two from John) eagerly join Jesus with strong christological confessions.

- Jesus launches a new era of nuptial bliss and stirs hope for a purified new temple.

- Jesus offers new birth and eternal life to Nicodemus.

- Jesus welcomes Samaritans to living water.

- Jesus heals a Gentile official's son.

These events evoke hope of messianic fulfillment, in multimedia portrayal.

John 5 begins similarly. Jesus heals a paraplegic in Jerusalem, one waiting thirty-eight years to be healed. The catch that clouds the healing is the timing: Jesus heals on the Sabbath. The healed man carries his mat and walks, as Jesus the healer told him to do. Jesus breaks one of the Sabbath rules. *The Jews*, here the religious leaders, spring into action, accusing Jesus of violating Sabbath law *["The Jews," p. 520]*.

Jesus' first defense is to identify his work with God's work, for God does not cease to do good on the Sabbath. The evangelist informs the reader that the conflict is serious: they are *seeking all the more to kill him* (5:18a). The Jews then accuse Jesus of *making himself equal to God* (v. 18c).

The remainder of the chapter bears the marks of a trial, consisting of Jesus' defense of his actions and calling in witnesses that support his work and his claims. The key point is unity and mutuality of the Son and the Father, not equality (as the Jews charge) nor subordination only (our too-easy alternative). Jesus speaks of his interdependence with God, and as Son he declares his dependence on the Father, both in what he says and what he does. The Gospel consistently emphasizes the unity and oneness of the Son and Father. The Jews charge Jesus of claiming *equality* with God, but Jesus subverts the charge, asserting that as his Father continues to work, so he does also. The Jews are unable to fathom this, let alone believe in him *["The Jews," p. 520]*.

While John 5 marks a new phase in the conflict between Jesus and Jewish leaders, the "testing" or rejection of Jesus' claims harks back to the beginning, as in 1:10-11, 19-34, and again in 3:11-21, 31-36.

OUTLINE

Jesus Heals on the Sabbath, 5:1-15
They Decide to Prosecute, 5:16-18
Jesus Goes to Trial, 5:19-47

EXPLANATORY NOTES^W

In chapters 5–10, John structures Jesus' ministry around the Jewish feasts. "The celebration of a Jewish *feast* is called a *zikkārōn* (a noun derived from the Hebrew word *zākar*: '*to remember*'), a memory that recalls God's active presence to the Jewish people in the past, rendered present in the celebration of the feast" (Moloney 1998: 164–65). Feasts *remember* God's salvation history. Chapters 5–10 feature Jesus' place in salvation history. Moloney reminds us that not only John, but also Judaism as a whole, was seeking new understandings of the feasts in the posttemple period when the Gospel was written. Within his chiastic analysis of virtually all of John's Gospel, Miyazaki has identified these six chapters as "The Feast Narrative": Sabbath (ch. 5), Passover (ch. 6), Tabernacles (ch. 7), and Dedication (ch. 10). John presents "Jesus as the fulfillment of key symbols of these feasts" (18–20, esp. 19) *[Feasts, p. 516] [Chiasms, p. 507]*.

Another pattern emerges in the Gospel: Jesus' actions are regularly followed by contentious discourses. In chapter 2 Jesus' signs are oriented to Jewish institutions: the Passover is the context for Jesus' prophetic action in the temple (2:12).

Jesus Heals on the Sabbath 5:1-15

5:1-9 Jesus Heals a Paraplegic on the Sabbath

In most healings in the Gospels, Jesus responds to one who seeks him out for healing. But in this story, as he goes up to Jerusalem to celebrate an unnamed feast, Jesus sees a crippled man at the Bethesda Pool at the Sheep Gate and initiates dialogue. The name of the pool varies in different translations, due to variants of this Aramaic term in the Greek manuscripts *[Textual Variants, p. 532]*.

The Sheep Gate (Gr. *probatikos*) is located in the northeast Jerusalem wall. Close to this gate is a sheep market, even to this day. In the first century, festival pilgrims coming into the city purchased sheep here for sacrifice. The evangelist's naming of the gate may

---

w   Where the superscript w occurs after headings, please see the commentary's online Web Supplement for additional material. Go to: http://www.heraldpress.com/bcbc/john.

thus allude to sacrifice (cf. *probata* in John 2:14-15; Isa 53:7; Ps 43:23 LXX [44:22 ET]; Suggit: 68), thus subtly suggesting that Jesus' action here will set into motion his own sacrificial death (v. 18!).

Recent archaeological finds have yielded another layer of meaning. Both the pools of Bethzatha and Siloam (ch. 9) were huge pools, larger than two 75-foot-frontage city lots, in trapezoidal shape. Bethzatha, the northern pool, measures 164 feet on the north, 131 feet on the east and west, and 174 feet on the south (Reich and Shukron). The pool was located just north of the temple. With archaeology's findings on both pools, we now know these pools were constructed (Bethzatha in the Hasmonean Period) to function as purification pools (*mikva'ot* [*miqwa'ot*]) for the many pilgrims coming to Jerusalem for the festivals (von Wahlde 2009: 155–74; Gibson 2005, 2009; Burge 2009: 2–3). This evidence is significant for John's historicity: he knew these pools and their functions. Eusebius, in his *Onomasticon* (early fourth century) also did, for he speaks about the "two pools" with Bethzatha having five porticoes, known as the Sheep Pool. He also says the pool had a reddish color, which may indicate its waters were tinted by the blood of the sacrificed sheep. John 5:2 is one of those incidental yet accurate topographical descriptions of the pool and its five porticoes, described in present tense, which leads some scholars to argue for an early date for John, before Jerusalem's fall (Wallace; Robinson 1976). While many scholars view the verb here (*estin*) as a historical present, numerous fourth- to sixth-century sources describe the porticoes in past tense (Wallace: 188–89).

John presents Jesus as integrally related to Jewish purification rites (recall John 2:6; 3:25). The new layer the author adds to Jesus' relation to the Jewish institutions (temple, sacrifice, Sabbath) and festivals is *purification*. What is Jesus doing in relation to Jewish purification rites? Further, how do these two stories located at pools contribute to John's *water* theme and symbolism? Is there a subtle contrast here between the water of the purification pool, in which there is a "stirring" at certain times, and the never-ending *living water* Jesus promises to the Samaritan in John 4?

Jesus *knew* the man had been there *a long time*, specified by the narrator as *thirty-eight years* (vv. 5-6). In one respect this story is similar to that of the Samaritan woman: Jesus seeks out both. But the outcomes of the two narratives differ sharply, even though both narratives advance important aspects of Jesus' ministry. The Samaritan woman's faith response leads many Samaritans to confess Jesus as *the Savior of the world*. The healed paralytic *tells* the Jews that *Jesus* healed him. Because it happened on the Sabbath, contro-versy ensues, and Jesus' christological identity unfolds, offends, and ruptures—similar to what happens in John 9. It appears that the miracle on the Sabbath occurs in order for Jesus to set forth his christological challenge to "the Jews," who seem determined to persecute and prosecute Jesus. The narrative is not construed explicitly as a *must* (*dei*) event (as was Jesus' journey through Samaria), but its cause-effect design seems to infer an unavoidable *necessity* for the conflict.

Jesus opens the conversation with the infirm man by asking, *Do you want to be made well?* The *sick man* responds with a lengthy answer, which both excuses himself for why he is not already well and avoids a direct answer (v. 7). Jesus does not trifle further but commands him, *Stand up, take your mat and walk.* The man obeys, is made well, and begins to walk. The narrator then drops the bomb-shell: *Now that day was a sabbath* (v. 9). *Now also* the storm of opposi-tion gathers. and ominous clouds threaten Jesus' future.

5:10-13 The Jews Interrogate the Man

The Jews—whoever they are—are immediately onto the case [*"The Jews," p. 520*]. They accuse the man of violating the Sabbath by carrying his mat. They insinuate that he should know better: it is strictly forbidden on the Sabbath. The man's response in effect is "I did what some Jewish man told me to do; when one waits thirty-eight years for healing, why not risk it, Sabbath or no Sabbath?" The Jews pursue the matter and want to know who told him to carry his mat. The healed man does not know his name, for Jesus has *disap-peared in the crowd that was there.*

5:14-15 Jesus Finds and Instructs the Man, Who Announces His Healing Publicly[w]

Jesus finds the man in the temple. Again Jesus takes the initia-tive. Jesus must have told the man who he was, or someone else told him, for the man reports that the healer's name is Jesus. Jesus finds the man to warn him: *See you have been made well! Do not sin any more, so that nothing worse happens to you.* Then, for whatever reason—the text gives no hint—the man goes to the Jews and tells them it was Jesus who healed him.

What are we to make of this man? Was telling the Jews a betrayal of Jesus? Did Jesus scold him when he said, "Stop sinning"? Many commentators (e.g., R. Brown 1966; Brodie; Schneiders 2002: 191,

200) assess the man's character and response to Jesus negatively. The man makes excuses for his long infirmity, never asks Jesus for help, and never makes any christological confession as does the man born blind in chapter 9; then when he learns the healer's name, he tells on him to the Jewish authorities. Jesus' command, *Do not sin any more, so that nothing worse happens to you* (v. 14), suggests personal culpability, in contrast to the man born blind (9:2-3).

Is this negative assessment tenable? Patricia Bruce thinks not. While earlier holding a negative assessment, she has changed her mind and lists reasons why. She (45) agrees with Lindars (1972: 216) that the man sets Jesus' authority above the *halakic* (Jewish embellishment of the law) prohibition of carrying a mat on the Sabbath. The man's willingness to obey Jesus' command (v. 9) means the man is a risk taker, obeying Jesus' Sabbath-breaking command. The man's disclosure of Jesus' identity to the Jews is a desire to witness, even at some risk; he is not a traitor (P. Bruce: 45; Staley: 60, 63; contra R. Brown 1966: 209; et al.). Bruce contends that the man in verse 15 is *proclaiming* (*anangellō*), a term that always has a positive connotation in John (4:25; 16:13, 14, 15; cf. 25, *apangellō*, a related word used only here in John; also has *anangellō*, as a textual variant, which fits John's characteristic style).

Pursuing this point further, the nearest textual use of *anangellō* occurs in 4:25. Strikingly, the Samaritan woman uses it to describe what the Messiah will do when he comes: *proclaim all things to us*. The three (or four) uses in John 16 describe what the Holy Spirit will do when he comes: *declare* to you that which Jesus taught. Another verb with essentially the same meaning (*angellō*) appears twice in John (as a text variant to *legō* in 4:51 and more importantly in 20:18). In 4:51 it is used by the servants to *proclaim* (or *tell/told* in most translations) the good news that the royal official's son, *at the point of death*, is alive, pursuant to Jesus' command. Its use by Mary Magdalene in 20:18 is noteworthy: she *announces* to the disciples, *I have seen the Lord*.

The case is even stronger in light of the fact that the manuscript tradition is divided in 20:18 between *angellō* and *apangellō* (some support also for *anangellō*), with the stronger manuscript support for *angellō* (as in the current Nestle-Aland's 27th ed.). Forms of *angellō* thus connect the man's *proclaiming* (in ch. 5) to Mary Magdalene's joyous announcement (in ch. 20). This similarity has been overlooked by commentators, though Schneiders lauds Mary Magdalene for her *announcing*, "*I have seen the Lord*" (2003: 222–23, 238, 243, 254).

Bruce references nine other occurrences of *anangellō* in the NT: they are always positive (cf. a possible exception in Acts 19:18). Since this event is one of Jesus' seven signs in John, it intends to elicit a believing response (P. Bruce: 45–46). Why would the author(s) include a sign that puts the recipient in a negative cast, jeopardizing the Gospel's stated purpose in 20:30-31?

Despite the attraction of negatively comparing this lame man to the blind man's positive response in John 9, as Schneiders (2003: 163) and others have done, the case for a positive view of this miracle is more compelling. The purpose of this healing is not to psychoanalyze the man's character, but to see Jesus' miracle as a sign that elicits faith in Jesus by those who hear and/or read the story. Contributing to the evangelist's central concern, it *declares* Jesus' identity with God: Jesus does God's work, even on the Sabbath.

P. Bruce and Rensberger (38) concur that this man and the blind man—both anonymous—carry positive significance for the Johannine community and ideal readers. The blind man has credentials that the paralytic does not have. Compared to this man's disability and status as a beggar, the blind man has parents and neighbors and belongs to the synagogue, from which he is driven out. The lame man, however, has no one to care for him. He fits into a different category, and his situation portrays Jesus' manner of responding to those who are marginalized, poor, and without hope—an important point for the readers of the Gospel. Karris (44) points out that John's word for sickness here (*astheneia*, 5:5) appears to be understood in the Septuagint at least four times as meaning "poor." Jesus' healing the *nameless* man (simply *anthrōpos* in vv. 5, 7, 9, 15) intensifies his plight. He is bereft of family, group, and community (Pilch 2000: 130). Jesus' desire that this man be healed (*hygiēs* in vv. 6c and 9a) marks out what Jesus sees as his mission: to bring wholeness and wellness to the lame (ch. 5) and the blind (ch. 9), a *sign* of Jesus' messianic mission (Isa 35:5-6; cf. the miracles in the Synoptics and Luke 4:18-19). This event, on a Sabbath, opens the narrative to a most crucial declaration by Jesus: *My Father is still working and I also am working* (v. 17)! This is *Divine Sabbath Work* (Burer's book title).

They Decide to Prosecute 5:16-18

5:16 First Charge: Jesus Violates Sabbath Rules

This charge of Sabbath violation against Jesus appears throughout the Gospels. Jesus' healing of the paralytic in Mark 2:1-12 has features of the typical story about Sabbath violation. The accusation continues in Mark 2:23–3:6, when Jesus' disciples pluck grain on the

Sabbath and he heals a man's withered hand. The persistence of this accusation in each of the Gospels points to a fundamental collision between Jesus and the Jewish religious leaders regarding appropriate activity on the Sabbath. Jesus' view builds on Deuteronomy 5:12-15, where Sabbath celebration affirms liberation from bondage and a leveling of society to build community. Healing on the Sabbath fits both goals. In principle Judaism concurs, but the Pharisaic hedge of laws (613, according to *b. Makkot* 23b), developed to protect against desecration of the Sabbath, was fused with the Torah itself. Thus Sabbath prohibitions proliferated. Jesus sees the difference and defies the "fence of protection" that has stripped the Sabbath of its life-giving function. The charge of Sabbath violation often appears to be mixed with deeper issues, and this is the case here.

5:17 Jesus' Defense: My Father Is Still Working

Jesus' response to the accusation cuts deeper than simply quarreling over what he did in healing and commanding the man, *Stand up, take your mat and walk.* He anchors his work in God's work. That God continues to work in giving life even on the Sabbath was accepted by Jewish rabbis: babies are born, rain falls, and natural healing continues. On the Sabbath God's work of judging continues as well (Newbigin: 65). The fact that Jesus participates in God's Sabbath work, both giving life and judging, raises the hackles of the Jews even more than the alleged Sabbath violations did. Moreover, in linking his work with God's work, he claims a special relationship to the one God of heaven and earth: *My Father is still working, and I also am working.* To appreciate the force of Jesus' claim, recall the OT prefiguration of human relation to God as Father: God's promise to David includes "I will be father to him" (2 Sam 7:13-14//1 Chron 17:13-14; Ps 89:26); faithful servant, remnant Israel, calls on God as "our Father" (Isa 63:16; 64:8). The Jews conclude that Jesus is arrogating to himself divine prerogatives!

5:18 Second Charge: Jesus Claims Equality with God

Jesus' response offends because the Jews see it as threatening the Shema confession: "Hear, O Israel: the Lord our God, the Lord is one," and also the first commandment, "You shall have no other gods before me" (Deut 6:4 NIV; 5:6; Exod 20:3; Newbigin: 65). The Jews are incensed and *seeking all the more to kill him, because he was not only breaking the Sabbath, but was also calling God his Father, thereby making himself equal to God.*

The Jews accuse Jesus of claiming equality with God, yet it is not Jesus' own claim *["The Jews," p. 520]*. In light of 10:30 the accusation is partly ironically true, but not in the sense that Jesus is usurping divine position (cf. Phil 2:5-6; McGrath). The same type of accusation occurs at least twice later in the Gospel: in 10:33, where the Jews intend to stone Jesus for blasphemy; and in 19:7, where Jesus' death is justified because he has made himself God's Son (Meeks 1990: 310). Jesus' claims to be doing the work of God his Father, even on the Sabbath, arises out of his "love and obedience" as the faithful Son (Newbigin: 66). Jesus indeed claims unique intimacy with God; his relationship to God is *unity*.

A Jewish proverb says that "a rebellious son is one who makes himself equal to his father," but this is not what Jesus is; rather, he is the opposite, a Son fully obedient to his Father. Self-assertion to equality signals independence, leading in this case to rival status as god (Newbigin: 67; cf. Isa 14:14). Newbigin points out that this flawed understanding, that Jesus asserts equality, leads to the second-century christological debates and the Jewish and pagan charges that Christians have two gods.

The charges, which fail to recognize Jesus' inclusion into his Father's identity (Bauckham 1998a), later mix with Platonic thought to give rise to the "two natures" (divine and human) debate. Nestorian Christians unwittingly sided with the Jewish charge, failing to grasp the true claims of John's Christology: Jesus is one with God, was with God from the beginning, and indeed was God. Newbigin links Jesus' claims here with the evangelist's portrayal of Jesus' identity in 1:18 (the Son reveals the Father) and 5:30 (the Son Jesus seeks his Father's glory, not his own glory).

Another view sees irony in the charge of the Jews: they speak a truth they cannot comprehend, but one the evangelist intends. Jesus' followers know the truth they speak, but they understand equality differently. Carson interprets:

> The ensuing verses set out some of the parameters by which we may rightly understand that Jesus is equal with God (cf. Paul's remarks, also with respect to *isos*, in Phil. 2:6). Jesus is not equal with God as *another* God, or as a *competing* God: the functional subordination of the Son to the Father, the utter dependence of the Son upon the Father, are about to be explicated. (250)

Carson thus regards the charge as irony: "The Jews take umbrage at Jesus' implicit claim to deity" (cf. Truex: 192–200). Their understanding is faulty, however, and "needs serious modification, for

Christians will not accept di-theism or tri-theism any more than the Jews themselves" (Carson: 250). Christians, too, affirm monotheism.

In Jesus' discourses *two* strands of Christology emerge side by side (Meeks 1990): Jesus is presented as subordinate to God, his Father, *and* Jesus is presented as one with God, his Father (a binitarian view). On the one hand, Jesus claims that he does nothing on his own, but only what he sees his Father doing; he does only *the will of the one who sent him* (cf. 4:34). This is the subordinate Christology. On the other hand, however, Jesus claims authority to do what God alone does: raise the dead and judge. Furthermore, he has life in himself (Meeks 1990: 311). Some commentators lean more to the former, and some more to the latter. Talbert (125) holds the two in tension: "Any language about the unity of Father and Son (5:17-18; 10:30: 'I and the Father are one') is conditioned by the persistent motif of the Son's subordination to the Father." Talbert also stresses that the Father *transfers authority* to the Son, with the motive of love and the goal *that all may honor the Son, even as they honor the Father.* Failure to honor the Son is also failure to honor the Father (5:23). Indeed, both unity and subordination—or better, submission, to avoid a hierarchical world-view—are essential to an orthodox Christology.

Jesus Goes to Trial 5:19-47

The trial motif begins explicitly in this chapter. Lincoln (2000: 57–138) regards John 5 as the third stage of "truth on trial," in which the lawsuit motif permeates the Gospel narrative. Moloney translates verse 16 with "persecuted and prosecuted." The trial motif evokes the lawsuit genre often appearing in the OT prophets, especially in Isaiah 40–55 (Lincoln 2000). God is accused and acquitted, and then God prosecutes Israel. In both Isaiah and John *I AM* recurs *["I AM," p. 518].* Key terms in this trial language here are *judge* (*krinō*, in 5:22, 30), *judgment* (*krisis*, five times, in vv. 22, 24, 27, 29, 30), *witness* as verb (*martyreō*, seven times, in vv. 31, 32 [2x], 33, 36, 37, 39), and *witness* as noun (*martyria*, four times, in vv. 31, 32, 34, 36; cf. Lincoln 2000: 73). Jesus is first the defendant, but in verses 41-47 Jesus is the prosecutor. As Lincoln deftly puts it, "At the heart of the cosmic lawsuit is the death of Jesus as the witness and judge" (201). The "trial" continues to the end of Jesus' public ministry (ch. 12) and resumes in chapters 18–19.

5:19-30 Jesus Describes His "Criminal" Work

Jesus claims to be one with the Father. His oneness with God means that he has the right and authority to give life (vv. 21, 26-27a) and the right and authority (*exousia* in v. 27) to judge (22-24, 27b, 30). As verse 27b asserts, Jesus has authority for judgment *because he is the Son of Man*, a title that makes Jesus God's Viceroy on earth, drawing on Daniel 7:13-14 and the Similitudes of *1 Enoch* (Truex: 202–14, 222–24). The Father gives authority to the Son, which counters the charge in verse 18 that he is *making himself equal to God*. Similar to the *Logos* in the prologue, Jesus as Son of Man works the works of God because he is one with God, ontologically and functionally. John 8:15-16 reverses the point: Jesus judges no one; rather, the Father judges. Hence the mutuality: the Son does what the Father does.

The heart of the conflict is Jesus himself, identified with the divine Logos that brings light into the world, though many love darkness rather than light (1:4-5, 14; 3:19-21). In John's Gospel four dimensions of opposition, or duality, are interwoven with each other: christological, ecclesial (believers versus the world), moral, and political (Swartley 2006a: 278–89). The christological duality, opposition to the Son and the Father, is primary. The other three are derivatively intertwined with this primary duality. Jesus becomes a prototype of the believers' stance toward the world, the second duality (e.g., in 15:18-25). The christological conflict is intertwined with the ecclesial. People's response to Jesus, the Son, is the same as to the Father, since as Jesus says, *The Father and I are one* (10:30; cf. 8:28b-29; 5:17-18, 30) *[Duality, p. 511]*.

Opposition to the Son is also opposition to the Father. No wedge can be driven between the Father and the Son; they work, give life, and judge in concert *[Father, p. 515]*. Thompson summarizes the unity of the Son and the Father, demonstrating that God's actions as Father "are distinctly and peculiarly concentrated toward and through Jesus the Son" and "God's activity with relationship to the Son is all-encompassing . . . [expressing] God's life-giving powers and activity in past, present, and future." Indeed,

The Father . . . loves the Son (5:20; 10:17; 15:9; 17:23, 26); shows the Son what he is doing (5:20); raises the dead and gives life (5:21); gives authority to the Son to have life (5:26) and execute judgment (5:27); gives his works to the Son (5:36); sent the Son (5:37, 38; 6:29, 39, 57; 8:16, 18, 26; 11:42); testifies to Jesus (5:37; 8:18); set his seal on the Son of man (6:27); gives true bread from heaven (6:32); gives "all" to the Son (6:37; 13:3; 17:2, 7); "draws" people to him and teaches them (6:44-45, 65); judges (8:16); instructs Jesus (8:28); is with Jesus (8:29); seeks Jesus' glory (8:50, 54); knows the Son (10:15); consecrated the Son (10:36); hears the Son (11:41); honors those who serve Jesus (12:26); glorifies his name (12:28); will come and "make his home" with believers (14:23); will send the Holy Spirit (14:26); prunes the vine (15:2); loves the disciples (16:27; 17:23); glorifies Jesus (17:1, 24); "keeps" what has been given to the Son (17:11, 15); and sanctifies believers in the truth (17:17). (Thompson 2001a: 69)

In culminating his public ministry, Jesus says, *The one who rejects me . . . has a judge; . . . the Father who sent me has himself given me a commandment about what to say and what to speak. . . . His commandment is eternal life. What I speak, therefore, I speak just as the Father has told me* (12:48-50; cf. 5:42-43; 8:42-43). Jesus as Son is one with the Father precisely in his authority to give life (5:26; Thompson 2000: 135, 141–48, 152–54). This unity is also the foundation of the so-called high-priestly prayer: *And this is eternal life, that they may know you, the only true God, and Jesus Christ whom you have sent* (17:3). God's gift through Jesus is extended to all *those who will believe in me through their [the disciples'] word* (17:20).

5:31-38 Jesus Cites Witnesses

Commentators vary as to the number of witnesses Jesus cites to support his claims. Clearly there are at least three: John the Witness (5:33-35), the Father (vv. 37-38), and the scriptures (v. 39). Rather than identifying *the scriptures* as such, Keener specifies *Moses* as the third witness (1.659–60). A case can be made for five witnesses, since 5:36 specifies *the works* Jesus does as evidence for believing his claims. Jesus' appeal to *scriptures*, certainly the prophets, functions then as the fourth witness, and Moses as the fifth. It is not clear to whom verse 32 refers. Does it anticipate verse 33 (John), or does *another* refer *to the one who sent me* (v. 30), God the Father? Since the answer here is not clear, we limit the number to five: John, Jesus' works, the Father, Scripture, Moses. Jesus' defense is persuasive, a tour de force. Jesus defends himself well, exposing the attitudes of the prosecutors: *You have never heard his voice or seen his form, and you do not have his word abiding in you, because you do not believe him whom he has sent* (vv. 37b-38). Jesus' counterprosecution continues in the next paragraph.

5:39-42 Jesus Prosecutes His Opponents

Verse 39 is one of John's gems: *You search the scriptures because you think that in them you have eternal life; and it is they that testify on my behalf.* Similar to Luke 24:44-45, this verse is one of the NT's clearest expressions that (OT) Scripture points to Jesus in his messianic identity. The first verb can be indicative (NRSV, RSV, NIV,

NEB, REB) or imperative (KJV, CEB, Rheims NT, and others). In either case, Jesus affirms his opponents' searching the Scripture and their belief that they give life (cf. Ps 119). But then in verse 40 Jesus rebukes their search because it has not led to their accepting him *to have life*. This skillfully authenticates Scripture as witness to Jesus even as he critiques his opponents for missing the point.

Jesus' accusations against his opponents continue: *I know you do not have the love of God in you*—if you did you would believe the One to whom the Scriptures bear witness. In a chiastic structure, this and the next paragraph are one unit (adapted from Keener: 1.658):

A They reject God's word in his "sent one" (Heb. *shaliach* [*šaliaḥ*]), Jesus, (5:38).
   B Scriptures witness to Jesus (5:39-40) (life in the Scripture [5:39], in Christ [5:40]).
      C Jesus does not receive glory from people (5:41).
         D Jesus knows them (5:42a).
            E They do not love God (5:42b).
            E´ Jesus comes on his Father's behalf (5:43a).
         D´ They do not receive Jesus (5:43b).
      C´ They receive glory from one another, not from God (5:44).
   B´ Moses testifies to Jesus (5:45-46) [Moses accuses (5:45), Speaks of Christ (5:46)]
A´ They reject God's word in His *šaliaḥ* Moses (5:47)

In this analysis the Hebrew word for *sent one* (*šaliaḥ*) is crucial: the first argument proceeds on the basis that if you earlier rejected the one whom God has *sent*, then it is no surprise that *you* will do the same again. Indeed, *send/sent* (*pempō* or *apostellō*) is a keyword in John (Oyer: 446). The term occurs in 5:23, 24, 30, 36, 37, 38 in relation to Jesus' claim that he (the Son) does the Father's work. The actions are raising the dead (vv. 21, 24, 25, 28, 29), giving life (21, 24, 25, 26, 29, 39, 40), judging (22, 24, 27, 30), and testifying or witnessing (31, 32, 33, 34, 36, 37, 39)—all in order to elicit *believing* (24, 37, 44, 46, 47). These actions proceed from the mutual indwelling of the Father and Son. The *works* (*erga*) Jesus does, which have provoked the accusation of *the Jews*, are rooted in this Father-Son relationship (vv. 20c, 36b, 36c).

5:43-47 Jesus Identifies the Causes of Their Missed Catch and Closes the Case

Second, you do not seek God's glory, but glory from one another (v. 43). Third, *Your accuser is Moses* (v. 45b). *If you do not believe what he wrote, how will you believe what I say?* (v. 47). Since Moses is the lawgiver, this reference reflects a positive view of the law, consistent with my interpretation of 1:17. Torah law is presented positively when interpreted rightly (Pancaro; Motyer 1997: 42–43; Lincoln 2000: 54).

In all three of these charges (vv. 38-47 AT), Jesus states or infers the opposite: *I love God. I seek not human glory but only God's glory. And I believe what Moses wrote—and, be sure, it witnesses to me* (esp. v. 46). Jesus' defense and countercharges are sharp and must be seen in the context of verse 16a: *The Jews started persecuting Jesus*, reaction triggered by Jesus' Sabbath healing (v. 16b). Jesus' defense of his Sabbath action, linking his work to the work of *my Father* (v. 17b; cf. vv. 26-27), further exacerbates the polar positions of Jesus and *the Jews*. They regard Jesus' claim, *making himself equal to God*, tantamount to blasphemy and therefore are determined to kill him (v. 18). Truex (225) explains that Jesus' *breaking* or *releasing* Sabbath law prompts the charge that he is *making himself equal to God*. By claiming in his trial-defense "God's *creative power*" (what Sabbath symbolizes in God's covenant with Israel) and power as Son of Man to judge, Jesus opens himself to the charge of "sinning with high hand" (Num 15:30-36) and thus blaspheming God.

THE TEXT IN BIBLICAL CONTEXT

Restoring to Health[w]

Jesus' initiative to heal the lame man exemplifies the priority of healing in Jesus' ministry. About one-fifth of the narratives of the four Gospels are devoted to stories of healing (including release from demons). Usually sick people *come* to Jesus for healing, but Jesus *goes* to the pool of Bethzatha to heal the paralytic. In the Synoptic Gospels, healings function prominently in either Jesus' keynote sayings or actions inaugurating Jesus' mission and ministry (Matt 4:23-25; 9:35; Mark 1:21-34; Luke 4:18-19) and also in the mission of Jesus' disciples, in their apprenticeship (Matt 10:1-4; Mark 3:13-19) to proclaim the kingdom's arrival (Matt 10:5-8; Mark 6:13; Luke 9:1-2; 10:1-9). Jesus specifies his healings as one of his messianic credentials when messengers from John the Witness in prison ask whether he truly is the one to come (Matt 11:2-5; Luke 7:18-22).

When King Herod hears about Jesus' and his disciples' healings, he becomes alarmed and thinks John the Baptizer, whom he imprisoned, has been raised from the dead (Mark 6:14). In Acts 10:38 Peter summarizes Jesus' ministry: "He went about doing good and healing all who were oppressed by the devil."

Jesus' response to the lame man and to those with illness or disability echoes OT sentiments (P. Bruce: 50). Job describes himself as "eyes to the blind, and feet to the lame" (29:15). God commands Israel not to curse the deaf or cause the blind to stumble, but rather to fear God (Lev 19:14). God censures Israel's leaders for not strengthening the weak, healing the sick, or binding up the injured. God, as true Shepherd, will look after them and raise up "one shepherd, my servant David," to feed the flock (Ezek 34:4, 15-16, 23). Jeremiah speaks of raising up other shepherds to replace the destroying shepherds (23:1-4). Return from exile is the context for both promises. Israel's future after exile includes bringing home those with mobility impairments (Jer 31:8). The lame and the blind will be healed in the coming messianic age (Isa 35:5-6). Further, Jesus reverses OT policies that restricted the lame and the blind from the temple (2 Sam 5:8). Instead, in his Palm Sunday entry to Jerusalem, he cures the lame and blind who come to him in the temple (Matt 21:14). Jesus transforms the enmity toward the lame and blind into a state and relationship of shalom (Swartley 1994: 174n58).

Give Glory and Honor to God—Also to Jesus?

Jesus reproves his interlocutors because they accept glory from one another and do not seek the glory that comes from the one who alone is God (v. 44). Earlier, in verse 41, Jesus says, *I do not accept glory from human beings.* These verses disclose another dimension of the christological issue running through the Gospel. In what way is Jesus God (1:1, 18), and in what way is Jesus distinct from God? Throughout the Gospel, Jesus claims that his work and mission are to bring glory to God. Identified with God and as God, Jesus is nevertheless vicegerent of God. He lives to glorify the Father (ch. 17). He is Son; God is Father.

The Jews take offense that Jesus calls God his Father. But a similar theme appears already in Wisdom of Solomon 2:12-22, in describing the unjust treatment of the righteous person. Among the actions and words offensive to the accusers of the righteous one is when he "boasts that God is his father" (Wis 2:16d). The early church fathers regarded this Wisdom text, like Isaiah 52:13–53:12, as a prophecy of Jesus' rejection and shameful death. In John 5:39 Jesus says that Scripture bears witness to him. The entire Gospel demonstrates this truth since Jesus and the Gospel appeal regularly to Scripture—especially to Isaiah and Psalms, the worship book of Jesus, his disciples, and the church through the ages. Conversations between Christians and Jews can begin with common focus on selected OT texts, seeking to understand them in Jewish and Christian contexts.

Because of Jesus' Son relationship to God his Father, the logic follows that those who refuse the Son also refuse the Father. Derivatively, if the Jews seek glory only from one another, they refuse the Son, who gives all glory to God. If they refuse to believe Moses (vv. 45-46), they refuse also to believe the One whom God sent, Jesus (v. 47). They fail to glorify God as well as the One whom God vindicates and exalts to the highest heaven (Phil 2:9-11). Elsewhere in Scripture both God and Jesus Christ worthily receive glory: "To the King of Ages, immortal, invisible, the only God, be honor and glory forever and ever. Amen" (1 Tim 1:17); then in 6:15 the Lord Jesus Christ "is the blessed and only Sovereign, the King of kings and Lord of lords." Jesus Christ is denoted final judge, linked to his role as Savior (2 Tim 1:10; Titus 1:3; cf. 1 Tim 6:13-16). In Revelation, God receives "glory and honor" (4:11); likewise the slain Lamb receives "power and wealth and wisdom and might and honor and glory and blessing" (5:12; Talbert: 126; Swartley 2006a: 252).

These titles of deity for Jesus Christ have not only christological but also political import, even in the pastoral letters. These and similar titles rival those of first-century emperors, five of whom claimed these deity titles; in the East even more received such acclaim (Swartley 2006a: 85, 252). John's Gospel culminates in a trial before Pilate, where Jesus' kingship clashes with Caesar's. Even *the Jews*, cornered by Pilate's skillful maneuvering, choose Caesar as their king (blasphemy!), repudiating Jesus as King of the Jews (19:14-15, 19-22; see comments on John 19).

THE TEXT IN THE LIFE OF THE CHURCH

Prosecution and/or Persecution

As John 5:16-18 indicates, the Jews begin to persecute Jesus and even seek to kill him. Some commentators (Moloney 1998: 169–70; Lincoln 2005: 61–64, 198–200) suggest that the Jews both prosecute and persecute. It depends on the vantage point from which the conflict is viewed. The Jewish leaders regard it as justified prosecution because in their view, Jesus perpetrates heretical beliefs that cause those who follow him to violate cardinal beliefs of Judaism, such as belief in one God only. Anyone who claims God status must be prosecuted, for such belief has political consequence. It undermines cardinal tenets of the community's identity, causes confusion and conflict, and becomes a subversive influence in the peace and order of the community.

However, if one views the situation from the perspective of Jesus and his followers, the response of the Jewish leaders is persecution, as described in John. Jesus, however, not only defends himself against the prosecution—the accusations against him—but he also exposes the implications of their prosecution. Their unbelief stands condemned because key witnesses verify Jesus' claims. Jesus' words stand in judgment as prosecution of the Jewish leaders. Jesus rests his case with the Father. He does not rally forces to fight the leaders. He defers to the One, final Judge.

Chapter 5, with chapters 7–8 to follow, is a prototype for perceiving and evaluating religious persecution, killing, and martyrdom in following centuries. For the first three centuries Christians were prosecuted by the Roman Empire because they were "atheists" in that they did not accept the gods of the empire, and especially the emperor as God or Son of God, a status five emperors claimed in the first century—and many thereafter. The Christians regarded this as persecution, frequently culminating in martyrdom. But the empire regarded killing these Christian pests essential to keeping order and peace in the empire.

Even when the emperor converted, prosecution and persecution did not cease, as Tripp York (71–83) vividly describes: the Catholic leaders of Carthage prosecuted and killed the Donatists, whom they regarded as heretical. Augustine, the first influential voice to "justify" torturing heretics to force them to recant, killing them if they did not, approved the killing of Donatists, even though he opposed capital punishment for criminals. Later, when the Donatists came into power in northern Africa, for similar reasons they prosecuted and killed Maximian and his followers, who were a radical, gypsy-like wing of the Donatists. The rationale for such proceedings is that the church must prosecute heretics because false beliefs damn the souls of the heretics and cause many more to be led astray and be damned. Hence the religious wars of the centuries multiplied, most notably in the sixteenth century, with the Protestant and Radical Reformations. Catholics killed Protestants, Protestants killed Catholics, and both killed Anabaptists—for reasons similar to why pagan emperors killed the early Christians. False belief is a subversive influence in society, and only fire and sword can stop it—so the people thought. Except for the Jan Leyden Anabaptists in Münster, who fought with swords to inaugurate the new Jerusalem, most Anabaptists had no territory to defend and refused use of the sword in principle. They committed themselves to peacemaking, practicing nonretaliation and love of enemy.

Prosecution seeks to maintain sociopolitical and religious power; persecution is experienced by victims of the prosecution. What does it take to stop violence done in the name of God? Jesus *is* the intervention. His nonretaliation and renunciation of worldly political power together with his speaking truth and showing forgiving love offers a new way. It does not need sword to defend or massacres to cleanse the social order. Jesus broke the spiral of violence in his refusal to retaliate (John 18–19). The faithful follow his way. Indeed, as Tertullian put it, "The blood of the martyrs is the seed of the church" (*Apology* 50). That made sense when the prosecutor was the pagan Roman Empire. But when the prosecutors are Christians killing other Christians to eradicate what they deem to be heresy, those with power appear to win. John 5, however, asks us to reassess who really wins and who really is judged by God. In the church-state context of the sixteenth century, religious and political factors were interwoven. In the twentieth and twenty-first centuries, the two factors also coalesce. York rightly subtitles his book *The Politics of Martrydom.*

In John 5 *the Jews* are not all the Jewish people, for all the disciples and key characters befriending Jesus, including Mary, Martha, and Lazarus, are Jews [*"The Jews," p. 520*]. In John's narrative the Jews represent established religion. Also, "they represent us. If the cross is the bearing of the sin of all . . . , and not just of the Jews; if the question 'Were you there when they crucified my Lord?' must be answered with an awestruck and whispered 'Yes' by every human soul, then—equally—these words of Jesus are addressed not to Jews only, but to all" (Newbigin: 62).

Jesus' Relationship to the Father

Since *equality* is not the best word to describe Jesus' relationship to the Father in John, commentators suggest different perspectives on how to conceive and describe the relationship. The matter is crucial for teaching and preaching since implications result for Christology and possibly, derivatively, for male-female relationships. Talbert sees it as "both-and": unity or oneness between Son and Father *and* the Son's voluntary submission to the Father. The latter arises from Jesus' repeated claim that he speaks and works as the Father directs. This submission, however, does not imply a lesser worth, status, or role—and this emphasis is imperative both for John's Christology and for the relationship of women to men. My preference for John's Christology emphasizes interdependence, unity, and mutual indwelling, which the Gospel as a whole represents and stresses (1:1, 18; ch. 17; 14:7-12, esp. 9b, *Whoever has seen me has seen the Father*).

Whether the male-female relationship should be construed analogically from the Son's relationship to the Father is a much-debated issue in some circles today (e.g., in well-argued articles in *Priscilla Papers*, a journal of Christians for Biblical Equality). In John, the Son participates in the inner life of God, the Father. In 1:18, the Son is "turned toward" the *bosom of the Father*. The Son is *Revealer* of the Father. "The Son receives his very being from the Father, he possesses nothing that is not from the Father" (Rossé: 22). The Son has a unique relationship with the Father from eternity. His works are the works of God. John stresses unity: "The testimony of Jesus is truthful because it is based on his being that is turned permanently toward the bosom of the Father. He can make God known because he is God" (Rossé: 13). Nonetheless, the Father-Son designation connotes distinction, even though later Jesus says to Philip, *Whoever has seen me has seen the Father* (14:9c). The paradox, even mystery, of the Father-Son distinction *and* complete unity, *oneness*, are to be maintained. Given this unique relationship between Father and Son in John, using this as a model for the male-female relationship in marriage is only approximated even by the best of marriages. Is it possible to know the thoughts of the marriage partner as the Son knows the thoughts of his Father? Hardly.

In our time, however, with a huge spate of semipopular studies published on the "historical Jesus" quest (i.e., the many efforts to document Jesus' historicity by the canons of modern historical research, fallible though they be), the notion of identifying Jesus with God, or even with the creedal import "Son of God," encounters resistance, as Burge recognizes and laments. The resistance arises from the current pluralistic culture and postmodern stance, both of which object to "absolute claims to religious truth" (2000: 184–86). At the same time it is quite acceptable to regard Jesus as a great moral teacher, a "peasant rebel" proclaiming a "brokerless kingdom of God" (Burge 2000: 184, reflecting Crossan), a wandering charismatic or even an initiator of a peace movement. Most all these widely read "historical Jesus" scholars slight John's Gospel and its claims for Jesus' deity. In the quest for "the historical Jesus," many scholars regard such claims as the church's theological "overlay" to their notions of the historical Jesus. The pitfalls in such historical research are many, as the very *diversity* of the Jesuses produced by these methodologically precise quests over the last 170 years has shown (Schweitzer; Johnson 1996, 1999; Evans 2006; Dunn 2005).

Burge (2000) quotes C. S. Lewis on this point:

> Either this man was, and is, the Son of God: or else a madman or something worse. You can shut Him up for a fool, you can spit at Him and kill Him as a demon; or you can fall at His feet and call Him Lord and God. But let us not come with any patronizing nonsense about His being a great human teacher. (185, from Lewis, *Mere Christianity*, 41)

Canonically, Johannine Christology does not stand alone. Notably, Jesus is worshiped in Matthew, Luke, John, Paul, and Revelation (Swartley 2007: 213–37). Hurtado (2003, 2005) demonstrates this at length, rightly contending (against Wilhelm Bousett's tome of 1913) that this is not a late emphasis of Hellenistic Christianity (as Bousset argued), but derives from early christological understandings. Bauckham (1998a) rightly contends that the "identity" of Jesus in various New Testament writings matches God's identity, a point I have developed further (2007: 230–35; note the virtually unique appellation "God of peace" that matches "Christ is our peace"). It may not be popular to preach and teach this in today's academic world, but if as teachers we own our accountability to God rather than to popular sentiment, we will take up the challenge and proclaim the truth of the gospel.

SERMON STARTERS

1. "Healing the Sick Today." What are our attitudes and practices in regard to healing the sick? We may not have prohibitive Sabbath laws, but what about exclusion policies of USA health insurance companies (for preexisting conditions) and refusing patients who do not have insurance or Medicaid/Medicare? What about all the red tape connected with healthcare services? Are these any less onerous than Sabbath law restrictions? Are we less guilty than the Jews in this text? How do we restore the marginalized to life within the community of faith? (see Swartley 2012a: chs. 6 and 10).

2. "Who Is on Trial?" Arrange your sermon to convey the "trial" nature of 5:19-47 with various voices representing the "witnesses"

listed in verses 31-47. Plan ahead. Each witness identifies itself and shifts the wording into the voice of the witness: for example, "I am the Scripture. I testify that . . ." (John 5:39-40). The *me* shifts to *Jesus*.

John 6

Jesus Is the Bread of Life

PREVIEW

At our home in Elkhart, Indiana, it is not uncommon to receive two or three requests in the mail per day to give money to help feed the hungry. The total number of such agency requests per year soars to over a hundred. Of course, we respond first to local efforts to feed the hungry, such as Church Community Services in Elkhart and The Window in Goshen. But with all these efforts we only scratch the surface. The Millennial Development Goals (MDGs) of the United Nations includes eliminating world hunger by 2015. A Belmont Mennonite Church Sunday school class, inspired by Richard Stearns's *The Hole in Our Gospel* (Nashville: Nelson, 2009), has collected fifty cents per person per week to model action toward this vision: if every U.S. person would give seven cents a day, world hunger could be eliminated by 2015. It would be fine if we could do it otherwise, as Jesus did: feed five thousand men plus women and children with five loaves and two fishes. But we can't. Rather, what we can do is pledge not only to help feed the hungry, but also to point them to the water and food that Jesus gives for the life and salvation of humankind. We can begin with small steps and, with God's help, risk taking bigger ones.

Like John 5, John 6 begins with Jesus doing a marvelous *work* (*sign*), followed by a sustained discourse. This discourse has a wider audience. In John 5 the interlocutors are *the Jews*. In John 6 it is first the disciples, then a crowd (though these two groups were mixed in both scenes), then *the Jews*, and finally the disciples again.

The location for Jesus' miracle-sign and discourse occurs in Galilee, on *the other side of the Sea*. The Passover Festival is drawing near. This Passover marks the beginning of Year 2 of Jesus' ministry. John 6 also marks an important advance in the Gospel's purpose in presenting Jesus as divine Revealer, further disclosing Jesus' *I AM* identity *["I AM," p. 518]*. In Jesus' feeding the five thousand and discoursing on the *bread of life*, Jesus offers himself as true nourishment for human hunger and source of eternal life. The outline shows progression from widespread acclaim of Jesus—after his great feeding miracle, the crowd wants to make him king (6:14-15)—to a sifting among his disciples.

Jesus' extended discourse connects his feeding *sign* to God's manna gift through Moses. The discourse is framed by two storms—one at sea and one with the Jews contesting his claims. Two modes of peacemaking emerge: one is the sea as Jesus walks on it; another is Jesus' self-donation of his body and blood for the life of the world. Indeed, Jesus says his followers must eat his flesh and drink his blood to have life, eternal life (vv. 53-58). Just what this means has puzzled commentators and Gospel readers. Is it eucharist? Is it sacramental? Is this John's version of the institution of the Lord's Supper?

Many in the band of disciples choose to leave him, offended by the word (*logos* in v. 60, *rhēmata* in 6:63b and 68b). Jesus' word(s) are a stumbling block, and some disciples drop out (vv. 61, 66), a point never made in the Synoptics. Even the twelve must decide if they will stay with him. With Peter acting as their speaker, they answer yes: *You have the words of eternal life, . . . and . . . you are the Holy One of God* (6:68-69). But with this confession and commitment to follow, a shadow falls: one of them will hand Jesus over to the authorities, and Jesus already knows who will do this (vv. 70-71). This chapter is unfolding revelation! Jesus as *the bread of life* is at the center, but swirling around him are crowds of people and disciples tugged toward both faith and unbelief.

OUTLINE

Jesus Feeds the Five Thousand, 6:1-13
The People Respond, 6:14-15
Jesus Walks on the Sea, with *I AM* Self-Revelation, 6:16-21
Jesus Reveals the Meaning of the Sign: "I Am the Bread of Life,"
      6:22-40
The Jews Murmur and Challenge Jesus' Claims; More Self-
      Revelation, 6:41-59
Jesus Tests His Disciples; Some Leave, but the Twelve Confess
      Loyalty, 6:60-71

EXPLANATORY NOTES

The chapter's main points may be diagrammed in chiastic form:

A Jesus tests the disciples and feeds the five thousand (6:1-14).
  B Jesus reveals himself as *I AM* (6:15-25).
    C Jesus discloses, *I am the bread of life* (6:25-40).
  B´ Jesus further reveals, *I am the living bread from heaven* (6:41-59).
A´ Disciples express unbelief and belief (6:60-71).

The long portions of C and B´ manifest further chiastic features, such as Jesus' promise of eternal life occurring at the beginning (v. 27) and end (v. 40) of C. The same themes also occur within B´, in verses 47b and 54b [*Chiasms, p. 507*].

Jesus Feeds the Five Thousand 6:1-13[w]

6:1-4 Setting and Occasion

Three location-event signals head this chapter:

- The other side of the Sea of Galilee, designated here also as the Sea of Tiberius.

- Jesus went up the mountain and sat down there with his disciples.

- The Passover, the festival of the Jews was near.

The sudden shift from Jerusalem (ch. 5) to Galilee (ch. 6) has generated various scholarly theories on sources and dislocations. Since chapter 4 ends in Galilee, it would seem that chapter 6 should follow it. Then chapter 5 would immediately precede chapter 7, with both located in Jerusalem. Some scholars thus propose a switch between chapters 5 and 6. Even William Temple, normally averse to the theory of dislocations, grants that the Gospel reads better to put 6 before 5, and that 7:15-24 should *begin* chapter 7, following the end of chapter 5 (1940: xxxiii).

Despite numerous proposals for rearrangement, which often assume earlier stages in the development of John's Gospel, more recent scholars see narrative unity in the order as it now is. Reversing the order creates other problems: blurring the separate feasts in each chapter and making 7:1-13 nonsensical since Jesus is

---

w   Where the superscript w occurs after headings, please see the commentary's online Web Supplement for additional material. Go to: http://www.heraldpress.com/bcbc/john.

already in Jerusalem at the end of chapter 5. Also, the progressive unfolding of Jesus' self-disclosure is muted in a chapter reversal. In its present canonical order, chapter 6 advances Jesus' self-disclosure begun in chapters 4–5, and chapter 7 follows well from chapter 6.

Several authors point out that chapter 6 is an extended *midrash* on God's gift of manna to Israel through Moses (e.g., Borgen 1965: 20–27, 33–46, 61–98, 147–92; 1983: 23–31; Suggit: 70). Chapter 6 continues Jesus' claim that the OT, specifically Moses and the Torah, witness to him, intensifying the point in chapter 5: "John 6 therefore provides a good illustration of the argument of 5:21-47" (Suggit: 70; a key point in Borgen's extensive study). Jesus' words about Moses and the Torah in chapter 5 are followed by a Moses-like deed, feeding the multitude, expositing its meaning, and thus portraying Jesus as fulfilling the wilderness manna given by God through Moses.

The second directional signal has Jesus going *up the mountain* with his disciples. This is important: Moloney notes that since *mountain* has the definite article (*eis to oros*), the narrative already echoes Moses' ascent to the mountain to receive the law (1998: 195–96). While it is not clear just where *the other side of the Sea* is in location, it is likely close to Bethsaida (cf. Luke 9:10). Traditionally, however, the feeding of the *five* thousand is located on the northwest side of the Sea of Galilee, near Capernaum, which in John is their destination after the feeding (6:16, 22).

That chapter 6 is located temporally with Passover is most significant, since it provides the festival setting for understanding the entire chapter, oriented to bread.

6:5-13 Jesus' Sign Tests the Disciples

Jesus' question to Philip is *testing* (*peirazō*; vv. 5b-6a) him. This correlates with God's testing Israel in the wilderness. God sends the gift of manna to Israel in order "to humble you and to test you, and in the end to do you good" (Deut 8:16). Exodus 16:4 also links God's gift of manna to *testing*, to see if Israel would obey directions for gathering and eating it (cf. Ps 66:10). Other texts speak of Israel as "testing" God through their stubbornness and disobedience in the wilderness: "They tested God in their heart by demanding the food they craved" (Pss 78:18, 41, 56; 95:9; 106:14; Exod 17:1-7; Deut 9:8). Israel's wilderness experience emphasizes God's testing them and their murmuring and testing God (Coats; for parallels between John 6 and Num 11, see R. Brown 1966: 233; Burge 2000: 193). This throws light on John 6. Jesus tests his disciples; the Jews murmur and complain about Jesus' sign, or lack of signs, similar to Israel's response. Paradoxically, the manna tradition is both gift and test!

Philip's response (v. 7) and Andrew's hopeful but despairing comments (vv. 8-9) show lack of faith—that Jesus could handle this matter and supply food for the multitude. But Jesus is not ruffled. He commands the disciples to make the multitude sit down on the green grass, about five thousand men (v. 10). The *sitting on green grass* may recall well-known Psalm 23:2, "He makes me lie down in green pastures" (Moloney 1998: 198). Then Jesus does with the loaves as he did when instituting the Lord's Supper: he takes the five loaves, gives thanks, and then distributes them to those who are seated. He does the same with the fish. The people—five thousand of them—eat as much as they want. Similarities to the feeding miracle in the Synoptics are notable both in Jesus' words and the specific numbers.

As if that sign is not sufficient, Jesus tells his disciples to gather up the fragments from the five barley loaves. They *filled twelve baskets* with *the fragments* (v. 13). The numbers, as well as specifying *barley* loaves, are significant. The *barley* fits with the Passover season, thus underscoring the paschal significance of this event. But barley is also the bread of the poor, similar to today's pita bread (Burge 2000: 194). Elisha fed one hundred men with "twenty loaves of barley" and also had "some left" (2 Kings 4:42-44). This suggests that Jesus is building on and fulfilling the prophetic legacies of Moses and Elisha. The *twelve baskets* left over, which Suggit (72) notes is the main clause of the text and which Daube (38) calls the "supreme miracle," indicates it is enough for the whole community, be it the twelve tribes or the Christian church. The five loaves, like the five porticoes in 5:2, may allude to the five books of Torah. In Mark the numbers are significant: five and twelve in the first feeding, then four and seven in the second feeding. Jesus quizzes his disciples on the numbers during the boat ride (Mark 8:18-21; see Swartley 1981/1999: 115–30).

Commentators generally see this sign as portraying Jesus' fulfilling God's manna gift through Moses. Many regard it as eucharistic in some sense (see comments on vv. 51-58). As the chapter proceeds, eucharistic potential heightens. That this narrative occurs in all four Gospels witnesses to its importance in and to the early Christian church.

The People Respond 6:14-15

6:14 Jesus Is the Expected Prophet

Responses to this sign are mostly positive. The *people* receive the food with joy and exclaim that Jesus *is indeed the prophet who is to come into the world*. This fulfills Deuteronomy 18:15-19, where God promises to raise up a prophet like Moses. Jewish literature prior to Jesus anticipated a renewal of Moses's manna: "The treasury of manna will come down from on high, and they will eat of it in those years because these are they who will have arrived at the consummation of time" (*2 Baruch* 29:8, a late first- or second-century AD work; the statement is similar to an earlier pre-Jesus text; cf. also *Sibylline Oracles* fragment 3:46–49). Or, again from a Jewish midrash: "As the first redeemer caused manna to descend, . . . so will the *latter redeemer* cause manna to descend" (*Eccl. Rabbah* 1.9). Qumran covenanters also expected a prophetic Moses figure to come as part of their messianic hope (1QS 9.10-11; *Testimonia* [4Q175] 5–8). Jesus' discourse highlights the significance of this sign with regard to the expected *prophet* (Meeks 1967). Jesus is fulfilling the manna hopes that were expected signs of the messianic age. Burge (2000: 198) summarizes the significance of Jesus' deed and word, "With a stroke of genius, Jesus has done precisely what he has done throughout the Gospel: He exploits some feature of Jewish belief and ritual and reinterprets it to refer to himself. He is the manna from God's treasury for which Israel has been waiting."

6:15 Jesus Rebuffs Efforts to Make Him King[w]

Jesus perceives that the people are about to come and force him to be king. The Greek term used here (*harpazō*) is the same as in Matthew 11:12, where Jesus speaks of people entering the kingdom violently, by force (cf. Gardner: 187–88). Both texts may reflect Zealot-like efforts to bring about God's rule with force to end Rome's occupation of Israel, as the Maccabees did nearly two centuries earlier. They wanted a political messiah who would end Roman rule. They could not grasp Jesus' God-granted kingship, affirmed earlier by Nathanael (John 1:49).

In light of the distinction Jesus made in chapter 5 between seeking human glory and seeking God's glory, O'Day (1995) comments, "In that moment [Jesus'] glory was revealed, because true glory has nothing to do with worldly glory." As Jesus later puts it, *My kingdom is not from this world* (18:36a). Jesus refuses human glory and the political option to rule by crushing the enemy. His way to kingship goes through the cross, to God's glory!

Jesus therefore escapes, to be alone *on the mountain* (6:15b), a recurring use of *eis to oros*. How Jesus will fulfill messianic hopes depends on his communion with God, his Father. He will walk a different path from Zealot force. His retreat is brief, however, for soon he appears again to his disciples, in surprising form and with astounding words.

Jesus Walks on the Sea, with *I AM* Self-Revelation 6:16-21

John's account of Jesus' walking on the water differs from the Synoptics' account (Mark 6:47-52; Matt 14:22-33). Rather than emphasizing Jesus' stilling the stormy sea and the disciples' failure to understand (Mark) or their response of worship (Matthew), John emphasizes Jesus' guiding them to their destination. The story explains how Jesus guides the disciples across the sea to their destination rather than rescuing them from a sea storm (Talbert: 133; Giblin). John's account echoes God's leading Israel through the sea to safety on the other side (Exod 13–15). Numerous psalms celebrate Israel's deliverance as founding event, such as Psalms 77:11-20 and 107:25-32 (Burge 2000: 195–96). Verse 30 in Psalm 107 prefigures John's emphasis: "Then they were glad because they had quiet, and he brought them to their desired haven." Compare John 6:21: *Then they were glad to take him into the boat, and immediately the boat was at the land to which they were going* (RSV).

The notable punch line in this story, though, is not Jesus' walking on the water or leading them safely to the other side, but the word that Jesus speaks to his disciples. Yes, the disciples are frightened to see this ghostly form drawing closer to them on the water—who wouldn't be?—but what Jesus says astounds: *It is I; do not be afraid* (v. 20). The English reader might not catch it, but the declaration *It is I* echoes God's self-revelation to Moses in Exodus 3:13-15: "I AM." The Greek of verse 20b, *egō eimi*, echoes the Septuagint of Exodus 3:14, "I AM who I AM." The same divine self-identification recurs thirty times in Second Isaiah (chs. 40–55), emphasizing God's sovereignty and universality (see the significant studies by Harner [1970] and Ball, esp. Ball: 33–45). The disciples receive what the crowd, which was left behind when they sought to make Jesus king by force, could not begin to comprehend. The crowd received bread, but the disciples received his *I AM* presence, with its power, deliverance, and guidance. Moloney stresses the difference: "The reunion is marked by Jesus' coming to the disciples as Lord, revealing himself as I AM, and being received by them. None of this has happened to the crowds, who remain at the place of the miracle of the loaves and fish. The false messianic hopes of the crowds have been corrected by Jesus' self-revelation, and the disciples are willing recipients of that revelation" (1998: 203) ["I AM," p. 518].

Jesus reveals himself as *I AM* in John for the second time (see 4:26 for the first time). Jesus now turns to the meaning of the manna miracle.

Jesus Reveals the Meaning of the Sign: *I Am the Bread of Life* 6:22-40

6:22-24 People Search for Jesus as the Result of the Bread-Feeding

Resuming the directional signaling of 6:1-4, the Gospel's narrator now tells the time, *the next day*, and then when and where, and who is there. The disciples have reached their destiny (v. 21), but the crowd, on the other side of the sea, saw the disciples go away in a boat. They also saw that Jesus was not with them. So where is he? After some boats from Tiberias docked near them, *the place where they had eaten the bread after the Lord had given thanks*, the people take these boats and embark for Capernaum, seeking Jesus and his disciples. Their inner sense tells them where to find Jesus and his disciples.

While this temporal and geographical information is necessary for the flow of the narrative, the most arresting part is what is italicized above. The narrator is identifying the continuity between the miracle-sign and the discourse that is to follow. Further, *where they had eaten the bread* contains a eucharistic motif, *after the Lord had given thanks*. This suggests a two-level reading. One level emphasizes what the crowd remembers: eating the bread. The second level connotes what the evangelist wants readers to remember: the *Lord gave thanks* over the bread. A deeper meaning is at stake, soon to be revealed.

6:25-34 The Crowd Wants Bread; Jesus Wants Them to Understand the Sign

When the crowd finds Jesus, they express their first curiosity: *Rabbi, when did you come here?* This is the narrator's prompt. Jesus does not answer it but instead launches into a *Very truly (Amen, amen)* saying. Jesus exposes their true motivation: You came looking for me *not because you saw signs* [which would have been a good motivation], *but because you ate your fill of the loaves.* Jesus cuts to the heart. He continues to distinguish between *food that perishes* and *food that endures for eternal life* (v. 27). Jesus gives the crowd initial insight into his feeding sign, encouraging them to work for food that will not perish. Then Jesus "loads" his offer christologically: the food-gift that endures eternally is that which he, the Son of Man, will give. The offer is backed with warranty: *For it is on him that God the Father has set his seal* (v. 27d). This statement gives the clue: to understand the miracle as a *sign* means grasping its christological significance. The sign reveals! Its faith-meaning points to who Jesus is. He is the Son of Man, the one whom the Father sent and authorizes, with warranty (cf. the revelatory Christology of the feedings in Mark; Swartley 1981/1999: 112–23).

In response, the crowd asks, *What must we do to perform the works of God?* They do not get it. Jesus picks up on *works* and answers, *This is the work of God, that you believe in him whom he has sent.* Again Jesus' word beckons them to acknowledge his identity: one sent from God, doing the *work* of God. To do the work of God is to believe in him and the one whom God sent. But again the crowd wants another meal! So they hint clearly, *Our ancestors ate the manna in the wilderness, as it is written, "He gave them bread from heaven to eat."*

The next two verses begin Jesus' *midrash* on the text they quote. Midrash denotes a rabbinic way of reflecting upon Scripture, primarily the Torah, to draw meaning from it to inspire, exhort, and guide living in the present. It often includes subtle wordplays and a "not-but" sequence, exposing meaning beneath the surface of the text. As Borgen explains, verses 32-48 give a midrashic exposition on the first part of the scripture, *He gave them bread from heaven.* Then verses 49-58 continue that theme, but focus on *to eat*, the last word (*esthiō*) in the quotation. The verb *eat* does not occur in Jesus' first exposition (vv. 32-48), but only in the latter. The whole is a midrash on that text (Borgen 1965: 28–57; 1983: 24). Koester (2003: 95) points out that the discourse may be viewed in three stages, with the first, verses 32-34, expositing *He gave.* Borgen shows that the discourse follows the midrashic pattern found in Philo:

> Truly, truly, I say to you,
> it was not [*ou*] Moses who gave you the bread from heaven;
> but [*all'*] my Father gives you the true bread from heaven.
> For [*gar*] the bread of God is that which comes down from heaven
>   and gives life to the world.

Borgen cites the *not-but-for* pattern in both Jewish midrashic rabbinic texts on Scripture and in Philo (1983: 24–25). In this John 6 exposition, the bread points beyond itself to the Father, to God, and thus sets forth again the christological import of Jesus' feeding of the multitude.

Jesus' interpretation of the manna follows rabbinic lines perfectly. First, the true source of the manna was not Moses but God. *It is God who sends bread.* Furthermore, the manna story goes beyond mere bread; it is a spiritual metaphor for how God feeds us his word. Deuteronomy 8:3 may well have entered Jesus' debate. "[God] humbled you, causing you to hunger and then feeding you with manna, which neither you nor your ancestors had known, to teach you that people do not live on bread alone but on every word that comes from the mouth of the Lord" (TNIV; Burge 2000: 198).

Jesus clarifies the source of the bread from heaven: it is from God. The *true bread from heaven* is Jesus. What the bread from heaven offers is *life to the world*: "That the giver and the gift are identical means that one does not receive something from Jesus without receiving Jesus himself" (Talbert: 136).

A significant contrast emerges in the narrative. Though their ancestors ate the manna that God sent from heaven, those who eat the true bread that Jesus is about to offer will live forever (6:31 echoes Exod 16:4, 15 and Ps 78:23; Burroughs: 81).

6:35-40 *Jesus Reveals Himself to Be the Bread of Life*[w]

Jesus makes his first specific *I Am* declaration in this discourse: *I am the bread of life* (v. 35). This is the first of seven (or more) *I Am* descriptors with a predicate nominative. Jesus is the bread of life that will eternally feed those who receive it.

The last two verses of this unit underscore Jesus' promise to *lose nothing of all that . . . [the Father] has given me, but raise it up on the last day* (v. 39). The Father wills that *all who see the Son and believe in him may have eternal life; and I will raise them up on the last day.* The repeated refrain *raise up on the last day* occurs a third time in verse 44, and again in 54. The verb for *raise* (*anistēmi*) is future in each case, whereas the gift of eternal life is in both the present and the future. A dual refrain runs through these verses: *come down from heaven* (33, 38, 41, 42, 51, 58) and *I will raise up it/them/the person on the last day* (39, 40, 44, 54). The one who comes down from heaven is the One who will raise the believers to eternal life (cf. Temple 1939: 88–89).

Another theme runs through this midrash: *Those who come to me* depend upon the Father, who *gives* (v. 37), *draws* (v. 44a), or *grants* (v. 65) them to come to Jesus. Emphasis falls not so much on Jesus' welcoming all people, but rather on "keeping people whom the Father has given into his care" (Burge 2000: 200). At the same time, however, Jesus' desire is that all come to him, yet the mystery of faith and unbelief teases the sovereignty and inscrutability of God. Judas illustrates the point. Even so, speech of the Father's sovereignty and the Son's keeping power still anticipates the exception (6:70-71).

John 6 and other texts in John (note 10:29) have been used to promote the doctrine of eternal security, linked to doctrines of election, predestination, and foreknowledge (cf. Rom 8:29-30). Whether based here in John 6 or in Romans 8, the eternal security doctrine is one sided. The Father's will is expressed clearly in the *whosoever* of John 3:16 (KJV) as well as in the recurring use of whoever in this chapter 6 discourse, especially in the *Amen, amen* saying in 6:47: *Whoever believes has eternal life.* The two points must be held in tension, both *whoever* and what the Father *grants*, as 17:2-3 indicates in speaking of both *eternal life* and people's *coming* to Jesus. The *will of the Father* is expressed clearly in 6:40: *This is indeed the will of the Father, that all who see the Son and believe in him may have eternal life; and I will raise them up on the last day.* The Father wills that all who see Jesus or hear the message (20:29) will believe and receive eternal life [Belief, p. 504] [Eternal Life, p. 513].

The Jews Murmur and Challenge Jesus' Claims; More Self-Revelation 6:41-59

Verses 41-58 affirm Jesus as *the bread that came down from heaven.* The center, verse 51, *I am the living bread*, can be presented in chiasm:

A *I am the living bread that came down from heaven* (v. 51a).
  B *Whoever eats of this bread will live forever* (v. 51b).
A´ *The bread that I will give for the life of the world is my flesh*
  (v. 51c).

6:41-48 Murmuring; Jesus, the Bread from Heaven, Gives Eternal Life

In the evangelist's presentation of Jesus' midrashic exposition of the quotation in 6:31, this portion focuses on *come down from heaven.* The phrase, repeated in verses 41 and 42, recurs also in the next unit in verses 52 and 58, which culminates the discourse. The *from heaven* emphasis is also implied in *the Father who sent me* (v. 44).

In verses 41-42 the Jews begin to complain about Jesus' claim that he came from heaven because they know him to be the son of Joseph. Therefore, *How can he now say, "I have come down from heaven"?* They imply that he is lying. Or they may be confused. Jesus admonishes them for complaining. He then complicates the matter as he explains his and his Father's role in offering the gift that leads to eternal life and resurrection on the last day. Here the ugly ditch between *from above* and *from below* that has emerged in John 3 with Nicodemus reappears. This is a basic and recurring contrast in John's Gospel (Meeks 1972). It readily results in two levels of speech and repeated misunderstandings by the Jews. They cannot comprehend Jesus: *No one can come to me unless drawn by the Father who sent me; and I will raise that person up on the last day* (v. 44). Jesus' follow-up citation from the prophets tantalizes: *And they shall all be taught by God* (Isa 54:13; cf. Jer 31:33-34). The *all* might give hope to the complainers since the promise then would include them. But then Jesus adds, *Everyone who has heard and learned from the Father comes to me.* That's a stopper in the debate, for that is exactly what his accusers resist.

This claim then presents a qualification, an invitation, and repeats Jesus' claim:

- Qualification: *Not that anyone has seen the Father except the one who is from God; he has seen the Father* (v. 46). This reiterates the last verse of the prologue: *No one has ever seen God. It is God the only Son, who is close to the Father's heart, who has made him known* (1:18).

- Invitation: With the *Amen, amen* formula, Jesus invites belief: *I tell you, whoever believes has eternal life* (v. 47).

- Basic claim repeated: *I am the bread of life* (v. 48).

This repeats the claim in verse 35: *I am the bread of life.* It bookends this part of the discourse. The next part takes a giant step into the claim's mystery and meaning.

6:49-58 Eating the Bread; Jews' Disputing; Eating Jesus' Flesh, Drinking His Blood[w]

The last word of the quotation in 6:31b, *eat*, is now taken up as the leitmotif of this final section of the discourse. Verses 49-58 emphasize *eating*, first the bread and then Jesus' flesh. Jesus reminds his interlocutors, *Your ancestors ate the manna in the wilderness* (v. 49). This prepares for his invitation that they, too, must eat the bread. But the invitation comes with two twists. Whereas your ancestors ate, *and died*, if you eat of the bread I give, you will live forever since *I am the living bread that came down from heaven. Whoever eats of this bread will live forever; and the bread that I will give for the life of the world is my flesh* (vv. 51-52). The crowd is eager to eat bread. But Jesus says, in effect, that bread is what the ancestors ate, . . . and they died! In contrast, if you eat the bread that I give, *now* come down from heaven (v. 50a), you *may eat of it and not die* (v. 50b). The next word offends: *The bread that I will give for the life of the world is my flesh.*

With this claim the Jews dispute among themselves: What could Jesus possibly mean? *How can this man give us his flesh to eat?* (v. 52a). Jesus answers with another profoundly puzzling Amen, amen declaration: *I tell you, unless you eat the flesh of the Son of Man and drink his blood, you have no life in you. Those who eat my flesh and drink my blood have eternal life, and I will raise them up on the last day; for my flesh is true food and my blood is true drink* (vv. 53b-55). Not only Jews but also most Christian believers are stunned by these words. Outside the Catholic and Anglican/Episcopal traditions, Christians in the West ignore these words, take them lightly, or spiritualize them. As Burge (2000: 202) puts it, "Now they are aghast as he makes the next step. Earthly bread—heavenly bread—Jesus as bread—Jesus as bread to eat—Jesus as sacrifice. It is all too much so their grumbling turns to argument (6:52)." Does Jesus *intend* to offend, making belief leap beyond the rational into the mystical or sacramental?

Verse 56 repeats the two key phrases a third time, *eat my flesh and drink my blood*, and then links them to union with Jesus (Christ): they *abide in me, and I in them* (anticipating ch. 15). Verses 57-58 repeat *eats* two times with the objects *me* and this *bread*. In verse 58b Jesus asserts that their ancestors *ate* and died. Jesus ends the discourse by saying, *But the one who eats this bread [that came down from heaven] will live forever* (v. 58c). In a ring structure these verses return to the language and emphases of 6:50-51.

Eating Jesus' flesh, if not already offensive in that it suggests cannibalism, is made more puzzling by the Greek verb in verses 54 and 56. The participle *eating* (*trōgō*) means *chewing* or *munching*. This verbal is in the present tense, signifying continuous *chewing* or *munching*. What does Jesus mean? What is Jesus saying with this commentary on the feeding miracle? Is this John's institution of the Lord's Supper? Burge (2000: 202) moves through these enigmas rather quickly, saying that this sounds like "religious cannibalism. Earthly symbols must be converted into spiritual truths."

"Spiritual truths?" Well, yes, but just what are these spiritual truths? It is virtually impossible to deny their eucharistic allusion, even denotation. The imagery certainly goes beyond Passover; eating human flesh and drinking blood is offensive to the Jewish mind. Jewish law forbids drinking blood (Lev 17:10-14), and Jewish Christians continued the proscription, even for Gentile believers

(Acts 15:20d, 29b). Can these words in John be taken literally? The point of connection with Jewish practice, however, is in *eating* the sacrifice that restores covenant relationship between sinful humans and God. The leap in thought, however, is the move from eating bread or roasted *animal meat* to eating *human flesh*. The missing link is the strange *glory* in John. When Jesus is lifted up on the cross, *sacrificed*, he gives himself for the life of the world. Indeed, the bread, *his flesh*—given through incarnation—is for *the life of the world*.

On these verses 51c-58 Johannine scholars dispute (echoing v. 52). Since it is difficult not to see sacrificial and eucharistic meaning in these verses, some notable scholars have regarded these verses as inauthentic, a later insertion into John's text, implying that for our theological comfort we can excise them and go on to the next section! Anderson (1996) argues against the "later insertion" thesis and for christological unity. Rensberger (1988: 77–81) surveys the arguments and decides also for the unity of the text. Its eucharistic meaning fits with John's larger understanding of the social experience of Johannine believers. Continually "abiding in Jesus" (ch. 15; also 17:18, 23; 20:21) and receiving life from Jesus as spiritual sustenance (14:19b-20) are hallmarks of John's community and its theology and life.

Many commentators accept some form of eucharistic meaning (R. Brown 1966: 284–85; Burge 2000: 202–3; Carson: 295–99; Rensberger 1988: 72–80; Moloney 1998: 223; Suggit: 71–72). Suggit contends that the eucharist is in the background—likely the *source* of the language—but here the focus is on the person of Jesus, his identity and work as the work of God (76; concurring with Borgen 1965: 61–97, 147–91). A key argument regarding Jesus' feeding of the multitude and the following discourse as eucharistic is that John does not have the institution of the Lord's Supper in John 13, where it would occur in the Synoptics. At least the tradition of the eucharist as practiced in the early church has influenced the telling of this event (Ellis: 101). Ellis and Suggit are correct that the chapter focuses on Jesus' identity and work, but this does not exclude eucharist!

Jesus' words on eating flesh and drinking blood, however, have negative hostile meaning in other uses (Ps 27:2; Zech 11:9; etc.). For them to have "favorable meaning" here, "they must refer to the eucharist." Otherwise they "cannot possibly be a metaphor for accepting his revelation" (R. Brown 1966: 284–85). Further, the eucharist is not dissociated from *Logos* revelation, but marks the apex of that revelation: in the eucharist Jesus gives his flesh for the life of the world. Those who believe and thereby live receive the fullest revelation of who Jesus is.

The case for a noneucharistic view has its proponents also. Morris (333) contends that the eucharist is not in view since all accounts of instituting the Lord's Supper speak not of *eating flesh* (*sarx*), but of *body* (*sōma*). In "every other New Testament passage referring to it [eucharist] the word is 'body' such as 'this is my *body* (*sōma*) broken for you.' . . . Jesus' language of eating and drinking Christ's flesh and blood thus appears to be a . . . graphic way of saying that people must take Christ into their innermost being" (335). Further, the verbs for *eat* and *drink* identify past point action (aorist) and thus signify Jesus' death. Morris (335n133) quotes C. H. Dodd, who says of 6:51: The bread that Jesus gives *for the life of the world is my flesh* and the imagery *drink my blood* (vv. 53, 54, 56) both *separately* signify violent death. Thus, Brant (2004) might agree with Morris, since hearing Jesus' words *dramatically* fits his inexorable march to death. Morris thus says *no* to eucharistic and/or sacramental views, however. Rather, Jesus is referring to his coming death. The continued *eating* (present of *trōgō*) in verses 54, 56, 57, 58 does not signify eucharist but "receiving Christ" (336). Even with this view some sense of eucharistic theology is present: Jesus' body (*flesh* in John) and blood continue to nourish the believer.

What metaphors support a noneucharistic interpretation? Matsunaga's answer is that while John has many symbols that suggest sacrament, he deliberately spiritualizes baptism and the Lord's Supper. John does not narrate Jesus' baptism or the words of institution for eucharist. The Gospel knows about the sacraments but avoids them in order to make central the "Johannine *Kerygma* that confessed the high Christology, and to give new qualifications of the true discipleship—the union of God-Jesus-disciples in love" (523). Footwashing demonstrates this love.

This is a creative explanation but not satisfying since it does not address Jesus' offensive commands to *eat my flesh and drink my blood*. Two features of the text, considered from the standpoint of John's larger theology, might explain why John uses *flesh* instead of *body* as well as why he has *drink my blood* rather than *drink the cup*, the term in the Synoptics and Paul. First, John's theology is incarnational. The Word (*Logos*) became *flesh* (*sarx*), and this calls for just such commands. They appear in this Gospel to highlight the incarnation and settle the docetic denial of Jesus' suffering and death [*Docetism*]. MacGregor (1962: 117) reminds us that both Justin (*First Apology* 66) and Ignatius (*To the Smyrnaeans* 7.1) speak of the eucharist as eating the *flesh* (*sarx*) of Jesus, and that the eucharist is not so much a rite commemorating Jesus' death as a bestowal of the "gift of eternal life."

A second consideration is how verse 56b (*abide in me, and I in them*) connects the text to John 15: Jesus is the true vine, and believers are the branches. Macgregor (1962: 112) informs us that "the Vine was a recognized eucharistic symbol at the time the Gospel was written," citing the *Didache* (9.2), "We give thanks to Thee, our Father, for the Holy Vine of David thy servant." While this does not account for the shock of the phrase *drink my blood*, it does connect the eucharistic language of John 6 to the larger Johannine emphasis on *mutual indwelling*. Blood here is a symbol of *life*: the life is in the blood. Hence the three distinctive Johannine motifs within this John 6 text—*flesh, eternal life, abide in me*—indicate that John has tailored the eucharistic motifs to his larger theology. Connecting verse 54 with *abiding in me* (John 15) indicates the verse is to be taken spiritually; it cautions against making this eucharistic language sacramental. Rather, it is the Spirit who gives life through the words of Jesus: "The primary emphasis is on Jesus himself . . . [as] the source and sustenance of eternal life" (Dunn 1971: 337). "The presence of eucharistic terminology does not necessarily imply the advocacy of institutional sacramentalism" (Anderson 1996: 130).

To pursue the issue we ask: Does John really speak here of the eucharist? After all, the continuous present for *gnaw* or *munch* (*trōgō* used four times in vv. 54-58) suggests not a rite celebrated on occasion, but a continuous partaking of Jesus who gives life (as Dunn affirms). Similarly, *drinking my blood*, taken literally, violates early Christian moral sanctions. If we think of this as sacramental, we need to rethink the meaning of sacrament. John's view of sacrament is not so much a rite or the institution of a liturgy. The outward rite is subordinated to Jesus' commandment to love one another, the identity mark of the new community that draws its life from Jesus (cf. John 15:10-13). MacGregor (1962: 118) regards both John 6 and 13 as sacramental: footwashing is the analogous sacrament in that Jesus alludes to baptism in saying *One who has bathed does not need to wash* (13:10a). The footwashing itself, standing in the place of the Lord's Supper, is not only a cleansing from postbaptismal sin but also denotes "a spirit of love and service that will unite them in fellowship with one another and with himself, and will be the badge of their discipleship." MacGregor takes Jesus' word *You also ought to wash one another's feet. For I have set you an example, that you should do as I have done to you* (13:14-15) as analogous to the eucharistic charge, "'Do this, as often as you drink it, in remembrance of me.' For as often as you eat this bread and drink the cup, you proclaim the Lord's death until he comes" (1 Cor 11:25b-26).

Given these varied views of this difficult text, we have these options:

- The text is not eucharistic but points to abiding union with Christ in his death (Morris; Westcott and Godet in the nineteenth century; Matsunaga; and also Dunn 1971: 335–337), in that the text cautions against using eucharistic language for sacramental effect: it rather calls for "union of the ascended Jesus with his believing followers through the Spirit."

- The text is eucharistic, but not sacramental, in the sense that *sacrament* points to an institutional liturgical rite in which Jesus' literal flesh and blood are ingested.

- The text is eucharistic and sacramental.

- The text is neither eucharistic nor sacramental.

- The text is sacramental, but not necessarily eucharistic. It makes all of life a sacrament, a life of union with Christ in love and service.

- The text is a combination of two or more of the above.

An example of this last view is advocated by Dumm: "It is obvious that the eucharist is the subject of John 6" (114). John places the eucharist here in proximity to baptism in 3:1–4:3. Baptism and eucharist are spiritual nourishment. Jesus offers this food because "it is on him that God the Father has set his seal" (6:27).

> Ultimately, the nourishment that Jesus offers is that truth to which his whole life has been dedicated, namely, the revelation, first, of the Father's unconditional love for us and, second, of our obligation and opportunity to offer, as much as possible, the same unconditional love to others. . . . This is the real meaning of the eucharist, which is all about God's love for us and of our love for others. As such, it is an epitome of the meaning of Jesus' life and teaching. (Dumm: 117)

What makes interpretation of John 6:52-58 difficult is not only the shocking imagery but also the different understandings of eucharist and sacrament fostered in the Christian body today. Because this matter is closely related to the diversity of understanding within various religious traditions, resolving the issue lies beyond these "Explanatory Notes." Much depends on how the term *sacrament* is defined (see TLC of this chapter).

6:59 The Synagogue in Capernaum

This brief verse closes the discourse that began when the crowd, searching for Jesus (vv. 22-24), found him in Capernaum (vv. 24-25), a city on the northwest shore of the Sea of Galilee. Further, it locates the discourse in the Capernaum synagogue, which may suggest that Jesus spoke these words on the Sabbath. It portrays Jesus and his disciples as integrated into the religious life of Judaism. Throughout Israel the synagogue was the place of teaching and learning, matching the temple in Jerusalem (cf. Luke 2:41-51). This detail is important as we seek to understand John 9:22 and 16:2.

Jesus Tests His Disciples; Some Leave, but the Twelve Confess Loyalty 6:60-71

6:60-65 Jesus' Claims Offend; Jesus Explains Further

These difficult words of Jesus, pointing to his death, offend many of his disciples. They complain about it and rhetorically say, *Who can accept it?* The NEB puts it memorably: *This is more than we can stomach! Why listen to such talk?* Jesus knows they are offended and takes the occasion to teach further, but this only adds fuel to the fire; many disciples turn back, no longer following him (v. 66). To accept the notion that following Jesus (discipleship) means continuously feeding on Jesus' flesh and blood may be analogical to Jesus' response to Peter's confession in Mark 8:27-38. Both signify costly discipleship!

In effect Jesus says, "If what I have said about eating my flesh and drinking my blood offends you, get this: What if you were to see the Son of Man ascending to where he was before? It is the spirit that gives life; the flesh is useless. The words that I have spoken to you are spirit and life. But among you are some who do not believe." Each of these five sayings distances rather than draws the hearers. The first and third (the flesh is useless) are difficult to comprehend, especially in view of 1:14, *The Word became flesh*, and what Jesus has just commanded, *Eat my flesh*. William Temple's perception here is helpful. He holds that the two sayings are quite different in connotation: eat my flesh signifies death; drink my blood signifies life. Flesh will die, but blood is life (even in OT sacrifice, "the life . . . is in the blood" [Lev 17:11]—and hence because it was an animal, the covenant people could not drink the blood, which was poured out for them). But Jesus' blood is to be drunk, figuratively speaking, so that you will have life in yourselves. John 6:63b, *The words that I have spoken to you are spirit and life*, does not mean that flesh equals spirit and blood equals life. Rather, it means that flesh and blood mean spirit and life.

Why not then start with *spirit* in the first place? Good reasons: to remember always the cross where *flesh dies*; to avoid some general *spiritual* mysticism that ignores the body broken and the blood out-poured; and lest we forget that outward acts are not efficacious in themselves, but always depend upon the death, resurrection, and ascension—the flesh and blood—of the Son of Man (Temple 1939: 94, 97–99).

Jesus' word on the Son of Man's ascending to where he was before further fogs the hearers (v. 62), much as Jesus' word to Nicodemus did (3:3, 5). So far in this narrative only Nathanael grasps the meaning of this descent and ascent language. Its meaning likely eludes the other disciples at this stage in Jesus' revelation of God and of his being with and in God. Despite 3:14, Jesus' first statement about being *lifted up*, the disciples do not yet comprehend that Jesus' death is his glorification and exaltation.

Jesus expects the *many* disciples (6:66) not to understand nor to continue with him (cf. Mark 4:11-12). The omniscient narrator unveils the all-knowing mind of Jesus. Jesus knew from the first who would believe (cf. John 2:24) and also who *was going to betray him* (6:71). And again, Jesus appeals to the sovereign Father, who manages the "gate" through which people come to Jesus. Those who come to him are those whom the Father grants (v. 65; see "Divine Sovereignty and Human Freedom" in the TLC).

6:66-69 Jesus Tests the Twelve; Simon Peter's Response

Now comes the parting of the ways among the disciples. Many turn back from following him (v. 66). So Jesus asks the twelve what they wish to do, giving them the freedom to choose: *Do you also wish to go away?* Peter responds in a way similar to his memorable con-fession in the Synoptics (Mark 8:29). John's version sounds a note of desperation: *Lord, to whom can we go? You have the words of eternal life. We have come to believe and know that you are the Holy One of God.* Manuscripts vary on the exact wording of how Peter names Jesus in this confession. Two variants to this NRSV/NIV reading are *Christ, the Son of the living God* or *Christ, the Holy One of God.* Though each of these two variants has support from several early manu-scripts, the reading *Holy One of God* has by far the strongest support. The variants add wording from the Messiah/Christ designation in the Synoptics. In John, Jesus has already been acclaimed *Messiah/ Christ* (1:41; 4:25).

Holy One of God appears in the Synoptics on the lips of the demons (Mark 1:24; Luke 4:34), who tremble in Jesus' presence. A similar phrase, "Holy One of Israel," appears often in Isaiah (41:14, 20; 43:14-15; 45:11; 47:4; 48:17; 49:7). In view of John's emphases on the Father's sovereign purpose and *granting* those who come to Jesus, this fits the narrative. Peter's confession and the evangelist's purpose link Jesus to God as holy and sovereign. This forms the context of the final remark.

6:70-71 Jesus Says One Will Deliver Him Over to the Authorities

Jesus' response affirms his choosing of the twelve disciples, presumably granted by his Father. But then he clouds their future by saying: *Yet one of you is a devil*—a harsh word indeed! Since Peter has just confessed Jesus' divine identity with words the demons disclose regarding Jesus in the Synoptics (Mark 1:24; Luke 4:34), one might think that Jesus speaks of *Peter* (cf. Mark 8:33, "Get behind me, Satan!"). But the narrator halts the guessing. He names Judas, son of Simon Iscariot, as the one whose future will so unfold.

Jesus names the exception to his declaration *No one can snatch it out of the Father's hand* (10:29). Or is it an exception? Was it Judas's own decision? Or was Judas thinking that if he would *hand Jesus over* to the authorities (cf. 6:71 NIRV), he would hasten the coming of the kingdom? These questions are difficult. What is clear is that Jesus knew that Judas would do this. It facilitates the culmination of Jesus' ministry: to be *lifted up* on the cross and thus *glorified*. Jesus' words in John raise agonizing questions, and the Gospel does not provide all the answers we might wish (Burge 2000: 207).

THE TEXT IN BIBLICAL CONTEXT

John 6 Anchored in OT Scripture[w]

John's Gospel often alludes to and quotes from the OT. Numerous verses in John 6 are a midrash on Exodus 16, as well as Psalm 78:24 (Borgen 1965), as shown in this chapter. But Jesus' manna miracle, his fourth sign, alludes also to other OT feeding miracles, placing Jesus in the prophetic Elijah-Elisha tradition.

Little wonder then that the crowd hails Jesus as a prophet after eating this manna-like miracle bread, affirming Jesus' fulfillment of Deuteronomy 18:15, "The Lord your God will raise up for you a prophet like me [Moses] from among your own people; you shall heed such a prophet." Trying to discern whether Jesus is that prophet, the people want another sign (6:30-31). Moses was known for his many signs and wonders. The evangelist presents Jesus in this Moses tradition but also wants Jesus' hearers to perceive what the manna sign points to: Christology, Jesus as Messiah (McGrath: 172–73).

The crowd wants to make him their Messiah-king since they knew traditions that told of the expected messiah opening the windows of heaven and raining down manna (see Explanatory Notes for this chapter; for quenching thirst, cf. Isa 48:20-21; Mic 7:15; John 6:35c). Jesus' words in John 6:63b, *The words that I have spoken to you are spirit and life*, joined to the manna miracle, echo Deuteronomy 8:3: "One does not live by bread alone, but by every word that comes from the mouth of the Lord" (cf. Wis 16:20, 26). While the people want to make Jesus prophet-king, Jesus broadens their vision and blunts their action. His claims—*I AM*, and *Son of Man ascending to where he was before* (cf. 1:1 and 6:62, in the context of 6:55-58; McGrath: 177–81)—stifle political thinking and offend. The people cannot comprehend (Pazdan 1991; Pamment 1985; Moloney 1976).

Jesus' walking on the water also echoes OT traditions. Jesus' *I AM* self-disclosure (6:20) blends Moses and Yahweh. In promising that the *bread that came down from heaven gives eternal life*, Jesus again blends Moses and Yahweh. But Jesus explicitly points beyond Moses to God, *my Father*, who gave them this manna (6:32). Jesus' work is one with his Father's, and thus Jesus and the Father give eternal life to all who believe, with promise of resurrection on the last day. John 6:41-44 alludes also to the OT: the Jews' *murmuring* (6:41, 43 RSV; 6:61 reflecting Jesus' claim in v. 58c) echoes Israel's murmuring (RSV: Exod 15:24; 16:2, 7-9, 12; 17:3; Num 14:2, 27-32, 35-36; 17:5). They *murmur* because Jesus claims he is both the *Son of Man* and the *living bread* come down from heaven. This bread contrasts to the *bread their ancestors ate* in the wilderness. Your ancestors *died* in the wilderness (Num 14:35), but by *eating* this *bread* you will *live* forever. Moses' manna could not impart life (cf. Burroughs: 83–90). Further, Jesus' *drawing* to himself those the Father gives him echoes the OT (Jer 38:3 LXX [31:3 ET], *elkyō*; see Dennis: 192–93; Freed 1965: 20; Keener: 1.685).

John 6:45-47 portrays Jesus' teaching as fulfilling "taught by God" in Isaiah 54:13 (cf. Jer 31:33). Jesus' statement in verse 45c, *Everyone who has heard and learned from the Father comes to me*, means that God's restoration day (Isa 54) has now come through Jesus the Messiah's words and deeds. The gathering of the twelve baskets of bread fragments connotes Israel's restoration. The restoration motif reappears in John 11:52, *to gather into one the dispersed children of God* (Dennis: 193–94). Jesus, who alone has seen the Father, *teaches* and *restores* them. Those who believe *have eternal life.*

Jesus' shocking exhortation to eat his flesh and drink his blood beckons people to feast on him, living by the Word come from and of God: *the Word was with God, was God* (1:1), and *became flesh* (1:14).

John 6 as Eucharist and Sacrament?

Is John 6:52-58 to be viewed as John's mode of instituting the Lord's Supper, eucharist? Both similarities and differences to the Lord's Supper in the Synoptics (and Paul in 1 Cor 11) are evident. The accounts of the "institution" in the Synoptics contain some words similar to John's account of Jesus' feeding the five thousand. Further, the emphases at the beginning and end of John 6 match the Synoptics' framing of the Lord's Supper accounts. Beginning: the Jewish Passover feast draws near; ending: a sifting and falling away of disciples. *But* John 6 is Passover a year earlier, located in *Galilee!*

Nonetheless, the similarity in language could indicate that John intends Jesus' feeding the five thousand to be his unique "institution" of the Last Supper (of the Synoptic accounts), shifting the accent from a "rite" to emphases on cleansing from sin and humble service in the footwashing (ch. 13). In all these texts there is either *blessing* the loaves or *giving thanks.* Two features in the feeding miracles of the Synoptic Gospels are absent in John, however: Jesus looks up to heaven before the blessing and breaking of the loaves, and Jesus gives the bread to the disciples to distribute. In John, Jesus himself distributes it directly to the multitude.

The next verses in the "institution" texts are quite different from John, though several crucial words occur in all: *my*, *drink*, and *blood.* The Synoptic "institution" texts have numerous additional words not in John:

- "body, cup, poured out for many or given for you"
- "covenant" ("new," in Luke and Paul)
- "(Father's) kingdom (of God)" in Matthew and Mark
- "forgiveness of sins" (Matthew only)

Even with the few same crucial words, striking differences occur:

- John's *eating* is the word *trōgō*, not the more usual word *esthiō*, as in Matthew.

- John links *drink* and *blood*, whereas the other four accounts link blood to "(new) covenant."

- John speaks of *eating my flesh* (*sarx*), whereas all the other accounts speak of "my body [*sōma*]" ("given for you" in Luke and Paul).

The differences are striking: thus an interpreter can hold that John 6:52-58 is *not* eucharistic. But the similarities are also significant: thus an interpreter can hold that John 6 is eucharistic. The debate is not easily settled, especially in light of John's theological distinctives otherwise. Different understandings of the eucharist as sacramental or nonsacramental—with this term understood differently by different Christian faith traditions—further cloud the debate.

My view is that the text is eucharistic and sacramental, but not in the sense of "institution." John's distinctiveness cautions us against making the text mirror the Synoptics and Paul. In light of John's uniqueness in having *Abide in me* and *Love one another* as the hallmarks of the believers' identity, John 6 calls us to the sacramental life, union with Christ in love and service (similar to Anderson's view, 1996: 130, contra Dunn 1971: 235–38). In short, eucharist as sacrament for John cannot be divorced from ethics. It is to be a lived eucharist and a lived sacrament, receiving grace (1:14, 16, 17) and drawing empowerment from Jesus, as a branch draws life from the vine (15:1-11). Since *eternal life* in John is *present* as well as *future*, the promise of 6:54 means that we live the gift of eternal life now, by abiding in Jesus and loving as he loved. Indeed, in chapter 17 believers join the Jesus-Father oneness, the very life and love of God [*Sacrament, p. 529*].

William Temple comes to a similar understanding (though his view of sacrament differs from mine). He rightly prioritizes *communion with Jesus* in the eating and drinking as "an end in so far as it is communion, but a means to an end in so far as it is sacramental." He regards the vine image in John 15 as suggestive of the wine of the cup (echoing John 2:1-10). John 15 is thus more explicitly eucharistic than John 6—the early church leaders linked the cup to the fruit of the vine. Further, *Eat my flesh* and *drink my blood* is surely figurative. The key point is feeding upon Jesus for life nourishment (1939: 95). Temple's quote from Ignatius (*To the Trallians* 8.1), "Renew yourselves in faith, which is the flesh of the Lord, and in love, which is the blood of Christ," sums up his view (81). John's language has three purposes:

- to point effectively to *spiritual* dependence on Christ;
- "to guard against materialism or magic in the use of the eucharist"; and

- "to secure that our sense of dependence on Christ is inseparably associated with His redeeming sacrifice"—so 6:51
  (Temple 1939: 99).

These I affirm.

THE TEXT IN THE LIFE OF THE CHURCH

Eating Jesus' Flesh[w]

Menno Simons treats at length the interconnection between John
1:1 and 1:14, bolstered by appeal to numerous verses and phrases in
John 6 (esp. v. 51), to stress that Jesus gives himself in his wholeness,
flesh included, for the life of the world. The recurring phrase "living
bread came down from heaven" is also of great importance. Menno
devotes over a hundred pages (in "Incarnation of Our Lord" and
"Reply to Micron," Menno: 794–913) to Jesus the Word becoming
flesh in Mary. But the flesh is not from Mary. If the flesh were from
Mary, Jesus would have been half Adam-type flesh. But he is not,
Menno argues. Further, he would have the character of two sons
simultaneously: one from Mary (fallen and sinful, as are all humans)
and the other from God (pure and holy). Menno regards this as
absurd. Menno argues against the Zwinglian reformers John à Lasco
(787–92) and Micron (835–913) and others as well, to assert that
Jesus the Word came down from heaven. The Word came from
heaven, and it became flesh in Mary. Menno stresses the heavenly
and not the human origin of the flesh.

Some Anabaptist historians question the orthodoxy of Menno's
doctrine of "heavenly or celestial flesh." But for John it is important
to hold the heavenly origin of the flesh, since it correlates with
John's *from above* (not *from below*) pervasive emphasis. Also, it gives
new meaning to Jesus' command, *Eat my flesh* and *drink my blood* (for
the views that Menno opposes, see 829, "second" point). Menno
often appeals to the recurring Johannine contrast between the
heavenly and the earthly (John 3:12-13; 6:62; cf. Eph 4:9-10), and correlates this with Paul's distinction between the first Adam and the
second Adam, Christ, who comes from heaven and will again ascend
to heaven. Menno argues for Christ's full humanity: he *became* flesh,
which dwelt in Mary. As Gerald Mast (177–78) says in his excellent
essay, drawing on Keeney's and Sjouka Voolstra's studies of Menno,
Menno holds that Jesus is not *from* Mary but *out of* Mary. Menno,
however, declares that Jesus was fully human, since the flesh *out of*
Mary "was derived from the same substance as that of Adam's
nature before the fall" (178).

However, when Menno exposits 6:63 and 6:54, he rants against those who think that "in the Holy Supper" they eat the "actual flesh" and drink the "actual blood" of Christ (153). He says, "It is useless to eat His flesh literally and to drink His blood. Nor could it be done, because He was about to ascend to the place where He was before" (153). Those who take 6:54 literally are "miserable" and "blind": the one who ascended up to heaven "cannot be masticated nor confined in alimentary tract nor be consumed by time, by fire or worms, as is the case with visible bread and wine as one can see" (153). He then speaks of the "spiritual" meaning in these words: "The words that I speak unto you, they are spirit, and they are life." Here is where Menno misses what could have been constructive to his "celestial flesh" view, since "eating Jesus' flesh" (in the Lord's Supper) is regeneration, affirming that believers live by that which comes *from above.*

In his extensive study of how Anabaptists Hubmaier, Marpeck, and Philips understood the Lord's Supper in the context of Christology, John Rempel (225–26) makes three important summary points. First, these authors correct the misunderstanding that Anabaptists and others in the Continental Reformation expressed when they "reduced the Lord's Supper to a human act of remembrance." Second, the Anabaptists did not focus primarily on what happens in the "elements" (transubstantiation or consubstantiation) nor did they spiritualize the meaning of the Lord's Supper. In a dynamic trinitarianism, "the Father works inwardly as the Spirit, and Son works outwardly. . . . They then become the means of the church's union with Christ, of its participation in his body and blood." Third, Anabaptist theology emphasizes "faith, reconciliation, community, and mission" in observing the Lord's Supper. "Anabaptism teaches that communion is the surpassing expression of reconciliation of Christians with God and with each other" (226).

Divine Sovereignty and Human Freedom

C. K. Barrett's article on "theological dialectic" in John applies to numerous themes (e.g., the present and future of eternal life). It includes the dialectic between human freedom and divine sovereignty. The text portrays people as *coming to* Jesus (6:15, 24) or Jesus as *inviting* them to come (6:35, 37). At the same time they come only "through the Father's enablement" (1972: 64). The dialectic appears in Jesus' dialogue with Peter. In his reply to Jesus' question *Do you also wish to go away?* (6:67), Peter confesses Jesus' unique identity, implying that he (and the twelve) will stay. But Jesus then says that *he* chose the twelve (v. 70), putting Peter's decision in tension with his sovereign election. In verse 65 Jesus declares, *No one can come to me unless it is granted by the Father.*

Four aspects of truth in this dialectic are to be held together:

- God in divine sovereignty initiates and predestines salvation (6:37, 44, 65).

- Humans choose how they respond to God's initiative (37, 45b, 64).

- The divine purpose is that all come to receive eternal life (39-40, 45).

- Jesus is the focal point where divine sovereignty and human freedom meet (passim in John; cf. Eph 1:4—God's adopts us in and through Jesus Christ).

I Am the Bread of Life and *I Will Raise You Up on the Last Day*

More than any other text in Scripture, John 6 promises that Jesus will feed our spiritual hunger now and will raise us up on the last day. Both are Jesus' gift of eternal life: present and future. Jesus satisfies our hunger for God now and promises final, future blessing—resurrection beyond our dying. Though difficult to visualize being *raised up on the last day*, what is foundational in this belief and hope is that God will vindicate those who believe in Jesus as the one whom God sent. This one *comes from above* as bread of life, gives his life for the life of the world, and *returns* to his Father to prepare a place for us (14:1-3). Jesus triumphs over sin and death.

John 7

Jesus: Living Water, at the Feast of Tabernacles

PREVIEW

Some decisions are extremely difficult. In January 1982 Mennonite Central Committee (MCC) sponsored a peacemaking seminar in Swaziland to draw leaders from churches in southern Africa, mostly South Africa, to come together and learn Jesus' peacemaking witness in an apartheid culture. Three resource persons were invited. One from South Africa was denied permission to attend; another from Germany (IFOR) was stopped at the airport with his visa strangely disappearing. As the third person, I made it because my wife and I went early, before Christmas. Later the local MCC leadership was able to get someone in Lesotho (though *from* South Africa) to come midway into the two-week seminar. But his coming tipped the Swazi police to investigate what was going on, since it was illegal to discuss anything political in public. The thirty attendees, who had risked security before—some spending time in jail—had a difficult decision to make. Do they continue with police monitoring the seminar, or do they stop, calling it quits? After hours of agonizing, the decision was to continue, risking punitive measures. For five days police monitored biblical teaching on peacemaking. Listen for analogies to this in John 7.

John 7 begins with Jesus and his disciples continuing in Galilee, with the rationale that he *did not wish to go about in Judea because the Jews were looking for an opportunity to kill him* (v. 1). *His brothers* (last mentioned in 2:12) now enter the narrative. They assume that Jesus

191

will go with them to the upcoming Feast of Booths (v. 2). Their blunt
rationale is pious and crass: *so that your disciples also may see the works
you are doing,* and for you to *show yourself to the world* (v. 4)! With an
aside to the reader, the narrator indicates that even his brothers do
not believe in him (v. 5). Jesus says *no* to going up to Jerusalem for
the feast and tells his brothers to go alone. Jesus' reason? Because
my time has not yet come, . . . [and] *the world hates me* (vv. 6-8). But
after his *brothers* go, Jesus goes, too.

Set mostly therefore in Jerusalem, chapter 7 complements chapter 6, set in Galilee. Similar themes appear—true bread and living
water—and increased misunderstandings by the crowds and *the
Jews.* Even while Jesus is still in Galilee, the narrator informs readers
that the Jews are looking for him at the festival. Hence he goes up
to Jerusalem *in secret.* Further, *murmuring* (*gongysmos,* v. 12 AT; cf. v.
32) continues within the crowd, which is divided in attitude about
him. Some think him *a good man;* others say he *is deceiving the crowd.*

Once Jesus arrives in Jerusalem for the feast, he speaks twice:
first, at the midpoint of the feast, on the *source* of his message and
authority. This elicits varied responses, and Pharisees send police to
arrest him (7:14-36). On the last day of the feast, Jesus speaks again,
teaching and fielding responses from *some of the people* (cf. vv. 25,
40). The authorities are befuddled and dismayed that the police
return empty-handed (7:37-52).

Division among the people occurs in both discourses as well (vv.
25-31, 40-44). At one point the crowd accuses Jesus of having a demon
because he asks forthrightly, *Why are you looking for an opportunity to
kill me?* (v. 19c, cf. vv. 1, 25). However, *many in the crowd* believe in him
(v. 31) because they cannot imagine that the expected messiah, if he
is still to come, would do more signs than Jesus is doing.

Jesus' statement on the last day of the feast, in verses 37-39, is
stellar. Stalling the rash impulse by the chief priests and Pharisees
to kill Jesus, Nicodemus controverts their plot, pleading that the law
requires due process, a hearing before judging. The others scoff at
this, asserting that Nicodemus must also be a Galilean, with the subtext, "You too must be one of his followers!" Their final write-off is
that if you search the Scriptures, you will see *that no prophet is to arise
from Galilee. Galilee* thus occurs at the beginning and end of the chapter. Opposition between Galilee (safety) and Jerusalem (danger)
appears. The Jerusalem Pharisees, however, demean Galilee (v. 52).

The heart of the chapter hinges on the significance of the Feast
of Booths and Jesus' relationship to it. Jesus claims for himself his
fulfillment of the festival's significance.

OUTLINE

EXPLANATORY NOTES

Jesus' Dilemma: To Go or Not to Go to the Festival 7:1-10

7:1-2a Reason for Jesus' Dilemma[w]

Galilee provides security for Jesus. Staying there postpones the looming crisis. The coalition forces seeking to kill Jesus are headquartered in Jerusalem, not in Galilee. Jesus knows that going to Jerusalem means starting the countdown to his arrest, culminating his ministry. This is his last trip south; according to John, he does not return to Galilee. A coalition of Pharisees, the Jews, and the chief priests are determined to rid the land of this miracle worker and revolutionary, dangerous teacher, whose popularity threatens Roman assault on the city (11:48). They must prevent an uprising (6:15).

From a Jewish theological perspective, Jesus is a self-appointed Messiah (6:15). Even worse, he claims a special relationship with God as Father, having been *sent* to do the *works* of the Father. This is blasphemy to Jewish ears; thus the Jews seek to kill him (7:19c). But is *now* the Father's timing for his ministry to end? Is now the time to face the consequences of his religious and political identity and let the chips fall where they will, on him? Not quite yet, for much is yet to be revealed.

The Feast of Booths, known also as Tabernacles or Ingathering, is at hand. As an adult male, Jesus' going to the feast is normal and expected (thus the Jews are searching for him, v. 11). This feast, like Passover, brings vast crowds to Jerusalem, spiking chances of a revolutionary uprising. Roman security is on alert (cf. Josephus, *Jewish War* 2.12.1). Jesus' discernment likely focuses on whether this feast symbolizes Israel's festival practices that connect with his mission. What word from his Father is to be spoken on this occasion?

This feast is authorized in three OT Scriptures (Exod 23:16b; Lev 23:33-43; Deut 16:13-15). The feast is seven days, Tishri 15–22, with

---

w   Where the superscript w occurs after headings, please see the commentary's online Web Supplement for additional material. Go to: http://www.heraldpress.com/bcbc/john.

the last (eighth day) a holy convocation (Lev 23:36; Num 29:35; cf.
www.hebrew4christians.com/Holidays/Fall_Holidays/
Sukkot/ sukkot.html). When the fifteenth falls on a Sabbath it thus
joins to another Sabbath, which may be the case in John 7. Always, the
first and last days are days of rest (Lev 23:39c-d), and the people are
to be altogether joyful. The feast is "a time of rejoicing" (Lev 23:40;
Deut 16:14). Everyone is to participate: sons, daughters, manservants,
maidservants, Levites, sojourners, the fatherless, and widows. The
occasion enacts social leveling and fosters communal solidarity. It
remembers God's delivering them from Egyptian bondage and providing booths for them to live in during their wilderness sojourn. The
people are to live in tents, set up on house roofs, in the courtyards,
and town squares (Lev 23:42).

The feast celebrates God's gracious provisions of fruit and grain
harvested in the fall (our mid-September). But it also celebrates
deliverance and liberation, as Hugo Zorrilla emphasizes in his doctoral study on John 7–10, summarized in his 1985 article. The social
leveling, with all living in tents, accentuates God's justice and liberation from the cultural walls of class and race that cause social
oppression.

Since Jesus decides to go up to the feast, we tune our ears to hear
how Jesus' words correlate with this feast's theology, especially the
two primary feast symbols, water and light. Expected as a Moses-type
messianic sign, water symbolizes "the gift of the well of the Torah."
"As the former redeemer made a well to rise, so will the latter
redeemer bring up water, as it is stated, 'And a fountain shall come
forth of the house of the Lord, and shall water the valley of Shittim'"
(Joel 3:18) (*Eccl. Rabbah* 1.8; Moloney 1998: 234–35). The manna bread
of John 6 and the water libations of the Feast of Booths in John 7
complement these messianic hopes.

The water ceremony reflects the people's gratitude for God's gift
of rain for good crops at this harvest festival, and it also recalls
Moses, the water giver. Even more, it reenacts Torah, the life-giving
well. The water rituals of the feast thus take on eschatological significance (Isa 44:3; 58:11; Ezek 47; Zech 14: see "Let the thirsty Come
to Me" in the TBC). The ceremony of lights complements the water
symbolism, when "men of piety and good work . . . danced under the
lights, while the Levites sang Psalms 120–134. This celebration lasted
most of the night for each of the seven days" (Moloney 1998: 235).
Four menorahs lit up the court of the women: "There was not a
courtyard in Jerusalem that did not reflect the light of the House of
Water Drawing" (*m. Sukkah* 5:3; cf. Zech 14:7-8). The phrase *House of*

Water Drawing comes from rabbinic sources that highlight the temple's role in this ceremony (Yeč 75–76). A rabbinic source describes both the water libation ceremony (*m. Sukkah* 4:9-10) and the ceremony of light (5:1-4).

Jesus' key declarations in John 7:37-38 and 8:12 are his water-and-light outcries, marking his messianic significance. The narrative of healing the blind man (John 9) culminates with his seeing the light.

7:2b-4 His Brothers Speak Their Mind

Jesus' brothers, knowing Jesus' signs done in Cana, changing water into wine (2:1-11) and healing the official's son (4:46-54), think the upcoming celebrative feast in Jerusalem is a good opportunity for Jesus to show his stuff, to show his works to the world—since Diaspora Jews and God-fearers come from all over the world. Their speech assumes that Jesus *wants to be widely known* (v. 4a; cf. Jesus' temptation to jump off the temple pinnacle to demonstrate his power in Matt 4 and Luke 4). If their brother Jesus does in Jerusalem the signs he has done in Galilee, chances are he will be a national celebrity, bringing honor to his family.

7:5 Narrator's Clue

The narrator tells us that *not even his brothers believed in him*. Like many in the crowd, they respond to the signs from a human point of view. They want popularity. They do not perceive the spiritual, messianic dimension of his signs (*sēmeia*, 7:31) and works (*erga*, vv. 3, 21). The narrator is harsh in his assessment. In the either-or of the Gospel's faith dynamic, his brothers are on the side of unbelief, not belief.

7:6-8 Jesus Speaks His Mind

In responding to his brothers, Jesus distinguishes between two times, *My time* and *your time*. Here the evangelist uses not the recurring *hōra* for *hour* (2:4; 4:23: 12:23), but the word *kairos* (7:6), which signifies a special moment—the *right* moment. The word is repeated in verse 8b, linked specifically to *this* feast. As Moloney (1998: 238) suggests, this infers that the *kairos* moment will come in association with a feast, and indeed it does, since Jesus is crucified, or sacrificed, at the very time the Passover lambs are slaughtered for the Passover offering, celebrating deliverance from bondage. Timing is crucial for Jesus, and this is not the moment for facing the world's hatred (v. 7). As for his brothers, Jesus tells them to go on up to Jerusalem now, because *the world cannot hate you*. Why is this so? It is because they do not believe in Jesus, whom the world hates (v. 5). Jesus gives reason for the hatred: *It hates me because I testify against it that its works are evil* (v. 7b). In John, Jesus is ever cognizant of the world's unbelief and hatred toward him. He needs more time to discern God's time and the right *festival* sequence (Tabernacles-Passover) for his divine claims to clash with the world's hatred. But as for his brothers, they may go anytime. *Go to the festival yourselves* (v. 8a).

7:9-10 Jesus First Stays in Galilee but Then Goes Up

After the brothers leave, Jesus remains in Galilee, but the text does not state how long. Verse 10 is constructed in such a way as to suggest that once the brothers' agenda no longer pressures him, Jesus receives a green light to go. But he goes *in secret, not publicly*, as his brothers hoped. This suggests that Jesus will buy time through this feast. He will make known his Father's revelation about himself regarding the feast, but he will avoid bringing issues to a climactic head prematurely. The *kairos* is not yet.

The Situation in Jerusalem 7:11-13

Three subjects are described: *the Jews, the crowd,* and *no one*. The Jews are looking for him (recall 5:18; cf. 7:1, 25), *seeking all the more to kill him* after his violation of healing the paralytic on the Sabbath. They see the festival as an occasion to arrest him (7:32). *The crowds* in the city are complaining (a form of the earlier murmuring) about him, with divided opinions: *He is a good man*, or *No, he is deceiving the crowd*. As Culpepper (1983: 92) writes, "Simultaneous movement happens in two directions: unbelief spreads, from the crowd even to the disciples, and those disposed to believe will not confess for fear of the Jews." Hence *no one would speak openly about him for fear of the Jews*. The subtext is that no one will publicly express loyalty to him. They do not confess belief openly even though they think him to be a good man.

Jesus' Middle-of-the-Feast Speech and Reactions 7:14-36

7:14-18 Jesus' First Declaration

In the *middle of the feast* (v. 14 RSV), likely the fourth morning, Jesus goes *up into the temple* and begins to teach. His teaching confounds the murmuring Jews, who *marvel* (RSV) or are *astonished* (NRSV) at his ability to teach. They cannot comprehend how he knows what he speaks about *when he has never been taught.* This phrase literally is *He does not know letters,* which implies that he is illiterate, in the view of some commentators. Most, however, conclude *certainly not,* since Luke 4:16 says he read from the Torah—and he likely did on this occasion also. The meaning is that he has not been schooled as a rabbi, such as Paul was, at the feet of Gamaliel. Jesus, explaining his teaching ability and authority, credits his teaching to God, his Teacher, who *sent* him (7:16-17).

Jesus shifts his response to a deeper level: the basis of epistemological insight and understanding. Epistemology is the science of knowing. Jesus speaks a unique word. Knowing whether his teaching is from God or just his own precocious audacity depends upon the disposition of the will. Understanding, says Jesus, comes not from proper rabbinic training or, in our day, from knowing the rules of biblical interpretation with various levels of critical inquiry, but from the heart's desire to do God's will. Augustine and Thomas are known for the maxim of "faith seeking understanding," but Jesus' word adds another angle: the desire to know and obey God's will opens the mind to understand. Resolving to *do* God's will *precedes faith.* Disposition to obey opens the mind to hear and understand, and thus believe. This in turn enables *knowing* the truth (8:32) that leads to eternal life (17:3).

Jesus' statement in John 7:17 parallels Jesus' reason for teaching in parables in the Synoptic Gospels. It helps explain Mark's *mystery*: some who hear will believe, but many will "see but not perceive, . . . hear but not understand" (4:10-12 RSV, a theme permeating Mark 4–10). Jesus in John 7:17 explains the *mystery* of failed understanding. *Knowing* is contingent on the desire of the will (see TBC and "Obedience and Knowledge" in TLC).

As Moberly writes in his excellent article, this statement reflects a larger motif in John, a polarity

> between that which is "from God," "from above," "from heaven," "from the Spirit," "not from this world," and that which is "from the world/ earth," "from the flesh," "from oneself." This polarity . . . [is of] prime structural importance (e.g., 1:12-13; 3:1-8; 31-32; 8:23, 28; 18:36-37). Thus the concerns of our passage are not marginal but central within the Gospel. (Moberly: 248)

Verse 18 clinches the point with another polarity: *Those who speak on their own seek their own glory; but the one who seeks the glory of him who sent him is true, and there is nothing false in him.* At the center of this pithy declaration are two uses of glory (*doxa*): "human esteem or the revelation of God" (Moloney 1998: 243). The latter recalls 1:14-18, where the Word (later, Jesus) reveals God's glory. Three aspects of opposition appear:

Speak on one's own ↔ speak as one sent
Seek one's own glory ↔ seek the glory of him who sent (me)
False ↔ true

Postmodern hermeneutics speaks of "deconstruction." Jesus deconstructs the thought world of the religious leaders, undermining their presuppositions, leaving them naked, in the classic image of "the emperor without clothes."

7:19-24 Jesus' Follow-Up Probing

Jesus follows up his deconstruction with application to the crucial topic of law, a topic his opponents relish and on which they have scored Jesus earlier because he healed on the Sabbath (v. 21 harks back to ch. 5, where Jesus heals the paralytic on the Sabbath). Jesus knows they seek to kill him because he did one work that astonished them. The word for *astonish* or *marvel* (*thaumazō*, v. 21; cf. 3:7; 4:27; 5:20, 28; 7:15, 21) here carries a negative. *Exasperation* best catches its connotation here. Jesus faces them squarely with the *law*, acknowledging its authority in Moses, the giver of the law. But then he holds it before them as a mirror and declares that they do not keep it. So *why are you looking for an opportunity to kill me?*

The *crowd* responds and disowns any intent to kill him. We note the shift in subject: those *seeking to kill him* in verses 1, 11, (25) are *the Jews*, but here *the crowd* denies the intent. Of course, the Jews are in the crowd, and Jesus' counter charges are aimed at them. So at this point in the narrative it is difficult to understand the crowd's accusation: *You have a demon!* Not until verses 43-44 do some from the crowd side with the Jews eager to arrest Jesus. Howard-Brook (1994: 179) explains the crowd's charge that he is "possessed, paranoid, delusional" (cf. Mark 3:22-27) as their response to Jesus' mind-boggling claims. They do not know of the conspiracy to kill Jesus. Jesus' response, therefore, is not aimed at the crowd per se, but to the conspirators in the crowd. For the most part, the crowd—until verses 43-44, when it is divided—functions as a buffer, thwarting the temple police from arresting Jesus (vv. 12 [2x], 20, 31, 32, 40, 43, 49). The *authorities* and *Pharisees* finally demean the *crowd*, saying they *are accursed* (v. 49).

First Jesus probes their pride in circumcision, saying its origin is not with Moses but with the patriarchs (Gen 17:9-14). Jesus drives home a point of consistency: if you circumcise on the Sabbath, why not also allow healing on the Sabbath—and rejoice? The final verse touches deeper than English translations catch. *Appearance* connects to the earlier seeking of *human glory* (v. 18); *right (dikaios)* judgment (v. 24) connects to *God's glory*. Howard-Brook (1994: 178–79) begins this unit with verse 18b, translating *adikia*, which occurs only here in John, as *injustice* instead of *false*. In his chiasm this matches *judge with justice* in verse 24. In seeking God's glory (v. 18) Jesus judges justly and truly, while those who seek their own glory judge unjustly (i.e., falsely), protecting their own self-interests. Further, the word *becomes angry* in verse 23 (*cholaō*) occurs only here in the NT, with the nuance of a "gut-level" unclean, impure thought (180).

Jesus has now deconstructed their understanding of the *law*, on which they considered themselves to be experts. He does not nullify the law one iota. Rather, he has interpreted it in accord with what glorifies God and honors that which is right (*dikaios*—an important word and value to *righteous* Jews). As Pancaro puts it in his extensive study of law in John's Gospel, "Whereas the Jews consider belief in Jesus a betrayal of the Law, [John] is tracing the Law back to its source and doing away with the opposition between the Law and belief in Jesus" (379). John presents Jesus as the fulfillment of both the *law* and Israel's religious festivals, notably the Passover in chapter 6 (cf. ch. 19) and here the Feast of Tabernacles. Earlier chapters made a similar point regarding temple (ch. 2), purification rites (chs. 2–3), worship (ch. 4), and Sabbath (ch. 5; also ch. 9).

7:25-31 Reaction: The Crowd in Agonizing Turmoil

Perhaps this paragraph is best titled "Confusion." Some Jerusalemites are astounded or dismayed that even though the Jews want to kill Jesus, here Jesus is speaking openly and no one is doing anything about it. The people are shocked that *the authorities* (*hoi archontes*) are allowing this to go on. As a result they surmise that they know he is the Messiah and therefore dare not take action against him. Verse 26b may be translated: *Can it be that the authorities have really come to know that he is the Messiah?* The word *mēpote* that heads the question implies a slightly negative answer (whether/perhaps). The implication is that Jesus can hardly be the Messiah, can he? Yet why don't they arrest and kill him, if that is what they are intent on doing? They answer their own query with a location/origin issue: *We know where this man hails from, but when the Messiah comes, no one will know his origin* (AT). Here is classic Johannine irony. A running issue in the Gospel is *where Jesus comes from* (*pothen*, occurring also in relation to the wine in 2:9, the wind/spirit in 3:8, water in 4:11, and bread in 6:5). The crowd struggles to know (vv. 27, 31). Jesus repeatedly says he comes *from above, from the Father, from heaven.* But the crowd, though they think they know, do not know what the reader knows and what the Johannine community knows.

Jesus' response in 7:28-29, as he is teaching openly in the temple, picks up on this irony and reiterates what he has said earlier in the Gospel. Jesus declares, *You know me, and you know where I am from.* Jesus speaks words they do not comprehend; he claims he is from the one who sent him. Verse 30 presents another enigma: *Then they tried to arrest him, but no one laid hands on him, because his hour had not yet come.* Here the usual word for *hour* (*hōra*) occurs, with temporal control of Jesus' mission throughout the Gospel (2:4; 7:30; 8:20; 12:23, 27; 13:1; a similar idea is expressed by *when such and such occurs*: 3:14; 8:28; 12:32; 13:31). Clearly human intent is constrained by divine timing and purpose. As a result of this conundrum, *many in the crowd* believe in him because they are convinced that the signs he has already done vindicate messianic identity (v. 31). When response of *belief* occurs, *signs* (*sēmeia*, pl.) is used, as in verse 31b.

7:32-36 Authorities Send Police to Arrest Jesus; Jesus' Response; "Jews" Confounded

This unit also portrays three character groups in relation to each other:

1. The *Pharisees* collaborate with the chief priests, who take action based on the crowd's earlier muttering.

2. The *temple police* are sent by this coalition of authorities to arrest Jesus.

3. The *Jews* are confounded.

Jesus' word (vv. 33-34) confounds all three groups. At the end, the Jews ask about Jesus' sayings. The police report is held until 7:45, opening a lapse of time in which Jesus gives brief discourses, with momentous significance for the Jews.

The first sayings apparently continue the *middle* day of the feast's activity (7:14). When Jesus sees the officers approaching, he speaks what makes sense when we know the Gospel's entire narrative plot. But at this point his words are puzzling: *I will be with you a little while longer, and then I am going to him who sent me. You will search for me, but you will not find me; and where I am, you cannot come.* The Jews are perplexed and confounded. Where in the world does he intend to go? If we cannot find him or go where he goes, he must be going to the Jews in *the Dispersion* (*diaspora*). Perhaps he will *teach the Greeks!* The narrator has the Jews repeat Jesus' words for effect (v. 36). They are most perplexed. This brief interchange with its confounding impact results in a narrative hiatus—silence on what happens the next three days.

Jesus' Last-Day-of-the-Feast Speech and Reactions 7:37-52

7:37-39 Jesus' Living Water and Spirit Speech: The Truth of the Festival[w]

Jesus reappears on the last, great day of the festival, and with stunning words: *Let anyone who is thirsty come to me, and let anyone who believes in me drink*, or, *If anyone thirst, let him come to me and drink* (RSV). The water imagery fits perfectly the elaborate water ceremony of the seventh day, virtually a continuous pouring of water (seven times) and wine upon the altar, so that water flows out of the temple area. Yet if the last day is to be a day of rest (Lev 23:39c-d), Jesus' words have the effect of continuing what has ceased, since the water and lights ceremonies ended on the seventh day. Jesus offers an unceasing flow of water, echoing his promise to the Samaritan woman: *a spring of water gushing up to eternal life* (4:14).

The Sabbath was marked by rest and continued festival readings. Coloe (2001: 129) argues for the eighth day since it is the *last* day: this day "may have provided a vacuum in which Jesus' offer of water and light (ch. 8) would have been more keenly appreciated." If Jesus gave this moving invitation on the Sabbath, it undoubtedly fueled the fire of those seeking to kill him.

Whether the *last, great day* is the seventh or eighth day, Jesus identifies himself as the source of water for all who thirst. The water libations symbolize God's faithfulness in sending rain upon the earth and quenching spiritual thirst. The words echo Isaiah 55:1a: "Ho, everyone who thirsts, come to the waters." Isaiah's invitation matches Jesus' words on this last great day of the Feast of the Tabernacles:

- Offering water and wine that money cannot buy
- God's people becoming a light to the nations
- Call to forsake wicked ways and turn to the Lord
- The categorical difference between human and divine thoughts

- The reliability of the seasons, with rain and snow matching the reliability of God's word going forth to accomplish its purpose

- The joyful, bountiful response of all creation—a memorial to the Lord and an *everlasting sign* of God's faithfulness that will never cease

The multiple threads of meaning and emotion converge in him: "Thirsty? Come to me!" "No longer is there need to hold daily ritual lustrations, daily carrying of water in a golden pitcher from the pool of Siloam. Jesus is the source of living water for *all* who believe in him . . . ; he transcends the Jewish feast" (Moloney 1998: 252). His offer is more precious than gold. While the hearers seek to grasp Jesus' great invitation, Jesus asserts scriptural warrant for his claim: *As the scripture has said, "Out of the believer's heart shall flow rivers of living water."*

Here we face three interpretive challenges. To grasp the issues, consider a literal translation of verses 37b-38 that sets off the dangling phrase in Greek (using pl., *them*):

> *If anyone thirsts, let them come [to me] and drink.*
> *The one who believes in me,*
> *   as the scripture said, "Rivers of water shall flow out of his*
> *   [autou] belly."*

The problems here are several. (1) What is the proper punctuation? Does the middle line go with what precedes or with what follows? The NRSV and RSV differ. (2) To whom does *his* (*autou*) in the last line refer? From whose belly does the living water flow? Jesus' belly or the believer's? And (3) to which Scripture is Jesus referring in verse 38?

First challenge. Since the earliest Greek text has no punctuation, translators must decide where and how to punctuate. Does one put the dependent phrase with what goes before, *Let the one who believes in me drink* (NRSV)? Or does one put the phrase with what goes after, *He who believes in me, as the scripture has said . . .* (RSV)? The RSV (also TEV, NIV, NAB, and Nestle-Aland's 27th ed.) puts a full stop after *drink* and links *the one who believes* with the quoted Scripture. *His* (*autou*) refers to *the believer*. Line breaks in p[66] and p[75] and numerous early church fathers support this punctuation.

Second challenge. Out of his belly shall flow rivers of living water (v. 38c KJV). When the English translation puts a full stop after *Let him come to me and drink* (RSV), it suggests that *his* (*autou*) refers to the believer, since *the one who believes in me* is joined to *As the Scripture says* ... Yet the NRSV, JB, and NEB include *the one who believes in me* with *drink* (also Kilpatrick; R. Brown 1966: 320; Kerr: 231; et al.), making lines 1 and 2 parallel:

> *If anyone thirsts, let him come [to me];*
> *And let the one who believes in me drink.*
> *As the scripture says:*
> *"Out of his belly shall flow rivers of living water."*

The possessive pronoun *his* in line 4 then refers to Jesus, and thus back to *me* in lines 1 and 2. This *christological* interpretation, which sees *his* (*autou*) as referring to *Jesus*, is widely held. However, *to me* (*pros eme*) is lacking in some early manuscripts [*Textual Variants, p. 532*].

Considering numerous lines of argument, Kerr (237) concludes that *autou* refers to Jesus: the *rivers of living water* flow out from Jesus. This view fits the Gospel's christological emphasis: Jesus is the source of the Spirit. Both interpretations have rationale and appeal. F. Mann (287–91) argues for both meanings. John's Gospel brims with double entendre and misunderstandings (see "Composition History and Literary Features" in the introduction). John may have constructed these sentences to fuse the believer with Jesus (cf. 15:1-11; 17:20-24), so that water flows out from Jesus and becomes a gushing spring of living water in the believer. By the believer's union with Jesus, the life-giving water originates from Jesus and flows out from the believers. This double referent thus matches Jesus' bestowal of the Spirit upon the *believers* (v. 39). *His* (*autou*) refers thus to *both*, Jesus *and* the believer. In the feast's libations, water connects with the Spirit in the OT (Isa 44:3; Joel 2:28) and even more clearly in the Jerusalem Talmud (*Sukkah* 5:1; Talbert: 149; *Gen. Rabbah* 70.1; Moloney 1998: 253).

Third challenge. Which Scripture is Jesus quoting? The OT source is unknown. Lindars (1972: 301) proposes Isaiah 12:3, "With joy you will draw water from the wells of salvation." Drawing "water from the wells of salvation" connects to the Tabernacles' "House of Drawing." Ezekiel 47:1-12 and Zechariah 14:8 speak of water flowing from the temple. These two texts were already linked in messianic prophecy (Moloney 1998: 256; Hoskins: 164–65) and thus bode well for the referent. Jesus' saying evokes eschatological hope, with water flowing out from the temple, nourishing the earth and giving life to the people. These texts are the likely sources (Kerr: 239–40), even though the singular *as the scripture (graphē) said* suggests a specific

Scripture. Another option is Psalm 46:4 (45:5 LXX; 46:5 MT), "There is a river whose streams make glad the city of God, the holy habitation of the Most High" (suggested by Jim Longley in email to me). In support, Psalm 46:4 speaks of *making glad*, matching the *rejoicing* of the Tabernacles Feast. The same Septuagint word in Psalm 46:4 for *rejoice* (*euphrainō*; the noun form occurs in Isa 12:3 also) appears in the OT prescriptions for the feast's celebration (Lev 23:40; Deut 16:14a, 15c)!

Proposed sources are many. Some cite Isaiah 58:11, "You shall be like a watered garden, like a spring of water, whose waters never fail." Kerr (239n98) cites numerous scholars who appeal to the water gushing from Moses' riven rock (Num 20:11; cf. Isa 48:21). The imagery is eschatological: "Christ is the fulfillment of that of which the rock was a type" (Hanson: 110). Isaiah's water texts utilize exodus traditions and thus connect the riven rock with the eschatological water flowing from the temple.

An earlier use of water imagery in 3:5 (with 4:14) foreshadows Jesus' death in John 19. Speaking of the Spirit, John 7:39 anticipates 20:19-23, where Jesus breathes the Holy Spirit upon his disciples. Both 3:15-17 and 7:38 contain invitations to come to Jesus by believing in him. The first text promises *eternal life*; the second, the gift of *the Spirit*. The final line in 7:39, *because Jesus was not yet glorified*, points to Jesus' crucifixion and resurrection as a precondition for Jesus' bestowal of the Spirit.

Since Jesus' teaching occurs on the last, great day of the Festival of Tabernacles and concludes by anticipating the gift of the Spirit, Jesus and the Spirit are the true tabernacle (Kerr: 245), where God meets humans and dwells among and within them (recall 1:14; Coloe: 2001, 2007). Jesus and his gift of the Spirit are thus *signified* in the Tabernacles Feast, in its liturgy and theology.

7:40-44 Reaction: Again, the Crowd in Turmoil

The reaction of the crowd to Jesus' stunning teaching varies. Some affirm him *the prophet*; others, *the Messiah* (echo the Samaritan woman). But *some* contest this, for the Messiah is *not to come from Galilee*. Micah 5:2 specifies Bethlehem, and of Davidic lineage (2 Sam 7:14; Ps 89:3-4, 19-37; Isa 11:1, 10). Moloney sees irony here:

A Christian reader is aware of the tradition that Jesus was from Bethlehem, and Galilee is a place he visits to go away from his own country (cf. 4:42 *sic* [4:43-44]). But the irony runs deeper, as Jesus is "from God," not "from Galilee." There is a uniqueness about who Jesus is and what he is doing that cannot be resolved by Jewish messianic categories. Faced with this uniqueness, the people can only fall into disarray. (1998: 254)

Moloney (1998: 254) summarizes the categories into which the people put Jesus, to assess his messianic portraiture:

- The hidden Messiah (the Jerusalemites, vv. 26-27)
- The miracle-working Messiah (many of the people, v. 31)
- The Messiah who provides living water (some of the people, vv. 37-41a)
- The Davidic Messiah (some of the people, vv. 41b-42)

The people or crowd end up divided: Some *wanted to arrest him, but no one laid hands on him.* This is not yet the hour: those sent to arrest Jesus are impeded.

7:45-52 Police Return; Authorities in Agonizing Turmoil

The temple police, powerless like those in the crowd who want to arrest him, return to the chief priests and Pharisees empty-handed. The authorities interrogate them: *Why did you not arrest him?* The police answer, *Never has anyone spoken like this!* The police's response is testimony to Jesus' uniqueness! They likely know that if they had arrested Jesus, the crowd would protest and a riot might ensue.

The Pharisees respond, echoing a judgment made earlier (v. 12d): *Surely you have not been deceived too, have you?* (v. 47). The Pharisees use their *authority* to trump the police, using an ad hominem argument: *No one among the authorities has believed in him, have they?* (AT). This retort demeans the police's integrity. The Pharisees judge the crowd to be ignorant and *accursed* (v. 49). They intimidate. Verse 48 might also be viewed as the Pharisees' effort to psych out any among the authorities who harbor empathy toward Jesus and his teaching. It has just this effect, for in verse 50 Nicodemus speaks up and halts any quick disposal of Jesus. Nicodemus reminds his colleagues, in the form of a question about normal juridical procedure, *Our law does not judge people without first giving them a hearing to find out what they are doing, does it?* His colleagues bristle and belittle him publicly: *Surely you are not also from Galilee, are you? Search and you will see that no prophet is to arise from Galilee.* Both questions begin with the negative *mē* and thus expect a negative response. The word *stupid* between the two sentences of the council (question and reprimand) would help convey the tone.

This is the second time the law is mentioned in this chapter. Jesus appeals to the law when he accuses them of not keeping the law given by Moses (v. 19; cf. 5:45-46). Jesus then exposes their inconsistent appeal to the law (v. 23). The Pharisees appeal to the law to *prosecute* but fail to see the law as ordering life for human shalom. Nicodemus appeals to the law to aid Jesus' case. These law authorities, except Nicodemus, are trying to circumvent the law to rid the land of this Jesus. Seeking to halt this irregular procedure, Nicodemus risks his reputation to seek a just legal procedure for Jesus. He also knows from his nighttime encounter with Jesus that Jesus claims to have come from above and that his signs are done by God's power. Nicodemus is on the verge of belief, even if secretly.

THE TEXT IN BIBLICAL CONTEXT

Willing God's Will and Glory

Verses 17-18 articulate the core of Christian commitment. This is John's discipleship (cf. Mark 8:27–10:52; Swartley 1981/1999: 135–63). The ELLC (English Language Liturgical Consultation, 1988) translates Psalm 119:36 well for this point:

Bend my heart to your will
and not to love of gain [human glory in John].

The following verse (Ps 119:37) matches the sentiments in John 7:18; 8:31-32:

Keep my eyes from what is false;
By your word give me life.

Moberly links Jesus' teaching here in John to the oft-recurring "fear of the Lord" motif in Israel's Scriptures (Ps 111:10; Prov 1:7; 9:10; 15:33; Job 28:28), saying, "'Fear of God' is the Old Testament's primary term for appropriate human responsiveness to God and so plays a role within the Old Testament somewhat analogous to that of 'faith' in the New Testament and Christian parlance" (2003: 256). "Fear of the Lord" describes one's disposition toward God. It is the foundation for "knowledge of God" (Ps 111:10; Prov 1:7, 29; 2:5; cf. 3:7-8). It is openness to God, a leaning toward God, a bending of the heart Godward. Psalm 86:11 expresses well the sentiment:

Teach me your way, O Lord,
    that I may walk in your truth;
    give me an undivided heart to revere your name.

In his classic article, Norman Porteous (152) expresses similar sentiment. He proposes that "knowledge of God" is interdependent on the formation of a community in intimate covenant relation to God and seeking to be obedient to God. The apostle Paul asserts that "the wisdom of God" is folly to the human intellect (Greek philosophy in that context). *God's* wisdom proclaims "Christ crucified" (1 Cor 1:18–2:16). Earlier, Paul articulates the same polarity between the human and divine word that John expresses in 7:17-18: "We also constantly give thanks to God for this, that when you received the word of God that you heard from us, you accepted it not as a human word but as what it really is, God's word" (1 Thess 2:13).

Let the Thirsty Come to Me

Water is essential to life. The Scripture, spanning thousands of years, is filled with water imagery, from an unnamed river with four branches (Pishon, Gihon, Tigris, Euphrates) flowing out of Eden (Gen 2:10-14) to the last chapters of Revelation: "To the thirsty I will give water as a gift from the spring of the water of life" (21:6b), which echoes John 7:37. And again, "Let everyone who is thirsty come. Let anyone who wishes take the water of life as a gift" (Rev 22:17b). Since this invitation is the voice of the Spirit *and* the bride to the faithful believers, it links to the whole of John 7:37-39. The Spirit and the bride extend the same invitation to those who thirst!

THE TEXT IN THE LIFE OF THE CHURCH

Obedience and Knowledge[w]

In *Homily 29* Augustine exposits John 7:16-18 to make two crucial points. First, when Jesus says, *My teaching is not mine but his who sent me*, he is saying, *I am not from myself*, echoing John 1:14. He is of the Father and *from* the Father. This in turn serves Augustine's trinitarian emphasis. Second, he takes verse 17 to support his dictum that faith leads to understanding. Here he quotes Isaiah 7:9b, which in the Septuagint reads, "If you do not believe, you will not understand" (*ean mē pisteusēte, oude mē synēte*)—a meaning different from the Hebrew, which may be rendered, "If your faith is not sure, you will not be secure" (AT). *Stand firm* in Hebrew (*te'amenu*) becomes *understand* in Greek, a point serving Augustine well (Moberly: 243–44). Both emphases fit John's theology. Moberly (245) agrees with Augustine but says Augustine fails to grasp the central point of Jesus' teaching in these verses.

In his 1814 Bampton Lectures at Oxford, the early nineteenth-century Oxford professor William Van Mildert chose this text as the focus for his second lecture. His angle of approach addresses the origin of religious error. His main point is that the human *will* explains departure from truth. Van Mildert holds that knowing the truth arises from the disposition of the will to do God's will: "The first requisite in the study of Divine truth . . . is a genuine singleness of heart, which has one main object in all its researches, that of knowing and obeying the will of God" (quoted by Moberly: 246). Moberly (254–55) espouses Van Mildert's emphasis and contributes further insights. He suggests that the polarity in verse 18 between *one's own honor* and *God's honor* determines if one lives *of this world* or *of God*. The Greek word for injustice (*adikia*) correlates with falsity: it is opposed to truth. Affirming the truth of Jesus' teaching is possible only when believing results in a "certain kind of self-dispossession." This is what is meant by the "fear of the Lord" in the OT.

Several centuries earlier, Anabaptist hermeneutics voiced a view similar to Van Mildert's and Moberly's. Moberly's "self-dispossession" is a helpful rendering of the Anabaptist *Gelassenheit*, an attitudinal stance toward God and the community. This disposition assumes obedience and may involve obedience unto death. Suffering, at least for Hans Denck and Hans Hut, was essential to *Gelassenheit* (Ollenburger: 55). The well-known dictum of Hans Denck expresses the point: "No one may truly know Christ except one who follows him in life."

Obedience is a key motif in discipleship and is essential to knowing the truth. Menno makes the point, summed up by Henry Poettcker:

> The prerequisites of understanding are seen to lie in the attitude of the one who comes to the Scriptures. Very briefly this attitude must be marked by obedience (willingness to submit to the cross), a willingness to be instructed both by the Spirit and by the brethren [*sic*] and a personal application in seeing the truths as they apply to everyday life. (65)

Irvin Horst, in an insert for defending his dissertation on Anabaptism and the English Reformation, makes the epistemological point:

> The concept of discipleship (*Nachfolge Christi*) among the Anabaptists, and to some extent among Martin Bucer and the Strasbourg reformers, has epistemological importance in connection with right thinking (*vera theologia*) and is thus more than a question of piety and ethics. (Proposition V)

C. J. Dyck (1984: 37) describes this epistemology: "Knowing and doing became a reciprocal experience of understanding and obedience, obedience and understanding. . . . It was impossible to understand the Scripture and the living Word apart from a love for Christ and a longing to do his will." J. H. Yoder (1984: 27) memorably says, "Only . . . [one] who is committed to the direction of obedience can read the truth so as to interpret it in line with the direction of God's purposes. '*If* . . . [one] will(s) to do the will of my father, [that one] shall know of the doctrine.'"

In *Anabaptist Ways of Knowing*, Sara Wenger Shenk emphasizes these same perspectives (46, 114, 136–39). Shenk rightly says that "loving and doing" contribute to *knowing*. In John, these emphases are commands, essential to obedience to Jesus' teaching. John's Gospel supports this Anabaptist understanding of epistemology.

In the twenty-first century in North America, obedience is a hard hermeneutic. What does obedience mean for the relatively wealthy in relation to the world's population? How do we value *security* in an increasingly violent world? The Christian practices of hospitality and mutual aid speak to both issues. The Anabaptists practiced both. Government officials detected Anabaptists by observing people who did these things. Thus these practices became "tests" for arrest, "trials," and death.

Water and Spirit

Dirk Philips understood *Out of his belly shall flow rivers of living water* (John 7:38 KJV) as referring to both Christ and the believer, with the water gushing from the rock when Moses struck it with a rod.

> The spiritual drink, that is, the water that flowed out of the rock which followed Israel [1 Cor 10:4], through the stroke of the rod of Moses [Exod 17:6], signifies to us the living waters of the Holy Spirit which spring out of the spiritual rock, that is Christ Jesus through the power of the most high, and runs for the cooling and quickening of all thirsty souls, who are thereby refreshed in their faith, to eternal life, John 4:10; 7:37[-38]. (Philips: 97)

(For more on the importance of water and Spirit, see McDermond: 242, 245–46.)

John 8

Truth on Trial: Jesus, the Pharisees, and the Jews

PREVIEW

Appealing to John 3:16 and 1 John 4:7-16, one could make the case as Rob Bell has done: *Love Wins.* In some ultimate sense it may be true. But what do we do with John 8 and the flyting battle (exchange of insults) between Jesus and the Jews? Who are these particular Jews? This is one of John's puzzles. *Judgment* permeates this text. Who is the judge? And *why* is there judgment? How does judgment correlate with *Love Wins*?

In John 8 tension mounts between Jesus and the Pharisees, and then between Jesus and *the Jews* ["The Jews," p. 520]. The chapter has generated anti-Judaism and even anti-Semitism among Christians. It seems to reflect some sort of church-synagogue rift (9:22; 12:42; 16:2). Since John is the Jerusalem Gospel, it zooms in to magnify Jesus' conflict with the Jewish temple authorities, attested also in the synoptic Gospels. The twelve verses of 7:53–8:11, "Jesus and the Woman Taken in Adultery," present a textual problem since most early manuscripts lack it, and some manuscripts locate it elsewhere *[Textual Variants, p. 532].*

In the first half of the remaining chapter (vv. 12-30), Jesus teaches any who would listen. This discourse continues from 7:1 to 7:39, with the Pharisees as the primary audience. Jesus makes a new identity claim, inspired by the Feast of Tabernacles: *I am the light of the world.* Light, like water, adorns the festival.

The second half of the chapter, verses 31-59, consists of accusation and counteraccusation between the Jews and Jesus, even though
the word *accuse* (*katēgoreō*), used in verse 6b, does not occur in this
portion. One is inclined to ask, as we do when children get into a
spat, "Who started it?" The children often do not agree; so also in
this scene in John. The Jews would say Jesus started it; Jesus would
say the Jews started it. A third option is that John, the Gospel writer,
started it. A fourth option is that the early church started it, with its
increasing conflict with the synagogue. Or fifth, the synagogue
started it by persecuting believers in Jesus as Messiah, which led to
sporadic expulsions of those believers from the synagogue in some
localities. A sixth explanation is that the first century's twin births
of Rabbinic Judaism and Orthodox Christianity led to sibling rivalry
(Boyarin 1999: 6, 15). Since these options are not mutually exclusive,
the conflict likely reflected several of the factors above. John 8 presents sharp conflict between Jesus and "the Jews."

Most scholars hold that John writes toward the end of the first
century, when Jewish-Christian relations became heated, at least in
some geographical areas (Robinson disagrees, contending that John
was written in the 60s). In the Synoptics severe conflict between Jesus
and the Pharisees arises early in Jesus' ministry (Mark 2:1–3:6). The
conflict theme unites Jesus' time with this Gospel's later time.

While John 13 and 17 are high points in Jesus' moral teaching,
with love as hallmark, John 8:13-59 is John's low point in moral
exemplar. However, 8:31b-32 is a gem: *If you continue in my word, you
are truly my disciples; and you will know the truth, and the truth will make
you free.* This word, however, triggers the bitter dispute.

OUTLINE

[Jesus and the Woman Taken in Adultery, 7:53–8:11]
Opposition Mounts between Jesus and the Pharisees, 8:12-30
Opposition Intensifies between Jesus and "the Jews," 8:31-59

EXPLANATORY NOTES

[Jesus and the Woman Taken in Adultery 7:53–8:11][w]

This story is located here in some manuscripts but appears elsewhere in other NT manuscripts. Without it, there is a seamless flow

---

w   Where the superscript w occurs after headings, please see the commentary's online Web
Supplement for additional material. Go to: www.heraldpress.com/bcbc/john.

from 7:52 to 8:12: the Pharisees are Jesus' interlocutors before and after (7:47; 8:13). The narrative moves from its setting in the temple (8:2)—the institution that functions for God's forgiveness of sins—to an undesignated location where the scribes and Pharisees accuse a woman they caught in the act of adultery (8:3). These religious leaders are testing Jesus as judge (8:4-6a). In bringing this case to Jesus, the leaders inadvertently testify to Jesus' authority regarding the law. The story enacts Nicodemus's plea in 7:51: Do not judge without a hearing.

In response to the accusation, Jesus stoops down and writes *on the ground—in the dust*, to use Rowan Williams's phrase (8:6b). When Jesus stands up, the testers press the question again (v. 7a). Jesus then addresses the crowd, calling for legal witnesses according to the law—but only those who are without sin. They alone are thus qualified to cast the first stone (v. 7b). This may indirectly point to Jesus' own christological claims, implying that he alone is qualified, but the narrative does not go there. Jesus does not execute retributive judgment. Rather, Jesus bends down and writes again on the ground while the crowd disperses, leaving the woman alone with Jesus (8:8-9). Jesus then stands and addresses the woman for the first time, releasing her from condemnation, liberating her to *go and sin no more* (8:11 KJV).

Numerous hypotheses have been suggested as to what Jesus wrote. Some think it may have been the Ten Commandments. Or perhaps Jeremiah 17:13, which says, "Those who forsake you will be inscribed in the dust, for they have rejected the source of living water, the Lord" (REB; echoing John 7:38). Or was it Deuteronomy 17:6-7, which specifies that charges against a person must be corroborated by *witnesses*? No one knows, but one of my Korean students has offered an attractive explanation, arising from Eastern cultural sensitivity. By writing on the ground Jesus redirects the shaming gaze of the accusers away from the woman to himself, an act respecting her dignity. Jesus thus establishes solidarity with her in taking the accusing gaze upon himself. His writing on the ground gives time for the accusers to cool down, feel the guilt of their own sins, and melt before the integrity and love of Jesus. After all, in adultery a man is also involved, and surely those smitten by Jesus' word would have thought about that!

Jesus' response to the woman does not minimize the seriousness of the alleged sin nor does it undermine the law. It frees her from death and makes possible a new life and sinning no more. Forgiveness is not mentioned but is implied. Jesus extends God's mercy to both the woman and the crowd. The story is not really about the woman: it exposes the sinister intent of the accusers in trying to trap Jesus. It opens a future for both the accusers and the accused.

Opposition Mounts between Jesus and the Pharisees 8:12-30

8:12 Jesus' Identity Claim: I Am the Light of the World

Jesus continues teaching at the Festival of Lights (Tabernacles). Jesus' new claim, *I am the light of the world*, draws upon the festal imagery of light, complementing the water in 7:37-38. On the evening of the first day of the festival, four large lampstands are lighted in the temple's Court of the Women, and celebrants dance in the joy-giving light (*m. Sukkah* 5:2-3). Light permeates the entire temple area. In this identity claim Jesus is indeed "the true fulfillment of Tabernacles joy when he declares himself to be the light of the world" (O'Day 1995: 632). While the lights celebrate this Jewish festival, Jesus universalizes the symbol for the whole world.

8:13-20 Jesus' Testimony: Truth on Trial[w]

Lincoln's *Truth on Trial* (2000) highlights this feature of John's Gospel, which figures prominently in this part of chapter 8 through verse 32 as Jesus responds to the Pharisees' efforts to best him. Homare Miyazaki has shown structurally how this theme stands at the center of Jesus' conflict encounters with the Pharisees or the Jews in chapters 5–10. His inclusion of 10:30 and 38, as well as John 5–6, indicates that this six-chapter feast narrative spans several feasts: an unspecified feast in 5:1, Passover in John 6, Tabernacles in 7:1–10:21, and Dedication in 10:22-39.

Three motifs flow through the text of the Feast Narrative: the "trial" of Jesus, the exodus, and the unity of the Father and the Son (see diagram on p. 214). The trial controversies and the feast motifs effectively witness to the oneness of God and Jesus.

Jesus' *I Am* declarations occur in this section and throughout the Gospel into chapter 15 and his *I AM* self-claims (absolute form) climax in 18:5, 6, 8 *["I AM," p. 518]*.

Another helpful analysis of 8:13-59 by Adam Tice (AMBS student paper) outlines the chapter in three units (vv. 13-20, 21-30, 31-59), each with cycles of opening statement, accusation (the Jews), response and counteraccusation (Jesus), accusation (the Jews), counteraccusation (Jesus), protests in verses 31-57 (the Jews), and a verdict closing each section (Jesus).

Chapter 5	Chapters 6–8	Chapters 9–10
The Bethesda Pool Event		**The Siloam Pool Event**
Flow 1: The Trial Motif		
The Prosecution of Jesus (5:16-18) Jesus is on trial.	The trial dialogues (chs. 5, 7, 8) Witnesses: Jesus, the Father, work, John the Witness, Bible, Moses, Abraham	**The Judgment** for the World (9:39-41) *I came into this world for judgment* (v. 39). The world is guilty: *Your sin remains* (v. 41).
Flow 2: The Exodus Motifs as Moses' Witness		
Moses wrote about Jesus. (5:46-47) Your prosecutor is **Moses** . . . *if you do not believe what* **he wrote** (5:45, 47).	Passover The going through the sea Manna—the bread of life The law of Moses The living water The light of the world The Feast of Booths	*We are disciples of* **Moses** (9:28). *God has spoken to* **Moses** (v. 29).
Flow 3: The Oneness of the Father and the Son		
Charge Jesus is *making himself equal to God* (5:18).	*I AM.* (8:24, 28, 58)	**Conclusion of the Feast Narrative** *The Father and Jesus are one* (10:30). Mutual indwelling (10:38)

The NRSV word *valid*, occurring in 8:13, 14, 16, 17, translates Greek adjectives for *true* (*alēthēs*; in v. 16, *alēthinos*). The related terms *truly* and *truth* appear as Jesus' gem words in verses 31-32. As in chapter 5, Jesus' testimony is the crux of the debate. The issue hinges on Jesus' provocative statement in 8:12b: *Whoever follows me will never walk in darkness but will have the light of life.* The Pharisees, who do not follow him, thus counter his claim to be *the light of the world* with the charge of false testimony or witness (*martyria*, v. 13). Jesus responds, reiterating the source of his authority:

> *Even if I testify on my own behalf, my testimony is valid because I know where I have come from and where I am going, but you do not know where I come from*

*or where I am going. You judge by human standards; I judge no one. Yet even
if I do judge, my judgment is valid; for it is not I alone who judge, but I and the
Father who sent me. In your law it is written that the testimony of two witnesses is valid. I testify on my own behalf, and the Father who sent me testifies
on my behalf. (8:14-18)*

This defense, appealing to where Jesus came from and their judging by human standards, echoes 3:11-13; 5:30, 37; and 7:17, where
true testimony is also on trial. Jesus then appeals to *your law* (!),
which requires two witnesses for valid testimony (8:17). He cites two
witnesses, his own and *the Father who sent me*, declaring that he
makes no judgment alone but that *I and the Father who sent me*
together judge (8:18, echoing 5:27, 30). This leads to the next round
of the Pharisees' contest: *Where is your Father?* Jesus responds, *You
know neither me nor my Father. If you knew me, you would know my Father
also* (v. 19). The die is cast for the quarrel to develop bitterly, hinged
on the key term *Father*, which proves credentials of identity.

The next verse (8:20) describes the state of the situation: Jesus is
still teaching in the temple, and no one has arrested him! Why?
Because his hour had not yet come (cf. 7:6; his teaching in the temple,
7:14-31; and precluded arrest, 7:32, 45-46). This timing motif,
already in 2:4 and recurring throughout the narrative, tolls the bell
anticipating the plot's denouement, when Jesus' hour does finally
come and he is lifted up on the cross in death, glorified.

8:21-30 Jesus of Mystery: Departure, I AM, Lifted Up

Jesus continues to instruct his hearers. He mystifies them by
referring again to his imminent departure (echoing 7:33-34) and
declares, *But you will die in your sin. Where I am going, you cannot come.*
But the Jews now respond with new speculation. In chapter 7 they
surmise that he will leave them and minister to those in *the
Dispersion among the Greeks* (7:35). Now they wonder if he intends to
kill himself (v. 22).

In the next two verses Jesus mystifies them further by sharpen-
ing a point implied earlier (3:31; 5:37-38; 7:28-29): *You are from below,
I am from above; you are of this world, I am not of this world* (8:23).
Bluntly put, Jesus and the Jews have different *world orientations*:
Jesus is from *above*, but the Jews are *from below* and thus have a this-
worldly mentality. This duality, with its cosmological ring, reveals a
difference in moral orientation *[Duality, p. 511]*. It lies at the heart of
John's Gospel, as Meeks (1972) has persuasively shown. This per-
spective factors into all of Jesus' disputes with the Pharisees and the

Jews. It offends them, and Jesus deepens the offense by declaring again, *You will die in your sins unless you believe that I AM* (v. 24 AT).

The Jews pointedly ask, *Who are you?* Jesus responds, *Why do I speak to you at all? I have much to say about you and much to condemn; but the one who sent me is true, and I declare to the world what I have heard from him* (vv. 25b-26; cf. RSV, which renders the first line of Jesus' response literally: *Even what I have told you from the beginning*). The narrator then informs readers that the Jews, on hearing this, do not understand that he has spoken to them of the Father (v. 27). Again, *the Father* is the crucial hinge on which John 8 turns. Jesus' origin and authority—as well as his identity—are in dispute, soon to be sharpened even more in verses 31-59.

The next two verses (28-29) correlate two previous motifs: Your *lifting up the Son of Man* with *You will know that I AM*. Both these declaratives have occurred earlier in John, but now for the first time they are connected, with Jesus speaking to *the Jews*. The implication is that *your role in my being lifted up on the cross will disclose to you my true identity* (v. 28). This is John's vintage theology: Jesus' identity is disclosed fully and clearly through his simultaneous death and glorification on the cross. But do the Jews perceive that? Likely not, for in John 18–19 the Jews do not confess Jesus' identity. Later, as Jews read the Gospel with its stated purpose in 20:31, some may affirm this truth (the thesis of Motyer 1997).

Jesus then speaks of his unity with the Father, as in 5:18 and 10:30: *I always do what pleases the One who has sent me. That One has not left me alone!* (8:29 paraphrased). Surprisingly then, the paragraph concludes by indicating that *many* [who heard him] *believed in him* (v. 30). This is a riddle, for the next round of dispute appears incongruous with their belief!

Opposition Intensifies between Jesus and "the Jews" 8:31-59

8:31-38 Truth and Freedom

The link between verses 30 and 31 is *Jews who believe*, but with different Greek tenses. Verse 30 uses the simple past, whereas verse 31 uses the perfect participle (with the pluperfect sense): *the Jews who had believed in him*. Griffith proposes that two different groups of Jews are in view: new believers are in the verse 30 group; *those who believed in him* are in the verse 31 group. This harks back to the group that turned away from following Jesus in 6:66 (i.e., those who had become apostate).

This distinction is helpful in that it prepares the reader for the sharp exchange in verse 37 and heated rhetoric that follows through chapter 8. In short, this means that Jesus excoriates not all believing Jews but only those who had believed in him and then turned against him (Griffith: 185–88). Other Jews remain faithful believers. O'Day (1995: 637) also cautions against continuity between verses 30 and 31. The exchanges between Jesus and the Jews in chapters 7–8 portray (and potentially elicit) a spiraling hostility between Jesus and unbelieving Jews (cf. the narrator's comment in 2:23-24: *Jesus . . . would not entrust himself to them*).

While 8:31b-32 exhorts believing Jews toward growth in faith, the next verses charge and countercharge, so that the Jews in verse 37 resist whatever Jesus says. This group of Jews justifies itself by its genealogical claim to be children of Abraham. But Jesus speaks of spiritual continuity with Abraham as judged by faith response to him. The Father, who called Abraham and to whom God promised many descendants, now speaks through me (Jesus). Griffith's explanation helps resolve the shock of Jesus' accusation: *You look for an opportunity to kill me* (v. 37b). Jesus judges their Abrahamic claim false. Thus Jesus stresses truth in later verses (40, 44-46). This parting between Jesus and a particular group of Jews fits with the evangelist's later description of Jews putting believers out of the synagogue (9:22; 12:42; 16:2) *["The Jews," p. 520]*.

Truth and freedom are the key motifs of the debate at this stage. Clearly Jesus and the Jews are on different wavelengths in comprehending the meaning of Jesus' declaration: *If you continue in my word, you are truly my disciples; and you will know the truth, and the truth will make you free* (v. 32). The first half specifies what it means to become a true disciple, implying perhaps that their *believing in him* is not firm. They still need to *continue* (remain, *menō*) in Jesus' word (i.e., *abide* in his teaching; cf. 15:4, 7, 10).

But the Jews resist the *freedom* of Jesus' truth. Instead they claim to be free already. Their claim indicates that they understand Jesus to speak of spiritual freedom—not freedom from Roman rule. They ground their claim in their heredity: *We are descendants of Abraham* (v. 33). Thus they need no further *truth* to be *free*. To this Jesus replies that all who sin are slaves to sin (v. 34). Jesus then distinguishes between slave status and son status: *The slave does not have a permanent place in the household; the son has a place there forever* (v. 35). A slave has no security and can be evicted anytime.

Building on his Son status, Jesus then declares: *So if the Son makes you free, you will be free indeed* (v. 36). The Son has the power to set free. Jesus *reveals truth*, and this *truth* has power to free people from their slavery to sin. What Jesus says threatens his opponents' comfort with God's mercy. Wrong human conduct enslaves people in God's household, and slaves can be ejected (Barclay: 2.28). Jesus concedes that the Jews may be the genealogical descendants of Abraham, but they are not the true descendants. Jesus' next declaration, *You are descendants of Abraham, yet you . . . [want] to kill me*, lays the foundation for the next phases of the debate (v. 37). Jesus is implying what he later says clearly: the actions of the Jews do not match those who are true descendants of Abraham. Jesus counters their actions with his own: *I declare what I have seen in the Father's presence* (v. 38). Jesus listens to the Father; his accusers are urged to do the same (38b): listen to the Father, heed the Son's teaching, and stop seeking to kill him.

One of John's major themes is *truth*. *Truth* appears seven times in verses 31-47. Continuing in Jesus' word and knowing the truth are interdependent. Truth is the foundation of freedom. Related themes connect the subunits within the larger literary unit of 8:31-59. The Jews do not hear the *truth* because they are not from God. Jesus says they are not from God because they do not understand. If they truly listen to the Father, whom Jesus the Son has seen, they do what the Father desires (v. 38).

Freedom comes from Jesus' truth: Jesus is the *light* that reveals sin. Jesus takes this verbal path because the Jews do not recognize their sin and their bondage to that sin. They believe they are free. Not until they acknowledge their slavery to sin will they be free. Jesus guides them and us to the truth about sin(s) to set them and us free. This slavery to sin "expresses the way in which humans tend to avoid the truth and to kill the would-be free person in themselves and in others" (Brodie: 330).

8:39-47 Identity Crisis: Jesus and the Jews

The discourse-debate proceeds to another stage, with the *truth*-test continuing and Jesus' *words* unveiling the *truth*. As O'Day points out (1995: 637), the *word* (*logos*), crucial in verses 31-32, continues through all phases of this debate (vv. 37, 43, 51-52, 55), as well as three *Amen, amen* occurrences (*Truly, truly, I say to you*; vv. 34, 51, 58 RSV) and repeated references to Jesus' speaking (vv. 38, 43, 45-46, 55).

In this round of the debate, the Jews boast two protest claims. In the first they claim Abraham as their father (v. 39a). Jesus counter-accuses sharply: *If you were Abraham's children, you would be doing what Abraham did, but now you are trying to kill me, a man who has told you the* truth that I heard from God. This is not what Abraham did. You are indeed doing what your father does (vv. 39b-41). After this answer, the Jews protest with another claim: We are not illegitimate children; we have one father, God himself (41b). The first We is emphatic; their protest thus may imply Jesus is of illegitimate birth, in contrast to theirs. The Jews strengthen their claims by discrediting Jesus, nullifying his judgment against them. This is the last word from the Jews in this paragraph.

Verbally, Jesus is on the offensive, and the Jews are on the defensive. In action, however, the Jews are on the offensive to kill Jesus (vv. 37b, 40b). Jesus then sets forth criteria that test their claim that God is their father (vv. 42-43):

- If God were your Father, you would love me, for I came from God and now I am here.

- You would also believe that I did not come on my own, but he [the Father] sent me.

- You do not understand [me] . . . because you cannot accept my word.

The logic of the first test is that since the Father loves the Son (5:20), you would also love the Son if the Father were really your Father. The second criterion reiterates a point made earlier. The third describes the Jews' present response and predicament. Because you fail these tests, Jesus says, You are from your father the devil, and you choose to do your father's desires (v. 44). Jesus validates this harsh judgment by declaring that the devil was a murderer from the beginning. That explains your desire to kill me! The devil does not stand in the truth, because there is no truth in him. The devil's nature is to lie. He is a liar and the father of lies (all in v. 44). Jesus continues, But because I tell the truth, you do not believe me. Which of you convicts me of sin? If I tell the truth, why do you not believe me? Whoever is from God hears the words of God. The reason you do not hear them is that you are not from God (vv. 45-47).

As paraphrased, Jesus' accusation is, "You, 'the Jews,' cannot accept the truth I tell you because you do not believe me. Your father is not God the Father who sent me, but the devil, who lies and instigates the desire to kill" (cf. 1 John 3:10). Declaring the devil to be the father of lies, Jesus "implicitly contrasts God as the Father of truth and the devil as the father of lies" (O'Day 1995: 643). Jesus' rhetorical question Which of you convicts me of sin? is reminiscent of the earlier scene in the temple with the adulterous woman. No one was without sin, and thus none could punish her for her sin. Now Jesus makes a similar point. Jesus' conclusion to these charges against the Jews is this: *The reason you* do not hear *the words of God* that I speak is *that you are not from God.*

This paragraph is harsh, hurting language. Again, it must be stated, *the Jews* here do not represent all the Jewish people. All the named characters in John, as well as the man born blind and his parents, are Jews. In this Gospel the true believers are Jews. *The Jews* appear to function as a foil against which Jesus calls forth true faith, from *Jews*, Samaritans, and Gentiles (see Motyer 1997). It is most difficult to identify who *the Jews* are historically, even though many attempts have been made (Lowe; Howard-Brook 1994; D. M. Smith 2005, 2008; Boyarin 2007) [*"The Jews," p. 520*]. The harsh invective reflects a recent or portending schism between believers in Jesus and some synagogues.

Jesus' sharp critique of Jewish legalistic practices, however, is evident also in the Synoptic Gospels. An underlying historical factor from Jesus' own ministry grounds this vituperative language. It is important that these two levels be distinguished, however, and that Christian believers today grasp John's *positive* portrait of Jews, contra *the Jews*, and base their relations with Jews today on these positive Jewish portraits (Jesus, his disciples, and Bethany friends), rather than on what Jesus says to *the Jews*, whoever or whatever this phrase signifies [*"The Jews," p. 520*].

A theological dimension is also present and transcends any specific historical explanation. In John and 1 John "the world" and "the devil" are intertwined with defiant political powers that seek to kill the love and truth that Jesus personifies and teaches. In that dimension *the Jews* transcend specific history and represent all humans who collude with those who oppose Jesus as the revelation of God his Father. The unbelief of *the Jews* is "not simply a result of their own decision; it is traced back to the ultimate power of evil, the devil" (8:44a; Schnelle 2009: 662–63). Jesus thus exposes what is ultimately at work in the authorities or powers, including also Pilate, who crucify him. This is the *revelation* of light and truth coming into the fallen, alienated, arrogant *world*, as John uses that term to designate the realm of unbelief, that which is *from below.*

8:48-59 The Rupture: Three Final Rounds in the Debate[w]

The heated debate now spirals. Understandably, the Jewish believers are upset at Jesus' word. While earlier the Jews were on the defensive verbally, they now go on the offensive (O'Day 1995:

644), accusing Jesus of being a Samaritan and having a demon (returning Jesus' charge that their father is the devil!). Jesus does not respond to the charge that he is a Samaritan, likely indicating that Jesus and the Johannine community welcome Samaritans. Jesus does refute the "demon" charge by stating, *I do not have a demon*; rather, *I honor my Father, and you dishonor me* (v. 49; cf. 5:23). To clinch his defense Jesus restates his claim that he seeks not his own glory (8:50; cf. 5:41-44; 7:18); instead, *There is one who seeks it and he is the judge* (8:50b; cf. 8:14-18). Further, Jesus says, *Very truly, I tell you, whoever keeps my word will never see death* (v. 51), echoing Jesus' earlier teaching. But the Jews cannot hear or accept this offer of life.

Never see death fuels the fire, and the Jews are now certain that Jesus has a demon, so they repeat the charge. The tables turn. The Jews claim that Jesus' charge flies in the face of what we know about Abraham: he died, and so did the prophets. They scorn Jesus' promise, repeating *never taste death* (v. 52c). Sarcastically they ask, *Are you greater than our father Abraham, who died? The prophets also died. Who do you claim to be?* (v. 53). *Who do you think you are?* (AT).

Jesus now uses his relationship with Abraham as his defense—a reversal from the previous subunit (O'Day 1995: 646). Jews believed that God had shown Abraham all of history, including the coming of the Messiah. Thus Jesus says, *Your ancestor Abraham rejoiced that he would see my day; he saw it and was glad* (v. 56). Jesus thus claims to fulfill in himself Jewish messianic hope. He also distances himself from the Jews and their heritage, saying, *Your ancestor*. These people are no longer his own! The Jews no longer accept the Scripture he fulfills. This raises a key question: Is John's Jesus distancing himself from Jewish identity, or does *your* emphasize that the listeners do not know God? Is not your law and your ancestor the true law and the true Abraham?

Wanting to discredit this claim, the Jews zero in on the absurdity of Jesus' statement, pointing out he is not yet fifty years old, then asking with sarcasm, *And have you seen Abraham?* (v. 57; this is their third offensive retort). The retort magnifies the Jews' spiritual blindness and deafness, so prominent in John's Gospel. Jesus stunningly clarifies, *Before Abraham was, I AM.* This is the "climax of [the] entire chapter" (Burge 2000: 263). Jesus, the *Logos* in the prologue, who *was in the beginning with God* (1:2), *came to his own, and his own did not receive him* (cf. 1:11 RSV).

Jesus' identity, crucial to the fourth evangelist, dominates chapter 8. Jesus makes striking *I AM* claims: *I am the light of the world* (8:12); *I am from above* (v. 23); *I am not of this world* (v. 23); *I am he, the Son of Man* (v. 28). These claims crescendo in verse 58: *Very truly, I tell you, before Abraham was, I AM.* This chapter makes explicit a recurring motif: the Jews are not of God. Truex (263–64) cites a series of verbal attacks that make this point, with 8:47 the most explicit:

- You are teachers, yet you do not understand (3:10).
- You have never heard God (5:37).
- You do not have the love of God (5:42).
- You seek your own glory (5:44a).
- You do not seek God's glory (5:44b).
- Your accuser is Moses (5:45).
- You do not believe Moses (5:46).
- You do not keep the Torah (7:19).
- Your father is the devil (8:44).
- You are not from God (8:47).
- You are blind and live in darkness (9:39-41).
- You are idolaters (19:15).
- You sought to kill Jesus (5:18; 7:1; 8:59; 10:31, 39; 11:8; 18:12).

The Johannine accusations are hot-tempered, to say the least, but it is obvious from the language that it reflects the concerns and passions of *Jews speaking to other Jews.* Nevertheless, from the perspective of the Judean authorities, such attacks would have been regarded as *blaspheming the leaders and the God of Israel.*

With this revelation, debate ends. Truex explains why and how this debate is understood as *blasphemy*, in light of numerous OT narratives and thus why there is good reason to excommunicate Jesus and his followers from synagogues (264–65; cf. Lincoln 2000: 49). "Jesus is greater than Abraham because Jesus is one with God" (O'Day 1995: 646). Jesus is the Son, the Messiah. He uses language that God used to describe Godself to Moses. This revelation is more than the Jews can handle, and they pick up stones to throw at Jesus (v. 59, echoing 8:5; 5:18; cf. 10:31). In their minds and hearts, Jesus' words are heresy: he compares himself to God and claims to be the Messiah and the eschatological Son of Man. The sin of blasphemy is punishable by death.

The lawsuit motif (*rib*), as Lincoln (2000) shows, permeates the Gospel. In John, since Jesus is the human face of God, the Jews are putting God on trial (cf. Lincoln [2000: 36–56] on Job and Isa 40–55). Reading this passage from a Christian perspective, it is hard for us to see the Jews' side of the debate. Why do the Jews want to kill Jesus? They believe they are defending God and monotheism. Because they "believe [Jesus] was blaspheming, . . . stoning is the legal response" (Burge 2000: 263). The evangelist uses witnesses in this lawsuit narrative to testify to Jesus' divinity (5:31-47). In chapter 8, however, Jesus' claim, *I AM*, reveals Jesus as *God* on trial.

With hostile action imminent, Jesus hides to escape stoning to death. John thus reminds readers of Jesus' humanity, the Word made flesh.

8:31-59 One Literary Unit

This battle regarding identity focuses on who are the true children of God. *The Jews* and Jesus both stake claims to special relationship with God. The Jews claim Abraham for their identity; Jesus claims "God my Father" for his identity. This debate covers all three subunits of this text. This diagram by Rachel Siemens depicts the argument's intensifying heat:

	The Jews	Jesus
8:31		The ones who believe are gathered together with Jesus in the temple. There is a physical closeness between them.
vv. 31-38	*We are descendants of Abraham.* This is an assumed identity for the people of Israel. As previously noted, there is some distance from Abraham.	*I declare what I have seen in the Father's presence . . . what you have heard from the Father.* Jesus is close to the Father, he has been in his presence. There is also a closeness with the Jews since "the Father" is the Father of both Jesus and the Jews.
vv. 39-47	*Abraham is our father.* The Jews are moving themselves closer to the religious patriarch. *We are not illegitimate. . . . We have one father, God himself.* Moving as close to God as they can, they too claim God as their father.	Jesus disagrees with this. Their actions would be different if they were Abraham's children. *I came from God. . . . You are from your father the devil.* Jesus is creating distance between himself/God and the Jews.

vv. 48-58	*You are a Samaritan and have a demon.* The Jews are turning the tables and are separating Jesus from God and from themselves.	*. . . but I honor my Father.* *It is my Father who glorifies me . . . your ancestor Abraham.* Jesus is adding to the distance between himself/God and the Jews. "My Father" occurs twice in this section (vv. 49, 54).
v. 59	*So they picked up stones to throw at him, but Jesus hid himself and went out of the temple.*	There is now physical separation between them.

In this identity debate, each side appeals to Abraham to prove their case. The Jews appeal to their physical and religious heritage. But Jesus speaks otherwise: beliefs and actions determine salvation. "Blood lineage does not guarantee spiritual lineage" (Burge 2000: 259). Our actions and response to him whom God sent reveal our true identity. Abraham listened to God (mark of his true heritage), but the Jews did not listen to the One whom God sent. How do we know who is from God (a major issue in 1 John; see McDermond)? Those who know God keep God's word (8:31, 37-38, 39, 42, 47, 51, 55). *Knowing* God frees from sin and death and gives eternal life. We cannot rely on religious heritage for salvation. Each generation must learn anew God's word and obey it.

THE TEXT IN BIBLICAL CONTEXT

Jesus the Light

In John's prologue, light appears at the beginning of God's creation (Gen 1:3-4). Light enshrouds God's self-manifestation (Gen 15:17; Exod 19:18; Pss 27:1; 36:9; 43:3; 104:2; Isa 2:5; 10:17; 60:1; Ezek 1:4). In the wisdom tradition, light symbolizes the law, God's word (Ps 119:105; Prov 6:23; Wis 18:4) (O'Day 1995: 632). The lights of the Tabernacles Festival recall God's miracle of light in the "pillar of fire" that guided Israel through the wilderness (Exod 13:21). Israel's later recitals of God's leading them through the wilderness mention God's special light: "In the daytime he led them with a cloud, and all night long with fiery light" (Ps 78:14). Another psalm speaks of "fire to give light by night" (105:39; cf. Wis 18:3). The divine presence in the cloud of glory (Shekinah; see prologue) focuses God's light on

Moses, the tabernacle, and the temple. True worship "declares God's glory among the nations" (cf. 1 Chron 16:24; Ps 96:3). Glory is a major motif in John [Glory, p. 516].

In the OT, light functions also as an image of messianic hope. Isaiah foresees that "those sitting in darkness will see a great light" (cf. Isa 9:2), a text quoted by Matthew (4:16) to keynote Jesus' ministry and by Zechariah, announcing Jesus' coming and ministry (Luke 1:79). Matthew identifies Jesus' followers as "the light of the world" (5:14, 16; cf. 6:23; Luke 8:16-17). John's prologue identifies the Word with light (1:4, 5, 7, 8, 9). The theme continues in John 3:19-21; 5:35; 8:12; 9:5; 11:9-10. In 12:35-36, 46, light is a climactic motif for Jesus' public ministry.

In the larger Johannine corpus, light streams through 1 John and plays a culminating role in Revelation. In 1 John light carries ethical connotation in 1:5, 7; 2:8-10, though 2:8 refers to Jesus as "the true light . . . already shining." In these ethical connotations, walking in *darkness* is the antonym of walking in the light. In Revelation *light* will flood the new city inhabited by the servants of the Lamb, "for the Lord God will be their light" (22:5; cf. 21:23). Even "the nations [of the earth] will walk by [this] light" (21:24).

Paul's epistles abound with light imagery also. The gospel is *light* shining in the *glory* of Christ. The light that appeared when God said, "Let light shine out of darkness," now shines in "our hearts to give the light of the knowledge of the glory of God in the face of Jesus Christ" (2 Cor 4:4-6; also 3:17-18). Paul's testimonial defense before King Agrippa describes those receiving the gospel as turning from darkness to light (Acts 26:18-19). A notable clarion call is "Put on the armor of light" (Rom 13:12; cf. Eph 5:14-15) and walk in the light (Eph 5:8; cf. Col 1:12; 1 Thess 5:5; 1 Tim 6:16).

Light imagery literally laces Scripture with numerous connotations, forming a bookend to the canon (Gen 1:3-4; Rev 22:5). It signifies divine revelation, guidance, presence, hope, and purity. It opposes and dispels darkness, replacing the sins of the flesh (Eph 5:3-14). It symbolizes the power of the gospel of Jesus Christ: conversion is turning from darkness to light (Col 1:12-13; Acts 26:18-19). In John 8, Jesus' declaration *I am the light of the world* extends the OT imagery. Jesus is the light and calls his followers to walk in the light (1 John 1:7). On the eighth day (ninth day in Diaspora) of the Feast of Tabernacles, Israel celebrated God's gift of the law (Simchat Torah; cf. www.hebrew4christians.com/Holidays/Fall_Holidays/Sukkot/sukkot.html). As the light, Jesus saves from sin; fulfilling the law, Jesus instructs and guides his followers. "Shine, Jesus, shine!"

Jesus, Truth on Trial

John 8 continues the lawsuit genre. Jesus' final *I AM* closes his defense. The trial resumes, however, in John 10 and culminates in John's trial narrative (chs. 18–19). John 8 interweaves the lawsuit form with major Johannine themes: Christology (*I AM*, 8:24, 28, 58), light (8:12), life (8:12; cf. 10:10; 17:3), truth (8:32, 40, 44, 45), glory (vv. 50, 54), and judgment (vv. 15-16, 26a, 54) (see Lincoln 2000: 193–201) *["I AM," p. 518] [Light, p. 527] [Eternal Life, p. 513] [Glory, p. 516]. Light/glory* and *truth/judgment* span the canon. Isaiah 40–55, also a lawsuit (*rib*) form, prefigures Jesus' court case against God's covenant people (Lincoln 2000: 38–51).

Truth describes God's moral life for the covenant people: "O send out your light and your truth; let them lead me; let them bring me to your holy hill and to your dwelling" (Ps 43:3). Here *light* and *truth* join. The two scriptural words for truth are *'emet* (Heb.) and *alētheia* (Gk.). The Hebrew word carries not only the notion of factual truth (as in 1 Kings 10:6; Isa 43:9) but, more frequently, reliability and relational faithfulness. Thus Psalm 89:14 describes the "foundation of God's throne" as "righteousness and justice, . . . steadfast love and faithfulness" (*'emet*). Truth and faithfulness characterize God's persona. Derivatively, God's righteous ordinances are true, for the truth is in God's word (Ps 119:160; cf. vv. 42-43, 142, 151; Prov 30:5; Neh 9:13). God's people are to practice truth and righteous living with justice (Deut 16:20; Isa 48:1; 59:14; Jer 4:2; 5:1; Zech 7:9). Psalm 86:11 is one of my devotional mainstays: "Teach me your way, O Lord, that I may walk in your *truth*; give me an *undivided* heart to *revere* your name" (emphasis added).

Truth occurs twenty-four times in John; another twenty times in 1, 2, and 3 John; and about thirty-eight times in Pauline writings. In John, truth is Jesus himself and his testimony. Witnesses testify to the truth. Jesus' high-priestly prayer links truth with holiness and God's word: *Sanctify them in the truth; your word is truth* (17:17, also v. 19). Jesus is the truth: *I am the way, and the truth, and the life* (14:6). In his final trial, Jesus confronts Pilate with truth: Jesus answers Pilate's question, *What is truth?* by simply standing there—*truth* in his face (18:37-38). Truth is "on trial" in John, anticipated already in 1:14, 17, but most prominent in chapters 5–8 and 18–19 (Lincoln 2000). In John 8 truth, revealed in Jesus' works and words, faces down unbelief. Jesus' identity as *I AM*, God's revealed name to Moses (Exod 3:13-15; 6:3), is truth incarnate ["*I AM*"; see the nine absolute uses of "*I AM*"].

Paul appeals to truth to defend his integrity against those who belittle his credentials as apostle (2 Cor 11:10; 12:6; 13:8); those who twist and swerve from the gospel (Gal 2:5, 14; 3:1); and those who suppress the truth by their ungodly and wicked practices, worshiping the creature rather than the Creator (Rom 1:18, 25). In differing contexts, Paul identifies truth with Christ (Eph 4:21; Rom 9:1). In the pastoral epistles, "truth" (used fourteen times) defends against false beliefs. Truth describes speech (2 Cor 6:7; Eph 4:15) and heads the list of Christian virtues in Philippians 4:8 (cf. Eph 4:15, 25; Stassen and Gushee: 50; Swartley 2006a: 412–13).

TEXT IN THE LIFE OF THE CHURCH

Jewish and Christian Relations[w]

The related essay *["The Jews," p. 520]* should be read alongside this discussion. The negative light in which the Jews are cast in the Gospel must not be projected onto the Jewish people. Jesus' sharp condemnation of "the Jews," whoever they are or represent, is conditional on their opposition to Jesus, their refusal to recognize in Jesus the true light of the world, and their blindness (John 9). The text reflects the specifics of a situation that we can no longer fully understand. They could not see Jesus as valuing, fulfilling, and transforming the Law and the Prophets. They refused to believe that God sent Jesus to bring them salvation. Jesus was not anti-Jewish. He himself was a Jew, as was the bearer of the gospel tradition *[Beloved Disciple, p. 505]*. John's ambiguous use of *the Jews* calls attention to the fact that the enemies of the truth can be of our own kind, those who are close to us, of our own clan and culture—any who do not accept the work(s) or words of God. Rather than making Jesus anti-Jewish, this contentious chapter is better understood as Jesus' heartbreak over some Jews' rejecting truth and salvation (cf. Motyer's argument, 1997).

The horrible history of Christian anti-Semitism must end. Motyer (1997: 386–87) describes some of its most horrible expressions in Christian writers, such as John Chrysostom and Martin Luther (1543). Luther called synagogues "nothing but a den of devils," urging Christians "to exercise 'a sharp mercy' by setting fire to synagogues and schools, . . . destroying Jewish homes, confiscating all their sacred books" (Motyer 1997: 2–3). Such expressions of hatred are also of the devil, culminating in the indescribable horror of Auschwitz and similar death camps. Motyer reports the efforts of various writers (Rosemary Radford Ruether, Clark Williamson and Ronald Allen, and James Dunn) who seek to free Judaism from this damning attitude by either bracketing the authority of John's Gospel for Christian believers (Reuther), showing it as inconsistent with John's love ethic (Williamson and Allen), or regarding it as a rhetorical symbol for the world's hostility toward Jesus (Dunn). I favor the latter two approaches and am in debt to Jewish scholars Adela Reinhartz and Daniel Boyarin, who open up other understandings of the conflict within the context of first-century Judaisms ["The Jews," p. 520]. In Romans 9–11, Paul, a messianic Jew, helps us toward a better understanding of Jews in first-century developing Christianity. In "The Bible and Israel" (Swartley 2007: 155–82) I discuss the impact of this Scripture on Christian-Jewish relations.

When Heritage Blinds to Light and Truth[w]

If we focus only on *the Jews*, on the problems this chapter poses historically, and on its impact in anti-Semitism over the years, we miss its key point. It actually calls us to examine our own responses to Jesus' claim to be the light of the world. Has the truth set *us* free? Or are we blinded by our tradition, our precious heritage, or simply being good people? Those who do not believe fail to experience the gospel's gift: through believing that Jesus is the Christ, the Son of God, they can *have life in his name* (20:31). What Jesus says to the Jews applies to us today. We cannot rely on our heritage for salvation. Rather, we need to accept God's gifts of light, truth, freedom, and life that Jesus offers.

One reason it is hard to be a missional church, to welcome newcomers into our congregations, is not only that we are to a lesser or greater extent set in our ways of doing things, but also that we are off-putting toward people who don't carry a family name from our church's heritage. If we are missional, we will not go searching for such connections but rather enthusiastically welcome and socialize with newcomers. They enliven the church fellowship and often become the congregation's foremost evangelists. We must free ourselves from ethnic-name addictions. In a missional congregation we talk about other things and extend the table.

Let the Jews in John remind us of that part of ourselves that obstructs love for Jesus, the mission power of the gospel, and welcoming "Samaritans" with joy. Let us hear John 3:16 with gratitude for God's love for us and extend that love to others in our mission practice. Let us hear Jesus' call to discipleship and explore what that entails:

1. By continuing in Jesus' *word*, we will know the *truth* that sets us *free* from sin's bondage. Then we rightly claim a place in God's household (John 8:31-36).

2. Whoever is from God hears the words of God (v. 47).

3. We do not seek our own glory, but we live and work to glorify God (v. 54).

4. By keeping Jesus' word, we are assured that we will never see death (v. 51) because Jesus' word gives us life.

Jesus' claim *"I am the light of the world"* continues as chapter 9 focuses on *blindness/sight.*

John 9

Blindness and Sight: Who Is Jesus?

PREVIEW

Most of us know a friend or relative who is losing their eyesight, often due to macular degeneration or occasionally a medical error in an attempted corrective surgery. Few of us know current stories of people miraculously healed from blindness though the power of Jesus Christ and the Holy Spirit, though such there are (read Crystal's story, in Pfeiffer: 49–53). Many of us know Ken Medema, who is blind physically but spiritually *seeing*. His ability to compose on the spot, play piano expertly, and sing movingly has been a blessing to many. We live in a world where we celebrate different types of miracles (Crystal's and Medema's) and yet also groan for complete healing in God's kingdom's coming in fullness (Swartley 2012a: 36, 75–76).

In John 9 Jesus heals a man born blind. It is a strategic story in John's Gospel. The healed blind man symbolizes mature faith and true sight. While Nicodemus may be a *secret* believer (19:38-39), the blind man who receives his sight miraculously is the *model* believer, witnessing publicly and courageously to the truth. His zeal for Jesus his healer turns the interrogation of the Pharisees and the Jews on its head, taunting the interrogators and exposing their infidelity both to Moses and Jesus *["The Jews," p. 520]*. Further, the blind man's faith in Jesus as *Son of Man* leads him to *worship* Jesus, linking Jesus to God.

The chapter climaxes with Jesus' judgment of the Pharisees. Jesus pronounces them blind: "You remain blind because you *do*

230

not see!" Blindness is not only a physical malady; it also symbolizes a spiritual condition, a result of resisting belief in Jesus. "In John 9 sight and blindness, physical and spiritual, are subtly and complexly played off against each other in an overarching paradox" (Schneiders 2003: 156).

This story of the blind man is an interpretive code to this iridescent Gospel:

- More than any other, this story showcases the bifocal lens of the Gospel: the time of Jesus and the time of the Johannine community's (threatened) loss of continuity with the synagogue and resultant hostility from Jewish leaders.

- John 9 "fuses the horizons of the pre-Easter Jesus, the post-Easter Johannine community, and the readers of the Gospel" (Schneiders 2003: 154).

- This "story sums up in a remarkably lucid and compact way what the fourth evangelist had to say about his community's relationship to Jesus, to the synagogue authorities, and to the secret believers" (Rensberger: 41).

- The Jews' inquisition of the parents, who may be crypto-Christians (R. Brown 1979: 71–73), "reflects the life of the Johannine community threatened with expulsion from the synagogue for confessing Jesus as one who comes 'from God'" (Schneiders 2003: 154, concurring with Martyn 1968/1979/2003; R. Brown 1979: 66–69, 166; Rensberger 1988).

- The blind man's washing in the pool of Siloam *(which means Sent)*, useful as a baptismal homily, reminds "every Christian" in John's community of the cost of following Jesus, *the Sent One* (Schneiders 2003: 149–50, 157).

- "The man's testimony is a quintessentially Johannine witness to the truth" (mirroring Jesus' encounter with Pilate in chs. 18–19; Schneiders 2003: 158).

A notable feature of John 9 is its extensive use of irony, most prominent in verses 16a, 24, 27b, 39, 41. The evangelist or the speaker is the ironist, and the Pharisees are the victim of the irony (see Ito's extensive discussion).

Numerous commentators arrange this chapter in a seven-scene chiasm. Mine also is seven but different from others.

OUTLINE[W]

A Jesus and His Disciples Discuss Why the Man Is Blind: "Who Sinned?" 9:1-5

> B Jesus Heals the Blind Man, 9:6-7
>> C The Neighbors and Pharisees Quiz the Blind Man, 9:8-17
>>> D The Jews Interrogate the Blind Man's Parents, 9:18-23
>> C´ "They" Grill the Blind Man a Second Time: Jesus "a Sinner"? 9:24-34
> B´ Jesus Leads the Blind Man to Christological Sight, 9:35-39

A´ Jesus and the Pharisees on Blindness: "Your Sin Remains," 9:40-41

We might well include 10:1-21 in this narrative unit, as O'Day (1995: 651) proposes, since 10:21 refers to Jesus' healing the blind man. Moloney (1998: 232, 306) regards 7:1–10:21 as one section, oriented to the Feast of Tabernacles (September; 10:22 shifts to the Feast of Dedication, in December). Talbert, however, contends that chapters 7–9 are one section, united by water and light imagery. Because none of these proposals is conclusive, I treat each chapter separately, recognizing multiple threads of unity in chapters 7–10 [*Unsettled Matters, p. 534*].

EXPLANATORY NOTES

Jesus and His Disciples Discuss Why the Man Is Blind: "Who Sinned?" 9:1-5

Continuing the Jerusalem location of the previous two chapters, but no longer in the temple, Jesus sees a blind man as he walks with his disciples. The lack of an article, *the* (*ho*) or *a certain* (*tis*) for specification, may be significant. The blind man represents *every person* (Painter 1986: 42). It has the effect of "de-emphasizing particularity and hinting that for John all humankind is born blind" (Duke: 118). Indeed, "we all share in the condition of the *anthrōpon* (humanity) by the side of the road" (Howard-Brook 1994: 215). We are not observers of the drama: instead, we enter into it as participants who rightly ask, With whom do I identify?

Jesus' disciples, entering the narrative for the first time since chapter 6, query Jesus about the cause of the man's blindness. They assume that someone has sinned (cf. Ps 41:3-12). "Working from a

---

w   Where the superscript w occurs after headings, please see the commentary's online Web Supplement for additional material. Go to: http://www.heraldpress.com/bcbc/john.

biblical principle that God cannot be credited with the evil that happens to people (cf. Exod 20:5; Num 14:18; Deut 5:9; Tob 3:3-4), the disciples pose a logical question" (Moloney 1998: 291). Whose sin caused the blind man's condition, his own or his parents'? The disciples don't think about the blind man's need for healing, only who is to blame. Jesus doesn't play the blame game: *Neither he nor his parents sinned* to cause this blindness. While the disciples moralize, Jesus acts to relieve suffering and thus manifest the works of God (cf. Rensberger 1988: 44; cf. Luke 4:18-19; Mark 8:22-26). Rowan Williams (75–76) aptly says, "Christians have every reason to say no to any system . . . that uses suffering to prove things: . . . guilt as a sinner being punished, or . . . innocence as a martyr." Rather, the man's condition opens up a space "where communication from God occurs."

In the ancient world, sin and suffering were conceived as cause and consequence (witness Job's friends). In John 9, however, this man was *born blind so that God's works might be revealed in him.* The clause in 9:3b is the typical Greek *hina* clause, best translated *so that* . . . . The *so that* emphasis is context for 9:4, *"We must work the works of him who sent me while it is day."* The so-that clause avoids the troubling theological implication that God has created suffering in this man in order to glorify himself (Burge 2000: 272–73). The troubling dimension is also answered by separating cause and purpose. The man was not made blind for God's glory to be revealed, but in the face of his blindness, the *purpose* of Jesus' action is to reveal God's glory (cf. 11:4, 40). The situation serves Jesus' revelatory gift.

In this healing, Jesus does God's work: he was sent for that purpose (see Burer, *Divine Sabbath Work*). Hence, *now* it is *day*, when *we must work the works of him who sent me.* Here is the divine *dei* that occurred last in chapter 4 (vv. 4, 20, 24; cf. its occurrence in Jesus' passion and resurrection predictions in Mark 8:31; 10:32-34). The use of the plural *we* is rare. The use of *dei* occurs usually in relation to Jesus' call and mission, but here Jesus includes the disciples in his mission (Howard-Brook 1994: 216). *Day* is the time for this mission because *night is coming when no one can work* (v. 4); this mission is *now* while it is light. This prompts Jesus' christological claim: *As long as I am in the world, I am the light of the world* (v. 5; cf. 12:35-36). Chapter 9 continues chapter 8, with Jesus' *I am the light of the world* (8:12). The end of John 9 exposes the blindness of the Jews (vv. 18-34) and some Pharisees (vv. 13-17, 40-41).

Day means the time of God's salvation favor, the time when Jesus as the *sent one* reveals God's saving works to those who have eyes to

see and hearts to believe. But *night* is also coming, as Jesus repeatedly alerts his disciples: *You will search for me and you will not find me*
(7:36b; 8:21), speaking of his departure (cf. chs. 14–16). Jesus' promised gift of the Spirit (20:19-23) also prepares them for his departure. His *I AM* identity claim, *light of the world*, is vintage John (cf. 1:5,
9; 8:12; 12:46).

Curtain. Scene 1 ends.

Jesus Heals the Blind Man 9:6-7[w]

Jesus continues as the main character, but the blind man appears
onstage. The healing itself is narrated with surprising brevity. First
Jesus spits on the ground and mixes his saliva with mud. Then Jesus
anoints the man's eyes with the spittle. Burge (2000) notes that "in
antiquity there was enormous superstition surrounding the 'spittle'
of a renowned person. Both the Greek healing cult of Asclepius and
Jewish popular belief gave spittle magical power" (273n3). Jesus'
use of spittle, however, is not magic but testifies to his identity with
the human. Touch is significant, "essential for the well-being of the
community, expressing intimacy of love." Lee (2010: 124) notes
Jesus' other uses of touch. It shows how each of the five senses is
important in John (cf. also Jesus' healing the deaf man in Mark 7:33
and the blind man at Bethsaida in Mark 8:23). Jesus' action perhaps
echoes Isaiah 64:8-11 (7-11 LXX): "O Lord, you are our Father; we are
the clay [*pēlos*]; we are all the work of your hand." The word *pēlos*
evokes Genesis 2:7, where God fashions the human being from the
soil. In the early church, healing was viewed as re-creation
(R. Brown 1966: 380–81). With the symbol of *light* (v. 5) the healing
connects also to the creation motif of John's prologue (Day 1 in
Gen 1).

Echoing Elisha's healing of leprous Naaman (2 Kings 5:10-14),
Jesus tells the man to go and wash in the pool of Siloam *(which means
Sent)*, invoking also perhaps the theme of Jesus as *the Sent One* (the
themes of healing and sending fit together also at the symbolic level
in John). The author of the fourth Gospel knows this pool and its
function. Similar to the Bethzatha pool in John 5, which is north of
the temple mount, Siloam is south of the temple mount and also a
purification pool, a *mikveh* (*miqweh*), to accommodate the many pilgrims coming to Jerusalem for the festivals. The Siloam pool of
Jesus' time had three sets of five steps, each set separated by a wide
landing, with waiting areas for descent and resting areas for ascent.
A few of these steps were discovered in 1898, but the dig was then
abandoned. Only in 2004 did the pool's true size and function come

to light (Reich and Shukron 2005). It is not to be identified with the much smaller "pool of Siloam" that tourists see today (91–96).

An original phase of the pool's construction began in the Hasmonean period, since coins from Alexander Jannaeus (102–76 BC) were found there. But the limestone coverage of the steps attests to a second phase as part of Herod's vast construction projects. The pool was destroyed in AD 70 with Jerusalem's fall to the Romans.

Jesus orders the man to go and wash in this purification pool (*mikveh*), and he comes *back able to see!* Does Jesus regard purification significant, since this story is similar to his telling the healed leper in Mark 1:44 to go and show himself to the priest? Or is this a witness verification? In either case, it is Jesus who heals, and the priest and the purification water *attest* the healing. It is done: the man now sees. But much interrogation—indeed, a "trial"—is yet to ensue, and there is more to *see* about the healer!

Curtain. Scene 2 ends.

The Neighbors and Pharisees Quiz the Blind Man 9:8-17

In verse 8 we learn that this blind man was a beggar, a detail of continuity with the man before he was healed. But he is beggar no longer: now he becomes a *witness*. The neighbor voices ask three questions:

- *Is this not the man who used to sit and beg?* (v. 8).
- *Then how were your eyes opened?* (v. 10).
- *Where is he*—this Jesus who healed you? (v. 12).

The neighbors' answers to the first question are divided. The tense (past continuous action) indicates that these three questions are repeated several times, as are the former blind man's response. Some are saying, "Yes, it is he"—that's the man, to be sure! Others are saying, *No, but it is someone like him* (v. 9). The man himself keeps saying, *I am the man*. As the man repeats his identity, the neighbors keep asking, *How did he do it?* (AT). As the man keeps repeating his story, the word passes along to others, and the crowd of neighbors grows. *The man witnesses to Jesus: The man called Jesus made mud, spread it on my eyes, and said to me, "Go to Siloam and wash." Then I went and washed and received my sight* (v. 11). The man heeds Jesus' command, is healed, and is a model disciple [*Disciples, p. 509*].

Wanting to see just who this man is who healed the blind beggar, the neighbors pose a third question: *Where is he?* The man responds simply, *I do not know*.

The *they* that begins verse 13 refers to the neighbors. Perhaps they think that since the blind man doesn't know where the healer is, the Pharisees as the religious leaders should be informed. Or, the fact that the healing has occurred on the Sabbath (v. 14) may have led the neighbors to report it to the Pharisees, since the healing has violated Sabbath law. Thus verse 14, *It was a sabbath day when Jesus made the mud and opened his eyes*, identifies the "stone of offense." *Kneading*, involved in making a *spittle*, "was one of the thirty-nine categories of work explicitly forbidden on the Sabbath" (*m. Šabbat* 7:2; O'Day 1995: 654, 656). Healing thus on the Sabbath, Jesus is provocative (cf. 5:9, where the healed man carries his mat on the Sabbath). In both cases the Pharisees' laws fencing the Sabbath commandment forbid healing chronic conditions on the Sabbath since they could wait until another day (*m. Šabbat* 14:3; *m. Yoma* 8:6). Jesus' actions challenge Pharisaic oral interpretations of Jewish laws, that likely lie behind the Mishnah sources.

The Pharisees begin their "trial" by asking the man how he received his sight. The man gives a brief explanation: *He put mud on my eyes. Then I washed, and now I see.* The Siloam pool is not designated, but enough has been said to incriminate Jesus. Some of the Pharisees, who won't even say Jesus' name(!), declare, *This man is not from God, for he does not observe the sabbath.* Their response identifies a situational conflict—one level of potential irony. What they say implies that at some level this miracle worker has come from God. But since they cannot accept this fact, they discount it by citing his Sabbath violation. The statement lands the Pharisees in *self-betrayal*: they are not able to grasp the truth they fear. The evangelist is the ironist, the Pharisees the victim, and the readers those entertained (Ito: 324).

Other Pharisees (v. 16c-e) respond more positively to Jesus, querying, *How can a man who is a sinner perform such signs?* The word *sinner*, now applied rhetorically to Jesus to critique the opposition, resumes the motif of 9:2-3 and will appear again on the lips of the now-seeing man who was born blind (v. 31). The disciples, Jesus, the Pharisees, and the healed man all use the same term, *sinner*. Verses 24c, 25, 34, 41 bring the sin theme to a climax, setting straight who is a sinner and just what counts as sin. This division among the Pharisees might signify "Nicodemus-style secret believers among the authorities" (Rensberger: 43).

The "trial" now proceeds to another stage of inquiry: namely, to Jesus' identity. This is a dramatic turn in the narrative. The Pharisees set up the question (v. 17) that begins to disclose Jesus' identity through the voice of the blind man. At this early point in the narrative, the healed man confesses, *He is a prophet.*

Curtain. Scene 3 ends.

The Jews Interrogate the Blind Man's Parents 9:18-23

In this new scene, both sets of characters change. Onstage we see the Jews and the parents of the blind man. Some commentators hold that the Jews are interchangeable with the Pharisees (e.g., Rensberger: 42; O'Day implies the same, in 1995: 658). But other matters must be considered also [*"The Jews," p. 520*]. The next scene, verses 24-34, begins with the subject *they,* who interrogate the man a second time, harking back to verses 13-17, the first time of their interrogation.

This scene (vv. 18-23) begins with an admission of the Jews' resistance to believe the man's testimony, but frames it with the word *until,* which implies that after they call his parents and interrogate them, they might believe the man's witness. The parents report that, yes, he was born blind and he is their son. For more certainty they would, however, need to ask their son. The phrase *the parents of the man who had received his sight* (v. 18d) complements the parents' identification of him (v. 20): *We know that this is our son, and that he was born blind.* Here the *before* and *after* of his healing stand in bold relief. It is the middle term, the connector, or how both these statements are true that dogs the Jews' probing. The parents will not be put on the trial stand, so they refuse to witness further, saying, *But we do not know how it is that now he sees, nor do we know who opened his eyes. Ask him; he is of age. He will speak for himself.* The parents abandon their son to his interrogators, who, like Saul before conversion, think they see well but are blind, with sin remaining (vv. 39-41; cf. *1 Enoch* 90:6-8).

The text states the reason for their refusal to be forthright, which is the key that unlocks the double referent of the Gospel story: the time of Jesus and the time of the persecuted Johannine community. The narrator states the reason baldly: *His parents said this because they were afraid of the Jews; for the Jews had already agreed that anyone who confessed Jesus to be the Messiah would be put out of the synagogue* (v. 22). The parents will not risk public identification with Jesus. They push the burden back on their son. The man's parents, models of *secret Christians,* "present an even more negative image than Nicodemus" (Rensberger 1988: 48).

Much ink has been penned on verse 22, *For the Jews had already agreed that anyone who confessed Jesus to be the Messiah would be put out of the synagogue,* and its significance in understanding the fourth

Gospel (cf. 16:2). J. Louis Martyn's thesis (1968/1979/2003), accepted and modified by Raymond Brown (1979) and Rensberger (1988), proposes that this verse reflects the late first-century religious circumstance of the Johannine community. Believers in Jesus as Messiah were excommunicated from the synagogue. Many Johannine scholars now regard this view as tenuous *["The Jews," p. 520]*. Truex's study of blasphemy may provide a more durable understanding of the factors leading to this situation.

In 9:28 the Pharisees revile this new testifier to Jesus and pit *disciples of [Jesus]* (more specifically, the blind man) against *disciples of Moses* (the Pharisees). Burge (2000: 275) explains, "These words point not merely to the division within Jesus' audience, but [also] to the later harsh division that will erupt between the synagogue and church in coming decades." Burge thus implies some line of continuity between Jesus' time and the period when the Gospel was written, much later, a link that I suggest moves from dispute and tension in Jesus' time to communal separation of some sort by Gospel-writing time, at least in some geographical areas. This separation, whatever its nature, is represented by the Johannine community. At the same time, Jewish scholars (Adela Reinhartz 1998: 121–38; 2001a: 42–53; 2001b: 222–27; and Daniel Boyarin 2002) and others point out that many narratives in John reflect solidarity between Jews and Jesus' followers, notably Mary, Martha, and Lazarus, as well as Jesus' own disciples. Hence the quest for understanding this difficult and delicate matter continues *["The Jews," p. 520]*.

The scene concludes with a voice-over in which the narrator repeats the parents' final word, thus underscoring their distancing themselves from the dispute and danger: *Therefore his parents said, "He is of age; ask him"* (v. 23).

Curtain. Scene 4 ends.

"They" Grill the Blind Man a Second Time: Jesus "a Sinner"? 9:24-34[w]

The subject *they* of verse 24 combined with *second time* refers to the Pharisees who in verse 13 began the "trial" of the blind man. Whether *the Jews* of verse 18 are included in *they* is problematic, as noted above. In stage production, it boils down to whether the same interrogating "characters" show up in verses 18-23 as in 13-17, 24-34. More likely it is a different set in verses 18-23, though in resolving the identity of the Jews in John, some overlap with Pharisees occurs.

The Pharisees admonish the healed man: *Give glory to God!* What irony! Jesus' entire mission is to glorify God, but *this* the religious leaders cannot accept. They regard it blasphemous to credit Jesus for this healing; instead, give God the *glory* (Truex: 222–24). The Pharisees want to rid the land of Jesus, who confronts them with words and actions they limit to God (cf. Mark 2:7-10). Instead, they label Jesus *a sinner* from the outset—before the trial begins! What an irony! Because the readers by now know more about Jesus than the Pharisees do, that gap in knowledge results in another type of irony: *dramatic* irony (Ito: 376). The cotext of this text (the larger narrative) has already informed the reader who Jesus is. The Pharisees have no difficulty in believing theoretically that God can heal the blind. But to witness such, done by a miracle worker, is more than they can comprehend or admit into their scheme of sorting out good from evil, the divine from the human. Their presupposition determines their conclusion (John 9:34). Jesus does not fit into their box—no way, not ever! And this exasperates. As religious leaders today, we too may be good Pharisees, in the best sense of the word, but we are confronted and confounded by this Jesus, who breaks the limits of our human experience.

The mounting tension now reaches its breaking point (double entendre)! Culpepper lays out the developing opposition, with contrasting ethos (1998: 177):

Contrasting Responses in John 9

The Blind Man	The Pharisees
I do not know. (v. 12)	*This man is not from God.* (v. 16)
I do not know whether he is a sinner. (v. 25)	*We know that this man is a sinner.* (v. 24)
One thing I do know, that though I was blind, now I see. (v. 25)	*We know that God has spoken to Moses, but as for this man, we do not know where he comes from.* (v. 29)

The next stage in the downward spiraling dialogue between the Jews and the man who can now see is stunning in its literary genius, its christological acuity, and the rapaciousness of unbelief. See it here in stage production form, since it lends itself well to that medium (in contrast to the long discourses in John):

BLIND BEGGAR (with sarcasm): Why do you want to hear it (my story) again? Do you also want to become his disciples? (v. 27)

PHARISEES (reviling tone): You are his disciple, but we are disciples of Moses. We know that God has spoken to Moses, but as for this man (Jesus), we do not know where he comes from. (vv. 28-29)

HEALED MAN (ridiculing amazement, then passionate affirming voice): Here is an astonishing thing! You do not know where he comes from, and yet he opened my eyes. We know that God does not listen to sinners, but he does listen to one who worships him and obeys his will. Never since the world began has it been heard that anyone opened the eyes of a person born blind. If this man were not from God, he could do nothing. (vv. 30-33)

PHARISEES (accusatory tone—ad hominem attack, with scorn): *You were born entirely in sins, and are you trying to teach us?* (v. 34)

The riposte concludes, narrating the man's loss of community: *And they drove him out* (v. 34).

Verse 27b is delicious irony. As Bultmann (336) puts it, "He treats the insincerity of their inquiry with the greatest possible irony." This healed blind man of low status in the community challenges the authorities in high position (Ito: 378). The man also models discipleship, which Schnackenburg regards as boldly ironic (1980: 1.251).

The *sin/sinner* theme runs through this paragraph: verses 24d, 25, 31, 34. The healed man voices the word (vv. 25, 31) in opposition to the religious leaders' charges. The accusing voices first label Jesus a *sinner* (v. 24d) and end with discounting the man's witness to Jesus as one *born entirely in sins* (v. 34). In their thinking his blindness marks him as a *sinner*, which is also the mentality of the disciples at the beginning (vv. 2-3). But in his rejoinders to their questions, the healed blind man moves from defense to offense.

The authorities, fed up with this man's zeal and verbal skill, halt the "trial" by ejecting the man from the synagogue (v. 34), the consequence the parents dodged (v. 22). Current scholarship tends to see the man's exclusion not as permanent excommunication, though Burge (2000: 275) allows for that too, saying, "We are not told if the discipline extends over a few days, a month, or permanently. Each may have been possible (though the latter seems unlikely)." Whatever the answer to these options might be, what we hear are authoritative voices, and what we see are arm gestures that push the healed and born-anew man offstage—indeed, out of the community.

Curtain. Scene 5 ends.

Jesus Leads the Blind Man to Christological Sight 9:35-39

Jesus reappears in the narrative for the first time since verse 11. He has been absent in 25 of the 41 verses of the chapter. In this long meantime, while the healed man bears the ostracism of his community, we can only guess what Jesus was doing. Was he furtively watching, or hiding for his own safety? In any case, he hears *that they had driven him out*. This is an opportune time in the man's experience when new things can be grasped, understood, and affirmed. The man receives spiritual sight, while Jesus judges the temple leaders to be spiritually blind. The paragraph is a bookend to 9:1: *a man blind from birth* who receives sight now advances to *spiritual sight*.

Jesus' first question astounds: *Do you believe in the Son of Man?* The man asks, *Who is he?* so he can believe. In Jewish thought *Son of Man* carries two connotations: one who comes from heaven ("on the clouds," Dan 7:13-14) and one who comes as eschatological judge (1 Enoch 49:4; 61:9; 69:27). Jesus' statement (John 9:39) indicates that the eschatological judgment has come in himself (cf. 3:18-21). Echoing his words to the Samaritan woman (4:26), Jesus identifies himself as the Son of Man: *"You have seen him, and the one speaking with you is he"* (9:37). The Greek is more emphatic: *That one is he.* The man's response is instantaneous: *Lord, I believe.* How much the Enochic or Danielic "Son of Man" traditions play into John's conceptions (the blind man is surely not informed) is difficult to assess (Boccaccini 2007) *[Christology, p. 507]*.

What *Lord* (v. 38) intends to communicate is unclear. Minimally, it is a respectful title: *Sir.* But it might also denote more than that: *Lord*, as he recognizes Jesus' divine authority. The evangelist may intend it to match what Logos signifies in the Aramaic *Memra* for the sacred name, establishing continuity with *The Name* and the *Memra-Logos* (Boyarin 2001: prologue). The man's response attests: he worships Jesus (cf. Ezek 1:28; Dan 8:17; Rev 1:17).

While some reliable manuscripts (p^{75} א W) lack verse 38, most manuscripts, including early reliable ones, include it *[Textual Variants, p. 532]*. Seeing the light and worshiping Jesus fit together in John's theology. (On "worship of Jesus," see Swartley 2007: 213-37.)

Verse 39 is an ironic climax. In usual thinking, Jesus enables those who already see to see more clearly, and those who do not see to become even more blinded (cf. Mark 4:10-12). The irony arises from counterfactual propositional opposition: John 9:41 reverses normal ways of thought (Ito: 379, 381). The readers are able to see the truth, but the authorities do not.

This chapter unfolds Jesus' christological identity. As Peter's confession is pivotal in Mark, so here the blind man's confession (9:35-38) is crucial, unveiling Jesus' identity for his disciples, the religious leaders, and ordinary people (parents and neighbors). Jesus as Son of Man (already in 1:51) connects heaven and earth. He comes from above, becomes incarnate, human, and yet reveals God. Burge (2000: 278) sums up the mounting Christology of this narrative that culminates in Jesus' *I AM* self-claim (v. 37), enacting *I am the light of the world*: "Rabbi (9:2), Jesus (9:3), the light of the world (9:5), Sent (9:7), from God (9:16), prophet (9:17), Christ (9:22 [RSV]), Son of Man (9:35), Lord (9:38)" (cf. the Samaritan woman's similar progressive understanding of Jesus' identity). The healed man *worships* Jesus as divine One in human form. The man does not immediately come to a proper recognition of who Jesus is when he is healed, but the authorities' resistance and the christological conflict that ensues finally bring him to see Jesus properly.

Jesus' coming into the world brings judgment that subverts conventional judgment. His judgment exemplifies *The Upside-Down Kingdom* (Kraybill). Jesus comes *so that those who do not see may see, and those who do see may become blind* (9:39). This phrase is another *so-that* clause, designating here not so much purpose, but the potential *result* of Jesus' coming. As the reader enjoys this ironic and dramatic narrative, one becomes aware of *also* being on trial: Do I truly see, or do I remain blind?

Curtain. Scene 6 ends.

Jesus and the Pharisees on Blindness: "Your Sin Remains" 9:40-41

This final scene has a more limited audience: *some of the Pharisees.* What is the significance of identifying these Pharisees as those *who were near* [lit., *with*] *him*? We have not heard of this group before. Perhaps they are to be distinguished from those who have expelled believers in Jesus as Messiah from the synagogue, as Howard-Brook proposes (1994: 229-30). Hearing Jesus' words (v. 39), they query hopefully, *Surely we are not blind, are we?* If they are a different group, thinking they would fare better than the persecutors of the blind man, their hopes are dashed categorically. Jesus' response cuts. They are going the wrong direction, from self-claimed sight to Jesus-pronounced blindness. If, however, they would own their blindness, they would be candidates to receive Jesus' gift of sight. A similar theme occurs in 1 John 2:8-11, which concludes that whoever "hates another believer" thus "walks in the darkness, and does not know the way to go, because the darkness has brought on blindness" (McDermond: 99).

In 9:41 Jesus pronounces the trial verdict with irony: what the religious authorities normally assume is counterstated. Again the evangelist is ironist. The religious authorities are the victims. And the readers are entertained. This irony gives support to Brant's thesis (2004) since it lends itself so well to dramatic stage production [*Drama, p. 510*].

However, this verse may hold open a choice for the religious leaders, since the narrative continues in 10:19-21. Here the Jews divide in their response to Jesus. Some respond favorably and others negatively, judging Jesus to be in league with the demons.

But the dialogical drama ends here, with the final haunting voice-over verdict of the true "trial" judge (9:41):

> *If you were blind, you would not have sin.*
> *But now that you say, "We see," your sin remains.*

Curtain. Scene 7 ends.

THE TEXT IN BIBLICAL CONTEXT

John as Drama, for Theater[w]

While many commentators recognize dramatic features in John, such as its masterful use of irony and other literary techniques (Culpepper 1983), Jo-Ann Brant's contribution (2004) goes a step further. Brant contends that John may be understood not only as drama in a general sense, but also as drama written for theatrical performance. One of the literary techniques more evident in John than in the other Gospels is the prevalent use of *deictic* language, such as *come* and *go*—words that *signify* or *point out*, such as *that* (*one*) [*ekeinos*] and *this* (*one*) [*houtos*]—and frequent use of intensives: *I* (*egō*), *we* (*hymeis*), and *you* (*sy, hymeis*). This fits with stage production.

Still further, the sign-discourse structure maximizes use of flyting, a technique characteristic of discourses in both Greek tragedies and John [*Drama, p. 510*]. In flyting, opponents duel, besting the other's position and reasoning. The discourses in John 5, 6, 8, and 10 depict flyting between Jesus and "the Jews." In Greek tragedy the winner in the linguistic flyt-duel often ends up losing the battle, since the opponents resort to mortal violence—exactly what happens to Jesus. Brant (2004) builds on this insight to understand Jesus' excoriation of the Jews. In performance a person, perhaps representing a group, plays the antagonist role in order to create the dynamic of the plot in the theatrical production. Characters present the play, but roles in real life differ significantly from that depicted in the text. Thus Jesus' harsh words to the Jews and the Jews' hostility toward Jesus do not necessarily reflect actual life relations *["The Jews," p. 520]*.

In John's Gospel, chapter 9 lends itself particularly well to Brant's thesis (2004). In the seven scenes shown in this chapter, John's Gospel is one that must be *seen*. This chapter exhibits the point with double entendre. Other NT literature may be viewed similarly, especially Mark and Revelation. While such Scriptures lend themselves to oral production, this feature does not mean actual staging for theater. Other factors need consideration, especially the question of the early church's acceptance of and relationship to the theater in Greco-Roman culture. To what extent general cultural ethos, including the theatre and its dramatic genre, influenced Gospel writing for communicative purposes is an open question.

John 9 in the Church's Liturgy

The dramatic quality of John 9 makes it a beautiful and powerful story. The healing of this man born blind connects at numerous levels with the experience of coming to faith. Other healings of blind people convey similar meaning: Mark 8:22-26, a healing symbolic of the disciples' coming to faith and following Jesus; Jesus' healings of the blind in Matthew 9:27-31; 20:29-34; and Luke 18:35-43. Certainly the placement of healings of the blind at both the beginning and end of Mark's famous "on the way" section (8:22–10:52) signifies that discipleship means *seeing* who Jesus is. Jesus' healing blind Bartimaeus (10:46-52) ends up with him following Jesus "on the way," which thus connects *seeing* and *following* Jesus (Swartley 1981/1999: 158).

Schneiders's essay on John 9 observes that it "has been linked to chaps. 4 and 11 (the Samaritan woman and the raising of Lazarus) in the church's initiation praxis" and that today the Roman Catholic lectionary schedules chapters 4, 9, 11 for every third year (Cycle A) "on the third, fourth, and fifth Sundays of . . . Lent . . . in connection with the scrutinies of the catechumens preparing for baptism" (2003: 149; Hoskyns: 363–65 describes their use in early Christian lectionaries). Chapter 9 lends itself to "enlightenment" through baptismal washing. Jesus' raising of Lazarus—from death to new life—prepares also for baptism. Schneiders (2003: 150; cf. also her 2002 essay) notes that the "'baptismal' lens provides a hermeneutical entrance into this sphere of Johannine spirituality." John 3 with its *born from above/again* homily may function similarly (cf. Acts 2:32-39; Rom 6:1-14; 1 Pet 1:3-9, 22). All these instruct for baptism so that eyes will be open to see Jesus.

Early catacomb art depicts the stories of the Samaritan woman (John 4), the healed paralytic (ch. 5), and the blind man (ch. 9) to exemplify conversion and baptism. Water is the agent of regeneration. At least as early as the third century, John 9 was read aloud as the third test in the examination preparing candidates for baptism, usually celebrated on Easter Sunday (Burge 2000: 279). The reading climaxes with the emphatic *I do believe* (9:38). The candidate's confession witnesses to the Christian faith.

Sin in Scripture[w]

In 1 John *sin* functions differently than it does in John 9. In John 9 sin is unbelief, failure to believe Jesus' *I AM* claims and to recognize Jesus as *the Lamb of God who takes away the sin of the world* (1:29, 36). In 1 John, sin is not walking in the light: "If we walk in the light as he himself is in the light, . . . the blood of Jesus his Son cleanses us from all sin" (1:7). But then sin also is disobeying God's moral law: "If we say that we have no sin, we deceive ourselves, and the truth is not in us. If we confess our sins, he who is faithful and just will forgive us our sins and cleanse us from all unrighteousness. If we say that we have not sinned, we make him a liar, and his word is not in us" (1:8-10; see McDermond). These verses declare that no one is without sin, but the next verse states that this letter is written to you so that "you may not sin" (2:1a). Later the author defines sin as "lawlessness" (3:4). To further complicate the matter, the one who walks in the light is now viewed as sinless (cf. 3:6, 9; 5:18). First John appears to give conflicting signals on sin (see McDermond: 65, 74–81, 311–12). Living in love (1 John 4–5) points toward the resolution.

Luke 15 and Matthew 18 are relevant also to the NT's instruction on sin. In Paul, God's answer to sin is *grace*. Permeating Paul's letters, *sin* occurs sixty-four times, forty-eight in Romans ("Sin in Romans," Toews: 409–11). As Toews puts it, "The reign of Sin and Death is replaced by the reign of Grace, Righteousness, and Life" (411).

In the OT, sin is whatever breaks covenant relationship with God, separating humans from God (Isa 59:2). Three of many terms are used most frequently, and each has its own connotation: *ḥaṭṭ'at*, missing the mark, or abandoning the straight road; *ma'al*, unfaithfulness; and *pešaʻ*, open rebellion against God (Jacob: 281). This OT perspective is helpful in understanding sin in John. Since Jesus comes to renew God's covenant with Israel, refusal of him and his word is sin in all three OT senses.

THE TEXT IN THE LIFE OF THE CHURCH

Whatever Became of Sin?

Some years ago Karl Menninger wrote a book by this title, chiding liberal Christian preaching for ignoring sin. His concern was motivated by mental health. A leader in treatment for mental illness, he began a leading mental health center, Menninger Hospital, in Topeka, Kansas, now in Houston, Texas. John 9 is about sin, and may be a good text to address this issue. It cautions us against labeling people "sinners."

To address Menninger's concern, other Scriptures need to be considered in the sermon or teaching. One important emphasis from the OT perspective is that of relational unfaithfulness, first to God and then also to other people. The perspective of 1 John judges failure to love and, similar to John's Gospel, failure to live in the light. Romans reminds us that "all have sinned and fall short of the glory of God" (3:23). Yes, all "lawlessness" is sin (1 John 3:4); good laws protect the welfare of other people. Violating those laws causes much grief and heartache both for oneself and for others (e.g., driving under the influence . . .). Various forms of sexual perversion are also sin. In our time, greed in business, lying, hoarding wealth, deception of all sorts, and corruption in government—all fall into the sin category. Scripture does not whitewash sin—hear the prophets—but beckons us to come to God (OT) in Jesus Christ (NT) for forgiveness, cleansing, and renewal. *Jesus* means savior from sin (Matt 1:21). Understanding Jesus as Savior from sin is essential in preaching and teaching.

Healing Stories in the Congregation

How does one preach/dramatize this story or other healing stories in one's congregation without offending persons with disabilities? This calls for sensitivity. The congregation may include a person with the disability the biblical text describes. One guideline would be to invite persons with disability to testify how Jesus has made them whole, so that their disability has not condemned them, but may be a means of witness to Christ.

Does miraculous healing occur? Definitely yes, and this point should not be avoided though it cannot be prescribed (see Pfeiffer; Swartley 2012a: 14, 34-36; and sources listed by Burge 2000: 280). We pray for healing, and if cure comes, we accept it as God's gift of grace in Jesus Christ. At the same time, through prayer we may be healed in spirit and attitude toward our disability or illness. For all of us eventually, complete healing of our mortal bodies awaits the resurrection (Rom 8:21-26).

John 10

Shepherds: True and False

PREVIEW

Many children's books introduce readers to a character they like and trust, while other characters (the bad ones) are not trustworthy and contend against the story's hero. The notorious Harry Potter series falls into this category but unfortunately opens young minds to the world of magic and witchcraft, which in some cases can play out negatively in teen years and beyond. In John 10 we meet a Shepherd true, but also false shepherds, not unlike what we encounter in our world today, whether in religion, business, or sports. The challenge is to learn to distinguish between the true and the false.

In John 10 Jesus is the Good Shepherd. In its John 9 context this imagery sharply critiques religious leadership; it judges between true and false shepherds. Jesus' judgment echoes OT prophetic critique of Israel's religious leaders (e.g., Ezek 34). John 9 indicts some Pharisees and Jews as blind leaders; John 10 continues the topic.

At the end of John 9, the Jewish leaders fail the test of good leadership by casting out the blind man Jesus healed. John 10:1-21 continues Jesus' discourse at the Feast of Tabernacles (chs. 7–9). Verse 21 ends by referring back to chapter 9, when some of the Jews, disagreeing with others who demonized Jesus, exclaim, *Can a demon open the eyes of the blind?* The imagery of sheep appears also in 10:27-29, suggesting structural continuity.

New narrative markers appear in 10:22, where we find a new feast and time of year. Whereas 7:1–10:21 occurs at the autumn Festival of Tabernacles, 10:22-42 is hinged to the winter Feast of Dedication, Hanukkah. Burge (2000: 286) puts all of John 10 with the Hanukkah Feast because both parts contain shepherd and sheep imagery. But chapter 10 is hinged to chapter 9 since the false shepherds mirror the blinded reactions of the Jews in chapter 9 and has the same audience (Moloney 1998: 312). Thus 10:1-21 thematically relates both Feasts: Tabernacles and Dedication/Hanukkah [*Unsettled Matters, p. 534*].

John 10 continues christological disclosures and claims (vv. 11, 14-15, 24, 36-38), extending the blind man's confession of Jesus as Son of Man (9:35-38) and Jesus' bold *I AM* claim in 8:58. The final three verses (10:40-42) culminate the testimony of an earlier witness. Since Jesus retreats *across the Jordan to the place where John had been baptizing earlier*, the fourth evangelist invokes John the Witness a final time. He contrasts Jesus' signs to John's ministry, which did not include signs but only a testimony affirming Jesus' "greater" role. Everything John said about him was true! As a result, many regard Jesus' ministry positively: *Many believed in him there.*

OUTLINE[w]

Jesus' Speech Figures: Gate, Shepherd, and Strangers, 10:1-6
Jesus: The Gate and the Shepherd, 10:7-10
Jesus, the Good Shepherd, 10:11-15
More Sheep, but One Flock, One Shepherd, and One Father, 10:16-18
The Jews' Response, 10:19-21
Time and Location of Discourse: Feast of Dedication, 10:22-23
The Jews' Key Question: Jesus' Answer, 10:24-30
The Jews and Jesus in Physical and Verbal Altercation, 10:31-39
Jesus Retreats; Hear Again John's Witness, 10:40-42

EXPLANATORY NOTES

With the shift to a new feast in 10:22-23, this chapter consists of two parts (Miyazaki):

---

w   Where the superscript w occurs after headings, please see the commentary's online Web Supplement for additional material. Go to: www.heraldpress.com/bcbc/john.

Texts	Title	Issues
Part 1	**Jesus: The Good Shepherd**	
10:1-6	Parable of a gate and a shepherd	• True leadership; Thematic link between 10:1-21 and the Feast of Dedication
10:7-14	Jesus, the gate, and the shepherd	• Jesus' self-revelation as the gate and shepherd • The nature of the life-giver • The relation of sheep with a shepherd, and the Son with the Father
10:16	Evangelistic character of the Johannine community	• Community, boundaries • Social setting: expulsion from the synagogue (formerly blind man cast out) • Evangelistic character
10:17-21	Love commandment of the Father.	• Jesus' voluntary life-giving • Life-giving power of the cross and resurrection • Love commandment of the Father
Part 2	**The Father and I Are One**	
10:22-30	The Father and I are one	• Feast of Dedication: expectation of messianic deliverer • Unity of Father and Son, as well as sheep and shepherd
10:31-39	Jesus, the consecrated one	• Jesus the consecrated one replaces the Feast of Consecration • Blasphemy • Temple motif
10:40-42	The witness of John	• Inclusio with the testimonies of John (chs. 1–3) • The issue of structure

Jesus' Speech Figures: Gate, Shepherd, and Strangers 10:1-6

The chapter begins with no indication of a shift in audience, time, or location. Jesus' discourse continues with his *Amen* signature, *Very truly, I tell you* (v. 1)—its fifteenth occurrence in John. It exclaims:

Pay attention! This is important! In light of Jesus' punchy maxims (9:39, 41), we might expect Jesus' discourse to highlight or explain in some way the failure of the religious leaders to believe (recall they are judged *blind* and their *sin remains*). The *thief* and *bandit* mirror those who deviously seek control of the sheep. Unlike the *good shepherd* (vv. 11, 14), they do not enter through the *gate*.

In the imagery of this "parable," *gate* and *shepherd* overlap in verses 2 and 3a. While earlier translations read *door*, newer versions rightly choose *gate*, the entrance to the sheepfold then and now. The *gate* metaphorically identifies the shepherd (vv. 1b, 1c, 2): the shepherd enters through the gate (v. 2). Shepherds build walls at the end of a canyon or valley to protect the sheep. They put thorny branches on the wall for safety so that a thief cannot climb up the wall (Burge 2000: 289). The gate is the only entrance for sheep to come and go safely and through which the true shepherd enters.

The *shepherd* imagery is deeply rooted in Israel's faith traditions. The OT uses shepherd metaphors three ways:

- God as shepherd (Gen 49:24; Pss 23; 78:52-53; 80:1; Isa 40:10-11);
- The leaders of God's covenant people as shepherds (Isa 56:9-12; Jer 23:1-4; 25:32-38; Ezek 34; Zech 11);
- Unrighteous leaders as false shepherds (1 Kings 22:17; Jer 10:21; 23:1-2). (See R. Brown 1966: 397; Burge 2000: 288.)

Jesus' significant phrase *The sheep hear his voice* (v. 3) recurs often in this chapter (vv. 3, 4, 5, 16, 27; cf. 14, 15). Shepherds used special calls or the sound of a short flute to guide sheep (Burge 2000: 288). Miyazaki's modified chiastic parallelism for verses 3b-4 shows the intimate relationship between the sheep and the shepherd. Repetitive phrases accentuate the relationship:

A *Sheep hear his voice* (v. 3b, voice, hearing).
　　B *He calls his own* [Gk. *idia*] *sheep* (v. 3c, own, belonging).
　　　　C He *leads them out* (v. 3c, guidance).
　　B´ *When he has brought out all his own* [Gk. *idia*] (v. 4a, own, belonging)
　　　　C´ He *goes ahead of them, and the sheep follow him* (v. 4b, guidance, following)
A´ *Because they know his voice* (v. 4c, voice, knowing).

The relationship between the speaker and hearer of the voice is parallel to the relation between the speaker and hearer of the word. Jesus' word enables people to belong (8:31), recognize (8:43), follow

(8:47), and have life (8:51), just as the voice of the shepherd calls the sheep that belong to him (10:3-4), know his voice (10:4), follow (10:3-4), feed (10:9), and have life (10:10).

The hearers (*some of the Pharisees*, in 9:40) and likely others (the audience of 9:40) fail to understand what Jesus says. The failure to understand links Jesus' speech of 10:1-5 to the evangelist's character-ization of *the Jews* in 9:39 and *some of the Pharisees* in 9:41 (Busse: 8). Misunderstanding, double meanings, and irony are recurring rhe-torical techniques in John's Gospel. The evangelist presents the story of Jesus this way to warn readers against misunderstanding and unbe-lieving, thus urging the readers to continue believing in fulfillment of the Gospel's purpose (20:31; Motyer [1997] contends the Gospel was written to persuade Jews to reconsider and believe) [*"The Jews," p. 520*].

Jesus: The Gate and the Shepherd 10:7-10

Completing the speech-figure of the gate and shepherd (vv. 1-6), Jesus applies these metaphors to himself in verses 7-18. Using the *I am* (*egō eimi*) phrase, Jesus claims to be the *gate* and *the shepherd*. Thus the theme of true and false leadership extends into this passage. Four *I am* phrases introduce four short units (vv. 7c, 9a, 11a, 14a) [*"I AM," p. 518*].

The Gospel evangelist composes verses 7-14 with parallelism and well-crafted clauses. Each unit has antithetical parallelisms: gate/shepherd and thief/hired hand. This antithetical parallelism highlights the distinctiveness of the life-giver (Jesus) from those who seek self-preservation (Burge 2000: 291). The antithetical par-allelism moves to a climactic point, from unit 1 to unit 3 (as Miyazaki's diagram of the key content shows):

	I am . . . (Jesus)	**Thieves, bandits, the hired hand**	**Theme**
Unit 1	The gate, unto salva-tion	Thieves and bandits	I (Jesus) versus they
Unit 2	*I came that they may have life, and have it abundantly* (v. 10).	*The thief comes only to steal and kill and destroy* (v. 10).	Life-giver (I) versus killer (they)
Unit 3	*I am the good shepherd* (v. 11). *The good shepherd lays down his life for the sheep* (v. 11).	*The hired hand, who is not the shepherd and does not own the sheep . . . leaves the sheep and runs away—and the wolf snatches them and scatters them* (v. 12).	Shepherd's self-giving act versus hired man's self-preserving act

In unit 1, Jesus the *gate* is the way to salvation, as verse 9 clearly states: *I am the gate. Whoever enters by me will be saved, and will come in and go out and find pasture.* The imagery may reflect Psalm 118:20-21: "This is the gate of the Lord; the righteous shall enter through it. I thank you that you have answered me and have become my salvation." It also accords with John 14:6, *I am the way, and the truth, and the life.* The *gate* is parallel to *way* in 14:6; *I came that they may have life, and have it abundantly* (10:10) is parallel to *life* in 14:6. Jesus' gift of life streams through the Gospel (1:3-4; 3:16, 36; 4:14; 5:24-29; 6:47, 53, 68; 12:50; 17:3; and the purpose statement, 20:31). In 10:10b, life—indeed, *life more abundantly*—is the Shepherd Jesus' gift. It contrasts to the *thief,* who *comes only to steal and kill and destroy* (v. 10a). Jesus' promise of abundant life, unfortunately, has been prostituted to serve all sorts of other ends (see "Abundant Life" in TLC). Jesus' gift of life, however, is rooted in the sheep-shepherd relationship and cannot be known except through personal relationship marked by trust, knowing, and loving. This is John's discipleship (cf. 13:31-35).

Jesus, the Good Shepherd 10:11-15

10:11 Jesus' "I AM" Claim

Unit 1 in the diagram to the left introduces Jesus the *gate* and thieves as antithetical figures. Unit 2 describes Jesus as the life-giver, while the false leaders are thieves who steal, kill, and destroy. Unit 3, beginning with verse 11, develops unit 2 and describes Jesus' life-giving method: *I am the good shepherd. The good shepherd lays down his life for the sheep* (v. 11). The term *good* (*kalos*) can be translated as *noble* (Burge 2000: 291) or *model* (R. Brown 1966: 395). Marlin Miller preferred *model.* Schnackenburg (2.294) hears in this term a chiming with *true* (*alēthinos*; cf. 6:32; 15:1), especially as an antithesis to the hired hand (vv. 12-13). However, he also notes that this emphasis blurs the force of verses 11b and 15b, where the shepherd's *laying down his life* fits better with *good.* The Greek *hyper* in *"for"* his sheep suggests a sacrificial emphasis (Burge 2000: 291, who says *hyper* is exclusively sacrificial in John's Gospel).

A most significant OT text for the John 10 shepherd image for Jesus is Numbers 27:16-18, where God foretells Moses that he will die on a mountain in the Abarim range. Moses then asks God to provide a *shepherd* to lead Israel:

> "Let the Lord, the God of the spirits of all flesh, appoint someone over the congregation who shall go out before them and come in before them, who shall lead them out and bring them in, so that the congrega-

tion of the Lord may not be like sheep without a shepherd." So the Lord
said to Moses, "Take Joshua son of Nun, a man in whom is the spirit, and
lay your hand upon him."

This is perhaps the earliest OT text where a human, instead of God,
is called the shepherd of God's people (however, Isaiah refers to
Moses as shepherd, 63:11). *Joshua* in Hebrew matches *Jesus* in Greek.
Both mean *savior*, and in context, *savior* of the people (cf. Matt 1:21).
This OT passage may thus be viewed as a messianic prophecy
evoked by Jesus in John 10.

Many metaphors in the feasts narrative (chs. 5–10) have roots in
the exodus *[Feasts, p. 516]*. The Feast of Tabernacles *remembers* Israel's
wilderness wanderings and their living in booths. The Lord was their
guiding shepherd. In Numbers 27:17 the tasks of the shepherd in leading the people are described with four verbs also used here: *lead out*
[exagō] (John 10:3; cf. *agō* in 10:16) and *lead in [eisagō]* (cf. *agō* in 10:16)
[so that God's people] go out [exerchomai] (10:9) and *come in [eiserchomai]*
(twice in 10:9). Of the many OT references to shepherds, two points
are notable in applying the title to Jesus. As applied to God in the OT,
the metaphor connotes one "who leads, protects and gathers together
his people, looking after them solicitously and lovingly"
(Schnackenburg: 2.295). The term in the OT was applied to various
political and military leaders, even Cyrus, king of Babylon (Isa 44:28–
45:1; for use of shepherd-king in Israel's ANE cultures, see Lind: 274).
Schnackenburg (2.295) says it was not applied to any of Israel's reigning monarchs, only to the *future* Davidic messiah-king (e.g., Ezek
34:23-24). However, 2 Samuel 5:2b speaks otherwise: "The Lord said to
you [David]: It is you who shall be shepherd of my people Israel, you
who shall be ruler over Israel." Other texts also speak of David as
shepherd (Ps 78:71-72, inferred also in 2 Sam 24:7). Tribal leaders in
2 Sam 7:7 are referred to as shepherds, but they are not *Israel's* monarchs as such. Indeed, for David *shepherd* connotes royalty, in the
prophetic future and in his historical role.

Second, none of the OT texts say the shepherd voluntarily gives
his life for the sheep (R. Brown 1966: 398). This is unique to Jesus,
the *good* or *model*, even *beautiful* (the most usual word for *kalos*)
shepherd. However, Zechariah does speak "about a shepherd of God
who is put to death and whose death brings about a turning point"
(13:7-9). Schnackenburg (2.295) sees this text as messianic and correlates it with "the mysterious 'pierced one' for whom the people
mourn (Zech 12:10)," which John cites in 19:37. Both thus refer to
Jesus' death (cf. Mark 14:27).

10:12-13 The Hired Hand's Actions

The portrait of the hired hand is antithetical in every way to the *good* shepherd. He deserts the sheep when the wolf comes. He runs away, leaving the sheep vulnerable to the wolf's snatching and carrying them away. Why? The hired hand does not *care* about the sheep. This imagery connects with the false and wicked shepherds depicted in Israel's history. Ezekiel denounces the religious leaders and rulers who do not care for their sheep but use the shepherd role only to fleece them in every way possible (34:2-8). False shepherds frequently mark Israel's leadership (1 Kings 22:17; Jer 10:21; 23:1-3). Therefore God will judge those shepherds (Ezek 34:9-10), raise up a true Davidic shepherd-king (Ezek 34:11-16, 23-24; cf. Isa 40:9-11; Mic 5:2, cited in Matt 2:6), and make with the people a covenant of peace that banishes wild animals and pours down blessing upon them (Ezek 34:25-26). More recently in Israel's history, the "hired help" imagery matches priestly leadership, evoking memories of the Hasmonean priests who purchased their leadership from the Seleucid rulers (Jason usurps it from his brother Onias III). To add evil to evil, Antiochus IV murdered his brother, Seleucid IV, to grasp the Seleucid Empire's rule over Israel (cf. Boccaccini 2002: 52–56, 114–17, 131–33).

10:14-15 Jesus' Relation to His Sheep and to His Father

A *I am the good shepherd.*
  B *I know my own*
     C *and my own know me,*
     C′ *just as the Father knows me*
  B′ *and I know the Father.*
A′ *And I lay down my life for the sheep.*

These verses climax John 10:7-15; they also recapitulate the heart of the message in verses 1-13. Here verses 14b and 15a contain a dual parallelism. The NRSV, NJB, and NIV translate these phrases, each as a chiasm: *I know my own and my own know me* (v. 14b). *The Father knows me and I know the Father* (v. 15a). These two chiasms parallel each other. Further, this dual-parallelism is framed by the main theme statement: *I am the good shepherd. The good shepherd lays down his life for the sheep* (in vv. 11, 14a, 15b). This

> *inclusio* . . . establishes the essential goodness of the shepherd in contrast to the hireling, showing the shepherd's solicitude for his sheep. Being a shepherd entails a constant living for one's sheep. The shep-

herd-status of Jesus the shepherd . . . makes itself manifest in the sacrifice of his life (*psychē*), so that he may . . . [grant] his sheep the gift of true life (*zōē*). (Schnackenburg: 2.294–95)

This section in chapter 10 is a masterpiece, describing the richness of the gospel of Jesus Christ. The two different words used here for *life* suggest that the first is that of a person giving his life ("living soul," Gen 2:7 KJV), whereas the second is John's eternal life, the gift of Jesus now and in the life to come *[Eternal Life, p. 513]*.

Finally in this paragraph, Jesus makes clear his relationship to his Father (v. 15a), elaborated in verses 17-18. Just as Jesus knows his own sheep and his own know him, so the Father knows Jesus and Jesus *knows the Father*. The verb *know* (*ginōskō*, vv. 14-15) means relational knowing, grounded in the mutuality of love (vv. 17-18).

More Sheep, but One Flock, One Shepherd, and One Father 10:16-18

10:16 Jesus Speaks about Other Sheep, but One Flock, One Shepherd

This verse can be displayed as a chiasmus:

A *I have other sheep that do not belong to this fold.* (Two groups of sheep)
  B *I must bring them also, and they will listen to my voice.*
    (Commitment for mission)
A´ *So there will be one flock, one shepherd.* (Unity of flocks)

Verse 16 picks up from verses 1-6 emphases on *sheepfold, flock,* and listening to the *voice*. Verses 1-6 and 16 appear to deal metaphorically with *boundaries* in the Johannine community. Verses 1-6 (A in the v. 16 chiasm) depict an in-group and an out-group, signifying the community boundary. Through accepting and following the voice or word of Jesus (B in chiasm, v. 16b), however, the outsiders become part of the community (A´). Verses 1-6 have overtones of a sectarian boundary, but verse 16 has an inclusive missional emphasis. Compare this inclusive emphasis with 11:52, *gather into one the dispersed children of God.* Both texts strike a missional emphasis that critiques the boundary. Jesus is not only for us, but also for others.

The term *must* (*dei*; v. 16b) describes the necessity for Jesus to include those outside the fold. The same term was used in the story of the Samaritan woman, *But he [Jesus] had to [dei] go through Samaria* (4:4). This necessity is not only a geographical necessity but also Jesus' vocational necessity to lead Samaritans into faith (O'Day 1995:

36). In the same manner, the fourth evangelist describes this mission to the *other sheep* as crucial for the Johannine community.

Burge (2000: 292) asserts that *other sheep* refers to Gentiles (cf. 12:20). But does Jesus himself envision a mission to the Gentiles? Or is this the conviction of the later church (Acts 8; 10–11; 13)? Raymond Brown suggests (1966: 396) that some elements of mission are evident in Jesus' ministry. In John, *the other sheep* could hark back to the Samaritans in chapter 4, or to the dispersed children of God in 11:52. But in a later work (1979: 81–91, esp. 90, 169) Brown suggests that *other sheep* refers to the other apostolic churches (generally under Peter while in John the beloved disciple appears over Peter!). Within John's narrative the term *other sheep* anticipates the coming of Gentiles (God-fearers?) to see Jesus in 12:20 (cf. Jesus' petition *on behalf of those who will believe in me through their word*, in his farewell prayer: 17:20-21). A possible reference though to dispersed Jewish Christians in 11:52 cannot be ruled out.

The last sentence of 10:16 memorably sums up John's passion for unity: *one flock, one shepherd*. Jesus' image of *flock* is corporate, the believing community. As Paul Minear explains in *Images of the Church in the New Testament* (1960), the NT has ninety-six images for "church." Virtually all of them are corporate: the believer is in community. This is important to John's conception of the church (a term, however, he does not use). John "does not offer an individualistic spirituality to anyone who accepts his revelation" (Rossé: 44, 54–57). The image of vine and branches (John 15) and Jesus' prayer for unity (ch. 17) view believers as personally and corporately in communion with Jesus and God. Just as there is *one flock*, so there is *one shepherd*: the *Word*, Jesus Christ, Son of Man and Son of God, Lamb of God, *My Lord and my God* (20:28).

10:17-18 Jesus' Dying and Living Again for His Sheep, the Command of the Father

Miyazaki presents a chiastic structure for 10:17-18 (paired emphasis shows paired expressions):

A For this reason *the Father* loves me (v. 17a),
    B because *I lay down* my life in order to <u>take it up</u> again (v. 17b).
        C <u>No one</u> <u>takes it from</u> me, but *I lay it down* of my own accord (v. 18a).
    B´ <u>*I have power*</u> to *lay it down*, and <u>*I have power*</u> to <u>take it up</u> again (v. 18b-c).
A´ I have received this command from *my Father* (v. 18d).

When Jesus speaks of *laying down his life* for his sheep, he clarifies that his death is voluntary, not compelled (vv. 17b-18b). Jesus does not die as a victim of conspiracy or persecution; instead, he dies in a self-giving act (R. Brown 1966: 398). This unit clearly states that Jesus' death is for the purpose of resurrection, but many commentators weaken this notion. However, R. Brown (1966: 399) correctly warns against the weakening of the resurrection in verses 17 and 18: "This is a failure to understand that in NT thought the resurrection is not a circumstance that follows the death of Jesus but the essential completion of the death of Jesus. . . . So resurrection is truly the purpose of his death."

Some interpreters stress that Jesus earns the favor of God (v. 17a) by his obedience to the Father's commandment (v. 18c; Burge 2000: 292). "Obedience can be an expression of honor, so that honoring one's father means doing what he asks" (Koester 2008: 50). Indeed, Jesus does what the Father commands. However, Jesus does not need to win the Father's love because Jesus is already in unique intimate relationship with the Father: *As the Father has loved [agapaō] me, so I have loved [agapaō] you; abide in my love [agapē]. If you keep my commandments [entolē], you will abide in my love [agapē], just as I have kept my Father's commandments [entolē] and abide in his love [agapē]* (15:9-10, cf. 13:34-35, 15:12-17). Raymond Brown (1966: 399) rightly describes 10:17-18 as a "bond of love" rather than "earning the love" of the Father.

The Jews' Response 10:19-21

The Jews again fail to recognize the message of Jesus, and a division occurs. Some say Jesus is demon-possessed (v. 20). This accusation appeared before (7:20, 8:48). These references allude to Jesus' death and Jewish conspiracy (7:19; 8:44).

In biblical times people thought that suicidal acts were caused by demons. In the Synoptic Gospels a possessed man was driven into fire and water by a demon (Matt 17:15). Jesus' voluntary death, however, is distinctively different from suicide. His death is a life-giving act for others (John 10:10), for the purpose of resurrection (vv. 17-18), in the will of God (v. 18), out of love (v. 17).

Time and Location of Discourse: Feast of Dedication 10:22-23

These verses register a change in time and location, but the following verses continue the sheep-shepherd theme, focusing now on the christological questioning of Jesus by the Jews. The trial contin-

ues. The new season is winter (December), when the Feast of
Hanukkah occurs. Jesus is again *in the temple, walking . . . in the portico
of Solomon.*

The Feast of Dedication, Hanukkah, is the fourth feast story in
this long feast narrative unit (chs. 5–10). This feast originated in 164
BC. With the conquest of Alexander the Great (332 BC in Palestine),
Greek influence spread rapidly among Jews (Burge 2000: 288). When
one of Alexander's successors, Antiochus IV Epiphanes, came into
power in Syria in the second century BC, he expanded his authority
and rule, impinging upon Palestine (Moloney 1998: 313). Some
Jewish people, like the Hasidim, resisted Hellenistic influence.
Others, like Jason and Menelaus, assisted Greek soldiers in defiling
the Jewish temple by sacrificing pigs on the altar and erecting
images of pagan gods. After several attempts the Maccabees suc-
cessfully wrested the temple from Antiochus's control.

The Feast of Hanukkah celebrates the rededication of the temple
from defilement by Greek occupation, and it warns God's people
against corrupting outside influences. The Feast of Dedication commemorates the cleansing and rededication of the temple after Judas
Maccabeus succeeded in liberating the temple from the Syrians in
164 BC (1 Macc 4). Fuller political independence was achieved in 142
BC (1 Macc 13:41). This feast also honors the heroic figure Judas
Maccabeus (Burge 2000: 286–88).

In winter (John 10:22) a cold east wind often blows. Solomon's
colonnade (v. 23) provides protection from the wind and warmth.
When Judas gained control of the temple in 164 BC, the people celebrated the victory with many lights throughout the courts, including Solomon's portico (for history of origin, see Keener: 1.823).
Hence the festival's light symbolism links it to the earlier Feast of
Tabernacles; chapters 7–10 cohere as one long unit, even though
other divisional markers within these chapters are evident.

Since this is an extrabiblical feast and not a pilgrimage feast,
some scholars regard the feast as less important than other feasts in
John (Keener: 1.832). But like Passover and Tabernacles (Sukkoth),
the feast extended for seven days, a significant time period for
Jesus' ministry. At this feast Jesus reveals more fully his identity
claim: *I and the Father are one* (v. 30 NIV, RSV). The passage locates
this christological claim *in the temple,* which during the Maccabean
period was most important to Judaism. The identity of *the Jews,* on
one level at least, is as "temple keepers." In John 10 Jesus indicts the
temple leaders as false shepherds. Hence Hanukkah plays a significant role in John's Gospel. Whatever view one adopts regarding the

structural markers and sectional breaks, the narrative depicts Tabernacles as blending into Dedication [*Unsettled Matters, p. 534*], both celebrating God's gracious provisions for God's people.

The Jews' Key Question: Jesus' Answer 10:24-30

10:24 The Jews: *Are You the Messiah?*

The Jews ask Jesus whether he is or is not the Christ. R. Brown (1966: 406) regards this question to be a reflection of the messianic expectation inherent to Hanukkah, which honors Judas Maccabeus as a deliverer of the nation. The association of a Davidic figure with the shepherd-leader in Ezekiel 34 and other OT texts may support this notion. Yet Ezekiel 34:24 refers not to a Davidic *messiah* but to *my servant David* as *prince among them.* John's Gospel appears careful not to link Jesus' unique sonship to the messianic "son of David" tradition (Howard-Brook 1994: 92), though it does affirm Jesus as King. But "son of David"? That's not good enough, as John 10:36 declares.

10:25 Jesus' Response: *My Works Testify to Me, but You Do Not Believe*

Here Jesus reiterates what he said earlier in 5:38, 40, 46. In 5:37b Jesus says, *You have never heard his voice*: the sheep know the shepherd's voice and follow him (10:4b). As in chapter 5 Jesus appeals to *his works* for belief, but just as they did not believe then, so again they do not believe. And here is the reason!

10:26 You Do Not Belong to My Sheep; Thus You Do Not Believe

Earlier, in 10:5, Jesus has said his sheep will not follow strangers because they do not know their voice. The obverse side of the coin in essence is "You who do not belong to my fold of sheep cannot believe my good shepherd claim or the other 'I AM' claims I have made." *Belonging* here is prior to *believing.* This is the reverse of what we might expect (in John 3 *believing* seems to be the entrance requirement). *Belonging* reflects the Johannine community's sense of necessary boundaries and perhaps provides a rationale for why opponents of their belief cannot come to belief. In short, the opponents are not willing to risk their lives, even unto death, with identifying themselves as members of this community. It also reflects the truth of 7:17, *Anyone who resolves to do the will of God will know whether the teaching is from God or whether I am speaking on my own.* In John, knowing and believing, often synonymous, are both dependent on commitment and obedience. Identifying with Jesus' sheep-fold opens the eyes (ch. 9!) to see and believe.

10:27-29 Jesus and His Sheep: They Hear and Know; Their Gift and Security

Both the first and last phrases of verses 27-29, *My sheep hear my voice. . . . No one will snatch them out of my hand*, echo Psalm 95:7 (94:7 LXX). John's first phrase echoes the end of verse 7, "O that today you would listen to his voice!" and its preceding phrase, "the sheep of his hand" (Keener: 1.825). John 10:1, 8, (10), speak of "thiefs and robbers" (RSV; cf. "wolf" in v. 12) seeking to seize the sheep. Hence the security of the sheep is strategic. Both Jesus and his Father guarantee the security of the sheep that belong to Jesus' fold (vv. 28-29). This contrasts with those who do not belong. Verse 27 affirms, *My sheep hear my voice. I know them, and they follow me.* The first and third phrases of verse 27 describe the *hearing* and *following*, recapitulating emphases in verses 2-5. The middle phrase repeats verse 14b.

Miyazaki diagrams the flow of thought in verses 28-29 as follows:

A *I give them eternal life, and they will never perish* (v. 28a).
    B <u>*No one will snatch them out of my hand*</u> (v. 28b).
A´ *What my Father has given me is greater than all else* (v. 29a),
    B´ *and* <u>*no one can snatch it out of the Father's hand*</u> (v. 29b).

The A and A´ lines specify what Jesus gives the sheep and what the Father has given to Jesus (for a discussion of the four textual variants, see Schnackenburg: 2.307–08). Similarly lines B and B´ specify first that no one will snatch sheep out of Jesus' hand, and second that no one can snatch sheep from the Father's hand. This parallelism "underscores the fact that Jesus and God do the same work: what is true of the work of one is true of the work of the other" (O'Day 1995: 676–77; Burer). Hence the climactic declaration in 10:30: the oneness of Jesus and the Father. Like the Father, Jesus holds the sheep of his flock in his hands (cf. Rev 1:16).

While these verses are used to bolster the eternal security doctrine, that is not the intent of the passage, at least not in the way that teaching has been construed. As believers in and followers of Jesus, we are eternally secure in his hands (cf. 1 John 3:18-24). If we truly belong to the flock, we will remain secure (1 John 2:19-20). But 1 John indicates that some who were with the flock left (2:19) and then says, "They did not belong to us" (see McDermond: 146–49).

James 5:19-20 indicates that it is possible to wander from the truth, leave the flock, and also to be restored to the flock through confession of sin. On balance, we do not doubt Jesus' and the Father's keeping power, nor do we underestimate the allurement of the world to draw us away. We dare not presume upon this assurance or devalue the seriousness of sin, from which none is exempt, lest we wander from the truth and jeopardize our *belonging* to the flock.

It is not clear how Judas is to be understood in relation to this strong keeping power of Jesus and the Father. John's Gospel seems to regard his sorrowful end as preordained (6:70-71), yet Jesus shares the bread and cup with him (13:26-30). Oddly, in 18:2-9, where the evangelist recounts Judas's action of handing Jesus over to the authorities, he cites a quotation, *I did not lose a single one of those whom you gave me*, which alludes to 10:28-29. The quotation is applied to the eleven after Jesus turns himself over and urges the soldiers to let his followers go free. There is no easy resolution to these dual emphases of the flock's security and Judas's status. Between his exposition of John 9 and 10 Schnackenburg (2.260-74) has a lengthy excursus on the relation of personal choice to divine predestination, reflecting the difficulties raised by these twin emphases in John (see also Kysar 2005: 45-52, with summary chart on 52).

10:30 The Father and I Are One

Flowing from statement(s) in B and B´ above asserting that *no one will/can snatch them from my* [or] . . . *the Father's hand*, Jesus' claim here stresses first of all functional unity (cf. v. 37). Jesus' and the Father's keeping power are one. This claim, *I and the Father are one*, may be used to bolster later trinitarian theology, which emphasizes the unity/oneness of the Father, Son, and Spirit. It also affirms the monotheistic Jewish Shema confession (Keener: 1.826). The emphasis that *my sheep hear my voice* (v. 27) recurs often in the narrative (10:3, 4, 5, 16, 27; cf. 14, 15) and conceptually corresponds to "Hear, O Israel" (Deut 6:4). *Hearing* permeates this chapter, as *seeing* does in chapter 9. These twin emphases from Isaiah 6:9 appear often in the NT (see TBC for John 12).

The central confession of the Shema is the oneness of God, "Hear, O Israel: The Lord our God, the Lord is one" (Deut 6:4 NIV, RSV). Hanukkah is a rededication of the temple to the God of Israel, cleansing and sanctifying it for the Lord God. The verb in 10:30 for the *I AM* (*egō eimi*) claim is plural: *I and the Father are one* [*egō kai ho patēr hen esmen*]. Jesus claims for himself the *I AM* meaning: *I and the Father are one* (NIV, RSV). This word is Jesus' clearest statement of self-identification (which seems to verify ironically the Jews' accusation in 5:18). Keener points out that since *one* is neuter, the likely meaning is "identity of purpose rather than identity of person" (1.826; Keener cites Borchert: 341). Even so, the phrase recalls the Gospel's first sentence, *In the beginning was the Word, and the Word was with God, and the Word was God* (1:1). Purpose and person blend in John. No wonder this claim impels the Jews to grab stones! (10:31; see TBC; the essay "Trinity in John"[w]).

Moreover, the juxtaposition of the phrases *one flock, one shepherd* (v. 16) and *the Father and I are one* (v. 30) is significant, as shown in the parallelism of verses 26-30. R. Brown (1966: 407–8) says that the Father and the Son bind people to themselves as one: Jesus prayed to the Father *so that they* [his followers] *may be one, as we are one* (17:11, 22b). Indeed, the declaration *The Father and I are one* has multiple layers of profound meaning. Originally the self-identifying *I AM* phrase was used for the Lord (Exod 3:14; Isa 42:8; chs. 43-46). Jesus' *I am* (with predicate) claims plus his absolute *I AM* assertions (of which I count seven to nine each) link Jesus' identity to the Lord in OT usage *["I AM," p. 518]*.

The Jews and Jesus in Physical and Verbal Altercation 10:31-39

10:31-33 The Jews Attempt to Stone Jesus

This is the second time (8:59) the Jews aim to stone Jesus. It comes after Jesus' startling declaration of his identity through his works that unites him to his Father. Jesus' response is calculated to stall for time and make them think, even just a little. He points again to *his works*, and asks, *For which of these are you going to stone me?* The Jews are ready with a response. They shift the "crime" from works to his word, accusing him of blasphemy. Why? *Because*, they say, *you, though only a human being, are making yourself God.* This replays 5:17-18, implied in 8:57-58 also. Now clearly stated, the crime is *blasphemy* (cf. Mark 14:58-64 par.).

10:34-36 Jesus Appeals to Scripture with Regard to His Sonship and Consecration

Jesus knows his Scripture well. As Howard-Brook aptly puts it, "In the heat of the moment, Jesus coolly gives them . . . an exegetical challenge as clever as that of any Pharisaic rabbi" (1994: 216). Psalm 82 is rather obscure, not well known. Verse 6 is set in the context of God's judging the nations' gods for not judging rightly because they do not deal justly with the weak, the orphan, the lowly, and the destitute. Howard-Brook insightfully comments:

> The psalm offers the same condemnation of Israel's bad judges [their gods] as Jesus does of bad shepherds, and in imagery fitting easily within the Johannine worldviews. Those who exercised the power of God's Law are acting as gods, yet they will "die like mortals." At the moment when Jesus is threatened with death for apparently claiming to be more than a mortal, he invokes a psalm calculated to remind these would-be judges of their own mortality! (1994: 246)

This interpretation assumes that the psalm is addressed to Israel's judges (representing Israel) who act as gods in their legal decisions. But in view of "the divine council" setting in 82:1a and 8 the psalm addresses the gods of the nations, similar to the way the major prophets direct extended oracles to the nations. In pagan nations, the ruling monarchs were often considered divine. But *the word of God* regarding these *gods* is they will *die like mortals.* The link between the foreign gods and Jesus' accusers diagnoses their moral condition: "They have neither knowledge nor understanding, they walk around in darkness" (Ps 82:5a-b; cf. Isa 44). Recall John 10:6: *They did not understand.* They remain blind (John 9:39, 41).

Jesus' response (10:34-37) is closely argued:

> *Is it not written in your law, "I said, you are gods"? If those to whom the word of God came were called "gods"—and the scripture cannot be annulled—can you say that the one whom the Father has sanctified and sent into the world is blaspheming because I said, "I am God's Son"? If I am not doing the works of my Father, then do not believe me.*

Jesus blends three strands in his defense: an inviolable Scripture statement in which national leaders are called *gods* (*major* claim); the fact of Jesus' special relation to and commission from God—thus the basis for his claim to be *God's Son* (*diminutive claim* for his status); and then an "out" for the accusers by stating negatively what he stated positively earlier in his debates with his accusers in this long, hot trial: "If you *judge* my works not to be of my Father, then do not believe me. But before you make up your mind, just remember God's judgment of the gods in the psalm." Jesus' response stuns enough to give him more time to state his case.

10:38 Further Homily on His Works and Union with the Father

Jesus now turns the argument in his favor, assuming that they— now *stunned*—just might allow the caveat that his works are of the

Father. If so, you do not need to believe my claims about who *I AM*—just *believe the works, so that you may know and understand that the Father is in me and I am in the Father*. From another angle, Jesus solicits their belief and deepens his claim. The mutuality of *the Father in me and I in the Father* states both the distinction and the inseparable union of Father and Son. This is vintage Johannine Christology and spirituality, the *mutual indwelling* of Father and Son (John 15, 17).

10:39 They Try to Arrest Jesus

They presumably are "the Jews" [*"The Jews," p. 520*]. Their effort to arrest him fails when he escapes *from their hands*. The reader wonders why and how Jesus manages this, now for the third time (see 7:32-46; 8:59). The answer is *My time has not yet come* (2:4).

Jesus Retreats; Hear Again John's Witness 10:40-42[w]

The Gospel evangelist intentionally links this last unit with the earlier ministry of John the Witness (1:19-36; 3:22-30; cf. Burge 2000: 298). *The place where John had been baptizing earlier* loops the reader back to where the story began. The phrase *across the Jordan* appears in 1:28 and 3:26, and now again (1:28 also specified *Bethany*). *Across the Jordan* thus provides an inclusio (envelope) that encapsulates the long narrative related to Jewish rituals and feasts (2:11–10:39). Yet there is another Passover to come (chs. 12–19). Chapter 11 is freestanding, a climactic sign anticipating Jesus' resurrection (ch. 20).

What is the significance of *he remained there*? It denotes a gap of time before the strategic *sign* in chapter 11. The reason for this is not only to escape from the Jews but also to time Jesus' next action, raising Lazarus.

Miyazaki outlines this short paragraph as a chiasm:

A *Many came to him, and they were saying* (Many came, 10:41a),
   B *"John performed no sign* (John's act, v. 41b),
   B´ *but everything that John said about this man was true"* (John's witness, v. 41c-d).
A´ *And many believed in him there* (Many believed, v. 42).

B and B´ make a parallel comparison: John's "act" and John's "witness." This comparison highlights John's significance. The chiasm's emphasis that people believe because of John's witness matches the description of John's role in the prologue: *He came for a witness, that he might witness concerning the Light, that all might believe through him* (1:7 AT). This reiteration of John's *witness* to Jesus as

Jesus' public ministry ends affirms that the voice and testimony of John ring true. John is truly a crucial witness, yet he remains *only* a witness. Believe in Jesus, therefore, as the true Revealer, the Son sent from the Father.

THE TEXT IN BIBLICAL CONTEXT

Shepherd and Sheep Imagery in Scripture[w]

Of the many connections to OT Scripture for shepherd and sheep imagery, Ezekiel 34 is the most extensive. See Lind's excellent treatment in *Ezekiel* (273–87), his TBC essay "Ezekiel 34 and John 10," and the TLC essay "A Shepherd Leadership." Shepherd leadership in Israel is not based on "violent power politics" (279).

More texts also merit mention. Israel's primary worship book, the Psalms, often employs shepherd-sheep imagery. Beautiful Psalm 23 portrays God as the model Good Shepherd who graciously and lavishly cares for God's people, the sheep. God provides green pasture and refreshing water for the sheep as they follow the shepherd (see James Waltner's BCBC exposition of this Psalm [127–33], and especially his TBC/TLC section "The Pervasive Shepherd Metaphor," 129–30). Other Psalm texts also inspire. Often used as a call to worship, Psalm 95:6-7a (KJV) says, "O come, let us worship and bow down: let us kneel before the Lord, our Maker. For he is our God; and we are the people of his pasture, and the sheep of his hand." Psalm 28:9, in the morning prayer from the Book of Common Prayer, petitions God, "O save your people, and bless their heritage; be their shepherd, and carry them forever" (here NRSV).

God as Shepherd, together with God as Father and the people as sheep, functions as a major motif in Matthew, in 2:6; 9:36; 10:6, 16; 15:24; 18:12-14; 25:32 (cf. 14:14; Swartley 2006a: 79–84; Yokota: 170–203). The union of these two images in John 10, with Jesus as Shepherd and God as his or *my Father*, is striking and suggests a theological similarity between John and Matthew (see diagram on Matthew in Swartley 2006a: 84). Peter, who received his commission from Jesus (John 21:15-19) to *feed my lambs/sheep*, utilizes the shepherd and sheep imagery in 1 Peter 2:25, "For you were going astray like sheep, but now you have returned to the shepherd and guardian of your souls." Again in 5:2-4, he exhorts the elders "to tend the flock of God that is in your charge" and "not lord it over those in your charge, but be examples to the flock" so that "when the chief shepherd appears, you will win the crown of glory that never fades away" (see E. Waltner's BCBC exposition: 158).

The oft-used benediction in Hebrews 13:20-21 also designates the "God of peace" as "the great Shepherd of the sheep" and like John 10 connects it to sacrificial language, "by the blood of the eternal covenant." This text in Hebrews links together "God of peace," "great Shepherd of the sheep," and "eternal covenant," reminiscent of Ezekiel 34, which links the promised "one shepherd, my servant David," with God's making "a covenant of peace" with the people (vv. 23-25). Ezekiel 34 concludes, "You are my sheep, the sheep of my pasture and I am your God, says the Lord God." Revelation 7:17 identifies "the Lamb at the center of the throne" as "their shepherd," who "will guide them to the springs of the water of life, and God will wipe away every tear from their eyes."

The image of gatekeeper in John 10 is employed in Mark 13:34// Luke 12:39 as a symbol of watchfulness and warning to the faith community to be always alert and expectant (R. Brown 1966: 392). See E. Waltner's TBC essay "Church Leadership as Shepherding" (166–67) for other pertinent NT texts (Acts 20:17, 28-29; implied in Luke 15:4-7; 19:10) and use of the shepherd image to describe leadership in the church.

John's Christology: Jesus as One with God the Father

On this topic see the exposition for 5:18 and the TLC section in the same chapter, "Jesus' Relationship to the Father." The Gospel abounds with a rich array of titles, with *Logos, Son of God, Son of Man, Lord,* and *I AM* outstanding [*Christology, p. 507*].

Though John's Christology is rich with many titles, "Son of David" is notably absent. Wayne Meeks's book title, *The Prophet-King* (1967), links John's view of kingship with the Moses and prophetic traditions in the OT, not the Davidic. Discussing numerous titles, Mealand identifies what he perceives as the major titles in the plot development, those with significance distinctive to John: *Son of Man* (associated with suffering and glorification); *Son of God, the Son* (overtones of royalty); God as *Father* and Jesus as *Son*; the *Logos with God and . . . was God* (*God* in 1:18 implies both sonship and *uniqueness*) (457–64). Mealand (464–65) links Jesus' *I AM* declarations to God's frequent announcements in Exodus and Isaiah: "I AM the Lord." This is a *major* christological feature of the Gospel.

We might ask why John is so distinctive in his christological portrait, in comparison to the Synoptic Gospels. More than one factor plays into the answer. First, the Johannine community's experience dates from the late first century: it establishes a distinctive identity within Judaism and perhaps also apart from Judaism. A second is the need for the believers to know Jesus as their Savior, King, Son of God, and Lord, in distinction from and in contrast to emperors who claimed the same titles. Jesus as the great *I AM* responds to basic human needs (bread, water, life, truth) that emperors promised to provide, but at the cost of violent rule.

In addition to these socioreligious and political factors is the importance of worship—not worship of the emperor, but of their Savior, Lord, and God. Oscar Cullmann (1953) rightly proposes this angle of approach, perceiving in John the lens of worship (see also Swartley 2007: 227–28, 230–35). In this regard John's Gospel shares a trait in common with Revelation (Swartley 2006a: 339–55, esp. 341n57; 2007: 239–62). Mary's apostolic announcement, *I have seen the Lord* (20:18), and Thomas's confessional exclamation, *My Lord and my God!* (20:28), say it all.

THE TEXT IN THE LIFE OF THE CHURCH

Shepherd and Sheep

Several second-century writers employ the shepherd metaphor. In the *Martyrdom of Polycarp*, the author (the church at Smyrna writing to all believers) claims that the martyred Polycarp, bishop of Smyrna, is now blessing the Lord as "the Shepherd of the . . . church" (19.2). Hermas, in his lengthy work, *The Shepherd*, features Jesus as Shepherd.

John 10:27-28 is frequently cited in the *Martyrs Mirror* by Anabaptists as they affirm their identity: *My sheep hear my voice. I know them, and they follow me.* They gain assurance of being safely in their shepherd's protecting arms, out of which they cannot be snatched (van Braght: 37, 422, 453, 513, 537, 604, 648, 820 / 475, 689, 743, 822).

This frequent use of shepherd and sheep imagery in Anabaptism is closely related to their understanding of discipleship. Discipleship elements appear in Howard-Brook's chiasms for 10:1-5 and 7-10. In each the central theme is "open, listen, call, lead out" (v. 3) and *I am the door. Anyone entering through me will be saved* (v. 9 AT). The center of each chiasm is attentive devotion to the shepherd and willingness to go out under the shepherd's direction. The "going out" linked with verse 9 entails mission, since others are invited to come in through the door, Jesus the Shepherd true. As later verses indicate, this shepherd lays down his life for the sheep. Following the true shepherd is a metaphor for discipleship, hearing the voice of the shepherd, the shepherd's call, and then going out to welcome others to come into this sheepfold (10:16). Discipleship is rooted in relation to and obedience to the shepherd and in the commissioning of the shepherd, which directs the sheep in their following.

Abundant Life

A Google search for *life abundant* or *abundant life* turns up millions of entries. On Amazon.com a similar search turns up thousands of book titles. Clearly this winsome, inviting phrase has not escaped the commercial wizardry of our culture. Few of Amazon's entries have any connection to Jesus or John 10:10. It appears that *abundant life* connects to a deep yearning within, to something missing in our culture. Advertisers know this and thus pander to that deep human desire and need. The book titles range from feminist theological concerns to wealth to biography to homeschooling. These titles cater to the hungers and thirsts of our culture . . . but they point in the wrong direction. I wonder how often pastors preach on this text and point to Jesus as the true source of abundant life. Pastor, this is your challenge.

The Shepherd True

The music of the church is rich with the shepherd metaphor. One of the oldest hymns in *Hymnal: A Worship Book* comes from Clement of Alexandria, from the late second century. Titled "Shepherd of Tender Youth" (#480), it begins, "Shepherd of tender youth, guiding, in love and truth, through unknown ways."

A nurturing prayer reading is "Loving Shepherd" (*Sing the Story*, #152). Also, "I Will Come to You in the Silence" (*Sing the Story*, #49) echoes John 10:2 / Isaiah 43:1: "I call you each by name."

John 11–12

Culmination of Jesus' Public Ministry

OVERVIEW[w]

These two chapters culminate Jesus' claims about his person through sign and word; they also anticipate the future. Thomas's resigned word of fate (11:16) strikes a motif that marks the journey ahead. Jesus' friendship with those whom he loves (the Bethany three) anticipates the intimacy of his farewell discourse. Anticipating his raising Lazarus from the dead, Jesus speaks his climactic *I AM* claim to Martha, *I am the resurrection and the life* (11:25). This stunning claim, made good by Jesus' raising Lazarus, catalyzes the chief priests and Pharisees to hold a special meeting of the *council* (Sanhedrin) to plot Jesus' demise. The Lazarus narrative of 11:1–12:11 reflects the Passover theme, "through death to life." The discourse and sign in chapter 11 dramatize Passover.

Jesus' great sign generates a popular response of such proportion that the religious leaders perceive him to be a threat to the nation's political security (11:48). Unless Jesus is stopped, the populace will embrace Jesus as king, causing a messianic uprising that will galvanize Roman troops into action to crush what they perceive as political rebellion. They will come and destroy our temple (*our holy place and our nation*, v. 48; echoing 2:19-22), the symbol of

---

w   Where the superscript w occurs after headings, please see the commentary's online Web Supplement for additional material. Go to: http://www.heraldpress.com/bcbc/john.

Judaism's national life and tenuous freedom. Hence the leaders heed Caiaphas's advice that *it is better for you to have one man die for the people than to have the whole nation destroyed* (11:50). The evangelist interprets this in accord with God's purpose: Jesus *was about to die for the nation, and for not the nation only, but to gather into one the dispersed children of God* (11:51c-52). The leaders plot Jesus' death (11:51-53, 55-57; 12:10-11).

Chapter 12 contains five portions, each signaling culmination. In the first, Mary anoints Jesus' feet for his anticipated burial, continuing the narrative of chapter 11. The characters are the same: Martha, Mary, and Lazarus. Several units appear in chapter 12:

- Mary anoints the feet of Jesus, for his burial (12:1-8).

- The chief priests plot against Lazarus (12:9-11)

- Palm Sunday people laud Jesus' royalty (12:12-19).

- Greeks come to see Jesus, prompting the hour's arrival: *My hour has come* (12:20-26).

- Jesus briefly struggles as he faces his imminent death (12:27-36a).

- Jesus and the author-narrator provide final interpretation of Jesus' public ministry and the people's responses (12:36b-50).

Themes and Motifs

Both chapters echo themes and motifs of earlier narratives. In 11:9-11 Jesus is again the *light of the world*, evoking chapters 8 and 9. In 11:37 some of the Jews hark back to Jesus' healing of the blind man, querying, *Could not he who opened the eyes of the blind man have kept this man from dying?* Similarly, in 12:9 the narrative refers back to the raising of Lazarus. Hence the chief priests plot to kill Lazarus (12:10). Why? Jesus' raising Lazarus has led many Jews to believe in Jesus (12:11).

Mary's anointing of Jesus together with Judas's response (12:5-6) announce that the passion has begun. Jesus' entry into Jerusalem is marked with all the trappings of royalty. Palm branches are strewn on the path to greet his royal debut. Outcries from messianic Psalm 118 proclaim Jesus *King of Israel!* And Jesus chooses a lowly colt in fulfillment of Zechariah 9:9, the context of which is ending warfare and commanding peace to the nations.

Most striking, Greeks come to see Jesus, and this prompts Jesus' startling response, *The hour has come for the Son of man to be glorified* (12:23). Jesus' declaration, *Now is the judgment of this world, now shall the ruler of this world be cast out* (12:31 RSV), is indeed climactic. Judgment culminates Jesus' claim that he has authority to judge (5:27; 8:16; cf. 3:19, 36). Jesus' claim, *I, when I am lifted up from the earth, will draw all people to myself* (12:32), echoes several themes running through chapters 3–10: *lifted up* and *glorified*. Jesus' words in 8:12 resound: *You are going to have the light just a little while longer. Walk while you have the light, before darkness overtakes you. . . . Put your trust in the light while you have it, so that you may become children of light* (12:35-36 NIV 1984).

Jesus' Call to Believe

John's citation of two Isaiah texts in 12:38-41 emphasizes *revelation, blindness, seeing,* and *healing* (salvation). Jesus' final words reiterate his call to believe. He has come into the world as the light—coming not to judge, but to save. He grants eternal life and all his words and works accord with what the Father commanded (12:44-50).

With Jesus' last *sign* in chapter 11, the long string of believing responses (2:11, 23; 4:39, 41, 50, 53; 6:69; 8:30; 9:38; 10:42) and unbelieving responses (2:24-25; 5:41; 6:64; 7:33, 45; 8:45, 48; 10:19) come to a head (11:45; 12:11 contrasts with 11:55; 12:42 contrasts with 12:37-39). No further references to *many believed* or *they did not believe* occur. The signs are done, the die is cast. The Son of Man will soon be lifted up—by the "powers" from below and the Power from above!

John 11:1–12:11

Jesus' Climactic Sign: Lazarus's Death, Raising, and Aftermath

PREVIEW

In 1957 a minister in the Shenandoah Valley close to Harrisonburg, Virginia, had a vision and believed there would be a resurrection of one of his church saints on a certain date. The expected miracle was heralded on local news media, and a number of believers went to see the miracle at the announced morning and time. But, alas, no resurrection occurred, and the minister and his followers were greatly disappointed. In John 11 Mary says that if Jesus had come earlier, the ill Lazarus would not have died. But neither she nor Martha nor anyone except Jesus expected a man to rise who was already dead for four days. But with Jesus, watch out! Miracles occur.

Jesus' raising of Lazarus is the Gospel's climactic sign. It culminates the crisis (*krisis*) of John's Gospel. The *signs* elicit some kind of response—either belief or unbelief. Jesus' miracle of raising the dead Lazarus in John 11 prefigures his own future: death and resurrection. With the new *Bethany* setting in 10:40 (the Bethany beyond the Jordan; recall 1:28), Jesus interacts no longer with *the Jews*, but with Jewish believers. Jesus dialogues with his disciples and with Martha preceding the sign. The dialogues interpret the sign. Jesus interacts not with the people at large—though their presence is noted—but with his inner groups, the Bethany family

273

(the Bethany two miles from Jerusalem) and his disciples (see Preview of 12:12-50).

Two episodes precede Jesus' great miracle and two follow. Once the problem of Lazarus's illness is described, Jesus interacts with his disciples and then with Martha. Though Jesus wants to meet Mary—she does speak to him and weep—Jesus does not speak to her. Rather, he weeps with her and the Jews who have come to comfort her.

After the miracle the narrative shifts to the problem this miracle poses for the authorities. Many of the Jews believe (v. 45), but some inform the authorities (v. 46). Jesus' miracle provokes fear among *the Jews*, sealing his cross destiny *["The Jews," p. 520]*. Which side does one take in this drama? In 11:37 some Jews query, *Could not he who opened the eyes of the blind man have kept this man from dying?* Jesus' sign galvanizes the opposition. The authorities know (vv. 46-48) that they must plot to kill Jesus. The narrative therefore shifts to an extended description of the authorities' conniving how to save their "holy place" from destruction. They fear Jesus' miracle power will arouse a Roman crackdown on the popular support of Jesus as a messianic claimant.

The final event of this unit is located in the home of the raised Lazarus and Martha and Mary. In this vignette Mary is the lead character, anointing Jesus' feet out of her great devotion. Judas's negative response is sandwiched between three emotionally moving exchanges: Mary and Jesus; Jesus and Judas; and Jesus and Mary; with Jesus' own final word forecasting his imminent death. Finally, in 12:9-11 Jesus faces accountability to the authorities for Lazarus being alive!

Some key questions arise in this Bethany narrative. *Lord, he whom you love is ill* (v. 3). The word *love* may anticipate the figure who first appears two chapters later, *the disciple whom Jesus loved* (13:23). What relationship does Lazarus have to the Gospel's authorship, since the beloved disciple is linked to the Gospel's authorship (19:35; 21:24)? These questions mystify *[Beloved Disciple, p. 505]*.

Jesus' self-disclosure to Martha (11:25-26), *I am the resurrection and the life,* followed by her confession, *Lord, I believe that you are the Messiah, the Son of God, the one coming into the world* (v. 27), reaches a revelatory apex, both in Jesus' self-disclosure of his divine personhood and power and in the human perception of Jesus' christological identity. Martha's confession expresses the stated purpose of the Gospel (20:31); the belief to which she witnesses in her confession is most significant. The earlier Samaritan woman's confession, now supplemented and extended by Martha's confession, are high points in the unfolding Christology of the Gospel. Both astounding perceptions of Jesus' identity are from women. This raises intriguing questions. What status do women have in the community? Does this community have female leadership, or is the Gospel mustering support for this reality? Or does this simply reflect the historical reality of Jesus' ministry [Women, p. 536]?

This climactic sign-narrative continues earlier themes. When Jesus hears that Lazarus is ill, he says, *It is for God's glory, so that the Son of God may be glorified through it* (11:4). The Jews try to stone Jesus (v. 8), echoing 8:59 and 10:31. And in 11:9-11 Jesus is again the light of the world, carrying forward emphases of chapters 8–9.

OUTLINE

Lazarus's Death, the Problem, 11:1-16
Jesus' Miracle, the Answer, 11:17-44
The Jews' Reactions, 11:45-46
Caiaphas's Role as the Council Plots Strategy, 11:47-57
Mary Anoints Jesus at Bethany, 12:1-8
The Consequence of Lazarus's Raising, 12:9-11

EXPLANATORY NOTES

Lazarus's Death, the Problem 11:1-16

11:1-6 Setting and Characters

The location and setting is Bethany—not the one in Perea, across the Jordan, but the Bethany just two miles outside Jerusalem (v. 18). Jesus' three friends—Mary, her sister Martha, and Lazarus, whom Jesus loves—live there. In verse 2 the narrator points ahead to what happens in 12:1-8, even using past tense (aorist) participles *anointed* and *wiped* (Moloney 1998: 325). This proleptic technique appeared earlier, when Andrew was introduced as Simon's brother before the narrative introduces Simon, whom Jesus names Peter (1:40-42). This indicates that the names of these people were well known to the first-century readers, from oral tradition and teaching and preaching at Lord's Day gatherings (O'Day 1995: 685). After verse 2 Martha carries the primary role in chapter 11, while Mary does in 12:1-8. The *sisters* send the news of Lazarus's illness and request: *Lord, he whom you love is ill* (v. 3). They expect Jesus will come.

Jesus' response in verse 4 is not pastoral consolation. Rather, it turns tragedy into an opportunity for triumph. Saying the illness is not unto death, Jesus gives his disciples hope, however briefly. He announces to them that Lazarus has *fallen asleep* (v. 11). Since sleep may be either literal or a euphemism for death, misunderstanding ensues. Then Jesus speaks prophetically, announcing the significance of Lazarus's—and his own—death: *This illness . . . is for the glory of God, so that the Son of God may be glorified by means of it* (v. 4 RSV). Striking is the christological claim that Jesus participates in God's identity: what glorifies God also glorifies the Son of God (v. 4d). The glory (*doxa*) theme in the prologue (1:14) and at his first sign in Cana (2:11) now moves again into narrative focus. God's glory shines in Jesus' teaching and deeds (5:41, 44; 7:17-18; 8:50, 54). Newbigin (140) comments, "From now on the theme of glory will move more and more into the foreground (e.g., 12:16, 23, 28, 41)."

Verse 5, short but sweet, tells of Jesus' loving relationship with this family. While the Greek *phileō* is used in verse 3 for Lazarus, and the Greek *agapaō* is used in verse 5 for all three family members, distinction in meaning is debatable. O'Day (1998: 686) sees no distinction, but see the comments on 21:15-19.

In light of Jesus' endearment to this family, one would think Jesus would go immediately, but he delays for two more days (v. 6). Does this prefigure Jesus' time in the tomb, waiting for God to resurrect him on the third day? Later we learn that Lazarus has been in the tomb four days (v. 17). Jesus' delay likely occurs to guard against any question as to whether Lazarus is dead. Jesus wants no easy out for those inclined to disbelieve. He knows that going to Jerusalem—especially after raising his dear friend—will lead to a fatal clash with the Jerusalem authorities. He counts the cost. Jesus' behavior is determined by the hour his Father has set for him.

11:7-16 Exchanges Between Jesus and His Disciples

After two days of delay, Jesus announces his decision to go to Bethany, ending his retreat across the Jordan (10:40). The disciples are perplexed and upset: they know that Jesus is putting his life on the line. They know Jesus' past conflicts with the authorities and their efforts to stone him (8:59; 10:31). Addressing him as *Rabbi*, the disciples say bluntly, *You know what the Jews are up to! Do you want to go and get killed?* (v. 8 AT). Jesus responds in *time* language, referring to day and night, which in turn signify his mission. *Day* contrasts to the *night* actions of stumbling and unbelief (vv. 9-10), which may allude to Jeremiah 13:16, "Give glory to the Lord your God, before he brings darkness, and before your feet stumble." Within the Gospel narrative it carries forward his claim in John 8:12, *I am the light of the world. Whoever follows me will never walk in darkness, but will have the light of life.*

In the next verses (11-15), Jesus repeats his resolve to go and says that Lazarus has *fallen asleep* (v. 11; the Greek *koimaō* may mean either *fall asleep* or *die*, as in 1 Thess 4:13-14; cf. KJV and NRSV). The disciples misunderstand the double meaning of *koimaō*, so they say, *He will recover*, thinking he will rejuvenate by sleeping (v. 12 RSV). So Jesus puts it baldly: *Lazarus is dead* (v. 14b). Jesus then declares a purpose, justifying his delay: *For your sake I am glad I was not there, so that you may believe. But let us go to him* (v. 15). A shocker is in this verse. Jesus says, *For your sake I am glad* (John's oft-used *chairō, rejoice*) that Lazarus is dead. Jesus' *rejoicing* is modified by the phrase *for your sake*, as if to say, *He is dead in order that I might show you something marvelous, and for that I am glad!* (AT). The disciples are perplexed. They know Jesus loves Lazarus. Why then Jesus' cold response to his death?

Thomas, the Twin (in Aramaic, Didymus), finally says resignedly, *Let us also go, that we may die with him* (v. 16). Thomas's response is ironic for what he says appears to be out of touch. But he is more in touch than he knows. Duke (59) asks, "Does this previously invisible character have a deep sense of understanding of the call of discipleship, or is he simply 'one with an eye for the grim facts, but no perception of glory'?" The narrative says nothing to explain this perplexing word. We are left with suspense, puzzlement, and curiosity as to what will happen next. Thomas's dour comment prepares us for Caiaphas's "solution" (v. 50)!

In church tradition the notion arose—especially in the East—that Thomas was a twin to Jesus. Quite likely their fates in martyrdom contributed to this belief in the church. Howard-Brook (1994: 259) suggests we read the Lazarus story from a martyr perspective since, based on his chiastic analysis of the 10:40–12:11 segment, "the raised Lazarus . . . become[s] the subject of the same murderous conspiracy as is Jesus" in the last verses of the unit, 12:9-10.

Jesus' Miracle, the Answer 11:17-44

11:17-27 Jesus and Martha[w]

The imminent astounding miracle has narrative anticipation. *Tomb* (v. 17) is the same word used in the plural earlier, in 5:28-29a, and translated *graves: Do not be astonished at this; for the hour is coming when all who are in their graves will hear his voice and will come out.* Further, what Jesus seeks to teach Martha also had precedent in

---

w   Where the superscript w occurs after headings, please see the commentary's online Web Supplement for additional material. Go to: http://www.heraldpress.com/bcbc/john.

earlier public discourse in Jerusalem: *Very truly, I tell you, the hour is coming, and is now here, when the dead will hear the voice of the Son of God, and those who hear will live. For just as the Father has life in himself, so he has granted the Son also to have life in himself* (5:25-26). The reader has been prepared for this greatest sign.

Mary stays home while Martha goes out to meet Jesus (v. 18). Mary's interaction with Jesus is deferred to verses 28-33a. Martha's bold initiative, together with her role and response, has prompted divergent perceptions among commentators. Some hedge or hesitate to affirm Martha's faith response as true Johannine faith (Burge 2000: 314; O'Day 2002: 87–88; Minear 1977: 119); a few denigrate Martha's faith confession (Moloney 1998: 328; more guardedly, Lee below). O'Day's hesitation (2002) comes with verses 39-40, where Martha protests Jesus' command to remove the stone and Jesus upbraids her, *Did I not tell you that if you believed, you would see the glory of God?* These verses can be viewed as putting Martha down, but they need not be read that way (and O'Day doesn't in 1995). Rather, they add suspense, intensifying the significance of the revelatory event. Jesus' statement is "an amalgam of his earlier words in vv. 4, 15, 25-26" (O'Day 1995: 691). It carries forward the narrative plot. Lee (1994: 205–6) regards Martha's faith as incomplete until after Jesus raises Lazarus. Martha and Mary are on a journey toward faith, culminating in 12:1-2. Thus although 11:27 represents incomplete and imperfect faith, chapter 12 shows Martha's full faith, *after* Jesus raises Lazarus. Martha and Mary host Jesus with devoted service in 12:1-3, 7-8, witnessing to their full faith—with the living Lazarus there!

Martha's faith response in verse 27 is certainly positive. Her initial statement indicates her openness to Jesus' unlimited power to solve this dilemma (vv. 21-22): *Lord, if you had been here, my brother would not have died. But even now I know that God will give you whatever you ask of him.* Jesus then says, *Your brother will rise again.* This affirms what Jesus taught in 5:25-29. She does not expect Lazarus's raising now but in the end-time resurrection. Jesus then challenges her to make later operative now. He asserts his sovereignty over the powers of death, even of dead Lazarus: *I am the resurrection and the life. Those who believe in me, even though they die, will live, and everyone who lives and believes in me will never die. Do you believe this?* Martha responds, *Yes, Lord, I believe that you are the Messiah, the Son of God, the one coming into the world.* Her *yes* affirms Jesus' saying; she confesses its logical implication.

Martha is not shifting the subject to a lesser statement of faith, but rather *grounding* her belief that Jesus can raise Lazarus *in her belief in Jesus as the Messiah and Son of God*, the stated purpose of the Gospel

(20:31). If Martha's confession were understood negatively, the author's purpose statement in 20:31 would express imperfect faith, an oxymoron most perplexing! Jewish Pharisaic hopes for the messiah included resurrection of the dead (Dan 12:2-3) *[Eternal Life, p. 513]*. Martha's confession is stronger than Peter's in Mark 8:27-30. It matches Matthew's version (16:16), which includes both "Messiah" and "Son of the living God." Martha's confession exemplifies the Johannine community's true faith, with a follow-up demonstration in 12:1-2. Esler and Piper (120), seeking to understand what the text would mean to believers in the Johannine community, express it well, "The confession of Martha is surely the confession of the true Johannine believer, and her actions in a challenging and perplexing situation depict obedience to the one whom she calls *Kyrie*, 'Lord.'" Conway concurs:

> Nowhere else in the Gospel does an individual character's confession conclude a conversation the way that Martha's does. The confessions of Nathanael (1:49), Peter (6:69), and Thomas (20:28) are all followed by some sort of reprimand by Jesus, and even the profession of faith by the formerly blind man (9:38) is followed by a judgment from Jesus. In contrast, Martha's confession is allowed to stand on its own. The only other place where this occurs is in 4:42 where the Samaritan villagers declare their understanding of Jesus as Savior of the World. (143)

Indeed, Martha's positive faith response is one with that of the Samaritan woman's and her villagers' confession, as well as with the later confession of Mary Magdalene in 20:18. All are fully positive. All also occur in the concluding chapters of the Gospels' three main structural divisions (chs. 1–4, 5–11 (12:8), 12–20). The christological clarity of Jesus' identity is carried by women's confessions. This structural pattern reflects the prominence of women's faith in the Johannine community *[Women, p. 536]*. Commentators demurring to Martha's confession are hesitant to own this stunning aspect of John's Gospel (see comments on ch. 20 with Mary Magdalene's role as first witness to Jesus' resurrection). Martha's *I have believed* (11:27 AT), which is formal confessional language, invites readers to confess the same. It is congruent with the Gospel's purpose (20:31).

Jesus' answer to Martha, *I am the resurrection and the life*, is most important as the climactic *I AM* claim of Jesus' public ministry. O'Day points out its double paradox (1995: 688; cf. Ridderbos: 396):

> the one who believes in me and dies → yet lives
> the one who lives and believes in me → never dies

Jesus' promise of resurrection means death has lost its power; eternal life (cf. John 3:15-17, 36; 5:26) is realized now *and* in the life to come. New life begins now; dying physically does not end this gift of life that extends eternally through Jesus' and God's resurrection power [*Eschatology, p. 512*] [*Eternal Life, p. 513*].

Jesus' teaching is visualized by Howard-Brook (1994: 256, adapted here) in chiastic analysis:

A MARTHA: *Lord, if you had been here . . .* (11:21-22)
   B MARTHA and *rise* (vv. 22-24)
      C JESUS: *I am the resurrection and the life* (vv. 25-27)
   B´ MARY and *rise* (vv. 28-31)
A´ MARY: *Lord, if you had been here . . .* (v. 32)

11:28-37 Jesus and Mary and the Jew[w]

Martha initiates Jesus' contact with Mary, saying, *The Teacher is here and is calling for you. Teacher* (or Rabbi) indicates Jesus' earlier relationship with the Bethany family. That Mary makes no comparable confession need not be viewed negatively, even though she blends with the Jews who had come to her house earlier to mourn with her (v. 19). The Jews follow her to meet Jesus.

Mary's response to Jesus shines: *falling down at his feet* (v. 32 AT), *weeping* (v. 33a), and confessing, *Lord, if you had been here, my brother would not have died.* Falling at Jesus' feet discloses her heart of devotion, recognizing Jesus' special identity. Mary *believes* Jesus could have healed her brother. Her weeping, however, indicates that she missed Jesus' *I AM* claim that Jesus has just disclosed to Martha. Only after her brother is restored to life does her action in 12:1-3 show complete faith and trust in Jesus.

Seeing Mary weeping, and the Jews who had come with her also weeping, Jesus is distraught in spirit. The Greek word (*embrimaomai*) translated by the NRSV as *greatly disturbed* (RSV, *deeply moved*) connotes some degree of anger. In secular Greek (as by Aeschylus) it denotes displeasure, expressed by an angry "snort." Psalm 7:11 (7:12, Aquila Gr.) and Isaiah 17:13 (Symmachus Gr.) employ the word in the sense of "indignant." When used with the dative and Jesus as the subject (Mark 1:43; Matt 9:30), the NRSV translates it as "sternly warned" or "ordered." The word reappears in John 11:38 as Jesus approaches the tomb. *Deeply moved* is inadequate. Some element of irritation or aggravation is present. The term is combined with *tarassō* (NRSV, *deeply moved*; RSV, *troubled*).

What causes this irritation? Four explanations have been given for Jesus' tears, which occur in the context of his angered and troubled spirit (Talbert: 174-75):

1. As a human, Jesus was simply grieved to tears.

2. Jesus is grieved over human sin or lack of faith.

3. Jesus experiences intense emotion in light of the situation, especially Mary's and the Jews' wailing and unbelief (the most common explanation).

4. John presents Jesus as a counter to the Stoic wise man, who never shows emotion.

Ridderbos (402–5) and R. Brown (1966: 435) suggest that Jesus' anger arises from facing Satan's grip over humanity through death.

In the thought sequence a straightforward answer is that Jesus is *disturbed in spirit* because of the disparity between the loud wailing (*klaiō*, v. 33) and his own confidence regarding the outcome of this situation. The verb near the end of verse 33 (*tarassō*) is best translated *troubled* (NIV, RSV) or *distressed*. Jesus then asks, *Where have you laid him?* They respond, *Lord, come and see.* Then Jesus himself begins to *weep*. But here the word used for Jesus' weeping is different from the one used for Mary's and the Jews' wailing. Jesus *weeps* (*dakryō*). It is the difference between loud wailing (v. 33) and silent weeping (v. 35). Talbert (175) explains the difference between the tears of Jesus and the wailing of Mary and mourners: "Jesus' tears are tears of sorrow; wailing signifies dejection without hope." Jesus' irritation and troubled spirit thus react to their hopeless dejection.

Lee makes a persuasive case in linking Jesus' *anger*, mentioned twice by the verb *embrimaomai* (vv. 33b, 38), to the rejection that follows in verses 46-53, since his anger sparks first in the context of the weeping and wailing, and second as he approaches the tomb. Lee (212) links Jesus' anger not to the wailing, his grieving at Lazarus's death, Mary's misunderstanding, or to Jewish unbelief in general, but to the specific rejection that will follow his raising of Lazarus: the rejection that impels the plot to kill him. The anger and troubled spirit segues to Jesus' passion and death. Jesus' *soul* is again *troubled* (*tarassō*) as he faces imminent death (12:27) and Judas's handing Jesus over to the authorities (13:21, 31).

Thus far in this story the Jews are portrayed in neutral terms. They make two responses: *See how he loved him!* And some say, *Could not he who opened the eyes of the blind man have kept this man from dying?* Both are true. The grammar of the question in Greek tilts toward a *yes* answer: Jesus could have prevented the death. But the larger purpose, that of manifesting Jesus' glory, is about to be revealed.

11:38-44 Jesus Raises Lazarus

As Jesus goes to the tomb, the narrator repeats that he is *deeply disturbed* (v. 38, *embrimaomai*, as in v. 33). Why? Certainly he is confident of the outcome, in light of verses 4, 15, and 40. Is it because he is facing down death? Or is it because the emotion of the episode and the wailing—an expression of unbelief—prompts an *upbraiding* spirit within him? Burge (2000: 318) says, "Jesus is angry at death itself and the devastation it brings." This explanation fits in part, but seems dissonant with his earlier confident responses. If Lee is correct, Jesus' own imminent passion prompts the emotion. As he comes to the tomb, he sees his own tomb! The narrative symbolizes Jesus' imminent passion. But why would Jesus feel anger at this point? Does Jesus groan with a snort of indignation at the prospect of his own death? Perhaps this is put too sharply, but if we allow for even a touch of this—and it can hardly be denied—then no longer can it be said that John's Jesus has no Gethsemane-type agony over his death, as Jesus does in the Synoptic Gospels. He does, here and in 12:27 and 13:21.

Whatever the answer, Jesus takes charge and commands that the stone be taken away. Martha protests, reminding Jesus of the stench since Lazarus has been in the tomb already four days. The *four days* is significant since it was commonly believed that the spirit may reenter the body at any time within the first three days after death, in which case the person could be resuscitated. After three days, return to life is possible only through raising from the dead. Jesus waits long enough so that the resuscitation time period has passed and all will know that what is about to happen is more than resuscitation. It is the miracle—a sign indeed—of Jesus' power over death!

Jesus responds to Martha by repeating the word he has given to the messengers who gave him the report of Lazarus's death: *Did I not tell you that if you believed, you would see the glory of God?* They then take the stone away, and Jesus prays aloud, looking upward: *Father, I thank you for having heard me. I knew that you always hear me, but I have said this for the sake of the crowd standing here, so that they may believe that you sent me* (vv. 41b-42). Jesus' prayer shows no lack of confidence in his Father's power to do what he is about to command, nor does he need special assurance from his Father to calm his troubled spirit. Rather, the axis of concern is *that they may believe that you sent me.* This indicates that the unbelief of those about him is what troubles him (Talbert's third option). He knows his disciples, who are *silent* onlookers for this entire scene, are lacking faith appropriate to the occasion. No one speaks up to express confidence that Jesus can solve the problem. The prayer is a public declaration of Jesus' identity with God in that he works what his Father works, giving life (5:25-26).

It happens with three words. Jesus commands in a loud voice, *Lazarus, come out!* The *dead man* comes out. Lest any doubt that this is a bona fide raising, the text says *dead man!* He comes out, appearing just as they have prepared him for burial: *his hands and feet bound with strips of cloth and his face wrapped in a cloth*, yet walking out of the tomb. Jesus commands, *Unbind him, and let him go.* That's it! New life it is—and trouble there will be (12:10-11)!

This story has numerous levels of meaning. On one level it is an astounding miracle, the greatest *sign.* On another, Jesus' manifest *glory* elicits *faith.* On another, it is proleptic of Jesus' resurrection. On another level, it elicits an existential encounter with this greatest sign: unbind *your* graveclothes of sin, fear, and death's power!

The Jews' Reactions 11:45-46

11:45-46 Many Jews Believe, but Some Report to the Pharisees

This extraordinary sign causes division in the crowd. *Many* believe, but *some* report the event to Pharisees, who apparently report it to other members of *the council*, the Sanhedrin Seventy (plus the high priest as chair), who call a special meeting to determine their course of action. Significantly, the *many* who believe are the Jews who came to mourn Lazarus's death. *Many* Jews are *not* opposing Jesus. We must not understand the Gospel's polemic against *the Jews* as referring to *all* Jews. The loved Bethany household and all the disciples, even Jesus, are also Jews! *["The Jews," p. 520].*

Caiaphas's Role as the Council Plots Strategy 11:47-57[w]

The rationale for keeping these verses together as one unit is that both verses 47 and 57 begin with *the chief priests and Pharisees,* even though for Stibbe (129) the unit is verses 45 to 54. The phrase provides matched bookends for the unit as it continues to verse 57.

11:47-48 The Council's Fear: The Romans Will Destroy[w]

The council's fear is palpable. The Romans will *destroy* the nation and its people if they let Jesus go on like this. Once before in John the people wanted to make Jesus king (6:15), but he fled to prevent it. Jesus has popular appeal. This time, as a result of Jesus' raising Lazarus, the rulers of this Jewish client state of the ruthless empire fear that Jesus' popular appeal through his *sign* miracles will lead the empire to intervene to prevent a feared populist coup. The immediate fear, however, arises from Jesus' undermining the authority of the Jewish leadership, even the council—with its tenuous coalition of the chief priests (largely Sadducees) and Pharisees. Any populist movement would threaten first their own authority, which in turn would then expose the nation's vulnerability to Rome's intent to keep all subject nations in tow by brutal force. The temple—the very symbol of fragile Jewish self-determination and religious identity—is at risk. Israel exists within a "delicate balance of power between Rome and Jewish political authorities" (Moloney 1998: 334). The Jerusalem authorities are running *scared*!

In this atmosphere of fear and desperation, the *high priest*, the symbolic head of Israel's covenant relation to the Lord God, offers a solution, proposing a plan that ironically expresses the heart of John's theology.

11:49-50 Caiaphas's Solution

Caiaphas plays a crucial role, not merely as high priest, but as high power within the temple hierarchy, the de facto ruling elite over the Jews, who are vassals under Roman rule. Caiaphas's perception and fear that the Roman army will come and destroy the nation shows more his political clout than his religious function. Some understanding of the Jewish vulnerability to Roman crackdown through Pilate, a scheming and unpredictably violent ruler, aids our grasp of just how strategic this "solution" is. Tom Thatcher has mined the political dimensions of John's Gospel. His insight is sharp and perceptive regarding Rome's constant power umbrella over Palestine.

Caiaphas's "solution" brings into focus "the three-headed dog of Rome" (Thatcher 2009: 11–17, 43–53). The "three heads" are first Caesar (Rome) with Pilate as his present local face: *the Romans will come*. Second, the cross is evoked in the counsel that *one man die for the people*. Third, the Jewish authorities, *the chief priests and the Pharisees* with Caiaphas, serve as the voice and accomplice of Caesar

(14). "John slays all three heads with the same narrative sword" (15). While Pilate is not mentioned in this episode, verse 48 infers that he will squelch any populist uprising. Jesus' imminent death on behalf of the nation and for others as well forespeaks cross. The chief priests—with emphasis on Caiaphas—and the Pharisees are the religious authorities. Perseverance against the beast that is ultimately doomed (12:31; 14:30; Rev 13, 18) defines John's view of the believers' relationship to the empire.

John's Christology presents Jesus in every way "superior to Caesar and his agents" (Thatcher 2009: 14). John's narrative sword strikes especially in this Caiaphas section and also in the trial narrative, with Pilate represented as more subtly shrewd and hostile than in the Synoptic Gospels. This point of view may strike the reader as dead wrong, especially if John has been perceived as apolitical, as a spiritual Gospel, or as only an evangelistic tract. Yet in chapters 2–11 some incidents are overtly political:

- Jesus confronts the authorities in the temple (2:13-22).

- The people want to make Jesus king (6:14-15).

- Jesus flees from hostile authorities who are trying to arrest and/or kill him (7:32, 45-52; 8:59; 10:39; 11:45-53).

A subtext permeating the Gospel is Jesus' control over successive waves of opposition. Jesus is not daunted, even before Pilate, where he questions the procedures against him several times, finally saying, *You would have no power over me unless it had been given you from above* (19:11).

The high priest that year, Caiaphas, knows the principle of offering one on behalf of the many. That is the annual task of the high priest: to present the blood of the animal sacrifices to the Lord by sprinkling it on the ark of the covenant, the mercy seat (*hilastērion*). With a straight course of logic, why not make this troublemaker a *sacrifice/scapegoat* so that the nation need not perish? Indeed, *It is better for you to have one man die for the people than to have the whole nation destroyed.* Caiaphas's word contains a key *fear* word, *destroy* (*apollymi*), applied to *this nation*.

The *substitution* element in this saying is motivated purely by concern for political security, voicing a widely accepted sad political maxim: "The sacrifice of an individual is never too high a price to pay for national security" (Dodd 1962: 138). Of all the people on the council, Caiaphas knows atonement theology. Its enactment is his job. In the next verses his solution becomes prophecy in the religious dimension of this solution.

The reasoning behind this solution is a classic biblical illustration of René Girard's explanation (112–24) of how escalating conflict
is resolved through channeled violence: choose a surrogate victim,
a scapegoat, to assuage the portending calamity—in this case a clash
of the empire with occupied Israel. Rather than risk the nation's
security, get rid of one who is enough like us to satisfy the powerful,
violence-hungry destruction machine threatening to attack us.
Jesus, a Jew, is one of us, but he is also different enough—he is a
miracle worker upsetting the loyalty of the people to our governance—so that he is readily and logically expendable. Hence, choose
this better option, *have one man die for the people*. It is transparent
political theory, practiced by this world's political leaders through
the centuries. Armies execute this procedure as a regular course of
action through CIA espionage and the secret sabotage of enemy
ranks. Thus politics justifies the use of violence to avert greater
violence. By its nature, political leadership usually pursues an ethic
fitting for "immoral society" encumbered with the responsibility of
making sure we and our nation survive (cf. Reinhold Niebuhr).

But is this the way of Jesus? Or does Jesus turn this logic and
course of action on its head by offering himself as Lamb to expose
and boycott the spiral of violence and bring the sacrificial scapegoat
system to its knees? Not all sacrifice is of the scapegoat type, as is
clear when Jesus voluntarily gives himself as sacrifice to end the
scapegoating. Even in his death Jesus and God are one, a deathblow
to any notion that Jesus' death witnesses to a violent God. Rather,
Jesus' death is God's sacrifice to and for us.

What happens here in Caiaphas's logic shapes the course of
action in the trial narrative (chs. 18–19). Indeed, Caiaphas's solution
is, ironically, prophecy. It confronts the reader with "the paradox of
Jesus' raising of Lazarus as the catalyst for his death sentence"
(O'Day 1995: 698). Even so, the authorities "are powerless in the
presence of the one who is the resurrection and the life" (699).
Caiaphas's political collusion with Rome is shocking. He is high
priest, representative of God to the nation, and representing the
nation to God. Jesus, God's viceroy on earth, is a profound, imminent threat to Caiaphas.

Reading the Gospel from the standpoint of AD 90, a painful
memory emerges. Twenty years earlier the vassal nation *did* perish.
The people were destroyed and scattered. The Romans did come
and destroy the nation, brutally, under Roman army generals Titus
and Vespasian, both of whom became emperors. In AD 71 they
marched captive Israelites through the streets of Rome, parading

them as vanquished victims. The scapegoat mechanism worked against the nation. Jerusalem, with its loved temple, became Rome's scapegoat to keep the peace of the empire. Caiaphas's solution evokes dual memories: prophecy of Jesus crucified and the tragic bloody history of Israel's national destruction.

11:51-52 Caiaphas's Solution, a Prophecy

That Caiaphas's solution is prophecy is irony of ironies. A high priest's prophesying fits Jewish tradition, which regards it as appropriate for a high priest to prophesy. It appears in a half-dozen citations from Philo and Josephus (see also Tosefta *Soṭah* 13.5–6; Dodd 1962: 138–40, citing A. Schlatter). The irony runs deep: the Lamb of God is sacrificed, but actually he sacrifices himself for the people. By being lifted up on the cross in death, God is glorified through an act of divine, selfless love that will draw all people to Jesus, to God (12:32).

This sequel to Jesus' raising of Lazarus plays a strategic role. It prepares for Jesus' own passion, death, and resurrection. The point of one man's dying for (*hyper*, in behalf of) the nation is Johannine atonement language (cf. 3:14; 12:32-33; "atoning sacrifice," *hilasmos*, occurs twice, in 1 John 2:2 and 4:10). The death of Jesus is thus not *for himself* but for others (Moloney 1998: 335). John the Witness introduces Jesus as *the Lamb of God who takes away the sin of the world!* (1:29, 36). The political (Caiaphas's solution) and the theological (John's theology) blend in this ironic manner.

The narrator's striking extension of this prophecy to *the dispersed children of God* fits Johannine theology. The chiastic center of the prologue (1:12) speaks of becoming *children of God*. The phrase *to gather into one* (11:52) pertains to the *other sheep that do not belong to this fold* (10:15-16) and anticipates Jesus' prayer *that all may be one* (17:21, 23). It may also symbolically correlate with the *gathering up* (*synagō*) of the twelve loaves left over in 6:13 (Dennis: 194). This gathering together *into one all the dispersed children of God* includes not only dispersed Israelites but also Gentile "God-fearers" and other Gentiles, an emphasis within some Jewish messianic anticipations. In the Gospel's setting of AD 90, the "'eschatological Israel' is the Church and thus the gathering here is the gathering of the Church" (Dennis: 194, citing Klaus Wengst, with support from J. Blank and from W. Meeks). While restoration of Israel's scattered sheep is here prophesied, the *gathering together* extends beyond Israel to include all of Jesus' followers, the expanding disciple band that Caiaphas seeks to dissolve. The good shepherd lays down his life for the sheep to bring together into one fold both Jewish and Gentile believers, faithful Israel's restoration and a "new creation."

11:53 All Agreed: Put One Man, Jesus, to Death

The council agrees to Caiaphas's solution: put Jesus to death. Next they must devise a plan that does not spark political protest or an uprising that defies the Sanhedrin's authority. They must pursue a plan that keeps the "peace" of the Pax Romana, a peace quite different from the peace Jesus promises to his disciples (14:27; 16:33; 20:19-23).

11:54 Jesus' Retreat to Ephraim near the Wilderness

Jesus hides to prevent the council from immediately fulfilling its decision. He goes to a little town named Ephraim (cf. the OT Ephron in 2 Chron 13:19), about a dozen miles north and slightly east of Jerusalem, an obscure town that readily provides a secure getaway (Burge 2000: 322–33). His disciples go with him. They *remain* there (again, *menō*). The Lazarus event and this retreat occur between the Festival of Dedication (10:22; December) and Passover (late March, early April). Some time now elapses.

11:55-57 Passover Near, Watch for Jesus

The clock keeps ticking. Passover is near. Jesus and his disciples, as observant Jews, will attend, though Jesus' popularity puts the security risk so high that some people wonder if he will appear. Many go up into the city before Passover to have ample time to undergo purification rites, so they, God's holy people, are ready to celebrate undefiled. They speculate on what will happen if Jesus comes, and are *asking one another as they stood in the temple, "What do you think? Surely he will not come to the festival, will he?"* (v. 56). The form of the question expects a negative answer. Conventional wisdom concludes that he will not come, that it is too dangerous. The chief priests and the Pharisees have put the people on alert to watch for him. They wish to execute the Sanhedrin's plan, just as they have precipitated it in the first place. With many people on the alert, the temple authorities hope to find and immediately arrest him, if he shows up. Jesus could stay in hiding, but six days before the festival, he ends his retreat.

Mary Anoints Jesus at Bethany 12:1-8

12:1-2 The Setting

This event continues from chapter 11, with Jesus again in the home of Martha, Mary, and Lazarus (until now Jesus was only on the way to their home [11:30]). Mary's anointing occurs six days before the Passover. The Gospel's festivals begin with *Passover near* (2:13), an unnamed feast (5:1), a second Passover (6:4), and now again, a *Passover near*. Other major festivals include Tabernacles (7:1–10:21) and Dedication (10:22-42). John 11 occurs between Dedication and Passover. Jesus dramatically transforms Passover. His Jerusalem ministry forms an inclusio:

Destroy this temple (2:19).
The whole nation [may be] destroyed (11:50).

Jesus and Caiaphas speak similarly, but on different wavelengths. Jesus knows what Caiaphas fears, and his *signs* reveal *life* that does not perish when temple and nation collapse. Caiaphas thinks conventional politics; Jesus thinks and acts neo-Christopolitics. Even Pilate's power is subservient to God. With these rival perspectives, Passover draws near. Jesus is at his friends' home in Bethany. They make dinner for him. Martha serves Jesus, the honored guest. The once-dead Lazarus, now restored to life, celebrates with Jesus, *the resurrection and the life*.

12:3 Mary Anoints Jesus' Feet

Mary anoints Jesus' feet with costly perfume worth *three hundred denarii* (v. 5), which is one year's wages for a day laborer—calculate the sum in your culture! Mary then dries her Lord's feet with her hair (v. 3). The fragrant perfume fills the room. Whether known or unknown to Mary, she is preparing Jesus for his imminent burial (v. 7). Not only is her anointing of Jesus a royal act, an acknowledgment of Jesus' lordship; it is also a prophetic act, anticipating the next days' events. Howard-Brook (1997: 89) believes that Mary knew exactly what she was doing:

Through her deed Mary reveals a clear understanding of what is about to unfold, an understanding totally lost on those at table with Jesus later the same week. She exhibits the attitude of a disciple who has learned the lesson of Lazarus: the prospect of death is not to be avoided or denied but to be prepared for.

Verse 3 does not state a motivation. Howard-Brook *could* be right, but only in verse 7 is this act explicitly connected to Jesus' death and burial by Jesus' own words.

12:4-6 Judas's Response, with the Narrator's Explanation

Judas is upset by this costly devotion. He accuses Mary and complains to Jesus and the disciples that this is a waste of precious money that could have been used for the poor. Concerned about the common fund, Judas's response marks a bad turn in events. What are Judas's motives? Jesus does not accuse Judas but pursues his mission, which ironically includes Judas's handover of Jesus to his opponents.

12:7-8 Jesus' Response[w]

Jesus protects Mary from Judas's criticism and commends her devotion, interpreting it as the "right" action for this moment: it is anointing for his burial! Unlike the Synoptics, in John women do not bring spices for his anointing, either on the eve of his burial or on Easter morning. Two men anoint Jesus for burial (19:38-40). In this light, Mary's act is strategic in John: at the beginning of Passion week, it prepares for the end! Verse 8 is not to be understood as Jesus' indifference to the poor. The contrast is between the appropriate and important action now versus the opportunity and mandate *always* to assist the poor (cf. 6:5; 13:29; OT laws and the prophets' passion; e.g., Amos 2:6-7).

The Consequence of Lazarus's Raising 12:9-11

A great crowd of the Jews flock to see Jesus as well as Lazarus, whom Jesus raised from the dead. The authority of the chief priests is threatened by this *sign*-miracle of raising the dead because more and more Jews are believing in Jesus. The plan announced in 11:53 is now reiterated, with the engineers of its implementation here narrowed to the chief priests. However, 12:10 ends with *as well.* This means that killing Lazarus, the now-visible key witness, also figures into their strategic plot. The concluding verse specifies the rationale and need for this plan to succeed—and swiftly if at all possible—*since it was on account of him [Lazarus] that many of the Jews were deserting and were believing in Jesus* (12:11). Jesus has threatened the Jews' precarious security on teeter-totter with Rome. The chief priests, politically accountable to Pilate, Caesar's deputy, choose to ensure the Jews' submission.

THE TEXT IN BIBLICAL CONTEXT

Similarity of Lazarus Stories: John and Luke

Luke's Gospel contains the story of one named Lazarus: "The Rich Man and Lazarus" (16:19-31). A poor man named Lazarus lies at the gate of a rich man and begs, but the rich man does not help him. After they both die, the rich man, tormented in Hades, looks up and sees Abraham far away, with Lazarus at his side. The rich man cries for mercy and asks Abraham to send Lazarus "to dip the tip of his finger in water and cool my tongue." Then Abraham pronounces judgment upon the rich man for his callous treatment of poor Lazarus in their lifetime. In agony, the rich man asks Abraham to send someone back from the dead to warn his five brothers of his (and their) plight if they do not change. Abraham replies, "They have Moses and the prophets; they should listen to them." The rich man says, "No, father Abraham; but if someone goes to them from the dead, they will repent." Abraham then says, "If they do not listen to Moses and the prophets, neither will they be convinced even if someone rises from the dead."

Luke's story resembles John's narrative in its appeal to Moses (ch. 5), Abraham (ch. 8), and "someone [who] rises from the dead" (Lazarus, ch. 11; Jesus, ch. 20). Resurrection figures into both stories. Raymond Brown (1966: 428–29) thinks John's story draws on Luke's, whereas Dodd (1963: 228–32) regards John's story as distinctively Johannine. Contrary to majority sentiment, Dunkerley (322–23, 326–27) argues that Luke's story developed from John's. More likely, these are stories from different geographical traditions, with John's account coming from Jesus' Jerusalem ministry (cf. Meier: 2.800–801). In John, Jesus is the raising power that provokes both belief and resistance to Jesus (12:9-11). Galvanized by this resistance to Lazarus's raising as witness to the truth of Jesus' teaching and signs, the chief priests seek *to put Lazarus to death* (12:11).

Mary and Martha in the Gospels

Mary and Martha appear in Luke also, but in a different portrait. (Lazarus is not mentioned with them.) All three names have been found in ossuary inscriptions near Bethany (Blomberg: 165). While the Mary and Martha story in Luke 10:38-42 does not locate the event specifically at Bethany, it says "a certain village." The roles of Mary and Martha are presented differently in the two narratives, though perhaps not as differently as usually thought. Nevertheless, the connection is significant enough to bolster arguments that John has affinity to and may have known and utilized Luke—or that Luke was influenced by John (Matson: 153; Shellard: 78–79). In both accounts their home provides hospitality for Jesus and his disciples, and in both Mary and Martha are deeply devoted to Jesus. They belong to Jesus' larger disciple circle, though they are not itinerant. They provide a "hospitable home" and have loyal love for Jesus and his itinerants. John 11:1-5 implies that Jesus knows this family well. This is his Jerusalem home, providing hospitality and support of Jesus and his disciples (Esler and Piper).

John is the only Gospel that *names* the woman of Bethany who anoints Jesus' feet (cf. Mark 14:3). She is not to be identified as the sinful woman in Luke 7:36-50. Rather, she appears in Luke when Jesus visits their home (10:38-42). In Luke, Martha serves while Mary sits at Jesus' feet. In both Luke and John, these sisters represent commendable roles. John, however, portrays Martha in a strong confessional role, and Mary in costly devotion, anointing Jesus' feet with *expensive perfume* (John 12:3 NIV). Both Martha and Mary function in exemplary roles in John, climaxing John's second major structural section. Neither sister is to be depreciated. Martha is not reprimanded for *serving*. Jewish scholar David Flusser, in dinner conversation at our home, said that Jesus is telling her that "only one *dish*" is necessary. Her role, nonetheless, is important. In John's Gospel both women are crucial to the unfolding drama in the Christology and spirituality of the Gospel [*Women, p. 536*].

One Man Dies on Behalf of the Nation or People

The phrase *on behalf of* (*hyper*) in 11:50, 51, 52 (reiterated in 18:14) occurs in similar expressions elsewhere in John: 6:51b, *The bread that I will give for* [*hyper*] *the life of the world is my flesh*; and in 10:11, 15, where Jesus the good shepherd says that he *lays down his life for* [*hyper*] *the sheep* (cf. 15:13). This use of *hyper* is a good example of both substitution and representation (see Snyder Belousek for careful exposition of the meaning of *for* [*hyper*] in this text and others (281–84, 289, 527).

John's view of Jesus' death on the cross is not primarily that of sacrifice, but rather of death leading to glorification and exaltation (Appold; Dennis: 16–21; et al.). But the numerous hyper texts I have noted above cannot be discounted (Dennis: 20). Matera rightly sees three themes in Jesus' death in John: (1) on behalf of others; (2) cleansing (as in the footwashing); and (3) glorification, with return to the Father. Dennis (20–21, 198–201) agrees, regarding John 11:50-52; 10:11, 15b; 6:51 as too crucial to be discounted. A fourth emphasis should be added: taking away sin's power reveals "the power of God's love in giving Jesus" (John 3:16), who through death destroys "the enslaving power of the false 'ruler of this world'" (Coloe 2001: 199). God's love, Jesus' love, is the power of salvation in John (see John 13:1; 17:26). In both texts Jesus' death is grounded in the Father's love for the Son, and their love for all who believe (17:23b, 26) and for the world (3:16). Love prevails.

In wider NT writings *hyper* functions as a key term in Jesus' death on behalf of others, notably in a pre-Pauline formula, "Christ died for [*hyper*] our sins" (1 Cor 15:3). Similarly, Jesus "gave himself for [*hyper*] our sins to set us free from the present evil age, according to the will of our God and Father" (Gal 1:4; cf. 1 Pet 2:24, "He himself bore our sins in his body on the cross"). Jesus' words of institution at the Lord's Supper—"my blood of the covenant, . . . poured out for [*hyper*] many"—are most significant (Mark 14:24; cf. Matt 26:28; Luke 22:20, "new covenant" "for [*hyper*] you"). The phrase echoes Isaiah 53:12, "He poured out himself to death, and was numbered with the transgressors; yet he bore the sin of many, and made intercession for the transgressors." The substitution/representation in *for* (*hyper*) involving participatory relationship between the Redeemer and redeemed, permeates numerous NT atonement texts (Snyder Belousek: 265–91, 331–61).

A subtext of Caiaphas's prophecy of Jesus' death matches Mark 10:45: Jesus gives "his life a ransom [*lytron*] for [*anti*] many." Mark uses a related preposition, *anti*, with similar but also distinctive meaning, signifying both substitution and face-to-face relationship (i.e., imitation). Discipleship is linked inherently to atonement (Swartley 2006a: 110–12nn39–41). In Hebrews, Jesus by his death becomes the high priest, of the eternal order like unto Melchizedek, who thus satisfies and ends sacrifice *once and for all* (2:17; 7:27; 10:10, 12).

THE TEXT IN THE LIFE OF THE CHURCH

I Am the Resurrection and the Life[w]

This topic could also be TBC discussion. But this commentary defers to the forthcoming BCBC volume on 1 Corinthians since that Epistle contains a complete chapter on resurrection (1 Cor 15). In both the early church fathers and Eastern Orthodoxy, the resurrection (*anastasis*) lies at the heart of theology, worship, and spirituality. A selection of resurrection texts for funeral services is readily available in any minister's manual. *Resurrection* has had resurgence within OT studies, owing to the influence of Jon Levenson, Jewish professor at

Harvard University, with two books on the topic (see also Greenspoon).

Psalm 17 is the Saturday morning reading before Easter in *An Anabaptist Prayer Book* (ed. A. Boers). It ends hopefully, "As for me, I shall behold your face in righteousness; when I awake I shall be satisfied, beholding your likeness" (v. 15). The psalm selections for the Easter section, as well as the OT and NT readings, morning and evening, speak of God's triumph over evil and death; they stress hope and resurrection (A. Boers et al.: 414–83). For both Menno and many Anabaptist martyrs, John 11:25-26 is foundational. These verses inspire and embolden the martyrs' witness before the authorities and secure their hope of life eternal.

Mary's Anointing: Preparing for Passion[W]

John's characterizations of Caiaphas and Mary in this unit represent extremes. Caiaphas is Jesus' enemy, whose political savvy sees it as necessary and prudent that this one man gaining unstoppable popularity be put to death. The 1941–42 novel by Dorothy Sayers, *The Man Born to Be King*, portrays Caiaphas as a calculating and unfeeling leader, religion notwithstanding—a cipher perhaps of Hitler, with scapegoat roles reversed—Caiaphas's saving the Jewish people at the price of one person, and Hitler's exterminating Jews as the price to save some Aryans. While this puts the onus of responsibility on the Jews, Sayers in her last chapter puts the responsibility on all of us: we crucified Jesus (cf. J. S. Bach's *St. Matthew Passion*). Jewish rabbi Sholem Asch's 1939 novel, *The Nazarene*, portrays Caiaphas more charitably, a man driven by political necessity (Reinhartz 2009: 160–78). In contrast, Mary is connected to Jesus' death (unknowingly?), preparing him through love's tender, tearful anointing of his feet for his burial.

Mary's devotion of love to Jesus inspires us to let go of all that hinders our freedom to love Jesus. Mary invites us to kneel at Jesus' feet, placing there our heart's treasures, even our earthly possessions. Ambrose and Augustine both regard giving to the poor as our tears anointing Jesus' feet.

> Anoint the feet of Jesus. By living well, follow in the footsteps of the Lord. Dry them with your hair. If you have superfluity, give it to the poor and you have dried the feet of the Lord; for hair is understood to be the superfluity of the body. You may do with your superfluities [as you desire]: they are more than you need, but they are necessary to the feet of the Lord. Perhaps on earth the Lord's feet are in need. For whom will he speak at the end if not of his members: When you did it to one

of these least of mine, you did it to me? You bestowed your superflui-
ties, but it was to my feet that you were gracious. (Augustine, *Tractates
on the Gospel of John* 50.7)

Jesus says we always have that opportunity; he encourages us to
give to those who cannot give in return (Luke 14:12-14). In our
anointing the feet of Jesus through giving to the poor, we enact
Jesus' parable (Matt 25:40). We pour our costly perfume on Jesus'
feet. (See Ambrose's similar view and those of other church fathers
in Swartley 1998: 29–34.)

Jesus' Tears, Mary's Tears, and Our Tears

Jesus' tears and troubled spirit witness to Jesus' humanity (Thompson
1988: 3) and his emotional solidarity with those mourning Lazarus's
death. His weeping is connected to his *troubled* spirit and thus cannot be understood simply as empathy or sympathy. Whatever our
explanation of Jesus' irritation and troubled spirit, the narrative
says, *Jesus wept!* Jesus' emotion enables us to express our emotion
when life is hard. We pour out our feelings to God (cf. the lament
psalms, J. Waltner 2006). Jesus is not a Stoic, unmoved by human
emotion.

Mary's washing Jesus' feet with her tears expresses her lavish
love for Jesus with freed emotions. The text does not apologize.
Rather, it lauds her and regards her as *the one* person who responds
in an exemplary manner. Martha's, Mary's, and the Jews' exasperation shows emotion also: *If you had been here, my brother would not
have died.* This is human experience in the face of loss. We too ask,
"If this or that would (not) have happened or if I had (not) done this,
would the situation now be different?" The text instructs us that
Jesus cares for us despite those questions. The "if" question yields
to trust and hope.

Jesus' and Mary's tears show us that faith and emotion are compatible, that one who believes not only feels emotion, but may
freely express it. *Their* weeping frees *us* to weep, cleansing pent-up
emotions that burden our lives (cf. Gen 45:14-15). Tears heal. If you
preach or teach from this unit of John, do not overlook Martha's and
Mary's roles.

John 12:12-50

The Final Scene in Jesus' Public Ministry

PREVIEW

What is daylight saving time? My father thought it a strange notion since we cannot make the days longer or shorter. John 12 (cf. 9:4; 11:9-10) values daylight, not only in Jesus' claim *I am the light of the world*, but also in his last-bid invitation for people to *walk while you have the light* (12:35) and *while you have the light, believe in the light, so that you may become children of light* (v. 36). This is quintessential daylight saving time, with a *saving* twist—*so that you may become children of light*.

John 12 concludes the Book of Signs (chs. 1–12). The seven great signs were to lead people to faith, indeed to salvation. In correlation with these signs, Jesus has identified himself as the *Son of Man* (1:51), *water of life* (4:14), *bread of life* (6:35), *light of the world* (8:12; cf. *the true light . . . coming into the world* in 1:9), *the good shepherd* (10:11, 14), and *the resurrection and the life* (11:25). Many believe in Jesus and follow (4:41; 6:14; 7:31, 8:31; 10:42; 11:45). Many also hide their belief for *fear of the Jews* (7:13; 9:22; 20:19). Others reject Jesus as a fanatic (6:60), even demon-possessed (7:20; 8:52; 10:20). They pejoratively label him *from Galilee* (7:41), a demonized Samaritan (8:48), a *sinner*, certainly not one sent from God (9:16). This Savior is not the messiah whom Jews anticipated (6:15; 12:34).

In John 1–11, Jesus' *hour has not yet come* (2:4; 7:6; 7:30; 8:20). Suspense builds as Jesus' followers anticipate Jesus' hour, what it entails, and how it will unfold. Momentous events pressure the coming of Jesus' *hour*: Jesus declares that he is *the resurrection and the life* (11:25); Jesus raises Lazarus; the chief priests and the Pharisees plot to kill Jesus (11:53); Mary anoints Jesus for burial (12:3, 7); Judas takes offense, with ominous consequence; and the chief priests plot to kill Lazarus also (12:10). Now Jesus enters Jerusalem, with crowds proclaiming him king (12:12-13); Pharisees bemoan that the world has gone after Jesus (12:19); and climactically, Greeks come to see Jesus (12:20-21). Now Jesus declares, *The hour has come for the Son of Man to be glorified* (12:23).

Five days before the Passover festival, the crowds hear that Jesus is coming to Jerusalem. They proclaim Jesus as *King of Israel* with joyous, hopeful shouts of *Hosanna!* They wave palm branches, greeting Jesus as Messiah come to free them from Roman rule. Jesus mounts a donkey, which has OT royalty precedents (cf. 2 Sam 19:26; 1 Kings 1:33, 38, 44; Zech 9:9). He does not come on a warhorse and chariot, thus averting the potential image of a military leader (cf. 6:15). He is proclaimed King. Seeing this royal procession, the Pharisees realize their powerlessness, and thus exasperate, *Look, the world has gone after him!* (v. 19). Determined, they retaliate (18:3). "Once set upon the course of violence, the world's engines of power run on their own momentum" (Howard-Brook 1997: 89).

Jesus' triumphal entry follows: Greeks coming to see Jesus heightens his identity as *Son of Man* and *King of Israel* sent from above. Chapter 12 then ends with three related discursive units: a sandwich of sorts, in which the narrator's interpretation of the people's response to Jesus' ministry, quoting Israel's Scripture (12:36b-43), is tucked between Jesus' final words of appeal to the people to believe (vv. 34-36a and 44-50).

OUTLINE

Jesus' Triumphal Entry, 12:12-19
The Greeks Come to See Jesus, 12:20-22
Jesus Responds: "The Hour Has Come," 12:23-26
The Meaning of Jesus' Hour Unveiled, 12:27-36a
John Explains the Jews' Response to Jesus' Ministry, 12:36b-43
Jesus' Summative Final Appeal, 12:44-50

EXPLANATORY NOTES

Jesus' Triumphal Entry 12:12-19[w]

The setting is no longer Bethany, but Jerusalem. Jesus enters the city on a donkey, greeted enthusiastically by a great crowd that heard he was coming. They go out to meet him (v. 13). The crowd spreads palm branches on the road, signifying a royal procession. Palm branches were used in earlier momentous celebrations: to symbolize life and fertility at the dedication of Solomon's temple (1 Kings 6:29, 32, 35); rededication of the temple in 164 BC (2 Macc 10:7); celebration of political independence under Simon Maccabeus in 141 BC (cf. 1 Macc 13:51); and palms appearing on coins struck by the Jewish insurgents during the first and second revolts (AD 66–70 and 132–35; F. Bruce: 259). These traditions shape the people's hope for a royal national liberator; they prepare the way for Jesus' entry into Jerusalem.

But to announce the nature of his royalty, Jesus chooses a donkey (*onarion*, v. 14; *pōlon*, v. 15 from quote, a lowly animal), a colt of a donkey, rather than a warhorse. This is not without OT precedent. Solomon rides into Jerusalem for his coronation on a mule, the king's mule (1 Kings 1:33, 44). The quoted Zechariah text carries several connotations: "an enthronement, a victory celebration, or a call to battle. . . . Jerusalem is summoned to welcome its king" (Kinman: 241). Jesus' means of entrance could signify either his nonpolitical stance, Jesus' meek and humble kingship (Matthew's accent)—or *warfare, battle* (cf. Isa 21:7). That John presents Jesus as *sitting* (v. 15c) on the donkey rather than "riding," as in Zechariah 9:9, tilts against the battle motif. It accords with John's overall presentation: Jesus is victorious, even as he enters Jerusalem to face the denouement of the plot to take his life. This, however, does not mean that no battle was fought, since shortly thereafter Jesus casts out the ruler of the world. Jesus wins the battle, but not with military weapons (cf. 18:36).

The cry of the crowd, *Hosanna! Blessed is he who comes in the name of the Lord, even the King of Israel!* (RSV), expresses the people's hope and expectation. The acclaim comes from Psalm 118:25-26. The text speaks of festal branches. *Hosanna* means "save us," expressing the people's desire to be delivered from Roman oppression. The crowd appeals to "Jesus to accept the role of a nationalistic deliverer"

---

w   Where the superscript w occurs after headings, please see the commentary's online Web Supplement for additional material. Go to: http://www.heraldpress.com/bcbc/john.

(Talbert: 185). They acclaim Jesus as *King of Israel* (cf. 1:49). In addition, parts of Zechariah 9:9-10 are quoted.

Slight shifts and additions in John are significant: (1) *King of Israel* is added to the Psalm 118 text; (2) *Do not fear* replaces "Rejoice greatly"; (3) *sitting* on a donkey replaces "riding." The omissions are startling as well: (4) "triumphant and victorious is he"—imagery possibly of military conquest but followed by—"humble and riding . . ."; and (5) "he shall command peace to the nations" (plus related imagery).

The alteration in points 2 and 3 affect the overall interpretation of the event: point 2 aligns the acclamation with the OT war oracles, often beginning with "Do not fear." That orients the event to Israel's hope of liberation from Rome. Point 3, however, reorients the liberation, not to military means, but to Jesus' victory already won by God's decree. *Sitting* symbolizes reigning: the victory of Zechariah 9:10 is already achieved, as John unequivocally affirms. Indeed, Jesus presents himself as a humble prince of peace, not a violent warrior or monarch (Ridderbos: 423). Finally, it is important to recognize, as John Collins (206) points out, that "Zech 9:9 is never used as a messianic prophecy in the Scrolls or the Pseudepigrapha." Though Collins (207) says that in Zechariah 9:10 "this king will bring about universal peace, apparently by military victory" (as in 4Q246 2.1-8), John does not quote the lines from Zechariah suggesting that view. John's use of Zechariah's prophecy for Jesus' messianic portrait fits his nonviolent Christology. However, as John 12:16 indicates, Jesus' *disciples did not understand* this until later. At the moment they and the crowd are not thinking of Jesus as fulfilling the Zechariah text (Coakley: 463). In the Synoptics (Mark 11:2; Matt 21:2; Luke 19:30), Jesus initiates this event by sending two disciples to find the colt. John lacks this (a "most obvious . . . difference," says Coakley: 477). This might reflect Jesus' resistance to kingship (6:15). But in John, Jesus does accept the title *King of Israel!* (12:13c; Nathanael's approved acclaim in 1:49; cf. 18:37; 19:19-22).

The unit concludes by circling back to the opposition. It thus serves as the matching bookend to 12:9-11, where the crowd wants to see Jesus and Lazarus, but the chief priests react by planning to kill them both since many Jews believe in Jesus. In verses 17-18 the crowd, having witnessed this royal event, comes to see Jesus who, they heard, has performed this spectacular sign of raising Lazarus. This inclusio of *chief priests/Lazarus* and *Lazarus/Pharisees* builds unity with chapter 11, protesting any notion of sharp cleavage between chapters 11 and 12.

The Pharisees then lament, *You see, you can do nothing. Look, the world has gone after him!* This, precisely and ironically, happens next!

The Greeks Come to See Jesus 12:20-22

In John 12:20, some Greeks (*Hellēnes*) come to Jerusalem to worship at the Passover festival. Scholars debate whom these *Greeks* represent. Are they Greek-speaking Jews from the Diaspora? This is unlikely since specific terminology (*Hellēnistēs*) occurs in Acts 6:1 and 9:29, where these people are called "Hellenists," Jews who speak Greek or follow some Greek customs. Or does John 12:20 mean proselytes, Gentiles converted to Judaism? Since *Gentiles* (*ta ethnē*, pl.) is never used in John (cf. Robinson 1985: 60), these people are likely God-fearing Gentiles who attend Jewish festivals in the outer Court of the Gentiles (cf. the Ethiopian eunuch who came to Jerusalem to worship, Acts 8:27-28). Paul speaks of Greeks who "fear God" (Acts 13:16, 26).

Here *Greeks . . . wish to see Jesus.* Seeing in John is linked to believing, coming to the light (cf. the blind man in John 9). Suddenly the *world* is coming to Jesus, to the dismay of the Pharisees (12:19). "The Greeks signal the closing of a chapter for Jesus. His ministry in Judaism is finished and he now belongs to the wider world" (Burge 2000: 343). Israel's covenant God is no longer Israel's sole possession. Greeks now wish to see Jesus.

The Greeks approach Philip. Howard-Brook (1994: 278) emphasizes the importance of Philip and Andrew in 12:21-22. Philip is mentioned in all the Gospels, but here Philip plays a specific role (see also John 6:5, 7; Acts 8). John seldom highlights specific disciples except to illustrate something particular about their character or role in the larger story, as is here the case. Philip, from Bethsaida in Galilee (1:44), the one who brought Nathaniel to Jesus (1:45-47), has a Greek name that makes him more approachable. Andrew, too, is a Greek name. Andrew, Simon Peter's brother, is always connected with Philip in John's Gospel (1:44; 6:8). Andrew brings Simon Peter to Jesus, and now Philip is approached to bring non-Jewish Greeks to Jesus. That Philip and Andrew play this role in John signifies the union of Gentile believers with Jewish believers—the *one flock* of 10:16.

Jesus does not respond specifically to the Greeks' request, but rather to the situation. The coming of the Greeks signals to Jesus that the climactic hour has dawned. Before, *My hour has not yet come* (2:4; 7:30; 8:20). But now with the coming of the Greeks, Jesus' *hour has come.* Through his death-resurrection-glorification, all peoples will be drawn to Jesus (v. 32). It is not clear, however, if the Greeks get to see Jesus. Carson's proposal (438) may play into this mission delay:

> Even if they met with Jesus at this point there is a sense in which they could not yet "see" him, they could not yet belong to him, until the "hour" is over and Jesus has been "lifted up from the earth" (v. 32). That is what is necessary for the gospel to be fully operative, the gospel that encompasses Jew and Gentile alike and draws together a new covenant community whose locus is no longer constrained by the parameters of Sinai.

Jesus Responds: "The Hour Has Come" 12:23-26[w]

Beginning with the strong phrase *Very truly, I tell you*, Jesus explains what this *hour* will mean (v. 24). Jesus' death is like a grain of wheat (*kokkos tou sitou*) that falls into the ground and dies in order to bring forth a rich harvest. Jesus' parable of the sower in Mark 4:1-20 presents a partial parallel: the manner in which God's reign comes is like the seed that falls into the ground, sprouts, and produces a harvest in those who hear the word. In John, Jesus is the person (the grain) that must die for harvest to come. This is Jesus' glorification, enabling the harvest of nations and peoples.

Jesus' death is immediately linked to discipleship, for verse 25 says those *who love their life will lose it*, but those *who hate their life in this world will keep it for eternal life*. This suggests martyrdom for the gospel's sake, anticipating Jesus' final word to Peter (21:18-19). We can think of the book of Revelation, Christians in the first three centuries, Anabaptists, Martin Luther King Jr., Archbishop Oscar Romero, and many other less well-known persons in situations where Christians are persecuted (China for many years, now Nigeria, and other countries). When we do so, we might remember also how Tertullian's word exemplifies the import of this text: "The blood of the martyrs is the seed of the church." Verse 26 extends Jesus' call to serve and follow him with willingness also to give one's life for the gospel. These verses are directed to Jesus' disciples; they call to costly discipleship, with the promise that *the Father will honor* those who follow. "What appears by all worldly standards to be utter and shameful defeat will in fact be an honorable coronation, the establishment of a new kind of reign amid the reign of darkness" (Howard-Brook 1997: 89).

The Meaning of Jesus' Hour Unveiled 12:27-36a[w]

In 12:27 we encounter Jesus in his humanity, expressing the anguish related to the present *hour*. Commentators vary on how John presents Jesus' suffering and death. Some see Jesus' death only as a prelude to glory and minimize his death's significance. Because Jesus is divine from the beginning in John, his suffering is minimal. Some regard it as a "show."

Most scholars disagree. Jesus is deeply troubled (cf. 11:33-35; 13:21). Jesus' agony cannot be minimized. The strong verb for *troubled* (*tarassō*) in 12:27 "signifies revulsion, horror, anxiety, agitation" (Carson: 440). Jesus' suffering participates in a universal human battle: Jesus "struggles with the very human characteristic that he urges his disciples to resist, to cling to his soul/life" (Howard-Brook 1994: 281). Minimizing Jesus' suffering and death fails to appreciate John's dominant emphasis on Jesus' glorification and oneness with the Father, revealed consummately in Jesus' suffering and death (Thompson 1988: 87–105). Ruprecht's disparaging opinion (106–17) that John is "mocking" Jesus' Gethsemane agony in Mark is far off the mark.

Jesus' struggle is not without hope for those who would follow. "This passage is tied to the themes of glorification (v. 28) and of the hour (v. 31), and provides incentive to follow (v. 26) the one whose death we must in some measure emulate, assured he did not find the path easy himself" (Carson: 440). *Troubled* in verse 27 portrays genuine anguish followed by resonant obedience as Jesus accepts the will of God (cf. 5:19-23; 6:37; 8:29, 38; 14:31; Heb 5:7-10). Jesus' final yes to his Father even unto death is continuous with how he has lived his whole life for others to glorify his Father. John introduces Jesus' passion with *Father, glorify your name* (12:28). This entails Jesus' suffering and death.

The Father's audible voice sounding from heaven points to the glory that already exists in the incarnation and in Jesus' works, as well as in the glory that is to come through death and resurrection. Only here in John's Gospel does a voice come from heaven. In the Synoptic Gospels, God speaks at Jesus' baptism and transfiguration (cf. Mark 1:11; 9:7; Matt 3:17; Luke 9:35). This distinctive feature of John's Gospel further highlights the crucial significance of his suffering and death. *This* is when heaven speaks.

The crowds seem not to understand God's words (12:29). Some don't recognize the sound as a voice: "Typically, the world can barely comprehend the magnitude of what is transpiring in Jesus Christ. Thus, naturally, there is misunderstanding. This voice, Jesus says, is for those listening, not for him[self]" (Burge 2000: 345). The misunderstood voice adds urgency and authority to the words of Jesus that follow.

In verses 31-32 Jesus unpacks the significance of verses 20-30. Carson (442–45) lifts out five crucial points. First, judgment occurs both at the end of the age and also in the Christ event here and now (3:17, 19-21; 5:22-30; 7:24; 8:16). The cross passes judgment on the world. Second, the prince or ruler of the world is driven out. The cross is Satan's defeat. As Jesus is enthroned, Satan is dethroned (14:30; 16:11, 33). Jesus' death is a cosmic battle (Kovacs). Third, Jesus will be lifted up from the earth on the cross and exalted to glory. Jesus' death is the pathway integral to his glorification (cf. Isa 52:13). Fourth, Jesus will draw all people to himself (cf. John 6:44; 5:19; 12:32; Eph 1:10). Jesus unites humanity. Finally, the coming of the hour (John 12:23, 27) indicates a revelatory axis of the ages. The meaning of history hinges on this turning point in the Gospel. The end time has begun; the impending events are eschatological.

Jesus the light (vv. 35-36) exposes the hidden darkness. As the light shining in the darkness, Jesus casts out the world's ruler. This is John's cosmic exorcism. While Howard-Brook (1994: 283) cautions against equating *ruler* (*archōn*) with Satan or the devil, saying these do not necessarily equate (cf. 3:1; 7:26, 48, where *archōn* refers to Nicodemus and the rulers of Judea). The "face" of the ruler of this world is *the Jews* and the Sanhedrin, who cast out Jesus and his followers from the synagogue (cf. 9:34). However, in John it appears that the various faces of resistance to Jesus are linked to a power beyond themselves, especially in John's references to Satan behind Judas's handing Jesus over to the authorities (6:70-71; 13:27). Nor do the authorities act on their own. In their opposition to Jesus, they and Satan play into the higher power of God, as in Gamaliel's solution to sacrifice the "troublemaker," which ironically is prophecy! Jesus later contrasts Pilate's earthly power as ruler to power from above (i.e., God's; 19:11). Both God and Satan participate in this earthly drama: Satan is the prince, head, or chief ruler of the world's evil; God in Jesus is victor over evil.

Neither pole of power is to be minimized. Lesslie Newbigin (159) rightly claims that the *archōn* of this world (v. 31) represents all the false shepherds of the world who function on the basis of self-interest: "The law represented by the scribes, religion represented by the high priests and the Sadducees, worldly '*realpolitik*' represented by the Roman governor, and popular revolutionary enthusiasm represented by the Passover crowds will all combine in a strange and unique coalition to condemn and destroy [Jesus]. And by this act they will write their own doom." Indeed, but what is *cast out* in 12:31 is more than these false shepherds. In John, *world* and unbelief go hand in hand *[World, p. 538]*. God the Sovereign rules over the ruler (*archōn*) of this world. God's sovereign rule is *now revealed* in and through Jesus (cf. 3:18-21).

He said this to indicate the kind of death he was to die (v. 33) is an explanatory note to the reader. The crowd does not have the benefit of such an explanation and thus struggles to understand. Their confusion is apparent in verse 34, as they seek to align their messianic expectations with what Jesus is saying about himself. Hence, what does *the Son of Man will be lifted up* mean? The crowd is looking for a politically triumphant messiah (cf. 12:12-19) to establish a political-power kingdom. However, Jesus is speaking of glorification coming through his being "lifted up." The crowd does not understand and queries, *What kind of Son of Man is this?* [AT]. The crowd cannot reconcile the messianic expectations of their religious tradition with Jesus' words.

Jewish eschatological expectations varied widely, even on the duration of the messiah's reign. In 2 Esdras 7:28-30 the messiah is expected to reign for a period of time, then die. In *2 Baruch* 30:1 the messiah is taken directly into heaven. In *1 Enoch* 49:2 and *Psalms of Solomon* 17:4 the messiah reigns eternally. The *Life of Adam and Eve* (first century AD) envisions the restoration of Israel without any messiah at all. The community at Qumran apparently expected two messiahs (1QS 9.11; *Damascus Document* [CD], passim). However, the Johannine community knows that the Messiah's reign is eternal and *not from the world* (18:36 RSV).

Jesus does not directly answer the questions of the crowd, nor does he engage in their faulty theological debates. Rather, he refers to his coming death and calls the people to choose and walk in the light before it is taken away and the darkness overtakes them (12:35-36a). Jesus' words (12:36a; cf. 8:12; 12:46) echo the imagery of light in the prologue. Those who *believe in the light . . . become the children of light* (cf. 1:12). "Rather than get into squabbles about the Law, Jesus offers the basic choice, . . . to choose life rather than death in order to continue as God's children" (cf. Deut 30:19; Howard-Brook 1994: 284).

John Explains the Jews' Response to Jesus' Ministry 12:36b-43

This final section of Jesus' public ministry consists of two parts: first, the evangelist's commentary on why many of the Jews did not receive Jesus, and second, Jesus' own summative gospel appeal. There is no apparent audience for this final summation. In terms of John as drama, we have a final soliloquy, with the spotlight focusing narrowly on Jesus, who is on the stage alone. This final commentary by the evangelist and the summary by Jesus that follows represent an opportunity for the narrator to address the reader directly.

John frames his explanation of why many of *his own people did not accept him* (1:11) with Jesus in *hiding* (12:36b; cf. 3:22; 6:15; 7:1; 8:59; 10:39-40)! With Jesus not speaking, the evangelist tells why he is a hunted man and why his own people, especially the leaders, have not received him: *Although he had performed so many signs in their presence, they did not believe in him* (12:37). John then quotes and uniquely blends two OT scriptures, Isaiah 53:1 and 6:10 (Schuchard: 85). Elsewhere in the NT, only Paul also quotes Isaiah 53:1a in Romans 10:16b, with exactly the same Septuagint wording. Isaiah 6:10 (also v. 9) is cited in part in the Synoptic Gospels (Mark 4:12; Matt 13:13; Luke 8:10b) and by Paul in his concluding words in Acts (28:26-27). The *idea* also permeates Paul's argument in Romans 11, with 11:10 quoting part of Isaiah 6:10. Paul, however, views this rejection as God's design (cf. Toews: 276)—to open the door for Gentiles to become grafted into the Jewish olive tree, to also receive God's mercy (Rom 11:31). Early Christian preaching appealed to Isaiah 6:9-10 for a stock explanation for the widespread Jewish failure to believe Jesus' signs, words, and claims about himself. Even in this section, however, we hear that many Jews, *even of the authorities, believed in him* (v. 42)! Most of them are apparently *secret* believers, personified by Joseph and likely Nicodemus, who cooperate for Jesus' burial (19:38-39).

The evangelist presents three main reasons for unbelief. First, Isaiah prophesied that God *has blinded their eyes and hardened their heart.* Second, even those disposed to believe could not openly confess Jesus as Messiah, Son of God, for fear of synagogue reprisals. Third, *they loved human glory more than the glory that comes from God.* Only the first reason in its appeal to Isaiah is new in the Gospel. Reason two appears in 9:22 to explain why the parents of the man born blind would not testify to Jesus' healing their son (see also 16:2). Reason three occurs more often in the narrative, to explain resistance to Jesus and unbelief (5:41; 7:18; 8:50 implied). In a chiastic structuring of this 12:12-50 unit, 12:36b-43 aligns with 12:20-26. The two portions contrast: the Jewish religious leaders don't see (cf. 9:40-41), but Gentiles *wish to see Jesus*. "Ironically, whereas Israel as a whole failed to 'see' (12:40), the Gentiles came to 'see' Jesus" (Keener: 2.884).

John emphasizes the *seeing* and omits the *hearing* part of the Isaiah prophecy. The quotation includes the line on *understanding*. It substitutes the Isaiah Septuagint phrase of *shutting their eyes* with *blinding* the people, a much more serious condition (cf. 9:39-41; Painter 1994: 448–49). John 12:37 begins the paragraph by noting the *signs* of Jesus rather than his words. Throughout the Gospel the people have *seen* Jesus' signs (2:11; 6:2, 14; cf. 9:39; 11:45). The next verses (12:44-50), Jesus' own summation, focus more on Jesus' words (cf. Whitacre: 326).

In earlier chapters *seeing* and *knowing* (understanding) are key emphases. Four different Greek *seeing* verbs appear in John, with a total of seventy-eight uses. The Gospel *reveals*, with *seeing* as the primary mode of understanding, though *hearing* also plays an important role (Thompson 2001a: 104–9), apparent in Jesus' final summative appeal. The accent on *reveal* occurs in the evangelist's first Isaiah quotation: *To whom has the arm of the Lord been revealed?* John links this to *seeing*, since the second quotation occurs in Isaiah after he *saw* the glory of the Lord in his vision of call to be a prophet. Revelation, seeing, and understanding are the criteria measuring proper response to Jesus. Many fail the test, but some pass.

The second and third reasons coalesce: seeking human glory resists public confession and belief in one who threatens the prevailing socioreligious order. As O'Day (1995: 717) puts it, "Because of a fear of political power and loss of prestige ('human glory') and security ('be put out of the synagogue'), some choose against the experience of God revealed in Jesus."

Verse 41 is the hinge verse of the unit: *Isaiah said this because he saw his glory and spoke about him.* Isaiah functions here with other faithful witnesses to God's glory: Moses (5:44-47; cf. 1:14, 16); Abraham (8:54-56); and John the Witness (1:6-9, 14-15, 26-36; 3:27-30). Those who believe also testify to God's glory manifest in Jesus (2:11; 11:40) [*Witness, p. 534*]. John declares that in his vision of God's glory, Isaiah saw the glory now revealed in Jesus the Christ. The verse preceding the quoted Isaiah 53:1 plays into the significance of Jesus' glory, since it says the Servant "shall be exalted and lifted up" (52:13), imagery that perfectly fits John's theology of Jesus' glorification, reflecting the Father's glory (cf. Keener: 2.885) [*Glory, p. 516*].

Jesus' Summative Final Appeal 12:44-50

Jesus recapitulates words he spoke earlier. *Jesus cried aloud* (v. 44a) this final appeal in his public ministry. He *shouts* a final call to believe, with the usual divine sanction: *Whoever believes in me believes*

*not in me but in him who sent me. And whoever sees me sees him who sent
me* (vv. 44-45). Believing entails response to Jesus' words: *hearing*
and *seeing* are complementary positive responses to Jesus' *revealing*
his Father.

Next Jesus reiterates his claim to be the light of the world, and
the ramifications of this for judgment and salvation, the burden of
3:17-21; 8:12-17. Verses 48-49 repeat emphases in 5:17, 19-30. The
final shout voices the Father's desire for all to hear: *I know that his
commandment is eternal life. What I speak, therefore, I speak just as the
Father has told me* (v. 50). Jesus' offer of eternal life echoes chapters
3 and 5. Jesus' words are authorized as the words of the Father. He
claims that his Father sent him into the world. This is the crux of
the case against him: blasphemy (5:17-18; 10:30).

These words are Jesus' final call; the *hour* of decision has come!

THE TEXT IN BIBLICAL CONTEXT

The Greeks Come to See Jesus

Each of the Gospels has its own distinctive way of including Gentiles
as recipients of the gospel of Jesus Christ. The point is essential to
each Gospel's Christology and view of worship. In John, the *hour*
comes only after the Greeks come and declare, *We wish to see Jesus.*
In Mark, Jesus journeys to Gentile territory and ministers there
(Mark 7:24–8:10), after which Jesus quizzes his disciples on the boat
ride. Only then do we understand the symbolism of the two feedings: the feeding of the five thousand with twelve baskets left over,
and the feeding of the four thousand with seven baskets left over
(8:14-21). This is followed by Jesus' *double* touch to heal a blind man
at Bethsaida (8:22-26). In this context—the geography, the two sides
of the sea, the symbolic numbers, and the double touch—Jesus
broaches the question, "Who do people say that I am?" The Gospel
then discloses Jesus' imminent passion, death, and resurrection.
When Gentiles are included (the east side of the sea; four thousand
people; seven baskets) in Jesus' ministry, Jesus prompts Peter's messianic confession (8:27-30), similar to John's narrative, with its
hinge in 12:20-23. Their political Christologies are similar: no
Gentiles, no Messiah! Jesus is Messiah only in the context of extending the gospel to include Gentiles (cf. Swartley 1981/99: 112–30).

Matthew's strategy on this point differs significantly. The
beginning and end of Matthew's Gospel shows Gentile inclusion in
God's salvation story. First, outsiders—women such as Rahab,
Ruth, Bathsheba, the wife of Uriah the Hittite—are included in the

genealogy. Second, wise men from the east come to see Jesus, and they worship him (2:1-12). Third, in the Gospel's conclusion Jesus directs the disciples to go to the nations of the world to proclaim the good news, baptizing and teaching all he has commanded. Fourth—in a strikingly similar strategy by John and Mark—a significant "turning" occurs in chapters 10 and 12. In 10:5-6 Jesus commands his sent disciples to "go nowhere among the Gentiles, and enter no town of the Samaritans, but go rather to the lost sheep of the house of Israel." When Jewish hearers refuse the gospel, Matthew indicates a turning to Gentile inclusion, citing two pertinent OT Scriptures (12:15-21: "He will proclaim justice to the Gentiles" and "in his name the Gentiles will hope"). These middle chapters inform readers of Jesus' judgment on "deaf" Jewish hearers while Jonah and the queen of the South are exemplary counterpoints (12:38-42).

Luke's "great omission" of Mark's journey into Gentile area—and hence the second feeding—is likely to be explained and correlated with his postponing the inclusion of Gentiles until his second volume, Acts. But like John he judges against hostility toward the Samaritans (Luke 9:51-56), extols the moral compassion of Samaritans in the classic story of the Good Samaritan (10:29-37), and lauds the expressed gratitude of one healed leper, a Samaritan (17:11-19). Further, the Gentile centurion beneath the cross exclaims in his confession, "Certainly this was a righteous man" (23:47 KJV), and praises God, joining the chorus of followers praising Jesus in 19:37. Luke's explicit inclusion of Gentiles is saved for his second volume, Acts, which narrates the kingdom gospel's expansion (Acts 1:8; chs. 8–28). Many times in Acts (cf. 13:46-49), Paul is "turning to the Gentiles." At the Jerusalem conference, James cites OT texts on Gentile inclusion (15:15-18). Saul (known as Paul in the Hellenistic world) is apostle to the Gentiles (9:15; 26:17-18). Peter's baptizing of Cornelius also witnesses to God's inclusion of the Gentiles (ch. 10).

The entire Pauline corpus has at its heart the Gentile mission. Paul describes himself as "an apostle to the Gentiles" (Rom 11:13; cf. Gal 2; Eph 3:1-7). The turn to the Gentiles is supported with OT Scriptures in every one of these cases except Mark. The early church reads the OT to see in it God's purpose of Gentile inclusion (Swartley 1981/1999: 112–30; 2007: 213–37). Jesus' primary commitment likely was to restore Israel (cf. Matt 15:24; 10:5-6; Rom 1:14-15), but Jesus' journey in John 4 points clearly beyond Israel. Brightly shining are the Gospels' christological disclosures and their subtle strategies to bring the Gentiles into each Gospel's narrative structure. Michael Bird argues rightly that in numerous strands of messianic hope, the restoration of Israel envisions also the inclusion of Gentiles. In John 12, Jesus' ministry to Israel is completed; those outside the "sheepfold" of Israel (10:16) also come to Jesus (Burge 2000: 352). The Greeks' query signals that Jesus' *hour* is come; he lays down his life for the life of the world (1:29; 3:16; 6:51; 10:18; 12:32).

Cross as Glorification[w]

Schnackenburg devotes a lengthy excursus to Jesus' glorification in John (2.398–410). I summarize his superb contribution. He emphasizes that John's image of being "lifted up [is a] symbol full of meaning for the believing beholder." Jesus' posture as he accepts and submits to the cross is anything but that of victim. Although we may use Girardian theory to explain how the violent conflict between the Romans and the Jews was averted by sacrificing Jesus (cf. Caiaphas's political maxim interpreted by the author(s) of John as prophecy; 11:49-52), the Gospel does not portray Jesus as a victim (see Verhey in the Web supplement to this commentary's introduction, p. 26): Jesus does not go to the cross as a victim, but as a servant glorified in self-giving love. Glory laces the Scripture. Books in which glory is significant are Exodus, Psalms, Isaiah, Ezekiel, John, the Corinthian Epistles, and Revelation [*Glory, p. 516*].

When *I Am* Lifted Up[w]

The imagery of John 12:32 is derived from Numbers 21:4-9, where Moses erects a pole with a snake fastened on it to eradicate the deadly venom of snakes biting and killing Israelites. John uses and transforms the imagery in 3:14-21 and in 12:32. The common features of the two stories are "lifted up" and "salvation from death," which in John yields *eternal life*. George Brunk III's Lenten meditation leads us in this symbolic trajectory from *snake* to *salvation*. Just as in the older story the lifted-up serpent becomes a means of salvation from death, so in the new story the Son *lifted up* on the cross, symbol of humiliation and shame, becomes the means of salvation from death. Those who benefit "look up" to the serpent, and in John *see* Jesus and believe his words and signs. The impact of the new event is stupendous: *the ruler of the world is cast out*, and Jesus *draws* all people to himself for salvation and eternal life (cf. 12:31-32 RSV).

THE TEXT IN THE LIFE OF THE CHURCH

The Gentiles Are Knocking at the Door[w]

John 12:20-23 exhorts the church to open its doors to welcome outsiders. The link between 12:20-23 and 12:24-26 indicates that Jesus
gives his life to welcome the Gentiles. Jesus gives himself, knowing
God's promise of eternal life is *now* to be fulfilled through his passion—his *hour* of death and his glorification—which with his resurrection is also exaltation. Jesus' fruitful death is the firstfruits: many
disciples will follow in its train (see the thirty-two named first-
century Christian martyrs in *Martyrs Mirror* [van Braght: 67] and
Tertullian's "seed of the church" quotation on page 161). Jesus'
death brings life to others. By believing, his followers receive eternal life *[Eternal Life, p. 513]*.

One loses one's life when one is focused idolatrously on oneself,
for such self-centeredness denies God's sovereignty. The instruction to hate one's life is not an antilife statement, but rather a command similar to Mark 8:34, "If any want to become my followers, let
them deny themselves and take up their cross and follow me." As
humans, we are unable to save our lives. We are invited to a discipleship where our lives are constantly given away and received
anew through Jesus' outpoured love for us (cf. Newbigin: 157). Self-
sacrifice and service mark this life of discipleship. Despite the difficult road, faithful discipleship leads to honor from the Father.

Dramatic Ending of Jesus' Public Ministry

We might view 12:36-50 in theatrical terms. Jesus exits at 12:36; the
narrator pulls the curtain on his public ministry:

> In vv. 37-43, the evangelist, "the playwright," reveals himself directly
> to the audience and comments on the dilemma with which the first
> "act" ends: Why do Jesus' own reject him? After he completes his
> speech, he, too, disappears behind the curtain, and the stage is com-
> pletely empty and dark. The voice of Jesus is then heard (vv. 44-50),
> crying out to the darkened theatre from the wings, his own voice pro-
> viding the final commentary on the drama that has played itself out
> before the audience. When Jesus finishes speaking, the audience is once
> again alone in the darkness, with Jesus' offer of salvation ringing in
> their ears. (O'Day 1995: 718)

As the audience reflects, they recall different sayings of Jesus
that burn into their hearts. *I, when I am lifted up from the earth, will
draw all people to myself* (12:32). Does the *all* include me, people from

every nationality and language, and people from across the generations and centuries? "Chrysostom explains that he needs to *draw* us
because we are fettered by a tyrant (*Homily* 57.3). . . . Athanasius
writes that the arms of the Cross enable Christ to embrace the
World (*On the Incarnation* 25). . . . Many, with Erasmus, understand *all*
to mean 'of all races and degrees' (1525: 254)" (M. Edwards: 128).
This is a universal vision without parallel in the Synoptic Gospels,
but present elsewhere in John (1:12, 16; 3:16; 5:24; 6:37, 47), despite
the unbelief. The invitation is for all to come. "The Fourth Evangelist
allows no possibility of hedging this decision; to believe is life, to
reject Jesus is to incur judgment" (O'Day 1995: 718).

Jesus' public ministry ends in John 12 as his direction and focus
shifts from the crowds to his circle of disciples and to the path set
before him. The path leads through the ongoing struggle between
light and darkness. As the struggle and tension mount, the people
must choose their side (12:35-36a). Throughout John, the choice is
between light and darkness, now with greater urgency as Passover
approaches.

Anabaptist Appeals to This Text

As they faced martyrdom, Anabaptists frequently took solace in two
verses in this unit:

- *Those who love their life lose it, and those who hate their life in this
  world will keep it for eternal life* (12:25).

- *On the last day the word that I have spoken will serve as judge*
  (12:48b).

The first verse (12:25) is cited five times in *Martyrs Mirror* (433,
434, 439, 836, 856) as explanation of why a martyr willingly gives up
life (e.g., Vigil Plaitner, in *MM* 432–33), or as a prisoner's final declaration to rebuke any who entreat them to recant rather than suffer
martyrdom. Especially moving is the testimony of a fourteen-year-
old lad, who with seven brothers is martyred at Gmuend, Swabia, in
1529. The lad had been put into a tower, "where he lay very severely
confined almost a year, suffering many an assault, but always
remaining immovable," however often they sought to induce him to
recant. When the day came for the martyrdom by sword, "a ring
was . . . drawn on the spot, as is customarily done for executions,
with the sword." A count rode by and promised the lad a subsis-
tence allowance and safety in his personal care if he would recant.
The lad replied:

Should I love my life (John 12:25), and therefore forsake my God, and thus seek to escape the cross? This I must certainly not do; the wealth can be of no help to either of us, but I expect a better in heaven, . . . in the kingdom of my Father, who has chosen me, and who can order and equalize all things as is best. Hence cease these entreaties. . . . To Him we must call from the bottom of our heart, when the hour is at hand, that we may depart with good cheer out of this world. (434)

The second text (12:48) is cited seven times in the English translation of *Martyrs Mirror* (358, 383, 638, 658, 915, 970, 972). In some cases it functions as self-assurance for the martyr facing death, in others as exhortation in letters written to family members or congregations, or as gospel reminders to the authorities about to kill them. The latter occurs in one of a series of letters by Lauwerens van der Leyen, July 10, 1559, at Antwerp, addressed to "the Lords of the Law at Antwerp, and the Dean of Ronse" (636): "The Word of the Lord, which was before ever your church existed shall judge men in the last day; it shall judge all men. Jno. 12:48" (638). A letter of another martyr, Jan Thielemans, combines lines from John 12:46, 48, and 50, emphasizing both judgment by Jesus' Word and "the commandment" of "life everlasting" (734). Another is a letter of Jan Wouterss (Dordrecht) to his only daughter, "The Word of Christ is always the Judge; hence let no one think hard of me" (915). These verses are chart and compass for the martyrs, to guide them into their promised heavenly haven.

Part 3

Denouement: Final Passover, Passion, and Resurrection

He was despised and rejected by others; . . .
     he was wounded for our transgressions, . . .
By a perversion of justice he was taken away.
     Who could have imagined his future?
For he was cut off from the land of the living,
     stricken for the transgression of my people.
They made his grave with the wicked
     and his tomb with the rich,
although he had done no violence,
     and there was no deceit in his mouth.
—Isaiah 53:3a, 5a, 8-9

John 13

Jesus Begins His Farewell

PREVIEW

Most of us can recall crucial turning points in our lives. It may have been a decision to change locations, moving from our local area and becoming translocal, living in multiple places over time. Sometimes these changes are difficult. Loss of relationships is one of the hugest hurdles. In John 13 Jesus moves into a final phase of his life's mission. Nothing will be the same again. Farewells are difficult, and Jesus faces a major one: parting with his dear disciples, his loved Bethany family, and his mother.

In the Synoptic Gospels, Jesus' Palm Sunday entrance into Jerusalem begins Jesus' final week of ministry (Mark 11:1-12//Matt 21:1-11//Luke 19:28-40). Mary's (only John names her) anointing of Jesus begins the Passion (Mark 14:1-9//Matt 26:6-13). In John both events occur together already in chapter 12. Chapter 13 is often seen as beginning the second half of the Gospel. Many commentators (e.g., Burge 2000) divide John into two main parts: the Book of Signs (chs. 1–12) and the Book of Glory (chs. 13–21). But in John the passion begins in chapter 12. And why wait until 13:1 to begin the Book of Glory when *glory* and *glorify* are emphasized in 12:23, 28 (2x), and already in 11:4 and as early as 2:11? John's *Gloria* in 1:14 is the overture to the entire Gospel.

The case for beginning the second half at chapter 13 is arbitrary. Miyazaki begins the second half with chapter 11 since the raising of Lazarus prefigures Jesus' resurrection in chapter 20, with the two resurrections serving as thematic bookends. The case for the division between chapters 12 and 13 rests on three narrative shifts.

First, Jesus no longer addresses the crowds or the religious leaders in discourses; he now focuses on his disciples. Second, chapter 12 ends with summary emphases on the belief/unbelief pattern basic to the first half of John. Third, the introduction in 13:1-2 intones a new solemn aura. Readers *feel* they enter a new vista of Jesus' self-disclosure and teaching on costly discipleship. Hence Culpepper (1991: 331) sees here "the most significant transition in the Gospel, introducing not only the footwashing but [also] the entire second half of the Gospel" (cf. Chennattu: 82). The footwashing, Jesus' special sign done for his disciples (Dunn 1970: 248), is unique to John (cf. 1 Tim 5:10 and in OT, 1 Sam 25:41). Parallel to Mark 10:42-45, it signifies "Jesus' voluntary death on behalf of his own" (249) and is John's call to discipleship, even unto death, as Peter intuitively grasps in 13:36-37 (cf. Segovia 1982: 50).

Another significant factor in the decision to begin the second half of the Gospel with chapter 13 is the unity of chapters 13–17. As O'Day says,

> Taken together, 13:31 and 17:1 establish the framework in which all temporal references in the farewell discourse are to be read. This frame explicitly locates all of chaps. 13–17 within the consummation of the "hour." The "hour" of glorification is *now*, played out in the words of the farewell discourse. All notions of present and future in the discourse are recast against the arrival of the hour. All adverbs of time, particularly adverbs of temporal immediacy (*nun, arti, euthus*; e.g., 13:31-33; 16:22, 31-32; 17:5, 13) reinforce the arrival of the hour. (O'Day 1991: 158)

Unlike the Synoptic Gospels, John has no institution of the Lord's Supper as part of the evening meal in John 13. Rather, John—and only John—narrates Jesus' washing his disciples' feet. This unique Gospel event is followed by Jesus predicting Judas's action to turn him over to the authorities. Unlike the Synoptic Gospels, John includes a significant interchange between Jesus, Peter, and the beloved disciple. John 13:31-38 contains three key emphases:

- *Now is the Son of Man glorified.*
- *Loving one another* is the mark of discipleship.
- Jesus foretells Peter's denial.

Jesus' command to love one another as the mark of true discipleship is unique to John. The command complements the servant meaning of footwashing (13:12-17) and is thematically linked to the beloved disciple's appearance in 13:23. Serving one another and loving one another are hallmarks of John's view of discipleship and ecclesiology (though he never uses the word *church*). John exposits this theology with a dramatic example: Jesus washes his disciples' feet. Jesus then gives the new commandment: *Love one another.*

Throughout the chapter tension mounts between Jesus' love, eliciting loving discipleship (13:1b, 6-10, 14-17, 34-35), and "the betrayal and rejection of that gift by those whom Jesus loves" (13:2, 11, 18-19, 21-30, 36-38; O'Day 1995: 720). Not only does Judas, a major character in the chapter, move outside the love circle, but also Peter stumbles around on the border. Jesus' footwashing combines radical hospitality, the prerogative of the host, with humble service, the role of the house servant. To accept Jesus' paradoxical double role as host and servant means sharing in his being and mission. This *sharing* in Jesus through footwashing "opens the believer to Jesus' eschatological gift of eternal life" (O'Day 1995: 723), promising abundant life and joy complete (10:10; 15:11).

OUTLINE

Jesus Washes His Disciples' Feet, 13:1-17
Jesus Predicts Judas's Action, 13:18-30
Jesus' Glorification, Love Command, and Peter's Denial, 13:31-38

EXPLANATORY NOTES

Jesus Washes His Disciples' Feet 13:1-17

13:1 Time and Motivation

The time is just *before* the third Passover festival in this Gospel, a marker that distinguishes this meal from the one in the Synoptic Gospels, the Passover seder. This timing difference from the Synoptics may be understood in light of three other distinctive Johannine features. First, both the meal and Jesus' teaching set the stage for the entire farewell discourse, with the accent on the discourse. In contrast to both Jesus and the "omniscient narrator," the disciples do not know Jesus is about to begin his farewell speeches. *Jesus knows* (v. 3) God the Father has *put everything into his hands* (NJB). Jesus therefore *chooses* to wash his disciples' feet at this time—to begin not only an action but also a new relationship and community, with love its distinguishing mark.

Second, John 6, set right before the Jewish Passover Festival, interprets Jesus' feeding of the five thousand with intensified Lord's Supper significance. Jesus *is* the *bread* of life (6:35, 48, 51). Jesus' followers eat his flesh and drink his blood. See John 6 commentary [Sacrament, p. 529].

A third reason John has no Lord's Supper institution at the evening meal is that Jesus' crucifixion occurs *before* the Passover meal. John apparently follows a different calendar than that of the Synoptic Gospels. The Passover was observed on Nisan 14 (Exod 12:6). In John that day begins *after* the lambs are slain in the afternoon. Jesus is the slain Lamb of God (1:29, 36) for the Passover that begins Friday evening. Jesus thus dies when the Passover lambs are being slain, around three o'clock in the afternoon before the Passover seder. The Thursday evening meal in John thus precedes the Passover seder and is a fellowship meal (*ḥaburah*). When Jesus' disciples then participate in the Friday evening Passover seder, they eat the flesh of the Lamb (John 6)! In John the *day of Preparation* refers to *Preparation for the Passover* (19:14) and *Preparation* for the Sabbath (19:31, 42). (For further treatment of the differences in chronology, see the comparative diagram in O'Day 1995: 704-5; Burge's extensive discussion: 2000: 364–67; Culpepper 1998: 200–201 [Chronology, p. 508].)

Three emphases permeate this chapter: Jesus knows *that his hour ... to depart out of this world* and go *to the Father* has *come* (13:1b RSV); his love for *his own to the end* (13:1c-d); and the devil's instigating Judas's tragic action. Jesus' "time having come" is the narrative marker of the second half of the Gospel, announced as imminent in 12:23 as the dawning hour of Jesus' glorification (12:23, 27-28). The hour has come for Jesus to vanquish death in his lifted-up glorification and departure from this world to his Father.

The second emphasis is Jesus' passionate *love* for his disciples. Jesus' love in 13:1 (and v. 34) frames the farewell narrative. It recurs at the midpoint (15:9-17) and at the end of the farewell discourse (17:26). In the footwashing Jesus shows his perfect and unending love for his disciples. Jesus *showed the full extent of his love* (13:1 NIV 1984). Jesus' love for his disciples enables love of one another, the mark of discipleship (13:34-35).

Third, Judas's handover of Jesus to the authorities is a prominent theme in this chapter. These themes, including Jesus' departure, punctuate Jesus' farewell address. His disciples cannot now go where he is going (13:36-38)—to death. Nor can they go with the resurrected Jesus into his ultimate glorification in his return to his Father (20:17).

13:2-11 Footwashing as Cleansing[w]

John 13:2 indicates that the footwashing occurs *during* the meal, likely at the beginning. (Newer ETs follow the more reliable MSS: *ginomai*, "during"; older ETs follow less reliable MSS: *genomai*, "after"; Metzger 1994: 203.) In verse 12, after footwashing, Jesus resumes his place at the table for a teaching session. Footwashing is thus preparatory for the meal (13:23-26). Occurring before the meal, footwashing readily signifies hospitality (to guests who arrive after walking on dusty roads in sandals), as in an earlier narrative of Abraham welcoming three strangers by offering to wash their feet (Gen 18:4; Coloe 2006: 74–76; Thomas 1991: 35–36; Hultgren: 541–42). Coloe emphasizes footwashing's hospitality; it welcomes persons into the household. She identifies five phases of the action in John's account that are typical of welcoming one in the "tradition of the Greco-Roman banquet/symposium." These phases of action "allow the footwashing to be seen for what it is—a gesture of welcome into 'my Father's household' (14:2)" (2004: 414). Footwashing expresses the host's *hospitality* to the guest(s). Although the host provides *the means* for footwashing, the host would not do the footwashing. In ancient cultures a slave does this menial chore for the guests (1 Sam 25:41), or if the guests are lower in rank, they would take the basin and water and wash their own feet (Gen 43:24; Judg 19:21).

No wonder Peter strongly objects to Jesus washing his feet: his Master and Lord cannot possibly wash his feet! The intensity in the interchange between Jesus and Peter is understandable. Peter emphatically refuses (13:8), expressed by the Greek negative *ou mē*: *No! Never!* Jesus' response is an emphatic *I*, with emphasis also on *you*, designating Peter: *If I do not wash you, you have no part in me* (Burge 2000: 369). Through participation in the footwashing and the supper that follows, Jesus seals his covenant relationship with solemn discipleship vows (Chennattu), even though the disciples do not fully understand until after Jesus' glorification (v. 7; Segovia 1985: 87).

When we reflect on Jesus' command to wash one another's feet, we usually think of humility and lowly service. Servant humility is surely one dimension of meaning, for Jesus teaches this explicitly in 13:12-17. But the first portion of this text, verses 3-10, speaks specifically about cleansing. We detect four reasons for Jesus' stress on cleansing:

---

w   Where the superscript w occurs after headings, please see the commentary's online Web Supplement for additional material. Go to: http://www.heraldpress.com/bcbc/john.

1. The statement, *but you* (pl.) *are* [already] *cleansed* in 13:10 points to an earlier act of cleansing, most likely baptism. In John, Jesus' first disciples earlier belonged to John the Witness's baptizing movement. They were certainly baptized (1:35-39). John the Evangelist also says that Jesus baptized (3:22), even *if it was not Jesus himself but his disciples who baptized* (4:2). Footwashing updates baptism (Coloe 2006: 81). This adds meaning to 13:10: *One who has bathed does not need to wash, except for the feet, but is entirely clean. Bathing* refers to their earlier baptism; it need not be repeated. The phrase, *except for the feet,* lacking in some manuscripts, including Sinaiticus, is likely original (Thomas 1987: 97–99), which sharpens the next point.

2. Verse 10 uses two different Greek words for *wash*. The first word, *louō,* is here translated *bath,* but it can also mean *wash.* Bathing is of the whole body. The second word, *niptō,* is used here in verse 8 (2x) and in other verses (5, 6, 12, 14 [2x]) for the washing of the feet. The narrative thus distinguishes between washing the whole body and washing only the feet. This distinction is important when Jesus insists that Peter (representing also the other disciples: pl. *you, hymeis,* in v. 10) need not be washed or bathed all over. He has already been cleansed and now needs only to have his feet washed.

Cleansing through washing is thus of two kinds: *baptism* (denoted by *louō*), not to be repeated; and *footwashing* (denoted by *niptō*), which is to be repeated. Footwashing is *cleansing* from *post*baptismal sin. It updates the cleansing of baptism. Many early church leaders refer to footwashing in just this way—a cleansing from sin occurring since baptism or the last footwashing. Theodore of Mopsuestia (*Commentary on Gospel of John* 6.26-30) says of footwashing: "This is not baptism in remission of sin (which they surely received once for all), neither again is there need for another baptism, for total cleansing is received the first time (it is performed). Now it is needful to wash only their feet in order to cover [sins], which things are committed again [i.e., after baptism] as you well know" (in Thomas 1991: 164).

3. First John is much concerned about postbaptismal sin: "If anyone does sin, we have an advocate with the Father, Jesus Christ" (1 John 2:1). "If we confess our sins, he who is faithful and just will forgive us our sins and cleanse us from all unrighteousness" (1:9). First John's use of *cleansing* fits the emphasis of Jesus' footwashing in John.

4. Jesus says to protesting Peter at the end of John 13:8, *Unless I wash* [*niptō*] *you* [your feet], *you have no part* [*meros*] *with me.* What

does this mean? Certainly part of the meaning is that Jesus expects Peter to accept him in the role of a humble servant, as a model for the disciples. But for Peter especially, it also means that he must accept this action as Jesus' cleansing him from sin; otherwise he will no longer remain with Jesus, given what Jesus knows will soon befall him (13:36-38). As Dunn (1970: 250) states, "The washing of the feet has signified the completed cleansing of the cross. Peter has seen only the symbol and not the significance, and in his ignorance has asked for what cannot be—a more complete cleansing." In verse 4, the Greek for *took off his outer robe*, or *laid aside his garments* (KJV), uses the verb that occurs in John for "laying down one's life in death on behalf of others" (10:11, 15, 17, 18; 13:37, 38; 15:13; 1 John 3:16; Dunn 1970: 248; cf. O'Day 1995: 722). Jesus' *laying aside* (*tithēmi*) his garments (John 13:4) prefigures his laying down his life (R. Eslinger: 43). Only later will Jesus' disciples understand this symbolic action (v. 7b).

Peter, first resisting and then accepting footwashing, contrasts to Judas, whose role in the passion frames the footwashing event (13:2, 10b-11). Peter will deny Jesus but will be forgiven and restored. Jesus also washes Judas's feet, showing his love for Judas *to the end* (v. 1d). But Judas was overcome by another power. His plight is described bluntly in 13:2, *The devil had already put it into the heart of Judas Iscariot . . . to betray him* (RSV), and then with more pathos in verses 10b-11, *You are not all clean* (RSV).

The English word *betray* is a loaded translation of the Greek *paradidōmi*, which simply means "to hand over" (Klassen 1996). In Mark's passion account, the word occurs ten times: for Judas's *handing* Jesus *over* to the chief priests (14:10, 11, 18, 21, 41, 42, 44), for the chief priests' *handing* Jesus *over* to Pilate (15:1, 10), and for Pilate's *handing* Jesus *over* to be crucified (15:15). Only in Judas's case does the NRSV use the translation *betray*. The verb appears in Luke 10:22, where Jesus claims that the Father has "handed over" all things to him: "All things have been handed over to me by my Father; and no one knows who the Son is except the Father, or who the Father is except the Son and anyone to whom the Son chooses to reveal him." This sounds vintage Johannine! Also, in Romans 8:32 the verb is used to describe God's handing over Jesus to death: If God "did not withhold his own Son, but gave him up for all of us, will he not with him also give us everything else?" Here the verb is translated as "gave him up."

The verb itself is neutral. Paul uses it when he says, "I commend you because you remember me in everything and maintain the traditions just as I *handed* them *on* [*paradidōmi*] to you" (1 Cor 11:2, emphasis added). Even though many other citations in the NT indicate that *betrayer* is a tendentious translation, almost all English versions use it. Greek verbs that mean "betray" more specifically (e.g., *exautomoleō*) do not appear in the NT at all. Klassen contends that to translate *paradidōmi* as "betray" does Judas a disservice.

In Matthew 26:50 Jesus addresses Judas as "Friend." In John's account both Jesus' apparent washing of Judas's feet and dipping bread with him at the Last Supper indicate love and friendship. In light of these considerations, how do we understand John's strong language of Judas's act linked to *the devil*? Is Judas a willing or unwilling vessel of the devil? John uses a form of the verb *to throw* in 13:2 (*ballō*; lit., *had thrust it into him*). Another form of the same verb (*ekballō*) is used by Jesus in 12:31 for the *casting* [throwing] *out of the prince of this world* (AT, cf. KJV; cf. uses in 9:34, 35; 6:37). As Howard-Brook (1994: 294) writes, "Whether we should understand this as meaning that the devil forced his way into Judas or whether Judas was somehow open to this violent entry is not clear." Translating *paradidōmi* as "hand over" does not soften the devil/Judas alliance.

John is more explicit than the Synoptics about Judas's actions done under the power of the devil (already in 6:70-71), but the Synoptic Gospels also witness to Satan's entrance into Judas as causative of the outcome (Luke 22:2). Furthermore, the statement "It would have been better for that one not to have been born" (Matt 26:24c//Mark 14:21c echoing *1 Enoch* 38:2-3) judges Judas's motives as sinister (Matt 26:15 and par.). We might wish the Gospels had treated Judas more kindly. One might contend that his action was necessary in order for Scripture to be fulfilled (Matt 26:24a; John 13:18b, quoting Ps 41:9; 40:10 LXX) and that Judas is a hapless victim. Even so, the Gospel narratives do not attribute innocence to Judas (even if one accepts the view that he intended to spark Jesus to "strike" his opponents with victorious power and win God's liberation battle). My sympathy for Judas arises when I ask whether he could have resisted Satan's entry. John's statements seem to answer no. My only response, with the help of the Lord's Prayer, James 4:7, and putting on the Christian armor (Eph 6:10-18) is to cry to God: Protect me—protect us—from diabolic power entering me and any in Jesus' disciple band today!

So how does "cleansing from sin" connect with humility and lowly service? The two meanings are not to be separated, for it is precisely in being freed from sin that we are empowered to live as servants of one another. Living this way protects us from sin (1 John 5:18). Through the cleansing of footwashing, we are empowered to serve one another, to renew and fulfill our baptismal pledges to follow Jesus [Sacrament, p. 529].

Those who emphasize Jesus' raising up a new temple (2:19; 7:38; 14:2) regard footwashing as preparation for entering into that new temple, which Jesus' death, resurrection, and glorification make possible (Kerr: passim; Coloe 2007: 123–66). Footwashing thus symbolizes Jesus' "act of eschatological hospitality." Jesus welcomes his disciples into the house that his Father is preparing for them (Hultgren: 542). As host of the banquet, Jesus breaks the custom of household servants washing the guests' feet. Jesus, the host himself, washes their feet, a powerful symbol welcoming them into *my Father's house* (2:16), anticipating *I go to prepare a place for you* in *my Father's house* (14:2).

13:12-17 Footwashing as Humble Service

In these six verses Jesus teaches a further meaning of footwashing. Since 13:7-10 emphasizes cleansing, why does Jesus, in this didactic session with his disciples around the table (v. 12), stress humble service? Two sequences indicate the flow of thought:

> You call me Teacher and Lord . . .
>   If I . . . have washed your feet, you also ought to wash one another's feet. . . .
> Truly [RSV], truly, I tell you, servants are not greater than their master. . . .
>   (13:13-14, 16)

> So if I, your Lord and Teacher, have washed your feet . . .
>   For I have set you an example [hypodeigma]. . . .
> If you know these things, you are blessed if you do them. (13:14-15, 17)

The textual clue to the meaning of humble service is that *servants are not greater than their master*. This statement makes the footwashing preparatory for Jesus' death. If the master must face the cross, so must the servants—and a good part of chapters 14–16 addresses the issue of imminent persecution in and by the world (cf. Matt 10:16-30). In context, this emphasis is rightly linked to hospitality and cleansing. These several meanings intertwine in this rare NT use of *example* (hypodeigma). As Culpepper (1991: 142–43) has shown, this term recurs in Jewish literature to designate fidelity to Torah even unto death. Martyrs are noble examples (hypodeigma) "of how to die a good death willingly and nobly for the revered and holy laws" (2 Macc 6:28, 31; 4 Macc 17:22-23; Sir 44:16). With this teaching Jesus' footwashing segues into the farewell discourse, with deeper meanings of Jesus' *example*: Jesus' love command in John 13:34 (cf. 15:12-15, 20-21a; 21:15-19).

Jesus' radical hospitality in washing his disciples' feet embraces cleansing and humble service. These are interlinked in Jesus' example (*hypodeigma*), culminating in his death. Washing another's feet signifies at the deepest level a love for the other that is willing to die for the other. "We know love by this, that he laid down his life for us—and we ought to lay down our lives for one another" (1 John 3:16). The entire farewell discourse prepares the disciples for Jesus' death as well as his departure to return to his Father. The Maccabean Eleazar, who "founded" the Feast of Dedication, speaks of his imminent death as a *hypodeigma* in his farewell discourse (2 Macc 6:28, 31; Howard-Brook 1994: 299). Jesus transforms the significance of the feast: his death, with water and blood from his side (7:37-39; 19:34), liberates from the prince of this world those who believe in him (6:37-40; 12:31). He puts *rejoicing* into their hearts through the gift of his Spirit (7:39; 20:22-23).

Faithfulness in radical discipleship, even unto death, provides a cohering center for John 13 (Culpepper 1991). This act connects footwashing to Mary's anointing since both prepare for Jesus' death (Weiss: 310-14). Sadly, Jesus' commitment to his friends galvanizes the chief priests to violence against Lazarus and Jesus (12:9-11). Jesus does not relent. Commanding love for one another, he calls his disciples *friends* (15:13-15). Jesus' footwashing enacts his friendship (Thompson 2003: 258, 264-72).

In this act, Jesus' friendship becomes a "sword and shield" against violence. "Footwashing is a profound and Christocentric act of friendship, an act that is our faithful response to the cycles of violence, dominion and oppression" (Schertz: 5). Friendship embraces both the soteriological and ethical meaning of footwashing. Footwashing disarms the disciples' messianic hopes of subjugating enemies. Footwashing opens us to "the Lord's love; for every Do this of the Lord goes back to his *I have done it*" (von Speyr: 35). Heeding Jesus' command, *Do this*, makes peace.

Jesus Predicts Judas's Action 13:18-30

This unit contains three interlinked themes: the one lost to the circle, Judas; the sudden appearance of a new figure, the beloved disciple, and his relational role to Peter and Jesus; and the meal itself, overshadowed by the dominance of the first theme.

13:18-20 Introducing Judas's Desertion[w]

Some translations and commentators include these verses in the preceding unit (as does the third edition of the UBS Greek Testament), but the Nestle-Aland Greek text (27th ed.) rightly makes it a separate (transitional) paragraph. The opening line, *I am not speaking of all of you*, exempts one disciple from the blessing of verse 17 and loops back to the somber comments in verses 10b-11. Jesus knows those whom he has chosen and also what must happen to fulfill the Scripture (Ps 41:9): *The one who ate my bread has lifted his heel against me.* While the Septuagint (Ps 40:10) uses *esthiō* for *eating*, in quoting this Scripture, John uses *trōgō* for *eating* (13:18), matching Jesus' earlier invitation to *munch* or *chew* on his flesh (6:54) to have eternal life (6:58). Jesus foretells what will happen, authorizing his foreknowledge with the revelatory *I AM* (13:19c)!

Even in this sad moment the narrative trope of *believing in Jesus* is not lost. The fact that one falls away could cast doubt on Jesus' mission and credibility, but Jesus' forecast of this event as being to *fulfill Scripture* protects against this doubt (note Jesus' prayer in 17:20). Jesus' prophetic knowledge of the future assures the disciples that he continues as trusted leader, even as Lord. Verse 20 underscores the importance of staying linked to Jesus, first by the emphatic *Very truly, I tell you*, and second by linking the disciple with Jesus in a union with *the one who sent me* (NIV). To receive Jesus' words, hard though they be, and cling to Jesus as his disciple validates what Jesus' mission has accomplished in training them for discipleship, except for one.

This tragedy of the one lost (Judas) permeates the narrative (13:2, 11, 18-19, 26-31a). Jesus' teaching on cleansing, service, and love for one another is haunted by a shadow figure—one who is not clean, one who though he eats the bread *has lifted his heel against me* (v. 18e). The devil's grasp of Judas (13:2) makes *his* footwashing experience hollow. It does not stop his collusion with plans for violence, though it is uncertain what his intent is at this point—opposing Jesus or helping Jesus launch his messianic triumph.

13:21-26a The Meal and Disclosure: Which One?

No sooner does Jesus speak these words than a sword pierces his own heart. Jesus is deeply troubled, agitated, angered in spirit. As O'Day (1995: 730) says, the "critical players in the betrayal are Jesus and the devil, not Jesus and Judas." What Jesus says is intensified by *testified* (NIV, *martyreō*) and another *Truly, truly, I tell you* [AT]. Then the bombshell drops: *One of you will hand me over.*

The disciples are dumbfounded, staring at one another (NIV). They have no clue about whom Jesus is speaking. At this desperate moment, upon hearing this crushing word, a new figure appears, *the disciple whom Jesus loved* (NIV): the beloved disciple. This one is reclining at Jesus' breast (*kolpos*, v. 23), the very image of Jesus' closeness to God in 1:18. *Love* links key relationships in John. Since Peter is usually the speaker for the disciples, he *nods* to the beloved disciple to query Jesus to discover of whom he speaks. Reclining at Jesus' right and leaning left toward Jesus in a customary seating position at the table, *that one* (Gr.) asks Jesus, *Lord, who is it?* [Beloved Disciple, p. 505].

13:26b-30 Judas Identified

Jesus answers through an act of hospitality, linking this critical moment back to the footwashing: "*That one* [Gr.] *to whom I give the bread I have dipped.*" *Dipping the bread then, he gave it to Judas, son of Simon the Iscariot* (AT). Immediately upon receiving the morsel, Satan entered into *that one* (Gr.).

Whether Judas ate the bread is not clear. Jesus, in charge of the situation, commands him to *do quickly* what he is to do. Judas obeys Jesus' command and immediately leaves. *And it was night* (v. 30), evoking the light-darkness motif lacing the earlier narrative. O'Day (1995: 730) refers to Satan's entry into Judas as *possession* and observes that Jesus' battle with "the demonic forces and evil is saved until the consummate battle of Jesus' own hour." This is true, but Jesus entered that battle in 12:27-30 (possibly already in 11:33-35 or even in the hot dispute of 8:31-59) and declared, *Now the ruler of this world will be driven out* (12:31). While John recounts no exorcisms, as in Matthew, Mark, and Luke, John treats evil and the devil on a cosmic scale, focused ultimately in Jesus' glorification through death and resurrection. Judas's role, allied with the hostile unbelief of *the Jews*, appears necessary to the denouement of Jesus' mission! ["The Jews," p. 520].

Verses 28-29 intervene between "Satan's entrance" and "Judas's departure." The narrator informs readers that the other disciples have no clue as to what is going on. They think that Judas, since he keeps the purse for the group, has left to purchase food for the upcoming festival or to give an offering to the poor, an act of customary charity concluding the meal. This indicates that the other disciples do not consider Judas as less faithful to Jesus than themselves. In the Synoptics the two sons of Zebedee draw the hostility of the other ten when they vie for top seats in the coming kingdom (Mark 10:35-45; Matt 20:20-28; Luke 22:24-27).

The meal is overshadowed by events surrounding it. The supper theologically seals Jesus' covenant relationship with his disciples (Chennattu), though sealing the covenant relationship is more prominent in the footwashing than in the meal.

The literal translation *that one* from the Greek highlights the role of the beloved disciple as a contrasting counterpart to Judas. The beloved disciple epitomizes an unconditional love union with Jesus. Judas represents defection and exclusion from the disciple circle. But Jesus loves even Judas, one of his own, to the end (13:1)! But because of the devil, Judas cannot return Jesus' love.

Jesus' Glorification, Love Command, and Peter's Denial 13:31-38

This unit is transitional. Some commentators link it to chapter 14 as the beginning of Jesus' farewell discourse. Rationale for this is strong, since themes in 13:31-35 recur and tumble over each other numerous times, with new dimensions through chapter 17.

At the same time, this final unit in chapter 13 functions as a significant conclusion to the footwashing meal and Jesus' teaching. Verse 31a, *When he had gone out, Jesus said,* continues directly from verse 30, Judas's exit. Further, Jesus' glorification is rightly rooted in the hospitality and humble service of footwashing. Jesus' last meal with his disciples anticipates the parting of the farewell discourse. Another consideration for beginning a new unit with chapter 14 is the shift in Jesus' dialogue partners: in 14:1 Jesus addresses the disciples as a group (*your* is pl.). Thomas, Philip, and the other Judas, not Peter, are Jesus' dialogue partners.

13:31-32 Jesus' Glorification

Jesus identifies himself as the *Son of Man* in this emotive declaration. In John *Son of Man* is associated with eschatological announcement (5:27; 8:28; 12:23), which itself is linked to Jesus' coming from and returning to his Father (1:51; 3:13-14; 6:62; 12:33-34; O'Day 1995: 732). *Glorify* recurs five times, uniting Jesus as Son to God as Father, and vice versa (cf. 12:23, 28). The chapter 12 sayings on *glorify* accentuate Jesus' leaning toward the cross, *to be lifted up*. *At once* (end of 13:32) expresses urgency and consummation in Jesus' fulfilling his mission. John 13:31-32 discloses Jesus' unity with his Father and the revelation of his divine glory.

13:33 (36-37) Jesus' Departure

Shifting from the ecstasy of God's glorifying Jesus, and Jesus' glorifying God, Jesus tenderly addresses his disciples as *Little children*. This address is used only here in John, though it appears frequently in 1 John (2:1, 12, 28; 3:7, 18; 4:4; 5:21; McDermond).

Jesus tells his disciples plainly, *I am with you only a little longer*. He reminds them that he said this before in public, to *the Jews* (7:33-34; 8:21), John's only use of *the Jews* in the farewell discourse. In those earlier uses addressing his opponents, Jesus stressed judgment and condemnation. Now he presents his departure "to his disciples as the seal of their new relationship with God, with Jesus, and with one another" (O'Day 1995: 732). He also tells them that they cannot come where he is going; then he shifts to the mark of their identity as his children, living his new commandment.

13:34-35 A New Commandment: Love One Another

This is the major specified commandment that Jesus gives directly to his disciples in the entire Gospel: *love one another. Just as I have loved you, you also should love one another* (see the varied forms of this commandment in "Commandments in John" in the TBC for John 15). This usual translation is too weak, for Jesus is not just a model of the past to be imitated: the command also makes Jesus' love contemporary, empowering believers to love, then and now. A better translation stresses this: *Love one another with the love with which I have loved you* (AT). This expresses the continuing relationship between Jesus and the believers (Rossé: 70).

By this everyone will know that you are my disciples, if you have love for one another. This declaration "opens up the possibility of community with God and Jesus and community with one another, but it is not an easy word to keep" (O'Day 1995: 734). The new commandment is the foundation and impulse of the hospitality and humble service permeating the chapter. The commandment here and in 1 John is vintage Johannine ethic, internally directed, with positive impact upon the church's mission to the world (*Everyone will know* . . .; TLC of this chapter). Much of 1 John is directed toward encouragement, with warnings. Keeping this commandment means practical obedience: remembering the orphans and widows in their affliction and giving to those in need (e.g., James 1:27; 1 John 3:17). Then believers are assuredly led by God's Spirit and protected from the world (McDermond: 86–87, 119–21).

328   John 13

However, this is not the only commandment that the fourth evangelist mentions. Chapter 12 ends with Jesus' declaring another commandment from God to Jesus, thus uniquely his to fulfill through his words and deeds. That commandment is *eternal life* (12:49-50; cf. 17:3). This commandment arches over the entire Gospel; it measures fulfillment of Jesus' mission. As Jesus' disciples enact his love commandment, they also enable Jesus' fulfillment of the eternal life commandment.

13:36-38 Peter's Promise, Jesus' Prediction

Peter wants to follow his Lord anywhere, so he asks where Jesus is going. But Jesus cuts short his eager pledge, saying, *Where I am going, you cannot follow me now; but you will follow afterward.* Peter replies with determination, *Lord, why can I not follow you now? I will lay down my life for you.* Peter uses the verb (*tithēmi*) that Jesus used earlier to forecast his future. Jesus repeats Peter's words, so he can hear them, but in the form of a question: *Will you really?* (AT). Jesus' final words, beginning again with the emphatic *Truly, truly, I say to you* (AT), later haunt Peter as he indeed experiences Jesus' prediction, *Before the cock crows, you will have denied me three times.* Peter's faith journey passes through the valley of tears, learning the hard way that unless and until Jesus paves the way through death, overcoming the power of the evil one, he does not have the strength to follow. The devil partially wins Peter.

The profiles of Judas, Peter, and the beloved disciple emerge paradigmatically in this narrative. Judas moves outside the love circle. Peter doggedly stays in but slips outside for a while, only to move in again as foremost shepherd of the new love covenant (21:15-19). Throughout, the beloved disciple (who he is we do not yet know) models the key criteria of the love community. His stature and authority is not in any official position, but in the charisma of love. He guides us through the remaining narrative, as *eyewitness* to the traditions of the Gospel and as faithful follower, not flashy but ever present, charged with love's mutuality in care of Jesus' mother, who also lovingly cares for him as son (19:26-27). He is the first to *believe* the resurrection miracle (20:8). Chennattu (83) sums up these paradigms of discipleship memorably: "The disciples and the subsequent readers are provided with three possible ways of responding to a covenant relationship, . . . expressed by . . . [*his own, hoi idioi*, 13:1] total rejection (Judas, 13:30), temporary denial (Peter, 13:36-38), and total faithfulness (the beloved disciple, 13:23)" [*Beloved Disciple, p. 505*] [*Disciples, p. 509*].

THE TEXT IN BIBLICAL CONTEXT

Judas in John and the NT[w]

In Mark (3:13-19), Matthew (10:1-4), and Luke (6:12-16; cf. Acts 1:13, 16), Judas Iscariot is listed as one of twelve disciples. In these Gospels he is listed last, with an added note about him as the one "who handed him over" in Matthew and Mark (AT), but in Luke, "the one who became the handover agent" (AT). Virtually all translations use "betray" despite the fact that in other places "betray" is not used in translating this Greek verb. John identifies Judas not as Iscariot but *the son of Simon Iscariot* (13:2). If the Gospels were written in the chronological order of Mark, Matthew, Luke, and John—as is commonly accepted—then Judas receives a greater amount of attention as time passes, with Luke excepted: in Mark, 169 words; Matthew, 309; Luke and Acts, 233; John, 489 (Klassen 1996: 13). Word count is one factor, but *how* each account presents Judas's role is more significant.

Despite what Judas does in turning Jesus over, Jesus fulfills his mission in John, which presents Judas's action as necessary to fulfill Scripture and accomplish Jesus' mission. Howard-Brook (1994: 293) points out that in John 13:1-3 Jesus "surrounds" the devil, for "verses 1 and 3 speak of Jesus' knowledge and planning, while verse 2 speaks of the devil's own activity." Similarly, in 13:12-35 Judas's action is bookended by Jesus' friendship sop on the one side and Jesus' love commandment on the other. Jesus' mission goes forward, despite the one lost.

None of the Gospels ascribes to Judas any particular negative character trait, nor is any clear about Judas's motives, except for the editorial comment in John 12:6. Judas keeps the common purse, but in John the disciples do not suspect him of deception (13:28-29). They think he leaves to do a good deed. Perhaps Judas thinks his action will hasten the messianic deliverance his Teacher Messiah will accomplish. When that fails, he repents (Matt 27:3-4). Even so, he takes his own life (Matt 27:5; cf. Acts 1:16-20c). All three Synoptic Gospels include Jesus' statement "But woe to that one by whom the Son of Man is betrayed!" (Matt 26:24; Mark 14:21; Luke 22:22). This distressing *woe* word does not appear in John. In Matthew (26:24) and Mark (14:21), Jesus continues, "It would have been better for that one not to have been born."

John 13 and the (New) Covenant

John 13 is a structural parallel to Matthew 26:26-29; Mark 14:22-25; and Luke 22:17-20, where Jesus makes a (new) covenant with his disciples. In the Synoptics Jesus' covenant with his disciples is made at the table, the Last (or Lord's) Supper event. Jesus speaks words of institution, using the term *covenant*, which in Luke and Paul's citation of the Supper, is designated "*new* covenant" (Swartley 2006a: 177–88).

Is John 13 to be understood also as a covenant-making parallel? Chennattu's answer is clearly yes, and she devotes her entire book to understanding discipleship as a covenant relationship, beginning with John 1:19-51. The farewell discourse in its entirety is Jesus' making and sealing the covenant, which begins with a meal and new commandment in chapter 13. John 13:17, *If you know these things, you are blessed if you do them*, is as close as we come in John to Jesus' words of institution in the Synoptics and Paul. In John, Jesus' covenant-making concludes with his high-priestly prayer for his covenant followers.

Chennattu is correct, but vast differences in emphasis regarding the meaning of the (new) covenant are apparent. The heart of the parallel is that John has a meal and gives a new commandment, features of covenant-making in the OT (Gen 26:26-30; 31:43-54; Exod 24:5-11; Deut 27:6-7). Indeed, the whole of Exodus 19:1–24:8 is God's covenant-making act with Israel, with emphasis on Moses's giving of the law, the Decalogue (20:1-17) and the Covenant Code (Exod 20:22–23:19). If one regards Jesus' covenant intentions as renewing the covenant that God established with Israel, then the OT covenant-renewal ceremonies are pertinent (e.g., Josh 24:1-18). Chennattu (70–71) cites this Joshua 24 text as a model for understanding John's covenant emphases, but she also emphasizes *newness* in John's *new commandment* (96–98). After God initiates covenant relationship with Israel on Mount Sinai, God gives commandments for covenant relationship. John 13:31-35 (and much of 1 John) parallels OT covenant moral stipulations. The OT Mosaic covenant entails not only the Ten Commandments but also several love commandments: "Love the Lord your God with all your heart, and with all your soul, and with all your might" (Deut 6:5-7). "Love your neighbor as yourself" (Lev 19:18b). "Love the alien as yourself" (19:34). Jesus sums up the entire law in the Synoptics with the double love command: love of God and love of neighbor (Matt 22:34-40//Mark 12:28-34//Luke 10:25-28; see Furnish for exposition). Matthew and Luke include also Jesus' command to love the enemy (Matt 5:44-45; Luke 6:27-36; see essays in Swartley, ed. 1992).

Jesus' new love commandment in John (13:34) is *Love one another just as I have loved you*. The larger discourse (15:1-18; 17:20-23) grounds the community's love for one another in Jesus' love for them and in *God's love for Jesus*. Love for one another is the new community's identity mark of faithful discipleship: *By this everyone will know that you are my disciples, if you have love for one another* (13:35).

Rather than connecting the covenant with the usual atonement motifs, as in the Synoptics and Paul through the words of institution, John seals the connection between covenant and new identity through the *practice* of the new love commandment. Though John is often regarded as lacking in ethical rigor, this new covenant-*signature* ethic connects *being* children of God with *doing* love actions, as 1 John makes plain. Thus you show that you are children of God (cf. Matt 5:44-48). Further, *love of God* welcomes the disciples into the oneness of the Son and the Father (John 17).

Footwashing in John enacts this distinctive theology through sacrament, sign, ordinance, or practice—whichever term one's theological tradition chooses. It symbolizes the *doing* of the new commandment. Thus viewed, John 13 is a tightly unified and theologically coherent unit, with Peter, the beloved disciple, and Judas exemplifying differing responses to the new covenant relationship. Knowing Jesus is epistemologically grounded in love and deeds of love. In John, the beloved disciple leads the other disciples into this new knowing, including Peter in every subsequent scene where they both appear [*Beloved Disciple, p. 505*].

THE TEXT IN THE LIFE OF THE CHURCH

Love for One Another

Tertullian appeals to John 13:35 for the distinguishing mark of the early Christians in his *Apology* (39.7) for the Christian cause: "The practice of a special love brands us in the eyes of some! 'See,' they say, 'how they love one another . . . and how they are ready even to die for one another'" (FC 10:99). The same prevailed for sixteenth-century Anabaptists, since their trials before magistrates often probed with whom they shared food, clothing, money, and lodging. But these trials, resulting in many martyrs, did not dissuade them from doing what was essential to their new commandment identity. They continued to practice this love command in obedience to Christ (Hiett Umble: 103–11).

Anabaptist sources weigh in especially on John 13:15 and 35. Menno's writings appeal to 13:15 twice, verse 16 once, and verse 35 three times. *Martyrs Mirror* references 13:16 once, 13:17 thrice, and 13:35 six times! The Anabaptists' appeal to *love one another* is the scriptural rationale for why they believe, live, and die. *By this shall everyone know . . .* is played out in martyrdom.

Menno Simons links John 13:15 with Matthew 11:29 to stress Jesus' example of humility as "true testimony of the Holy Spirit" (Menno: 441). Jesus' example is amplified in Menno's *Epistle to Micron*, where he laments how Christians "hang or put on wheel, or place on stake" other Christians: a "strange and unbecoming [act] in light of the compassionate, merciful, kind nature, disposition, spirit, and example of Christ, the meek Lamb—which example He has commanded all His chosen children to follow" (921). In his *Reply to Gellius Faber*, Menno cites "unfeigned, brotherly love" (John 13:35) as the fourth of six "signs" by which "the church of Christ may be known" (740, 743).

Last letters written to spouses, children, and congregations often appeal to John 13:35. One such case is that of Hans Symons, in prison at Antwerp (Sept. 13, 1567). To his children—Vincent, Kaerle, Willem, and Hans—and his wife, Tanneken, he says, "And I pray you, that you show love to one another all the days of your life, for Christ says: 'By this shall all men know that ye are my disciples, if ye have love for one another.' John 13:35" (*MM* 711). Toward the end of the letter, after many appeals that his congregation remain faithful and holy, he writes, "And above all, I pray you, keep the Lord before your eyes above all else, and love one another fervently; thereby men shall know that you are children of the Most High, for love abides forever, it never perishes. John 13:35; 1 Cor. 13:13, 8" (*MM* 712).

Another prisoner, Jacob the Chandler, addresses his children similarly (*MM* 803). In the martyr testimonies, editor van Braght includes a Confession of Faith, dated about AD 1600. The nineteenth article identifies "six signs of the church of God, by which it may be distinguished from all other peoples" (*MM* 393). In the sixth sign, "unfeigned godly love" describes Christ's true followers. The long description, replete with Scripture, concludes with texts from John and 1 John on love for one another, citing John 13:34-35 in full (*MM* 394).

How does love for one another show itself today in our congregations, homes, and actions in our larger society? Love works through practicing mutual aid, institutionally or spontaneously; caring for the poor, aliens, homeless, widows, and orphans among us (in church or society); speaking out on justice issues (e.g., healthcare access for all); and taking time to listen to hurting people. Burge 2000 (383) speaks of Henri Nouwen as testimony to living for others: "Here . . . we have a man whose life has been so deeply touched by the gospel that it transformed him and gave him the joy of service. He had been washed by Jesus, and so he was washing others' feet." We must first be bathed in God's love, Jesus' love, before we can share it with others (381–82). We must be washed, cleansed, then freed to love. Some of us like Peter protest and want to stay in control. Love disarms and enables us to reflect Jesus' limitless love, poignantly shown in John 13, which includes Judas in the disciples Jesus loves!

The Practice of Footwashing Today[w]

The ritual power of the embodied practice of footwashing is well illustrated by a story from Katongole and Rice's *Reconciling All Things*. The (extra)ordinary event occurred at the Lausanne Forum on World Evangelization in Pattaya, Thailand, in 2004. Thirty issue groups were formed for discussion and to report back at the end. Group 22, focusing on reconciliation across societal barriers and polarization, washed feet:

> When the time for our report came, we set up on the convention floor twelve people with basins and towels. Then as two people narrated what happened in our group during the week, the twelve people washed each other's feet: a Catholic priest, an Orthodox priest, and an evangelical pastor; an Israeli and a Palestinian; a black, a white, and an Asian American; Hutu and Tutsi; male and female.
>
> At the end of the presentation, the polite silence was interrupted by a standing ovation. . . .
>
> We did not meet to fix the many divisions and conflicts represented by the members of our group, . . . [but] what was poignantly revealed and confirmed to us in the gesture of footwashing was the nature and mission of the church in reconciliation. (110–12)

Love for One Another as Witness to the World

This distinctive Johannine emphasis on love for one another differs significantly from that of both the Synoptic Gospels and the Pauline literature. It has often been judged to be sectarian, not suited to vital witness to the world. However, various scholars have reassessed how sectarian identity may contribute positively to living within a pluralistic world. David Rensberger, Robert H. Gundry, and Miroslav Volf address the issue in complementary perspectives (Swartley 2006a: 289–96).

Rensberger (1988: 141–49) argues persuasively that the community out of which John's Gospel arose was in all probability what we today call sectarian, mostly because of its social location. It was expelled—or threatened with expulsion—from the synagogue, as reflected in 9:22, 34; 12:42; 16:2. John's high Christology is "directly related to the communal experience of the Christians for whom it was written" (119). Christology and community, while perhaps appearing to be "of no relevance to the social and political struggles of oppressed people" (118), enable a countercultural witness to the larger religious community and the sociopolitical power of the world:

> Above all, the meaning of John's sectarianism is that *because it was sectarian* it challenged the world on the basis of the love of God and the word of God. No religion that sees itself as the backbone of a society, as the glue that holds a society together, can easily lay down a challenge to that society's wrongs. A cultural religion is all too readily told to mind its own business, because it has a business, a well-known role in maintaining society's fabric unmolested. It is the sect, which has no business in the world, that is able to present a fundamental challenge to the world's oppressive orders. Precisely because it sees itself alienated from the world, its commitment to the world's orders is attenuated, if not abolished altogether. Thus it is able to take a stand over against the world and to criticize that which the world holds most dear. (142)

Rensberger thus regards Johannine Christianity, with its ethic of love for one another, a paradigm for a faith community that is "set free to criticize the world's injustice and violence in the name of the world's Creator" (143). The Amish, and to a lesser extent Mennonite and Brethren churches today, represent this paradigm. But these groups must heed the Revelator's critique to the church in Ephesus, "You have abandoned the love you had at first" (Rev 2:4).

O'Day (1995: 734) appeals to the models of Dr. Martin Luther King and Bishop Oscar Romero for examples of those who witnessed to God's love, Jesus' love—not because they consciously denied themselves freedom or because they chose to give their lives for others, but because they "chose to live the love of Jesus fully." The new commandment calls us to love one another for the same reason: to live God's love in Jesus as Christian brothers and sisters and thus glorify God. This is the fruit of Jesus' mission and the foundation and goal of ours.

John 14–17

Jesus' Farewell Discourse and Prayer

OVERVIEW

Discourse on Departing, Abiding, and the Paraclete[w]

Jesus' farewell discourse extends from John 13:31 to 16:33. Jesus' prayer in chapter 17 is bifocal. It consummates the discourse theologically, but in genre it differs from 13:31–16:33. The disciples are not present; Jesus prays to his Father on their behalf.

Jesus' farewell speech has precedents in Judaism and Greco-Roman literature: Jacob's farewell speech in Genesis 47:29–49:33; Moses's in Deuteronomy; Joshua's in Joshua 22–24; Cicero, *Divination* 1.30.63 (for more precedents, see Talbert: 200–201; Acts 20:17-38; Mark 13). The content of John 13–17 is unique, expressive of this Gospel's proclamation: Jesus is Revealer of the Father (1:18). Jesus is the One who loves. Jesus is the way, the truth, and the life. Jesus will send the Paraclete to comfort, guide, and empower the disciples. With Jesus' departure, the Holy Spirit will indwell the believers.

The Holy Spirit will come to dwell in them. They are also to dwell or *abide* in Jesus, enjoying a mutual indwelling, a love-union with Jesus and the Father (chs. 15–17; 17:20-26). Recurring themes are tightly interwoven, with eleven, by my count, tumbling over each other (not chronologically). Here I arrange them in a chiastic

---

w   Where the superscript w occurs after headings, please see the commentary's online Web Supplement for additional material. Go to: http://www.heraldpress.com/bcbc/john.

pattern, with the promised Paraclete at the center and assurances and peace as the envelope:

A Assurances for the Future
    B Departure (I am going away) and consolation (I will not leave you alone)
        C Injunctions to love
            D Keep my commandment(s)
                E Abide in me (in my love) as branches in the vine, mutual indwelling
                    F Fivefold promise of the Paraclete/Holy Spirit to come
                E´ Jesus, the way to (know) the Father: mutual glorification
            D´ Ask, and it will be done (14:13-14; 15:7, 16; 16:23-24)
        C´ Warnings of the world's hatred (persecution)
    B´ Promise of Jesus' return
A´ Gift of peace

Since most of these themes are repeated in chapters 14 and 16, numerous commentators propose that a final editor joined two sources together. The ending in 14:31c, *Rise, let us be on our way,* appears to anticipate chapters 18–19 directly. Scholars have proposed numerous explanations. We will appreciate the speech in its canonical narrative unity, however, dispensing with notions of disparate materials joined together by a final editor, or the idea that 14:31 ends one speech and chapters 15–16 are another, or that chapter 17 is tacked on as a farewell prayer. Jesus' farewell speech is best appreciated as a narrative unit, united by numerous key themes and rhetorical development.

The overlap of themes has progression, as this diagram illustrates:

13:31-35 (36-38)	14:1–15:17	15:18–17:26
Glorification	World	Conflict and tribulation
Departure (absence)	Paraclete (presence)	Unity and mutual indwelling
Love command-ment	*Obey my word* and *abide in my love*	Love and unity; *see my glory* that *world may believe*

The movement is down for column 1, up for column 2, and down for column 3. Hence the theme in the third position comes first in 14:1–15:17 (obey, abide). New dimensions of exhortation appear as the narrative progresses. As this diagram indicates, chapters 13 and 17 are linked thematically to chapters 14–16. Both, however, are distinct in certain aspects:

- Unique actions of Jesus: Jesus washes feet in John 13 and prays a sustained prayer in John 17.

- The central characters: John 14–16 features serial dialogues: Jesus with Thomas, Philip, and Judas (not Iscariot); Peter and Judas (prominent in ch. 13); and Jesus and his Father (ch. 17).

- Their distinctive beginning (ch. 13, footwashing) and ending (ch. 17, Jesus' prayer).

The fivefold mention of the promised Paraclete is most significant. These texts are sandwiched between other themes, especially persecution in the latter cases.

Theological Emphases in Jesus' Farewell Speech[w]

John 13–17 may be viewed as Jesus' covenant-making ceremony. Jesus' action, teaching, and prayer tie together many earlier Gospel themes, such as election, abiding in Jesus, and keeping God's commandments. Jesus speaks and does what the Father instructs him. The union of Father and Son, a sticking point between Jesus and "the Jews," now reaches its zenith in Jesus' prayer to his Father.

In addition to these themes, two major Johannine emphases emerge, striking for their diverse yet complementary perspectives. The first major theme stresses Jesus' prediction of persecutions and the threat of apostasy, in light of the political reality that the Johannine community faces in the empire. Thus it is important to be closely bonded to Jesus, to love one another, and to be assured that Jesus will not forsake his disciples; he sends the Paraclete. In this context Jesus' declaration, *He has no power over me* (14:30), assures their security (cf. 16:33 RSV, *I have overcome the world*). The *he* in 14:30 is *the ruler of the world* (AT; see 12:31). Jesus also prays, *Keep them from the evil one* (17:15 RSV). Here the evil one is *Satan* (named in 13:27). These forces collude in the politics of the Gospel (Cassidy: 40–41; cf. Carter 2008). Believers will stand victorious against these evil powers because Jesus faces them down and gains victory over them in his death. *Arise, let us go* (*egeiresthe, agōmen*; 14:31 AT) matches exactly the parallel in Mark 14:42, when Jesus ends his Gethsemane agony and goes via Judas's signal to face the

Roman soldiers, the political power arresting and crucifying Jesus. This exclamation is a "delayed exit" to death (see comments on 14:30-31). It builds narrative suspense by anticipating Jesus' death and also provides for continued farewell teaching.

The second major theme of Jesus' farewell speech is spiritual formation. This formation prepares the disciples to live in the hostile world after Jesus leaves them. They comprehend this, though, only after Jesus' resurrection. Brodie, who is strong on spiritual formation, sees narrative unity and development of interrelated emphases (428–29). The disciples' spiritual formation moves through three stages: cleansing, purification, and sanctification. This pattern charts the changes necessary for the disciples also to face down the world and the ruler, or prince, of this world—Satan—and to live victoriously. (For Brodie's exposition of these chapters, see Swartley: 2006a: 301–2.)

John 14

Jesus' Love; the Way, the Truth, and the Life

PREVIEW

Two Scriptures people marginal to the church know best are often Psalm 23 and John 14:1-3. This is the case of a young Christian (age fifty-two) whom I currently nurture. While such persons may know these texts and regard them as their favorites, they likely are not able to recite them. People in nursing homes, as is this young man, can soon memorize these texts; we recite them in my visits. Psalm 23:6a, "Surely goodness and mercy shall follow me all the days of my life," is most precious to those with terminal illness. It enriches John 14:1. Psalm 23:6b, "I will dwell in the house of the Lord forever" (KJV), interprets John 14:2-3. These texts assure us that God-in-Jesus prepares for us an eternal home.

Jesus' farewell speech begins in 13:31. This portion focuses on Jesus' glorification, his love commandment, and his imminent departure. It sets the stage for what Jesus says in chapter 14. John 14 begins with Jesus' eye to the future—where he will go and what he will do for his disciples. He goes to prepare a *place* for them, a place that has many rooms, ensuring space for their security and comfort. But to get to that *place* and *space*, they need to know and follow the way! *Place* and *way* are interrelated, and both are to be understood under the umbrella of the mutual glorification of the Father and the Son, with the disciples living the new commandment: *Love one another.*

The disciples cannot understand the map that leads from the present to the future. Through Philip's voice, they think in the present and ask to see the Father now (14:8). Jesus helps them understand what he earlier spoke publicly: his words and works testify to his Father. Jesus also promises his disciples, You *will do greater works than I have done* (AT), leaving them stunned. Jesus then expands 13:34 with new dimensions: *If you love me, you will keep my commandments* (vv. 15, 21). Loving Jesus will manifest itself in keeping his commandments, which certainly includes his new commandment in 13:34: *love one another.* The thought line is *Just as my words and works show my unity with and in the Father, so your greater works and love that keeps my commandments will show your unity with and in me* (AT). Then Jesus tells his disciples that he will *pray to the Father* to send them what they need in his absence: *another Paraclete* (AT), who will guide them in knowledge and stay with them forever. In contrast, the *world* cannot know Jesus and the Father because *the Spirit* is not in them.

The next paragraph (14:18-24) recycles similar themes. Jesus describes the Holy Spirit's work: to *teach you all things, and bring to your remembrance all that I have said to you* (v. 26c RSV). Jesus bestows the gift of *his* peace, to quell their fear and make them secure in his absence. His final words reflect urgency: his departure is near; *the ruler of this world is coming. . . . Rise, let us go hence* (vv. 30-31 RSV).

OUTLINE

Jesus Prepares a Place and Shows the Way, 14:1-11
Jesus and the Father Ensure the Future, 14:12-24
Jesus Consoles His Disciples in View of His Departure, 14:25-31

EXPLANATORY NOTES

Jesus Prepares a Place and Shows the Way 14:1-11

14:1-3 Jesus Prepares a Place[w]

Verse 1 consists of three commands: *Do not let your hearts be troubled. Believe in God, believe also in me.* The verb *believe* (*pisteuete*, used twice) could be an indicative in either case: *You believe.* But likely both are intended as imperatives, rather than an indicative followed by an imperative, as in the KJV. Three times earlier we encountered the verb *troubled* (11:33; 12:27; 13:21), describing Jesus' agitated spirit as he encounters death—Lazarus's and his own. His

---

w   Where the superscript w occurs after headings, please see the commentary's online Web Supplement for additional material. Go to: http://www.heraldpress.com/bcbc/john.

self-giving love, even of his life, promises to overcome this death enemy. In this case, Jesus senses that his disciples will also *be troubled* as he tells them of his departure and hard times ahead. So he confidently commands them to not let their hearts be overcome with anxiety, dread, and fear. Rather, *believe in God, and believe also in me* (AT). The intended meaning may be *You believe in God, don't you? Then believe also in me*. This matches Jesus' emphases in 14:6-11, where Jesus and the Father are linked in union, with Jesus revealing the Father (cf. 14:13, 20, 21c). In verse 11 Jesus again calls his disciples, *Believe in me*. This eleven-verse unit is bookended by Jesus' call to believe (vintage John).

Two related points emerge in the next two verses. Jesus promises them that his *Father's house* has *many rooms* (*monai*, *mansions*, KJV; *rooms*, RSV, NIV; *dwelling places*, NRSV). The Greek *monai* is related to the verb *menō* (*abide*) in chapter 15. It thus connotes "be with" or "be at home with." Jesus and his disciples will dwell together. Some scholars, notably Dodd, regard this as fulfilled in Jesus' resurrection and the coming of the Paraclete (1953/1968: 395, 403–6). Jesus *abides* with them through the Spirit, a notion similar to Paul's "in Christ" emphasis. Gundry (1967: 70) agrees that the contexts of *menō* in John and 1 John make *monai* refer to "not (a) mansion in the sky, but spiritual positions in Christ." Gundry affirms this present aspect but contends that this does not exhaust the meaning of *going away* when combined with *I will come again and will take you to myself* (14:3b). Jesus speaks of going to prepare *a place for them* (vv. 2b-3). Jesus speaks of present and future. Jesus' resurrection and the Paraclete's coming "prefigure Jesus' second coming (14:18, 23, 26; 16:16-22)" (71).

Second, the word *place* in this context elicits a special nuance of meaning. In the Jewish world of that time it was customary for the bride upon marriage to move into the home of the bridegroom's father. Here, in John, we do that permanently, eternally. We know where and with whom we will be. As the bride of Christ, we move with the bridegroom (recall 3:29) into the Father's house; here there is room for all God's children of love (13:35). Jesus promises to provide for us, the bride of his love, plenty of space or room for us in an eternal home. We move into the divine space that is the bosom (*kolpos*) of the Father, from which the Son came, and the Son's bosom on which the beloved disciple leaned at the Last Supper. Our final passage in dying and living (11:25b-26a) is moving into the bosom of the Father and Son of love.

Some scholars contend that *house* refers to an eschatological *temple* (e.g., Bryan). The image evokes three previous uses of *temple* or *holy place* (2:16; 4:20; 11:48). But *place* and *body* (2:21) are not readily compatible. Jesus speaks of a *place* to which he is going and to which the disciples will come later. How then is 14:2 connected to 2:16? Bryan contends they are two separate uses and meanings of *temple* imagery, both connected to *my Father's house*: "John's readers knew that the Jewish leaders' fear for their 'place' (11:48) was more well-founded than they could have guessed. But, unlike the leaders, the followers of Jesus need not 'let their hearts be troubled' (14:1), for Jesus has gone to prepare a more enduring 'place,' a heavenly and eschatological Temple, in which his followers will one day dwell" (195–96).

Neither use of the temple imagery should be dissolved into the other; it is entirely possible that John views the concepts of the heavenly sanctuary and Jesus' glorified body as entirely harmonious (197). That "the New Temple of the risen Jesus provides access to the heavenly temple of the Father's house" is argued well by McCaffrey (21):

> In Jn 14:2-3 we have the simple image of a spacious house, with many rooms. It is easily intelligible within the Jewish tradition with reference either to the Jerusalem temple, or the heavenly temple, as the eschatological goal of universal redemption; and even with reference to both the Jerusalem temple and the heavenly temple at the same time. . . . In this house, whether it be the Jerusalem temple or the heavenly temple, there are rooms . . . enough for a great number to dwell there. (75; cf. 109, re Jewish tradition on "journey to a place")

Because of the possible dual references of this imagery in Jewish tradition, it is understandable why the disciples are confused. The *many rooms* in this heavenly place assure the disciples that they will have a place and space, close to Jesus and to the Father: *I will come again and will take you to myself, so that where I am, there you may be also* (14:3b). The climax of Israel's journey in Exodus 15:18 might be inferred in the declaration "The Lord will reign forever and ever," a prominent motif in Revelation (11:15d).

14:4-11 Jesus Shows the Way

In John 14:4 Jesus shifts the imagery from *place* to *way*. The NRSV's *to the place* is not in the Greek text, but it captures the proper sequence of imagery since *way* leads to *temple-place* in Israel's faith traditions. The *way* the Lord guides the covenant people leads to the holy sanctuary (Swartley 1994: 32–33). Since Deuteronomy serves well as the covenant model for Jesus' farewell speech (Chennattu;

Lacomara), its imagery of *way* and *place* in the same sentence is pertinent: "The Lord your God . . . goes before you on the way [LXX *hodos*] to seek out a place [*topos*] for you to camp, in fire by night, and in the cloud by day" (Deut 1:32d-33; cf. Howard-Brook 1994: 314). McCaffrey shows the connection between numerous OT texts and John 14:2c-3a with the word *go* (*poreuomai*) and the promised land or temple as destination (76–93). He does the same for *prepare* (*hetoimazō*) and *place* (*topon*; 97–103). The *way* image echoes the *way* (*derek*) in the OT (Exod 23:20; Ps 119:1, 3, 5, 27, 33; Isa 40:3; Mal 3:1; Prov 2:8, 20; cf. 1QS 8.14), the context for its use in John.

The *way* image trips the disciples. Thomas, whose intuition has earlier sensed what lies ahead in his dour comment, *Let us also go, that we may die with him* (11:16), now levels with Jesus, *Lord, we do not know where you are going. How can we know the way?* This question, put with some frustration, prompts Jesus' memorable pronouncement, *I am the way, and the truth, and the life. No one comes to the Father except through me.* Jesus, the Son, is the way to the Father. This is not new in John; it is already implied in the prologue, especially in the claim that Jesus *is in the bosom of the Father*, and *he* will *exegete* the Father, for all to know him (1:18; 3:16; 6:35). The claim is inferred also by Jesus' oneness with the Father (chs. 5, 8, 10). What is perhaps new is the angle of emphasis. Until now in John, Jesus reveals the Father. But now Jesus is *the way* to the Father. Jesus is also *the truth*, the contentious point in Jesus' controversies with the Jews (chs. 5 and 8). It reappears in Jesus' trial by and of Pilate (18:36-38). Jesus as *way* and *truth* gives *life*, a theme struck in 3:14-17, 36; 5:1-29; 6:32-53; 11:25-26; and will appear again in 17:2-3. Jesus ends his public ministry, saying, *And I know his* [*the Father's*] *commandment is eternal life* (12:50). To know Jesus is to know the Father (14:7).

Philip, on the verge of ecstasy, presses for the grand show: *Lord, show us the Father, and we shall be satisfied* (oh? cf. 16:29-30, finally!). Jesus then speaks baldly, disappointed that his disciples flounder on why he has come into the world (paraphrased):

- Philip, you see me, you see the Father, and you still do not know me? (v. 9).

- I am in the Father and the Father is in me. Do you not believe this? (v. 10a).

- I do not speak on my own authority, but I speak the words of the Father (v. 10b).

- The works I do, the Father does in me (vv. 10c-11; cf. Burer).

Therefore, *believe me that I am in the Father and the Father is in me; but if you do not, then believe me because of the works themselves* (v. 11). This reiteration of themes benefits the disciples and all who later hear these words addressed directly to them. It anticipates the Father's and Son's mutual indwelling.

It also reiterates the point that Jesus' words come from the Father. Jesus gives what he receives, a point made nineteen times in John's Gospel. Jesus' words and works are possible because he has first heard and received them from the Father. This is also a pattern for his disciples. They *receive from* Jesus in order to give, speaking and doing what Jesus now says will be even greater works than he has done. How is this possible?

Jesus and the Father Ensure the Future 14:12-24

14:12-14 Greater Works, Asking in Jesus' Name, All to Glorify the Father

In verse 12 Jesus introduces a new theme with the emphatic *Truly, truly, I say to you* (AT). This term, used twenty-five times in John, stresses a saying's importance. In this case, it is the *greater works* the disciples will do in Jesus' name. How do we understand such a statement in light of the stellar works that Jesus does in his ministry? Is it a greater number of works and in many different places worldwide—thus a *quantitative* sense of *greater*? Or is it a greater *type* of work, a point difficult to imagine? After all, Jesus raised dead Lazarus! What could be a greater work than that? Who today can do that?

Verses 13 and 14 indicate *Jesus will do it*, not *we* by *our* capabilities. *Greater* means that the works the disciples will do in *Jesus' name* "belong to the new eschatological age ushered in by Jesus' hour" (O'Day 1995: 746). They thus glorify God through Jesus, who is now also glorified by these works (14:13b; cf. 1:14; 2:11; 5:44; 11:4; 17:4). The works will be a multiplication of glory to the divine, Jesus and the Father. In this sense, with Jesus' disciples all over the world doing these works of love and power, *greater* is quantitative and qualitative (*double* glory—Jesus and the Father in their oneness and mutual love!).

14:15-17 Love and Obey; The Father Will Give You Another Paraclete[w]

Earlier Jesus spoke of one commandment for the Son (12:50) and one *new* commandment for the disciples (*Love one another*); now Jesus speaks of *commandments* (pl.) that the disciples are to keep (vv. 15, 21). This plural use is interchangeable with the *word(s)* Jesus has spoken (vv. 23-24). *Keeping Jesus' commandments* thus means obeying

Jesus' teachings (5:38; 8:31, 37, 51; 12:47-48). But all this is framed by a conditional, *If you love me. Keeping Jesus' commandments* and *loving me and one another* are the heart of Jesus' farewell discourse. The two emphases soon reappear in verses 22-24. They recur in 1 John (McDermond: 86–87, 273–74).

In this context of love and obedience, Jesus promises to send a special gift to his disciples: the Paraclete, who *is the Spirit of truth.* This is the first of five homilies (14:16-17, 26; 15:26; 16:7-11, 12-15) on the promised Paraclete, though the last Scripture does not use *Paraclete*, but *Spirit of truth.* The Paraclete is designated only once as *the Holy Spirit* (14:26) and three times as *the Spirit of truth* (14:17; 15:26; 16:12; a phrase known in the DSS, 1QS 3:18-19; 4:21). The verbal form of Paraclete, *parakaleō* (noun, *paraklēsis*) occurs many times in the NT. The special noun form *paraklētos* (masc.) appearing here is not found elsewhere in the NT nor in the Septuagint (though the Aquila and Theodotion Gr. versions use it in Job 16:20) except to designate Jesus in 1 John 2:1. But the usual noun and verb forms occur many times in the Septuagint, usually translating the oft-recurring Hebrew word *naham*, meaning "comfort" (Ps 23:4; 86:17; Job 29:25; Howard-Brook 1994: 320).

In the NT the verb *parakaleō* in its active and passive forms has a range of meaning: "comfort, console, encourage, counsel, exhort, admonish, advocate, beseech (appeal), call for help." The NRSV (also NAB, NIV 2011) translates *paraklētos* as *Advocate* (RSV, NIV: *Counselor*; KJV: *Comforter*; NASB, NKJV: *Helper*). *Advocate* is close to the literal meaning: "one called to the side of." An advocate is one who aids in times of need or trouble. This advocate may assume various roles (see more in ch. 16). In John the legal sense of *Advocate* is strong, either defending the disciples or reproving or convicting the world (16:7-11). Since the *paraklētos* is designated as *Spirit of truth* three times, advocacy is dominant, especially when truth is on trial, as Lincoln (2000) puts it.

Two unique emphases occur in this text's promise of the Paraclete. First, the Paraclete is *another* Paraclete. This means that he will continue the presence and work of Jesus, who is with them now as Paraclete (cf. 1 John 2:1). Jesus' work is to do the work of the Father, so he now asks the Father to send *another* Paraclete in the face of his imminent departure. Most of the meanings for Paraclete apply to Jesus' words and works: "comforter, helper, sponsor, advocate, exhort, counsel, and admonish."

The second important emphasis here is the last line of verse 17: *You know him, because he abides with you, and he will be in you.* In the first two clauses, *know* and *abides* are present tense; in the last part, *will be* is future tense. The first clauses are thus in tension with 7:39: *Now he said this about the Spirit, which believers in him were to receive; for as yet there was no Spirit, because Jesus was not yet glorified.* Hamilton clarifies the eschatological timetable of the Spirit's work among God's people. First, he relates the work of God's spirit in the OT to the Spirit's role in the NT, specifically to John 3:4-6; 4:23; 7:39; 14:17; and 20:22. In short, God's spirit *dwelt* in the temple and would come *upon* individuals for special tasks in the OT. The Spirit could also be experienced in rebirth and regeneration (John 3), as Jesus proclaimed the kingdom, but would *indwell* the disciples only after Jesus' glorification through death and resurrection. Hence the promise here in 14:17 prefigures 20:22, when Jesus *breathes into them* [*emphysaō*] *and says to them, "Receive the Holy Spirit"* (AT). This marks the *indwelling*, the disciples' way of *abiding* in Jesus (15:4-5). Rather than dwelling in a physical temple, the Spirit now indwells Jesus' disciples who as the new temple mediate God's presence and forgiveness of sins (Hamilton: 116–22, 154–60; TBC for 16:5-33). This *indwelling* complements 14:20, 23 and 15:4-5; 17:23.

The final phrase of 14:16 is precious: the Advocate/Comforter *will be with you forever.* These words are similar to Jesus' in Matthew 28:20, "And remember, I am with you always, to the end of the age." The Spirit is Jesus Christ's eternal presence with his disciples. The Spirit represents the Lord Jesus. In Jesus' absence the Spirit is his presence (cf. Parsenios: 82; Johnston: 86). Seeing this connection between Jesus and the Spirit puts Paul's word in brighter light: "Now the Lord is the Spirit, and where the Spirit of the Lord is, there is freedom. And all of us, with unveiled faces, seeing the glory of the Lord as though reflected in a mirror, are being transformed into the same image from one degree of glory to another; for this comes from the Lord, the Spirit" (2 Cor 3:17-18).

14:18-21 Assurances and Promises Recounted[w]

These verses reiterate the heart of Jesus' assurance to his disciples. What was said in the positive in 14:1-3 is now reaffirmed by negating the opposite: *I will not leave you orphaned* [*desolate*]. Jesus will *not desert* his disciples. Then Jesus promises the positive: *I am coming to you* (v. 3b; cf. 17:13). But this also implies *departure.* Hence 14:19-20 explains, *In a little while the world will no longer see me, but you will see me; because I live, you also will live. On that day you will know that I am in my Father, and you in me, and I in you.* This is a conundrum. "With the eyes of the world, you will no longer see me, but with eyes of faith, you will see me again." Why? Because Jesus lives, you will live also! *That day* appears to refer to Jesus' resurrection, not his parousia (his second coming), as in the Synoptic Gospels and also in John 14:1-2. This mutual indwelling recurs in chapters 15 and 17; it assumes Jesus' resurrection. John 14:21 extends 14:15-17, anticipating 15:9 and 17:20-26. Jesus explains the indwelling with pithy components:

- *Because I live, you also will live* (14:19c).

- *You will know that I am in my Father, and you in me, and I in you* (v. 20).

- *If you keep my commandments* [pl.], *then you are those who love me* (v. 21a AT).

- *And you are those who will be loved by my Father* (v. 21b AT).

- *And I will love them and reveal myself to them* (21c).

Since 14:23b says, *We will come to them and make our home with them,* echoing the *house* of verse 2a, it is clear that an eschatological distinction between imminent postresurrection appearances and a future parousia is blurred in John.

14:22-24 Jesus Manifests Himself to His Disciples, Not to the World; Judas's Query

Judas (not Iscariot) listens well. Why the distinction between us and the world? *Lord, how is it that you will reveal yourself to us, and not to the world?* Jesus' answer, profound as it is, requires the reader to make some inferences. His answer nuances what he has said earlier. *Those who love me will keep my word, and my Father will love them, and we will come to them and make our home with them.* Love and obedience, keeping Jesus' word, are the means of *knowing* and *seeing!* The Father loves those who love and obey Jesus. Together the Son and the Father will come and make their *home* with them. The word for *home* here is *monēn*, the accusative singular of the same word (*monē*; as nominative pl., *monai*) in verse 2a, which NRSV translates as *dwelling places* (RSV: *rooms*; KJV: *mansions*). Dwelling together in the same living quarters is *how* Jesus' disciples will see him. What does this mean? Is it literal or figurative language? The disciples are mystified.

Verse 24 sheds little more light on the puzzle in enunciating the negative counterpart: *Whoever does not love me does not keep my words.* Jesus then follows up with what he has often said before: *The word that you hear is not mine, but is from the Father who sent me.* Again, the time and place of this *home* where Jesus and the Father dwell together with the disciples are not described clearly. Eschatology is fuzzy. We have no house blueprints, no location, and no building schedule. All are left open. But there is a down payment, coming soon!

Jesus Consoles His Disciples in View of His Departure
14:25-31

14:25-26 Gift of the Paraclete, the Holy Spirit

Verse 25 is transitional, referring back to things Jesus has said. Jesus underscores their importance with *while I am still with you*. Departure is implied to be imminent, not far in the future.

In verse 26 Jesus promises a down payment of his future presence. *The Father will send in my name . . . the Paraclete, the Holy Spirit* (AT). Jesus *promises* the gift of the Spirit. But Jesus does not give the Spirit until after the resurrection, when Jesus breathes *into them* the Holy Spirit (AT; see 20:19-23). Unlike in Paul's letters, where the promised Spirit-already-come is the down payment of the full inheritance (Eph 1:14), here the *promise* of the Spirit's coming points to what Jesus has spoken about in John 14:23b. This is how the Father and the Son *will dwell* with them. They will make themselves *at home* in their being, personally and corporately. Yes, they will see Jesus again after he departs and after he is raised from the dead, and Jesus will abide with them through his Spirit, which he breathes and the Father sends into them.

This is the second of the five Paraclete promises. Only here is the Paraclete identified as the *Holy* Spirit. The Spirit's work is twofold: teaching (all things) and reminding (what Jesus has said). None of the English translations of *paraklētos* (as noted previously for v. 16) denotes this particular role, though most can be stretched to include it. To grasp the meaning of Paraclete in John, we must hear what all five texts say the Paraclete will do.

The second part of this Paraclete text begins with *that one* (Gr. *ekeinos*). Both the designation and work of the Paraclete are personalized. The word *Paraclete* is masculine (though *Spirit* [*pneuma*] in Gk. is neuter; *Spirit* in Heb. is feminine). Considering these three language uses, it is appropriate to refer to the Spirit in either gender while realizing that the Spirit, like God, transcends gender. Since *Paraclete* (masc.) is dominant in John, this commentary will use *he* for the Spirit. The Paraclete personally continues Jesus' work.

In Jesus' promise to send the Paraclete and to introduce his disciples to the work of the Spirit-Paraclete, Jesus "builds a bridge between the Spirit and the Father, *and*, because the Father sends him *in his name*, between the Spirit and himself as well" (von Speyr: 146). Jesus' teaching on what the Spirit will do guides believers in their discernment regarding Spirit-claimed manifestations. Do they accord with the Spirit's teaching of Jesus and the Father?

14:27 Gift of Peace: Do Not Be Afraid

Peace was an expected accomplishment of the expected messiah. The peace of that messiah was a peace that followed war and subjugation of enemies. But Jesus in his triumphal entry (John 12) chooses a different path to kingship. Jesus speaks of his death, as a seed falling into the ground, dying, and then bearing much fruit (12:24). Jesus promises a special messianic peace.

Jesus' messianic peace is not the peace that *the world gives*. It is a peace that comes with the Spirit, a peace that gives an inner- and outer-centeredness amid the chaos and even the persecution that Jesus' disciples will endure from the world. Jesus' peace is an alternative power to worldly power and domination. In John, peace is Jesus' bequest to his followers in the midst of a hostile world (14:27; 16:33). Segovia, in his study of discipleship in John, remarks on Jesus' twofold promise of peace: "The peace of the disciples is a peace which comes from knowing that *they* . . . have . . . access to the Father through Jesus and the Spirit. . . . This peace is also a peace which implies and entails rejection, open hostility, and even the possibility of death. It is, therefore, in every way possible, a peace 'not of this world'" (1985: 94).

My peace is contrasted to the world's peace. Jesus' peace contrasts also to troubled hearts controlled by fear (Minear 1984: 60). Jesus as revealer, life-giver, light, way, and truth gives peace that dispels fear and assures his presence. At this point, as before in the narrative, the disciples do not fully comprehend Jesus' teaching. Not until Jesus' resurrection and his breathing *into them . . . the Holy Spirit* (20:22 AT) do they understand this and numerous other teachings of Jesus (cf. 2:17, 22; 12:16; 4:31-38).

Both peace and love (13:34-35; 15:12) stand in opposition to the world's character. Jesus' daring tour through Samaria shows that Jesus' peace extends also to the enemy. Love for one another and peace that transcends the world's conflicts and its persecution become marks of Jesus' followers so that all may recognize Jesus' disciples and be drawn to Jesus and into his new community of love and peace.

Jesus then repeats his command in 14:1, *Do not let your hearts be troubled*. But now he adds, *and do not let them be afraid*. Here Jesus is the original Paraclete (cf. 1 John 2:1). He comforts, encourages, and exhorts his followers not to be troubled or afraid as they continue in the world after he leaves. *Another* Comforter will continue the role Jesus began. The dual "comfort-assurance" declaration echoes Isaiah 41:10, "Do not fear, for I am with you, do not be afraid, for I am your God; I will strengthen you, I will help you, I will uphold you with my victorious right hand." God's covenant promise continues in Jesus and the Holy Spirit.

Jesus' gift of peace is interwoven literarily with four recurring themes in his farewell: (1) love one another; (2) Jesus' going away; (3) the promised gift of the Holy Spirit; and (4) preparing the disciples to live in a hostile world, which will persecute them. The gift of peace flows out of the oneness, the mutual indwelling of the Father and the Son, a pattern also shaping the farewell prayer when Jesus first prays for himself (17:1-8), then for his disciples on the basis of the Father-Son mutual indwelling (17:9-19), and then for those who will come to believe through the disciples' witness (17:20-27). John 20:19-23 fulfills Jesus' promise of the Holy Spirit's coming and shows the inherent connection between Jesus' bestowal of peace and the gift of the Spirit. Indeed, "Jesus' gift of peace is 'from God,' a gift that the quantifiable and fragile peace produced by the politics of this world can never match" (Moloney 1998: 401). Jesus' gift of peace extends John's earlier emphases on Jesus as God's gift of light, life, and love. The promised gift of the Paraclete, the Holy Spirit, the Spirit of truth, will transform Jesus' followers. Peace and Paraclete integrate Jesus' salvation and ethics in John.

14:28 Departure; Love; Going to the Father

This verse adds a new dimension to Jesus' announced departure: *If you loved me, you would rejoice that I am going to the Father, because the Father is greater than I.* Jesus solicits empathy! He says, rephrased, "Look, though this news is hard for you, if you really loved me [the phrasing indicates they do not!], *you would rejoice* for my sake. I am going to my Father, who is greater than I. I will be secure, having fulfilled my commission from the Father." Instead of sorrow, you should *rejoice that I am going to the Father, because the Father is greater than I* (14:28).

A similar statement in 16:22 promises joy to the disciples—something impossible for them to fathom as they try to come to grips with Jesus' leaving. Yes, "his return to the Father should lead them to joy, not sadness, since the departure fulfills his work, and marks the successful completion of his mission" (Parsenios: 95, who points out that joy is a trope in Hellenistic and Roman consolation speeches of departing heroes as well). All this, put upon the disciples, leaves them with conflicted emotions. In that circumstance, Jesus says, "Time is up" (14:30a AT). The *ruler of this world is coming* (v. 30b).

14:29-31 Now That You Know, Believe; Watch Out, Let Us Go[w]

Each of these three verses provides closure to the discourse. First, Jesus explains that he has said all these things *before* his departure occurs, *so that when it does occur, you may believe.* That has been Jesus' goal all along—that his disciples *may believe* in him! This goal laces the entire discourse, which though apparently ending here continues after all! The *hour* is close to fulfillment. Second, since time is running out, Jesus tells them that *the ruler of this world is coming. He has no power over me.* Jesus' collision with this world's ruler, Satan, whose face appears in the empire (which Pilate represents), is at hand; yet be assured that Satan will not win this final round but will be conquered (cf. 16:33c; 1 John 5:4-5, 19).

Third, be assured that all is going as the Father commanded *so that the world may know that I love the Father.* This is an unexpected twist. Not only are the disciples in the scope of Jesus' mission, but the world, even in its hostility against Jesus and the disciples, also remains the object of God's love and salvation (John 3:16)! As Jesus faces down the world in his crucifixion-glorification, his desire is that the world may come to know that *I love the Father.* Even though the world hates Jesus and his disciples, Jesus knows that God loves the world and desires the change of heart needed to believe in Jesus and to respond to Jesus and the Father in kind, love for love. This unfailing love for the Father, even now appealing to the world to recognize that Jesus loves the Father, frames the passion narrative, with its intense opposition between Jesus and the world.

Rise, let us be on our way (14:31c). In the context of the preceding closure motifs, this appears to end the discourse. But it doesn't. Jesus continues speaking. How is this problem to be resolved? Parsenios puts the dilemma memorably: "If John's Gospel is the most enigmatic of the Gospels, then among the most enigmatic items in the Fourth Gospel is the curious narrative fissure that cuts between chapters 14 and 15. Jesus announces at 14:31 that he will leave the Last Supper, but at 15:1 he does not appear to have gone anywhere, and simply continues speaking" (49).

Scholars have proposed numerous theories, but only Parsenios's satisfies, in my judgment. Parsenios contends that the solution to this enigma is what is known as the "delayed exit" drama technique in Greek tragedy. The hero knows his imminent end and hears an announced exit. But he continues his farewell words, in some cases to great length. This means that the exit motif in 14:31 is to be seen as an *exit* that leads to *death*, which adds to numerous narrative preparatory indicators in chapters 2–13 (cf. *the hour*, antagonists try to kill Jesus, Mary's anointing, Jesus' own teaching about his death and departure). The dissimilarity with Greek tragedy is that Jesus announces his exit, whereas in Parsenios's cited parallels, another person announces the hero's exit to death (50–75).

Two other features from Greco-Roman tragedy and cultural practice corroborate Parsenios's thesis. First, the "delayed exit" is followed by speaking that often intends to console those who remain, which Jesus certainly does in his continuing discourse. The promised Paraclete will be Jesus' successor (as Joshua was for Moses), even Jesus' double. He will console and counsel as Jesus himself does (78–109). Second, the "symposium meal-word" cultural practice is analogous to that depicted in John's farewell discourse. The symposium begins with a meal but soon moves into extended discourse and conversation. The similarities between Parsenios's description of the symposia and what occurs in Jesus' farewell speech are striking. Parsenios's final paragraph to his chapter titled "And the Flesh Became Words" (111–49) describes the original and enduring purpose of the discourse: "The very writing of the Gospel— especially the Farewell Discourses—serves as a basic way in which the keeping of the words is accomplished. Consequently, Jesus continues to speak even after he has returned to the Father. . . . The Word who became flesh is now present in the words" (149).

With Parsenios's contribution, 14:31 is no longer enigmatic. It enlightens the reader. As a delayed exit signal, it sets the stage for more *word* from Jesus that prepares his followers for his imminent departure and death. The entire unit fits the word-supper (*logodeipnon*) of the Greek symposium. Instead of a prime example of a botched editorial job, we have a prime example of the evangelist's narrative skill.

THE TEXT IN BIBLICAL CONTEXT

"My Father's House" and the New Temple[w]

The word for *house* in *my Father's house* (*oikia* in 14:2a; used also in 4:53; 8:35; 11:31; 12:3) is not the same as that used in *my Father's house* in 2:16 (*oikos*, 2x; also in 2:17; 7:53; 11:20). Since *oikos* is more common for the Jerusalem temple in the Septuagint, John's use of *oikia* in 14:2 tilts toward heavenly temple, though the distinction is blurred in John's shift from one to the other in 11:20 and 31 (McCaffrey: 177–78). In 8:35 *oikia* connotes *family* of God; both 8:35 and 14:2-3 are linked to discipleship. Jesus' invitation, *Abide in me* (John 15), fits with this new temple image. The risen Jesus (2:21-22) and his disciples are the new temple. Numerous images complement this perception:

- The new temple of [grace and] truth (John 1:14)
- The new temple as the meeting-place between God and humans (1:51)
- The new temple of worship (4:20-24)
- The new temple as source of the Spirit (7:37-39)
- The sanctification of the new temple (10:36)
- The goal of the new temple (11:47-53)
- The glory of the new temple (12:41)
- The "sign" of the new temple (20:19-29; McCaffrey: 177–255)

After careful analysis of these themes, McCaffrey concludes his study:

> The perspective of the New Temple which emerges in our interpretation of Jn 14:2-3 clearly dominates the fourth gospel and the parting discourses. It is hardly surprising that the gospel ends with a final provision of the risen Jesus as the "sign" of the New Temple (20:19-29). (245)
>
> The purpose of the earthly mission of Jesus to bridge the gap between God and [humans] by his passion-resurrection is effective in the new Temple of the risen Jesus, where God and believers are one. (252)

John's new-temple imagery accentuates the believers' intimacy in union with the Son, who is one with the Father. It contributes to John's mutual indwelling emphases.

This theme links with many OT and NT Scriptures. Psalm 84 praises "the Lord of hosts" for the beauty of God's temple (cf. Pss 48; 15; Psalms of Ascent, 120–134). Beloved Psalm 23 ends with "And I shall dwell in the house of the Lord for ever" (RSV). The fall of Solomon's temple lies behind many laments in the Psalms (e.g., 74) and Prophets (e.g., Jer 12–15). Many NT writings envision Jesus and his community as the new temple (Mark; John; Paul; Eph 2:19-22;

1 Pet 2:4-6). Revelation (21:22) culminates the image: the holy city
has no temple; its temple "is the Lord God Almighty and the Lamb."

THE TEXT IN THE LIFE OF THE CHURCH

Jesus as the Way, the Truth, and the Life

Jesus defines himself as *the* access route to God, the Father, contrasting himself to the false shepherds in John 10. Believers through
the ages know and value this truth.

At the same time, we must be careful not to use this text to club
other religions. Rather, we bear testimony to Jesus as truth in our
Christian experience. We value noble ethical insights of other religions and affirm those devout in their faith (Jewish, Muslim, Hindu,
and others). This does not mean compromising our beliefs. Rather,
witness to Jesus as way, truth, and life for Christians is essential to
honest interreligious dialogue.

When people of other faiths visit our churches, their presence
can sharpen our awareness of what is distinctive about our Christian
faith and provide opportunity for us to know more clearly what our
words and practices signify. The early apostles professed their
beliefs in interaction with other religions. In our pluralistic world
today, we have opportunity to do the same. Paul's respect for the
religious practices of other devotees is evident in his Areopagus
speech, where he quotes Aratus, a renowned Greek philosopher. He
does so not to judge the saying negatively, but to provide an opening for proclaiming the gospel of Jesus Christ (Acts 17:18-32). For
further reflection on the sensitive issues involved here, see O'Day
(1995: 743–45).

John 15:1–16:4

Mutual Indwelling of Jesus and Disciples: Abiding and Loving, Facing Hatred

PREVIEW

Several years ago, my son and I, separated by miles, were engaged in similar tasks, picking fruit. He and his daughters picked apples from one tree rich in fruit, generating 140 quarts of applesauce. I picked blackberries from a wildly grown expansive patch and found few berries. My son pruned his Iowa apple tree; the old dying canes in the Michigan berry patch (not my own) had not been cut off. Hence the berry crop was meager. The fruit outcome was about 140 quarts of applesauce from one tree and only 14 cups of blackberry jam from one huge patch! Our stories connected by email over the intervening weekend.

John 15 welcomes us into a beautiful new world of living on the vine with pruned vines, abiding in Jesus, and learning regenerated relationships through obeying Jesus' new command to love one another. The chapter consists of two distinct parts, with the first (15:1-17) built on the imagery of Jesus as the true vine and his disciples as the branches. The second, beginning at 15:18, prepares Jesus' followers to face the hatred of the world. *Abiding* in Jesus and *loving* Jesus and one another are central to Jesus' *revelation* of God and God's redemptive, transforming power. These emphases fortify the disciples as they face Jesus' departure and the hatred of the world.

The image of the vine and branches is a strong metaphor for John's mutual indwelling emphasis. The *vine* part of the image has a rich OT background that highlights God's nurturing care for the people of the covenant. It comes at an auspicious place in the farewell discourse: after the covenant is formed in the footwashing and the meal, with both in the context of Jesus' delayed exit to death. The disciples' solidarity with Jesus, their necessary union with Jesus, and the pruning that goes with growth in discipleship—all are foundational to this second part of Jesus' farewell speech.

The third recurring promise of Jesus to send the Paraclete occurs at the end of chapter 15, with emphasis on the Spirit's role as *Advocate*, the one who *testifies, bears witness* to Jesus, who soon will face the unleashed hostility of the world. Yet not only the Spirit, but also you, the disciples, will *testify* on behalf of Jesus (15:26-27). The final paragraph of the unit (16:1-4) speaks of persecution from the synagogue. By Gospel-writing time this apparently has happened; it contributes to John's presentation of Jesus' conflict with *the Jews*, as in chapters 5–8.

Several emphases in this unit occur earlier and again later in the speech. They include abiding in Jesus' love and keeping his commandments (15:7-10), especially loving one another (vv. 12, 17), bearing fruit (vv. 4-5, 16), *asking the Father in my name* (v. 16d), and the world's hatred (vv. 18-25). This last portion ends with a quotation from Psalm 69:4 (cf. 35:19) to provide scriptural warrant. Jesus' third promise of the Paraclete reinforces its thematic centrality in Jesus' farewell. Jesus beckons his disciples to take giant steps forward in Jesus' spiritual formation program though his teaching on the vine and the branches, necessary pruning, fruit-bearing, joy made complete, and a new identity: *friends* of Jesus. Jesus prepares his disciples for what lies ahead, for the passion crisis and the postresurrection era of the Holy Spirit, when the disciples will carry forward Jesus' testament of love, sealed by his laying down his life for them, and for all who will believe and follow Jesus. Under the umbrella of love, with the Spirit indwelling them, these words testify to Jesus' and the Father's "mutual indwelling." These teachings will strengthen the disciples as they face the world's hatred and persecution.

OUTLINE

Abide in Jesus, the True Vine—Pruned and Bearing Fruit, 15:1-11
Jesus' Commandment, 15:12-17
Facing the World's Hatred, 15:17-25
The Advocate and You Testify to Jesus, 15:26-27
Facing Expulsion from the Synagogues, 16:1-4

EXPLANATORY NOTES[w]

John 15:1-25 may be viewed as a chiasm (Ellis: 225–26; Howard-Brook 1994: 329). Here is a chiasm pattern similar to theirs, modified and extended:

A Jesus, the true vine; disciples, the branches (15:1-6)
    B Keep my commandments: love and bear fruit (vv. 7-10)
        C So that your joy may be full (v. 11)
    B´ Keep my commandment: love, friends, and fruit (vv. 12-17)
        C´ The world's hatred (vv. 18-25)
A´ The promise of the Advocate (v. 26)
    B´´ The disciples testify (v. 27)
        C´´ Persecuted by the synagogue (16:1-4)

The chiasm provides a useful visual scan of the whole unit. A and A´stress Jesus' initiative; B, B´ and B´´, the disciples' actions; C´ and C´´, the negative responses. Joy (v. 11) and Paraclete/Spirit of truth (v. 26) are special positive emphases in this chapter.

Abide in Jesus, the True Vine—Pruned and Bearing Fruit 15:1-11

15:1-3 Jesus, the Vine; My Father, the Vinegrower

I am the true vine, and my Father is the vinegrower. Jesus identifies himself by another precious *I Am* image: *I Am* the true vine. This is the last *I Am* declaration Jesus makes in John. Since God's covenant people are often identified with vine imagery in the OT (see TBC), Jesus is declaring that he is the true fulfillment of that vine imagery. *He*

---

w   Where the superscript w occurs after headings, please see the commentary's online Web Supplement for additional material. Go to: http://www.heraldpress.com/bcbc/john.

embodies faithful, true Israel. Further, God's promises of an eschato-logical era of a renewed covenant people are now being fulfilled. Jesus' self-identification as the true vine announces the arrival of the long-awaited Messiah.

As true vine, Jesus is the source of life for the disciples. This tes-timony of the Johannine community as faithful disciples means that we depend upon Jesus for our life, for sustaining nourishment. This is Jesus' only *I Am* claim that qualifies the predicate noun: *true* and *belonging to* the vinegrower, the Father (cf. R. Brown 1970: 659). The Father-vinegrower oversees the life-giving process. "There would be no life in the vine and no care for the branches (cf. v. 2) if the vinegrower did not tend it" (Moloney 1998: 422).

That Jesus refers to the *true* vine infers rival vines. Beasley-Murray, concurring with Bultmann (1971: 529–30), says, "Seeing Jesus as the true Vine . . . contrast[s] with whatever also claims to be the Vine" (1999: 271). Israel is often suggested as the other vine, but this obscures a key point: Jesus personifies true Israel. O'Day (1995: 757) sees *Jesus* as the true vine because he is from the Father, just as he is the true light (1:9) and the true bread from heaven (6:32). As true vine, Jesus is *true* Israel. Verses 1 and 5 together depict the community of the vinegrower, the vine, and the disciples (branches in the vine).

> When Jesus speaks of himself as the vine, then, his words are not only self-revelatory, but are [also] revelatory of the interrelationship of God, Jesus, and the community in the life of faith as well. All three elements—gardener, vine, and branches—are essential to the production of fruit. The repetition of the "I am" saying in vv. 1 and 5 positions Jesus as the middle ground between God and the community. (O'Day 1995: 757)

This relationship makes the Gospel's distinctive emphases on "mutual indwelling" central to understanding Jesus as the *true* vine. The word *true* does imply counterfeit vines. But more important, it denotes the new community that participates in the life and being of Jesus and the Father.

Verse 2 introduces two new themes in John: pruning and fruit-bearing. *He removes every branch in me that bears no fruit. Every branch that bears fruit he prunes to make it bear more fruit.* The Father prunes. These two sentences are linked in Greek by two main verbs, both from the same stem: *removes* (*airō*) and *prune* (*kathairō*). The Father cuts off the branch that does not bear fruit and prunes the branches that remain in the vine, so they can bear more fruit. Jesus also iden-tifies the pruning shears: *the word that I have spoken to you* (v. 3). The same word stem for *prune* in verse 2 appears in verse 3 as *cleansed* (*katharos*), recalling the *clean* (*katharos*) of the footwashing and Jesus' word *You are clean* [*katharos*], *though not all of you* (13:10-11). This puts Jesus' *footwashing* and Jesus' word on pruning into a complementary *cleansing* relationship. The words for pruning in John are not natural to their context but are carefully chosen to highlight the wordplay with cleansing (R. Brown 1970: 660).

These verbal relationships show that Jesus' *vine-and-branches* imagery is continuous with Jesus' dramatic action of footwashing (ch. 13). This narrative unity also augurs for one unified discourse. If footwashing updates the original *cleansing* through baptism, pruning is an analogous *cleansing*, done by the Father. Jesus' and the Father's works are one. Cleansing from sins and cutting off dead wood are similar actions. In the latter, the action enables the branch, living from the vine, to bear more fruit. Footwashing and fruit-bearing exemplify discipleship.

Pruning is necessary for living on the vine. Its purpose is to enable the vine to bear more and better fruit. Pruning is "abiding, even under the knife" (Wink: 413). In John's larger narrative, bearing fruit could be *testifying* that leads unbelievers to follow Jesus (4:35-38; 15:27; 20:30-31). Or it could mean bearing the fruit of the Spirit (Gal 5:22-23), the fruit of living on the vine (cf. Kenneson): "love, joy, peace, patience, kindness, goodness, faithfulness, gentleness, and self-control" (RSV). In this dual expression of fruit-bearing, love is the hallmark of their identity. Through this fruit-bearing the world is drawn to Jesus.

15:4-5 *The Vine-Branch Union*[w]

Jesus and his Father work mutually in verses 1-3; in verses 4-5 Jesus and the believers are linked in mutuality to produce fruit (cf. Beasley-Murray 1999: 271). The relationship of Jesus to his disciples is both simple and complex in this powerful imagery.

> *Abide in me as I abide in you. Just as the branch cannot bear fruit by itself unless it abides in the vine, neither can you unless you abide in me. I am the vine, you are the branches. Those who abide in me and I in them bear much fruit, because apart from me you can do nothing.* (15:4-5)

As a branch depends upon the vine to live and bear fruit, so disciples must abide in Jesus to live and bear fruit, especially in a hostile world (14:17, 27; 15:17-24).

As noted previously, John uses *abide* (*menō*) with special intent, already in the call of the first disciples (1:38-39, there translated as *staying*) and again when the Samaritans ask Jesus to stay with them, which he does for two days (4:40). In 11:54c Jesus goes to a remote town and *remained* [*emeinen*, past tense of *menō*] *there with his disciples*. The Gospel from the beginning anticipates this key teaching in chapter 15. John's use of *menō* (40x) far exceeds that of any other NT writing: the Synoptics, twelve times; the Johannine Epistles, twenty-seven times; all other NT books together, thirty-nine times (Burge 1987: 54). The Gospel's model relationship for Jesus and his disciples is that of *staying* or *remaining* together. With chapter 15 the awkward use of *menō* in earlier contexts finds its true sense, meaning to *abide* not only *with* but also *in* each other. The imagery unites Jesus to his disciples inseparably. If separated, the disciples will no longer be disciples. They will live no longer in the *heavenly order* (*from above*, from where Jesus has come) but in the *earthly order* (*from below*, where the world lives).

Abide is not a common word these days. It is rather out of style, archived, I suppose (except in the old hymn "Abide with Me"!). In our fast-paced computer culture, we do not know what *abide* means. We stay with other people only for a short time. Friendships that abide are hard to come by. If they *abide*, they require commitment and nurturing. That is the direction Jesus takes his disciples in this lengthy discourse. Jesus teaches them to live in *communion* with him.

In John's culture, *abide* has resonance. But in this Gospel other layers of meaning beyond the cultural are loaded onto this term. Those layers include growing levels of understanding what it means to follow Jesus, to be his disciples. At one point they, too, almost turned away from Jesus (6:66-69). Another layer of meaning arises from the unfolding revelation of who Jesus is in this Gospel. The disciples began with impressive christological declarations in their first days of meeting Jesus (1:37-51). But the meaning of these confessions has to be fleshed out in life, when they encounter the offense of Jesus' words and actions, when the religious leaders oppose Jesus, when a powerful group of *their own people*, some Pharisees and Jewish religious leaders, want to kill Jesus. Would they *stay, remain* with Jesus? All this drama of real-life relationships pours meaning into Jesus' word *Abide in me as I abide in you* (John 15:4). This is not a sweet, sentimental relationship. After all, this is at the heart of the farewell discourse, which Jesus delivers to prepare for his imminent departure, indeed his death. What does it mean to *abide in one* who is about to leave you in death? What does it mean to be told, *Apart from me you can do nothing*? But if you continue to *abide in me*, you will *bear much fruit*?

It means *mutual abiding* of the disciples in Jesus, and Jesus in the disciples, a point that augurs for the present subjunctive in 20:31 (see comments there), thus emphasizing continuing to believe, sticking with Jesus. It stresses a discipleship that "takes up the cross"—to borrow Mark's phrase (8:34)—and as *a grain of wheat falls into the earth and dies* (John 12:24b). Abiding in Jesus is double-edged: it is the only way to survive as a disciple, but it is a costly relationship. Abiding in Jesus means joining the "disciples-unto-death" corps.

15:6 The Negative Consequence of Not Abiding in Jesus

Not bearing fruit has a fatal consequence: getting chopped off by the gardener, who throws the branch into the fire to be burned. This is a tragic ending for the branch but essential for the tree's health; the dead branch is good for nothing else. While interpreters tend to identify the dead branches with heresy, apostasy, or false messiahs, it is *everything* that severs relationship with Jesus, *abiding in Jesus*. Since *bearing fruit* in the farewell discourse refers to works of love (14:12, 15, 21, 23)—and these testify to Jesus (cf. above)— union with Jesus hinges on this very point: "The unproductive branches . . . are those people *within* the Christian faith community who do not bear fruit in love. This verse is not a polemic against Jewish apostasy, nor does it point back to Judas's betrayal. Its concern is with those people who are already in relationship with Jesus ('every branch in me')" (O'Day 1995: 757).

With such strong language of destruction for branches that bear no fruit, it is easy to think of fruit-bearing as a test of faithfulness. But this is a misinterpretation. If one is linked to Jesus, as a branch to the vine, life will flow through the branch and produce fruit. The test is whether or not we abide in Jesus (cf. Burge 2000: 418). When we do, we avoid this tragic end.

15:7-11 The Benefits of Abiding—Joy Made Complete

Fruit-bearing *is* loving Jesus and loving one another. *Abiding in Jesus* is parallel to *keeping his words* (v. 7a-b). Verse 10, a hinge verse, together with verse 11 in the larger section of 15:1-17, reiterates this point and makes *keeping my commandments* the condition and certainty of *abiding in my love*. The benefits of abiding in Jesus the true vine and keeping his commandments are fourfold:

- You may *ask for whatever you wish, and it will be done for you* (v. 7c).

- *My Father is glorified by this* (v. 8).

- You enter into the mutuality of Jesus' relationship to the Father (vv. 9-10).

- Your joy will be full and complete (v. 11).

The first two benefits reiterate recurring themes in the Gospel. The last two introduce new emphases. Also in verse 8, the disciples join Jesus in glorifying the Father.

The first benefit sounds dangerous. Do we really want God to give us whatever we ask for? The conditions of *keeping my commandments* and *abiding in my love* are essential to properly understanding Jesus' promise. With these conditions, what we *ask* is guided by desiring to be faithful disciples and receiving only what is fitting to life on the vine. We may ask to be delivered from *all* that prevents fruitful living on the vine.

The second theme anticipates what Jesus prays for in 17:20-26. Believers are included in the life relationship that the Father has with the Son. By bearing fruit and becoming Jesus' disciples, those first followers (and we) glorify the Father, just as the Son has glorified his Father. Like the Son, we also love, obey, and glorify the Father. Just as the Father reciprocally glorifies the Son, so disciples in their obedience will be glorified; faithful testimony means laying down one's life for the gospel (15:13-14; cf. 21:15-19) *[Glory, p. 516]*.

The third theme, with similar emphases, focuses on the mutual indwelling. The embrace of love goes full circle. It begins with the Father's love for Jesus, then moves to Jesus' love for his disciples, and then cycles back to the disciples' abiding in Jesus' love and Jesus' abiding in the Father's love. But for each, the disciples and Jesus, *keeping my* or *the Father's commandments* is the means and mark of love's flow. The mutual abiding of each in the other implies a relationship of obedience and glorification. Biblical interpreters sometimes speak of a "hermeneutical circle." In John we encounter an ontological (ultimate being) circle of love and obedience embracing the Father, the Son, and the disciples. Living on and from the vine, Jesus, is our entry into this circle of divine being.

The fourth benefit is joy. Joy! Just as John the Witness experiences joy in fulfilling his calling to be the friend of the bridegroom (3:29), so now Jesus' disciples experience full and complete joy through Jesus' embrace of them into the divine circle of love. Throughout this discourse Jesus speaks to and of his disciples with the plural *you*. With a personal commitment to discipleship, we become the community of love, for the hallmark of Jesus' disciples is love for one another. This loving and obeying is joy in community, reflecting the joy of the divine, the interrelationship of Father, Son, and Spirit. The Trinity is a community of love. "The oneness of the Father and Son is grounded in love and expressed in giving for the sake of others" (Koester 2008: 202).

When we visualize what a vine and branches look like, we see branches linked to each other, growing out of other branches. As Jesus' disciples, we enter into this branch community, where no branch is devalued, but all draw ultimately on the vine, Jesus Christ. In Eastern Orthodox theology the term *perichōrēsis* describes a "circle dance" among the members of the Trinity. Reflecting mutual indwelling among the three persons, the Trinity is an image of community. Each member of the Trinity embraces the other two in love, purpose, and being. This divine mutuality now embraces the disciples as they abide in Jesus the true vine and love one another, keeping Jesus' commandments. This gives joy: *My joy . . . in you, . . . that your joy may be complete.*

Jesus' Commandment 15:12-17[w]

15:12-15 Love One Another; Friends of Jesus[w]

Between verses 10 and 12 the narrative shifts from plural *commandments* to the singular *commandment*. The singular commandment is to *love one another*, the new commandment that Jesus gave his disciples in 13:34, the badge of their identity.

Jesus then makes a new remarkable announcement: *You are my friends if you do what I command you. I do not call you servants any longer, . . . but I have called you friends.* This breakthrough in identity hinges on the introductory line, *No one has greater love than this, to lay down one's life for one's friends* (15:13). This basis for the new identity—a love so great that one will die for friends—harks back to footwashing. Footwashing and friendship are interconnected (cf. Schertz).

Then in verse 15 Jesus gives a dual causal explanation for this new identity: *because the servant does not know what the master is doing; . . . because I have made known to you everything that I have heard from my Father.* The subtext of this explanation is that Jesus has revealed to his disciples his imminent death, and this is the logical outworking of the new commandment, love for one another (v. 13). O'Day sees this motif already in Jesus' footwashing example. She suggests a paraphrase of 13:8, "Unless I wash you, you are not my friend" (2008a: 38). She proposes that friendship is "the theological center of the Gospel of John" (a key point of Ringe's *Wisdom's Friends*). When one sees the link between friendship, love for one another, and dying for one's friend, discipleship brightens, for it reflects Jesus' mission, which leads to his glorification on the cross.

Based on her study of friendship in Greek and Roman antiquity, O'Day points out two common features of friendship, both stated in these verses: bold speech at the "symposium dinner," where friends interact frankly and openly with willingness to die for one another (cf. Ford 1997: 168–72). This one might expect, but the second, from a secular source, surprises. "In the *Symposium*, Plato writes, 'Only those who love wish to die for others.' Aristotle writes, 'But it is also true [that] the virtuous man's conduct is often guided by the interests of his friends and of his country, and that he will if necessary lay down his life in their behalf'" (O'Day 2008a: 35; cf. Brant 2011: 218–19, 228). Illumined by this context, Jesus' designating his disciples as *friends* intensifies his call to follow unto death.

What is remarkable about Jesus' teaching is not so much its rhetorical similarity to this Greco-Roman context. Rather, Jesus' calling his disciple-friends to lay down their lives for one another is not grounded in patriotic loyalty to country or emperor, but is an alternative based on seeing "the world from above" that judges all earthly kingdoms (cf. John 18:36, where these distinctions are sharp and clear). When friendship is viewed as John's theological center, this distinction is crucial. Friendship in John is faithful *witness* that leads to martyrdom for the gospel and the community of love (cf. Minear 1984). This becomes clear when Jesus is arrested (18:10-12) and interacts with Pilate (18:33–19:11). But as Ford points out, Jesus is not devoid of sovereignty. The entire passion narrative is, as it were, a consecration ceremony of a monarch, with Mary's anointing for kingship (12:12-19), an inclusio with anointing the crucified Messiah at the tomb (19:38-42). The entire narrative presents regal glory through the lens of the cross. The Master dies for his friends—for their salvation. The Greeks wish to see Jesus (12:20-23). Will they join the friendship? Pilate is baffled by Jesus' kingship and rightly fears (Ford 1997: 176–86).

15:16-17 Christological Foundation for Bearing Fruit[w]

Jesus' emphasis on friendship is crucial to understanding verses 16-17, as O'Day explains:

> Verse 16 is also pivotal in understanding what it means for the disciples to be Jesus' friends. . . . Jesus chose the disciples, not the other way

around. Friendship with Jesus is not affective or elective on the community's part. Rather, friendship with Jesus derives from Jesus' own initial act of friendship—his enacted love in his life and death creates friendship. Anything that the disciples do subsequently is a response to Jesus' initiating act of friendship. As a result of Jesus' choosing them as friends, the disciples are appointed by Jesus to bear fruit. (2008b: 62)

Compared to friendship in Greco-Roman writings, *bearing fruit* is Jesus' new motif to associate with friendship. For John, bearing fruit is possible only by *abiding* in Jesus, staying connected as branches to the vine. *Abiding* in another and *bearing fruit* are distinctive Johannine perspectives on *friendship*. They are deeply embedded in John's Christology—who Jesus is—and in his sociology—a community of love, suffering for Jesus as it lives in a hostile world (see below).

Highlighting the christological foundation of bearing fruit that will last (v. 16c), the narrative reiterates two basic motifs: *The Father will give you whatever you ask him in my name [and] I am giving you these commands so that you may love one another.* The word *commands* points back to all that Jesus has taught them, although what is immediately specified is the one commandment, to *love one another.* It appears that the plural commandments function to undergird, highlight, and empower the one command, *love one another.* This means willingness to lay down one's life for the other and thus be Jesus' friend.

This new identity of the disciples as Jesus' friends—abiding in him, bearing fruit, loving one another, even dying for one another—re-creates their social world, how they understand the outside world, and how they relate to it. Since the disciples are now friends of Jesus, they are to love as he loved, entering into a life-giving *abiding* in Jesus. In this light the spirituality of John's Gospel encompasses discipleship and empowers it with divine friendship. This invitation is sacred, beckoning us who teach discipleship to go deeper and further into intimacy with Jesus, an intimacy that Jesus experienced in his relationship to God. "Lord Jesus, help us!"

Facing the World's Hatred 15:17-25

15:18-21 Disciples Will Be Hated as Jesus Is Hated

In this farewell speech, Jesus clarifies the nature of the two worlds in which his disciples will live. Jesus' teaching in 15:1-17 instructs the disciples to live in the world from above, which Jesus mediates from his Father to them. Now in these verses the "world below" confronts the disciples. Jesus warns his disciples that the world that has hated him will hate them also (v. 18). The world below does not love, but hates (15:18-19). It does not know the One who sent Jesus, but the disciples do, because *you do not belong to the world*, [for] *I have chosen you out of the world* (v. 19).

Echoing the footwashing teaching of servants not being greater than their master (13:16a), Jesus now applies it to the hatred and persecution his disciples will face from the world. If their Master is persecuted (v. 20), so will his disciple-friends be persecuted (v. 20c; cf. Tan: 176-77). But the hating world below no longer controls the disciples because they live in accord with and by the empowerment of the world above. Jesus mentions another option of response from the world: *If they kept my word, they will keep yours also* (v. 20d). This thread of possible positive response from the world seems, however, to be too short to knot for hopeful expectation.

15:22-24 Jesus' Accountability to the Father

While verse 21 explains that the world's hatred is *on account of my* [Jesus'] *name*, these next verses address and judge the world's action as ultimately accountable to the Father. Jesus' coming from the Father and bearing witness in the world makes the world culpable for its sin (vv. 22a, 24a-b). Since Jesus, in his word and works, brings deliverance from the world of hatred, and the world refuses his word and works, those who are of the hating world are without excuse (v. 22b). *They have seen and hated both me and my Father* (v. 24c). The final phrases in both verses 23 and 24 specify that the world is accountable for its hateful response to the Father. This is so because Jesus has been faithful in accountability to the Father, both in his words and works, which the world has not accepted.

15:25 The World's Hatred Fulfills Scripture

The world's hatred does not mean that God is not in charge, nor does its antagonism to Jesus undermine Jesus' saving mission; rather, it shows the necessity for that mission. In fact it fulfills Scripture (*They hated me without a cause*: John 15:25; cf. Ps 69:4; cf. also Tan: 177; Talbert: 216). Scripture prophesies the world's response. Thus the disciples can endure and be assured that all is well when facing hatred, persecution, and death. The peace that Jesus gives them (14:27) enables them to have courage because Jesus has conquered the hostile world (16:33). As Jesus conquered the world, so can the disciples as they abide in him (cf. 1 John 5:4-5).

The Advocate and You Testify to Jesus 15:26-27

In the flow of the narrative, this portion on the Paraclete is sandwiched between Jesus' words about the world's hatred and the synagogue's persecution. *Advocate* is an apt translation here, for the believers need another (parallel witness) to assist them in testifying to Jesus in the face of hatred and persecution. "In secular usage *paraklētos* seems to have carried judicial overtones" (Hamilton: 64), and that fits the function described here. The Paraclete, the Spirit of truth, will testify with and through them. The Spirit of *truth* is power when truth itself is on trial. In this situation he, as the voice of Jesus, will present their case. In that sense Jesus continues to be present with them as they face adversity and hostility. This testimony to Jesus is intensified since Jesus will send the Spirit (*when the Advocate comes*). In 14:26 (also 14:16) the *Father* will send the Spirit. The Spirit will testify to Jesus, as John the Witness (1:15; 3:27-30), "the woman at the well (4:39), the Father (5:32; 8:18), Jesus' works (5:36), the Scriptures (5:39), Jesus himself (8:18), and the crowd (12:17) [have] done" (Hamilton: 85).

This text (15:26-27) provides the key to understanding the Paraclete's role in the Johannine community. It parallels Matthew 10:19-20 in that the Holy Spirit guides the speech and witness of those persecuted for the gospel. Matthew reads, "When they hand you over, do not worry about how you are to speak or what you are to say; for what you are to say will be given to you at that time; for it is not you who speak, but the Spirit of your Father speaking through you" (R. Brown 1970: 685, 699). Luke's parallel (21:14-15) to Matthew does not mention the Holy Spirit; Jesus will give them wisdom to speak. In the Olivet discourse, Mark's parallel is closer, both in wording and chronological location: "When they bring you to trial and hand you over, do not worry beforehand about what you are to say; but say whatever is given you at that time, for it is not you who speak, but the Holy Spirit" (13:11). John does not say it is the Holy Spirit speaking in you, but he likely infers that. Both the Spirit of truth and *you* (the disciples) will *testify* to Jesus. John's religious context appears to be more specific (cf. Burge 1987: 29, 31), for the world hates and persecutes, and the *synagogue* casts you out.

Facing Expulsion from the Synagogues 16:1-4

Verses 1 and 4 frame verses 2 and 3. Jesus explains why he *has spoken* these things to his disciples, reflecting back upon what he said to them. Verse 1 gives the reason: *to keep you from stumbling*. This suggests that Jesus refers back mainly to the coming reality of their need to face the world's hatred. But verse 4 ends with another reason why he did not speak about this earlier: *because I was with you*. It also states why he did not say *these things* from the beginning. Lindars (1981: 64) points out that *I have spoken these things to you* [*tauta lelalēka hymin*] (AT) is a rhetorical technique marking "a transition in thought and brings the subject back to the present situation" (cf. 14:25; 15:11; 16:25, 33). In 16:2-3 Jesus speaks of *an hour* that is coming (v. 3) *when those who kill you will think that . . . they are offering worship to God*. Being put out of the synagogue is one aspect of the coming testing, but facing hatred that kills followers of Jesus is the ultimate hour of darkness. This is the deeper explanation of why Jesus frames verses 2-3 with verses 1 and 4.

Verse 16:2, together with 9:22, has received much scholarly attention, especially in light of J. Louis Martyn's 1968 landmark construction of a setting for the Gospel's origin: the experience of sporadic Jewish persecution of Christians, though not formal excommunication from the synagogue (see "Setting and Occasion" in the introduction and the related essay *["The Jews," p. 520]*). Martyn proposes that the Gospel must be read on two levels: Jesus' time and the Johannine community's time, with considerable distance between the Judaisms of those two periods. Persecution from "the Jews" reflects the setting of the latter time. Similar warnings of persecution occur in the Synoptic Gospels (e.g., Mark 13:9; Matt 10:17, 23; Luke 21:12-24). Acts also testifies to Paul's experiencing persecution in the synagogues. Is the Johannine situation really unique, or does it represent local reprisals similar to those in Acts (13:50–14:6, 19; 17:1-10; cf. 21:10-14)?

Further, the fourth Gospel is immersed in Jewish feasts and institutions. It breathes Judaism. Jesus does not replace this valued Jewish culture. Instead, he *reveals* his Father's purposes to fulfill God's salvation purpose through the symbols and religious significance of these Jewish traditions. The expulsion from the synagogue, hardly excommunication, does not characterize Jewish-Christian relations as a whole at that time (the term *Christian* never appears in John), nor does the term *the Jews* refer to all Jews, nor to all Judeans, indicated clearly by Mary, Martha, and Lazarus of Bethany, whom Jesus loved, as well as his *Jewish* disciples, including Mary Magdalene. Most came from Galilee. Jesus, too, was a Jew *["The Jews," p. 520]*.

THE TEXT IN BIBLICAL CONTEXT

The Vine Imagery[w]

John 15 has its home in the many OT references to Israel as a vine planted by God. Isaiah 5:1-7, set in the nuptial imagery of a love song, says, "Let me sing for my beloved my love-song concerning his vineyard: My beloved had a vineyard on a very fertile hill. . . ." This reference is telling (cf. the wedding motif in John; in that light John 15 may take on a nuptial nuance as well). Hosea 10:1 and Psalm 80:8-13 also present Israel as a vine. "The song of the vineyard (Isa 5:1-7) offers the parade example of 'vine' as a symbol for the people of God. . . . [Judah's failure] to live in justice and righteousness is expressed through the metaphor of yielding fruit: God, the planter, expected grapes, but Judah produced only wild grapes (vv. 2, 4)" (O'Day 1995: 757).

Isaiah 5:7 is sharp in its judgment for Judah's failure to produce fruit: "For the vineyard of the Lord of hosts is the house of Israel, and the people of Judah are his pleasant planting; he expected justice [mišpaṭ], but saw bloodshed [mišpah]; righteousness [ṣedaqah], but heard a cry [ṣeʿaqah]." The wordplay stuns and sears judgment into Israel's memory.

Numerous OT passages (Hos 10:1-2; Isa 3:14-15; 5:1-7; Ezek 15:1-5; 17:1-21; 19:10-14; Ps 80:8-18) depict Israel as God's vine or vineyard. Josephus (*Ant.* 15.395) writes about a large golden vine set at the sanctuary entrance in the temple built by Herod. The vine appears on coins and ceramics as well. Beasley-Murray (1999: 272) links judgment to this imagery: "It is striking that in every instance when Israel in its historical life is depicted in the OT as a vine or vineyard, the action is set under the judgment of God for its corruption, sometimes explicitly for its failure to produce good fruit" (e.g., Isa 5:1-7; Jer 2:21). Although this is true of *many* OT texts, other uses (as in Isa 11:1; 27:2-6; Hos 14:4-7; cf. 1QH 14.15; 16.6, 20; *Jubilees* 1:16-18; *1 Enoch* 32:4-5) anticipate a blissful union between God and Israel, with both vine and bridal imagery (Song of Sol 8:12). Jesus, the true vine in John 15, connects to Jesus' *good wine* for the wedding in 2:7-10!

Commandments in John[w]

John 15:10-15 is the Gospel's last reference to the Father's commandments to Jesus (v. 10) and to the commandment (v. 12) and commands (v. 17) that Jesus gives to his disciples. *Commandment(s)* occurs eleven times, divided almost equally between singular and plural, as follows (adapted from von Wahlde 1990: 11–20):

Commandments	
Given by the Father to Jesus	**Given by Jesus to the Disciples**
10:18, The commandment to *lay down* his life and *take it up again.*	
12:49-50, Commandment: *what to say and speak.* Commandment: [to give] *eternal life.*	
	13:34-35, A new commandment: *Love one another as I have loved you.*
	14:15, *If you love me, you will keep my commandments.*
	14:21-24, Whoever keeps my commandments loves me.
14:30-31, *I do as the Father commanded me* (refers to facing *the ruler of this world* [and laying down his life]), . . . *so that the world may know that I love the Father.*	
	15:10, *If you keep my commandments, you will abide in my love.*
15:10, *I have kept the Father's commandments and abide in his love.*	
	15:12, *This is my commandment, that you love one another as I have loved you.*
	15:17, *I give you these command[ment]s so that you love one another.* [AT]

While some commentators say that Jesus gives only one commandment (13:34-35), the situation is more complex. The noun appears in the plural six times; in the singular, four times. In 14:15 *commandments* (pl.) refers to both doing *greater works* and *asking the Father* in Jesus' name. In 14:23 *love me* and *keep my word* are specified as the *commandments* of 14:21 (a combination in Dan 9:4c; Deut passim; Josh 22:5; Neh 1:5). Add these four to *love one another*, and we have five commands Jesus gives his disciples. Reducing them to one violates the text. The command in 10:18 is readily harmonized with the dual command of 14:30-31 yet retains its own specific emphasis.

The Father's commands to Jesus are varied also. In 12:49-50 Jesus fulfills *two* commandments of the Father: to speak what the Father tells him and to give eternal life. The verb in 14:31 appears to embrace two actions also: face *the ruler of this world* (v. 30) and act so *that the world may know that I love the Father* (v. 31b). Jesus' obedience in giving his life *for the life of the world* (6:51) counters the world's unbelief and violence. Consider the forgiveness offered by the Amish to Charles Roberts, who shot ten Amish schoolgirls in the 2006 Nickel Mines tragedy. That Christlike love stunned the world!

In 1 John the term *commandment* occurs eighteen times, with similar emphases. One distinctive emphasis appears there: "that we should believe in the name of his Son Jesus Christ" (3:23). This is coupled with "love one another." The meaning of "love one another" is put into practical terms (2:3-11), where the term *commandment* occurs six times (von Wahlde 1990: 54–55). Obeying Jesus' *commandments* (2:3b) and "obey[ing] his word" (2:5a) show that God's love has reached perfection in the believer. It proves that the believer abides in Jesus and that we "walk just as [Jesus] walked" (2:6). Later, in 4:21–5:5, the term *commandment(s)* (used 4x) sets up a reciprocal relationship between loving the brother and sister as evidence of loving God, as well as knowing that we are children of God because we love God and keep his commandments. First John 5:4-5 extends this solidarity of God and the believers into the sphere of power to conquer the world, somewhat analogical to John 14:30-31 read with 15:9-12.

The relationship between John 15:10 and 11 is most significant. Keeping the commandments yields *joy . . . complete* joy! *Joy* (noun *chara* and verb *chairō*) occurs twenty-five times in the Gospel and Epistles of John: eighteen times in the Gospel and seven times in the Epistles.

Jesus' commandments in John are related to Jesus' double commandment in the Synoptic Gospels: love of God and love of neighbor (see "John 13 and the [New] Covenant," in TBC for John 13). John's love commands affect the believers' witness to the world. As Minear (1984) emphasizes, John is the *Martyr's Gospel*, since both Jesus and his disciples are called to lay down their lives for the other.

TEXT IN THE LIFE OF THE CHURCH

Keeping the Commandments

In John 14 and 15, *keeping my commandment(s)* is linked to loving Jesus (14:15, 21-24; 15:9-12, 17). First John emphasizes the same. McDermond (86–87) devotes a major TBC section to this topic, with extensive citation from Anabaptist writers.

The Holy Spirit as Advocate

Most hymns that speak of the Holy Spirit depict the Spirit as a source of power, peace, and comfort, but in John 15:26 the accent differs. It speaks of truthful *testimony* to Jesus in the face of the world's hatred and synagogue persecution. Two lines from "Fire of God, Undying Flame" (*Sing the Story*, #103) capture in part the work of the Spirit as presented in this text: "Strength of God, your might within / conquers sorrow, pain, and sin. Fortify from evil's art / all the gateways of my heart." But the biblical text more sharply focuses on truthfully *testifying* to Jesus in the face of hostility and trial, both legal and political. The Spirit and the disciples join together in this testimony.

We seldom think of the Holy Spirit as our defense counsel. Yet in the stories of the martyrs, we hear that the Spirit aids the speech of the persecuted as they testify to Jesus before authorities. In describing the testimony of fifteen-year-old Jacques Dosie, who was imprisoned at Leeuwaerden in 1550, van Braght writes, "The faithful God, according to His promise (Luke 21:14; Matt 10:19; Mark 13:11; Luke 12:11), gave him a mouth and wisdom, which they (the Lord and Lady of Friesland) could in no wise resist or quench" (*MM* 498). The Lady, impressed with the young lad's knowledge and speech, called him in many times to hear him (499). The authorities used the tongue screw, an instrument of torture, to try to stop the martyrs' bold witness. Sixteenth-century Anabaptists readily identified with "being put out of the synagogue" (16:2). The Yoder/Hochstetler index of Scriptures (200) lists thirteen citations of 16:2 in *Martyrs Mirror*. This aspect of the Paraclete-Spirit's work—true and bold testimony empowered by the Spirit—merits more emphasis in our homilies and hymnody.

Life on the Vine: Living Love

In his insightful book *Life on the Vine*, Phil Kenneson devotes a chapter to each fruit of the Spirit. He identifies obstacles to fruit-bearing latent in our culture. Kenneson correlates the obstacles to love with promotion of self-interest; in a market economy this puts a price on everything and reduces relationships to contracts. These obstacles to love are like the birds, squirrels, and deer that eat the fruit from our trees.

Kenneson says that our joy fruit is choked by manufactured desires, cravings for more, and anxiety and fear. Such cultural forces are like the tiny invisible insects that get into the fruit and spoil it. These pervasive cultural forces keep us from joy. Joy is hard to come by in our culture. Just when we think we are about to enjoy the fruit from our trees, a late frost comes and freezes our blossoms, and joy once again is snuffed from our lives. So we become hardened to life's routine and give up on joy—until the Spirit breaks through anew and melts our hearts. Then even in the hardest of times, we rejoice in God's love and salvation.

Bearing the fruit of peace, Kenneson says, is thwarted by numerous cultural forces: the separation of life into private or public spheres; the compartmentalizing of life (professionalism and specialties that make community discourse difficult); the strangling of politics by special interest-groups; the defense of rights (e.g., malpractice suits in medical practice); and the sanctioning of violence that shortcuts conflict transformation. These block peace in both personal and communal dimensions. Such forces are like the hurricanes, hail, and tornadoes that strip the fruit off the branches. To abide in the vine and bear the fruit of love, joy, and peace in our culture is difficult and hazardous. We need countercultural empowerment, prayer, meditation on Scripture, and even fasting to enable us to withstand the cultural threats to our fruit, which sap our nourishment from the vine.

To bear the fruit of peace, our peacemaking must draw nourishment from abiding in Jesus, or in Paul's language, from our "in-Christ" identity. John's metaphor of Jesus as vine and his followers as branches stresses *mutual indwelling* in two ways: drawing life from Jesus and abiding in Jesus. In John's "great commission" (20:19-23), Jesus' oneness with his disciples is sealed by his *breathing* the Holy Spirit *into them* (AT). The Spirit is the abiding and indwelling presence of the divine: the Spirit in us, we in Jesus, and the Son in the Father.

Jesus' teaching on abiding raises the question of the relationship between doctrinal belief and spiritual union. Burge asks, "Is discipleship a commitment to doctrinal beliefs concerning God and Jesus? Is it a way of 'love' perhaps that sets disciples apart from the world? Or is it an experience, a mystical spiritual encounter that transforms?" (2000: 423). Burge answers by saying it is all three: "Discipleship is a way of thinking (doctrine), a way of living (ethics), and a supernatural experience that cannot be compared with anything in the world" (423). Abiding in Jesus and receiving his life-giving nourishment as a branch receives nourishment from the vine is deeply spiritual. Burge concludes: "Without some dimension of an interior experience of the reality of Jesus, without a transforming spirituality that creates a supernatural life, doctrine and ethics lose their value" (423). Werner Packull's and C. Arnold Snyder's (2001, editor; also 2012) studies of Anabaptism (cf. C. J. Dyck 1995) concur that the discipleship of the leaders of first-generation Anabaptism was deeply rooted in spirituality, drawing from the spiritual mystical tradition of medieval Catholicism.

This is what we need in our time.

John 16:5-33

The Paraclete's Work, Jesus' Departure and Consolation: Joy and Peace

PREVIEW

When a parent or pastor is about to leave this world through imminent death, parting words to children or parishioners are difficult. Emotions of love and care for those receiving the parting words are intense, and words come with difficulty. In his farewell speech, Jesus has much to say to his disciples, but some of it is difficult to understand. In these final words to his disciples, Jesus pastorally engages his disciples in dialogue, comforting their sorrowful hearts. In the first part Jesus informs them of coming events with two motifs: *not see/see again* and the riddle of *a little while*. The disciples are puzzled. Knowing their perplexity, Jesus guides their thought and emotion through the stages of their groping for understanding.

Human emotions rise to the surface in Jesus' last dialogue with his disciples. Acknowledging their *hearts of sorrow*, Jesus introduces new imagery to explain the significance of his leaving. He speaks of a woman going through the pain of childbirth, then rejoicing when the baby is born. Jesus uses maternal imagery to explain to his male disciples the crisis they will soon face. While the pain and joy in 16:21 may refer to Jesus himself, in verses 22-23 Jesus uses these images for the disciples. First they will experience pain, and then later joy.

Jesus acknowledges that he is speaking to them in *figures of speech*. But he also promises that *on that day* he will *speak plainly of the Father*. Now the disciples say they understand: *Yes! Now you are speaking plainly!* (v. 29). They then say that *you*, Jesus, *know all things*—and really don't need anyone to question you! This is strange in light of their questions in chapter 14. Then the disciples make an important confession: *We believe that you came from God.* Finally! But is this sudden shift to *understanding* ironic? Do they really understand? This is the last time the disciples collectively speak to Jesus in the Gospel of John.

Jesus has final words for them. He affirms their belief but questions it—a clue to the ironic intent. He says, *Do you now believe?* Jesus then predicts that they all will be scattered, and he will be left alone, *except* for my Father who is *with me*. To close his farewell to his disciples, he enfolds all he has said with the purpose *so that in me you may have peace*. Then, looping back to the theme of 15:18-25, he reminds them of persecution to come. *But take courage; I have conquered the world!*

OUTLINE

The Work of the Paraclete, 16:5-15
Final Dialogue on Departure and Its Ramifications, 16:16-33

EXPLANATORY NOTES

The Work of the Paraclete 16:5-15

Although the work of the Paraclete is the main focus of this section, other aspects of Jesus' relationship to his disciples, now and in the future, are addressed as well. Many commentators put 16:4b with this section, and there are good reasons to do so. It is indeed transitional. Parsenios comments on verse 4b and sees analogies with the "supper symposium" in the Greco-Roman world. He enlightens these crucial words in Jesus' farewell speech:

> Jesus' admonition at 16:4b insists that the sole purpose of his entire set of discourses is to allow his followers to hear his voice when they no longer see his countenance. . . . Where Plutarch claims that Socrates' dinner conversations are a feast for later generations not originally present with Socrates, Jesus similarly insists that his words from the Last Supper are spoken for a time when he is no longer present. Preserved as they are in a *logodeipnon* [words spoken at the supper],

later generations can share in the feast long after Jesus departs. "I did not say these things (*tauta*) to you from the beginning because I was with you. But now I am going to him who sent me. . . ." Indeed, with this comment, Jesus is already partially displaced by his words. His earthly presence in his *flesh* is already becoming a presence in his *words, tauta*. (142)

Jesus' disciples must both *remember* and *keep* these words (146). *Eating* and *hearing* constitute Jesus' legacy for his disciples, then and now.

16:5-6 Departure: No Questions? Hearts Filled with Sorrow

Verse 5 has played a key role in efforts to understand the unity and disunity of the farewell discourse. Some scholars regard the verse as conclusive evidence of a "compositional problem," in light of the closure byte in 14:31, *Arise, let us be on our way*. The apparent contradiction between chapter 14, where the disciples ask questions, and 16, where Jesus scores them for not asking questions—might argue for chapters 15 and 16 as separate discourses (e.g., R. Brown's chart parallels, 1970: 589–93). Some think the discourses were poorly stitched together by an editor in the development of the Gospel's final form.

But this view misses the insights that accrue from seeking to understand the discourse's narrative unity in its present form. While Jesus' words *Yet none of you asks me, "Where are you going?"* seem to contradict chapter 14 and thus be a different discourse, they can be understood differently. These verses portray the disciples as coming to grips emotionally with what Jesus has been saying. They are in shock, given what Jesus has just said about imminent hatred from the world and persecution from the synagogue. Further, his three forecasts of *another* Paraclete and his own absence are taking their toll. They are not asking (the verb *erōtaō* is in the present tense) where he is going. Their hearts are filled with sorrow, which Jesus knows (v. 6). Hence Jesus' comment that they are not asking any more questions is not a reprimand nor a complaint, but an empathetic identification with their inner journey. What else might they ask?

O'Day (1995: 770) explains this difference between chapters 14 and 16 by regarding the former as oriented more to "assurance and consolation" and the latter as focused more on the future. Yes, chapter 16 is focused on the future, but it also addresses assurance and consolation for the present. However, O'Day (771) affirms Schnackenburg's (3.126) explanation, which is more persuasive:

Jesus' word here "is primarily a rhetorical device. Jesus is not really concerned with the disciples' [lack of] questions about his departure, but refers to their present speechlessness as a way of introducing their 'situation of sorrow.'" Dodd (1953: 413) links their sorrow to their dismay about the future. This may be true, but the emotional overload from all that has been said is an important factor in understanding these two verses. In verse 7 Jesus identifies pastorally with their emotion—their "hearts of sorrow" *and* their joy (15:21-22).

16:7-11 *The Paraclete's Work Concerning the World*

Verse 7 is transitional. Jesus holds their sorrow in his heart and shifts to hope in the presence of another *Comforter* (AT; the best translation for this context). He helps them to see that not all is lost by his going away. *It is to your advantage that I go away, for if I do not go away, the Advocate [Comforter] will not come to you; but if I go, I will send him to you.* The Comforter will care for you in your distress. *"The requisite departure of Jesus does not refer to his necessary absence when the Paraclete appears. It refers to the preliminary death and glorification of Jesus for which the Spirit must wait (7:39)"* (Burge 1987: 133, italics original).

Verses 8-11 focus on the work of the Paraclete as (legal) prosecutor in relation to the world. The world that hated Jesus will hate the disciples (15:18-19, 23). The prosecuting work of the Paraclete in relation to the world is three-dimensional, with each dimension introduced by the same Greek word (*peri*), which the NRSV and NIV (2011) translate as *about* (RSV, *concerning*; NIV 1984, *in regard to*). The KJV deleted the word in translation and used *reprove of* with three objects: *sin, righteousness, judgment.* By this choice the KJV accentuates the lead verb in verse 8, *reprove* (*elenchō*, which NRSV and NIV 2011 translate as *prove wrong*; RSV, *convince*). While *reprove* fits well with *sin*, it does not connect well with *righteousness* and *judgment*. A parallel use of the verb occurs in 8:46, where Jesus asks, *Which of you convicts me of sin?* Since *sin* is first in 16:8, the verb-object parallel matches exactly. *Convict* (cf. NIV 1984) is perhaps the best translation for the three-dimensional task in 16:8-11; it fits the image of prosecuting advocate. O'Day (1995: 772), however, prefers *exposing* as the primary meaning. In the cross event, the Spirit *reveals* or *exposes* sin, righteousness, and judgment. The Paraclete will expose the world's culpability *because* it prosecuted and crucified Jesus.

Just as sin, righteousness, and judgment are each introduced with the same preposition, *concerning* (*peri*), so each of the three accusatory terms is followed by a reason in a *because* (*hoti*) clause. The world's sin is refusal to believe in Jesus. The world's conviction concerning *righteousness* or *justice* is *because I go to my Father, and you will see me no longer*. This twofold explanation is puzzling. Does the return of Jesus the righteous one to his Father represent his vindication (another sense of *dikaiosynē*) and glorification? Unlike Jesus' promise *You will see me* [again] (14:19), this *see me no longer* phrase is not followed by such a promise. Rather, Jesus stresses his departure and absence, though in 16:16-19 he says three times, *You will see me* [again].

The world's *judgment* is certain *because the ruler of the world* has already been cast down (12:31 AT; cf. Hamilton: 86–89; O'Day 1995: 771–72). The TNIV translation of the last causal line, *because the prince of this world now stands condemned*, conveys the durative sense of the perfect tense. What happened already in 12:31 now stands; the devil's defeat by the cross and resurrection (glorification and vindication) exposes the ruler's doom. Jesus' imminent death on the cross as Lamb of God displays his *righteousness* or *justice* in revealing his Father's love for the world, exposing the rationale for the world's judgment, displayed for all to see (cf. Col 2:15).

But will the *world* be convicted or convinced of any of this, as 16:7 seems to say? Or is this to be understood as the Spirit's revealing to and empowering the disciples in their *witness* to the world? The disciples' witness will have an impact upon the world, convicting people of their sin, potentially leading them to join the new community of love. This seems more likely. If the former interpretation—that the *world* experiences *conviction*—is intended, the impact on the world is an *eschatological* crisis, the work of the Spirit to be exposed fully and culminated on the last day.

16:12-15 The Paraclete's Work in You, the Disciples

These verses reiterate previous emphases (paraphrased):

- I could say more, but you cannot bear it all now.

- The Spirit of truth, when he comes, will guide you into all truth.

- The Spirit of truth will not speak on his own, but he will speak what he hears, declaring what is to come (cf. the *testifying* in 15:26).

- The Spirit will thus glorify me, declaring what is mine to you.

- The chain of revelation is from Father to Jesus, from Jesus to the Spirit of truth, from the Spirit of truth to the disciples.

The word for *bear* (*bastazō*) in the first line normally means "to carry something" (*stones* to throw at Jesus in 10:31; *money*, which Judas carried in 12:6; cf. Howard-Brook 1994: 347). But here the word has a psychological sense. Jesus is sensitive to what the disciples are able *to carry emotionally*. The word for *guide* (*hodēgeō*) in verse 13 is a compound of *lead* (*agō*) and *way* (*hodos*). This verb often appears in the Psalms (LXX) when calling on God for guidance—leading the way (Pss 25:4-12, [note esp. v. 9]; 27:11; 119:33). "Teach me your way, O Lord, that I might walk in your truth" (Ps 86:11) fits well John's theme. Jesus said, *I am the way, and the truth, and the life* (14:6), and now the Spirit will resume the work of Jesus. The OT motif of looking to God for instruction and guidance through word and Spirit, prominent in the wisdom tradition, is here carried forward by the Spirit of truth (cf. Howard-Brook 1994: 347; O'Day 1995: 773).

The word for *declare* (last phrase in vv. 13 and 14) is especially striking since it has the sense of *announce* or *proclaim* (*anangellō*). It is used in that sense in 4:25 and appears again in 16:25c (also fifty-seven times in Isaiah; Howard-Brook 1994: 347–48). Most striking, however, a similar word (same root) is used for Mary Magdalene's proclamation of Jesus as the resurrected one (20:18). Hence the Spirit will continue the *proclaiming* work of Jesus. Although the Spirit serves as prosecuting attorney in relation to the world, for Jesus' disciples his role is instructional guidance and gospel proclamation. Indeed, the term *Paraclete* has an iridescent meaning, with the context providing its connotation.

The Spirit's work witnesses consistently to Jesus and the Father (v. 15). This "ring of truth" occurs also in Revelation: "Worship God! for the testimony of Jesus is the spirit of prophecy" (19:10c-d). Neither *declaring what is to come* nor *prophecy* means forecasting events to happen through the ages. Instead, they mean bearing witness to Jesus' triumph through and over death—indeed, his glorification in John. God, Jesus, and the Spirit speak the same truth, exposing and convicting of sin, righteousness, and casting the "plumb line" of righteous judgment (cf. Amos 7:7-9).

Final Dialogue on Departure and Its Ramifications 16:16-33

16:16-19 Not See/See Again: A Little While (Mikron) Puzzle

This portion of the discourse is a bit of comic relief: *mikron*, which means *a little while*, occurs seven times. If presented by Jesus and his disciples onstage, the scene would elicit laughter. The narrator is master of skillful repetition: Jesus speaks, using the word two times (v. 16). Then *some of his disciples* repeat what Jesus said and discuss it among themselves, also using *mikron* twice (v. 17). Then the narrator formulates their puzzlement into a query to Jesus, with the definite article concretizing the query into a *mikron* riddle (*this* "*a little while,*" v. 18). Jesus knows they are wanting to ask him about it, so he repeats it again, but this time as a question: *Why are you discussing . . . ?* (v. 19 AT). Does Jesus solve the riddle for them? No, Jesus introduces another memorable and distinctive reality that his farewell will bring into their lives.

Now the readers of the Gospel know what the disciples cannot comprehend. Jesus *is with them* just *a little while* longer. Then they will not see him for *a little while*. The text has two words for *you will see*: *opsesthe* (in vv. 16b, 17, and 19b) and *theōreite* (in vv. 10, 16a, and 19a). This verb *theōreite* (present imperative) is used with *no longer do you see me*, while *opsesthe* (future indicative) is linked to *after a little while you will see me again* (AT). Distinction in meaning here is difficult. Mark 16:7 also uses *opsesthe* to describe *seeing* the post-resurrection Jesus. In John that *seeing* will be *after a little while* coupled with *again* (*palin*). The play on words seems to indicate that while the disciples can behold him now as incarnate Son of the Father (1:14), when they *see* him after his death and resurrection they will see him as the glorified One!

16:20-24 Jesus' Answer: Pain and Joy

Jesus begins his answer with the memorable *Truly, truly* saying (its first use since 14:12, repeated in 16:23, his last use in speaking to his disciples as a group [cf. 21:18, to Peter only]). His words are filled with pathos, evoking that of Israel's great prophets (see Heschel: 221–32). Jesus' departure will have opposite effects on them and on the world. They, the disciples, will grieve; the world will rejoice. *You will have pain, but your pain will turn into joy* (v. 20). Jesus then illustrates by a woman's experience in childbirth: first great pain, then great joy. This imagery also occurs in the prophets, as Israel bears the travail of Yahweh's discipline and punishment (Isa 26:17-19) and then later knows the joy of restoration and promise of a joyful future (66:7-8, 10; see Howard-Brook 1994: 351). Verse 22 reiterates: *So you have pain now; but I will see you again, and your hearts will rejoice, and no one will take your joy from you.* The final line of verse 24, *that your joy may be complete*, renews Jesus' promise in 15:11, *I have said these things to you so that my joy may be in you, and that your joy may be complete.*

With the overall dour tone of the farewell discourse, at least from its depiction of the disciples' clueless responses, it is easy to miss these upbeat emphases. Yes, the Paraclete is compensation for their loss of Jesus. This the disciples do not grasp. Perhaps the three-fold repetition of the noun *joy* and verb *rejoice* does get through to them. There is a future for them, even though Jesus is soon to leave them.

The image of *birthing* evokes earlier Gospel emphases also: those *born of God* are God's *children* (1:12). Jesus promises Nicodemus that by being *born again/from above*, he will enter into the kingdom of God (3:3-10). And Jesus promises *life* throughout the Gospel. Josephine Ford comments on the birthing and mothering imagery—as well as that of Redeemer and Friend—in John's Gospel:

> I suggest that Jesus goes to his passion not as a victim, nor as a scape-goat, nor as a bloody sacrifice, not to appease a deity, nor to trap or pay a debt to the devil, but as a woman to give birth to her child through blood and water. Neither does he implement this alone but in total mutuality with the Father, in whom and for whom he is glorified, and the Spirit, the *alter Christus*. In John 19:34 the soldier pierces the side of Christ, and water and blood gush out. The rebirthing of God is consummated. (198)

Ford links together numerous themes pertinent to understanding how Jesus' words in the farewell discourse connect with the rest of the Gospel (e.g., 19:34). Further, in John 7:38-39 the disciples could not receive the *indwelling* Spirit until after he was glorified. The pain-bearing *mikron* is necessary for the joy-experiencing *mikron*; both are God's death-resurrection birthing the love community through water and blood (cf. 1 John 5:6-8; McDermond: 244).

Another theme that recurs in John is *asking and receiving* (16:23-24b). Some commentators say this is the only NT text authorizing *asking in Jesus' name*: "Nowhere else in John or in the New Testament is it said that things will be given in Jesus' name" (R. Brown 1970: 723; Howard-Brook 1994: 352). But John 15:16c says much the same. Here the emphasis is double: [*Ask*] *for anything in my name* (16:24a) and *If you ask anything of the Father in my name, he will give it to you* (v. 23b). Asking *Jesus* matched with *his* promise to give (14:14) is now shifted: no longer will you ask *me, Jesus*, but you will ask *the Father*. Jesus is the Internet provider to request the Father. This text is a model for prayer to the Father "in the name of Jesus" (cf. Eph 5:20; Col 3:17; James 5:13-14).

Most Christians would be hard-pressed to identify where in Scripture this formula is prescribed. Since John stresses the mutual indwelling of God in Jesus and Jesus in God, one would think that *either* God or Jesus may be addressed in prayer: our requests may be sent heavenward to either the Father or the Son. Other texts in John (14:13-14) speak of asking Jesus, though verse 14 adds *in my name*, which implies that the Father is the object. The command to *ask* in 15:7 does not specify *whom* to ask. The point here in 16:23-24 is in keeping with John 14:6: Jesus is *the Way* to the Father! Perhaps the clue to the difference is *on that day* and the different verb for ask (*erōtaō* in 16:23a versus *aiteō* in 16:23b-24). O'Day says, "'On that day' the confused, anxious, and stammering questions that have marked the disciples' relationship to Jesus during his ministry (e.g., 6:9; 11:8; 13:6, 25, 36) and especially during the farewell discourse (14:5, 22; 16:17-18) will cease" (O'Day 1995: 1780).

Perhaps also *erōtaō* requests (16:23a) reflecting confusion will cease, but boldly asking (*aiteō*, vv. 23b-24) the Father in Jesus' name will be normative. *On that day*, the day of Jesus' glorification through death and resurrection, the disciples' "what-do-you-mean?" questions (*erōtaō*) will cease; the Spirit will enable his disciples to ask the Father directly *in my name*. In the flow of the narrative, with this invitation to ask, Jesus is turning over guidance in prayer to the Spirit.

16:25-28 Jesus' Answer: I Will Speak Plainly of the Father[w]

Just as there is a shift in the manner of asking, so there will be a shift in Jesus' manner of speaking: *I have said these things to you in figures of speech. The hour is coming when I will no longer speak to you in figures, but will tell you plainly of the Father.* Some commentators take *figures of speech* to indicate the mode that Jesus uses throughout the Gospel. But the referent is more restrictive. The word used here for figures is *paroimia*. In John it is used only here (16:25, 29) and in 10:6, in Jesus' metaphor of the sheepfold, the shepherd, and the sheep. The only other NT use is in 2 Peter 2:22, where it connotes "proverb," as does its occurrence in the wisdom literature of the Septuagint (e.g., Sir 39:1-3).

How does the coming of *the hour*, which is almost at hand, make such a huge difference? Jesus says he will speak plainly, not in figures. Jesus turns *You will ask nothing of me* (v. 23) to *On that day you will ask in my name. I do not say to you that I will ask the Father on your behalf* (v. 26). The shift is slight, but it implies that Jesus' departure

---

w   Where the superscript w occurs after headings, please see the commentary's online Web Supplement for additional material. Go to: http://www.heraldpress.com/bcbc/john.

will make a difference in how both he and they pray. Perhaps the shift intends to jolt the disciples to prepare for the catastrophic change about to come. In chapter 17 Jesus does pray to the Father for his disciples, so his point in chapter 16 is tactical. The rationale for this shift is the direct relationship of the Father to the disciples and vice versa: *for the Father himself loves you, because you have loved me and have believed that I came from God.* In other words, you have passed the test: because you love me and believe that I came from the Father, now you have direct access to the Father, but *in the name of Jesus.* The word for *love* here in 16:27 is "friendship love" (*phileō*). This love connotes a reciprocal relationship of friendship, which Jesus welcomes in 15:15 (cf. Howard-Brook 1994: 355).

In the farewell discourse five clusters emphasize *asking* (14:12-14; 15:5-8; 15:14-17; 16:20-24; 16:25-28). Paul Minear identifies the "multiple filiations" of thought in Jesus' command to ask:

> The act of obeying this command is associated with believing, with doing the same or greater works than Jesus, with glorifying the Father, with carrying out a group appointment and ministry in the name of Jesus, with total dependence on him, with bearing fruit, with knowing God and conveying that knowledge, with persecution, and with witnessing by way of martyrdom. (1984: 89)

Jesus then drives home what he and the Gospel narrator have been saying many times in many ways: *I came from the Father and have come into the world; again, I am leaving the world and am going to the Father.*

16:29-32 The Disciples' Affirmation and Jesus' Counter-Affirmation[w]

Now the disciples speak their last (ironic?) corporate word in the Gospel: *Yes, now you are speaking plainly, not in any figure of speech! Now we know that you know all things, and do not need to have anyone question [erōtaō] you; by this we believe that you came from God* (vv. 29-30). How did they so suddenly get to this point? If taken literally, it means that Jesus' admission that he is speaking in figures has enabled them suddenly to see the deeper, true meaning of all he has been saying, and until now they have not understood. Some scholars see hilarious irony here: they say what they do not know.

O'Day (1995: 782) points out the disciples' "understanding" responds only to Jesus' origin from the Father and not to his departure. "The omission underscores the incompleteness of their bold confession, because they do not acknowledge the necessity of Jesus' death and departure to complete his revelation of God." Have the disciples come to the "tipping point" and *think* they are prepared for what is to come? Or are they simply "giving in" to their weariness and naively settling for the comfort of the supper? The sudden shift of the disciples (pl.) in the interchange is puzzling, at the least.

Jesus' response appears to confirm the disciples' inadequate, if not ironic, statement. Strikingly, dialogue stops here. Jesus responds with the Gospel motif *Do you now believe?* (v. 31b), but the disciples do not answer. Jesus' following words indicate that they need to hear more. They have more to learn before their naive (?) affirmation rings true. Jesus says, *The hour is coming, indeed it has come, when you will be scattered, each one to his home, and you will leave me alone. Yet I am not alone because the Father is with me* (v. 32). The Markan parallel is 14:27, where Jesus bluntly tells his disciples, "You will all become deserters," and then quotes some of Zechariah 13:7, "Strike the shepherd, that the sheep may be scattered; I will turn my hand against the little ones." The statement appears in all three texts (Zechariah, Mark, John). In John 10:12 where the *hireling* (RSV) abandons the sheep the wolf comes and *scatters* the sheep. In John 10 Jesus is the noble shepherd, who defends the sheep, but here the sheep will *abandon him* in his hour of trial (Howard-Brook 1994: 356).

The disciples do not speak again until after Jesus' resurrection, and the narrator gives no clue to how they react. Meanwhile, Jesus bestows an invaluable gift.

16:33 Parting Gift: Peace in the Face of Persecution

Verse 24 ends with Jesus' assurance *that your joy may be complete.* Here Jesus' words to his disciples end with *so that in me you may have peace.* In light of the emotional tangle between Jesus and his disciples throughout the discourse, this is truly an amazing ending! The themes of joy and peace may be viewed as bookends to this last part of Jesus' conversation with his disciples (Howard-Brook 1994: 357). The peace that Jesus promises is not sentimental or some escapist piety, but peace in the face of *persecution* (v. 33c). Recapitulating the hard admonition of 15:18-25, Jesus says, "The world will persecute, yes, but this will not destroy the stronger love that I, Jesus, give to you, and invite you to experience" (paraphrased).

Most important, *Take courage; I have conquered the world!* Jesus finishes the battle against the *ruler of this world* (12:31; 16:11; 19:30). Because Jesus overcomes the world's ruler, his disciples can have peace, even in the face of persecution, expulsion from the synagogue, and in every adversity (cf. Rom 8:37-39). The same Johannine theology breathes through 1–3 John (e.g., 1 John 5:4, 19) and Revelation, where the word *conquer* occurs sixteen times (2x in 3:21), with alternating scenes of who conquers whom (Swartley 2006a: 337–38). The Lamb's victory prevails. The disciples' work "is not theirs to achieve the victory but rather to live in the light which that victory casts on the world around them. In place of their fear, Jesus commands 'courage' [its only use in John]. . . . These are the final words that Jesus speaks to his fragile, confused, struggling community before the moment of the cross. What remains is a prayer, direct communion between Jesus and his Father, which both the disciples and we are privileged to hear" (Howard-Brook 1994: 357).

THE TEXT IN BIBLICAL CONTEXT

The Paraclete, or Holy Spirit[w]

While it is common to blend together the Paraclete, Spirit of truth, and Holy Spirit, these three terms fan out differently across Scripture. I print below the only Paraclete texts in the NT, next treat "Spirit of truth," and then "the Holy Spirit."

The Paraclete Texts

And I will ask the Father, and he will give you another Advocate, to be with you forever. This is the Spirit of truth, whom the world cannot receive, because it neither sees him nor knows him. You know him, because he abides with you, and he will be in you. (John 14:16-17)

But the Advocate, the Holy Spirit, whom the Father will send in my name, will teach you everything, and remind you of all that I have said to you. (14:26)

When the Advocate comes, whom I will send to you from the Father, the Spirit of truth who comes from the Father, he will testify on my behalf. You also are to testify because you have been with me from the beginning. (15:26-27)

Nevertheless I tell you the truth: it is to your advantage that I go away, for if I do not go away, the Advocate will not come to you; but if I go, I will send him to you. And when he comes, he will prove the world wrong about sin and righteousness and judgment: about sin, because they do not believe in me; about righteousness, because I am going to the Father and you will see me no longer; about judgment, because the ruler of this world has been condemned. (16:7-11)

I still have many things to say to you, but you cannot bear them now. When the Spirit of truth comes, he will guide you into all the truth; for he will not speak on his own, but will speak whatever he hears, and he will declare to you the things that are to come. He will glorify me, because he will take what is mine and declare it to you. All that the Father has is mine. For this reason I said that he will take what is mine and declare it to you. (16:12-15)

My little children, I am writing these things to you so that you may not sin. But if anyone does sin, we have an advocate with the Father, Jesus Christ the righteous; and he is the atoning sacrifice for our sins, and not for ours only but also for the sins of the whole world. (1 John 2:1-2)

The term *Paraclete* occurs in all of these passages except 16:12-15, which extends 16:7-11. While *advocate* is the most frequent translation in these texts (including 1 John 2:2), the sense of *comforter* and *guide*, *helper*, and even *teacher*, is present. The Paraclete is the indwelling presence of Jesus in the life of the believers. Although *paraklētos* denotes *advocate* in the Greek court, the Septuagint's related uses of the verb *parakaleō* translate the Hebrew term *naḥam* as *comfort* (see Hamilton).

Despite the disciples' fears and doubts, Jesus promises the Spirit to advocate for them, to defend, assure, *comfort*, and guide them through the dark days ahead (Howard-Brook 1994: 320-21). Franck's published doctoral dissertation on the Paraclete argues persuasively that we should not narrow the work of the Paraclete to one meaning only, but recognize at least three major functions: the forensic aspect (the Advocate who defends believers and reproves or convicts the world); the farewell assurance and comfort themes; and also the didactic function: the Paraclete *will teach you everything, and remind you of all I have said to you* (14:26); *he will guide into all truth* (16:13), the fruit of his teaching.

Franck privileges the *teaching* role (37-75). He regards *witnessing* or *testifying* (*martyreō* in 15:26) as part of the teaching function (Franck: 57). The Paraclete glorifies Jesus (16:14) when he proclaims what he receives from Jesus to the disciples (16:14b; Franck: 66-67, 73-74; cf. the Spirit's coming in Jesus' glorification in 7:39c-d). Franck's thesis further contends that this *teaching* role is taken up and embodied in the Paraclete's inspiration of the beloved disciple to write the Gospel (79-98). Hence the Paraclete continues to teach the church whenever and wherever the Gospel is read, taught, and preached. The Paraclete thus continues to *testify* to Jesus.

Spirit of Truth

John uses the designation *Spirit of truth* most frequently for the Paraclete. It fits with the Gospel's larger emphasis, "truth on trial" (Lincoln 2000). Truth exposes falsehood and is at the center of Jesus' high-priestly prayer (17:15-19). Jesus' concern in this crucial part of the prayer is for the believers' protection from the world and their sanctification (being made holy) in and by the truth. The word Jesus has spoken is truth. The ultimate collision between Jesus and Pilate is over the related issues of kingship and truth (18:33-38). Significantly, Jesus claims: *I am . . . the truth* (14:6).

Truth has a wide range of meaning in Scripture. It figures crucially in the argument in 1 John (McDermond: 62). Ephesians 4:15 has the remarkable phrase *truthing in love* (AT, literally), which prescribes the nature of relationships and discourse within the Christian community. In 4:20-21, after warning against the sins of the world, Paul calls believers to Christ, truth's embodiment: "That is not the way you learned Christ! For surely you have heard about him and were taught in him, as truth is in Jesus."

In the OT *truth* is fidelity in relationships, a twin to *righteousness*. Israel's downfall was its failure to walk in truth, to maintain fidelity in covenant obligations to God. Psalm 86:11, my personal treasure, embraces the way of the Torah for the people: "Teach me your way, O Lord, that I may walk in your truth. Give me an undivided heart to revere your name." *Walking in the truth* is a central motif of OT ethics. It is foundational for community life and faithful relationship to God. When truth is fudged, covenant love is feigned. Community falls apart and religion becomes a farce. The Paraclete's role is to guide believers into *truth*. Along with love for one another (13:34-35), truth is a hallmark of the believers' identity.

Holy Spirit

Elsewhere in the NT, the term most commonly used for the Paraclete is *Holy Spirit*, though it is mentioned only once in these texts (14:26). But as Hamilton and others have pointed out, it lies at the center of John's narrative, with crucial insights occurring in 3:3-10; 4:23-24; 6:53; 7:37-39, then climactically in John 20:22-23, when Jesus breathes the Holy Spirit into his disciples (cf. Gen 2:7). This is John's Pentecost. It forms the basis for the disciples' authority to forgive sins and to represent the mission of Jesus in the world. The Spirit is also a key motif in 1 John. The tests for knowing that the Spirit dwells corporately and personally within the community are whether believers truly love one another in word and deed and whether they keep Jesus' commandments (3:16-24).

In the OT the Lord's spirit came upon people for special tasks (Moses, Joshua, the Judges, Saul, David, and certainly in the calls of the prophets; see Hamilton). Isaiah 63:10-11 personalizes the holy spirit, saying Israel "rebelled and grieved his holy spirit." Several lines later, the prophet queries, "Where is the one who put within them his holy spirit?" In the Synoptic Gospels, the Spirit descends upon Jesus at baptism to authorize and empower his ministry (Luke 4:16-21) and his confrontation of the demons. By the Spirit of God (finger of God in Luke 11:20) Jesus exorcizes and frees people from Satan's bondage (Mark 3:21-29; Matt 12:22-32). Jesus' entire ministry in Luke and even more frequently in Acts is directed by the Holy Spirit. I concur with Hamilton that it is only with Pentecost that the *indwelling* of the promised Spirit becomes effectual. Even with that reality, there are times and occasions when people after Pentecost are especially filled, gripped, or empowered by the Spirit for a given task and mission (e.g., in Philip's encounter with the Ethiopian eunuch, Acts 8:29). In the Pauline letters the Holy Spirit is the seal of our redemption (Eph 1:13). We are not to "grieve the Holy Spirit" (Eph 4:30) or "quench the Spirit" (1 Thess 5:19).

Most crucial, our cry to God as our endearing, loving Abba is through the Holy Spirit (Gal 4:6; Rom 8:15). The Holy Spirit presents our groaning sighs, which we cannot voice, to the Father (Rom 8:26). The Holy Spirit assures us we are children of God as we keep Jesus' commandments and love one another (1 John 3:23-24). The Holy Spirit guides us in the Lord's Prayer and is God's best gift to believers (Luke 11:1-13). Concluding the call to don the armor of God in the believers' stand against the devil, we are to "pray in the Spirit at all times in every prayer and supplication" (Eph 6:18).

The Corinthians allowed the Spirit's gift of tongues to cause division among them. Paul's instruction to resolve the problem was not to deny that tongues are a gift of the Spirit but to set forth criteria by which to judge whether expressions are from the Holy Spirit or unholy spirits (1 Cor 12, 14). Love is one decisive factor (ch. 13). Building up the entire body is another (ch. 14). This panorama of Spirit activity in Scripture includes also the fruit of the Spirit (Gal 5:22-23 NIV 1984 and RSV): "love, joy, peace, patience, kindness, goodness, faithfulness, gentleness and self-control." With these evident in our lives, we are assured that we are God's children, with the Spirit dwelling in us. We participate in the trinity of love and mutual indwelling (John 15 and 17).

The Holy Spirit is named in Matthew's great commission in the baptismal pronouncement (28:18-20) and in a much-loved benediction, "The grace of the Lord Jesus Christ, the love of God, and the communion of the Holy Spirit be with all of you" (2 Cor 13:13).

Jesus' Gift of Peace

Key themes in Jesus' farewell discourse, including the Paraclete and peace, appear again in John's mission commission. Talbert (254, with modifications in brackets) shows the remarkable connections between the themes in John 14 and 16 and those in 20:19-23:

I am coming back to you (14:18, 16:22).	*Jesus came to them* (20:19).
Peace I leave with you (14:27) [16:33].	*Peace be with you* (20:21).
Then your hearts will rejoice (16:23).	*Then the disciples were glad* (20:20d).
As you have sent me,	*As the Father has sent me,*
I have sent them (17:18).	*even so I send you* (20:21).
If I go, I will send the Spirit to you (16:7b) [14:16, 26; 15:26].	*Receive the Holy Spirit* (20:22).

The peace that Jesus promises in John 14:27 and 16:33 is an inner calm, corporately and personally, when facing external hatred and persecution. Within the Gospel's larger ethos of conflict (cosmic, religious, and political), peace is an alternative power to other contending powers (Swartley 2006a: 313–14).

The linking of Jesus' postresurrection peace greeting to breathing the Holy Spirit into the disciples and giving them the mission commission in John 20:19-23 is significant. John 4 and chapters 14 and 16 indicate that the peace and mission of John's Gospel transcend cultural, racial, and religious boundaries. The fields ripe for harvest (4:38) include enemy Samaritans. The sequel in 4:46-54 portrays the splendid faith of the Roman official. Jesus heals his son. As a result, this man and his household become believers. In both cases, ethnic, religious, and national enmities are disempowered and transformed by the power of Jesus, Savior of the world.

In Ephesians, Jesus "is our peace" (2:14), which breaks down walls of enmity between peoples. Jesus' peace unites them (Yoder Neufeld 2002: 215–33). Many other NT texts speak also of Jesus' triumph over enmity, the world, sin, and death. In Luke 10:18 Jesus sees Satan falling from heaven when the Seventy proclaim the gospel of peace in the villages of Galilee (10:5-6). First John 5:4, 18-19 and Revelation emphasize Jesus' conquest of evil, with the saints praising and worshiping God Almighty for the Lamb's victory in liturgical crescendo ("Service of Worship," Swartley 2007: 239–62). Many NT texts (Rom 8:31-39; 1 Cor 15:54-57; Eph 2:11-15) proclaim

Jesus' victory over the powers (Swartley 2006a: 50–52; for ministry of Jesus' victory over the powers in social and personal deliverance from evil, see also 2006b: 24–40; 2006c: 96–112; 2009: 89–103).

THE TEXT IN THE LIFE OF THE CHURCH

The Holy Spirit in the Life of the Church

In 1977 the Mennonite Church in its biennial convention adopted a brief official document titled *The Holy Spirit in the Life of the Church*. The statement contains one good line in referring to Jesus' farewell discourse in John: "The Spirit interprets Christ (Jn. 14:16; 15:26; 16:13ff.)" (section 3B). Yet the role of the Spirit in guiding Jesus' disciples and empowering them to face persecution is muted.

However, the statement makes some good and helpful points about the Spirit's roles in the church, listed here in abbreviated, modified form (3B):

- The Spirit indwells every Christian. To belong to Christ is to have the Spirit (Rom 8:9).

- The Spirit undergirds the whole range of Christian experience from beginning to end, including spiritual gifts (1 Cor 12–14).

- The Spirit is closely tied to the person and mission of Christ [here the Paraclete *references* are cited].

- The Spirit is given that the church might truly be the body of Christ, sharing in his life, faithfully manifesting his character, and being fruitful in every good work (Rom 8:29; Gal 5:16-26).

- The Spirit is given to the church to empower it for the task of bearing witness to Christ (Acts 1:8) [true also of the Paraclete in John].

- It is the work of the Spirit . . . to interpret and vitalize the gospel in the lives of God's people.

In article 3 of *Confession of Faith in a Mennonite Perspective* (Mennonite Church 1995: 17–20), Paraclete texts are occasionally referenced (e.g., 16:8-10; 14:26; and 16:13, where *Spirit of truth* occurs). The article ends by saying, "The Holy Spirit . . . comforts us in suffering." This is as close as it comes to the Paraclete's role as *Comforter* and *Advocate*. In current theology the role of the Holy Spirit is accentuated more strongly (e.g., Moltmann 1997; Pentecostal contributions, well analyzed by Bruner). Too often Anabaptist his-torians and theologians have given short shrift to the role of the Spirit, especially that of the Paraclete. Two articles—by Shillington (31–39) and Snyder (64–73) in *Vision* (2012)—rectify this deficiency. Both are important along with other essays in this *Vision* volume, titled *The Holy Spirit and the Christian Life*.

Preaching and Teaching Peace

Three key texts on peace are John 14:27; 16:33; 20:19-23, 26. Jesus' journey through Samaria is a peacemaking event. *Peace* laces both OT and NT Scripture, with 250 occurrences of *shalom* (*šalom*) in the OT, and 100 of *eirēnē* in the NT (Swartley 2006a: 28n2). The wide range of NT peace emphases relates to at least twenty-one topics (indexed in Swartley: 2006, 2007). These may guide a two-year cycle of preaching and teaching peace. Here are three, related directly to John's Gospel:

- The Lord's Supper texts, even though John presents a puzzle here—for Communion Sunday (2006: 177–88; for John 6, see 184n16).

- *My peace I give to you, . . . not as the world gives* (John 14:27 RSV; cf. 16:33; 18:36). Link this to the indwelling of the Holy Spirit as Jesus' gift (2006: 284–89, 296–302). Jesus' three gifts of love, peace, and Paraclete "form the bedrock of the Johannine community of faith during Jesus' absence" (Neville: 182–83).

- "Peace and Mission" (John 4; 20:19-23; cf. Swartley 2006a: 304–16; 2007: 227–28). One might link this teaching and preaching also to worship (cf. Swartley 2007: 229–37; 265–66).

Jesus Prays to His Father

PREVIEW

As the early church leader Ignatius was taken to Rome as a prisoner headed for martyrdom, he wrote to his beloved churches in Asia Minor over which he was bishop. His pervading concern in these letters is that he be found *worthy*, a *true* martyr. That hope is correlated, however, with one key concern, that the churches under his leadership have unity. He prays, pleads, and longs that they be united in their belief and behavior in fidelity to Jesus Christ. Only if the churches over which he is bishop are united will he be *truly* a martyr (Swartley 1973).

As Jesus the Son pours out his heart to his Father before his arrest, he intercedes for his disciples. Some OT precedents for such prayers are Moses' parting words and blessing for the Israelites (Deut 33) and patriarchs Moses and Noah (*Jubilees* 1:19-21; 10:3-6; O'Day 1995: 787n562; cf. also Ezra 9; Neh 9; Dan 9). Jesus' prayer begins with his praying for himself, followed by prayer for the people. Aaron's order in making sacrifices is the same (Lev 16:11-16).

Numerous scholars consider this a prayer of self-consecration; Jesus prepares *himself* for death, glorification, and sacrifice. Others see it as sealing Jesus' unity with the Father and inviting his disciples into that unity. All three dimensions are present (cf. Burge 2000: 460–61). The prayer is toned with glory and mutual glorification [*Glory, p. 516*].

Jesus comes into the presence of his Father *as if* he is already in his glorified state, dwelling with his Father. As Dodd deftly puts it, "The prayer in some sort *is* the ascent of the Son to the Father"

(1953: 419), a narrative complement to the footwashing, when Jesus humbles himself in his Word-made-flesh ministry. As footwashing climaxes Jesus' intimacy with his disciples as *friends* (15:15), so this prayer climaxes Jesus' intimacy with his Father. The mutual indwelling in chapter 15, *Abide in me as I abide in you* (v. 4), crescendos as this prayer moves through three phases of Jesus' loving desire for his followers. It climaxes in Jesus' petition that his disciples—present and future—be one, united in him as he is with his Father (17:21-23).

The entire prayer breathes *glorification*—of Jesus and of God. The recurring and progressive use of *Father* (six times) in this prayer astounds: *Father* (v. 1; repeated in v. 5), *Holy* Father (v. 11), with *Father* repeated (vv. 21, 24), and *righteous* Father (v. 25). Other complementary expressions include *your Son* and *the Son* (in v. 1; then *me* recurs in the chapter), *your name* (vv. 6, 11, 12, 26), and *your word* (vv. 6, 14, 17). Recurring uses of *sent me* (vv. 8, 18 [plus *sent them*], 21, 23, 25) or *have given me* or *gave me* (vv. 2 [2x], 4, 6 [2x], then 7, 8, 9, 11, 12, 22, 24 [2x]), a giving that Jesus extends to his disciples (vv. 2, 8, 22), show the relational depth of this prayer. Other words or phrases (see vv. 11, 22) occur several times to describe the intimacy of the Father with the Son or of Jesus with his disciples. Both *sending* and *giving* are purpose oriented: *so that they may be one* (vv. 11, 21, 22).

Jesus prays for God's protection of believers from evil and that *all be one* in Jesus as Jesus is one with his Father. Believers today are judged by this prayer, split as we are into many different groups. It calls us to repent and grasp anew Jesus' desire for all believers to enter into the oneness and mutual love of the Father-Son relationship.

"Jesus reveals God to be a communion of persons; he dies in order to bring human beings together into unity," into union with him, and with the Father (Rossé: 44). Jesus' last will and testament energizes believers to live their unity in Jesus Christ.

OUTLINE

Jesus Prays to His Father for Himself, 17:1-8
Jesus Prays to His Holy Father for His Disciples, 17:9-19
Jesus Prays to His Father for All Who Will Come to Believe, 17:20-24
Jesus Sums Up the Purpose and Effect of His Coming, 17:25-26

EXPLANATORY NOTES

The prayer continues themes struck earlier in the Gospel and in Jesus' farewell:

Recurring Themes in John 17	17:1-8	17:9-19	17:20-26
Glorification	1, 4, 5	10	22, 24
Jesus sent by God	3, 8	18	21, 23, 25
Jesus has completed God's will	4, 6, 8	12	26
Address to the Father	5	11	21
God has given believers to Jesus	6	9, 10	24
The world	5, 6	9, 11, 14, 15, 16, 18	21, 23, 25
Believers have kept the faith	6, 7, 8		25
Unity of the believers		11	21, 22, 23
God's protection of believers		11, 12, 15	
Believers belong to God	6	9, 10	
Unity of the Father and the Son		11	21, 22, 23

Jesus Prays to His Father for Himself 17:1-8

17:1a Prayer Setting: Eyes toward Heaven; The Hour Has Come

A shift in location is implied between chapters 13–16 and 17. It appears that Jesus is no longer with his disciples in the room where they ate the Passover seder, but outside, perhaps on the Mount of Olives. While it may be Jesus is alone, his disciples may also be present (see 16:33; 18:1): "This prayer is said aloud before the disciples precisely so that they may share this union (21-23). Because there is an audience, the prayer is just as much revelation as it is intercession" (R. Brown 1970: 748).

Jesus lifts his eyes to heaven to pray to the Father. What he says first, *Father, the hour has come*, positions the prayer in its theological temporal stance. The *hour* has been anticipated from 2:4 onward. *Now* it has come. The Father's purpose in sending the Son is to be fulfilled. Jesus prays in full awareness of the events that are about to take place.

17:1b-5 Prayer Aura: Mutual Glorification—Eternal Life for Those Who Know Me[w]

In this unit, *glorify* forms a chiastic inclusio (Howard-Brook 1994: 359):

---

w   Where the superscript w occurs after headings, please see the commentary's online Web Supplement for additional material. Go to: http://www.heraldpress.com/bcbc/john.

A *Father, glorify your Son* (v. 1)
    B Power over flesh, *give life* (v. 2)
        C *This is eternal life* (v. 3)
    B´ On earth [= flesh], finished work [= give life] (v. 4)
A´ *Father, glorify me* (v. 5)

Jesus addresses God as *Father* (cf. the Lord's Prayer, where Jesus instructs his followers to do the same; Matt 6:9) *[Father, p. 515]. The hour has come* (v. 1) sounds the nearness of Jesus' death and the Son's glorification. This declaration first occurs in 12:23, when Greeks come to see Jesus. Mary's anointing of Jesus, also in chapter 12, forecasts the *hour* of the cross, just as Lazarus's death and resurrection prefigure Jesus' own.

Glorify your Son (v. 2) begins Jesus' request to his Father. The glory Jesus asks for is not for personal gain, but a glory that reflects back upon the Father: *so that the Son may glorify you* (cf. 5:44; 12:43). The Father's glory embraces the Son, and the Son returns glory to the Father. Jesus' request acknowledges that glory belongs to God: it comes from God, and Jesus returns it to God. Glory is "already present in God. . . . If God grants glory to someone, he grants that person to participate in his honor or power or divine radiance" (Talbert: 224–25). In bestowing the divine glory upon the Son (1:14), the Father also gives to the Son authority to grant eternal life (3:14-21, 31-36; 5:21-26). This life is the *authority* to become *children of God*, given to those who believe (1:12 AT). Giving life is God's prerogative. In John, the Father delegates it to the Son (cf. Moloney 1998: 461).

This gift of eternal life enables believers to *know God* (v. 3). In the direct address of prayer, Jesus' request is *that they may know you, the only true God, and Jesus Christ whom you have sent.* Moloney (1998: 461) sums up the theme in John: "Knowledge of God comes through the revealing words and actions of the Sent One (cf. 1:14, 16-18; 3:14-15, 16-17, 21-36a; 4:13-14; 5:24-25; 6:35, 51; 7:37-38; 8:12; 9:5; 10:27-29; 11:42; 13:18-20; 14:6-7)." This emphasis on knowledge counteracts an incipient gnostic-type claim that special knowledge saves apart from Jesus' glorification through death *[Gnosticism, p. 518]*. It is not *knowledge* that saves, but Jesus Christ, the one whom God has sent. "The reference to the 'only true God' is missionary language, . . . setting the disciples as well as Jesus apart for their missionary tasks" (Witherington 1995: 269).

Verse 3 correlates well with John's purpose statement in 20:31: believing in the Son is the way to true knowledge of God, for it is the only Son of God who has revealed God the Father (see comments on 1:18). Knowledge of God is a dominant motif in the OT: in the Exodus narrative, the Psalms, and the Prophets (for citation of texts, see Howard-Brook 1994: 360–61). In 17:4 Jesus prays his closure statement to his Father: *I glorified you on earth by finishing the work that you gave me to do.* Jesus is saying, *I have now completed the mission you sent me to do* (AT). The word for *finish* is important (see Howard-Brook's chiasm), for it appears again in verse 23 and in Jesus' final word on the cross, *It is finished* (19:30b).

Glorify me (in 17:5) bookends this first unit. The Son's granting eternal life is linked to the Father's and the Son's mutual bestowal of glory, each upon the other (vv. 2, 4, 5). Jesus entreats the Father as before (v. 1), but with two new perspectives on the word *presence* (NRSV uses it twice in v. 5). In the first, Jesus asks that the Father glorify him *in your own presence*; Jesus yearns to be with his Father. Second, Jesus reminds the Father of where and when it all began. He desires to be reunited to the Father *with the glory that I had in your presence before the world existed!* This loops back to 1:1, where the Word was *with God in the beginning.* Many scholars see an antiphonal relation between chapter 17 and the prologue. As the divine Word moves downward in the prologue, the Son's glorification moves it upward in this prayer, for the incarnate Son's work is finished.

In sum, the Son asks the Father to complete their mutual glorification, a prime motif in the Gospel. Like the term *Paraclete*, *glory* has many nuances (see TBC for ch. 12) *[Glory, p. 516].* Chapter 17 links *glory come down* to imminent *glory going up* through the cross and God's vindication of Jesus, the faithful Son, even unto death (cf. Phil 2:5-11).

17:6-8 Recall: What Jesus Has Done for "Those Whom You Gave Me from the World"

Jesus now rehearses what his mission has been: to *reveal*, to make *your name known to those you gave me.* A name reveals one's nature and character. Exodus 3:13-15 reveals the special *name* of God (YHWH), inherent in Jesus' revealing God's *name* to the disciples. Jesus reveals God's character, without which the disciples cannot be sent on their mission (Newbigin: 228). Jesus has made known God's name to a specific people: those whom God gave him (229). These have been given to me *from* [out of] *the world.* Jesus says that these whom you have given me *have kept your word* (v. 6c), a strong commendation of the disciples.

The long sentence in verses 7-8 makes three claims about what Jesus has done and describes the current status of his disciples in their spiritual formation: they know that *the words* I have spoken are *words that you gave to me.* They have received them and now know *in truth that I came from you.* And they have *believed that you sent me* (i.e., mission accomplished!). Jesus has done all that his Father asked and intended for him to do.

Jesus Prays to His Holy Father for His Disciples 17:9-19

An overview of this section is helpful to identify for whom Jesus prays, as well as for what or why (adapted from Talbert 234–35):

	For Whom or What	Why
17:9-11a	Jesus' present disciples	Because Jesus is going to the Father, and they will be left alone.
11b-13	That God will protect them and make them one in unity and loyalty	Because Jesus has done this during his ministry but will now be leaving.
14-16	That God will keep the disciples from the evil one	Because they are not of the world, the world hates the disciples. They need protection.
17-19	That God will sanctify them	So they will be set apart for God's service in the world.

17:9-10 May They Know Their Identity as Jesus' Own[w]

Jesus is not praying for the world, but rather for those whom God has given him (v. 9). Some commentators see this as Jesus' disinterest in the world and score John for representing Jesus thus. R. H. Gundry sees this detachment from the world positively, as a theological basis for arguing against the easy truce that evangelicals have made with the world (2002; see his book title!). Others disagree and interpret differently. Volf (2008: 39–45) refutes Gundry's argument and presents "the world" as the arena for God's love and salvation made known through Jesus. Jesus is not losing sight of this larger Johannine vision.

Jesus' work is nearing completion, so he prays for the believers to be equipped to live in the hostile world without him. Jesus prays that through the disciples' faithfulness, the world will be won into the community of love. Newbigin (229) passionately says that God's "purpose is that the world should be saved (3:17), but [Jesus] does not pray directly for the world because he is not carrying out this purpose otherwise than through the community which is the Father's gift."

Verse 21c pleads for the world to come to Jesus because of the mutual indwelling among Father, Son, and believers, since all are one. In this context, it is clear that verse 9a is not shutting the world out, but is a way of sharpening Jesus' focus on his disciples *so that* the world will be attracted through them to Jesus. These present-tense verbs draw readers, then and now, into the disciples' circle. Newbigin notes that the pronouns have shifted from the personal to the neuter, emphasizing that this prayer is universal in scope.

17:11-16 Protect the Disciples from the World[w]

Verse 11 portrays Jesus on the brink between the world and his Father. His teachings, his signs, and his spiritual formation of the disciples are now finished. Yet, as Jesus walks through suffering and death, the disciples have their most important lesson to learn, the way of Jesus' nonretaliatory love.

Jesus knows the disciples must continue in this world, so he cries out to his Holy Father to keep them *in your name* to protect those whom *you have given me*—and that for a specific purpose: *so that they may be one, as we are one.* This is the only occurrence of *Holy Father* in the NT. It suggests that Jesus' concern for the disciples' protection from the world depends on their vision and grasp of God's holiness. In the OT, God frequently appears as "the Holy One of Israel" (cf. Pss 71:22; 78:41; 89:18; and thirty-one times in Isaiah; cf. J. Waltner: 754; esp. see his essay "Holiness, Holy": 753–55). An encounter with God acknowledges God's holiness (Isa 6:3; note also Pss 96:9; 99:3, 5, 9; 111:9b). Later Jesus prays that his disciples be *sanctified* [made holy] *in the truth* (vv. 15-17, 19).

Jesus' earnest plea to his Father for the disciples' protection is even more boldly highlighted by reminding the Father—and the readers—that this is Jesus' own task while he is here on earth. Given the political composition of that first disciple band, which includes a pro-Roman tax collector and several Zealot types (who are bent on killing the Romans), we can imagine that Jesus' task is not simple. Jesus knows the long, hard lessons he has taught his disciples. Yet, at Jesus' arrest, Peter's sword flashes as he cuts off the ear of the high priest's slave (John 18:9-11; cf. Luke 22:47-53).

Now, Jesus prays to his *Father*, it is your task to protect these vulnerable disciples from *the world*. Jesus gives over this task to his Father, confident that he will do it. Jesus acknowledges Judas's defection (v. 12c), inevitably *destined* when Jesus reveals the Father's redeeming love among humans alienated from God. The nonretaliatory way to salvation *through the cross* exposes human evil and violence, even among the disciples.

Not all commentators agree that the *son of perdition* refers to Judas (v. 12 RSV). Who is *the one destined to be lost*? Witherington (1995: 270) and Talbert (227) say this is a clear reference to Judas. O'Day assumes the same (1995: 793). But Moloney (1998: 467) disagrees: "This expression must be given the meaning it has in the only other place it appears in the NT: Satan (2 Thess 2:3, 8-9)." Satan is the *son of perdition destined for destruction*, claims Moloney. As 13:2 indicates, Satan has entered into Judas.

Another view invites consideration: Howard-Brook (1994: 365) slices the pie by saying that since Satan, not God, gave Judas to Jesus, Jesus has therefore kept all that God gave him. "Jesus makes clear that that one was not in fact given to Jesus by the Father but was given by the devil, the father of lies and murder (8:44)." Klassen supports this view, saying that the Greek should be translated as a genitive of origin rather than a genitive of purpose (i.e., son destined for destruction) or an adjectival genitive (destroying son). Furthermore, "'son of perdition' refers to an eschatological figure, someone who will bring about a decisive change in the relations between humans and God. . . . Judas is a symbol of evil rather than a common betrayer. . . . He portrays not a man but Satan himself, the antagonist of God and the Revealer, Jesus Christ" (Klassen 1996: 153; cf. also 152).

This view fits Jesus' claim (10:28; cf. 10:10) as the good and true shepherd whose sheep *never perish* (10:28), though 17:12 notes the exception. This keen perception of Moloney, Klassen, and Howard-Brook makes sense of this difficult exception to God's keeping power. Yet it raises the agonizing question that Job presents: Why does God give a slice of power over to Satan—even if only for a time? This theodicy question has no answer except the explanation that some angels rebelled against the Almighty (Jude 6; 2 Pet 2:4; *1 Enoch* 6–16; 55:3-4; 64; 69; 100:4; developed from Gen 6:1-4). And they continue to rebel with the result that God's saving drama in Scripture from start to finish battles against this rebellion, known in the evil manifest in Satan, devil, demons, the powers, "the beast" (Swartley 2006a: 107n35, 222–45, esp. 230, 341n55).

Jesus (John 17:13) states the rationale for this prayer while he is yet *in the world so that they may have my joy complete in themselves*. The words translated *complete* in verses 13 and 23 are not the same. The verb in verse 13 connotes *fulfillment* (the perfect tense of *plēroō*). Jesus knows the disciples' joy will depend on their protection from the world and their unity in love. When one is pressured by the world, one does not have joy. But when one is protected from the world, unity and joy flourish.

The clincher to the petition comes with the reminder in verses 14 and 16 that *the world has hated them because they do not belong to the world, just as I do not belong to the world* (v. 14, partly repeated in v. 16). This recaps Jesus' teaching in 15:18-25, a key emphasis in John expressed also in the recurring *above/below* contrast (Meeks 1972). The frequency of *world* in this chapter reveals Jesus' major concern for his disciples.

Verse 15, however, sandwiched as it is between the repetitions in verses 14 and 16, adds new dimensions to Jesus' concern. First, Jesus explicitly says that his plea for the protection of his disciples does not mean *to take them out of the world, but* [rather, second] *I ask you to protect them from the evil one.* The tempter behind the world's temptations is now named. It is *the evil one,* elsewhere called *the devil* or *Satan* (13:2, 27).

17:17-19 Father, Sanctify the Believers in the Truth

This three-verse portion begins with *Sanctify them in truth* (v. 17) and ends with *so that they also may be sanctified in truth* (v. 19). The Greek *hagiazō* means "I make holy, sanctify," or "consecrate." The disciples are to *be set apart* from the world (AT), with their own identity, beliefs, ethics, and mission, even though they are *in the world.* In its only other use in John's Gospel, *hagiazō* means *set apart* as well (10:36 AT), and there Jesus speaks of himself. This is a fitting ending to Jesus' petition, which addresses God as *Holy* Father (v. 11).

Jesus' relationship to the Father is the foundation of his earlier request that the Father protect the disciples *from the world. Protection* and *consecration in holiness* relate hand in glove. Only as the disciples *live out* their consecration, their sanctification, their being made holy, only thus will they be able to stand against the world, the sphere of the evil one's power (v. 15b). So also it is with us.

Another key term in this unit is *in truth,* part of the bookend emphases. In this first use, it appears in the declaration *Your word is truth.* This denotes Jesus' oft-repeated assertion that he speaks only the *words that* the Father authorizes! The Father's word is truth, which Jesus represents. Lies and distortion of truth are the devil's gateway into the community of light, love, and truth, as 1 John declares. (This was the root of the error of the "secessionists," those who left the Johannine community for reasons of both ethics and belief, as the alternating sections of ethics and belief in 1 John illustrate; cf. Talbert: 7; McDermond: 28-31, passim.)

Jesus' *self*-consecration (v. 19) empowers the disciples' consecration: *And for their sakes I sanctify myself, so that they also may be sanctified in truth.* In Greek, *for their sake* is *hyper* (*on behalf of*), implying that Jesus' consecration is sacrificial on behalf of his followers. But Jesus does not die as a victim, "for he does not speak simply of setting himself apart for his death, but of joyously embracing the completion of his revelation of God *in the events of the hour*" (O'Day 1995: 794). Jesus consecrates himself so that his followers may receive his gift of holiness (Burge 2000: 467). Human holiness depends on God's holiness mediated through Jesus' holiness as gift. Holiness is *Gabe und Aufgabe*—a gift and a task. Scripture calls God's people (OT and NT) to be holy, as God is holy (Lev 19:2; 1 Pet 1:15). The holiness of the disciples is a prerequisite for Jesus' *sending* of the disciples (cf. John 10:36; 17:17-18; 20:21).

Verse 18 provides complementing rationale for the three-way relationship between the Father, the Son, and the disciples in consecration and holiness. It speaks of *sent* and *sending*: As the Father has *sent* the Son into the world, so the Son has *sent* the disciples into the world. The verbs here are past tense (aorist), indicating the accomplished actions that support the imperative in verse 17 and the present tense in verse 19. This word is directed to the Father; in John 20:19-23 Jesus directs it to his disciples with a sending imperative.

Jesus Prays to His Father for All Who Will Come to Believe 17:20-24

Jesus knows that his disciples will at some time also depart from this world. So, after praying for them, he prays for those who will become believers *through their word.* In verses 20-24, Jesus prays for four identity features of his future disciples:

1. For a unity that is visible through their love for one another; love that grows out of their relationship with Jesus, modeling the unity between the Father and Son.

2. For the spiritual intimacy of *indwelling.* The Spirit will make this mutual indwelling possible (Burge 2000: 468). Talbert notes that the glory given to the believers (vv. 22-24) will enable this spiritual intimacy (237).

3. For their presence and testimony in the world.

4. That they might see and share in the divine glory with Jesus and his Father.

17:20-23 May They Be Completely One

Jesus prays passionately for unity. The entire prayer moves toward and enhances this petition. Verse 20 defines those for whom Jesus now prays: not only his immediate disciples but also all who will come to believe, as the disciples' *word* of witness is passed from generation to generation and worldwide in every generation. Jesus prays *for* those *who will believe through their word*, closing the gaps among the disciples, the Gospel's readers, God's people through the ages, and us today!

Just as verses 17 and 19 emphasize *sanctify*, so verses 21 and 23 emphasize *unity*—that all might be made one, with verse 22 a historical (past perfect) recital similar to verse 18. Indeed, "the unity of the incarnate Son with the Father is the ground . . . of the unity of [the] believer and the Godhead, as well as of unity between the believer and other Christians" (Smalley 1978: 212).

A structural parallelism occurs between verses 20-21 and 22-23 (adapted from R. Brown 1970: 769; cf. Mardaga: 150):

> *that* [hina] *they all may be one* [17:21a]
> *just as* [kathōs] *you, Father, are in me and I in you* [v. 21b]
> *that* [hina] *they also may be* [one] *in us* [v. 21c]
> *that* [hina] *the world may believe that you sent me* [v. 21d]

> *that* [hina] *they may be one* [v. 22b]
> *just as* [kathōs] *we are one, I in them and you in me* [vv. 22c-23]
> *that* [hina] *they may be brought to completion as one* [v. 23b]
> *that* [hina] *the world may come to know that you sent me* [v. 23c]

Each block contains one *just as* clause and three *purpose* (*hina*) clauses. The first purpose clause pleads for the unity of the believers, and the third purpose clause expresses its effects upon the world. Jesus' prayer is thus both for the *church*, for its unity, and for the *world*, that it might come to know Jesus. So is Jesus *not praying for the world* (v. 9 RSV)? Yes and no. He prays for the world's salvation through the agency of the church's unity. This is a sobering truth, given the fractured church of our time (see TLC for this chapter).

In these verses Jesus' prayer is the basis for the historical twinning of missionary vision and ecumenical passion for the church's unity, evident in the origins of ecumenism. Youth Bible studies, missionary passion, and gatherings of diverse Christian bodies shaped the nineteenth and twentieth centuries' quests for *becoming one in Christ*, spiritually and organizationally. The same passion continues today in the face of new schisms and divisive issues *[Ecumenical Relations, p. 511]*.

17:24 Bring Them All Home to See My Glory and Know My Love[w]

The stunning "unity/oneness" theme of verses 22-23 continues in verse 24 as the focus of Jesus' prayer, now set in the present tense.

Jesus passionately desires the unity of the disciples with one another and thus union with him and in turn with the Father. Verse 24 recalls also the motif of those *whom you have given me* (v. 24b, repeated in v. 24d). The first petition refers to location for *those* the Father has given to him, and the second specifies their seeing *the glory* that the Father has given to the Son *before the foundation of the world*.

Jesus' *desire* is twofold: that the disciples *may be with me where I am*, and that they might *see my glory* (RSV: *behold my glory*, expressing the contemplative nuance of *theōreō*). Earlier narrative features, events, and dialogues, as well as narrative clues (1:14, 39; 2:11; etc.), anticipate Jesus' culminating desire and petition: that he and his disciples might dwell together (2:19, 21; 14:2)—that they might know and see his and the Father's glory. Here this reality is transposed into eschatological expectation. It will happen, but first they will walk through the "valley of the shadow." Jesus will die and the disciples will scatter. The resurrection miracle will put the desire back on course toward fulfillment. The disciples will pass through their own trials. Finally they will be with him to share his presence and behold his glory. When the disciples receive the Holy Spirit, imparted by Jesus (20:19-23), they will also know Jesus' presence, a foretaste of his glory. Knowing the glory shared by the Father and Son is the fruit of the unity for which Jesus prays. The branches, pruned to be sanctified and sent, bear the fruit of the true vine. Glory and unity, holiness and mission, all pulse in tandem. Each is crucial to the other *[Glory, p. 516]*.

Jesus Sums Up the Purpose and Effect of His Coming 17:25-26

Again Jesus addresses the Father, this time with the adjective *righteous*. Together with this echo of the sanctification-holiness theme, Jesus reiterates three motifs of the prayer: (1) he has made known the *name* of the Father to his disciples; (2) the Father-Son's shared *love* might be in his disciples; and (3) this love and Jesus himself might be in them, thus their *unity*. This bond of love "is not an end in itself, for by living out the love of God in oneness with each other, the faithful call the wider world to know the love of God" (Koester 2008: 202).

The *name* Jesus made known to his disciples (see also v. 6) is the *I AM* of the eternal God (von Wahlde 2010: 2.724–26). Jesus has revealed God fully to his followers. They have believed. And Jesus will continue to make God's name known to the world.

THE TEXT IN BIBLICAL CONTEXT

Jesus and Prayer

Prayer, essential to Jesus' spirituality, reflects his dependence on God. This prayer relationship is a constant in John's Gospel. Jesus often affirms that he can do nothing on his own. He speaks what the Father gives him to speak. His works depend upon his Father. John does not present Jesus in a Gethsemane *prayer* struggle before God as we read in the Synoptic Gospels (Luke 22:39-46). In John 17 Jesus, however, prays for himself and for his disciples. Jesus' prayers to his Father in John 11:41 and 12:27-28 anticipate the extended farewell prayer of chapter 17, with its emphasis on mutual *glorification.* These prayers portray Jesus' human struggle as he faces imminent death (cf. Heb 5:7). In John, Jesus' struggle with death interacts with divine love that leads to the *hour* of Jesus' *glorification:* Jesus carries and dies on the cross. His Father glorifies him as he is *lifted up* on the cross and vindicated by God in resurrecting him *[Glory, p. 516].*

In his farewell Jesus invites his disciples to *ask him* (14:13-14; cf. 15:7). In 15:16 and 16:23b-24, he urges his disciples to *ask his Father* for anything *in my name.* The disciples' prayers are intertwined thus with Jesus' prayer for their unity. Their praying expresses the mutual indwelling that marks Jesus' unity and love relationship with the Father. In their praying future believers also are incorporated into this divine indwelling, mediated through Jesus:

> To believe in Jesus . . . means being incorporated into this relationship of oneness and love that exists between Christ and God—that is, to experience the reality of Jesus' prayer: "may they also be in us!" (v. 21). And that relationship implies that believers in Jesus are part of the unique prayer experience between Christ and God, and so are caught up in his intercessory praying and share in it themselves when they pray in Jesus' name. (Lincoln 2001: 171)

Prayer to God in Jesus' name is participation in our oneness with Jesus Christ and God. It is a holy privilege expressing our identity, assuring us who and whose we are.

Jesus is portrayed as a person of prayer in the other Gospels as well. He retreats for periods of solitary prayer (e.g., Mark 1:35). Some Synoptic Gospel texts contain prayers, notably the Johannine Thunderbolt in Luke 10:21-22 (//Matt 11:25-27). Facing the cross, Jesus prays, "My God, my God, why have you forsaken me?" (Matt 27:46b; Mark 15:34). This echoes Psalm 22, a lament of the dying righteous one, but with vindication and praise at the end (vv. 22-31).

Luke highlights Jesus as a person of prayer. Nine texts (3:21-22; 5:16; 6:12-13; 9:18-20, 28-29; 11:1a; 11:1b-13; 22:31-32, 39-46) specifically say that Jesus prayed. Two of Jesus' three sayings from the cross are prayers. The first, "Father, forgive them; for they do not know what they are doing" (23:34), is unique to Luke and is a prototype of one faithful to God amid martyrdom (see Stephen's prayer in Acts 7:60b). The other prayer from the cross, "Father, into your hands I commend my spirit" (Luke 23:46), echoes Psalm 31:5 (a psalm of prayer and praise amid severe distress). In Luke, Jesus instructs his readers on the importance of persisting in prayer in his parable about the widow and the unjust judge (18:1-8).

In John, Jesus' final word on the cross, *It is finished*, may be a prayer culminating his relationship to the Father. The narrative of the Father and Son's mutual *glorification* through Jesus' death has now reached its goal (anticipated in 2:19, 21-22; 3:14). Beyond the Gospels, Scripture is filled with prayers (Swartley 2006d: 10–11).

Protected from the Evil One

This topic is discussed in the TBC section for John 13 in "Judas in John and the NT." Here in John 17 Jesus prays that his followers be protected from the evil one, focusing the issue more sharply. If the secessionist development in 1 John is what Jesus is praying about (McDermond: passim), then the issue revolves around the relationship between believing and ethical practice. Belief in Jesus as the Messiah who came in human flesh, who lived, died, and rose again, and is the glorified Son of God—these are the very beliefs on which the evil one preys. Using violence to achieve messiahship (John 6:15; 18:10, 36) is also Satan's way (note Peter's denials of Jesus and use of the sword). In John, the evil one's intrusion into the community takes varied forms, not only through Judas.

In addition to the issues raised by the secessionists, another catalog of "openings" whereby the evil one deceives the disciples appears in 1 John (2:15-17):

> Do not love the world or the things in the world. The love of the Father is not in those who love the world; for all that is in the world—the desire of the flesh, the desire of the eyes, the pride in riches—comes not from the Father but from the world. And the world and its desire are passing away, but those who do the will of God live forever.

On both sides of this text, Jesus' followers are faced with heresies: one claims it is possible to continue in sin and yet be God's children

(1:6, 8), and another "antichrist" (2:18; 4:3) denies Jesus' suffering in the flesh, his full humanity. Together these five expressions (three in the quotation) represent how alluring and divergent are the tactics of the evil one to circumvent the protection and disrupt the unity for which Jesus prays. See McDermond's exposition on these texts.

Prayer for protection from the evil one occurs in the Lord's Prayer: "Deliver us from the evil one" (Matt 6:13; better than the RSV's "from evil"). Jesus faced down the devil in his temptations (Matt 4:1-11; Luke 4:1-13). Temptation is common to all believers (1 Cor 10:13), but God is able to provide a way of escape, protection, and deliverance from evil. Hence Scripture is filled with cries to God for protection, deliverance from enemies, and help in times of distress. Psalm 91 is one such text (see vv. 1-6, 14).

The Psalms are replete with declarations of God's protection and care for those who put their trust in the Lord (e.g., Pss 3; 56; 57; 118:5-14; 125:1-2). In light of Jesus as the true, protecting shepherd in John 10, Psalm 23 also fits this category (esp. v. 4). The enemies are those who sabotage the safety of God's people. While these are frequently political enemies, this motif is generalized, so the cries of prayer to God connect with human temptation, dangers, and catastrophes of all sorts from the evil one. In his study of the complaint psalms, Mbon observes that the enemies are not usually identified; they transcend the original historical situation and often refer to the godless or the wicked (9). Thus the Psalms readily voice the prayers of God's people applicable to varied situations of distress, evil, and need for help. They ring true for Jesus' disciples through the ages.

In a similar manner, God promises to Joshua, "Be strong and courageous; do not be frightened or dismayed, for the Lord your God is with you wherever you go" (Josh 1:9). This call to trust God is applicable to situations in which Satan seeks to devastate us. God's marvelous promise through Isaiah, "Do not fear, for I am with you, do not be afraid, for I am your God; I will strengthen you, I will help you, I will uphold you with my victorious right hand" (41:10) provides us with strength and security against evil. It is a marvelous text to cite in the face of fear or temptation.

Paul's word to "put on the whole armor of God" to protect against evil is most pertinent (Eph 6:11-20). The struggle is defined as not against "blood and flesh, but against the rulers, against the authorities, the cosmic powers of this present darkness, against the spiritual forces of evil in the heavenly places." We therefore wear God's armor (see Yoder Neufeld 2002: 290–316):

- Belt of truth
- Breastplate of justice/righteousness
- Shoes shod to proclaim the gospel of peace
- Shield of faith
- Helmet of salvation
- Sword of the Spirit, the word of God

Another aspect of protection from the evil one is shown in Jesus', Paul's, and Peter's commands not to return evil for evil (Swartley 2006: 213–15; 2007: 49–53).

Most important, Jesus prays that we be protected *from the evil one* (John 17:15). Keeping this foremost in our minds closes the door to the evil one's prying it open, whatever tactic he tries to use. "Abiding in the vine" is likewise important—meditating on what *abide* (*menō*) means in the midst of daily struggles (John 15). The rich repertoires of John's metaphors that nurture relationship with Jesus also protect. Jesus' prayer for unity is a corollary to his prayer for protection from the evil one. As we open ourselves to Jesus' love and its "mutual indwelling" in and among us, we are strengthened in our resistance to temptation and evil.

The Church's Oneness in Jesus Christ

Numerous NT texts emphasize unity, notably Ephesians 4:3-6: Make "every effort to maintain the unity of the Spirit in the bond of peace. There is one body and one Spirit, just as you were called to the one hope of your calling, one Lord, one faith, one baptism, one God and Father of all, who is above all and through all and in all." This follows Paul's declaration that Jesus Christ breaks down the partition that separates Jews and Gentiles (2:11-22). In Christ they become one. In 2:13-18 the terms "both [groups] . . . in[to] one" and "peace" each occur four times. Since Jesus unites, the church claims unity (see Yoder Neufeld 2002: 110–24, 133–136, 172–75, 190–92).

Significantly, in 3:3 believers are called to *maintain* the unity, not to attempt to *create* it. The idea that Jesus' followers are to create unity would usurp Christ's gift and the very essence of what the church is. As C. Marshall states,

> It is hugely significant that Paul tells his readers in verse 3 not to create the unity of the Spirit in the bond of peace, but to *maintain* it (*tērein*). The unity of the church is not something its members manufacture by being unusually nice to one another. It is something that already exists.

It is an objective reality, effected by the Spirit of God. Notwithstanding the church's immense diversity and frequently fractious history, the truth is that there is only "*one* body" and "*one* Spirit" (4:4), just as there is "*one* Lord" (4:5) and "*one* God and Father of us all" (4:6). The word "one" recurs no fewer than eight times in three verses. It is desperately important to Paul. The oneness of the church is every bit as fundamental to Christian orthodoxy as the oneness of God and the lordship of Christ.

C. Marshall identifies four virtues much needed to maintain the unity of the church: humility, gentleness, patience, and loving tolerance. Without these the church is prone to factions, as history documents. The proper response is *lament*.

The church at Corinth was beleaguered with factions (1 Cor 1:10-19). Paul's response stresses "Christ crucified" as central to the gospel. This answered the imposters, who were diverting the Corinthian believers into other gospel versions (2 Cor 11:13; cf. Gal 1; 2:4). Paul's classic summary of the gospel as reconciliation counters schismatic influences and calls the believers not only to oneness in Christ, but also to be ambassadors of the reconciliation that results from God's work in Christ (2 Cor 5:17-21). In the midst of the Corinthian dissension over the gifts of the Spirit, Paul points to the more excellent way, where *love* triumphs. Love measures the value of the gifts to the body (1 Cor 12–14, with ch. 13 crucial).

THE TEXT IN THE LIFE OF THE CHURCH

Since the sixteenth century, John 17 has been known as Jesus' "high-priestly prayer," though already in the fourth century Cyril of Alexandria had designated Jesus as "high priest" in this prayer (O'Day 1995: 787n501).

What Is God's Desire for the World?[w]

Jesus' statement in John 17:9b, *I am not praying for the world* (RSV), seems to throw a curve into our thinking about God's relationship with the world. Many scholars have debated its meaning (see Explanatory Notes in this chapter and Swartley 2006: 289–95). To resolve this, a more basic question must be asked in this TLC section: What is God's desire for the world? If one joins 17:9a to 21d, it is clear that Jesus is passionate for the world. His repeated plea for unity is *so that the world may believe that you have sent me* (v. 21d), and again, *so that the world may know that you have sent me and have loved them even as you have loved me* (v. 23c). When Jesus petitions the

Father for unity among believers, the world is in view, since disunity discredits the Christian witness to the world.

The church's unity is important to its mission. Without unity, the church is deemed incredible by the world. Because Jesus' concern for the world depends on how his disciples lead the church, he brackets out direct prayer for the world and focuses on the disciples, who are *in the world* and yet not *of the world*. In John the *world* stands opposed to God, yet God loves it and gives his only Son to save all who believe.

The Lord's Prayer calls on God the Father to "rescue us from the evil one" and prays for God's name to be "hallowed" or "sanctified." (Jewish piety considered this a faithful vocation to God.) This emphasis authorizes nonconformity in the believers church and in the Pietist and Holiness movements of the last centuries: We are to be *in the world*, but *not of the world* (John 17:11, 14 KJV; cf. 1 John; McDermond: 52–53, 74–75, 134–36).

John 17:24 links the world firmly to the love that God had for Jesus *before the foundation of the world*. Praise and thanksgiving be to God Almighty who has purposed "to unite all things in [Christ]," and who has revealed this purpose in God's "fullness of time" (Eph 1:10 RSV; Gal 4:4-6)! The seven hymns in Revelation celebrate God's victory over human violence, natural calamities, and the perversity of the powers, accentuating this praise, thanksgiving, and jubilation to God Almighty. These hymns climax the seven worship scenes (Swartley 2007: 241–62). This, too, is John's theology and scriptural legacy.

Jesus' Vision of Unity for Today[w]

Church history is disappointing. Already within the Johannine community schism developed (1 John 2:18-27; 4:1-2). It continued in the early church (consider the Montanists, the Arians, and other groups regarded as heretical). The Reformation increased "splits" over perceived faithlessness. Anabaptists did not speak one voice either, as McDermond's treatment shows (see 160–64, "Schism and Doctrinal Truth," TLC on 1 John 2:18-27).

Difficult questions such as these arise: What is the nature of the church's unity when schism and denominationalism define the church's life in today's world? What hope is there for the church in our time to realize Jesus' prayer for us? If each of us reflects upon our life experiences, most of us can identify an experience or special event in which we felt "all are one" in Christ.

I recall leading a group of thirty-seven college students with my family of four for nine weeks in the Middle East and several

European cities. A high point came when over a million people—a rainbow of ethnic identities—gathered from all over the world in Saint Peter's Square in Rome in 1975. We heard Pope Paul VI bring Easter greetings of peace to this vast sea of people in five languages. We experienced a visual fulfillment of this prayer, a foretaste of the kingdom coming.

In my local context the unity and power of the Spirit are evident in our small church group, composed of members with Quaker, Pentecostal, Lutheran, Mennonite, and nondenominational charismatic backgrounds. These small illustrations of the church becoming one may be viewed as the macro- and microdimensions of Jesus' prayer *that they might all be one*. Hearts blend and are enriched when people with varied rich religious traditions share and pray together.

Efforts to define the nature of the church's unity value the spiritual and *koinōnia* fellowship or missional qualities more than formal creeds or organizational structures. Unity offers an attractive, attracting witness to the world; disunity does the opposite. The root of disunity is spiritual. The Tower of Babel exemplifies principalities and powers at work that prompt people to reject God's loving, saving grace. The cure for disunity is also spiritual: it is to participate in the unity of the Father and Son (Talbert: 236).

So how exactly does unity in a Christian community function evangelistically?

> It does so, in part, by being what it is. . . . The community of love is itself a part of the Gospel. . . . The Johannine community confronted the world not merely with a doctrine or a creed but, as all sectarian groups do, with an alternative society, a counterculture, in which its message of the messiahship of Jesus was realized. It sought to draw people out of the world and into the messianic community, and it did this not only by its words but [also] by being that community. (Rensberger: 147, 150)

We fulfill Jesus' prayer for unity in our sense of common calling, love, joy, holiness, and mission. These together mark a body of faith, a people who resonate with this prayer. Newbigin emphasizes calling, mission, and love, which Jesus demonstrates in his self-sacrifice (228, 231–32), stressing the importance of calling (228): "This community exists not because of decisions which its members have made. It is not constituted by the faith, insight, or moral excellence of its members. It exists because God has called its members out of the world by his own action and given them to Jesus. They are those whom God has chosen 'before the foundation of the world' (Eph 1:4)."

Jesus' prayer for unity is fulfilled when believers participate in the community of the Trinity:

> The same love that unites Father and Son and constitutes their being as communion also unites believers among themselves and introduces them into the life of the Trinity. [Thus the] mutual love lived out in community becomes itself a revelation of the divine *agapē* that has opened itself to humanity. . . . [The] unity in question is by its nature a transcendent reality because it is sharing in the divine unity. (Rossé: 84)

This also fulfills God's purpose *that the world may believe.*

Current efforts to seek Christian fellowship that transcends denominational lines are represented by the Focolare Movement (Chiara Lubick), Bridgefolk, the charismatic renewal, and Churches Together. Focolare and Bridgefolk complement each other in bringing together people from the Roman Catholic and other faith traditions. Focolare, rooted in the Roman Catholic Church, grew out of Chiara's "baptism of love" for all believers some fifty years ago. It is international in scope, includes many grassroots people, and embraces the sweep of denominations. In Bridgefolk, Mennonites and Catholics seek common ground and enjoy rich fellowship as they learn to know one another. Where Focolare privileges *loving, joyous fellowship*, the latter seeks understanding between and intersection of the faith traditions.

The Ecumenical Movement[w]

Lesslie Newbigin has been a prime energizer in the ecumenical movement, as was John R. Mott in the early part of the twentieth century. Both were inspired by missionary zeal and saw mission as the key to bringing disparate groups together—a reality that happens more often on the mission field. John H. Yoder (1958: 4-7) identifies three roots of the ecumenical movement: revival work combined with mission; the peace movement occasioned in part by World War I; and third, the distinctly American denominational situation. Yoder notes both the early conservative and later more liberal tendencies in the ecumenical movement (7-14). He rightly says, "The unity of all believers is a Scriptural command" (16) and "Christian unity is not to be created, but to be obeyed" (21). Yoder reminds us that disunity has dogged the church through the ages (19-27). He argues that the Anabaptists did not separate from the larger church but were forced out (28-35) [*Ecumenical Relations, p. 511*].

One important factor in seeking unity is to recognize that a local church is not an organism to itself, nor is any one denomination a complete embodiment of the church of Jesus Christ. For example, Christians in the USA and Canada are more fully complete when they relate to Christians in other parts of the world. Church bodies that constitutionally and in official doctrine transcend national fracturing are the Roman Catholic and Orthodox Churches, though their national "personalities" show diversity in practice. The Anglican Church might be included, but recent developments in moral practice threaten their global unity [Ecumenical Relations, p. 511].

The national fracturing of church bodies is especially evident in the history and practice of war, when Christians kill other Christians, even within the same denomination. This is sad and tragic. Participation in war is a litmus test as to how seriously we take Jesus' prayer (John 17). Christians at war against Christians mock Jesus' prayer for unity.

The proliferation of the church into many denominations harms the cause of Christian mission worldwide. Reflecting on a 2006 visit to China, John A. Lapp writes,

> I was taken by the Chinese church's self-definition as being post-denominational. Fifty years ago Herbert Butterfield called denominations a luxury of European dominance. The church in China, as well as the church in other locations, learned through bitter conflict, persecution, and suffering [that] the fragmentation of the church is a weakening of the God movement, . . . a violation of Jesus' prayer "that they may all be one" (John 17:21). (58)

Jesus prays for us, that we *may all be one, becoming completely one,* knowing that God's word is truth, in and by which the Father sanctifies us (vv. 21, 23, 17). As Paul illustrates in Ephesians, unity (3:1-6) together with "speaking the truth in love" (4:16) is not an oxymoron, but evidence of ecclesial authenticity. If we are completely one as Christ prays for in this heart-prayer, then we will renounce the spirit that generates disunity. As one Mennonite church leader put it, "Disunity is perhaps the greatest sin of all, for it is a rebellion against the heart and will of Jesus, and it snuffs out the glory of God. . . . Wherever unity is preserved, the glory of God flames up with a glow that will attract the . . . world" (Fred Kanagy in *North Central Conference Bulletin*).

John 18–19

Jesus Handed Over and Crucified

OVERVIEW

This unit is John's passion narrative, though many anticipations of it occur earlier. John 6 speaks of eating Jesus' flesh and drinking his blood. Religious leaders seek to kill Jesus. Mary anoints Jesus for his burial (12:8). Jesus' farewell (John 13–17) announces and prepares the disciples for his imminent departure. Jesus' passion fulfills the *hour*, a time capsule punctuating the narrative since 2:4. Jesus' *glorification* climaxes in his death on the cross.

John's account of Jesus' passion and death is also Jesus' hour of glorification and in that respect the narrative destination and climax of the Gospel (cf. O'Day 1995: 799). Jesus begins his prayer (17:1) by saying, *Father, the hour has come; glorify your Son so that the Son may glorify you.*

OUTLINE

This narrative readily divides into three major units:

Jesus' Arrest, Jewish Trial, Peter's Denials, 18:1-27
Jesus' Trial before Pilate, 18:28–19:16a
Jesus' Crucifixion and Burial, 19:16b-42

A chiastic analysis accentuates Jesus' trial before Pilate:

A Jesus' betrayal and arrest in a Garden (18:1-12)
    B Jesus' brief trial before the Jews (18:13-27)
        C Jesus' trial before Pilate (18:28–19:16a)
    B′ Jesus' crucifixion after Pilate hands Jesus over to the Jews
      (19:16b-37)
A′ Jesus' burial in a garden (19:38-42)

Peter and Pilate

This outline and the chiasm, however, do not show the role that Peter's denial plays in Jesus' arrest and trial before the Jewish high priest(s) that year (18:15-18, 25-27). This is important, since it is foreshadowed in 13:36-38 and culminates in 21:15-19. More than subplot, Peter's role is a lead motif with theological and political significance.

The trial of Jesus before Pilate, the larger textual unit, brims with theological and political significance. Jesus is in control throughout. He is sovereign. He is not the passive subject of the action or the suffering victim. Rather, he puts his interrogators on trial (cf. O'Day 1995: 799). When arrested, Jesus identifies himself in the garden. He is the true judge as he appears before *the Jews*. Before Pilate, Jesus is again the true judge, not Pilate. Jesus carries *the cross by himself. . . . He went out to what is called The Place of the Skull* (19:17). Jesus announces, *"It is finished." Then he bowed his head and gave up his spirit* (19:30).

Dramatic Irony

In keeping with the Gospel's style throughout, the trial narrative brims with irony and double entendre, especially in Jesus' trial before Pilate, evident in the chiastic focus on Jesus' hour of glorification. J. M. Ford compares John's dramatic irony with that of Greek literature:

> The victims of John's irony are Pilate, the tyrant, and the unbelieving Judeans *["The Jews," p. 520]*. In the passion account the Johannine technique of irony and misunderstanding reaches its culmination. The audience knows that Jesus rose from death; they may also have known of the tragic fall of Jerusalem in 70 CE and the disgrace of Pilate, banished for misconduct. It is the friends of Jesus who understand the meaning of this dramatic irony and the true consecration of the monarch. (1995: 115).

John 18:1-27

Jesus' Arrest, Jewish Trial, and Peter's Denials

PREVIEW

In the late 1970s as Belmont Mennonite Church was about to begin its service, two masked Communist Russian-dressed soldiers entered the sanctuary and riveted the congregation's attention. They demanded that everyone give up their Bibles or face arrest and imprisonment. Two stalwart saints refused, stood their ground amid a tussle, and finally intimidated the soldiers. These believers thought it was for real, and it took weeks for them to reconcile with those who planned this all-too-dramatic skit. They protected their Bibles. What or whom does Jesus protect as he faces arrest?

Jesus enters and exits the garden to meet the advancing soldiers, greeting them with a compliant question, *Whom do you seek?* They answer, *Jesus of Nazareth.* Jesus responds, declaring, *I AM* (three times; vv. 5, 6, 8). This response so shocks the interrogating Roman soldiers that they fall to the ground, repulsed by the power of Jesus' word.

John's distinctive purposes continue. Jesus asks the squadron of soldiers to let his disciples go, saying (in effect), *Take me and let my disciples go.* But Peter, determined to follow Jesus to death (13:37), puts up a fight, draws a sword, and cuts off the right ear of Malchus, a slave of the high priest. Jesus reprimands Peter with a memorable nonresistant declaration: *Put your sword back into its sheath* (v. 11). The soldiers then seize Jesus and take him, bound, to Annas, the father-in-law of Caiaphas. This begins to fulfill 11:49-52, where Caiaphas as high priest prophesies that Jesus will *die for the nation.*

The camera then shifts to Peter, who contrasts with *the other disciple*, who is known to the high priest (18:15-16). He brings Peter into the high priest's courtyard. But on the way Peter denies that he knows Jesus. As if not enough, a second scene follows, with Peter's denying Jesus a second time as he warms himself by the fire where *servants and officers* also stand. Peter publicly disowns his relationship to Jesus. As foremost disciple who twice earlier has promised loyalty to Jesus (6:68-69; 13:37), Peter likely represents the other disciples as well.

After the reader learns of Peter's first denial of knowing Jesus, the camera shifts back to the trial before the former and influential high priest Annas. Annas questions Jesus *about his disciples and about his teaching* (v.19). Since Peter has drawn a sword against Malchus and cut his ear off—no small aggression as another slave recalls the event later (v. 26)—the high priest has a right to be concerned, and his questions likely seek to determine whether Jesus, his disciples, and his teaching reflect revolutionary intent. Jesus' answer emphasizes having taught *openly to the world*. Many have heard my teaching, he says. Ask them, not me.

One of the officers slaps Jesus' face. Jesus' response zeros in on whether he lied or spoke the truth. Annas, having enough of this, sends him bound to Caiaphas the high priest. In light of the Synoptic Gospels' description of Jesus' trial before the Sanhedrin council, Jesus' "trial" in John appears nondescript: no charges, no defense. Why these appearances before these religious figures, with little trial substance? The Jewish trial functions mostly as a springboard to the trial before Pilate.

The unit closes with Peter's second and third denials. Immediately afterward, *the cock crowed*; Jesus' prediction (13:38) is fulfilled. After 18:12, the narrative consists of *interchanges* between Jesus' "trial" and Peter's denials.

OUTLINE

Jesus, with Judas and Peter, Manages His Own Arrest, 18:1-11
Jesus and Peter Go to Trial, 18:12-27

As a chiasm, this can be presented thus:

A Jesus appears before Annas, fulfilling Caiaphas's prophecy
    (18:12-14)
    B Peter denies Jesus (18:15-18)
A´ Jesus is "tried" before Annas (18:19-24)
    B´ Peter denies Jesus the second and third times (18:25-27)

EXPLANATORY NOTES

Jesus, with Judas and Peter, Manages His Own Arrest 18:1-11

The setting for Jesus' arrest is *across the Kidron valley* in *a garden*, unnamed in John, where Jesus has *often met with his disciples* (v. 2b). The Synoptic Gospels suggest that this garden is also known as Gethsemane, where Jesus anguished over his imminent death. (The actual phrase "Garden of Gethsemane" occurs nowhere in the Greek text, though the NASB has it as a heading in square brackets before Matt 26:36 and Luke 22:39.) In John that anguish has occurred in 12:27-29. Jesus' Gethsemane struggle in the Synoptics does not fit John's narrative, for Jesus' hour of death punctuates John's narrative from his first *sign* (2:1-11) onward. The decision to accept the cross is evident already in 3:14.

Jesus has dispatched Judas earlier, saying, *Do quickly what you are going to do* (13:27d). Jesus expects to see Judas now and is not disappointed. Jesus steps forward to meet Judas, who is accompanied by *a detachment of soldiers together with police from the chief priests and the Pharisees* (18:3). The "detachment" or "cohort" (*speira*) denotes a "band" (RSV) of Roman soldiers, either six hundred or perhaps a subunit of two hundred. The Roman soldiers and Jewish police now carry out what the Sanhedrin (chief priests and Pharisees in 11:47, 57) colluded to do: to arrest Jesus, whose astounding *signs, words,* and *works* have caused the religious leaders to fear that *the Romans will come and destroy both our holy place and our nation* (11:48b). They are ready to cooperate with Pilate to accomplish their goal. Political enemies join forces to halt the popularity of the Jesus movement (cf. Luke 23:12)! This sizable band comes at night with *lanterns and torches and weapons* (John 18:3b). The scene is a fake portrayal of Jesus' *I am the light of the world.* But Jesus' Son-light, *the light the world*, outshines this torchlit darkness.

Echoing 15:13, Jesus walks willingly to meet those arresting him, for the hour has come for him to lay down his life for his friends. As he said earlier, *No one takes it from me, but I lay it down of my own accord. I have power to lay it down, and I have power to take it up again* (10:18). Jesus, knowing all that is to happen, takes charge of the situation and asks, *Whom are you looking for?* (18:4, 7). Their answer, *Jesus of Nazareth*, sparks curiosity, for the word *Nazōraion* has more than one meaning (18:5, 7). On the lips of the soldiers, it denotes a city in Galilee. To believers who read this narrative, it may suggest Jesus' dedication to live the Nazirite vow (Judg 13:5) or that Jesus fulfills the messianic vision of the *neṣer*-branch of Isaiah 11:1 (cf.

R. Brown 1970: 809–10; Howard-Brook 1994: 375–76). Again, Jesus shines as light in the darkness.

Jesus' response to their quest stuns: *I am he*, or better, *I AM [egō eimi]!* (vv. 5, 6, 8) *["I AM," p. 518].* The arresting band falls to the ground (cf. "every knee should bow," Phil 2:10). The narrator stresses the point by repeating what Jesus said: *I AM* (vv. 6, 8), and also noting that Judas, who turned him over, was *with them!* The arresting band is dumbstruck and powerless, so Jesus asks again, *Whom are you looking for?* Again they give the same answer, *Jesus of Nazareth.* So Jesus answers again, *I told you that I am he*, the same stunning *I AM* declaration. Judas hears it again. With its double resonance, Judas' headphones are resounding *egō eimi!* I imagine that his heart melts, for in this Gospel we hear no more of Judas.

Jesus seeks a favor from the soldiers, saying in effect, *Take me, since I am he for whom you look.* But *let these men go.* Jesus pleads for the security of his disciples. John explains why: to fulfill the Scripture, *I did not lose a single one of those whom you gave me.* This faces readers with a conundrum: on the one hand Judas was one *who believed in Jesus* (2:12) and chose to stick with Jesus (6:71b; 12:4) and yet, on the other hand, the text also reflects the view that Judas is not one of those given by God to Jesus, but "intruded" into the disciple band at the instigation of Satan (6:71c; 13:2).

At this moment Peter's determination to protect his master flares into violence. He unsheathes a sword, striking the high priest's slave, Malchus. Fortunately his inexpert aim takes only an ear, which occasions Jesus' memorable saying, *Put your sword back into its sheath.* In this teachable moment, Jesus not only reprimands Peter but also declares what he has been teaching his disciples since 12:24: he is willing to undergo death so that God's purposes might be revealed and fulfilled. He affirms his Father's salvation purpose: *Am I not to drink the cup that the Father has given me?* The true essence of Jesus' gospel is exposed. Salvation, eternal life, and bonding with Jesus and the Father come through the cross. Jesus renounces violence. Howard-Brook says it well:

> Satan's representative has amassed soldiers, police, and weapons, but God's representative is the one who does the capturing, simply by the power of God's name. It is one of the strongest models of nonviolent resistance in the New Testament and presents the most difficult challenge to those faced with the world's power. Do we *really* believe that God's name is stronger than weapons and military forces? Jesus *does* believe it. (1994: 377)

Jesus is sovereign in facing violence. He does not cower before it, but triumphs over the powers that perpetrate violence. Jesus' sovereignty permeates the entire passion narrative, as Gench's title for chapters 18–19 says: "Sovereign in Life and Death" (117–27).

Jesus and Peter Go to Trial 18:12-27

18:12-14 [A] Jesus Appears before Annas, Fulfilling Caiaphas's Prophecy

These first A-B subunits consist of the first stage of Jesus' "trial" and Peter's first denial (vv. 15-18, below). The components are similar in A´-B´, the second set of paired subunits (vv. 19-27). Each set of paired subunits contains what John wants readers to see in relation to each other. The trial is the stage for the denials. Accordingly, Peter's denials stand out boldly. They carry an important dimension of Johannine theology and narrative purpose, consummated in chapters 20 and 21, where Peter emerges into the spotlight in the Gospel's final scene. The Jewish trial in John is nondescript compared to that in the Synoptic Gospels. It pales beside Jesus' trial before Pilate, or Jesus' trial of Pilate!

In Mark (14:53-65) Jesus' examination before the high priest brims with christological disclosure in the exchanges between an unnamed high priest, who speaks for the chief priests; the elders; and the scribes assembled with the whole council. In John, the high priests are mentioned, and they are two, not one. Annas is the high priest emeritus, the father-in-law of Caiaphas, the current high priest. Yet Annas wields considerable power over the religious affairs. Here he appears only for the narrator to introduce his authority and relationship to Caiaphas and to recall the point of 11:48-52, where Caiaphas unwittingly prophesies this situation: Get rid of the troublemaker to prevent the Romans from destroying *our holy place and our nation*. The narrator wants us to hear the prophetic edge of this saying once again: it is *better to have one person die for the people* (18:14b). That's it. The first stage of the trial is done.

18:15-18 [B] Peter Denies Jesus

The sequel to this is more revealing. First, there is *another disciple* (the beloved disciple?) who supersedes Peter's leadership role. He knows and is known to the high priest. He goes *with Jesus into the courtyard of the high priest*, Annas (18:13, 19-24). This striking detail is peculiar, not found in any other Gospel. Does this disciple have a priestly affiliation [*Beloved Disciple, p. 505*]?

The next verse highlights Peter's standing *outside* and the other disciple's coming out to fetch him, clearing his entrance with the *woman* guarding the gate! But as Peter passes the guard, she clarifies his identity, framed to expect a negative answer (a question beginning with the Greek *mē*): *You are not also one of this man's disciples, are you?* Peter welcomes the out and replies, *I am not.* Even in the presence of this other disciple, whose identity is linked to Jesus, Peter baldly says, *I am not.* Then Peter blends into the crowd of slaves and police who are standing around a charcoal fire, warming themselves. Yes, Peter is standing *with them!* The word for *charcoal fire* is *anthrakia* (v. 18); it will appear later, in a resurrection scene (21:9), when Peter stands again—for healing of this painful memory!

18:19-24 [A´] Jesus Is "Tried" Before Annas

The narrator shifts the plot back to the trial, where Annas, high priest emeritus, questions Jesus . . . but with no success. *He asks Jesus about his disciples and about his teaching* (v. 19). Jesus has nothing especially to say to Annas, so he reminds him (with Caiaphas likely standing by) that his teaching has always been public: *I have spoken openly to the world; I have always taught in synagogues and in the temple, where all the Jews come together. I have said nothing in secret. Why do you ask me? Ask those who heard what I said to them; they know what I said.*

This noncompliant response irritates the police, and one of them strikes *Jesus on the face, saying, "Is this how you answer the high priest?"* Jesus' response is part apologetic and part defensive. The first part opens the door to be proved wrong in so speaking, but the second strongly infers that the door (to being wrong) is closed with a challenge: *If I have spoken wrongly, testify to the wrong. But if I have spoken rightly, why do you strike me?* With this odd turn in the trial, Annas signs off and passes him on to Caiaphas, a nonplayer in the entire trial. He "played" earlier, in 11:48-52 when he wrote Jesus' death sentence. The only part Caiaphas plays here is to hold Jesus and the unfolding drama while the narrator highlights Peter's next sad encounters.

A certain confusion surrounds who really is the high priest in John. Both Coloe and Kerr suggest that the author uses this confusion to critique the Jewish high-priest system, inferring that *Jesus is the true high priest,* who through his trial and death intercedes for his people (Coloe 2001: 203–5; Kerr: 317). Support for this interpretation derives from three narrative emphases. First, Jesus' prayer that immediately precedes this arrest in the garden is a high-priestly intercession. Second, the term *high priest* occurs eight times in this brief narrative span (vv. 13, 15 [2x], 16, 19, 22, 24, 26). Third, the threefold *I AM* declaration in 18:5, 6, and 8 may connect to earlier occurrences where Jesus discloses his *I AM* identity. Shirbroun (332–33) contends that God gives *his name* to Jesus in 17:6, 11-12, 26, and that high priests in the OT bore the name of God in wearing a signet, "Holy to Yahweh." Kerr thus proposes that John presents Jesus as the true high priest. While this may appear speculative, John's Gospel does undermine and fulfill other authority structures of Judaism (e.g., temple, Sabbath, feasts). Hence critique of the priesthood fits this pattern.

Or does the confusion over the high priest's identity simply reflect the historical situation? Some scholars see this as a historical detail that exemplifies John's attention to historical details elsewhere. Taken together, these augur for historical reliability (Dodd 1953: 444–53; Bauckham 2006 passim [186–87]; Anderson 2011: 195–219 [206]). Do we have a "Jerusalem-based history" of Jesus' ministry that sheds historical light beyond Matthew, Mark, and Luke? An answer must appeal to wider Gospel evidence and Josephus's contribution also (see *Ant.* 18.2.1; 18.4.3; and "History and Theology" in the introduction of this commentary).

18:25-27 [B´] Peter Denies Jesus the Second and Third Times

In 18:25-27 the narrative shifts to Peter again, where he continues to warm himself by the fire. In the glow of the light he certainly looks like one of the disciples the police or bystanders have earlier seen with Jesus. So *they* ask the question, first by the guard: *You are not also one of his disciples, are you?* The Greek syntax implies a "no" answer. In Peter's favor—maybe they like his company—they make it easy for him to get off the hook. And he does: *He denied it and said, "I am not."* But the curiosity is not squelched. Now *one of the slaves of the high priest, a relative of the man whose ear Peter had cut off, asked, "Did I not see you in the garden with him?"* This is eyewitness evidence, incident- and location-specific! The interrogation expects a "yes." But Peter has already said, "No" twice, so it is easier to deny Jesus again. Peter does not want to be identified as a sword-bearing revolutionary, so he denies his disciple affiliation with Jesus a third time, *and at that moment the cock crowed* (v. 27). We are not told Peter's response, just as we learn nothing of Judas's response after his deed in verse 5. Peter's "redemption" must wait until after the resurrection.

Other Gospels tell us more, but for John, it is enough to portray both Judas and Peter playing their roles against Jesus. Jesus walks through the valley toward death alone; he carries his own cross

(19:17). Nonetheless, he is sovereign, in control of the calamity, for this awful mess leads to awe-filled glory and exaltation. Facing the cross, Jesus-the-truth sets free, judging violence. The dying One exposes violence for what it is, opening a new history, a new creation, and a new world where light, life, and love triumph over darkness, death, and destruction. Jesus is the way, the truth, and the life!

John 18:28–19:16a

Jesus' Trial before Pilate

PREVIEW

It happened in a town in the Midwest, during a late evening walk after a heavy day of work. Perhaps he did look suspicious as he walked back and forth in a fast-food parking lot. As he rounded the last corner of a long motel, three search lights beamed into his face and three police officers closed in on him, two in front and one in back. With his hands raised by command, their search of his body was thorough. When his nose began to run, he reached for his handkerchief, only to be stopped by command and gunpoint. His wallet and personal items were in the hotel room—thus no identification. After their thorough quizzing about his presence in the town and their scoffing at his true answers, he said, "I have only one thing on me, a small cross." They asked to see it. He reached into his overcoat pocket for a little wooden cross his son had made for him in summer camp, which was missed in the earlier frisking since it was small and not metal. As the police looked at the simple small cross, the guns lowered, and they began to apologize, believing his report on giving Bible lectures that day. Pilate, too, came face-to-face with a cross, and if second-century Gospels are to be believed, his heart changed at the sight of the cross and the righteous man he crucified.

John's Gospel presents a longer and more theologically acute account of Jesus' trial before Pilate—or Pilate's trial before Jesus—than any other Gospel. The chiastic structure of 18:28–19:16a is widely recognized for the back-and-forth movement between Pilate's vacillation *inside* his headquarters where he meets Jesus and *outside* where he meets Jesus' accusers. Whether Pilate is judged to be shrewdly calculating, sympathetic, or pitiful, his shifting from one stage to the other dramatizes his predicament. Pilate—and the Gospel readers—must take a stand regarding Jesus: yes or no to his self-claims and the divine authority in his signs and works.

The trial narrative is replete with irony. It presents both the Jews and Pilate in their self-incriminations on a double, downward spiral that ironically contrasts to Jesus' glorification as he is crowned, robed, and pronounced king on his way to the cross, to be "lifted up" in glorification and exaltation (cf. Duke: 127). This trial climaxes the pervasive trial motif of the Gospel. It also climaxes the theme of Jesus as judge and king, answering conclusively the over-arching question of the Gospel, "Where is Jesus from?" The answer to that question is of cosmic consequence.

John's account of Jesus' trial before Pilate in 18:28–19:16 excels in artistic distinction. In addition to Pilate's alternating movement from outside to inside his courtroom in seven scenes, both the structure and thematic flow effect completeness. The first paragraph of the next section, 19:19-22, is also part of the trial narrative, since it is an ironic conclusion to Pilate's confrontation with the Jews and a hinge to the following account of Jesus' crucifixion.

OUTLINE[W]

A The Accusation: Pilate and the Jews (*Outside*), 18:28-32

    B The Testimony: Pilate and Jesus on Kingship (*Inside*), 18:33-38a

        C The Verdict: Pilate Pronounces Jesus Innocent (*Outside*), 18:38b-40

            D Scourging and Mocking the King (*Inside*), 19:1-3

        C´ The Verdict: Pilate Pronounces Jesus Innocent (*Outside*), 19:4-8

    B´ The Testimony: Pilate and Jesus on Authority (*Inside*), 19:9-12

A´ The Sentence: Pilate and the Jews and Jesus (*Outside*), 19:13-16a

EXPLANATORY NOTES

The Accusation: Pilate and the Jews (*Outside*) 18:28-32

This unit begins with the officers moving Jesus from the Jewish court to the Roman court, Pilate's headquarters. The handover

---

w   Where the superscript w occurs after headings, please see the commentary's online Web Supplement for additional material. Go to: http://www.heraldpress.com/bcbc/john.

occurs *early in the morning. They* in verse 28 must refer back to the
officers in verses 12 and 22 (pl., in RSV correctly; NRSV's sg. is inac-
curate). These Jewish *officers* (generic *hypēretai*; cf. Luke 1:2, *servants*)
are under the command of the chief priests (cf. *the temple police* in
7:32, 45). They will not enter Pilate's headquarters lest they defile
their ritual purity before the Passover. Ironically, while they maintain their ritual purity, they enlist a Gentile ruler to prosecute this
Jewish *Nazarene*! Brown comments on this irony:

> The opening confrontation of Pilate and the Jews is described with
> subtle irony. Having cynically decided on the death of Jesus because it
> was more advantageous that one man die than that the whole nation
> be destroyed, the Jewish authorities are, nevertheless, scrupulously
> correct in their observance of ritual purity. They do not hesitate to
> make use of the Gentiles to destroy their adversary, but they will not
> enter the Gentile's house. Implicitly there may be another element of
> irony: they fear that ritual impurity will prevent their eating the
> Passover lamb, but unwittingly they are delivering up to death him
> who is the Lamb of God and thus they are making possible the true
> Passover. (R. Brown 1970: 866)

These officers of the Pharisees and chief priests meticulously and
religiously maintain their purity in order to celebrate the Passover
Feast that commemorates their deliverance from bondage to
Gentiles. But now they scapegoat one of their own to the whims of
this Gentile procurator (an echo of Joseph's brothers' selling Joseph
into Egyptian bondage). Again the one handed over will become the
Savior of the people.

Jesus is now in the hands of Pilate. Although Luke 23 and John's
narrative here may appear to portray Pilate favorably in his not-
guilty pronouncements, such is not the dominant assessment of
Pilate's rule and character (see Philo's analysis on page 429). In this
Johannine narrative, Pilate's role is that of a shrewd politician who
first plays Jesus off against the Jews and then plays the Jews against
Caesar, resulting in double calamity. In his interchanges with the
Jews, Pilate is antagonistic, but with Jesus he appears curious and
either kindly disposed or indifferent. Nonetheless, he represents
"world power" and is urged by Jewish authorities to put Jesus to
death (11:47-52).

To Pilate's initial question, *What accusation do you bring against
this man?* (18:29), the Jews respond evasively and inconclusively.
Throughout the trial the charges become more confused. Since
their accusation against Jesus is muddled, it soon becomes clear that
Jesus will not receive a fair trial before Pilate.

The officers give Pilate an evasive response to his query on the charge: *If this man were not a criminal, we would not have handed him over to you.* Pilate's shrewd response is to put the burden back on them, saying, *Take him yourselves and judge him according to your law.* Then *the Jews* (as the narrator now calls the accusers) reply, *We are not permitted* [presumably by Roman law] *to put anyone to death.* This is not exactly true, since according to their law they could *stone* an offender to death—as they wanted to do in John 8:5 (cf. 8:59; 10:31-32; 11:8; and R. Brown 1966: 337). The narrator okays the Jews' dubious statement because the fulfillment of Jesus' mission requires being *lifted up* (3:14; 12:32), specifying the kind of dying he must undergo. While the cross is public humiliation politically, it is also the means of Jesus' glorification through which he will draw all people to himself. Both Jesus' prophecy and Caiaphas's prophecy determine the course of events. Jesus is judge in this trial, with both the Jews and Pilate under his authority.

The Testimony: Pilate and Jesus on Kingship (*Inside*) 18:33-38a

As with Mark, this Gospel makes kingship central in the trial plot. Jesus is called king eleven times (18:33, 37 [2x], 39; 19:3, 12, 14, 15, 19, 21 [2x]). Although in John the charge "Jesus claims to be a king" (cf. Luke 23:2) is not mentioned, this is what Pilate immediately asks about. Pilate has dealt with other messianic claimants and knows what boils in the Jewish blood: freedom to live under their own king. Pilate's query identifies the accusation as political insurrection.

Jesus' response to Pilate's question, *Do you ask this on your own, or did others tell you about me?* (18:34) overtly turns the tables. This shift of topic subtly puts Pilate on trial. Pilate must choose what he will believe and testify regarding Jesus. Pilate's defense question, *I am not a Jew, am I?* (18:35) portrays himself on trial. He dissociates himself from the Jews, yet in the narrative, he allies himself more and more closely with the wishes of *the Jews ["The Jews," p. 520].* He has his own political goal: to disenfranchise the Jews of their covenant identity (19:15d). Pilate cannot take a neutral stand regarding Jesus. He gradually aligns himself with those opposing the One who reveals the truth, and in this process he subordinates the Jews to Caesar. He maneuvers the trial adroitly, but in the end he, too, is judged by the truth: Jesus.

Although Pilate tries to separate the politics of state from the politics of religion, the trial is of cosmic religious consequence.

Jesus' terms of *kingdom* and *kingship* (18:36 RSV) supersede Pilate's comprehension: *My kingdom is not from this world. If my kingdom were from this world, my followers would be fighting to keep me from being handed over to the Jews. But as it is, my kingdom is not from here.* Pilate is confronted with *power* and *kingship not from this world.* Jesus concretizes the point by denouncing *fighting.* The word used here (*agōnizomai*) is derived from athletic imagery and has the meaning of *contending* (as in 1 Cor 9:25; Col 4:12; Howard-Brook 1994: 400). In 2 Timothy 4:7a, the same term is used but is translated with military imagery, as fighting: "I have fought the good fight" (in athletic terms, "I have competed well in the contest"). Jesus' servants (*hypēretēs*) do not run a this-worldly race.

Jesus defines his reign in terms of *truth* (18:37-38), anchoring the trial and crucifixion to this important Johannine theme. The painful irony is that the one who is *full of grace and truth* (1:14), who is the giver of *grace and truth* (1:17), who is *the way, and the truth, and the life* (14:6)—this one will be judged by untruth, sentenced by those whose words are ironically true but who know not the truth they speak. Truth judges rightly and thus aligns Jesus' purpose statement here—*For this I was born, and for this I came into the world, to testify to the truth* (19:37)—with his earlier words: *I came into this world for judgment so that those who do not see may see, and those who do see may become blind* (9:39).

The Verdict: Pilate Pronounces Jesus Innocent (*Outside*) 18:38b-40[w]

Immediately following his question *What is truth?* Pilate moves again outside the headquarters, toward the Jews, and pronounces the verdict. This is the first of three times when Pilate pronounces Jesus innocent: *I find no case against him* (18:38; 19:4, 6). But the innocence of Jesus does not detract the Jews from their plan. When offered the release of the innocent, they reject the truth, demanding instead the release of Barabbas.

A double irony occurs in the Jews' request that Pilate release Barabbas instead of Jesus. First, the name *Barabbas*, translated literally, means "son of the father." So the Jews request a man's release whose very name matches how Jesus identifies himself in John: *the Son of the Father* (cf. 6:40). But instead of the true Son of the Father, the Jews choose a *bandit* (*lēstēs*, 18:40). In first-century Palestine, a "bandit" was not a common thief; Josephus uses the word *lēstēs* to speak of political insurrectionists! Jesus is declared innocent of political insurrection, yet his freedom is traded for the release of one held prisoner for revolt against the Romans!

It is probable that Pilate is not so much interested in Jesus or his innocence as he is in exploiting the situation to retain Barabbas, who *is* a real threat of insurrection. He offers to release Jesus, whom he perceives as harmless. He knows this will infuriate the Jews, but he is acting in character. According to descriptions of Pilate from other sources, especially Josephus (e.g., *Ant.* 18.3.1-2; 18.4.1-2; *Jewish War* 2.9.4), Pilate was calculating and antagonistic toward the Jewish population. "Philo [in] *Ad Gaium* 38.302 attributes to Pilate robbery, murder, and inhumanity" (R. Brown 1970: 847). This fits with Luke 13:1, "Now there were some present at that time who told Jesus about the Galileans whose blood Pilate had mixed with their sacrifices" (NIV 1984).

Neither *the Jews* nor Pilate *belongs to the truth* (18:37).

Scourging and Mocking the King (*Inside*) 19:1-3

The center of the chiastic structure of the seven-scene trial is a classic example of this Gospel's irony. Tersely put, the coronation, investiture, and proclamation of Jesus as *King of the Jews* mockingly and ironically testifies to Jesus' identity: "Pilate begins the inevitable process of glorifying Jesus" (Howard-Brook 1994: 403). The paragraph is sandwiched between Pilate's first declaration *I find no case* (18:38) and his second and third *no-case* pronouncements (19:4, 6). In John the mockery of Jesus is confined to the thematic center of the trial narrative (19:1-3); in the Synoptic Gospels the mockery continues through the trial and the crucifixion.

Pilate flogs Jesus with a barbed whip (*mastix*), a common torture practice of Roman officials as they soften up the accused for execution (cf. the similar practice in Exod 5:14 by Pharaoh, and in Deut 25:2-3 by an Israelite judge). The Roman soldiers then dress him for his mock appearance as king, following up Pilate's pronouncement of Jesus' identity as *King* in 18:39. They keep *coming up to him, saying,* "Hail, King of the Jews," and strike him on the face (the temple police also strike Jesus on the face in 18:22). These slaps on the face "prepare" for the violence of the crucifixion.

The one mocked as king is truly *King*, attired in royal *purple robe* and *crown*. Emperors wore a laurel wreath, also called crown (*stephanos*). Neyrey points out

> that the crown was made of "acanthus," a thistle type plant with broad saw-toothed leaves. A "crown" would easily be made by positioning the

leaves vertically around the head and securing them with a cord. The effect, then, mimics the rays of light springing from the head, an image used to portray gods and monarchs on coins. The point of this type of crown is mockery and dishonor, not torture. Again, shame, not pain. (302–3)

While Neyrey stresses the *shaming* of Jesus throughout the passion narrative (cf. Heb 12:2, "disregarding [KJV: despising] the shame"), the reality of pain from the thorns cannot be discounted. Jesus wears a crown suited to the spectacle that both Rome and the Jews want to make of him. In John what is intended to shame and humiliate Jesus is prelude to glorification, the Father's full revelation in the Son. In contrast to the Synoptic accounts, Jesus is not stripped of his royal robe, but apparently remains in royal garb throughout the trial, emphasizing ironically Jesus' journey as King to his glorification.

The Verdict: Pilate Pronounces Jesus Innocent (*Outside*) 19:4-8[w]

Pilate's second and third *no-case* pronouncements regarding Jesus occur in short succession. When Pilate first states that he finds *no case against him* (18:38b), he refers to *your* custom, noted above, of releasing *someone for you at the Passover* (in Mark 15:6 and Matt 27:15 it is *Pilate's* custom). But now the Jews refer to their law (*We have a law . . .*) as rationale for why Jesus must die (19:7). The rationale, not explicitly stated, seems to be Jesus' claim *to be the Son of God,* which the Jews consider blasphemy (see comments on 5:18; 10:31-38; Truex: 195–200). Pilate co-opts this custom, and the Jews appeal to their *law*—tools for both to achieve separate agendas. This contrasts with law based on *truth,* which leads to justice and to right judgment.

The tension between Pilate and the Jews mounts in this scene. John's Gospel continues to portray Jesus in control: *Jesus came out, wearing the crown of thorns and the purple robe* (19:5). Hence amid the trial and mockery, Jesus is ironically sovereign, while Pilate and the Jews are blinded to the truth of who Jesus is, in part by their antagonism toward each other.

Pilate presents Jesus as a pitiful, harmless spectacle, with his famous *Ecce homo/Behold the man!* (KJV, RSV). Mocking Jesus, Pilate also mocks the crowd. This not only intensifies the tension between Pilate and the Jews, but also deepens the resolve of the Jews to rid Jesus from their politics.

Although John's Gospel emphasizes seeing and believing, seeing does not always lead to believing. Jesus comes out *wearing the crown of thorns and the purple robe* (19:5). *When the chief priests and police saw him* (crowned and robed like a king; 19:6), they shout for his crucifixion. Seeing necessitates choice. The choice the Jews make repeatedly (5:16; 6:41-42; 7:1, 30, 32, 44; 8:59; 10:31; 11:47-53) culminates in their rejecting Jesus as King. Their choice is their indictment.

The demands for Jesus' crucifixion irritate Pilate, so he taunts them with a response they cannot carry out: *You take him and crucify him* (19:6 NIV). This is followed by Pilate's third pronouncement of Jesus' innocence: *I find no case against him* (v. 6d). But *the Jews*, also exasperated, intensify their case against Jesus, saying, *He ought to die because he has claimed to be the Son of God* (v. 7c).

While this may appear as a shift from a political to a religious accusation, it is not. At least five Caesars in the first century claimed divine status, calling themselves "the Son of God" (Swartley 2006a: 85). Since the emperors of both Jesus' time (Augustus, accepting the title with reticence) and John's time (Domitian, declaring his divine status boldly) claimed that title—which Jews detested—this is intended by the Jews to make Pilate understand the criminal severity of the case at hand.

Understandably then, Pilate is *more afraid than ever* (v. 8). Just what does he have on his hands—a rival emperor? Or is this a divine miracle worker, a role also known in the Greco-Roman world? So his questioning of Jesus in the next unit takes a different turn. For the Jews the situation becomes excruciating because OT messianic anticipations include the title "Son of God" (e.g., Isa 9:6; cf. Ps 2:7). So their rejection of Jesus is rejection of both Jesus as *truth* and *Son of God*.

The Testimony: Pilate and Jesus on Authority (*Inside*) 19:9-12

Pilate responds with fear to these words by returning to his headquarters to question Jesus further. Now Pilate asks, *Where are you from?*—the logical sequel to his fear about this man's "criminal" identity. In the narrative plot, this question climaxes a central theme of the Gospel: *I am from above* (8:23; Meeks 1972). Jesus' sudden silence before Pilate reminds readers once more of Jesus' role in the trial. Though power moves back and forth between Pilate and the Jews as they spar and grasp for possession, Jesus remains in control, not intimidated.

Although Pilate assumes he has power over Jesus to release or crucify him (v. 10), O'Day points out that Jesus' previous words indicate otherwise (1995: 821). In 10:18 Jesus says, *No one takes it* [my life] *from me, but I lay it down of my own accord. I have power to lay it down, and I have power to take it up again.* Jesus has power over life and death (5:26; ch. 11). His response to Pilate in 19:11 is stunning: *You would have no power over me unless it had been given you from above; therefore the one who handed me over to you is guilty of a greater sin.* Indeed, Pilate's political power does not reside within himself: it is given to him from another, *from above.* Jesus declares that God is the source of even Pilate's power. Jesus has already said that he is *from above.* Jesus and Pilate are contestants in *power from above.* But Jesus knows this and understands it: Pilate does not. Jesus' power from above denotes not only the source of Jesus' authority and power; it also challenges Caesar's power, manifest in the above titles ascribed to both Jesus and Caesar. *From above* is a double entendre.

Thatcher's thesis that John's Gospel presents Jesus as battling Rome's three-headed beast ("Pilate, the cross, and the Jewish authorities") is relevant (2009: 14–15), for in these verses Pilate is defeated: "Jesus now speaks as the representative of a monarch whose power radically supersedes that of Pilate's master. This episode clarifies . . . John's theory of the relationship between Christ and Caesar" (78). Pilate is put under God's sovereignty, which Jesus represents. While this verse may be read to stress the God-given authority of the empire—and thus the Christian's submission (as in Rom 13:1-7)—this narrative strikes another chord. It puts the empire and Pilate under divine judgment. It does not shift the *guilt* to the *one who turned him over* to Pilate. It declares both parties *guilty* under divine judgment (80).

The one who is guilty of the *greater sin* is either Caiaphas specifically (11:48-51; 18:24, 28) or the Jewish leaders, referred to collectively. Since the latter is likely intended, Jesus here judges the Jewish authorities. Judas is included as well since he sided with the Jewish authorities. In this drama the Jews reject the One who reveals the sovereign God. Pilate also bears guilt for his acquiescence to the execution of this man whom he judged. He aligns himself with the unbelieving Jews to keep "peace and order" by means of a scapegoat: Jesus.

The politicized words of the Jews in 19:12c, *Everyone who claims to be a king sets himself against the emperor,* are in tension with Jesus' words in 18:37, *Everyone who belongs to the truth listens to my voice.* The author places these statements in corresponding sections of the chiasm, emphasizing poignancy of the irony; the one on trial is the One by whom all others are tried and judged. In resorting to

Rome to accomplish their goals, the Jews have betrayed their own law. Crying out, *If you release this man, you are no friend of the emperor. Everyone who claims to be a king sets himself against the emperor*; they twist Pilate's arm. Pilate responds in kind, forcing them to disown their covenant God. They rapidly spiral downward into the depths of anguish and apostasy. The Jews' duplicity is exposed: they align themselves with Rome, disowning their Lord God as King. They value the preservation of their nation and law more highly than they value their covenant pledge to revere alone the Lord God's kingship.

The Sentence: Pilate and the Jews and Jesus (*Outside*)
19:13-16a

Contrary to his pronouncement of innocence, Pilate now acts as one powerless to execute right judgment. The Jews now accuse him of setting himself against the emperor if he does not kowtow to their demands to crucify Jesus. Pilate's power now is naked, pitiful, and impotent to bring about justice. He now shows his true character as a ruthless manipulator. He forces the Jews to disown their covenant God, through a judgment (*bēma*) scene (v. 13).

The Greek is ambiguous. It is not clear whether Pilate himself sits down on the judge's bench (*bēma*) or whether he sits Jesus down on it. In the highly symbolic and ironic style of the Gospel, the ambiguity in the Greek verb (*kathizō*) may be intended. The verb is sometimes transitive (cause another to sit down) and sometimes intransitive (to sit oneself down). R. Brown argues that it is most unlikely that a Roman governor would put a prisoner on the judge's bench (1970: 880–81).

But why does the author takes pains to include this detail? Verse 14 ends with Pilate's presenting Jesus to the Jews and saying, *Behold, your king!* (KJV, RSV) at the very hour (noon) when the slaying of lambs begins. The transitive meaning may thus represent yet another example of John's irony as Pilate sits Jesus on the bench in contempt. This also explains why the text is silent on what Pilate says from the "bench" as judge. Jesus sits on the *bēma* in royal purple at this hour, adding both to John's sarcastic portrayal of Pilate and to John's distinctive theology: the king-judge will be slain for the sins of the people. This also fits with John's dramatic (theatrical) presentation of Jesus (Brant). Either way, the very mention of the judge's seat and the ambiguity of the verb conjure up the enduring issue in this trial: Who really is on trial? Who is the true judge and king?

The name of the place, *the Stone Pavement*, is not a translation of the Hebrew word, *Gabbatha*, but simply another name for the same place. Many interpretations of *Gabbatha* have been suggested, but it most likely indicates an elevated place, a ridge, or a hump (R. Brown 1970: 882). This again suggests Jesus' glorification, certifying that Jesus in his glorification will be elevated for all to see. That elevation has begun.

Specifying the time as noon on the day of Preparation for the Passover is important, for this is when preparation for the slaughter of the lambs began. The timing is crucial since it harks back to the beginning of the Gospel, where John the Witness says of Jesus, *Here is the Lamb of God who takes away the sin of the world* (1:29), and again where John calls Jesus *the Lamb of God* (1:36). The purpose of this Lamb offering himself is to restore relationship to God by giving himself for the "sin" and the "life" of the world (6:51; cf. Snyder Belousek: 188–91). At this hour also Pilate, perhaps now himself on the *bēma*, presents Jesus to the Jews: *Here is your King!* (19:14).

Following their repeated demands for his death, Pilate turns from questioning Jesus to questioning the Jews: *Shall I crucify your King?* (19:15). The tension between Rome and the Jewish people is palpable with this ironic and direct confrontation: Pilate forces the Jews to choose. What will they choose to do with Jesus their King?

Pilate puts it to them one more time, around noon, when the priests began to slaughter lambs for sacrifice, saying to the Jews, *Here is your King!* (v. 14). Immediately they cry as before, *Away with him! Away with him! Crucify him!* Pilate then takes his delicious bite: *Shall I crucify your King?* The chief priests recant their holy covenant loyalty, saying, *We have no king but the emperor* (19:15). In these words they indict themselves as apostate. The *chief priests*—of all groups— confess allegiance to the emperor, denying their covenant loyalty as the people of God. Shrewd Pilate then hands *him over to them to be crucified* (v. 16a). As Howard-Brook observes, in this *handing over* (*paradidōmi*), "Pilate cooperates in the crucifixion; he is indeed a 'friend of Caesar.' But he does so by *handing Jesus back to the chief priests*. He has gotten out of their way by allowing them to share in the imperial power [at the price of their own covenant apostasy!]. The scene comes to an end with the placement of Jesus back in the hands of 'his own,' those who have never received him" (412).

Pilate manipulates the entire drama so that the Jewish leaders are forced into an unbearable situation, declaring loyalty to Caesar rather than to God, who called them into a covenant relationship, whose first command jealously declared, "You shall have no other gods before me" (Exod 20:3). Talbert describes it well:

Their words drip with irony. Instead of "May you be our king, you alone" (= eleventh benediction, *Eighteen Benedictions*), or "From everlasting to everlasting you are God; beside you we have no king, redeemer, or savior, no liberator, deliverer, provider, none who takes pity in every time of distress and trouble; we have no king but you" (= the hymn sung at the conclusion of the Greater Hallel by the high priests as part of the Passover Haggadah), Judaism's priestly leadership confesses, "We have no king but the Caesar." (241)

No more questions, accusations, or taunts. Pilate simply hands Jesus over to be crucified. Both Pilate and the Jews get what they want. Pilate averts the threat of uproar on his watch in his city. The Jews succeed in securing the sentence they want. However, the cost is high for both. Pilate has allowed himself and his authority among the Jews to be mocked and manipulated. The Jews have revoked the one characteristic identifying them as God's chosen people and nation. But what is empty victory for Pilate and the Jews is glorification for Jesus [*"The Jews," p. 520*].

Throughout this narrative Jesus is sovereign. He emerges as true King and true Judge. Both Pilate and the Jews are victims of Jesus' piercing judgment.

John 19:16b-42

Jesus' Crucifixion and Burial

PREVIEW

Have you ever carried a cross in a Good Friday procession? Church traditions in many countries perform such a procession through parts of the city. Someone carries a cross for all in the procession to identify more fully with Jesus, who in John carries his own cross to the place of crucifixion, *The Place of the Skull.*

John's account of Jesus' crucifixion scintillates with the last round of political positioning between Pilate and the Jewish chief priests. Pilate wins. Pilate's inscription on the cross, *Jesus of Nazareth: King of the Jews*, is in three languages and creates a stir among the Jews. It is enough to make the chief priests bargain once again with Pilate. This inscription audaciously declares in their face what they have done: crucified their King (recall that Pilate *handed him over to them to be crucified*, v. 16a)! *["The Jews," p. 520]*. What Pilate says in response to the chief priests' plea ironically seals the truth of what is written: *What I have written I have written.* The narrative then unfolds a series of events that *fulfill* what is written in Israel's Scriptures. Virtually everything that occurs connects to prophetic Scripture.

John also shows Jesus' humanity and informs us of three memorable last words of Jesus not found in Matthew, Mark, or Luke. Jesus' tender love for his mother and for the beloved disciple take center stage as his first words from the cross. His final word, *It is finished*, consummates the works, signs, and words of his ministry. When the

436

soldier pierces Jesus' side, producing blood and water, *eyewitness testimony* credentials the bearer of this Gospel's traditions (v. 35).

Citations of OT Scripture lace this narrative, so much so that the narrator is also in the face of the Jews regarding their Scripture. Jesus' death, which the chief priests were determined to carry out, now unlocks the prophetic significance of one Scripture after another, to the extent that each given event in the narrative is prophecy fulfilled. The calendar time, *the day of Preparation* for a particularly important *Sabbath* (19:14, 31, 42), also attests to the fulfillment motif. What is done to Jesus and *when* it is done accords with Scripture!

Jesus' burial is the occasion for Nicodemus to reappear (see ch. 3) as one who has not forgotten—and perhaps not forsaken—Jesus. It also introduces (another) *disciple*, a *secret* one, *Joseph of Arimathea* (19:38-39). This tantalizes the reader, for it leaves open the question of salvation for both. Did Nicodemus receive birth *from above*? Is his faith commitment now disclosed? Or did he do this noble deed to atone for his failure to comprehend the mystery of birth from above? Similarly, the status of Joseph puzzles. Are they part of Jesus' larger disciple band that, now with the political furor quelled, comes forth into *the light* that Jesus has brought into the world?

OUTLINE

Jesus Is Crucified, 19:16b-25a
Jesus' Words from the Cross, 19:25b-30
Jesus' Body on the Cross, 19:31-37
Jesus' Burial, 19:38-42

EXPLANATORY NOTES

Jesus Is Crucified 19:16b-25a

19:16b-18 The Cross Scene

Here in verse 17 for the first time the word *cross* appears in John's Gospel. Until now other figures or metaphors were used to foretell this event: *lifted up* (3:14; 8:28; 12:32); *I lay it* [my life] *down of my own accord* (10:18; cf. 6:51; 12:24); and *my hour.* All point to this moment and event: Jesus' dying on a cross, his glorification.

Like the other NT Gospels, John says this historic event happened at *The Place of the Skull.* Matthew and Mark point out that it is also called "Golgotha," but only John points out that this is its name *in Hebrew.* The reason for this name may be the skull-like shape of the hill on which crucifixions took place or because of the many skulls scattered on this hill northwest of Jerusalem, after vultures ravished the bodies of the dead while still on the cross. A further point, unique to John, is that the two crucified with Jesus (also in Mark and Luke) are described as *one on either side* (expressed by two uses of *enteuthen*, v. 18). The choice of words makes clear that Jesus is between them, alluding to his reconciliation of sinners, not only to God but also to one another. Howard-Brook (1994: 417) connects the imagery with the OT *mercy seat* between the two cherubs (Exod 25:22), thus highlighting Jesus' role as God incarnate, the place where the sins of the people are brought annually into the Lord God's presence by the high priest for atonement, cleansing, and forgiveness.

19:19-22 The Controversy over the "Title"

On a board to nail atop the cross, Pilate writes a fuller title inscription than what we find in the Synoptics: *Jesus of Nazareth, the King of the Jews.* Furthermore, he writes it in Hebrew, Latin, and Greek, symbolizing its universal appeal. Ironically, it proclaims the truth for the whole world. The three languages are those of Jewish Scripture (Hebrew); of the expansive Roman Empire (Latin); and the language of commerce and of the prevailing culture of the time (Greek). Whatever Pilate intended, the title witnesses the truth of Jesus' kingship, which mystifies and perhaps spooks Pilate (18:37-38). The words evoke Jesus' earlier prophetic prediction: *I, when I am lifted up from the earth, will draw all people to myself* (12:32). This trilingual confession draws all people to Jesus crucified.

Many of the Jews read this inscription. Pilate's twelfth-hour ploy has outwitted them and thus triggered the chief priests' dire plea (v. 21): *Do not write, "The King of the Jews," but, "This man said, I am King of the Jews."* Pilate answers, *What I have written I have written.* While Pilate's inscription may or may not be toned with sarcasm (cf. vv. 14-15), the Gospel narrator's deft use of irony is clear: "John conscripts Pilate's tongue to make a true confession" (Culpepper 1998: 231).

Pilate's trilingual title (*titlos*) imprints his ownership on this dastardly deed. As Koester puts it,

From a Roman perspective the placard identified Jewish messianism as a capital offense and reminded the populace that threats to Roman rule would not be tolerated. From a Jewish perspective, the placard created a demeaning caricature of Jewish national sentiment; therefore they asked that it be changed to read, "*This man said* I am King of the Jews" (19:21) so that the onus would fall squarely upon Jesus himself. (2003: 227/1995: 203)

The placard witnesses to the fact that the Roman and Jewish peoples shared in the crucifixion of Jesus (stated clearly in Acts 4:27). *They crucified him* (19:18). *They* includes *us*; we are Gentiles or Jews. Our acquiescence to this deed is our sin and with our repentance, also our salvation.

19:23-25a *The Soldiers' Disposal of Jesus' Clothes*[w]

The four soldiers take and divide Jesus' clothes *into four parts, one for each soldier.* They thus incriminate themselves as participants in the murder of this king *from above.* But one piece stops them, his *tunic* (*chitōn*). They notice that it is seamless, woven from top to bottom, and they do not want to ruin it by ripping it into four pieces. So they cast lots for it, thereby fulfilling the Scripture: *They divided my clothes among themselves, and for my clothing they cast lots* (see Ps 22:18; 21:19 LXX). This part of the passion narrative is important to John. As Culpepper (1998: 231) notes, in the Synoptic accounts the clothes and tunic are divided in six to twelve words, but John gives this sixty-seven words. The main point for John is likely that it fulfills Scripture. But it also carries symbolic significance: *it is seamless, woven in one piece from the top* (v. 23e). The symbolic significance may invoke Jesus' prayer for the unity of all who believe and will come to believe. Jesus' seamless tunic metaphorically draws all believers into "one body, one community. What God weaves, God weaves whole, from above. There is but one vine, one net, one flock, one shepherd, one Son, and one seamless tunic woven from above" (Culpepper 1998: 232).

This important unit ends with a somber note: *and that is what the soldiers did.* The brief declarative sentence functions somewhat like *Selah* at the end of a psalm, intensifying the episode: "Don't forget it, know it happened." Its significance lives on.

Jesus' Words from the Cross 19:25b-30

19:25b-27 *To His Mother; to His Disciple*

All four Gospels speak of women who watch Jesus as he dies on the cross. Luke alone does not name them but refers to "all his acquaintances . . . who had followed him from Galilee" (23:49). The Synoptics say they watch "from a distance" (Matt 27:55), but John

---

w   Where the superscript *w* occurs after headings, please see the commentary's online Web Supplement for additional material. Go to: http://www.heraldpress.com/bcbc/john.

(19:25) says they are *standing near the cross*. In John, the beloved disciple is also near, standing beside Jesus' mother. John names three or four women: Jesus' *mother, his mother's sister, Mary the wife of Clopas, and Mary Magdalene*. It is unclear whether Mary, the wife of Clopas, is the sister of Jesus' mother or is another woman. Matthew and Mark name Mary Magdalene first, then Mary the mother of James and Joseph, then the mother of the sons of Zebedee (Matt 27:56; Salome in Mark 15:40). Only John mentions Jesus' mother, but she may be identified in Matthew and Mark as "Mary the mother of James and Joses," since James and Joses are identified elsewhere as Jesus' siblings (Mark 6:3; Matt 13:55). In addition to those named, "many other women" are present, according to Mark (15:41) and Matthew (27:55). In John the naming and positioning of the women near the cross is a prelude to his addressing both his mother and the beloved disciple.

What Jesus says to his mother and the beloved disciple is unique to John and important as Jesus' first words from the cross, one of the multiple high points of the Gospel. These words speak the loving heart of Jesus precisely when he suffers on the cross. He is not *me*-oriented, but other-focused. In this double exchange Jesus links his mother and the beloved disciple into a loving and caring relationship.

As noted in John 2:1-12, Jesus' mother appears only there and here as bookends to Jesus' earthly ministry. Unnamed in both cases, Jesus addresses her as *Woman*. This is not because Jesus disrespects or demeans her. The beloved disciple is also never named, and certainly not because Jesus or the Johannine author or community demean the importance of either of them. The opposite is true. Jesus' mother and the beloved disciple emerge in the narrative as important types, symbolic of roles larger than themselves. To name them particularizes them and restricts their significance. John intends more.

A renowned Roman Catholic scholar, Raymond Brown holds that "Jesus' mother becoming the mother of the beloved disciple seems to evoke the OT themes of Lady Zion giving birth to people in the messianic age, and of Eve and her offspring. This imagery flows over into the Church who brings forth children modeled after Jesus, and the relationship of loving care that must bind the children to their mother" (1970: 926). Brown does not want to press the symbolism unduly but thinks there are enough lines of evidence to support this view. Brown regards Mary, the mother of the Lord, as mother of the Church. The beloved disciple's care of Jesus' mother elevates his role as a *type* of the true believer.

Brown points us in the right direction. On the one hand, we do not need to correlate this symbolism with any specific branch of the Christian church. On the other hand, historicity and symbolism are not alternatives. Both Jesus' *mother* and the *beloved disciple* are historical persons, but their roles in John's narrative are also symbolic *[Beloved Disciple, p. 505]*. That Jesus' mother bookends his earthly ministry and that the beloved disciple appears almost always in relation to Peter—comparatively superior in knowledge, love, and commitment—is telling. John is inviting us into a mystery larger than history and larger than ourselves, into corporate figures that symbolize the heartbeat of Jesus' followers, not yet called "church" in John. Before becoming church they need to know that mother begins the wedding; Jesus incarnates and consummates the union; and the beloved disciple transmits its bonds of love and joy from the first believers to later generations. We need to know his role in the Gospel *[Beloved Disciple, p. 505]*.

We need to hear these words, dear to Jesus' heart, expressing his deep love for both his mother and the beloved disciple: to his mother, *Woman, here is your son*; to his disciple, *Here is your mother*. His words create a mutual bond of love that shapes their future: *From that hour the disciple took her into his own home*. This precious and empowering love and care from Jesus symbolizes the life of the church yet to be born. Viewed from the time of the Johannine community, this care and love mark Jesus' true followers, who abide in him as branches in the vine: Jesus' mother receives her son; the beloved disciple receives his mother. Jesus' great love for both seals their love for the other.

19:28-29 "I Am Thirsty"

This second word from the cross testifies to Jesus' humanity, evoking human thirst for God (Ps 63:1; Isa 55:1). Jesus desires God's presence, even on the cross. John identifies this word as fulfillment of Scripture, likely Psalm 69:21b, "For my thirst they gave me vinegar to drink" (cf. Ps 22:15). Various elements of Scripture are fulfilled: Jesus the righteous one becomes thirsty, and *sour wine* (vinegar) on a *branch of hyssop is held to his mouth*. The wine-filled sponge on a hyssop branch echoes the exodus Passover tradition in which the Israelites put blood on their doorframes with the hyssop plant (Exod 12:22). In this light Jesus' death is a sacrificial salvation-liberation event (cf. John 6:51-58). Jesus' *blood* links Jesus' giving his life with the blood on the door that spared the Israelites.

Jesus' saying is set specifically in the context that he *knew that all was now finished* (John 19:28a). His word has figurative significance within John's narrative in which water gives life (4:13-15; 7:37-39). Both food and drink are symbolic in John, pointing to that which comes *from above* and satisfies *human* thirst. "Only in John does Jesus actually drink the sour wine, and in so doing he symbolically drinks the cup of suffering as he dies" (Culpepper 1998: 235). Jesus' thirst expresses his readiness to drink the last swallow sustaining him in his suffering. Does the wine of the cross bookend with the wine of the wedding?

19:30 "It Is Finished"^w

Jesus now speaks his third and final word, *It is finished*. He then bows his head and gives up *his spirit*. As the Latin states, *Consummatum est!* Jesus' words and works are finished. Each *sign* can now be seen as proleptic of Jesus' consummate gift, his being lifted up on the cross for his glorification. He is the Lamb slain "to take away the sin of the world" (1:29, 36). He is King (6:15) who gives his life as bread for the world (6:45-58). Jesus' pronouncement in 12:31-33 is fulfilled: "*Now is the judgment of this world; now the ruler of this world will be driven out. And I, when I am lifted up from the earth, will draw all people to myself.*" He said this to indicate the kind of death he was to die. The next verses in John 12 put starkly before all people the choice to believe or not to believe in Jesus, to walk in the light or to continue in darkness.

Every metaphor, sign, and action of Jesus finds its consummation in this event, Jesus crucified, breathing his last for the life of the world. He gives so we can receive; he dies so we can die to our old selves and receive eternal life. If we faithfully follow, we will have our own giving up and our own dying to the world, our own engagement with the powers, religious and political. We will also know that the gift of new life, despite present sufferings, opens the door to God's resurrection power for us and gives life to others.

Jesus' Body on the Cross 19:31-37

19:31a-c A Time Bind: The Day of Preparation for the Sabbath

The timing of the *hour* of Jesus' death on the cross is significant. The Passover is to be observed on Nisan 14 (Exod 12:6; Lev 23:5). Jesus' death is prior to Passover (19:14). Jesus is slain as Paschal Lamb during the afternoon and end of Nisan 13, *the day of Preparation for the Passover* (John 1:29; cf. 1 Cor 5:7). Apparently the Passover and

Sabbath are on the same day that year. The "sixth hour" (*noon*, John 19:14) is when the faithful begin slaying the lambs for Passover. In placing Jesus' death *before* the Passover meal, John diverges from the Synoptic Gospels. There the Last Supper is the Passover meal, but in John, Jesus is slain *before* the Passover meal. Any solution of the differing accounts is complex, though most scholars consider John's chronology more historical on this point [*Chronology, p. 508*].

19:31d-33 No Bones Broken

Judging by the amount of text allocated to it, what happens to Jesus next is important to John: it fulfills Scripture. The Jews ask that the legs of the crucified men be broken to hasten their death (19:31), so that the bodies can be disposed of (taken down from the cross) before the Sabbath begins. When the soldiers come to Jesus, they see that he is already dead, so they do not break his legs. Jesus' legs are not broken (John 19:33) just as the bones of the Passover lambs are not to be broken (Exod 12:10, 46; Num 9:12; cf. Ps 34:19-20). Even in this scriptural detail, Jesus is the unblemished Lamb slain for the sins of the people.

19:34 Side Pierced: Blood and Water[w]

Why *one of the soldiers pierced his* [Jesus'] *side with a spear* is not explained. Talbert suggests that the soldier "doubtless aimed at the heart to be sure of his death" (245). Maybe so, but John's point lies elsewhere, the importance of both *blood and water* gushing from Jesus' side. The blood testifies to Jesus' humanity, since in Greek mythology (e.g., *Iliad* 5.340–41) only blood-water issued from a goddess wounded with a lance (Talbert: 245). But here it is blood *and* water, which some see as symbolic of eucharist and baptism. More likely, the separate mention of blood cuts against gnostic views that deny Jesus' full humanity, specifically his suffering of death.

In 1 John 5:6 a similar issue is at stake: "This is the one who came by water and blood, Jesus Christ, not with the water only but with the water and the blood." McDermond (64, 244–46) proposes that those who seceded from the Johannine believers denied the blood. Their gnostic denial affirmed the water of baptism and cleansing but repudiated the blood (McDermond: 308–9). Jesus' baptism is by water and blood, the cup of suffering. The water, blood, and Spirit testify to Jesus' distinctive identity as Son of God, conqueror of the world, and giver of life (1 John 5:5-12).

John 19:34 is certainly related to 7:37-39, where Jesus promises living water and assures his disciples that water will flow out of his (Jesus' and/or the believer's) heart, but that cannot happen then since the Spirit has not yet been given, and Jesus has not yet been glorified. The water from Jesus' side prefigures the postresurrection gift of the Spirit. John's order is intentional: blood, signifying death, comes first; water, signifying life, comes second. Both witness to Jesus' gift *for the life of the world* (6:51), and both may evoke birthing imagery in which blood and water flow from the one who gives birth (Howard-Brook [1994: 428–29] suggests an analogy to Gen 2:21-22 LXX). Both texts use the Greek word *pleura* (Genesis: "rib"; John: "side"). The two also symbolize eucharist (blood) and baptism (water, likely also pointing to footwashing, John 13). Sin is washed away; believers are purified.

19:35 Eyewitness Testimony

Whatever we make of verse 34, Jesus' *blood and water* prompt the testimony of the eyewitness responsible for this Gospel, the author and/or bearer of this Gospel tradition. This verse together with 21:24 connects the Gospel with the beloved disciple. The Gospel claims eyewitness authenticity. In both verses John emphasizes the *truth* of eyewitness *testimony*. Bauckham proposes that this disciple is an unnamed Jerusalem disciple (2007) who was an eyewitness to Jesus' ministry, predominantly in Jerusalem in John. For other views, see the essays [*Authorship, p. 502*] [*Beloved Disciple, p. 505*].

19:36-37 Scripture Fulfilled

Jesus' death is presented as fulfillment of Scripture, shown by key citations or allusions:

- John 19:24, quoting Psalm 22:18 (21:19 LXX)
- John 19:28, quoting Psalm 69:21 (69:22 MT) or 63:1 (63:2 MT)
- John 19:36, quoting Psalm 34:20 (cf. Exod 12:10, 46; Num 9:12)
- John 19:37, quoting Zechariah 12:10

Thatcher expresses dissatisfaction with the manner in which John seems to tack fulfillment of Scripture to an otherwise coherent and potent narrative of Jesus' crucifixion and death (2009: 101–3). These prophetic statements, however, are crucial for John's overall purpose, just as are his locating most events and discourses of Jesus' ministry on the Jewish feast calendar. The Gospel cannot be read and fully appreciated until one views the entire presentation as scriptural fulfillment. Only then does one catch the irony in Pilate's declaration: *What I have written I have written*. If that doesn't ring the scriptural bell of Jewish readers, what would?

John cites two Scriptures to seal the eyewitness's testimony to what has occurred and why in this passion event to fulfill Scripture: *These things occurred so that the scripture might be fulfilled, "None of his bones shall be broken." And again, . . . "They will look on the one whom they have pierced."* The repeated unbroken bones highlights its scriptural importance. The piercing of Jesus elicits yet another Scripture (Zech 12:10), which continues with "they shall mourn for him, as one mourns for an only child, and weep bitterly over him, as one weeps over a firstborn." The Hebrew for child is *yaḥid*, used for Isaac in Genesis 22:2, 12 (your "only son"). Hence the context for the quotation is a sacrificial theme. The one they gaze upon on the cross, the pierced one, has truly given his life for the sins of the world: "God has been revealed in the pierced one, and this revelation of God continues in the flowing water and the spilled blood of baptism and eucharist as the worshiping community experiences the presence of the absent one" (Moloney 1998: 506). The testimony of the eyewitness—indeed this Gospel—mediates Jesus' presence.

Jesus' Burial 19:38-42

All four Gospels mention Joseph of Arimathea taking Jesus' body and burying it. Luke tells us that he is a member of the council, the Sanhedrin, "a good and righteous man, . . . who . . . had not agreed to their plan and action, . . . and he was waiting expectantly for the kingdom of God" (23:50-51). Matthew tells us he is "also a disciple of Jesus" (27:57). John tells us that he is a *secret disciple of Jesus!* Courage shines in his initiative. Pilate gives him permission to take Jesus' body.

In John alone, another courageous figure comes forward: Nicodemus, whom we met in chapters 3 and 7. He brings a lavish amount of spices, a *mixture of myrrh and aloes, weighing about a hundred* [Roman] *pounds* (*litra*), about seventy-five pounds in today's standard (19:39; Culpepper 1998: 238), worth about $12,000 in today's currency. We are not told that Nicodemus is a secret disciple, but his association with Joseph infers it. In this act Nicodemus expresses his love for Jesus. For John's Gospel this may also be a restoration scene for Nicodemus, akin to Peter's rehabilitation in chapter 21. Is the former "secret believer" now an open believer?

The two men wrap the body of Jesus *with the spices in linen clothes* in accord with Jewish burial custom. They then bury Jesus in a new unused tomb in the garden *in the place where he was crucified* (v. 41). The reason for burying Jesus close by is explained: *It was the Jewish day of Preparation.* An irony arises. The one accused of breaking the

Sabbath is now quickly buried as part of the *Preparation* for the Sabbath! Jesus is Lord of the Sabbath in both his life and his death.

THE TEXT IN BIBLICAL CONTEXT

Glorification[w]

Jesus' passion as the hour of glorification is peculiar to John's Gospel. The sheer number of times that some form of the word *glory* occurs in John, compared to the Synoptics, reveals its significance. The noun *glory* (*doxa*) occurs eight times in Matthew, three in Mark, thirteen in Luke, and eighteen times in John. In the Gospels the verb *glorify* (*doxazō*) occurs twenty-three times. It occurs thirty-nine times total in the remaining NT (but none in 1, 2, 3 John!) [*Glory, p. 516*] (count source, J. B. Smith: 92).

John interprets Jesus' passion as his hour of glorification. Glorification is linked with God's self-revelation in Jesus. Glory is shared among the Father, the Son, the Spirit, and those who believe in Jesus. The Father glorifies the Son (8:54); God is glorified in the Son (13:32); God's glorification of the Son enables the Son to glorify the Father (17:1); Jesus gives the glory to the believers that he has received from the Father (17:22).

Only in John is the Son of Man *lifted up*. Only John's Gospel does not use *risen* to describe Jesus' resurrection in chapter 20. In the Synoptics this verb (forms of *egeirō*) is used to announce Jesus' resurrection (Matt 28:6; Mark 16:6; Luke 24:6). The verb does occur in John 2:22 and 21:14 to describe Jesus' resurrection, promised and remembered. Jesus also speaks of resurrection in John 5:29 and claims it as his own identity in 11:25: *I am the resurrection and the life*. The expressions *raise up* and *live forever* occur as a promise to believers in 6:35-58.

Jesus' glorification echoes Isaiah's description of the suffering and glory of the servant: "See, my servant will act wisely; he will be raised and lifted up and highly exalted" (52:13 NIV). Here "lifted up" is an important link on the way between the "raised" of resurrection and being "exalted"—a link realized by the suffering servant and Jesus through suffering.

Jesus reveals God in his glorification on the cross. Jesus' self-sacrifice in his suffering reveals both his love of the Father and his love of *his own* (John 1:11). *But I do as the Father has commanded me, so that the world may know that I love the Father* (14:31). (See TBC for the prologue, "Glory Drama"; and TBC for John 12, "Cross as Glorification" [*Glory, p. 516*].)

John's Passion Account

About 90 percent of John's Gospel has no parallel in the Synoptic Gospels. Many of the 10 percent parallels occur in the passion narrative. The passion narrative is the longest continuous narrative in John with a basic similarity to those in the Synoptic Gospels (Jesus' arrest, Peter's denials, Judas's role, the trial, the crucifixion, and the burial). Other parallels are Jesus' cleansing the temple (John 2:13-22); Jesus' feeding the multitude, followed by Jesus walking on the sea (6:1-21); Mary's anointing of Jesus (12:1-8); and Jesus' final meal with his disciples (13:1-30). While there is similarity, many differences occur as well. The temple cleansing, put at the beginning of Jesus' ministry in John, is similar to Matthew's and Mark's accounts (Luke's account is quite short). Even in the passion parallels, John differs in significant details and has several distinctive features:

1. Judas brings the Roman cohort of soldiers, and Jesus advances for his arrest.

2. There is no kiss from Judas; Jesus identifies himself as *egō eimi* (*I AM*), shocking the soldiers.

3. No Jewish trial takes place at night. Since Jesus is crucified before Passover, the trial events take place in early morning. Jesus is taken to the former high priest, Annas, who sends him bound to Caiaphas, his son-in-law and *high priest that year*. Much of the trial is interchange with Pilate.

4. The unnamed *other disciple* appears in the account, is *known to the high priest*, and enters while Peter stays outside and denies knowing Jesus.

5. Jesus is mocked in the trial, but not when he is on the cross.

6. Pilate and Jesus carry on an extended dialogue on *kingship*, *kingdom*, and *truth*.

7. Pilate (or Jesus) sits on the *bēma* (judgment bench), with Pilate's declaring of Jesus, *Behold, the King of the Jews* (cf. 19:14, 19 KJV).

8. Jesus carries his own cross. In the Synoptics "Simon of Cyrene" carries it (Matt 27:32; Mark 15:21; Luke 23:26).

9. Pilate plays his power against *the Jews*, forcing them to disown the basic confession of their identity.

10. The beloved disciple is with Jesus at the cross!

11. Jesus' three "words" from the cross, words not found in the Synoptics.

12. The details surrounding Jesus' body on the cross (no legs broken; *blood and water* flowing from his pierced side).

13. Extensive citations of Scripture fulfilled (as also in Matt 26:31, 54, 56; 27:9, 46; Mark and Luke have several). John has more unique citations or allusions (e.g., 19:36, 37).

14. The appearance of Nicodemus to assist Joseph with the burial.

Viewing this comparison from the other direction, the Synoptics have a number of distinctive features that do *not* appear in John. Culpepper (1998: 228) lists eight, which I have modified and expanded to ten:

1. A longer Jewish trial, with content in Matthew and Mark. The chief priests' charge against Jesus is his saying, "I will destroy the temple . . . and in three days build another." This is followed by the chief priests' query whether Jesus is "the Christ, the Son of God" (Matt 26:63 RSV) or "the Blessed One" (Mark 14:61). In all three Gospels Jesus answers, "You will see the Son of Man seated at the right hand of the power of God" (with wording variations). Jesus' crime is then named: *blasphemy* (Matthew and Mark; inferred in Luke).

2. An extended scene of Jesus' struggle and agony in Gethsemane.

3. Jesus' being mocked while he is on the cross.

4. Jesus' cry of dereliction (likely quoting Ps 22:1).

5. The penitent thief (only in Luke 23:39-43).

6. Darkness at the crucifixion, even though John uses the symbolism of light and darkness.

7. The counting of the hours (except for *the sixth hour* in John 19:14 RSV).

8. The rending of the temple veil (esp. important in Mark 15:38).

9. The earthquake (only in Matt 27:51).

10. The opening of the tombs (Matt 27:52-53); yet Jesus opens Lazarus's tomb in John 11.

Mark, Matthew, and Luke also diverge significantly from each other. Most striking in Luke are Jesus' prayer from the cross "Father, forgive them; for they do not know what they are doing" (23:34) and what the centurion says when Jesus dies: "Truly this was a righteous man" (23:47 AT). Many other differences among the

Synoptics could be cited. Each Gospel writer bears testimony to distinctive strands of the oral traditions about Jesus. Each Gospel has its distinctive theology and purpose. Each contributes to the whole; none is of lesser importance.

In addition to the common outline of the passion events among all four Gospels, some of the sayings of Jesus or of his accusers in John appear also in one or more of the Synoptic Gospels, such as these:

1. Jesus' (military-type) command to one of his disciples (Peter is named only in John) who draws a sword against the arresting officers: *Put your sword back into its sheath* (John 18:11; cf. Matt 26:52). Jesus' follow-up sayings differ between the two accounts, with John emphasizing Jesus' divine purpose in coming into the world to *drink the cup the Father has given me*; and in Matthew, Jesus declares, "All who take the sword will perish by the sword," suggesting Jesus' followers should not bear the sword (Jesus had the power to call twelve legions of angels to defend himself but he did not; Matthew regards this also as Jesus' fulfillment of "the scriptures").

2. Pilate's question to Jesus in all four Gospels, *Are you the king of the Jews?* (John 18:33; Matt 27:11; Mark 15:2; Luke 23:3). In the three Synoptic Gospels, Jesus answers with the multilayered meaning of "You have said so." In John 18:33-38, Jesus' answer (unique to John) is fuller and leads to an extended interchange with Pilate: *Do you ask this on your own, or did others tell you about me?* The next round of conversation intrigues: Pilate grunts, *Am I a Jew? Your own . . . have handed you over to me* (RSV); and Jesus replies, *My kingship is not of this world* (RSV). This leads on to Pilate's encounter with truth.

3. The exchange of Barabbas for Jesus (John 18:39-40; Matt 27:15-18; Mark 15:6-11).

4. Jesus is mocked as soldiers adorn him with a purple (Matthew, scarlet; Luke, elegant) robe and a crown of thorns on his head. The people say, *Hail, King of the Jews!* (John 19:2-3; Matt 27:29; Mark 15:17-19; Luke 23:11). Luke does not mention the crown of thorns.

5. Pilate hands Jesus over to be crucified (John 19:16; Matt 27:26c; Mark 15:15d; Luke 23:25c).

6. The place of crucifixion: *The (Place of the) Skull* or Golgotha (Luke does not include *place of the*).

7. Pilate's inscription over the cross, "This is [Matthew adds "Jesus"] the King of the Jews" (Matt 27:37; Luke 23:38). Mark has just "The King of the Jews" (15:26), and John adds, *Jesus of Nazareth*.

8. Women watching as Jesus is crucified (John 19:25; Matt 27:55-56; Mark 15:40-41; Luke 23:49).

9. Joseph of Arimathea, a member of the council, comes, takes Jesus' body, and buries it (John 19:38-42, with Nicodemus assisting; Matt 27:57-61; Mark 15:42-47; Luke 23:50-56).

These events and sayings common to the four Gospels attest the political dimension of Jesus' death and show surprises in discipleship as well. Except for John's beloved disciple, all the men have fled the scene of crucifixion. In contrast, the women watch (John places them *near*; the Synoptics have them at "a distance"). A member of the council, whom John describes as a "secret disciple," buries Jesus. Discipleship comes from unexpected quarters!

Elements of John's passion narrative permeate other NT writings, notably the "slain Lamb" in Revelation, in which *Lamb* occurs twenty-eight times, although there *Lamb* is rooted in the martyr tradition (Johns 2003), with elements of the sacrificial as well (Swartley 2006: 333–34). Paul speaks of Christ as "our paschal lamb [who] has been sacrificed" (1 Cor 5:7).

THE TEXT IN THE LIFE OF THE CHURCH

The Meaning of Jesus' Death in John[w]

Each NT writer contributes a distinctive emphasis to the meaning of Jesus' death. John's contribution complements the larger NT testimony. To make the point, John does not speak of "justification" (Paul) or "sacrifice" (Hebrews), though John's image of *Lamb of God* has sacrificial overtones.

In John, Jesus' death occurs expressly as the fruit of the Father-Son union, in which Jesus as Son does the works of the Father, speaks the words of the Father, and obeys the Father's commands. The fruit of this relationship leads to Jesus giving his *flesh* [life] *for the life of the world* (6:51), extending *eternal life* to all who believe in Jesus and thus receive the Son and the Father, and promising believers victory over death and the devil. Jesus' death means light triumphs over darkness, life over death, and love over hate. Jesus' death is inseparably twinned with glory and the mutual glorification of the Father and the Son. Jesus reveals the will and purpose of the Father in his love for the world, seeking its salvation. Conversely, the failure to believe and accept that salvation is one's own judgment as one continues to walk in darkness.

Scriptures that complement John's emphasis on Jesus' death are Hebrews 2:9-11, 13b-15, 17; Philippians 2:5-11; and Ephesians 5:1-2.

The Politics of Jesus[w]

No other passage in the NT is more revelatory of Jesus' politics than John's passion narrative. The Gospel's portrait of Jesus is not *apolitical*, but *neopolitical*. It is a politics that transcends the political categories of the disciples, the Jews, and Pilate (representing Rome). Jesus' response to Peter's wielding a sword against Malchus in the garden (John 18:10) declares his nonviolent peacemaking stance: *Put your sword back into its sheath. Am I not to drink of the cup that the Father has given me?"* (18:11). Pilate, in his struggle to understand the Jewish charge that Jesus claims to be a king, cannot comprehend Jesus' words in 18:36, *My kingdom is not from this world.*

Unfortunately, John 18:28–19:16, the trial before Pilate, is listed only in Year C of the lectionary readings for Good Friday. In the believers church tradition, which has not historically followed the lectionary, this passage may be visited even less frequently. Powerful as the hearing of the Word is, hearing it only in this setting makes it an unlikely text for preaching. The result is that the church is shortchanged in the hearing and preaching of this important Scripture. Preachers must find creative ways to incorporate these texts into their preaching menu.

This text in particular, due to the difficult dilemma faced by Pilate, is an excellent choice to present in a character sketch. We can only wonder what Pilate really thought about Jesus. The text faces us with crucial questions: Who is Jesus? What does Jesus reveal about God? How does this affect our relationship to God? Getting into Pilate's skin can confront us with uncomfortable but important questions of our own duplicity.

John 20

The Risen Jesus Ignites Mission and New Community

PREVIEW

The story is told of a man resurrected from death in the Javanese Mennonite Church under the leadership of the gifted charisma of Soehadiweko Djojodihardjo (1918–88). Pak Djojo, as he was known by many endeared to him, united the three divided synods of the Javanese Christian Muria congregations. As the story passed into Mennonite circles in the 1970s and '80s, it raised a question: Was this a true resurrection, or was it a resuscitation? The debate usually came to a draw, sometimes with one questioning the other's degree of faith. Such stories have been reported by Christian healers through the ages. All such stories are miracles of *raisings*, but Jesus alone is resurrected to a new body that does not die. All miraculously raised people through the ages later die. Only Jesus is the exception; others must await resurrection to a new body on the last day!

Mary Magdalene is a key witness to the resurrected Jesus. Her story is unique to John. She comes to the tomb alone in the dark, in sorrow and love for the One who saved her and reoriented her life. When she announces to Peter and the beloved disciple that the stone is rolled away from the tomb, the two men race to the tomb. The beloved disciple arrives first; the two men's responses are true to character. As Mary lingers at the tomb, angels greet her in her deep grief. Then comes the dramatic recognition scene.

In John 20 the primary characters are Mary Magdalene, Peter, the beloved disciple, and Thomas, who climactically confesses, with adoration, *My Lord and my God!* With Mary's testimony, *I have seen the Lord*, these confessions voice the Christology that John wants his readers to believe and proclaim.

John's versions of the Pentecost and of the great commission provide distinctive perspectives in comparison to those of Luke (24:47-49; Acts 1:8; Acts 2) and Matthew (28:16-20). Jesus himself breathes the Spirit into the disciples, who are huddled together behind locked doors *for fear of the Jews* (20:19-23). Jesus first extends a peace blessing—twice: *Peace be with you* (vv. 19d, 21b)—and links it to his *sending* them as the Father has sent him (v. 21c). This Pentecost-like commission grants to the disciples authority to *forgive the sins of any* (v. 23). What they forgive is forgiven, and what they retain is retained (Matt 18:18; cf. 16:16-19 addressed to Peter). In John this authority and task is given to all the disciples present. Thomas is absent and needs special "convincing" a week later. When the disciples report to Thomas the surprise of Jesus' appearance to him, they repeat Mary Magdalene's confession: *We have seen the Lord* (v. 25b).

The chapter concludes with the Gospel's clear purpose statement (v. 31). This chapter, with its high drama, unravels the mystery of Jesus' signs and words in John and relieves the suspense generated by Jesus' figural teachings. The disciples begin to understand not only Jesus' plain words (16:29-33); they also see their meaning in Jesus' astounding actions. The "new commandment," given in 13:34, is now matched by a dawning new reality: Jesus is risen from the dead! He is alive! He is alive! His works, signs, and mission live on!

OUTLINE

The Shock of the Open Tomb, 20:1-10
Mary Magdalene's Encounter with Jesus, 20:11-18
Jesus Appears and Breathes the Holy Spirit on the Disciples, 20:19-23
Thomas Comes to True Belief, 20:24-29
Conclusion: Culmination and Purpose, 20:30-31

EXPLANATORY NOTES

John 20:1-18 is a narrative sandwich: Mary Magdalene sandwiches both Peter and the beloved disciple in that these verses begin and end with Mary (Hooker: 140). Verses 11-18 narrate her encounter with Jesus.

The Shock of the Open Tomb 20:1-10

20:1-2 Mary Magdalene and Her Response

Only John's Gospel tells us that Mary Magdalene goes alone to the tomb while it is yet dark. Why does she go? She does not take spices to anoint Jesus (Nicodemus has supplied enough of those). Most likely she is driven by love, a deep love for the best friend she ever had. Only in Luke (8:2) do we learn that Jesus has freed her from seven demons. In Jesus she has found the only life worth living. *Magdalene* probably indicates that she comes from the Galilean village of Magdala, by the Sea of Galilee, where today is a beautiful spread of flowering bougainvillea.

In John, Mary Magdalene is first introduced as one of the women who stood *near the cross* of Jesus (19:25). Named last there, she emerges first onto center stage, alone, in John 20. She is the first to discover the open tomb, surprised to see the massive stone rolled away. "The door of the tomb was heavy, wheel-shaped, anywhere from four to six feet tall, which was placed in a shallow trough and held upright by a short wall on either side of the tomb opening" (Burge 2000: 536). She assumes that someone took away Jesus' body.

Mary Magdalene apparently has no thoughts of Jesus' bursting forth from the tomb by God's resurrection power. Who would? As a result, she is dumbfounded. So she runs and reports the situation to the two leading disciples, Peter and the beloved disciple. She says to them, *They have taken the Lord out of the tomb, and we do not know where they have laid him.* The plural *we* is difficult to explain, but she may be speaking of other women who come to the tomb a bit later, but which John does not report. The Synoptic Gospels report the visit of several women who go together to the tomb at dawn, when the sun is just rising (Mark 16:1-2; Matt 28:1; Luke 24:1—Mark names three women; Matthew, two; and Luke's "they" refers to the women who have come with Jesus from Galilee, 23:55). John's narrative detail that Mary Magdalene goes to the tomb *while it was still dark* may echo Nicodemus's coming to Jesus *by night.* In either case the darkness contrasts to the light that shines in her ensuing encounter with Jesus.

Mary Magdalene is not Mary of Bethany (John 11–12; cf. Mark 14:3-9), or the sinful woman (Luke 7:36-50), and certainly not the woman taken in adultery (John 8:2-11). In John Mary Magdalene emerges as one who, next to the beloved disciple, best understands the heart of Jesus, and to whom Jesus grants special standing among his followers [Women, p. 536].

20:3-10 Peter's and the Beloved Disciple's Responses

The two awakened disciples—Peter and the beloved disciple—race to the tomb. True to form, the beloved disciple arrives first and Peter second (cf. 13:23). The beloved disciple allows Peter to enter first, as if moderating the event *[Beloved Disciple, p. 505]*. Peter enters and sees everything, *the linen wrappings and the cloth that had been on Jesus' head, not lying with the linen wrappings but rolled up in a place by itself* (an echo of Lazarus's unbinding, 11:44). Peter apparently does not comprehend the significance of what he sees. The beloved disciple, who has already seen what Peter sees by stooping down and looking in, then enters. Characteristically, *he saw and believed.* He is the first to believe Jesus' resurrection without seeing the risen Jesus, thus modeling the beatitude, *Blessed are those who have not seen and yet have come to believe* (v. 29b; Lindars 1972: 602).

The next statement of the narrator, *For as yet they did not understand the scripture, that he must rise from the dead*, might seem to contradict this, but not necessarily so. It may apply to Peter, but it also highlights the exceptional nature of the beloved disciple's faith. The two then go to their *homes* (cf. Luke 24:12d), where they were staying in Jerusalem. The beloved disciple knows what Peter does not know.

Mary Magdalene's Encounter with Jesus 20:11-18

20:11-13 Mary Lingers, Weeps, Is Greeted by Two Angels

Mary lingers by the tomb, weeping and bending over to look inside. As she does this, she sees *two angels in white*, sitting where the body of Jesus had been lying, one at the head and the other at the feet (v. 12). The angels speak to her and ask, *Woman, why are you weeping?* She explains, *They have taken away my Lord, and I do not know where they have laid him.* She likely has no thought of resurrection (only in 11:25 does Jesus link resurrection to himself, though *lifted up* in 3:14; 8:28; 12:34 signifies both cross and exaltation, which implies resurrection).

20:14-15 Mary and the "Gardener"

Now Mary suddenly sees a man and takes him to be the gardener—someone who might help solve her dilemma. He is indeed able to do so, but not as she anticipated. The man, *Jesus*, whom she does not recognize, asks her, *Woman, why are you weeping? Whom are you looking for?* Mary says to him, *Sir, if you have carried him away, tell me where you have laid him, and I will take him away.* Mary thinks she can carry away the body of Jesus? Thank God, she is not put to the test! Instead, another test confronts her, and she passes.

20:16-18 Mary Recognizes Jesus: From Turning to Announcing[w]

Gardener Jesus speaks the word that awakens Mary's spirit: *Mary*. Hearing her name and *turning*, she says to him, *Rabbouni!* (Aramaic for "my Teacher"). She tries to hold on to him, which he protests (v. 17), because, he says *I have not yet ascended to the Father*. Why does Jesus say this, since he has already been *lifted up* and glorified through the cross? Perhaps it is to seal for Mary the reality "from above." Rather than holding Jesus, she is to tell *my brothers . . . , "I am ascending to my Father and your Father, to my God and your God."*

Jesus does not leave Mary in the realm "from below." Hooker suggests that *ascending* shifts the mind *from below* to *from above*. What she is to tell the other disciples unites her to Jesus in his special relationship to God the Father, *my Father* and *your Father*. Her words mediate to the disciples this *above* reality: *ascending* to the Father. They are beckoned into this new reality, but they need their own encounter with the ascending and reappearing Jesus.

How should we understand Jesus' prohibition in verse 17? It may mean *Do not hold on to me* (NRSV, NIV), *Do not hold me* (RSV), or *Stop clinging to Me* (NASB); but less likely, *Touch me not* (KJV). The key point lies with *ascend to the Father*. Burge (2000: 556) explains that Mary needs this jolt to stop her from thinking that he will be as before the resurrection—in a normal human body. Schneiders proposes that the rationale in verse 17, *I have not yet ascended to the Father*, be taken as a rhetorical question (quite possible in Greek): *Am I as yet* [or *still*] *not ascended . . . ?* The answer then is "No, you are indeed ascended, that is, glorified." This, Schneiders says, "makes much better sense of the passage because Jesus' ascension to the Father, that is, his glorification, is precisely the reason Mary will now encounter him in the community of the church rather than in his physical or earthly body" (2003: 220). This explanation, however, seems to be jettisoned when Jesus invites Thomas to touch the nail prints in his hands and the scar in his side, which indicates the resurrected body retains those physical wounds.

Mary's movement in this narrative scene can be more fully appreciated by observing the sequence of three participles (in the

---

w   Where the superscript w occurs after headings, please see the commentary's online Web Supplement for additional material. Go to: http://www.heraldpress.com/bcbc/john.

Greek): *weeping* (v. 11, participle; v. 13, verb), *turning* (v. 14, verb; v. 16, participle), and *announcing* or *proclaiming* (v. 18; Schneiders 2003: 216–20). While *weeping*, she peers into the tomb through her tears and cannot see Jesus or the new spiritual horizon his absence might signify, even though she sees two angels, and their question to her might have tipped her off to a new spiritual breakthrough. Mary "is distraught, overcome with hopeless sorrow" (217). In stage two, "Conversion," two uses of *turn* occur. In the first use, with a finite verb in verse 14, she *turned around* or *back* (*eis ta opisō*), which means "toward the things that lie behind." She fails to see and recognize Jesus. She is turning around to see Jesus, but in not knowing him, she is still turning backward. However, with the participle in verse 16, Mary is *turning* to recognize Jesus. In the next and final stage, Mary is "the Easter apostle" (221). She is *announcing* or *proclaiming* the good news to the disciples (v. 18). The participle used here is significant. Considering the textual variant, it is either *angellousa* or *apangellousa* [*Textual Variants, p. 532*]. The latter infinite verb form is used twice in 1 John 1:2-3 with another similar word also in verse 5 (*anangellomen*) and is rightly translated *proclaim* (1 John 1:2-3 RSV, TNIV; *declare*, NRSV, though NRSV has *proclaim* in v. 5). The NRSV's *announced* in John 21:18a is better than the bland *told* in RSV and TNIV. Translators tend to fall short of conveying the full import of Mary's role. Here Mary is fulfilling the role of eyewitness, proclaiming what she has "touched," "seen," and "heard" (1 John 1:1-3 includes these three English verbs). She is the first Easter apostle and proclaims the good news of Jesus' resurrection! [*Women, p. 536*].

Jesus Appears and Breathes the Holy Spirit on the Disciples 20:19-23

20:19 Locked Doors, but Jesus Appears and Says, "Peace Be with You"

One would expect the transition from Jesus' appearance to Mary onward to Jesus' appearance to the disciples to be seamless. Mary has already proclaimed to them, *I have seen the Lord*. Why then are the disciples not filled with boldness, going out to proclaim that Jesus is alive, that Jesus has conquered death? Instead, they lock themselves in for the night to protect themselves from what the Jews might do to them. For those who plotted Jesus' death might now go after his followers (cf. 11:16; 12:10; Peter's denials to save his skin).

Their hideout strategy is suddenly foiled. Jesus appears in their midst, even though the doors are locked. He counters their fear with

Peace be with you, echoing 14:27 and 16:33. This peace greeting of the risen Jesus, recurring in v. 26, loops back to John's prologue, evoking Genesis 1. This allusion to God's peaceable creation is now manifest in the *Logos*-become-flesh, whose signs, words, and works culminate in his nonviolence in his trial and death (cf. Neville: 201–2).

20:20 Jesus Shows His Hands and Side

Jesus speaks the word of peace, then shows them *his hands and side*. While "we can hardly speculate how he has materialized among them" (Burge 2000: 558), Jesus' materiality cannot be doubted with his body before them. The disciples *were glad when they saw the Lord*. The persuasive impact is heightened precisely because "the showing of the pierced body . . . has no trace of apologetic" (Moloney 1998: 534). Even more astounding is that Jesus' "presence despite the locked doors is an indication of his victory over the limitation that human circumstances would impose" (530–31). Given these three factors—the human speech, Jesus' material appearance, and his presence despite the locked doors—the disciples must be confounded. But they express neither doubt nor dismay. Rather, they *rejoice*, thus fulfilling Jesus' promise in 15:11; 16:20-22 (three times; see Oyer), 24; as well as Jesus' prayer for them in 17:13. The labor pains are over; new life fills them with new hope.

20:21 Jesus Commissions His Disciples

Jesus reiterates his peace greeting, *Peace be with you*. This is a stunning "hello," given the circumstances, a reality that Jesus transmits to them so they can transmit it to others. This peace fulfills the OT royal messianic hope that anticipates the messiah's victory over evil. It is the eschatological victory, which in John finds its consummation in Jesus' triumphant word from the cross, *It is finished* (19:30). Immediately after this word of peace, Jesus commissions the disciples: *As the Father has sent me, so I send you* (20:21; cf. 3:16). This is John's great commission (cf. Matt 28:18-20).

Jesus joins his peace greeting to commissioning his disciples. Two earlier Gospel units (John 4 and chs. 14–16) show peace and mission crossing cultural and racial boundaries. The ripe fields in 4:35-38 include Samaritans. Their sequel portrays the splendid faith of the Roman official (4:46-54) in asking Jesus to heal his son. The man and his household become believers. Ethnic, religious, and national enmities are disarmed and transformed by Jesus, *the Savior of the world* (4:42), a rival claim to that of the Roman emperors. The sending of 20:21c, then, has the whole world as its horizon, with political implications.

Believers will be persecuted by the world's authorities (15:20; 16:33; 17:14-15; 18–19; 21:18-19). John links the sending to the bestowal of peace (also in 16:33). Believers bear the presence of Jesus and the Father into the world. In this peace mission, believers will be known by their love for one another (13:35) and by God's love for the world (3:16), even though the world does not receive the incarnate One whom God has sent (1:11; 5:40-44; 15:18-21). Empowered by Jesus' commission, this newly formed community of sent disciples embodies the salvation, peace, and reconciliation that the hating, persecuting world needs. Peacemaking through the transforming power of the risen Christ is mission.

20:22 Jesus Breathes the Holy Spirit[w]

Jesus' gift of the Holy Spirit to these distraught but now rejuvenated disciples enables the peace mission to begin. The manner in which the disciples receive the Spirit is unique, quite unlike the portrayal of Pentecost in Acts 2. Scholars intent on explaining why we have two differing Pentecost accounts have produced numerous explanations. Burge (2000: 559) cites three attempts to reconcile these accounts: in John the Holy Spirit gift is (1) a symbol, (2) a partial anointing, and (3) a genuine anointing. He prefers the last, saying, "That they would be empowered again, in a different way, on Pentecost does not eliminate the possibility that they were filled earlier" (561).

In John, Jesus himself breathes (out) the Holy Spirit for the disciples to receive: lit., *Jesus breathed and says to them,"Receive Holy Spirit"* (AT). The article is lacking in Greek and may have one of two implications. An anarthrous (no definite article, "the") construction is sometimes used to stress the quality of essence, as in John 1:1c, where God is anarthrous. Or the lack of the article may connote a more general, nonspecific meaning (e.g., Jehovah Witnesses hold that John 1:1c says "the Word was a god," whereas Christians more broadly hold to the "quality" meaning, "very God"—so also in Mark 15:39 for "Son"). In John 20:22 the lack of the article has the effect of stressing the unique quality of the Holy Spirit. Most English versions translate it as *breathed on them*, though these last two words do not appear. Even if we take the common view that the prefix *em* in the Greek *empysaō* means *breathed on* (BDAG, RSV, NRSV), *them* (*autois*) is the indirect object of *says*, though it could do double duty, the dative object also of *empysaō*. But if the LXX Genesis 2:7 is the prototype for this breathing (recall the prologue's echo of Gen), then *breathing into* would also be an appropriate translation, as suggested earlier.

The event in John is a *resurrection day* event. Jesus' breathing into them is birthing imagery (Gen 2:7) and evokes the call to new birth in John 3 (cf. 6:63) and the (eternal) *life theme* of the Gospel. The gift of the Spirit also fulfills Jesus' five-fold promise in his farewell speech. He promised to send the Paraclete to be with them after he departs. Now the Spirit remains with them after he suddenly leaves the room.

What Jesus says and does parallels Jesus' words in the farewell discourse (Talbert: 263):

As you have sent me, . . . I have sent them (17:18).	*As the Father has sent me, even so I send you* (20:21).
If I go, I will send [the Spirit] to you (16:7b).	*Receive the Holy Spirit* (20:22).

The coming of the Holy Spirit on Jesus at his baptism (1:31-34) empowered Jesus to do the works and speak the words of God. The same Spirit will now empower the disciples and unite them to the Son and the Father, fulfilling Jesus' prayer request to his Father, *As you, Father, are in me and I am in you, may they also be in us, so that the world may believe that you have sent me* (17:21). Hence the disciples participate in the mutuality of the Father and the Son, enabled by the Holy Spirit that has just been breathed into them, empowering them to carry on Jesus' mission.

The disciples receive Jesus' Spirit life and power, which now embodies the divine within each of them and enables them as Jesus' disciples to *love one another*. The word *Receive* [the] *Holy Spirit*, is potent, for they are to receive each other *as* they receive Jesus and God. The Holy Spirit is now embodied in each of them. This mutuality and reciprocity become the foundation of the new community of Jesus' followers.

This text harks back to John 7:37-39. Now that the Spirit is given, the living water flows from Jesus and the believers (echoing Ezekiel's vision in 47:1-12). Jesus' mission of giving living water (John 4:10, 14) and Jesus' anticipation of his disciples' carrying forward that mission now come to fruition. Hence they are *sent*, as the Father *sent* Jesus (Oyer: 349–53).

20:23 Jesus Grants Them Authority to Forgive Sins[w]

It is shocking to read of Jesus' bestowing upon the disciples the authority to forgive or retain sins. In John, Jesus is nowhere said to *forgive* sins (as he does, for instance, in Mark 2:5-10)! No one is explicitly *forgiven* their sins in John—not even the Samaritan woman or the woman taken in adultery! One might deduce the idea of forgiveness from 1:29 (*the Lamb of God who takes away the sins of the world*), or 8:11 (*neither do I condemn you*), but *forgiveness* as such is not stated. Since forgiveness of sins is a crucial component in the authority that Jesus gives his disciples we might infer that Jesus has been doing this for people all along in the Gospel, as the *sending* parallel in 20c might suggest, even though John never explicitly mentions forgiveness. Perhaps. This could explain why the Jews think he claims God's prerogative, as in Mark 2:7-10. But this rationale for the Jews' accusation in 5:18 (cf. 10:30-31) does not appear in John.

Even if Jesus did not need to forgive sins in his ministry, the disciples do in theirs. Jesus' disciples receive this divine prerogative to forgive sins only as the Holy Spirit is embodied in them. This authority is inherent to the Gospel's commission and proclamation, not to an office or personal charisma. O'Donovan explains it well: "This does not imply . . . that the apostles have the right to forgive and retain sins *arbitrarily*, but in accord with the preaching of the gospel, which invites all to repentance and forgiveness" (176). The authority is hinged also on Jesus' command to love one another and the Spirit's presence in the community (cf. O'Day 1995: 847–48).

The "retaining of sins" has caused perplexity, but "the mission of the Paraclete [is] to 'lay bare' the goodness and evil of the world (cf. 16:7-11)" (Moloney 1998: 536). Moreover, sin in John "is defined christologically, i.e., by a person's reaction to Jesus" (Oyer: 309). This makes the retention of sin a transparent act, and forgiveness and retention more clearly a function that defines Christian community. Oyer's proposed translation of *krateō*, NRSV's *retain*, as "prevail over," "control," or "overcome" transforms *retain* in verse 23 from a "pesky problem" (319) to "the bestowal of life [by] . . . the controlling of sin and/or the forces of evil" (330).

Although not developed further by Oyer, this suggests a potent paradigm: forgiveness applies to sins that are past and not correctible or capable of recompense, while "power to overcome" (*krateō*) applies to sins that still have a prospective element, where compensation or restitution is still possible (relevant in OT terms) or where there is ongoing damage or habitual sin. This indicates that forgiveness and *krateō* are no longer antitheses (as Oyer recognizes: 331). They are complementary in nature. They emphasize the dual achievement of forgiveness and victory over evil, which Jesus' victory on the cross fulsomely now confers to the community of faith.

In light of the history of the church, this power to forgive and to "retain" is too readily viewed as a power-based hierarchical relationship. Within the community of faith, truth and love are essential if forgiveness and overcoming (*krateō*) sin are to be truly reconciliatory and renewing through the Spirit's empowerment of the individual and community.

If this passage (and esp. v. 22, *he breathed . . . . Receive Holy Spirit*) is not the "climax to the entire Gospel" as Burge suggests (2000: 559), it is nevertheless the Gospel's supreme declaration on the primacy of the Holy Spirit, the Spirit counterpart to Thomas's supreme christological confession.

Thomas Comes to True Belief 20:24-29

20:24-25 Thomas Refuses to Believe without More Evidence

John introduces Thomas here as one *called the Twin* [Didymus], as in 11:16. Thomas missed the important event a week earlier, unless this story is from a later author (von Wahlde's "third edition," while the event a week earlier was from the "second edition"; 2010: 2.870–72), in which case the aporia (puzzling difficulty) does not mean that Thomas did not receive the inbreathed Spirit. This view is attractive but speculative. As the narrative sequence reads, the other disciples tell Thomas what Mary Magdalene has told them: *We have seen the Lord.* Thomas responds, *Unless I see the mark of the nails in his hands, and put my finger in the mark of the nails and my hand in his side, I will not believe.*

Thomas is not content to believe the witnesses—the other disciples, including Mary Magdalene. He needs his own encounter with the postresurrection Jesus, whom he cannot comprehend in terms different from how he has known Jesus before the devastating Friday crucifixion event. Earlier in the Gospel, in response to Mary's and Martha's request for Jesus to come and heal deathly ill Lazarus, Thomas was the first to support Jesus' decision to return to Judea, even though they knew the Jews were trying to kill Jesus. When Jesus finally says that Lazarus's sleeping is a euphemistic expression and that he really is dead, Thomas says, *Let us also go, that we may die with him* (11:16). His response expresses a resigned duty to follow Jesus. More positively, however, it advances the narrative plot in two ways. It leads to Jesus' greatest sign—raising Lazarus from the dead—and to Jesus' *lifted-up* glorification. His response then and now is realistic: he needs visible and tangible evidence.

20:26 Locked Doors, but Jesus Appears: "Peace Be with You"

This eerie scene of Jesus' suddenly appearing recurs a week later (RSV, *Eight days later*—inclusive Sunday to Sunday count) when the disciples are gathered together and Thomas is with them. It is déjà vu for the ten, but not for Thomas. The *doors are shut*, but Jesus suddenly comes and stands in their midst. Again he says, *Peace be with you.*

20:27-28 Thomas Becomes a True Believer

Jesus addresses Thomas directly, meeting him on the very terms he stated a week earlier: *Put your finger here and see my hands. Reach out your hand and put it in my side. Jesus continues: Do not doubt but believe.* At least three portraits of Thomas have emerged among interpreters. The first is the common one, designated by the epithet "doubting Thomas." A second links this doubt to his obstinate will and characterizes him as "stubborn" in his demand for material, physical proof. A third regards Thomas as genuine and sincere in his quest to come to belief.

None of these three is totally off the mark. The second one is advanced by Moloney and has merit, especially in light of verse 29. Thomas's strong statement in verse 25 may support this view. Jesus' command to Thomas is sharp, sparring with Thomas's strong language in verse 25: *Put* [lit., "throw," *ballō*] *your finger here ... put* [your hand] *into my side* (v. 27). This may connote rebuke of Thomas's obstinacy. Jesus' further command has perhaps an even sharper edge: *Do not be an unbeliever but a believer* (v. 27c, ET by Moloney 1998: 539n27). Or it could be translated, *Do not be faithless, but believing* (RSV). None of the Greek words for "doubt" occur in this text, a fact that calls the first interpretation into question.

The Greek in verse 27c is *apistos, unbelieving*; it is not *aporeō* (to be in doubt), *diakrinō* (to be uncertain), *diaporeō* (to be perplexed), or *distazō* (to waver or hesitate in doubt). Jesus confronts his lack of faith or slowness to believe. In keeping with the Gospel's overall intent, the text highlights *witness* and *testimony* as the crucial medium to elicit faith—and this is likely why this story segues into the Gospel's purpose statement. The story demonstrates the struggle to *believe* the *witnesses*, but also promptly overcomes that sin-prone weakness. Immediately Thomas bursts out with the crowning christological and confessional gem of the Gospel, declaring, *My Lord and my God!* (v. 28). If obstinacy was his problem (Moloney), his darkness has suddenly become light. Now he is a willing follower of Jesus, *knowing* whom he follows.

The third reading of the text sees Thomas as typical of how any seeking human would respond. O'Day takes this stance in her commentary (1995: 849–50; cf. also Johns and Miller). Thomas asks for evidence, genuinely searching to know Jesus and the meaning of his teaching, just as he did in 14:5, when Jesus spoke about going away to prepare a place for them: *Thomas said to him, "Lord, we do not know where you are going. How can we know the way?"* Jesus answers him memorably: *I am the way, and the truth, and the life. No one comes to the Father except through me. If you know me, you will know my Father also. From now on you do know him and have seen him.* Jesus then replies to Philip's query, *Lord, show us the Father, and we will be satisfied* (14:8): *Whoever has seen me has seen the Father* (14:9c). As O'Day states, "It is not touching Jesus that leads Thomas to this confession of faith, but Jesus' gracious offer of himself." O'Day disputes commentators who say that Jesus is shaming Thomas by his bold offer, reading his command to touch him as slightly sarcastic. O'Day asks, "Why would a character whom Jesus has shamed be given the most powerful confession in the Gospel?" (1995: 850). She rightly sees verse 27 as "another demonstration of the truth of 1:16: 'From his fullness we have all received, grace upon grace'" (850).

Whichever view one takes of Thomas, we must acknowledge that Thomas's response to Jesus is the "supreme christological pronouncement of the Fourth Gospel" (R. Brown 1970: 1047). As von Wahlde puts it, "Here we find one of the clearest and most powerful confessions of the divinity of Jesus in the entire NT: My Lord and my God!" (2010: 2.871). It complements as bookend what the Gospel says first in 1:1: *The Word was God.* Brown also rightly sees the political ramifications and the OT rootage of this confession. Emperor Domitian, during whose reign this Gospel was likely written, claimed the title *Dominus et Deus noster* (Latin for "our Lord and God"). *Lord* (*kyrios*) is the standard translation of the sacred name in the Septuagint. "Thomas combines the two titles used of God in the LXX: 'Lord' (used for the Hebrew *YHWH*) and 'God' (*used for Elohim . . .*), and then applies them to Jesus" (von Wahlde 2010: 2.868).

The potency of Thomas's confession lies in the comprehensive nature of the declaration, for it encompasses belief and obedience, worldview and relationship. It prefigures what Thomas's Lord will do with him as apostolic witness. The Mar Thoma Church of Syria and India knows this well, for they hold Thomas as their founding apostle. Thomas's supreme faith declaration is the foundation of true belief and discipleship. Thomas's special role in the Gospel lies at the heart of Charlesworth's thesis (1995) that Thomas is the beloved disciple, a view not widely held *[Beloved Disciple, p. 505]*.

Jesus meets Thomas where he is. This encourages us in our quest toward belief. Jesus comes, even on our terms, to reveal himself and the God he incarnates.

20:29 Jesus Acknowledges True Belief

Thomas's confession provides the occasion for Jesus' final word in this dramatic narrative. Jesus says to him, *Have you believed because you have seen me? Blessed are those who have not seen and yet have come to believe.* The first line of Jesus' declaration may be either a question (RSV, NRSV) or a declaration (NIV: *Because you have seen me, you have believed*). The bigger question is whether it slightly scolds. Much depends on what one provides in the reading of it! In neither case does Jesus undercut the validity and significance of the confession. Rather, his encounter with Thomas "prepares for the time beyond that of the eyewitnesses by commending belief that takes place without seeing" (von Wahlde 2010: 2.870). Those who hear and read this Gospel are beckoned to believe on the basis of its witness. The text is a postapostolic mission witness.

Some use this text—along with 2:23-25; 4:48; 6:26-27; 20:25, 27— to argue that signs are viewed negatively in John. But Johns and Miller (1994) persuasively counter this view. Jesus rebukes Thomas not because he has insisted on eyewitness evidence, but because he has failed to believe in the eyewitness evidence of those who *have seen* Jesus *[Belief, p. 504] [Signs, p. 529]*. Furthermore, since the second-century *Gospel of Thomas* was used much by gnostics (Pagels 1989; 2003) who denied Jesus' physicality and death, this climactic story in John is intended as a polemic against Gnosticism. In this respect, it uses the physical wounds in the hand and the scar in the side to argue, as 1 John does (cf. McDermond), that Thomas's faith is linked to the crucified Christ.

Verse 29 anticipates the culmination in verse 31. The story does not end with the (evidence of the) resurrection of Jesus; it begins there, with new life in the Spirit that enables *us* also to say to Jesus, *My Lord and my God!* Indeed, Thomas may be the first recorded example of the Holy Spirit's exercise of prevenient grace, which echoes John 1:16! John 20:29 is a comfort to believers of all ages; it "means . . . there are no second-class Christians *chronologically*" (R. Brown 1984: 109). It is a beatitude: *Blessed are those who have not seen and yet have come to believe.* Jesus' word segues to second- and subsequent-generation believers who could not see Jesus as the apostles saw him (Minear 1983). In this respect it links chapter 20 to 21, which provides models of apostolic faith that serve as paradigms for future generations—so they may come to saving faith in Jesus Christ and receive eternal life now in this world and in the age to come (cf. 3:16; 12:25; 17:2-3).

Conclusion: Culmination and Purpose 20:30-31

The signs support belief, leading to life in Jesus' name. A tiny textual variant—the presence or absence of an *s*—in this purpose statement has generated much discussion. The manuscript evidence is divided between the present tense (*pisteuēte*) and past (aorist) tense (*pisteusēte*) for the word *believe*. If the present tense is original—and there is strong evidence for this—then the Gospel's purpose is to assist believers to *continue to believe*, strengthening and deepening the faith of believers who are facing external pressure. If the aorist tense is preferred (many ETs have *may believe*, reflecting the ambiguity of the Greek), the text emphasizes the Gospel's missional posture and purpose. Strong early manuscripts have the present tense (*pisteuēte*), but a wider family and greater number (some early) support the aorist (*pisteusēte*) [Textual Variants, p. 532]. Because this reading has manuscript support from a wide geographical range in the early church, it is clear that most of the early church used the Gospel evangelistically, but certainly also for nurturing and spiritual formation.

The pervasive use of *sending* language in the Gospel provides strong internal evidence that John's Gospel is evangelistic in purpose. More than fifty forms of *apostellō* (*send*) appear in the Gospel. In her dissertation on John 20:19-23, Oyer tabulates the uses of the two Greek words for *send* (*apostellō* and *pempō*) in John (446; cf. Swartley 2006a: 322–23). The Father's love in sending Jesus reveals God's purpose: to save the world from its blindness and unbelief (sin, in John 9:41). Jesus' sending his disciples extends his work as the sent One. "Having been sent" is the empowering muscle of mission, based in the prior action of the Father and the Son. Given the persecution suffered by the believing Johannine community, the Gospel's function of enabling believers to continue believing is certainly also in view.

THE TEXT IN BIBLICAL CONTEXT

Peace and Mission in John and the NT: John 20:19-23 and John 4:1-42

In John's Gospel

These texts contain a strong call to mission: *As the Father has sent me, so I send you* (20:21c). Jesus' *Peace be with you* (v. 21b) prefaces this commission. Earlier Jesus says the same in his greeting when he suddenly appears to his fearful disciples (v. 19d). Jesus' mission charge stands under the umbrella of his peace greeting.

Verbal connections between 20:21 and 4:38 are striking. After his encounter with the Samaritan woman, Jesus speaks of his vocational food: calling the disciples to see *how the fields are ripe for harvesting* (4:35d). Jesus says, *I sent you to reap that for which you did not labor* (v. 38a).

Expositions of John 4 regularly slight the importance of what Jesus does in Samaria teaching not only *mission* but also *peacemaking*. The disciples and the woman are interchanged in the narrative. When the disciples leave to buy bread, Jesus meets and talks with the woman. When the disciples return, the woman takes her water jar and goes back to the city. Jesus then presents a minidiscourse to his disciples on mission. Peacemaking and mission are indeed the focal emphases of John 4, a precursor to Jesus' sending commission in John 20, which is linked to *Peace be with you*. In light of John 3:16 and 20:31, we cannot maintain, as some do, that John's Gospel represents a community turned in on itself, concerned only for intra-community welfare.

That Jesus joins the peace greeting to the commission in John 20 is significant in light of John 4. Together these texts portray the peace mission of John's Gospel, leaping cultural and racial boundaries. The ripe fields (4:38) include Samaritans and a Roman official and his son. As *the Savior of the world*, Jesus "kills" ethnic, religious, and national enmities (Eph 2:16b). The sending of John 20:21c has the whole world as its horizon.

We noted that in John 14 and 16 Jesus connects his peace text with the Spirit in the farewell discourse. We noted also the parallels to these motifs in 20:19-22 (Talbert: 254). Clearly the gift of peace, which Jesus gives, is linked integrally to Jesus' sending mandate in this first crucial postresurrection encounter with his disciples.

The Holy Spirit (advocate, comforter, empowerer) is a key player in this postresurrection text. In 20:22 Jesus *breathes* the Spirit on or into his disciples to empower them for the sending task. The term *breathe* (*emphysaō*) appears only here in the NT. It harks back to the

Septuagint of Genesis 2:7, where the Lord God breathed into the dust-formed body the spirit-breath that made the human a "living soul." In both Genesis 2:7 and John 20:22, God's/Jesus' breath is the source of life, peace (*shalom* and *eirēnē*), and mission now manifest in Jesus' gift of the Spirit, a "new creation" (cf. 2 Cor 5:17)!

While Matthew 28:19-20 is most frequently quoted to authorize the church in its worldwide mission, John 20:21-23 explicitly grounds the disciples' mission in Jesus' own mission. John Stott sees it as the "most neglected" but "crucial form of the Commission" in that it makes Jesus' mission the model for ours: "Our understanding of the church's mission must be deduced from our understanding of the Son's" (23).

Although Jesus' mission was certainly unique in some ways, *his* mission is the foundation of the *church's* mission. As Jesus brought salvation to the Samaritans and offered life to all who would receive it, so our mission today is the same. The authority bestowed upon the disciples in this "peace-breath" word enables them to release people from sin's bondage, grant them freedom, and live *abundantly* (10:10b).

Jesus' peace, Spirit-breath, and sending charge enables his disciples to embody the Father's love and salvation for the world. The Spirit-led bearers of this unique peace-mission will be known by their love for one another (13:35) and their love that incarnates God's love for the world (3:16), even though the world does not receive those whom God has sent (1:11; 5:40-44; 15:18-21). In the power of the Spirit, Jesus' *sending* is peacemaking—through the transforming power of Jesus as Messiah, Savior of the world.

Wider NT Witness

To what extent is this feature of the mission-commission normative? Does the mission charge really stand under the umbrella of the peace greeting? Luke 10 bears eloquent testimony to this in that the peace greeting of the seventy initiates and extends the gospel of the kingdom of God. The seventy go out on their gospel mission with the greeting "Peace to this house" (10:5). The result is that the demons lose their power; Jesus sees Satan falling from heaven like lightning as the disciples extend Jesus' mission (10:17-18).

Paul, the stellar evangelist who took the gospel to the West, affirms the same (Acts 26:17-18). Paul uses the unique title "God of Peace," as shown elsewhere (e.g., Rom 15:33; Swartley 2006: 208–16). At the center of his gospel is salvation, forgiveness of sins, peacemaking, and reconciliation through Jesus Christ (Swartley 2006a: 191–205; see also Yoder Neufeld's rich essay, "For He Is Our Peace," 2003: 215–33).

In Jesus' memorable beatitude in Matthew 5:9, Jesus exclaims, "Blessed are the peacemakers," and in 5:43-48, "Love your enemies." Peace and peacemaking are the identity markers of God's children (Swartley 2006: 56–58). In Matthew's great commission, Jesus authorizes his disciples to "make disciples of all nations, baptizing them in the name of the Father and of the Son and of the Holy Spirit, and teaching them to obey everything that I have commanded you" (28:19-20). Mark calls the disciples to renounce rivalry (9:33-37; 10:35-41) and learn to live at peace with one another (9:50d; 10:42-45). In James, 1 Peter, and Hebrews, peace is a cardinal feature of the gospel (Swartley 2006a: 254–75).

The Resurrection

Even though John 20 does not use the term *resurrection*, the narrator in his distinctive style makes resurrection the point of the narrative in a subtle and gradual unfolding of its reality. On the one hand, the tomb is empty (vv. 2-11). Then Mary Magdalene encounters two angels sitting in the tomb, but not Jesus. On the other hand, the risen Jesus appears three times: to Mary Magdalene, to the gathered disciples that same evening, and a week later to the disciples, including Thomas. The risen Jesus greets the disciples three times: *Peace be with you* (vv. 19, 21, 26). He also commissions them to apostolic mission, bestows the Holy Spirit on them, and gives them authority to forgive or retain sins. Mary Magdalene, the disciples, and Thomas encounter a visible postresurrection Jesus.

Each of the other three Gospels climaxes with Jesus' resurrection: Mark 16:1-8; Matthew 28:1-20; Luke 24:1-52. Each account is longer than the one mentioned earlier. Details vary. Each fascinates in its distinctive emphasis. Mark ends his narrative with expecting a meeting of Jesus and the disciples in Galilee, connoting commission to mission and/or parousia. The women, filled with fear, run from the tomb and tell no one what Jesus has told them to tell. (Their action and the implications of this way of ending the Gospel have elicited various interpretations!) Matthew has soldiers guarding the tomb to prevent Christian proclamation; later Jesus appears to his disciples on a mountain to authorize eternal proclamation of the good news to the whole world, with specific mission instructions.

Only Luke reports Peter's solo trip to the tomb and the great Emmaus walk, when the visible/invisible Jesus joins the two travelers and discloses his identity in the breaking of the bread. In Luke, Jesus explicates to them what the Scripture foretells about the Messiah—indeed, about himself. Jesus promises the coming of the

Holy Spirit and leaves the disciples *in Jerusalem* (unlike Mark and
Matthew), filled "with great joy, and they were continually in the
temple [of all places!] blessing God." In these experiences the disciples encounter epiphanies: a young man in the tomb in Mark,
heralding good news; an angel in the tomb in Matthew, announcing
the good news; two men in the tomb in Luke, saying the same; and
two angels greeting the weeping Mary Magdalene in John.

Amid, beneath, and above all the varied details of these four witnesses to the resurrected Jesus is consistently the proclamation of
good news—a good news that opens the door to prepare and equip
the disciples for ongoing gospel mission. Hope, faith, and Holy Spirit
(in all except Mark) punctuate these narratives. Although the resurrection culminates the story of Jesus' earthly ministry, it also opens
the door to the ongoing ministry of Jesus' first followers. It begins
what has continued for two thousand years: proclaiming the good
news of God's salvation through Jesus Christ to all the peoples of the
earth.

Jesus' resurrection is at the heart of the NT witness in texts such
as these:

- Peter's and Paul's sermons in Acts and in their testimony
  before authorities (2:32; 3:15; 4:10; 5:30; 13:30-38; 24:20-21).

- First Peter 1:3: "He [the God and Father of our Lord Jesus
  Christ] by his great mercy has given us a new birth into a
  living hope through the resurrection of Jesus Christ from the
  dead."

- First Corinthians 15: The gospel of Christ's death and resurrection.

- The parallel between Jesus Christ's resurrection and our resurrected living (Col 3:1-4).

- The baptismal exhortation in Romans 6:1-11 (cf. Col 2:13).

- The many NT acclamations of Christ's victory over the principalities and powers (e.g., Col 2:10, 15; Eph 1:19-32; Rom
  8:35-39; see Swartley 2006a: 229, the "normative" column
  and 230–45).

- The heartbeat of the saints' and the martyrs' triumph in
  Revelation (e.g., 5:6-10; Swartley 2006a: 332–55).

The OT has some precursors: Job 19:25-27; Psalms 16:11; 17:15;
Ezekiel 37; Daniel 12:1-3 (see also the TBC entry on ch. 11; and from
a Jewish point of view, Levenson 2006).

THE TEXT IN THE LIFE OF THE CHURCH

Hope, Joy, Faith, Peace, and Power

John 20 moves from despair to bewilderment to hope. Mary's sorrowful walk to the tomb shifts to bewilderment when she sees the tomb empty: Jesus' body is gone, but the burial wrappings are still there. She is overwhelmed with grief until Jesus reveals himself, calling her by name. Jesus, whom she had thought dead, is alive! But now he speaks of ascending to his Father. Mary Magdalene, eager to do Jesus' command, runs to the disciples (Jesus' *brothers*) to tell the good news: *I have seen the Lord!* Filled with hope and joy, she knows Jesus' resurrection signifies that he is indeed Messiah and Lord.

Peter and the beloved disciple similarly journey from despair to bewilderment, then to hope and joy. The beloved disciple is the first to see and believe, while Peter's response in chapter 20 is mute. When Jesus suddenly appears in their midst and greets the gathered disciples with *Peace be with you*, their mood shifts from fear to foreboding: What is going on? Their emotions are surely mixed, but the narrator tells us little about that. Instead, Jesus takes charge. Extending his peace greeting a second time to his disciples, he *sends* them as the Father *has sent* him. He breathes the Holy Spirit on and into them to guide and empower them for their mission. They move to hope, task, and empowerment.

Jesus' visible appearance to them as they are huddled together in the upper room enables their breakthrough to faith and joy. Realism strikes with Jesus' commission to continue the task the Father has sent Jesus into the world to do. Then Jesus' gift of the Holy Spirit recalls Jesus' teachings on the Paraclete. They now realize that the Holy Spirit continues Jesus' presence with them. He will guide and empower them for their mission to present the good news to all people. They become the bearers of the good news of peace, joy, faith, and hope. The response of people to this gospel determines whether their sins are forgiven or retained.

As the final character in this resurrection drama, Thomas journeys from despair and doubt to faith. He wants concrete evidence (cf. Jesus' "shroud" for enthusiasts today) that the good news that has transformed Mary Magdalene and the other gathered disciples on that Easter Sunday is not some phantom. When he sees the risen Jesus appear to the gathered disciples a week later and sees the wounded hands and side, he is jolted to faith. He does not need to touch Jesus. He simply exclaims, *My Lord and my God!* Thomas voices what many of us need in our modern and postmodern world. We harbor doubts that Thomas openly expresses. When Jesus in unex-pected ways encounters us in a dream, a vision, or a caring friend, our doubts dissolve as we grasp anew the heart of Christian faith: that Jesus is the Lord, God among us, and our faith leads to adora-tion, *my* Lord and *my* God!

Resurrection: Focal Lens for Christian Ethics

This topic may appear "out of order" in a commentary on John 20, since John has little to say about the "kingdom of God," a moral motif that permeates the Synoptic Gospels. John H. Yoder's genial *The Politics of Jesus* threw a cable across the chasm that had sepa-rated Christian ethics from NT ethics, specifically the teachings of Jesus in the Gospels (1994: 3). This is not the place to evaluate his spanning the chasm (see Swartley 2006a: 133–40; 2007: 116–25). But since the Gospel of John is often overlooked in such endeavors, its resurrection account is relevant, as Oliver O'Donovan suggests in his stimulating book *Resurrection and Moral Order*. While Yoder focuses mostly on the Gospels' core teaching on the cross, O'Donovan identifies the resurrection as the link that connects Jesus' teach-ings, life, and death with Christian ethics. The Holy Spirit, too, aids the interfacing between Jesus and ethics.

John contributes significantly to the interconnectedness of all these aspects of Jesus' mission: Jesus' life and teachings, his death, his resurrection, and his bestowal of the Holy Spirit—all fit together in one narrative flow. The liturgical year, however, follows Luke: Easter, then seven weeks later, Pentecost. John joins Jesus' resurrec-tion with Jesus' bestowal of the Spirit on Easter Sunday under the canopy of *Peace be with you*. The unity between John 20 and 21, with Jesus' questions to Peter, *Do you love me?* indicates that love is foun-dational to ethical reflection and moral action. In John, *agapē* (self-giving love) is not generic love that stamps approval on whatever one thinks is good for me or us, including a "just war." For that reason Hays refuses love as a focal image for moral decision (1996: 200–203). But when love is understood as the model that Jesus and the beloved disciple exemplify in John—as defined in John 12:24-26; 13:1-17, 31-35; 15:12-17, and much of 1 John, especially 3:11-24 (McDermond 2011: 273–74)—then love is a reliable guide to Christian ethics.

Not only are peace and self-giving love hallmarks in John's res-urrection narrative; profound christological confession also laces the narrative. This is crucial to the lens through which we consider Christian ethics. To see Jesus as the image of the moral character of

God is profoundly important in connecting Jesus and Christian ethics. Thus there can be no bifurcation between ethics that appeals to God as Creator, and ethics that appeal to Jesus' moral vision of the reign of God. The latter cannot be neutralized or refused under the warrant of the former, a move that Yoder criticizes. O'Donovan (20–21) likewise critiques this move in the Roman Catholic debates between advocates of a "faith ethic" and those who regard "autonomous morality" as a guiding norm for those of goodwill. O'Donovan (22–25) gives prominent place to the Holy Spirit as the guarantor of freedom and the One who leads us to follow in Jesus' step, for the Spirit witnesses to Jesus (throughout John).

Hays's three focal images of community, cross, and new creation provide criteria to adjudicate among moral options. These points and the three above—peace, love, and Holy Spirit—are all hinged to Jesus' resurrection. In them we have a foundation to chart the path from the NT to Christian ethics today. In John 20 the bestowal of the Holy Spirit forms and defines the new community. The risen Jesus, *ever bearing the marks of the cross*, leads Thomas to belief. The new creation restores God's Genesis creation (O'Donovan) and heralds a new creation, anchored in the love of Jesus and the beloved disciple's model of love *[Beloved Disciple, p. 505]*. The work of the Holy Spirit is described richly in Jesus' farewell discourse to his disciples *in ethical, moral terms* (16:8-17).

Numerous NT texts orient Christian ethics to Jesus' resurrection and the Holy Spirit. Colossians 3:1-4 anchors Christian living in Jesus' resurrection. Sinful practices are "put off," and one is to be clothed with love and peace (vv. 14-15, 17). Colossians explicitly identifies resurrection as the bridge between Jesus and the moral life. Other texts make resurrection central to the new life, the new creation (see 1 Pet 1:3; cf. Titus 3:4-7).

Many passages link resurrection to the new life (Rom 6:1-14; Phil 3:10-14; Eph 1:17-23; 2:4-10). The Holy Spirit empowers believers to live this new moral vision (Rom 8:1-17; Eph 1:12-14). The Anabaptists assumed these links. In *The Spiritual Resurrection*, Menno regards "the first resurrection" as the new birth (Menno: 51–62) that bears the fruit of a "genuine renewed nature and disposition [that] has put on Christ Jesus" (58). His work on the *New Birth* (89–102) continues the theme: "In baptism they bury their sins in the Lord's death and rise with Him to a new life. . . . They put on Christ and manifest His spirit, nature, and power in all their conduct" (93). Riedemann speaks similarly: "Participation in the new creation included involvement in concrete structures and vocations" (Riedemann, cited from Finger

2004: 528). A Marpeck quotation cited by Neal Blough (1994) regards the resurrection, Holy Spirit, and new birth as all part of one whole, producing the moral life that reflects Jesus Christ.

John 20 connects resurrection and bearing the marks of the cross with Jesus' bestowal of the Holy Spirit. All this occurs in the context of Christ's gift of peace and his making mutual love the identity marker of faithful discipleship. This anchors the Christian moral life in cross and resurrection. Thus the gospel empowers mission!

Jürgen Moltmann reflects on his theological journey in his first and last major publications, *Theology of Hope* (1967) and *The Source of Life: The Holy Spirit and the Theology of Life* (1997). His most recent book, *Ethics of Hope* (2012) in parts 4 and 5, addresses the very issues inherent in John 20:19-22. In his 1967 presentations at Duke University, he was grilled on whether he believed in the resurrection as an objective event that occurred historically or whether he saw it as a subjective belief dependent upon faith—a polarity then popular in theological scholarship (cf. van Harvey et al.). Many years later I can still hear his steady response to his persistent questioners: "I believe in the resurrection, that Jesus Christ has been resurrected and that is our faith's foundation" (my paraphrase). Moltmann would not budge to one side or the other. For him and for me, Jesus' cross and resurrection are the foundation for Christian theology and ethics. John fuses Jesus' resurrection with the gift of the Holy Spirit, whose indwelling presence and power (authority to forgive or retain sins) mediates Jesus to believers in every age across the globe.

Practice Resurrection, the title of Eugene Peterson's 2010 book, beckons us to grow into spiritual maturity through the power of Christ's resurrection working in us through the Holy Spirit. Jesus died to give us life. In his risen life we find our own. Popular prescriptions for spirituality do not suffice, and may even obstruct spiritual growth. Though Peterson's "conversation" is based on Ephesians, his diagnoses of what we need to do and how we need to do it flow out from resurrection ethics. Borrowing from Wendell Berry, he contends, "We live our lives in the practice of what we do not originate and cannot anticipate." Resurrection and the Holy Spirit enable us.

John 21

New Horizons and Destinies

PREVIEW

"Wow, that preacher surely missed a good ending five minutes before stopping!" Why does John not end with the purpose statement in 20:30-31? What more do we need? If this commentary had appeared in the 1980s, it may have said just that about John's Gospel. When Gail O'Day wrote her outstanding commentary on John for the *New Interpreter's Bible* in 1995, she reported that except for Hoskyns (550), the major commentators agree that chapter 21 is a later addition (O'Day 1995: 854). After all, isn't 20:28-29 an obvious climax and then 20:30-31 an obvious summary for all that John wants to say? Why preach longer when the sermon has already come to a satisfying end?

In 1983 Paul Minear wrote, "The jury of modern NT scholars has agreed with unparalleled unanimity on one issue in Johannine research: chapter 21 is not an integral part of the original gospel but was composed separately and probably by a redactor" (85). Using narrative analysis in her study of John, O'Day questions this consensus—and rightly so. Since the early 1990s the consensus has shifted to affirm John 21 as an integral part of the Gospel. Major themes developed throughout the narrative continue into chapter 21. Most significant, Peter and the beloved disciple are portrayed in two more scenes, where their relationship is confirmed and clarified. Chapter 21 is not a dispensable addition, as earlier thought. Rather, it is "meaningful and coherent in the Gospel narrative as it presently stands" (Segovia 1991: 67).

Chapter 21 consists of two main parts: verses 1-14 treat a failed fishing venture on the Sea of Tiberias (Galilee) that is rescued by a stranger on the shore who knows a lot about fishing and makes tasty fish-and-bread breakfasts. The second part, verses 15-23, is located on the seashore by a charcoal fire and presents one last depiction of Jesus in a question-and-answer session with Peter—to save his life as Jesus' disciple. The interchange is both gut-wrenching and soul-redeeming. Under the spotlight is the loyalty test that Peter earlier thought he had aced (13:36-38) but had actually flunked (18:15-18, 25-27)—just when Jesus needed him most.

If ever we need a story of God's graciousness and Jesus' forgiving love, we find it in chapter 21. Without it, Peter would remain in darkness, and the beloved disciple would remain a shadowy figure. But with chapter 21 the sun bursts brightly on the horizon, lighting these two main characters in the discipling and missional task implied in Thomas's confession and stated in the Gospel's purpose (20:28, 31).

The two main parts of John 21 are supplemented with two verses (24-25) that speak to the origin of the whole Gospel. What the Gospel has done many times, it does one final time: it links knowledge of the truth with authorization based on evidence. These final verses attest to the veracity of the author's witness to the words and deeds of Jesus while acknowledging that the Gospel's narration is necessarily selective.

OUTLINE

Time, Location, and Characters of the Story, 21:1-3
The Mysterious Miracle of a Great Catch of Fish, 21:4-14
Jesus Restores and Commissions Simon Peter, 21:15-19
Jesus and the Beloved Disciple, 21:20-23
The Beloved Disciple's Testimony, with Selectivity, 21:24-25

EXPLANATORY NOTES

John 21:1-14 lends itself to the following chiastic structure:

A Introduction: Jesus reveals himself to the disciples (v. 1)
    B Disciples gather and decide to go fishing (vv. 2-3a)
        C Fishing failure: a Stranger (Jesus) says, "Cast on the right side" (vv. 3b-6)
            D The beloved disciple recognizes the stranger: it is the Lord (v. 7)

     C´ Fishing success: disciples get abundant catch and
        recognize Jesus (vv. 8-12)
   B´ Disciples gather to eat a eucharistic meal of bread and fish
     (v. 13)
A´ Reiteration: how Jesus revealed himself to the disciples (v. 14)

Time, Location, and Characters of the Story 21:1-3

The opening words, *After these things . . .* (*meta tauta*), link chapter 21
to 20 and the entire Gospel. Earlier scholars regarded *meta tauta* as
the later redactor's connective. Even R. Brown (1970: 1067) dispar-
agingly describes it as a "stereotyped connective conveniently used
to attach extraneous matter." He then observes that the term is also
used to begin the longer addition to Mark's Gospel. However, *meta
tauta* appears elsewhere in John's Gospel (3:22; 5:1; 6:1; 7:1) at points
where there is a shift in location (7:1 is a wider scope of travel in
Galilee). On the evidence of narrative style alone, the phrase argues
more for the originality of chapter 21 than for a later addition.

    The verb *reveal* (*phaneroō*) appears immediately after the open-
ing phrase (v. 1a, repeated in 1b) and then again in verse 14 as an
inclusio (envelope) for this unit. It appears six times earlier in the
Gospel (1:31; 2:11, significantly in connection with Jesus' first sign at
Cana; 3:21; 7:4; 9:3; 17:6). Brown observes this, but adds that it is
used nowhere else in the NT to describe a postresurrection appearance except in the late addition to Mark (16:12, 14), which could
argue that Mark's addition is influenced by John 21! Moloney (1998:
548) also notes the verb's rarity in the Synoptics. It appears only at
Mark 4:22; 16:12, 14.

    These observations actually strengthen the case for the integral
relation of chapter 21 to chapters 1–20. *Phaneroō* fits well with
John's thematic emphasis on revelation. Forms of the verb occur
nine times in 1 John, making a total of eighteen uses in the Gospel
and Johannine Epistles (see the comments on 1 John 1:1-4 in
McDermond 2011). I do not share Moloney's skepticism regarding
John 21. Though acknowledging the trend to consider chapter 21 an
integral part of the Gospel, Moloney says, "The reader, who rises
from 20:31 under the impression that both Jesus (see 20:29) and the
narrator (see vv. 30-31) have had their last say, is surprised by the
laconic summary statement of 21:1 that Jesus revealed himself
again. After blessing those who believe without sight (20:29), are
there to be more appearances?" (1998a: 185).

    Already in 1994 Howard-Brook perceived the narrative unity
between chapter 21 and the rest of the Gospel. He identifies twelve

thematic connections, including the three named disciples, the charcoal fire, and more (446). Although John 21:1-19 coheres significantly with the rest of the Gospel, verses 20-25 likely *are* a latter addition, since they imply that the beloved disciple, the primary author of this Gospel, has now died.

The sudden shift in location, *by the Sea of Tiberias* (used also in 6:1 as an alternative designation for the "Sea of Galilee"), might suggest that Jesus' Galilean postresurrection appearances in Matthew have influenced a later redactor. But since Matthew is the only Gospel with such appearances in Galilee (though Mark also anticipates such in 16:7), it is difficult to argue that John's later redactor is copying a larger Gospel tradition. Furthermore, the content of John 21 is unique to John, as is virtually all of chapter 20. A more prudent stance is to withhold judgment on this matter and to seek to account for the narrative continuity between chapter 21 and the rest of the Gospel.

John 21 presents the denouement of the roles of Peter and the beloved disciple in the Gospel. Without this chapter, Peter is left in the (former) high priest's courtyard (18:16-27) denying his Lord. Peter never speaks in chapter 20; he only peers into the tomb. Nor does he speak when the disciples twice gather. The evidence for the structural continuity of chapter 21 with the Gospel is stronger than are "indicators" of a later redactor's addition, despite the earlier consensus. (Von Wahlde continues to regard it as independent material taken over by the third author: cf. 2010: 2.888, 884n1.)

Verse 2 identifies the seven gathered disciples: *Simon Peter, Thomas called the Twin, Nathanael of Cana in Galilee, the sons of Zebedee, and two others of his disciples.* This listing exhibits several striking features. First, only three are named: Simon Peter (the narrator uses both names); Thomas, denoted as *Didymus the Twin* (also in 11:16; 20:24), whose role in chapter 20 makes him a key disciple; and Nathanael, whom Jesus has declared *a true Israelite in whom there is no deceit* (1:47a AT) and to whom he said, *You will see greater things than these* (1:50b). Only now does Nathanael reappear in the narrative. His confession of Jesus' identity at the beginning of the Gospel as *Son of God* and *King of Israel* marked him a key disciple. Thomas's confession in 20:28 and Nathanael's confession in 1:49 function as bookends to Jesus' identity in John. Here Nathanael is said to come from Cana in Galilee, where Jesus' did his wedding-wine sign. Each of these three named disciples has made a significant confession about Jesus. On behalf of the disciples, Peter has confessed Jesus as *the Holy One of God* in 6:69. In addition, each has "revealed their doubts about their relationship with Jesus: Peter, by his denial; Thomas, by his demand for physical proof; and Nathaniel, by his doubt that 'good' could come out of Nazareth" (Howard-Brook 1994: 467–68).

It is not clear how the nameless four disciples are to be understood in relation to the beloved disciple in verse 7. The *two* unnamed sons of *Zebedee* appear here in John for the first time. Is the reference to the *two sons of Zebedee* preparing the reader to identify John with the beloved disciple in verse 7, and thus solve the mystery of his identity in the narrative? Maybe, but likely not. The familiar "James and John" of the Synoptics are never named in the fourth Gospel. In the Synoptic accounts they play negative ethical roles in crucial instances (cf. Mark 10:35-37; Luke 9:54). Their response to Samaritans in Luke 9:54 contrasts sharply to Jesus' in John 4.

The beloved disciple of verse 7 is more likely one of the *two others of his disciples*, since the beloved disciple is identified as *the other disciple* in 18:15-16 and 20:2, 3, 4, 8. In 20:2 the other disciple is explicitly identified as the beloved disciple, *the disciple whom Jesus loved* (AT), in 13:23 *[Beloved Disciple, p. 505]*. (Otherwise Andrew and Philip would be likely candidates for the *two others of his disciples*; cf. R. Brown 1970: 1068.) The evidence leans toward disconnecting John, son of Zebedee, from the beloved disciple. The mystery of the beloved disciple's identity continues in the narrative, even in 21:24, which seems to identify him as the eyewitness author(izer) of the Gospel.

The seven disciples decide to do what some of them were doing before they began following Jesus, though John's Gospel (1:19-44) never tells us that they had been fishermen. The number *seven* likely connotes completeness *[Numbers, p. 528]*. It "may suggest that this group is meant to be seen as representative of the entire community of Jesus' followers" (Lincoln 2005: 510). Howard-Brook (1994: 161) sees significance in a "conference" of seven disciples representing apostolic and Johannine communities.

When Simon Peter says, *I am going fishing*, they get into a boat, launch out into the water, and start fishing. They fish all night and catch nothing (v. 3b), despite the fact that fishing in the Sea of Galilee is generally best at night. Since night fishing is common, the disciples' failure may or may not connect with *night* symbolism elsewhere in John (3:2; 9:4; 11:10; 13:30; 19:39; cf. D. M. Smith 1999: 392). Since John's *darkness* motif (1:4, 7-9; 8:12; 9:5; 12:35-36) connotes unbelief, it is probably not applicable here.

How does one square the disciples' return to fishing with their new vocation in 20:19-23? Why go fishing after Jesus has breathed the Holy Spirit upon (or into) them, empowering them to carry on Jesus' ministry? Weren't they sent to do the works of God and to forgive or retain sins? But beneath the narrative surface, more than fishing occurs. *Fishing*, Peter's *hauling* or *drawing* in the net, and the count of 153 are probably all symbolic. Furthermore, the breakfast on the shore points to a deeper, most likely eucharistic, meaning. Brodie (582, cf. 576, 585) says the breakfast fits with John's enflesh-ing the divine in the ordinary. The "ordinary living" is that to which "the Spirit was directed." As a result, going fishing does not surprise.

Similarly, Richard Hays (2008a: 5–12) points out in discussing the nature of John's Gospel that the *materiality* of the Gospel is a feature of John's symbolic world. The significance of this fishing venture leads to postresurrection *seeing*.

The Mysterious Miracle of a Great Catch of Fish 21:4-14

21:4-6 First Elements of the Recognition Scene

At daybreak the vision is blurred. Jesus calls to his struggling, dismayed disciples out on the sea with no fish. The reader knows that the man on the shore is Jesus, but the disciples do not recog-nize him. Jesus' question, called out to the disciples, is phrased similarly to the woman's question to Peter in 18:17. Set up for a negative answer, Jesus asks, *Children, you have no fish, have you?* Answer, *No.* Jesus then directs them, *Cast the net to the right side of the boat, and you will find some.* The disciples do so, and the net fills with fish—so many that they are *not able to haul it in* to the boat! It is too heavy even for these muscular men! This comical scene dramati-cally illustrates Jesus' words on the need for branches to *abide* in Jesus the vine: *Apart from me you can do nothing* (John 15:5).

Jesus' address of the disciples as *children* is typically Johannine. In 21:5 the Greek is *paidia*. In 1:12 it is *tekna* (*children*) and in 13:33 *teknia* (*little children*). The shift between *paidia* and *tekna/teknia* is typical for John (cf. 1 John 2:1, 12, 14, 18, 28; O'Day 1995: 857; McDermond 2011: 171, 302–4). The term connotes endearment and may be the disciples' first clue to the stranger's identity. The huge catch of fish prompts recognition as in the recognition scenes in chapter 20.

21:7-8 Recognition and Revelation

In view of 20:28, one might think that Thomas would be the first to recognize Jesus. But in keeping with the character plot of the Gospel narrative, it is the beloved disciple, whose name embodies the heart of Jesus and who says to Peter, *It is the Lord!* Echoing John 13:23, the beloved disciple mentors Peter to understand Jesus' word! Peter is ever dependent upon the beloved disciple (cf. 18:15-16; 20:3-8) [*Beloved Disciple, p. 505*].

Simon Peter's response to the beloved disciple's disclosure is instant. He immediately puts on some clothes—a little dress-up to meet the Lord—and jumps into the sea. Simon, O Simon, impetuous and well meaning! While Peter slogs to the shore to meet Jesus, the other disciples bring the boat to shore, dragging the net full of large fish about a hundred yards (two hundred cubits).

21:9-13 Breakfast around the Charcoal Fire

Setting (21:9). What the disciples see on the shore surprises them: fish on a charcoal fire and bread. Jesus has prepared breakfast for them! Astounding! But what is Peter thinking? Charcoal fire, charcoal fire, charcoal fire—his thoughts are likely stuck, ruminating over the earlier charcoal fire and what happened there (18:18, 25). Has Jesus arranged this for Peter's sake? Likely so, in light of the dialogue that follows (vv. 15-19). The word for *charcoal fire* (*anthrakia*, from which we get the word "anthracite") occurs only these two times in John (18:18; 21:9) and nowhere else in the NT. As Peter gazes into the fire, feels its warmth, and hears Jesus inviting them to breakfast, the healing of his painful memories begins. See Richard Hays's moving sermon on Peter, "Standing by the Fire" (2008b).

Bring in the fish—153 of them (21:10-11).[w] Jesus commands the disciples to bring some of the fish they caught. Peter lurches out into the water and drags the net onto the shore. If the other disciples struggle to get the boat and net to shore while buoyed by the water, how does Peter by himself drag this net to the shore? Symbolic overtones here cannot be missed. Peter has a lead role in drawing the net to shore. The verb *elkyō* is significant for it is the same verb used in 12:32, *And I, when I am lifted up from the earth, will draw all people to myself.* Peter's action in response to Jesus' command, *Bring some of the fish that you have just caught* (v. 10), signifies his leadership role (21:15-19). In early church art the net and its many large fish symbolize the community of Jesus' disciples in one faith.

Is the number 153 symbolic? Some say no; it simply means that someone—most likely Peter—took the time to count them. Early church fathers offer varied explanations, with Jerome's the most

---

w   Where the superscript w occurs after headings, please see the commentary's online Web Supplement for additional material. Go to: http://www.heraldpress.com/bcbc/john.

attractive. In his commentary on Ezekiel 47:9-12, which this text may echo, he cites a Latin writing, *Halieutica*, in which the learned poet Oppianus Cilix says, "There are one hundred and fifty-three kinds of fish." Unfortunately, modern editions of Oppianus do not include this passage (Neyrey 2006: 337–38). However, this interpretation supports the meaning of this great catch: it symbolizes the mission of believers to all peoples, with Peter as "chief fisherman" (337, 334).

Throughout church history many other proposals have been offered (see R. Brown 1970: 1074–76), but the most persuasive is Richard Bauckham's, which utilizes a combination of a rare mathematical feature combined with gematria (where alphabetical letters have numerical values). Bauckham notes the gematria value of *believe*, *Christ*, and *life*, key words in John's stated purpose in 20:31, 153. Further, *signs* is 17, the rare *triangular* number of 153. Bauckham, however, says the Gospel's readers do not need to know the mathematical explanation of 153 to understand that the great catch of fish in the net means the gospel harvest will be plentiful. "The miraculous catch of fish . . . depict[s] symbolically the church's mission of bringing people to faith in Jesus and new life as children of God" (2007: 281).

Come and dine for breakfast, . . . and see (21:12-13). Verse 12 indicates that the disciples now know who this stranger on the shore is, and therefore *none of the disciples dared to ask him*. They know him through the miracle he has just performed, which evokes memory of Jesus' earlier signs. Most similar to Jesus' feeding the five thousand, it complements that sign with eucharistic significance: Jesus *took the bread and gave it to them*, and *the same with the fish* (cf. John 6). Both events (chs. 6; 21) disclose the divine in and through the *material* elements. In this scene the huge quantity of fish steals the show, but then in the eating the bread takes priority. The *order* and *content* of bread and fish match the pattern in John 6. The twelve baskets of eucharistic bread left over there, and now the 153 fish (instead of two)—both symbolize plenty. Jesus *draws* all (12:32), and *many* come.

21:14 Timing of Revelation

The explicit textual notation, this is *now the third time that Jesus appeared to the disciples after he was raised from the dead*, prepares the reader for what follows. The count of *three times* is important. Watch for it!

Jesus Restores and Commissions Simon Peter 21:15-19

21:15-17 Threefold Renewal[w]

This scene is one of the most poignant in the Gospel. Still *standing by the charcoal fire* (cf. 18:18), Peter's pain inflames. When Jesus approaches him, Peter likely expects reprimand for his denials. Instead, Jesus questions him about his love-loyalty. Simon Peter may have considered this Jesus' tactful way of reproving him for his failure. But when the interchange on *Do you love me?* is followed by a command to assume a leadership role among Jesus' followers, any sense of reproof yields to the prospect of promise. The question-and-answer drill has a conspicuous alternation and play on words. The word variation is more extensive than that of two verbs for *love*. Jesus addresses Peter as *Simon, son of John* each time. Each of Simon's answers begins with *Yes, Lord*, except for his last response.

Jesus' Question	Simon's Answer	Jesus' Commission
Do you love (agapaō) me?	*You know (oida) I love (phileō) you.*	*Feed (boskō) my lambs (arnion).*
Do you love (agapaō) me?	*You know (oida) I love (phileō) you.*	*Tend (poimainō) my sheep (probaton).*
Do you love (phileō) me?	*You know (ginōskō) I love (phileō) you.*	*Feed (boskō) my [little] sheep (probaton [some mss. probation]).*

In the Greek NT, *love* occurs as a form of either *agapaō* or *phileō*. *Agapē* love is self-giving, expressed ultimately in willingness to lay down one's life for another, which Peter promised to do for Jesus (13:37). *Phileō* love is friendship love—what is expected of friends who enjoy each other's company (cf. Jesus' calling his disciples no longer *servants*, but *friends* in 15:14-15). In questioning Peter, Jesus uses *agapē* the first two times, and Peter answers with *phileō*. Is this the most Peter can pledge? To match his tepid response, Jesus switches to *phileō* the third time he asks, *Do you love me?*

Jesus' first question includes *more than these. These* refers either to the other disciples (whether Peter loves Jesus more than they do, or whether he loves Jesus more than he loves them) or to his fish (representing his fishing career). It is impossible to know which is meant. Perhaps the narrator intends the reader to face the question: What is the "these" that competes with and threatens to undermine *my* love and loyalty to Jesus?

Interpreters disagree on whether these word variations for *love* are significant. Many say that what we have here is simply stylistic variety. O'Day, representing the majority view, says, "These verbs are used as synonyms throughout the Gospel, with no difference in meaning. Both verbs are used to speak of 'the disciple whom Jesus loved'" (*agapaō* in 13:23 and *phileō* in 20:2). Both are used of God's love of Jesus (10:17; 5:20); God's love for the disciples (14:23; 16:27); and the disciples' love of Jesus (14:23; 16:27). O'Day (1995: 860) concludes, "There is no reason, therefore, to ascribe gradations of meaning to their usage here" (as NIV 1984 does; NIV 2011, TNIV, and NRSV do not). John simply has a "propensity for synonyms." Talbert's similar view notes a wider interchange between two words. It conforms to his style (261; cf. also Culpepper 1998: 245–49; Witherington 1995: 356; Lincoln 2005: 516; Ringe: 65). Attempts "to find deeper meaning" in the variation and "connections among these words should be viewed with utmost caution" (Burge 2000: 587–88).

However, Howard-Brook sees significance in this variation. Against Burge he says that interpretations glossing over the significance of the variations should be viewed with utmost caution! He thinks it nonsensical to pass over the gradations in meaning, not only in the word for *love* but also in the ever-increasing shepherding responsibility to which Jesus appoints Peter, here called *Simon*. He also observes Peter's shift in choice of words for *know*. In his first two responses he uses *oida*, but in the last, *ginōskō*. In Peter's last response he actually uses both: *Lord, you know* [*oida*] *everything; you know* [*ginōskō*] *that I love* [*phileō*] *you*. While both Greek words may connote relational knowing, *oida* has also an *understanding* dimension. The shift to *ginōskō* in the third exchange may suggest that Peter is tempering his response to match Jesus' shift from *agapē* to *phileō*.

Howard-Brook (1994: 477) says this reduction of different terms to the same meaning is "hardly credible, given how carefully the text has been crafted. Why in this highly stylized interaction would the writer develop a mixed word usage just for the sake of variety? Why, given the centrality of both love and knowledge in the gospel's theology of discipleship, would such a change be made in word usage without there being an important reason?" Howard-Brook explains that while Jesus calls for self-sacrificing love, Peter is able to pledge only friendship love. In the third round Jesus accommodates, but nonetheless charges Peter with care of the disciple flock: "If Peter cannot understand the question in terms of his relationship with

Jesus, perhaps he can get it through his relationship with Jesus' sheep" (478).

Howard-Brook comments also on the *lambs/sheep* play. He correlates *lambs* (*arnion*) with Jesus as "the Lamb of God," despite the fact that John the Witness uses *amnos*, a different Greek word for *lamb*. *Lambs* allude to those who will die for the gospel, whom Simon is called to support. The *sheep* may signify those whom Simon will nurture in faith. *Poimainō* (to shepherd) in Jesus' second charge connotes this element of nurture and shepherd care.

What we have here is actually a fourfold wordplay (cf. the table on p. 483): (1) self-giving *love* (*agapaō*) versus friendship *love* (*phileō*); (2) *tend* (*poimainō*) versus *feed* (*boskō*); (3) *lambs* (*arnion*) versus *sheep* (*probaton*); and (4) *know* with understanding (*oida*) versus *know* (*ginōskō*). Given that this wordplay occurs within a tightly crafted dialogue of two persons, it surely seems that the Gospel writer intends significance in the variation. Shepherd (777–92) confirms this view by pointing out the dominance of the *agapaō/agapē* word group (verb and noun) in John 13–17. Jesus' dialogue with Peter in 13:5-10 and 13:36-38 frames 13:34-35, where *agapaō* occurs three times and the noun once. The concentration of *agapaō/agapē* words in 15:9-12 echoes 13:34-35. Jesus' rebuke of Peter in 18:11 represents Peter's failure to embrace the *agapē* love that lays down one's life.

These texts, related to Peter and marked by sacrificial *agapē* love, provide the narrative *dialogue* context for 21:15-19, which ends with Jesus prophesying Peter's future *agapē*-inspired self-sacrifice. In testing Peter for his *agapē* love and charging him to tend and feed the sheep, Jesus recalls his earlier statement, *I lay down my life for the sheep* (10:15, 18). Jesus' prophecy indicates that in his future role, Peter will do what his *phileō* love cannot now promise—an irony in light of Peter's promise in 13:37.

Brodie (591) agrees from another angle of consideration, "A do-you-love-me situation is not the time for meaningless variations." Brodie's perception of the variation on *lamb/sheep* attracts:

> The sequence "Feed my lambs.... Shepherd my sheep.... Feed my little sheep" [based on a questionable textual variant (*probatia*)] corresponds to looking after people in the three main stages of life—when people are young (lambs) and need to be fed; when people are adult (sheep) and need shepherding; and when people are old, yet in some ways are once more like children (little sheep) and once again need to be fed. This meaning finds support for the fact that the text which immediately follows implies three basic ages ("When you were young . . ."). (591)

Elsewhere in the Gospel's texts, the differing word choices for *agapē* and *phileō* reflect that both types of love appropriately describe discipleship. None of the variations cited by O'Day or Talbert, however, occur within a dialogue as in 20:15-17. The verb variation between 13:23 and 20:2 is perplexing. Why does the narrator use *phileō* love in 20:2 but *agapē* love in all other references to the beloved disciple, including 21:7 and 20?

In 11:3 Mary and Martha send a message to Jesus: *Lord, behold, the one whom you love [phileō] is sick* (AT). Then in verse 5 the narrator reports, *Jesus loved [agapaō] Martha and her sister and Lazarus."* The Bethany women choose friendship love to describe Jesus' bonding to Lazarus, but the narrator goes further, choosing self-giving love. Both *loves* are true here and also of the Father's love for the Son, the Father's and the Son's love for the disciples, and the disciples' love for Jesus. The *no greater love* that motivates laying down one's life for friends is striking in 15:13-16, which shows that friendship love and self-giving love are not antithetical: one responds to the other, as Jesus' questions to Peter exemplify. Jesus' love for Simon, even after the third round of question and answer is completed, is *agapē* love, though Simon consistently reciprocates with friendship love. Jesus' third question to *Simon, son of John*, has the effect of exposing Peter's realism in light of his earlier weakness and denials. Thus Peter is hurt: with mention of *the third time*, Peter hears the cock crow! In the third round, Jesus meets Peter at the friendship level of love. Nevertheless Jesus' *agapē* love will sustain Peter in his future role of shepherding Jesus' flock.

21:18-19 Prophecy of Peter's Future

Jesus' prophecy of Peter's future in verse 18 functions as analogue to 13:38, where Jesus prophesies Peter's denial. This is Jesus' last *Truly, truly [Amēn, amēn]* statement in the Gospel. This distinctive address occurs twenty-five times in John. It connotes Jesus' authority and in this case his prophetic word. Though brash and denying, Peter is redeemable. He will tend the lambs and feed the sheep. But this lead ministry role will not be without cost. To make the point, Jesus uses another bell-ringer word, *gird (zōnnyō)*, which harks back to the night Jesus *girded himself* (KJV, translating a related form) before stooping to wash Peter's feet.

The contrast between Peter's freedom to clothe or gird himself when he was young and strong to his later life condition, when another will *gird* him, is the significant surface meaning of the prophecy. But with *gird*, what Jesus has signified in his footwashing role is also what Peter will need to do and be. Just as Jesus' foot-washing is his last servant act before his death, so Peter, girded by another and carried *where you do not wish to go* as a faithful witness (*martyria*; cf. 19:35; 21:24) to the gospel, will also meet death, as his Master and Teacher did. Minear (1984: 158–59) says, "love = feeding = following," which in turn defines Peter's martyrdom. Peter's shepherding role will be modeled after the noble shepherd, who lays down his life for the sheep (10:11, 17-18).

The narrator in verse 19 explains, so the point cannot be missed: *He said this to indicate the kind of death by which he would glorify God* (cf. the similar statement for Jesus' death in 12:33). The phrase *Stretch out your hands* denotes crucifixion in antiquity. "Origen [in Eusebius, *Hist. eccl.* 3.1] and the *Acts of Peter* claim that Peter was crucified upside down" (Talbert: 262). With this prophecy and Jesus' final word, *Follow me*, Peter's future is set. He will do what his Lord has commanded—indeed, what he earlier pledged: *I will lay down my life for you* (13:37c).

Jesus and the Beloved Disciple 21:20-23

21:20-21 Narrative Bridge

These two verses function as a narrative bridge for movement from Peter to the beloved disciple. The Gospel cannot end with Peter. Since 13:23-26 he has looked to the beloved disciple for knowledge about Jesus. From then onward, the Gospel emphasizes Peter's dependence on the beloved disciple. Hearing his commission for the future, Peter turns reflexively to the beloved disciple and then asks Jesus, *Lord, what about him?*

21:22-23 The Future of the Beloved Disciple

Jesus then addresses a crucial issue regarding the beloved disciple and in so doing reiterates his call to Peter: *Follow me.* Apparently a rumor had circulated among Jesus' disciples between the time of Jesus and the time when the Gospel was written, claiming that Jesus said the beloved disciple would not die but would live until Jesus returned: *So the rumor spread in the community that this disciple would not die* (v. 23a). The narrator now corrects the rumored saying with an important caveat: *Yet Jesus did not say to him that he would not die, but, "If it is my will that he remain until I come, what is that to you?"* In essence, what Jesus says, *Why be concerned about him? If it is my will that he live on after you die, even until I return, what is that to you? Follow me* (AT).

The import of this correction is twofold. First, it unhooks Peter from the beloved disciple, upon whom he has depended since the Last Supper. Cutting the apron strings, Jesus tells Peter, *From now on, you are on your own* (AT). Your task is special; the beloved disciple has his own future. Peter has graduated into a direct love relationship with Jesus and will live out Jesus' prophecy soon enough. Second, this rumor likely generated dismay among early believers within the community when the beloved disciple died. They were not expecting this since the rumor said he would live till Jesus returned. The correction thus comforts the believers: the beloved disciple's death does not disprove what Jesus had said.

Furthermore, drawing attention to the beloved disciple opens the narrative to important information regarding the Gospel's origin and production.

The Beloved Disciple's Testimony, with Selectivity 21:24-25

Four personal references (three sg., one pl.) other than Jesus occur in these verses (cf. Carter 2006: 180-81): *This is the disciple who is testifying to these things and has written them, and we know that his testimony is true. But there are also many other things that Jesus did; if every one of them were written down, I suppose that the world itself could not contain the books that would be written* (emphasis added).

To whom do the terms *the disciple, we, his,* and *I* refer? The disciple most likely refers to the unnamed disciple *whom Jesus loved* (e.g., 21:7), mentioned six or seven times in various scenes and roles in the Gospel *[Beloved Disciple, p. 505]*. The identity of that person is enshrouded in mystery in the Gospel. The traditional author, John the apostle, is never mentioned as such in the Gospel. The only *John* mentioned (nineteen times) is John the Witness (as in chs. 1, 3, etc.). As the Gospel's eyewitness and author, the beloved disciple must meet the criterion of being an eyewitness to Jesus' ministry as narrated in the Gospel. Since the Gospel is Jerusalem oriented, the Galilean son of Zebedee hardly qualifies. The beloved disciple most likely lived in Jerusalem. One appealing solution is to identify the beloved disciple as Lazarus, since he qualifies on this score. It would be easy to understand why early believers would think that Lazarus, already raised from the dead, would continue to live until Jesus returns. Witherington (2006), J. N. Sanders and Mastin, Filson, Stibbe—all these advocate the Lazarus solution. But most scholars do not. The identity of the beloved disciple is more complex than meets the eye *[Beloved Disciple, p. 505]*.

According to conventional interpretation, the *we* in verse 24b refers to the believers in the Johannine community who have treasured the beloved disciple's testimony to the words and deeds (*signs*) of Jesus. This may refer to a special group within the Johannine community that contributed to the Gospel through their testimony and memory of Jesus, corroborating the beloved disciple's testimony. They certify as true the testimony of the beloved disciple (cf. 19:34). If the beloved disciple's testimony was already in written form, then verse 24b may be an editor's insertion. However, similar *we* phrases occur in 1:14, *We have seen his glory*, and 3:11, *We speak of what we know*. It is not clear that *we* in verse 24b is a later insertion into an earlier text (cf. also the "we" in 1 John 1:1-4).

Bauckham (2006: 370–72) argues against the predominant view that the *we* certification is a later insertion (which he espoused in his 1993 essay, revised as ch. 3, "The Beloved Disciple as Ideal Author," in 2007: 73–92, confirming his change in position: 91n24). He contends that *we* in verse 24b is "the we of authoritative testimony," similar to the "royal we." It refers to none other than the person speaking or writing. Hence in verse 24b the we means the beloved disciple who writes (or directs the writing of) the Gospel. Bauckham appeals to the use of "we" in 1 John 1:1-5; 4:11-16; 3 John 9-12; John 1:14-16; 3:10-13 (esp. v. 11); 21:24 (2007: 272–81).

Despite this welcome turn in Gospel research, some sense of certifying community may be present in all the texts Bauckham examines, including 1 John texts as well (see McDermond: 275–76). The probability that the beloved disciple had already died by the time 21:24-25 was written (cf. vv. 20-23) supports this view. Since verses 20-23 likely reflect an era later than the beloved disciple, verses 24-25 likely do as well. Although the Gospel uses *we* to attest the "authoritative testimony" that the beloved disciple bears (Bauckham 2007: 271–72), that does not rule out the corroborative witness of a "school" or "circle" that assisted in the production of the Gospel. Culpepper's critique of Bauckham is instructive. He regards the *witness* in 21:24 as an official "literary seal or certification of authenticity, in which the editor, speaking on behalf of the Johannine school, affirms the truthfulness of the community's Gospel" (2009: 363). However, the technical term for "literary seal" (*sphragis*) does not occur in verse 24, which weakens Culpepper's critique. If the author/editor intended that, why didn't he use the term *sphragis*? Bauckham's persuasive argument thus continues to attract.

Culpepper regards the first person *I* in verse 25 as referring to a later editor who hereby bears witness to the reliability of the beloved disciple as eyewitness author. This ending differs from John 20:30-31 in that 20:30-31 speaks about the signs that Jesus did, along with their purpose: to elicit and support continuing belief in Jesus as Messiah, the Son of God. In 21:25 the later editor reflects on the selectivity of the beloved disciple in writing what he did. Whether the author (the beloved disciple) or the later editor was aware of one or more of the Synoptic Gospels is not clear. In any case, this statement implicitly endorses a wider witness to Jesus' life and teachings. *The world itself could not contain the books that would be written* is hyperbolic, reflecting a customary end-signature in which *I* is used to end ancient writings, as detailed by R. Brown 1970: 1130 (cf. also Neyrey 2006: 343).

The ending (16.8) of the rabbinic tractate *Soperim*, attributed to Rabbi Joḥanan ben Zakkai (ca. AD 80), puts this Gospel's hyperbole in perspective: "If all the heavens were sheets of paper, and all the trees were pens for writing, and all the seas were ink, that would not suffice to write down the wisdom I have received from my teachers; and yet I have taken no more from the wisdom of the sages than a fly does when it dips into the sea and bears away a tiny drop" (R. Brown 1970: 1130; Neyrey 2006: 343).

Such an ending as John 21:25, whose purpose is *praise* of the One to whom the author *testifies* (Neyrey 2006: 343), reminds us of the great hymn stanza:

> Could we with ink the ocean fill and were the sky of parchment made;
> Were ev'ry stalk on earth a quill, and everyone a scribe by trade;
> To write the love of God above would drain the ocean dry;
> Nor could the scroll contain the whole, though stretched from sky to sky.
> —F. M. Lehman, ca. 1917, in *Sing the Journey*, #44

This imagery of God's fathomless, unfailing, and unending love fittingly concludes this Gospel of light, life, and love.

THE TEXT IN BIBLICAL CONTEXT

Peter

Peter is a rich character in the NT. John's Gospel gives us unique insights. Peter's journey with Jesus begins in 1:42 (with his name change). It matures in 6:68-69 and 13:37-38, then culminates in Jesus' final commissioning of him to be shepherd leader of the church (21:15-19). But during Jesus' passion, Peter falters and fails. Jesus' last word to Simon Peter is *Follow me* (21:22). In this last redemptive question-and-answer commissioning, Jesus addresses Peter as Simon, son of John, not as Peter. Jesus is taking Peter back to their first meeting, before Jesus changes his name to Peter.

Standing by a charcoal fire a second time, Peter relives his career (when he was Simon, son of John) through his entire journey with Jesus. Peter remembers his denials of Jesus (18:17, 25, 27), his sprint to the tomb (20:2-10), Jesus' appearances to the disciples (chs. 20–21), and the huge catch of fish he has just hauled in (21:11). Now he is again standing by a charcoal fire—this time to eat the breakfast Jesus has prepared: a breakfast of bread and fish!

Other Gospels in the NT present Peter's role differently. Mark names Simon first in Jesus' calling of the first four disciples (1:16-17): "Follow me and I will make you fish for people." Jesus and his four disciples dine in Simon's home on Jesus' first day of public ministry. Jesus heals Simon's mother-in-law, who is sick with fever. In 1:36 Simon leads the search for Jesus, who is off alone, praying. The "home" to which Jesus returns in 2:1 is likely Simon Peter's (cf. 3:19).

When Jesus appoints twelve on a mountain to be his core of disciples, Simon is mentioned first, and there Jesus changes his name to Peter (3:13-19). Next and crucially, Peter confesses Jesus to be the Messiah on the way to Caesarea Philippi. But what kind of Messiah? When Jesus (the Son of Man) then speaks of the necessity (*dei*) of his death and rejection by the religious leaders, Peter rebukes him. Then Jesus rebukes Peter and says, "Get behind me, Satan." Jesus will not be the Peter-expected messiah, a ruler of an earthly kingdom by military might (8:27-33; cf. John 18:36). Peter is named first as the inner three go with Jesus up the Mount of Transfiguration (9:2-8). Of the three disciples, only Peter speaks: "Let us build three booths up here to preserve our cool experience!" (AT). The narrator tells us, "He did not know what to say, for they were terrified" (9:6). Then God refocuses their attention on Jesus: "This is my Son, the Beloved; listen to him!" Though not named here, Peter is certainly present later in Mark 9–10 (e.g., 10:28) as Jesus teaches costly discipleship. Peter is again named first when four disciples ask about the destiny of the temple (13:3-4).

In Mark's trial narrative, Peter's role is similar to the role he plays in John: he vows to stick with Jesus even unto death (Mark 14:29-31) but then denies Jesus three times. Mark has a Gethsemane scene in which Peter along with the other disciples fall asleep rather than stay with Jesus as he struggles and prays through the night (14:32-42). The next mention of Peter after his denials is 16:7, where he is *named* as one to receive the news that the risen Jesus is going before them to Galilee. No "beloved disciple" appears in a role relationship with Peter in Mark, Matthew, or Luke.

Matthew's presentation of Peter is similar to Mark's except for three notable differences. First, in 14:28-31 Jesus saves Peter as he sinks while trying to walk on the water like Jesus—a notable scene showing Peter's intent to be like Jesus. Second, Matthew puts Peter in a more positive light in his great confession, "You are the Messiah, the Son of the living God" (16:16). Jesus affirms the confession, saying that this has been revealed to him by "my Father in heaven." Then Jesus commissions Peter for his special role as the foundation rock (*petra*, linking to the name *Petros*, "stone") on which the church is to be built. Jesus gives to Peter "the keys of the kingdom" and promises, "Whatever you [sg.] bind on earth will be bound in heaven, and whatever you [sg.] loose on earth will be loosed in heaven" (16:17-19; 18:18, you in pl.; for exposition of this important text see Gardner: 246–49; Swartley 1994: 118–22). But when Peter protests Jesus' announcement of his imminent suffering, Jesus' reprimand of him is even stronger than it is in Mark. Jesus says, "Get behind me, Satan! You are a stumbling block to me" (16:23).

Third, Peter is the point person when "the collectors of the temple tax" ask why his teacher does not pay the tax. A comic scenario follows, but the christological twist in the story is the subtext that Jesus as *King* frees his disciples ("sons" or "children") from tribute (17:24-27).

In the trial narrative (Matt 26:33-35, 69-75), Peter's pledge of loyalty and later denial is presented similarly to that in Mark. Also like Mark, Matthew includes the Gethsemane scene lacking in John. In the resurrection narrative, Peter is not singled out. Instead, he blends with the other disciples, whom Jesus calls "my brothers" (28:10). Along with the other disciples, Peter receives the great commission on the mountain (28:16-20).

Luke's narrative differs in that a fishing miracle occasions Peter's conversion and call (5:1-11). Neyrey (2006: 333–34) puts in parallel columns the core content of Luke 5:1-10 and John 21:4-8. The similarity is striking. In Luke 9:20-22, Jesus does not reprimand Peter after his great confession for his assumed nationalistic view of the messiah. The location of the confession is unspecified. At the transfiguration, Luke (9:32) has "Peter and his companions . . . weighed down with sleep" but they stay awake and see the glorified Jesus. Peter then requests "three dewellings." Luke's trial narrative clarifies why Peter's denial is not the end of his discipleship: Jesus says to him, "Simon, Simon, listen! Satan has demanded to sift all of you like wheat, but I have prayed for you that your own faith may not fail; and you, when once you have turned back, strengthen your brothers" (22:31-32). Peter then pledges to go with Jesus even unto death, though Jesus prophesies otherwise. Luke's most notable difference from the other three Gospels is that Peter runs to the tomb alone after receiving the news from the women that Jesus is risen (though 24:12 is lacking in some ancient MSS). Jesus' appearance to Peter is attested also by Paul (1 Cor 15:5).

First and 2 Peter are traditionally ascribed to Peter as author. Notable is 2 Peter's statement declaring Peter an eyewitness of Jesus on the holy mountain, the Mount of Transfiguration: "For he [Jesus Christ] received honor and glory from God the Father when that voice was conveyed to him by the Majestic Glory, saying, 'This is my Son, my Beloved, with whom I am well pleased.' We ourselves heard this voice come from heaven, while we were with him on the holy mountain" (1:17-18).

Love[w]

Jesus' questions to Peter and Peter's responses culminate John's profuse love emphasis in chapters 13-21. The distribution of the word *love* (counting both verb, *agapaō*, and noun, *agapē*) in John's Gospel is striking: It occurs eight times in chapters 1-12, then thirty-six times in chapters 13-21, with only one of these in the trial narrative (19:26). The verb (*phileō*) occurs thirteen times, but its distribution differs: it occurs four times in chapters 1-12, then three times in Jesus' farewell discourse (15:19; 16:27 [2x]), and six times in chapters 20-21 (20:2; 21:15, 16, 17 [3x]). All together, *love* (verb/ noun) occurs fifty-seven times in John. This compares with the many occurrences of *life* in chapters 1-12: the noun (*zōē*), thirty-two times (with only four after ch. 12, in 14:6; 17:2, 3; 20:31); and the verb (*zaō*), sixteen times (with only two after ch. 12, in 14:19 [2x]). John's Gospel is the Gospel of life and love, as *life* (verb/noun) occurs fifty-four times, and *love* appears fifty-seven times (verb/noun) [*Love Ethic, p. 527*].

In its various forms, *love* occurs over eight hundred times in the NRSV text of the Bible. Many of these describe God's love, as the oft-recurring *steadfast love* demonstrates (as in Ps 136). *Love* (noun/ verb) occurs 109 times in John's Gospel and Epistles together (see references for "love one another" in McDermond: 274-75) [*Love Ethic, p. 527*]. This extensive usage of *love* comprises over 10 percent of the total uses of *love* in the NRSV. The Greek word *eros*, which denotes erotic love, does not occur in the NT. The main Hebrew OT word for love (*'ahab*) has a wider range of meaning than the NT *agapē* word group (verb and noun), but most uses describe God's unfailing love, which the Septuagint translates with forms of *agapaō* (Hatch & Redpath: 1.5–7). The *first* and most significant OT love command is the Shema, "Hear, O Israel: The Lord is our God, the Lord alone. You shall love the Lord your God with all your whole heart, and with all your soul, and with all your might" (Deut 6:4-5, recited three times a day by the faithful). Second, the people are also to love their neighbors: fellow Israelites and aliens (Lev 19:18).

When tested by a lawyer as to which commandments are the most important, Jesus cites these two commands and says that they anchor the whole of "the law and the prophets" (Matt 22:40). Both Mark (12:28-34) and Luke (10:25-37) have longer versions of the same exchange: in Mark the scribe agrees with Jesus, but Luke's lawyer looks for a loophole in identifying his neighbor. Hence Jesus answers with the story of the good Samaritan. In this story the command connects with Jesus' *third* love command, "Love your enemies" (Matt 5:44-48; Luke 6:27, 35; cf. Lev 19:33-34).

Jesus' recurring command in John, *Love one another*, is the hallmark of faithful discipleship (13:34-35). It is Jesus' *fourth* love command. John states that one cannot say that one loves God if one does not show love to fellow believers by helping them in their time of need (1 John 3:16-18; 4:7-12, 16).

The second commandment, which Jesus says is "like the first," appears in three different settings in the NT: twice in Paul and once in James. Paul cites, "You shall love your neighbor as yourself" (Gal 5:14), as a guiding directive for the freedom believers have in Christ Jesus. In discussing the believers' relationship to evil and to government authorities whom God orders and who are to restrain evil, Paul cites this commandment, specifically in relation to those who collect taxes—possibly prompted by a brewing tax revolt (Rom 13:9, amid 12:18–13:10). James (2:8) cites Jesus' second love commandment when dealing with the disparity between how the rich and poor are welcomed and treated in the assembly. Partiality to the rich violates Jesus' love commandment. The range of practical issues to which this commandment is put in the NT is striking and instructive for us today in preaching, teaching, and counseling.

Other NT "heart texts" on love include these:

- Romans 5:8: "But God proves his love for us in that while we still were sinners Christ died for us."

- Second Corinthians 5:14-15: "For the love of Christ urges us on, because we are convinced that one has died for all; therefore all have died. And he died for all, so that those who live might live no longer for themselves, but for him who died and was raised for them." Here is the context for Paul's memorable call to reconciliation (5:16-21).

- Galatians 5:22-23: Love is the first among nine manifestations of the fruit of the Spirit.

- First Corinthians 8:1: "Now concerning food sacrificed to idols: we know that 'all of us possess knowledge.' Knowledge puffs up, but love builds up." This is essentially another contextual use of the love command.

- First Corinthians 13: The entire chapter is rightly known as "the great love chapter."

- John 3:16: One should be able to cite it by heart.

- John 13:34-35 and 21:15-17 (see above). The latter serves as the climax to John's Gospel.

- First John 4:7-16 represents a marvelous reflection on God as love and on our love for each other.

- Ephesians 5:1-2: "Therefore be imitators of God, as beloved children, and live in love, as Christ loved us and gave himself up for us, a fragrant offering and sacrifice to God."

In popular parlance we have heard that "love makes the world go around," but this misses the deeper meaning of love in Scripture: Love draws God to us and us to God.

THE TEXT IN THE LIFE OF THE CHURCH

Love, Foundational for Ministry[w]

Jesus does not belittle Peter for his denials. Rather, Jesus extends God's graciousness and gives him a second chance. He addresses him more familiarly as *Simon, Son of John*, going back to his family name rather than the name Jesus gave him: *Peter*. Standing not far from the charcoal fire, with all the memories it holds for Peter, Jesus invites him into a new relationship with moral distinction: *Simon son of John, do you love [agapaō] me more than these?* Peter is now aware of how weak his will is when his commitment is tested. Earlier he has said emphatically, *I will lay down my life for you* (13:37). Now he knows his weakness, that he could not do it when the chips were down. So he responds to Jesus, *You know that I have friendship love for you* (AT). Jesus then repeats his former question, dropping the last phrase, and Simon Peter responds as before. In the third round, Jesus meets Simon on his terms: friendship love. Nevertheless, Jesus commands him: *Follow me.*

In every case, Jesus calls Simon Peter to leadership ministry of Jesus' disciples. This encounter between Jesus and Simon is not only a restoration of Peter's promised discipleship, but also a renewed vision of God's grace and love. It enables him to face who he is and what he is to do. Jesus prophesies that Peter's future discipleship will not progress on the basis of his will, his natural gifts, or his lofty pledges. Nevertheless, Jesus chooses him and forgives his weakness. Having prophesied Peter's failure, he now prophesies Peter's future discipleship.

Love and ministry are essential partners, for love is the foundation of ministry. In John it is not the apostolic *Amt* (office, as in Matthew) that authorizes Peter's leadership, but the *charism* (empowering gift) of love (cf. Kragerud). In John we do not see a *rivalry* between the beloved disciple and Peter (as Kragerud infers and Ruprecht makes foundational to his interpretation of the Gospel), but rather complementary roles, in which each has his own respective calling.

Bauckham (2006: 87) notes that Peter's mode of discipleship leads to service and sacrifice, whereas the beloved disciple's receptivity fits his role as Gospel eyewitness and author. Peter's commission means he will learn the sacrifice of love's demands. The beloved disciple, who models love within the narrative, testifies in his own person to the primacy of Jesus' love for him and indirectly to God's love for the whole world [*Beloved Disciple, p. 505*]. Simon Peter certifies his readiness for ministry by his Yes to Jesus' threefold question: *Do you love me?* Jesus' prophecy of his future seals it. Let these two modes of love, Peter's and the beloved disciple's, be models for our ministries!

Outline of John

Part 3
Denouement: Final Passover, Passion, and Resurrection

Essays

AUTHORSHIP John the elder (in Ephesus) and John the apostle have been considered as "authors" of the Gospel. But is either of these *the disciple whom Jesus loved*, who in 19:35 and 21:24 bears eyewitness testimony? In sorting through ancient sources that provide external evidence for the Gospel's authorship, Bauckham begins with *The Letter of Polycrates*, written in the AD 190s to Victor of Rome: "Moreover, John too, he who leant back on the Lord's breast, who was a priest, wearing the sacerdotal plate (*to petalon pephorekōs*), both martyr (*martys*) and teacher, . . . has fallen asleep at Ephesus" (Bauckham 2007: 37, quoting Eusebius, *Hist. eccl.* 5.24.3; cf. also Josephus, *Ant.* 3.7.6).

Polycrates's comment about this John's wearing the sacerdotal plate (*petalon*) fascinates.[w1] As Bauckham (2007: 42) says, this is the high-priestly turban with the Tetragrammaton (*YHWH*) inscribed on the forehead band of gold. Polycrates explicitly identifies this John who was known as high priest, martyr, and teacher with the beloved disciple in John's Gospel.[w2]

The Muratorian Canon, which may date from the second or the fourth century AD, says this about John:

> The fourth of the gospels is of John, one of the disciples. To his fellow-disciples and bishops, who were encouraging him, he said, "Fast with me today for three days, and whatever will be revealed to each of us, let us tell to one another." The same night it was revealed to Andrew, one of the apostles, that all should certify what John wrote in his own name. . . .
>
> Why, then, is it remarkable that John so constantly brings forth single points even in his Epistles, saying of himself, "What we have seen with our eyes and heard with our ears and our hands have handled, these we write to you"? Thus he professes himself not only an eyewitness and hearer but also a writer of all the miracles of the Lord in order. (Bauckham 2007: 59)

---

w   Where the superscript w occurs after headings, please see the commentary's online Web Supplement for additional material. Go to: http://www.heraldpress.com/bcbc/john.

Several points in this ancient testimony are noteworthy. John is identified as one of the disciples, not as an apostle. This John is identified as "an eyewitness and hearer . . . of all the miracles of the Lord." He was encouraged by others to write, including Andrew, who is mentioned foremost in John's Gospel along with the other unnamed disciple (1:40). Also, this ancient writer describes John's Gospel as written "in order," a point made also in Papias's testimony in Eusebius, who identifies the content of John as complementing the reports of the Synoptic Gospels since they record mostly what happened *after* John the Baptist was arrested. John's Gospel records earlier events and presents a longer time span for Jesus' ministry (*Hist. eccl.* 3.33.5–8). Tatian's second-century *Diatessaron* (perhaps originally in Greek but extant only in Syriac and other languages into which it was translated) is the first attempted harmony of the Gospels, later repudiated by the church. It lists the Cana wine miracle as Jesus' first—before any of the Synoptic miracles—and contrasts "the lack of order in the Gospels of Mark [Papias says the same of Mark] and Matthew with the order to be found in the Gospel of John," though the original Hebrew Matthew—whatever that is—may have been in order. Tatian does not always choose John's order over the Synoptics, but does so when it comes to chronological order (likely referring to citing events within the order marked by consecutive feasts and a longer time span) (Bauckham 2006: 227–29).

Papias's quotation, cited in the introduction of this commentary, confuses the two Johns: the first is likely John the apostle (though here he is not called an apostle), and the second John is designated "the elder John." Bauckham privileges the other ancient sources to distinguish between the two Johns in this passage. Noteworthy here is Papias's preference to hear "the truth" and to listen to a "living and surviving voice."

In his exacting work with the pertinent sources, Bauckham has revived an earlier view held by some Johannine scholars that John the elder, not the apostle, was the beloved disciple eyewitness of the words and deeds of Jesus reported in John. Bauckham reports that Hengel in his careful research identified John the elder as author, but concedes that editors may have had a hand in shaping the final Gospel narrative. Further, Hengel suggests that the Gospel's enigmatic reference to an anonymous *beloved disciple* may have been intentional: to hint at either John the apostle or John the elder (Hengel 1989: 127–32; Bauckham 2007: 34). These concessions Bauckham regards as unfortunate, for Polycrates and Irenaeus (following), clearly point to John the elder as author.

Bauckham identifies six strengths in this identification, most notably "that the name of one of the greatest teachers of the early church," the beloved disciple eyewitness, is not lost to historical knowledge (for the other five advantages, see [w3]).

Irenaeus frequently refers to John the elder as "John, the disciple of the Lord" (nineteen times) or as "John" (thirty-four times), but only twice as an "apostle," and in those instances Irenaeus resorts to apostolicity because he is contending against gnostics who are challenging the Gospel's authority (Bauckham 2006: 452–69). In contrast, Irenaeus and others regularly refer to Paul as an apostle. Normally and almost consistently, Irenaeus refers to this author as "the disciple of the Lord," whom he links to the eyewitness of 21:24, which "is meant not so much to put John in a group as to distinguish him uniquely. It conveys his special closeness to Jesus, both historically during Jesus' ministry and theologically in his Gospel" (2006: 459). Because John presents Jesus' ministry as mostly in Jerusalem, the eyewitness disciple was likely a resident in the vicinity of Jerusalem. For internal evidence for authorship, see a later essay [Beloved Disciple, p. 505].[w4]

BELIEF/UNBELIEF Belief or unbelief is one of the dualities in John's Gospel, together with the duality of *from above* and *from below*. Belief or unbelief describes human response to Jesus as God's revelation. *From above* describes the origin of the Revealer, and *from below* describes the origin of those who do not receive the Revealer. Believing and knowing are inter-related in John ("Obedience and Knowledge," TLC for ch. 7); believing is a form of knowing. *Knowing* in John, as in the OT, includes covenant relation with God, receiving divine revelation, doing the commandments, loving one another, and practicing justice, mercy, and kindness (Mic 6:8). It is knowing God in creation, covenant, and the Spirit.

Believing (*pisteuō*) occurs one hundred times in John (J. B. Smith: 98; Schnelle 2009: 717). *Pisteuō* occurs in 1:7, 12, 50; 2:11, 22, 23, 24; 3:12 (twice), 15, 16, etc. John 1–12 shows a response pattern (*believe* or *not believe* does not always occur, but responses reflect such):

> Belief: 2:12; 4:39-42, 50-53; 6:66-69; 8:30, 31; 11:45; 12:42
> Unbelief: 5:38-47; 6:52; 7:32-35, 45-49, 52; 8:48-59; 10:19-20; 11:55-57; cf. 20:27c

Similar structural patterns occur in John 6:30-40; 8:25-35; 10:24-28a, which appear to consign the Jews to unbelief, sealed by the Isaiah quotations in 12:37-40 (von Wahlde 1984). However, the matter is not that simple. In John 6, 8, and 10 the initial belief of the Jews shifts to offense and unbelief, but in 11:45 *many* believe and only *some* tell the miracle to the Pharisees. Also, 12:42-43 contests the scheme by denoting "secret believers" (cf. Joseph and Nicodemus in 19:38-40). It is more accurate to say that many believe and many do not. The Isaiah texts apply to those who do not believe.

The *signs* and *works* play a strategic role as witnesses in John's Gospel (together with John the Witness, Moses, and the Father). They function within John's juridical plot to present testimony intended to persuade people to believe—in Jesus' time, the Gospel's time, and in the reader's time. Johns and Miller take up the issue, controversial in Johannine schol-arship, whether signs are to be viewed negatively or positively, or some of both. Source theories tend to resolve conflicting signals in the text by assigning an original positive function to signs—they lead to belief—whereas the final author (or redactor) regarded signs negatively.[w1] Johns and Miller persuasively contend that signs function positively, even within the mixed signals of the "problem passages": John 2:23-25 (extending to 3:21 in their exegesis); 4:48; 6:25-31; 20:24-29. Their careful exegetical explanations satisfy. In the first case, the problem is not signs per se, but "secret belief" that, while genuine, does not go far enough. In 4:48 the stated need for "signs and wonders" in order to believe is not a repudiation but a solemn pronouncement about the positive role they play in believing (cf. Moses' signs and wonders: Johns and Miller make fascinating comparisons here). Jesus thus gives *signs* to generate belief, both here and in 6:30. Thomas did not need a sign per se, but he did need evidence. Thomas is not rebuked for wanting evidence (the other disciples had seen Jesus' wounds a week earlier!), but for his failure to believe the testimony of others—a crucial issue for all who read the Gospel. Will readers *believe* on the basis of the evidence presented by the Gospel's host of witnesses? As Johns and Miller point out, nowhere in the Gospel is unbelief explained by lack of or inadequacy of signs, but to other causes (see the comments on 12:38-43). As 20:31 clearly states, signs are meant to elicit belief *[Signs, p. 529]*.

To *believe* in the Word sent by God into this world is to receive the *power to become children of God* (1:12). Believing in(to) Jesus leads to salvation and life; unbelief lands people in darkness (3:15-19). These two themes converge in Jesus' prophetic oracle at the close of his public ministry: *The light is with you for a little longer. Walk while you have the light, so that the darkness may not overtake you. If you walk in the darkness, you do not know where you are going. While you have the light, believe in the light, so that you may become children of light* (12:35-36). *Children of God* (1:12) are here children of light. "God is light, and in him is no darkness at all" (1 John 1:5b). In the double designation, believers receive a new status and new moral identity: *children of God who walk in the light of God.*

Belief or unbelief is one of John's *sensitivities* in interpretation (Motyer 1997: 57–62). The purpose of John's Gospel (20:31) is to evoke and nurture belief. Full belief leads to discipleship and is thus correlated with (eternal) life, which punctuates the narrative (60–61). Schnackenburg (1.571–72) emphasizes the *testing* of faith so that stages of faith are evident in the narrative reflected in christological confessions. Perhaps so, but believing and discipleship are twinned in John; believing christological confession and discipleship are one whole *[Disciples, p. 509]*.

John expresses "believe *in* Jesus" with the Greek preposition *eis*, which literally means *into*. It denotes "movement toward." Hence *belief* in Jesus leads to orienting one's life in the direction of Jesus, moving closer and closer to him. To refuse belief leads to the opposite: moving further away from Jesus. Thus the tragic disbelief of the Jews in the Gospel is explained as their having a *hardened . . . heart* (12:39-40), where John quotes Isaiah 6:10, a NT proof text for unbelief (Mark 4:11-12; Matt 13:14-15; Luke 8:10; Acts 28:24-27; Rom 11:7-11, 20). The unbelief of the Jews is not peculiar to John (cf. numerous episodes in Acts where Jews expel Paul from the synagogue, e.g., 17:1-10; cf. also 1 Thess 2:14-16). What is peculiar in John is the high-decibel use of the designation *the Jews ["The Jews," p. 520].*

BELOVED DISCIPLE The beloved disciple is the Gospel's eyewitness (19:35; 21:24). The traditional view identifies him as the author of the Gospel— either John the apostle or possibly John the elder, who resided in Ephesus and utilized the eyewitness testimony of John the apostle. Problems with this view have led to attempts to identify the beloved disciple as some other Jerusalem-based eyewitness. Some hold that the beloved disciple is an ideal figure in the Gospel narrative who embodies love.[w1] Searching for the historical identity of the beloved disciple is intriguing, but findings are elusive. The term *the disciple whom Jesus* [or *he*] *loved* occurs five times: 13:23; 19:26; 20:2; 21:7, 20. *The other/another* [*allos*] *disciple* occurs six times: 18:15, 16; 20:2, 3, 4, 8. (The unnamed disciple in 1:35-40 may or may not be the same person.) The identification of the *other disciple* as *the disciple whom Jesus loved* is clear in 20:2-4, in tandem with 20:8.

One other use of [one] *whom Jesus loved* occurs: for Lazarus in 11:3, 5. Some scholars thus propose that the beloved disciple is Lazarus, based on the evidence of John 11:1-5, 35-36. This view is advocated by Floyd Filson (1963: 22-25), Stibbe (72), Witherington (2006), and others. J. N. Sanders and B. A. Mastin (1968: 29-32) identify the beloved disciple as Lazarus, whose memoirs came into the hands of John Mark, the author. John and John Mark were often confused in antiquity (29-52; see further in Kysar 1976: 97n33).[w2] The textual link between 11:3 and 5 and the sudden appearance of the *disciple whom Jesus loved* at the Last Supper, seated next to Jesus, makes Lazarus a strong candidate for authorship.

If one seeks to solve this enigma of the beloved disciple's identity by naming a historical figure, the choice is between the Gospel's internal evidence and the external evidence as presented by Hengel (1989) and Bauckham (2006: 290-508; 2007) [*Authorship, p. 502*]. The external evidence points to John the elder, of Ephesus; the internal, to Lazarus, despite the comment of 12:10. In both cases the eyewitness (19:35; 21:24) is a Jerusalem disciple, given the Gospel's bulge on Jesus' ministry in Jerusalem. Perhaps the beloved disciple's "anonymity is deliberate—not to hide the identity of a historical person, but to present the beloved disciple as the ideal disciple" (Kügler: 485-86; affirmed by Evans [1990: 267-68] in reviewing Kügler's book). But Evans rightly says that such a narrative role for the beloved disciple is not fictive (Kügler), but based on a historical person, whose identity is intentionally ambiguous in the text. As many authors say, anyone who had identified himself as the beloved disciple would have been perceived as arrogant. The final editor, whatever the name, certifies the beloved disciple's testimony.

This is a carefully crafted narrative, designed to elicit faithful discipleship and belief in Jesus. Surely the author expects more from his readers than to name the beloved disciple! That *more* is to identify with the beloved disciple as an ideal believer or disciple of Jesus.[w3] John's Gospel gives us no clues that the apostle John is its author—he is not even named in the Gospel. *The twelve* (6:67-71; 20:24) are never named in John, as they are in the Synoptics (cf. Mark 3:16-19 and par.) [*Disciples, p. 509*]. Gospel titles were added in the second or third century. In the Synoptic Gospels (Mark 10:35-37; Luke 9:52-55), John's aspirations and behavior fall far short of emulation. The beloved disciple in the fourth Gospel models a role that draws readers not only to Jesus *lifted up* (12:32) but also to one's relationship to Jesus, defined as *love* and *abiding*. Love *believes* and *knows*. From 13:23 onward, Peter is dependent on the beloved disciple's closeness to Jesus.

Only after Jesus settles Peter's love for Jesus (21:15-19) is Peter unhooked from the beloved disciple and able to follow his own vocation.

Just as the beloved disciple draws us to the heart of Jesus, God's one and only Son, and to the Father, so the Jews in the Gospel represent the opposite, those who do not believe and do not know Jesus *["The Jews," p. 520]*. It is the reader's choice! Which model do I aspire to emulate?

In the end, the beloved disciple "retains his privacy, a privacy that even the most inquisitive commentator will do well to respect" (Michaels: 24).

CHIASM In a chiasm the first and last lines are related by similar words or themes, the second and next-to-last lines do so as well, continuing toward a center that highlights the major emphasis of the unit. Efforts to structure John in chiastic form, either in its entirety or specific parts, abound. Peter Ellis has a macrochiasm of the entire Gospel. He then exposits each section of the Gospel by heading the section with its own respective chiasm. However, scholars often see the chiastic structures differently. The most persuasive work overall is Homare Miyazaki's chiastic structure of the Gospel oriented to "The Feasts." He accepts criteria, developed by Blomberg, that identify chiasms as such (11–15). See his chiasms for chapters 18–19 and others by Miyazaki throughout this commentary and Web supplement.

The prologue and first four chapters have received much chiastic analysis. Culpepper's chiasm for the the prologue (1980–81: 2-6; 1998: 116) attracts because it has both economy of words and maximizes pictorial display:

The Chiastic Structure of the Prologue

1–2	18 The Word with God
3	17 What came through the Word
4–5	16 What was received from the Word
6–8	15 John announces the Word
9–10	14 The Word enters the world
11	13 The Word and his own people
12a	12c The Word is accepted
	12b The Word's gift to those who accepted him

This chiastic analysis, however may be questioned on two points. First, is the emphasis of v. 18 on the *Word* being with God? Yes, in that the *Son* (here not *Word*) is in the *Father's bosom* (*kolpos*), but the explicit emphasis falls on the Son's *revealing* the Father in his incarnate life (v. 14). Verse 12 nicely fits the center of the chiasm, with its emphasis on *to become children of God* (cf. John 1:47; 8:31-59).

For more examples see the Web essay on chiasms.[w1] For a fuller definition and more examples, see D. Miller: 224–26.

CHRISTOLOGY AND CHRISTOLOGICAL TITLES Titles for Jesus in John abound, about twenty in all:

The Word (1:1, 14)

Only begotten God (or *Son of God*, or *unique Son of God*) (1:18; 3:16, 18; cf. other versions)

Son of God (varied nuances in 1:34, 49; 11:4, 27; 20:31, among others)
The Son (3:16, 36; 5:19-27; passim)
Son of Man (1:51; 5:27; 8:28; many others also, with apocalyptic element)
Rabbi or *Teacher* (1:38, 49; 3:2, 26; 4:31; 6:25; 8:4)
Teacher come from God (3:2; 11:27-28)
Rabbouni (20:16)
Messiah, or *Christ* (1:41; 4:25, 29; 11:27; 20:31)
Prophet (4:19; 9:17)
Savior (4:42; cf. 1 John 4:14)
The Coming One (12:13)
Lamb of God (1:29, 36)
The Holy One of God (6:69)
The Shepherd (ch. 10)
The Sent One of God (3:16-17, 34; 5:30; 7:16-18; and esp. 10:36; others also)
I AM, absolute use (7x) and with predicate (ca. 9 modifiers) [*"I AM," p. 518*]
King of Israel (1:49; cf. 6:15; 12:13)
King of the Jews (19:19, by Pilate)
Paraclete (14:16 NJB)
(The) Lord (11:3, 21, 32; 20:25; 21:7; cf. 6:68)
My Lord and my God (20:28; cf. 1:1, 18 for *God*)
                      —Sources: Beasley-Murray 1999: lxxxi; Carson: 96; Mealand

Hengel (2008: 271) adds to this list: *the Anointed, the Elect, the only Begotten.*

Many of these titles appear already in John 1. In John 9 another sequence occurs, with *Lord* serving as the climax (v. 38). In light of Daniel 7:13-14, *Lord* may be implied in *Son of Man*. Reynolds holds that *Son of Man* in John is consistently apocalyptic, contra C. H. Dodd's "realized eschatology" [*Eschatology, p. 512*]. Explaining the theological meaning of these titles goes beyond the limits of this essay. Schnelle's *Theology of the New Testament* is a prime source for discussion of these titles (2009: 688–94). He rightly says that *I AM* in its absolute and predicate uses is a distinctive christological feature of John's Gospel.

Numerous discussions in the commentary (for chs. 1; 5; 10; 17) address the significance of Jesus' oneness with God, the Father. A fuller Christology does not *develop* as the Gospel unfolds (contra Mark), since 1:1 and 1:18 already disclose Jesus' divine identity: One with God. The absolute *I AM*, occuring first in 4:26, testifies to the same (see Exod 3:13-15).[w1]

CHRONOLOGY OF JOHN AND THE SYNOPTICS Three key differences dominate the discussion. First, the Synoptics present Jesus' ministry within a one-year cycle, whereas John structures Jesus' ministry as a three-year *feast* cycle. In the Synoptics, Jesus' public ministry is primarily in Galilee, with one trip south in the prepassion cycle of Matthew, Mark, and Luke (for a more extensive study of the Synoptics' structure, see Swartley 1994). Jesus arrives in Jerusalem in Mark 11:1; Matt 21:1; Luke 19:28.

The second main difference is how and why John and the Synoptics differ on the day of Jesus' death (see Culpepper's comparison chart, 1998: 200–201). Many scholars attempt to resolve or explain this difference. This issue was noted by early church writers and was intertwined with the paschal controversy. *The Letter of Polycrates*, written in the AD 190s to Victor of Rome during the paschal controversy over Quartodeciman observance, regards Nisan 14 as the day to put away the leaven; Passover thus begins on the eve of Nisan 15. Polycrates's letter indicates that he among other Asian church leaders observed Passover in accord with John's chronology. Jesus was crucified on the Day of Preparation for Passover—the day leaven is put away. Passover was celebrated that evening (Bauckham 2007: 39–41).

Several alternative interpretations exist. First, some hold that the Synoptic Gospels are historically correct. Thus John's placing the Passover meal on Friday night is theologically motivated. Second, others say that John is correct. Jesus died as Passover Lamb for the Passover evening meal. The Synoptics are theologically motivated in making the Last Supper a Passover meal. Third, perhaps both are correct but follow different calendars, since Qumran placed the evening of Nisan 14 and day of Nisan 15 on a different calendar day than that of mainline Judaism. This calendar was known and followed beyond the Essenes at Qumran (cf. Annie Jaubert 1965; 1990). Fourth, John's meal, too, was a Passover meal, since both John and the Synoptics speak of Judas's betrayal in conjunction with the meal. They "recline" in both cases, and they stay within the Jerusalem precincts (Gethsemane) after the meal, as the Passover law required. They also distribute alms after the meal (John 13:29), as required for Passover (Burge 2000: 365–66, harmonizing the two traditions). This resolution partially concurs with I. H. Marshall's: "Our conclusion is that Jesus held a Passover meal earlier than the official Jewish date, and that he was able to do so as a result of calendar differences among the Jews" (1980: 74).[w1]

Certainly John regards the Thursday evening supper as a special meal, but the Passover meal properly occurred on Friday, *after* Jesus dies as the slain Lamb. Jesus' death is on the *Day of Preparation* for the Passover meal, thus following the Asian calendar of making Nisan 14 the day to put away the unleavened bread and *prepare* for the Passover meal on the evening when Nisan 15 begins (Bauckham 2007: 40–41; O'Day 1995: 704–5; Kysar 1976: 5).[w2]

Finally, the third significant difference has to do with when Jesus "cleansed" the temple, since it is unthinkable that he might have done this twice. This issue is discussed in the comments on chapter 2.

DISCIPLES AND DISCIPLESHIP *Disciple(s)* occurs eighty-one times in John (74x in Matthew; 45x in Mark; 38x in Luke). The word *disciple* does not occur in the Johannine Epistles! The named disciples in John are Andrew, Simon Peter, Philip, Nathanael, Thomas, Judas (not Iscariot; 14:22), and Judas, *son of Simon Iscariot* (6:71). Unique to John, the beloved disciple appears in prominent roles. The *sons of Zebedee* are mentioned (21:2) but never named. John is always John the Witness (appropriately called John the Baptist in the Synoptics, but not in John). Seven of the disciples identified elsewhere in the NT (in Mark 3:16-17; Matt 10:2-4; Luke 6:12-16; cf. also Acts 1:13) are not named in John: two named James, Matthew, Thaddeus, Simon the Zealot, Bartholomew. Some commentators propose that Bartholomew and Nathanael are the same disciple. John speaks of *the twelve* in 6:67, 70, 71; 20:24.

John varies the number of disciples (cf. 1:35-51 with 6:60, 66 and 21:2). Only Philip is *called* at the outset, *Follow me* (1:43; for Peter, see 21:19); others are "transferred" to Jesus by John and become disciples gathering around Jesus (see "Gathering Disciples" in TBC for 1:19–2:12). Some of these are introduced to Jesus by friends (see comments on 1:35-51). Nathanael (1:45-51; 21:2) and the "beloved disciple" do not appear in the Synoptics. Commentators generally do not perceive discipleship as one of John's primary themes, though Chennattu's *Johannine Discipleship as a Covenant Relationship* is a wonderful exception. The essays by Segovia (1985) and Hillmer (1996) appear in volumes that address discipleship in the entire NT. Both are helpful, though Segovia excludes 13:31-35 and chapter 21, regarding them to be later additions. Hillmer recognizes the importance of discipleship in John. Discipleship involves both *relationship* with and *abiding* in Jesus. It means *following* Jesus and keeping Jesus' commandments, especially *loving one another. Believing in/into* and confessing Jesus encompass both relationship and action: discipleship interacts with Christology (84–93, 96).

Chennattu rightly sees discipleship as permeating John's entire narrative. In John 1:35-51,

> the disciples are initiated into a process of following Jesus. [In chs. 2–4,] the disciples are given various models of discipleship as Jesus reveals the presence of God. In chapters 5–10, . . . the disciples and characters in the story are provided with revelations of God in Jesus' words and work, and are confronted with choices for or against Jesus. Chapters 11–12 heighten the urgency of decision and set the stage for Jesus' hour. (71)

Her outline of Jesus' farewell speech carries forward the discipleship theme (82), focusing particularly on the beloved disciple (100–201). She titles John 17 as "A Prayer Consecrating the Covenant Community of the Disciples" (130). She also identifies "Covenant-Discipleship Motifs in John 20–21," emphasizing reclaiming in John 20:1-18, empowering in 20:19-31, and constituting the new covenant community in 21, to which she could add discipleship (140–79).[w1] Chennattu's contribution is particularly helpful for believers church communities of faith.

This commentary highlights discipleship at various places (1:35-51; 13:31-35; and ch. 21). Jesus' teaching his disciples is prominent (4:27-38; 6:1-21, 60-71). In 7:2-3 Jesus' brothers tell him to *go to Judea so that your disciples also may see the works you are doing.* Jesus' farewell addresses his disciples. After Jesus' resurrection, he appears twice to the disciples in 20:19-29 (a third time in ch. 21), giving them John's version of the great commission and eliciting Thomas's confession. The entire Gospel teaches true discipleship, with the beloved disciple as model.

DRAMA IN JOHN Brant proposes that John exhibits numerous features suggesting it was written for stage production. These features are evident especially in the discourses. One such feature is John's use of *deictic* language. Thus Brant observes that John frequently uses words *that point toward,* such as *come* and *go*, as well as words that *signify*, such as *that one* (*ekeinos*) and *this one* (*houtos*). John also has recurring intensives: *I* (*egō*), *we* (*hēmeis*), and *you* (*sy* [sg.], *hymeis* [pl.]). This is the kind of language that is most at home on the stage. Deictic language invites the listener or reader into the subjectivity of the characters. It emphasizes time, space, and modality.

Of the dozen "speech-action" features Brant discusses, the most fascinating is "flyting," which is characteristic of discourses in both Greek tragedies and John. Flyting is a form of argument in which opponents duel, besting the other's position and reasoning. The discourses in John 5, 6, 8, and 10 consist of flyting between Jesus and "the Jews." These discourses increase in intensity. Further, she observes that in Greek tragedy the winner in the linguistic flyte-duel often ends up losing the battle, since the opponents then resort to mortal violence—exactly what happens in John.[w1] Since dramatic roles are fictive, Brant proposes that seeing John in theatric mode frees us from regarding John as anti-Judaic. But theater presentation may also have the reverse effect.

DUALITY, NOT DUALISM Literature on John's Gospel (and Epistles) often regards dualism as one of its characteristic features, evident in the oppositions between light and darkness, death and life, belief and unbelief, and most foundational of all, *from above* versus *from below*. But are these oppositions really dualistic, or does the term *duality* better describe these Johannine emphases? Stephen Barton and Miroslav Volf in their perceptive essays (in Bauckham and Mosser: 2008) argue that, strictly speaking, John is not dualistic. Duality more accurately describes John.

The dualities in the Gospel do not set the Johannine community in complete opposition to those around them. Volf contends that John calls believers to a particular kind of sectarianism. These believers do not see only negatively or positively coded responses, but they do courageously name evil while also forgiving and showing their willingness to die for those who do evil.[w1]

Discussing John's "dualisms" ("above and below, true and false, love and hate, good and evil, life and death, light and darkness, Christ and the devil"), Culpepper says, "Christology, not dualism, is the real focus of each of the Johannine writings" (1996: 23, 24). John's dualities also have ecclesial, moral, and political dimensions (Swartley 2006: 280–89). The Logos is the light of the world; darkness has not, does not, and will not grasp or master it. This theme shines also in Revelation: "The city has no need of sun or moon to shine on it, for the glory of God is its light, and its lamp is the Lamb. The nations will walk by its light, and the kings of the earth will bring their glory into it" (21:23-24).

ECUMENICAL RELATIONS John H. Yoder (1958: 7–14) identifies both conservative and more liberal tendencies in support of the ecumenical movement. He rightly says, "The unity of all believers is a Scriptural command" (16) and "Christian unity is not to be created, but to be obeyed" (21). He reminds us that the epistles make it clear that disunity was evident already in the NT church. Indeed, it has dogged the church through the ages (19–27).[w1]

The challenge facing Christians in ecumenical efforts is greater today than it was several decades ago because denominations are fracturing over what Michael Root calls "fluid identities" (10–11). Polarization in mainline Protestant denominations over same-sex issues is but one illustration. Ecumenist Cardinal Walter Kaspar (2005) calls the church to renew its efforts toward unity, for the same reasons Jesus gave in John 17:

> Ecumenism is not an end in itself but subordinated to the fundamental mission of the church to go out into all the world and to preach the gospel to all peoples (*Matt. 28:19*). Thus the ecumenical movement is a response to the prayer which Jesus directed to his father on the eve of his death, and which we are to respect as his last will and testament: "That they also may be one in us, that the world may believe" (*John 17:21*).[w2]
>
> Ultimately only spiritual ecumenism will be in a position to overcome the present crisis. Jesus' word "That all may be one" (*John 17:21*) was not a command or an order but a prayer. Ecumenism means joining in this prayer in the certainty that when two or three—and so much the more when they are two or three churches—are united in prayer in the name of Jesus, they have the promise that they will be heard (*Matt 18:20*).

Snyder Belousek (604) passionately ends his discussion on "Christ Is Our Peace" with the following appeal:

> A church that would witness to the world concerning the gospel of God's salvation and peace in Christ must be *both* evangelical and ecumenical; indeed, we must be ecumenical in order to be evangelical. Through Christ and the message of the cross we are called to make peace with one another within the church for the sake of the gospel of Christ crucified. Through Christ and the power of the cross we are enabled by the gift of the Holy Spirit to break down walls of division between Christians before a watching world. Thus may the people of all nations—long divided by nationality, race, gender, and class—see a living, embodied sign of the reality of reconciliation with God through the peacemaking cross of Jesus Christ.

ESCHATOLOGY If any topic in Johannine studies has been on shifting sands, it is this one. The continuum of emphasis goes from Dodd's "realized eschatology" on the one hand, to "apocalyptic" on the other. The first occurrence of the christological title Son of Man speaks of *heavens opened* in the present tense (1:51). Between these two extremes of the spectrum, most Johannine scholars see present and future aspects of eternal life (see comments on 5:24-29). Thompson (2008a: 238–39) discusses the theological significance of both present and future realization in the wider context of 5:25 (present) and 5:28-29 (future). She identifies these two aspects in John 11 also, in Jesus' teaching and action. "John 11 testifies to the character of God as life-giving and shows the anticipation of a future life with God" (244) *[Eternal Life, p. 513]*.

In the introduction to his commentary, C. K. Barrett regards eschatology as one of eight major topics of John's Gospel. He recognizes both present and future elements (cf. Kysar's chart presenting both dimensions, 1976: 87). In light of both realized and future eschatology in John, I propose another term for John's eschatology: believers eschatology. In John believing into (*eis*) Jesus leads to eternal life, experienced here and now and flowing into the future. John 5:29c expresses the converse: . . . *those who have done evil, to the resurrection of condemnation.*

Believers eschatology weds the present and the future, with Jesus ever at the center, whether in Jesus' giving life; in the believer's "ingesting Jesus," to use Webster's term; in the Spirit's working in the believer; and/or in the union of peace and mission. John strongly emphasizes believers' bonding as *branches* to Jesus as the *vine* (15:1-17), then experiencing the hatred of the world (15:18-25)—all in one chapter—and being united with Jesus just as Jesus is one with his Father (ch. 17). These emphases point to what has been called *realizing* eschatology, perhaps better termed *believers eschatology*, experienced in the present and fulfilled in the future (see McDermond on 1 John 2:17). He correlates 1 John with Paul's eschatology, as in Elias's *Remember the Future.*

ETERNAL LIFE[W1] *Life* in noun, verb, and compound forms occurs fifty-four times in John, with most occurrences in chapters 1–12 and a concentration in John 3–6. *Eternal life* occurs seventeen times, in well-known verses: 3:15, 16, 36; 17:2, 3 (the other 12x in 4:14, 36; 5:24, 39; 6:27, 40, 47, 54, 68; 10:28; 12:25, 50). *Eternal life* denotes more a *quality* of life than it does endless time. It is both *present* and future (cf. McDermond: 153). Jesus' gift of *life* is a primary emphasis in John 1–12. The term *eternal life* rarely occurs in the Synoptic Gospels (Matt 19:16, 29; 25:46; Mark 10:17, 30; Luke 10:25; 18:18, 30). The Synoptics often speak of "kingdom of God/heaven," a term that John uses only in 3:3, 5 (*kingdom* occurs 2x in 18:36; cf. Paul's use of God's righteousness/justice).[W2]

Four perspectives contribute to understanding *eternal life* in John: (1) the OT anticipation for eternal life, or the life of the age to come; (2) the intertextual connections to the empire's promise of eternal life attached to the "eternal city" (Rome), boasting of Pax Romana; (3) John's eternal life and its relation to the empire and its Christology; and (4) the relation of eternal life to the material, social, and political dimensions of human experience, including bodily resurrection.

1. *The OT anticipation.* Several late OT texts and other Jewish sources speak of eternal life (Dan 12:2, 13, which relates intertextually with the "everlasting kingdom" in Dan 6:26; 7:13-14, 27). In 2 Maccabees 7:9, where seven sons undergo torture and martyrdom, one after the other, they and their mother express assurance that their martyrdom will be vindicated by God's resurrection of the faithful. Both *4 Ezra* (7:2-44; chs. 11–13; 14:35) and *2 Baruch* (chs. 26–30; 49–52; 72–73) envision a two-age scenario, with many tribulations followed by a four hundred-year reign on earth (in *4 Ezra*), after which "a new world is established" (Carter 2008: 220). These texts, together with *Psalms of Solomon* (esp. ch. 17) and *1 Enoch* 37–71, anticipate

an age to come under God's sovereignty that "blatantly and profoundly contrasts with, overcomes, and transforms material life in the present age under Roman rule" (220).

2. *The connections of John's eternal life to the empire's promise of eternal life.* Rome proclaimed itself the "eternal city," and the empire named itself Pax Romana. In the reign of Caesar Augustus from 31 BC to AD 14, the notion of "the golden age" emerged. As Carter writes, "Augustus's golden age was clearly not a future pie-in-the-sky vision: it was already here. It was 'realized eschatology'" (2008: 205). Although the elite in Rome and the *sebastoi* (city family hierarchs) flourished, the mass of the Roman population lived under oppression, frequently experiencing food shortages. They "slaved" for the benefit of the elite (Carter 2008: 205–8; Swartley 2006a: 35–40; Wengst 1987: 7–51). The vision of "the golden age" persisted through Augustus's successors. Under Claudius (AD 41–54) the citizens of Ephesus were assured "that the emperor 'has taken the whole human race under his protection.' With Domitian occurred a makeover and reinforcement as the eternal Domitianic golden age" (Carter 2008: 207).

Shortly after John's Gospel was written, Pliny, governor of Pontus-Bithynia in the north of Asia, indicated that provincials appeal to the emperor's *Salus* (prosperity) and *Aeternitas* (eternal existence) in making petitions (Pliny the Younger, *Ep.* 10.59, 83). The emperor assured people that Rome was here to stay (Carter 2008: 207–8).

3. *John's eternal life and its relation to the empire and its Christology.* John's distinctive use of eternal life is related to the promises of the empire on the one hand and to the Gospel's many christological titles on the other. Many of the titles for Jesus, including even those for his divine identity, were also claimed by Roman emperors during the first century (Carter 2008: 176–203; Swartley 2006a: 77–90). Is John's frequent use of *eternal life* the Gospel's way of subverting the claims of the empire? Or does the Gospel present Jesus with titles claimed by the emperors as a way of distancing the faithful believers from the empire and empowering them to live their community life in faithfulness to their Lord and Savior? Carter leans toward the latter (2008: 226–27), but both are surely in view. Carter recognizes and Webster's *Ingesting Jesus* suggests that the imagery of Jesus' *I AM* claims are connected with somatic (bodily) needs and realities.

4. *Relation of eternal life to material, social, and political dimensions of human experience, including bodily resurrection.* Examine the *I AM* claims with a predicate nominative *["I AM," p. 518].* Most of these relate to the basic sustenance of life: living water and food that endures to eternal life (John 4), bread of life (John 6), a shepherd who feeds and cares for his sheep (John 10), resurrection (John 11), and branches that produce fruit (John 15). Jesus' first sign in Cana fulfills OT anticipations of the feast of the new age (Isa 25:1-9; cf. Carter 2008; Webster). The Roman Empire's Golden Age promised abundant food and drink. Webster identifies eight meal events in John, with several expressly called *signs.* In John 6 the feeding of the multitude leads to Jesus' claim that he is *the bread of life.* This is connected with *I will raise them up on the last day* (6:39, 40, 44, 54; cf. 11:24-27). While Jesus' command to eat his flesh to live may shock, it speaks symbolically of *ingesting*

Jesus in all spheres of life—personal, corporate, somatic, material, and even political. It coheres with Jesus' introduction as *Lamb of God* in 1:29, 36, and with the later Passover meal (19:14). Believers eat Jesus and drink his blood to live—abundantly and eternally *[Sacrament, p. 529] ["I AM," p. 518]*.

FATHER AND SON Both the Lord's Prayer (Matt 6:6-9; Luke 11:2-4)—with its Aramaic *Abba* Father background—and Jesus' use of *Father* in John highlight *intimacy* as the essential relational quality. In John, God is called *Father* 118 times (4x in Mark, 42x in Matthew, 29x in Luke). *Father* occurs more frequently in John than in the other Gospels combined. Matthew's occurrences are concentrated in the Sermon on the Mount. In the Synoptic Gospels, Jesus rarely *addresses* God as Father. He does so in the Lord's Prayer (Matt 6:9//Luke 11:2), in his joyous outcry to his *Father* in Matthew 11:25-27//Luke 10:21-22, and in his word of forgiveness from the cross (Luke 23:34, lacking in some MSS).

Outside the eleven instances in John 17, Jesus' direct address of God as Father is sparse in John as well, but they are significantly placed: in raising Lazarus (11:41) and in facing his glorification on the cross (12:27-28, twice; cf. Thomas's climactic confession in 20:17). When Jesus speaks *about* his Father in John, the Father is the origin and source of life, one who has authority, and one who loves his children (Thompson 2001a: 58). This is similar to the character of God as Father in the OT (Swartley 1990: 13–14). In John, God as Father complements Jesus as Son in intimate loving relationship. The Son does the will of the Father, is obedient to the Father in all things, and yet shares the identity and authority of the Father. Jesus' claim to do the work of the Father and to make his identity one with the Father leads to opposition from the Jews (5:16-27; 8:15-20, 37-47; 10:17-18, 28-30) *["The Jews," p. 520]*.

In John 17 the intimate relation between Jesus as Son and God as his Father is poignant (17:21-23). Rossé's exposition of this theme is rich:

> Since Jesus is the Word permanently turned to the Father, to know Jesus is to discover the relationship existing between the Son and the Father; it is to discover God as a communion of persons. . . . "In his teaching and in his very life he reveals nothing else but the Father; he is the revelation of the Father" [quoting L. Cilia, from French]. . . .
>
> The realization that Jesus came from the Father, that he is the one sent by the Father, contains the answer to the question of his origin. Recognition of the divine origin of Jesus means grasping the bond that unites him to the Father and defines him as Son. . . . The divine identity of Jesus discloses a life of communion, a relationship that makes him the Son. (14–15; see Rossé further, chs. 1–2)

God as Father is not without parallels in literature outside the Gospels. Julius Caesar claimed the title of Father (*parens patriae* and *pater patriae*) late in life; Augustus acquired the title in 2 BC (D'Angelo; Swartley 2006a: 81–83, for Matthew). The effusive Father language in John troubles feminist scholars, for evident and valid reasons (see, e.g., the articles in Reinhartz 1999).

Unlike Matthew, however, John uses *the Father* more than *my Father*—the latter mostly in chapters 14–15 (ch. 17 is direct address: *Father*). Anderson's (1999), Lee's (1999: 180–81), and Thompson's articles (1999: 26–29) emphasize that in John *Father* is joined to two primary themes: *sending* and *intimacy*, a mutuality of and in love. Thompson (20–26, 29–30) rightly identifies the theme *giver of life* (John 5:26) as the foundational basis of this mutuality: the Father and the Son's "life-giving work" (30) is one. It gives life to believers and is life "for all the world." (See also the "summary and response" articles by Ringe and Young in this 1999 volume: 189–202.)

FEASTS Israel's major feasts form John's overall structure. Does John present Jesus as the replacement of both these feasts and the temple (Suderman), or does the Gospel highlight the importance of these feasts and their theological significance for Johannine believers? In this respect, John is similar to the Synoptic Gospels, which use Israel's major faith traditions for their structure (Swartley: 1994). John's feast structure "transforms" the feasts' theological significance in light of Jesus as Messiah. Jewish believers celebrate the feasts with the new meanings in Jesus' discourses at the respective feasts. John's Gospel, written after the fall of the temple where the feasts were celebrated, reinterprets these feasts to promote "the piety of his community as *Jewish* Christians" (Yee: 27). Yee notes the Pharisees' parallel efforts, under the leadership of Rabbi Yoḥanan ben Zakkai, to give new meaning to the feasts appropriate to synagogue worship.[w1]

FLESH AND GLORY *Flesh* (*sarx*) occurs thirteen times in John in five different passages, each with a different context that affects the nuance of the term: the prologue (1:14), the dialogue with Nicodemus (3:6), the bread of life discourse (6:51-56, 63), the Tabernacles discourse (8:15), and Jesus' high-priestly prayer (17:2). *Flesh* occurs in relation to *glory* only in 1:14 and 17:1-4. In 3:6 and 6:63 *flesh* contrasts with *spirit*. In all uses it connotes humanity (thus NRSV translates it as *human* in 8:15).

Other physiological terms in flesh's semantic field include *blood* (*haima*), *body* (*sōma*), *belly* (*koilia*, 7:38 KJV), *breast* (either *kolpos* or *stēthos*), *human being* (*anthrōpos*), Jesus' *thirst* (*dipsaō*), *blood* and *water* (*haima* and *hydōr*), the *mark of the nails* (*ho typos tōn hēlōn*), and the *wounded side* (*hē pleura*). These signify Jesus' humanity, as do references to Jesus' hometown (1:45; 7:41-42), his parents (1:45; 2:1-12; 6:42; 19:25-27), his brothers (2:12; 7:2-10), and his friends (11:1-3). The materiality of the signs demonstrates Jesus' incarnation (Lee 2002: 30).

GLORY AND GLORIFY Both the verb and the noun recur often in the Gospel. Crucial uses connect with Jesus' becoming flesh (1:14), Jesus as *lifted up* (12:28-32), and Jesus' prayer in which he anticipates his death, resurrection, and departure (ch. 17). *Glory* is stitched into the Gospel's narrative structure.[w1] Flesh and glory are not polar opposites. *Flesh* is perishable and transitory (Schnackenburg: 1.267). Jesus takes on flesh as the precondition and pathway to glory. The reality of Jesus' flesh cannot thereby be shortchanged; rather, it magnifies Jesus' glory and glorification (Thompson

1988/1993; contra Käsemann). *Glory* and *glorify* are a lens into John's Christology. For the relation of *glory* to the *Word-Logos*, see Evans 1993a.

Raymond Brown (1966: 503) defines *glory* as a visible manifestation of God's majesty in acts of power. Its frequency of occurrence in the NT is as follows:

The Synoptics	John	1–3 John	Revelation	Total Johannine	Total NT
23	18	0	17	35	165 (many of which are Pauline)

But Brown's eighteen for John does not include verbal forms, such as *glorify*, *glorified*, and *glorifies*—totaling twenty-three! The fourth Gospel depicts Jesus' very life, in his teachings and signs, as the revelation of God's glory. Moloney writes: "Jesus' life, teaching, and signs have been the revelation of the *doxa* [glory] of God. . . . The *doxa*, which is the love bestowed upon the Son by the Father, . . . is present in the human story in the *doxa* that Jesus has given to the believers" (1998: 474).[w2]

At the core of Jesus' controversy with the Jews in John is *glory*: whose *glory* one seeks (5:41, 44; 7:18; 8:50, 54). We see this in the ironic retort of the Jews, *Give glory to God!* (9:24), and in the narrator's prophetic interpretation of Jesus' *glory* (12:41-43). Several *signs* reveal God's glory (the first sign in 2:11 and the last in 11:4, 40!). The mutuality of the Son and the Father in *glorifying* one another is central to John (1:14; 12:28; 17:1, 5, 22, 24).

The theme of *glory* is not unique to John. It permeates the Psalms and Isaiah (Lincoln 2000: 48, 50): "Glory, the phenomenon of light that streams out as the majesty of God, is the manifestation of the Lord's holiness" (Pss 19:1; 29:1-2; Isa 6:3) (J. Waltner: 754). It is dominant in Exodus and Ezekiel. God's "fight" against Pharaoh is to manifest his glory (Exod 14:4, 17-18; 16:7, 10). God's gift of Torah to Moses is enshrouded in glory (Exod 24:16-17; 33:18-23). Isaiah testifies to God's glory in chapter 6 and again in 40–55 (Lincoln 2000: 48). In Ezekiel, God's glory stages his prophetic calling (1:27-28; 3:12). It also *moves*, leaving the Lord's house (10:18-22) and transporting Ezekiel to the exiles in Chaldea (11:22-25). Finally, it brings him and the exiles back home (39:13b, 21; 43:2-5; 44:4). In Daniel, God's glory is part of the dominion and kingship bestowed upon the "one like a son of man" (7:13 RSV). Thompson refers to some of these OT texts in her good discussion on *glory* in John (2001a: 121–25). Glory is also a dominant motif in Paul (notably in Gal 1:5; 2 Cor 3:10-18; and Rom 3:23, the summation of his preceding discourse on human sin).

Several TBC sections discuss *glory*: "The Glory Drama of Scripture" for the prologue; "Cross as Glorification" in John 12, which accentuates John's correlation of cross with glory (see the comments on 13:31-38; and "Glorification" for 19:16b-42). For essays on *glory* in other BCBC volumes,

see Janzen (*Exodus*): 447–48, who discusses this divine manifestation with
other OT companion motifs: name, face/presence, hand/arm; Friesen
(*Isaiah*): 443–44; and Lind (*Ezekiel*): 378–79. These essays complement one
another, presenting a mini-OT theology on glory. That the *New Interpreter's
Dictionary of the Bible* (Nashville: Abingdon, 2006–9) lacks an article on *glory*
is surprising.

GNOSTICISM In the mid-nineteenth century, F. C. Baur thought John was
written in the mid-second century and represented a sea change from the
Synoptics in its theology and influence in early Christianity. He thought it
was contemporary to the gnostic *Gospel of Truth*. But the differences
between these two Gospels are stronger than the similarities. Similarities
are praise to the *Logos* and Jesus as *revealer* of truth. But the differences are
acute. In the *Gospel of Truth*, esoteric knowledge with special passwords
releases one from the evil matter (*hylē*) of this world. The world came into
being through many emanations from the Father as the *plērōma* filling all
in all. After thirty emanations, Wisdom (*Sophia*) fights Silence (*Horus*), after
which *Sophia* produces seven powers, the head of which is Jaldaboth, the
inferior OT God who creates the cosmos and humans in three parts: spirit,
soul, body. Body is the evil *hylē*, from which the Revealer redeems, recap-
turing the "spark" of light. What a contrast and contradiction to John's *The
word was made flesh*! Despite Käsemann's view that John consists of a "naïve
docetic Gnosticism," later gnostic gospels breathe a suffocating air compared to John.

The discovery of p[52], which dates to around AD 125, has forced scholars
to conclude that the Gospel must predate its earliest exemplar (MS). The
discovery of the Nag Hammadi Codices in Egypt in 1946, with its manifold
gnostic documents, caused another sea change. Hill contends that in the
second and third centuries Christian orthodoxy developed a phobia to
John's Gospel because the gnostics used it to their advantage, a point with
some credibility.[w1]

Two reputed canon scholars, however—Bruce Metzger (1987) and
Robert Grant (1963, who changed his opinion from his 1942 article)—argue
that Ignatius (ca. AD 110) echoes John's Gospel and reflects its theology
(Metzger 1987: 46–48). Close analysis of Ignatius's letters corroborates
Metzger's view, since Ignatius's "imitation" texts appeal to Jesus' suffering
(hardly gnostic), love for one another, and faithful discipleship. In turn,
these features are linked to the unity of the churches over which he served
as bishop. Only if Ignatius is a true disciple and the churches are in unity
(cf. John 17) can he die as a true martyr. This is vintage Johannine theology:
suffering, love, discipleship, unity, and true witness/martyr (Swartley
1973: 99–103).[w2]

For other essays on Gnosticism in BCBC volumes, see Martin: 289–90;
Yoder Neufeld 2002: 346–47; Yeatts: 454; and McDermond: 308–9.

"I AM" John's unique use of *I AM* (*egō eimi*) occurs in the absolute (NRSV: *I
am he*) and predicate adjectival noun forms. The metaphorical *I am*-plus-
predicate phrases are *I am the bread of life* (6:35, 51); *the light of the world*

(8:12; 9:5); *the gate* (10:7-9); *the good shepherd* (10:11, 14); *the resurrection and the life* (11:25); *the way, and the truth, and the life* (14:6); and *the true vine* (15:1, 5.) The predicate nominative uses are seven, though O'Day (1995: 602; cf. Burge 2000: 199) lists two extras (elaborations of the traditional seven):

- *I am the living bread that came down from heaven* (6:51).

- *I am the good shepherd. I know my own and my own know me* (10:14).

The implied *I am the living water* also counts (4:14; 6:35c; 7:38-39). The *life* claim of 14:6 overlaps with 11:25, but *truth* is a separate claim. Hence this also makes nine even apart from O'Day's inclusion of 6:51 and 10:14. Both counts together make eleven! John's *I Am* affirmations are intertwined with the prologue's emphases on light, life, glory, and revelation.

John has seven text settings and nine separate occurrences of the absolute *I AM* (4:26; 6:20; 8:24, 28, 58; 13:19; 18:5, 6, 8). Contexts vary, with five different person groups addressed (AT):

- 4:26 *I AM, the one who is speaking to you* (the Samaritan woman).

- 6:20 *I AM, the one speaking to you* (to his disciples at sea).

- 8:24 *You will die in your sins, if you don't believe that I AM* (to Pharisees).

- 8:28 *In lifting up the Son of Man, you will realize that I AM* (to Pharisees).

- 8:58 *Very truly, I tell you, before Abraham was, I AM* (to the Jews).

- 13:19 *I tell you this now ... so that ... you may believe that I AM* (to disciples).

- 18:5, 7, 8 To the arresting *soldiers* and *police* (three times): *I AM.*

Jesus' *I AM* identity points unmistakably to Exodus 3:13-15, identifying Jesus as the Lord (*YHWH*, Tetragrammaton): "I AM who I AM." This is evident in John's "truth on trial" emphasis, with the Lord's lawsuit against God's people (Lincoln 2000: 40–43, 46–48). It reinforces *the Word's* identity with God in the prologue.

This does not threaten monotheism, but intensifies it. What God is, Jesus is. What God does, Jesus does (Bauckham 1998a; Hurtado 2003, 2005; Swartley 2007: 227–37). Jesus' *I AM* statements affirm Israel's monotheism. Harner's study of *I AM* shows the continuity with Isaiah's *I AM* in Isaiah 40–55 (Heb. *'ani hu'*, as in 43:10), emphasizing God's sovereignty and redemptive purposes (Harner 1970, 1988). Ball's full-length monograph considers other background uses as well (Greco-Roman, gnostic, and Mandean). Jesus extends the second exodus *I AM* statements of Isaiah 40–55. He also transforms those claims, since return to a material temple is eclipsed by Jesus as Revealer and recipient of worship of God (Kierspel).

Ball's literary and theological analysis of John notes the reactions of people to the absolute *I AM* in John 8:59; 18:5, 6, 8. "It provokes a strange response on the part of Jesus' narrative audience" (58). In John 4, Jesus reveals this self-identity to support the Samaritan woman's dawning perceptions of his identity: *a Jew, sir,* and *a prophet* (cf. Ball: 62). The comments in this commentary on John 4 note O'Day's point that Jesus not only mediates revelation, but also is God-revelation in his self-designation as *I AM*. In this respect the absolute uses carry forward the *Word's* christological claims in John's prologue. Jesus' *I AM* self-revelation in John 6:21 sparks the subsequent *bread-of-life* narrative. Similarly, in John 11, Jesus' *I am the resurrection and the life* prepares for Jesus' raising of Lazarus. As with the other signs in this Gospel, John handles this scene in such a way as to show that it is not simply a spectacular miracle, but also a christologically significant *sign*. Hence Jesus makes the dual promise to believers in 11:25b-26 (cf. Ball: 103).

The connection between Jesus' claim *I am the light of the world* and his healing of the blind man (8:12–9:41) has similar import. So also Jesus' claim *I am the good* [true, model] *shepherd* (in 10:11, 14) with 10:17-18, where Jesus speaks of his power to *lay down* his *life* (for the sheep) and *to take it up again*. Then Jesus raises Lazarus (ch. 11), prefiguring Jesus' own resurrection, a structural gem. Similarly, *I am the vine and you are the branches* is the heart of Jesus' tender farewell to his disciples (13:31–16:33).

Jesus' *I AM* declarations in the absolute form and his predicate adjectival noun claims are core to the Christology of John's Gospel.

"THE JEWS" The meaning of the term *the Jews* [*hoi Ioudaioi*] in John is enigmatic. The issues are complex and the literature is vast, with sundry proposals to resolve the conundrum. Jesus' invective against *the Jews*, especially 8:44, has contributed to the tragic Christian persecution of Jews. This occurred already in the early centuries and later. In the year Columbus "discovered" America (1492), Spain expelled the Muslims and the Jews, unless they converted to Catholicism. Martin Luther's 1543 tract *On the Jews and Their Lies* contains damning statements against Jews (see TLC for John 8).

In his article "Martin Luther and the Jews," Hillerbrand points out that in his early 1523 tract *That Jesus Christ Was Born a Jew*, Luther breathes a different air, hoping for conversion of Jews and counseling kindness to Jews. Hillerbrand demurs on posing any direct connection between Luther and the Holocaust (the Shoah). He sees the development of anti-Semitism as quite complex, with nineteenth-century Catholic Austria a seedbed for anti-Semitism (138) as well as for the development of ghettoes. Whatever one's interpretation of the intervening centuries and their influences, German Lutheranism was "unprepared for the challenge of Nazi racial ideology" (143). Using John to support anti-Semitism is sin; it contradicts John's major themes of light, life, and love. It makes the Gospel exclusive, opposing John's open invitation. It undermines the universality of John's Gospel (cf. Kysar 1976: 111–18).

This topic is complex and sensitive (cf. Bieringer et al.: 3–37; Ashton). Here I summarize it in four parts: (1) In a textual analysis I examine the argument between Jesus and *the Jews*. (2) I search for the referent: To whom does *the Jews* refer and why? (3) With narrative analysis I seek to determine the sense of the term in John: How does it function in relation to other characters and themes in John's narrative (symbolic) world? The term does not occur in the Johannine Epistles because the community is apparently no longer in significant relationship with the synagogue (McDermond:

143–49). (4) I pursue the hermeneutical and theological issues: Is John's theology anti-Jewish? Is it anti-Semitic?

1. *Textual analysis*. The term *The Jews* (*hoi Ioudaioi*) occurs seventy times in John (NRSV; seventy-one if the variant reading in 3:25, *hoi Ioudaioi*, is accepted). The term occurs only five times in Matthew (cf. Lieu 2008: 171), six times in Mark, and five times in Luke. Subtracting duplicate uses in Synoptic parallels, it occurs only four times in the Synoptics, including "the King of the Jews" (as in Mark 15:26). These uses are mostly on lips of Gentiles who refer to the Jews, as is true of other extracanonical literature (e.g., Philo; cf. Cook: 262–64). Applied to John, this would mean the Gospel is written from a Gentile perspsective, but that deduction is too facile, as Cook acknowledges. John is rooted in Judaism. Only Acts uses the term more often (82x in sg. and pl.). The NT uses a total of nineteen (11x in Romans, 8x in 1 Corinthians). Other designations for Jesus' interlocutors, such as *Pharisees, rulers, chief priests,* and even *Jerusalemites* (*scribes* and *Sadducees,* prominent in the Synoptics do not appear in John!) However, whenever the Johannine "narrative moves toward hostility, it also moves toward use of *hoi Ioudaioi*" (Lieu 2008: 171). The term occurs in the singular only twice (4:9, in the Samaritan woman's response; and 18:35, in Pilate's response). It is distributed unevenly in the narrative. It occurs forty-six times in 1:19–12:11. It does not occur in the prologue and it occurs only once in Jesus' farewell speech (Jesus reminds his disciples of what he said to the Jews, 13:33). In the passion narrative the term occurs twenty-three times, but only once in the resurrection narrative (*for fear of the Jews,* 20:19).

All but seven uses are by the narrator. These seven exceptions are 4:9 (the Samaritan woman); 11:8 (where the disciples repeat what the narrator said earlier in 8:59; 10:31); 18:35 (Pilate); and four uses by Jesus (4:22; 13:33; 18:20, 36; Lieu: 174). Of these four by Jesus, only two occur in direct discourse, one of which has a positive connotation. Over one-third are nonhostile in connotation. Thus not all references to "Jews" in John are adversarial (e.g., 11:31). Except for the Samaritan woman, the (likely Roman) official, the Greeks who come to see Jesus in 12:20, and Pilate and the Roman soldiers in chapters 18–19, all of the other characters in the Gospel, including Jesus and the disciples, are Jews, many of whom emerge in a positive light. D. M. Smith (2008: 8) identifies the NT texts where *Jews* occurs. The term *Jews* is absent from the catholic epistles, *even the Johannine Epistles*(!), the Pastoral Epistles, Hebrews, Ephesians, Philippians, 2 Thessalonians, and Philemon. First Thessalonians 2:14-16 comes closest to John's thirty-eight adversarial uses.

The Jews appears first in John as those who send *priests and Levites from Jerusalem* to inquire about John's identity (1:19). But then 1:24 says they were sent *from the Pharisees.* In the temple cleansing (2:12-22), "the temple authorities or leaders are identified as the *Ioudaioi* (2:18, 20)" (Carter 2006: 68–69). This collision between Jesus and the temple authorities sets the stage for continuing distinction between those who are for Jesus and those who are against him. John puts the temple cleansing at the beginning of the Gospel, perhaps to expose the divide between belief and unbelief early in the narrative. As the Gospel progresses, the dividing lines become clearer. Usually the Jews—whoever they are—are located in Jerusalem, but in 6:41, 52, they are in Galilee (cf. 1:19).[w1]

In chapters 5–8, where feasts structure the narrative, *the Jews* are the chief but not the sole interlocutors. They become increasingly adversarial toward Jesus. Striking shifts in Jesus' dialogue partners occur:

- John 5 uses *the Jews* throughout.

- John 6 shifts from *the crowd* (v. 22) to *the Jews* (v. 41).

- In John 7 *the Jews* appears interchangeably with *the crowd* (vv. 11-24), *some of the people* (v. 25), *Pharisees* (v. 32, alarmed by many *in the crowd* who *believed*, v. 31), *some in the crowd* in conflict with *others in the crowd* (vv. 40-44), and *temple police* who report to *the chief priests and the Pharisees* (vv. 44-49).

- John 8 [7:53–8:11, *the Pharisees*] has *the Pharisees* (8:12-21), *the Jews* (vv. 22-30), *the Jews who had believed in him* (vv. 31-47), then *the Jews* (vv. 48-59).

- John 9's narrative has a striking interchange between *the Pharisees* (9:13-17) and *the Jews* (vv. 18-23). When used, *they* appears to blend the *Pharisees* (inferred from quizzing the blind man a second time), *the Jews* (vv. 24-34), and then *some of the Pharisees* (v. 40). *The Jews* and *the Pharisees* appear to be interchangeable in principle. *The Pharisees* play a major adversarial role and appear to be conflated with *the Jews*, as Rensberger has noted (42). O'Day implies the same: "The authorities . . . have the dual identity of Pharisees/'Jews' in this scene, underscoring the fluidity of levels in the telling of the story" (1995: 658).

- In John 11 some Jews console Martha and Mary and are not adversarial (vv. 19, 31, 45). The adversaries are the *chief priests*, *Pharisees*, and *the council* (the Sanhedrin, vv. 46-47). Here the term *Jews* represents the broader landscape of Jews—most of the characters in the Gospel (see below).[w2]

2. *The referent.* The recurring references to *the Jews* and to specific parties also adversarial to Jesus raises the question of referent. To whom does *the Jews* refer? Proposed solutions differ:

a. Judeans (a minority opinion, but with confident voice).

b. The religious (temple) authorities (widely held).

c. Descendants of elite returnees from Babylon who controlled the temple and were an orthodox-confessional group, thus representing intra-Jewish division between returnees and those whose ancestors never went to Babylon. Diverse groups, including Samaritans and Christ-believers identified themselves as "Israelites." They, too, were Jews, but not *the Jews* who represent the opposition in John. John does not represent a "parting of the ways" beyond Messiah-believers and Jews, in the broader sense (Boyarin 2002: 222-38).

    d. Those who persecute believers in Jesus and put them out of the synagogue.

    e. Those who charge Jesus with blasphemy (Truex).

The various arguments in favor of these solutions are long and complex. See the Web supplement.[w3]

If Jesus' alleged blasphemy is the rationale for the Jews' putting some Jesus believers out of the synagogue (9:22; 12:42; 16:2), then John in principle concurs with the Synoptic Gospels, since Jesus' opponents in Mark 2:7 and 14:62 explicitly accuse Jesus of blasphemy. This would reopen the question of whether Mark's, Matthew's (9:3; 26:65), and Luke's (5:21) views differ that much from John's symbolic worldview regarding what led to Jesus' death. Although Mark never mentions expulsion from the synagogue, two features are somewhat analogous: already in 3:6 the Pharisees and Herodians collude to kill Jesus. Thereafter Jesus never returns to the synagogue except in his hometown of Nazareth, where he encounters unbelief (6:1-6)! Second, in his apocalyptic discourse, Jesus prophesies that his followers "will be beaten in synagogues" (13:9).

Luke presents Paul as calling together the Jewish leaders in Rome for his last defense (Acts 28:17). Luke differs from Mark and John on Jesus' relation to the temple (Luke 24:53) and to the synagogue leaders. Jesus' words about (against?) the temple are crucial in Mark, Matthew, and John. They lead to Jesus' crucifixion. (Luke speaks, however, of Jesus' claim to be the Messiah and Son of God in 22:66-70—even more Johannine—with the charge of blasphemy implied in 22:71.) John puts the temple cleansing first, as a lens through which to read the narrative. *The Jews* understand on one level, but Jesus means otherwise. This illustrates John's narrative skill in portraying misunderstanding and double meaning. The other two charges of blasphemy in John differ from the Synoptics, though John's *equal-with-God* charge is parallel to "forgiving sins" in Mark and Matthew. The rancor against the Jews (John 5–8) has no parallel in the Synoptics.

The similarities between the Synoptics and John raise the question of whether John's negative portrayal of the Jews has its roots in Jesus, since conflict between Jesus and the religious leaders occurs in all four Gospels (note esp. Matthew's woes against the Pharisees in ch. 23, which reflect conflict in Matthew's time *and* in Jesus' time).

Notably, the terms *scribes* and *Sadducees* occur nowhere in John, given that 7:53–8:11 is not original to this Gospel. The scribes were teachers of the law. Since proper understanding of the Law of Moses lies at the heart of the conflict between Jesus and the Jews in John's Gospel [*Law, p. 526*], perhaps *the Jew*s refers primarily to the role of the scribes as interpreters of the law. In the first charge of blasphemy against Jesus in the Synoptics, the scribes are the foremost accusers (Mark 2:6; Matt 9:3; Luke 5:21). Jesus does what is only God's prerogative: he forgives sins (something Jesus does not do in John!). The "scribes" oppose Jesus, and in coalition with other groups, seek to kill him—as do *the Jews* in John. John's parallel to the Synoptic "Sadducees" may be the *council* in 11:47-53.

    3. *Solutions from the sense of the narrative* (relational features of the narrative in characters or themes). In seeking the identity of *the Jews* based on

their narrative role, differing proposals emerge. Four considerations shape the debate:

a. Unbelief is a primary feature characterizing *the Jews.* Related to this, *the Jews* may be a cipher of John's negative use of *world.* To some extent, the terms are interchangeable.

b. Issues of Torah, temple, and purity mark the tiff between Jesus and *the Jews.*

c. Most of the cases where *the Jews* oppose Jesus are subtly ironic.

d. John's dramatic literary features suggest stage production script. *The Jews'* dramatic role is not actual life. Therefore readers should not castigate Jews, and certainly not demonize them.

Fuller representations of these arguments are available on the Web.[w4]

The search for better solutions continues, which O'Day calls for (1995: 507). Given the varied explanations of the term in "referent" and "narrative sense," Hakola contends that John intentionally makes the identity of *the Jews* ambiguous.[w5] While this is true, it is *the chief priests and the Pharisees* who call the council to determine Jesus' fate (11:47), and this combo also authorizes Jesus' arrest in 18:3. But not all "authorities" are included, since *many, even of the authorities,* believe in him (12:42)! Any definitive solution appears elusive. Von Wahlde (2010: 1.63–68, 91–93) solves the problem by allocating different meanings to *hoi Ioudaioi* in his proposed sequential editions of the Gospel. But this does not satisfy since his proposed editions are hypothetical.[w5]

4. *Hermeneutical and theological issues.* Whichever solution we espouse, the hermeneutical and theological ramifications are important. Hakola thinks the purpose of the designation was to "distance" Johannine believers from Judaism: "Christians were adopting a non-Jewish identity" (226). Hence, distinction between the Jews in authority and other Jews is not clear (cf. Culpepper 1983: 126). Concurring with Reinhartz (2001b) and Culpepper, Hakola holds that the blurring of distinctions of *hoi Ioudaioi* within the text leads to a "generalization" of Jewish identity as the author stereotypes those who reject Jesus. This results in "elevated . . . bitterness and hostility of the polemic to a new level" (226), which inspires alienation of Christians from Jews.

While this appears true, there are no *Christians* nor *church* in John. Believers remain part of Judaism. Only thus does threat of *being put out of the synagogue* make sense (9:22). All the people in the Gospel narrative are Jews unless otherwise specified. John's Gospel witnesses more to continuity than discontinuity with the Judaisms of the first century.[w6]

Instead of distancing the Johannine community from Judaism, a different function of this generalized, ambiguous use of *the Jews* in John may be considered. The fuzziness surrounding the identity of *the Jews* complements the anonymity of the beloved disciple, who is also a Jew. The Gospel narrative calls readers to identify themselves on a *continuum* of Jews in relation to *belief* in Jesus-Messiah and *love*: ranging from *the Jews,* Judas, the Pharisees, Nicodemus, the Bethany family, Peter, Nathanael, Mary Magdalene, Thomas, to the beloved disciple. The beloved disciple is

bonded heart-to-heart with Jesus in love (13:23). Whoever he was historically (and Bauckham provides a viable answer: 2006, 2007, 2008) *[Beloved
Disciple, p. 505]*, his elusive identity in the narrative, like that of *the Jews*, calls
readers to emulate the distinguishing quality of his identity: *love*. This
tones our attitude toward the "other," whoever that is in our setting. This
is Christians' best hope as they seek to atone for the bloody history of
Christians' persecuting Jews.

In Girardian theory (Swartley, ed. 2000), *the Jews*, no more or less than
other groups, fit within the *universal* cultural *desire* that *imitates* and leads
to *conflict* that spirals into *violence* and *scapegoating*, unless checked by law
or *another* religious imperative. In this approach John's Gospel *exposes*
human violence *and* the means of redemption from that violence, namely,
love for one another and welcoming the enemy (whether Samaritan or
otherwise) into that circle of love. In the face of hostile threats to kill him,
Jesus sharply castigates his opponents, but this is no sharper than that of
the OT prophets and the Qumran covenanters (Evans 1993b: 3–8). Some—
even many—change, but others do not. Readers must choose whom they
desire to emulate in character identification: whether Jews who, like *the
Jews, hate,* or whether Jews who, like the beloved disciple, *love*.

Peter's restoration hinges on Jesus' question *Do you love me?* a crowning
climax of the Gospel. If so, *Follow me*. Love (friendship love and self-giving
love) is the best bridge between Jews and Christians in today's world.
Hostility has ended (Eph 2:11-22). This is the hermeneutical road we must
travel as we bracket this aspect of John, not regarding it morally normative, along with OT war texts (see Swartley 1983: 229–34, with twenty-two
points of hermeneutical learning, esp. points 5, 9, 15, 16, 17). John's portrayal of the Jews must be put into intracanonical dialogue with other NT
biblical texts, notably Paul's treatment in Romans, where Jews and Gentiles
are one in Christ and God's covenant with Israel is binding. Gentiles are
grafted in. Some hold John (and Paul) to be supersessionist (the church
replaces Israel), and some contend that John is not supersessionist, since
the controversy is intra-Jewish. In either case, Christians today must cen-
sure the hostile language of both the Jews and Jesus in John (cf. also the
hostile language among and between Reformation and Anabaptist writers).
Instead, we should seek to emulate the beloved disciple.

Using the translational principle of dynamic equivalence, the CEV and
NLT present attractive translations. In all cases except 4:9 and 18:35 (texts
spoken by the Samaritan woman and Pilate), *hoi Ioudaioi* is consistently
translated the *people*. The exclusion-from-synagogue texts are softened.
The term *Jewish leaders* is preserved at appropriate places. (The LB uses
Jewish leaders for *the Jews* in all cases.) The CEV and NLT translations disarm
the *universal* scapegoat mechanism and merit consideration in halting the
disastrous history of effects this Gospel has had for Jews.

Hakola's conclusion, similar to other scholars, is persuasive: "I believe
that we should not take what John says of Jewishness and the Jews as a
foundation for building Christian identities in relation to the Jews and
Judaism in today's world" (242). One caveat, though: Jesus' word to the
Samaritan woman is *Salvation is from the Jews* (4:22).

LAW IN JOHN Comments on this topic vary greatly. Volf (among others) holds that law is not a factor in John's Gospel: the community is guided by the love command (2008: 45–46). Lincoln, however, contends that the lawsuit genre is central in John 5–12 and 18–19. Jesus refers several times to *your law* (8:17; 10:34). Their view of the law falls short of Jesus' perception of law. In 7:50-52, Nicodemus appeals to *the law* for a fair hearing (Lincoln 2000: 54–56). Jesus appeals to Moses the lawgiver as a key witness to his words (5:45-47). As noted in "Ethics of the Gospel" (see introduction, p. 38), Kanagaraj and van der Watt argue that John affirms the law—especially the Decalogue. Pancaro's 590-page monograph on law leaves no stone unturned.

In the conclusion to his discussion of law in John 7, Pancaro says, "In 7:19 Jesus accuses the Jews of not doing the Law because they seek to kill Jesus; Jn 7:51 further explains in what way the (condemnatory) judgement the Jews pass upon Jesus is against the Law" (156). As the law is understood by the Jews, Jesus opposes it. But as soon as "faith in the mystery of Christ's person" enters the picture, then "Law testifies in favor of Jesus; Jesus no longer appears as a violator of the Law, but as the one who fulfills it (cf. Jn 7:21-23)" (156). With regard to John 7, Pancaro emphatically concludes, "Jn brings this home at 7:51 by having the Law of the Jews establish conditions for the judgement of Jesus which can be met only by those who believe on him; by presenting faith in Jesus as demanded by the Law!" (156; the latter part of this quotation makes sense only in the context of the former quotation; it goes beyond what 7:51 explicitly says). This explains why and how in John 5 Jesus appeals to Moses as his witness: *It is Moses who accuses you* (v. 45b RSV). Following this comes Jesus' stinging accusation: *But if you do not believe his writings, how will you believe my words?* (v. 47 RSV). Pancaro's exposition of John 7 on law provides the lens for understanding 1:17, *For the law was given through Moses; grace and truth came through Jesus Christ* (RSV).

In summarizing Pancaro, Loader (434) says, "John sees no opposition between Moses and Jesus, Torah and gospel"; "Torah is absorbed into this higher reality represented by Christ" (Pancaro: 262). Loader (434–47) summarizes numerous scholarly views on the topic (Kotila, Martyn, Neyrey, Luz, Freyne, Thorbald, Scott, Pryor, Deine) before taking up his own study of John (Loader 447–91). Two points in this rich study are especially important. First, John's language (e.g., *gift of God* and *living water*) is reminiscent of language used of Torah. What Judaism claims for Torah, John claims for Jesus" (457). Second, John is saturated with the ethos of Judaism (law and feasts), and he "sees no need to attack it as such" (488), but it is "both inferior and preliminary to the realm of the Spirit opened up by Jesus" (490). Jesus' love command (13:31-35) does not appeal to the Jewish law but goes beyond it to a higher ethical realm. Even with a positive view of the law, John's Christology transforms it, and thus in essence is its replacement (488–91). Culpepper (2001: 81) concurs, saying that while John is thoroughly Jewish, it is also "trenchantly anti-Jewish." He regards John's theology supersessionist (i.e., it supersedes or replaces OT law, festivals, and institutions).

Jesus indeed transforms the law, but *replacement* is too strong since the discourse dialogues are intra-Jewish debate reflecting conventions of the time. To interpret John as "replacement" or "supersessionist" underwrites the misuse of the Gospel in the history of sad (anti-Semitic) effects through the centuries.

LIGHT AND DARKNESS This duality permeates the Gospel. The contrast appears in 1:4-5; 3:19-21; 8:12-59, with chapter 9 continuing the theme in the *blind/seeing* metaphor. The final words of Jesus' public ministry are *Walk in the light, not in darkness* (12:34-36, 46 AT). The imagery also appears in 1 John (McDermond: 30–33, 48–51). Light and darkness form one of John's sharpest dualities. It is related to the *from above* and *from below* duality. In John *children of light* (12:36) is a term opposed to the self-proclaimed label *disciples of Moses* (9:28), both within a social situation where the *light* community penetrates the dominant social groups who unwittingly live in darkness (Petersen: 58, 80–109).

The Psalms, the Prophets, and the Qumran texts also contain this duality. The duality of the "sons of light and the sons of darkness" in the Dead Sea Scrolls (as in 1QS 1.9-10) represents a particularly striking parallel to John's Gospel and bears witness to the contentious variety of Judaisms in the first century. In discussing Romans 13:11-14, Toews has helpful commentary (327–32). The new age dawning in Christ Jesus provides moral muscle for the call to walk in the light (cf. 13:13) and to wear "the armor of light" (13:12). A sharp moral duality appears also in Ephesians 5:8-10 (cf. Yoder Neufeld 2002: 230–38, 345–46): "In the Gospel of John, *light* and *darkness* function as mutually exclusive terms, which nevertheless interpenetrate. Thus in John 1 the 'light' . . . [the 'Word'] enters the 'darkness,' which can neither absorb it nor overcome it. . . . For both John and Ephesians, the transition point of persons moving from darkness to light is 'believing' (e.g., John 1:12-13; Eph 2:8)" (246).

LOVE ETHIC IN JOHN What is new in both the fourth Gospel and the Epistles is the primacy Jesus gives to the command to *love one another* as the Father loves Jesus and as Jesus loves the Father. In the essay "Love" (TBC for John 21), the statistical analysis showed that words from the *agap-* stem occur 96 times in the Gospel and the Epistles, and the verb *phileō* verb occurs thirteen times in the Gospel. Put together, the Greek words for *love* (noun/verb) in John and 1–3 John thus occur a total of 109 times, representing over 10 percent—though the text is only 2.5 percent—of the occurrences of *love* in the entire Bible (NRSV), even though the OT abounds with descriptions of God's steadfast love and other uses of love, including the double commandment.

As noted in "Ethics of the Gospel" (see introduction, p. 38), several scholars have judged John as sectarian, intracommunity oriented. Their judgment that John does not provide any viable love ethic (cf., e.g., Schrage; Meeks 1996) does not do justice to the Gospel. Because this Gospel speaks of love far more than any other Gospel, such a predisposed discount of love in John is unjustified. More, it is evidence of a negative moral bias regarding the Gospel. Käsemann's dismissal is lamentable: "The object of Christian love for John is only what belongs to the community under the Word, or what is elected to belong to it, that is, the brotherhood of Jesus" (65). This dismissal reflects the assumption that an "ethic"—to be called such—must directly address world issues (e.g., politics, economics, culture). The notion that the new community of the Gospel, characterized by a distinctive love ethic, is relevant to the world escapes consideration. Unfortunately, Käsemann's own weak ecclesiology prevents him from understanding—let alone appreciating—John's substantial ethical message.

Two articles open a path to a needed corrective. The first by Culpepper on "Inclusivism and Exclusivism" (2002) corrects the misperception that John is only sectarian and exclusivist. While such elements do appear, a strong thread of social and theological inclusivism pervades the Gospel (e.g., the prominent role of women, one a Samaritan [ch. 4]; and God's love for *the world* [3:16], which includes *other sheep . . . not of this fold*; 10:16 RSV): "The exclusiveness of the gospel of John is therefore balanced by an inclusiveness that sets the revelatory and redemptive work of Jesus in the mystery of God's love for the world" (105).

D. Moody Smith directly addresses the issue of the nature of John's love ethic. Smith reviews the arguments (2002: 110) against a love ethic that reaches beyond the proposed sectarian in-group and then proposes a different view: "John . . . distills out of his message the one ethical commandment to love one another (13:34)—not just your neighbor, but also not your enemy. Yet the commandment to love one another is capacious, capable of infinite expansion, so as to include all humanity. . . . The synoptic Jesus' command to love your enemy (Mt. 5:44) is not contradicted" (111).

Schnelle's theological exposition (2009: 726–34) presents John's ethic similarly, noting especially that Jesus' love commandment is twinned with his deed of footwashing: together they provide "normative content of the loving service the disciples are to do" (734). Rensberger's contribution exposits this love ethic as a valued form of sectarianism that has the capacity to critique and transform the world's hatred and indifference, thus witnessing to the world the costly love of God for the world, manifest in the Son on the cross. John's love ethic combined with its strong emphasis on mission and peace may be the best hope for transformation of the world's ways into the ways of the Father and Son, who in self-donation have given and give themselves for the life of the world!

See "Ethics of the Gospel" (in the introduction, p. 38); comments on 13:31-35; "Love for One Another" (TLC for ch. 13); "Commandments in John" (TBC for 15:1-16:4); "Life on the Vine" (TLC for 15:1-16:4); "Love" (TBC for ch. 21); "Love and Ministry" (TLC for ch. 21).[w1]

NUMBERS IN JOHN John has a penchant for numbers. While Menken's study may overdo the point, it is clear that seven is used with intent (traditionally, seven *I AM* texts in the absolute form and seven with predicates). John 1:19–2:11 presents Jesus' early ministry within a framework of seven days. Bauckham (2006: 387) sees seven witnesses in Jesus' first phase of ministry [*Witness, p. 534*]. John has seven disciples present at postresurrection

(21:2). Seven also appears often in Revelation: seven churches (chs. 2–3), seven seals, seven trumpets, seven bowls of wrath.

Is the number three significant in John? The wedding in Cana is on *the third day* (2:1)—presumably the third day after what was just reported on the fourth day (1:43-51). Jesus says, *Destroy this temple, and in three days I will raise it up*, signifying his resurrected body (2:19, 21-22). The Bethany family has three siblings (chs. 11–12). Peter denies Jesus three times (ch. 18), and he is restored as shepherd of the sheep with a threefold question: *Do you love me?* (ch. 21). We might even include God's fullness in John in trinitarian form: Father, Son, and Paraclete.

Three and seven appear to bear symbolic significance in John's Gospel narrative. Both symbolize completeness and perfection. Together they echo the seven days of creation (Gen 1:1–2:3) and the three angelic visitors to Abraham who announce Sarah's conception, enabling fulfillment of the promise that Abraham's family would become a blessing to the nations. (For Bauckham's [2007] proposal that the 153 fish caught in John 21 is significant, see the comments for that chapter.)

SACRAMENT Scholars are divided on whether John 6:51-58 is eucharistic and/or sacramental. I think it is eucharistic. It is also sacramental if sacrament is understood as embracing our moral life in union with Christ as branches to a vine and marked by loving one another. See "John 6 as Eucharist and Sacrament?" (TBC for ch. 6); "Footwashing Today" (TLC for ch. 13); "John 18:10-11; 18:36 and 19:34 in Anabaptism" (TLC for ch. 19).

In these entries my position concurs with Rempel's (225–26) three-point summary of the contribution of three Anabaptist leaders (Hubmaier, Marpeck, and Philips), as well as with Menno Simons as presented in "Eating Jesus' Flesh" (TLC for ch. 6). Anabaptist theology emphasizes "faith, reconciliation, community, and mission" in observing the Lord's Supper. Believers church theology broadens the meaning of *sacramental* to include the faith and moral life of the church. As Klaassen has shown, in Anabaptism the followers of Christ regard all of life to be sacred. Nothing is sacred in and of itself, but Sabbath, baptism, and the Lord's Supper are sacred when practiced obediently in the community of faithful discipleship (2001: 11–29). Believers churches do not celebrate the Lord's Supper as Roman Catholics do, in which the priest's pronouncement effects the change (transubstantiation) of the bread and wine into the body (flesh?) and blood of Jesus. Although believers church members consider communion to be a memorial celebration, they also consider it more than a memorial. Communion "re-presents the presence of the risen Christ in the church" (Mennonite Church 1995: 12). Communion celebrates and constitutes *koinōnia* (1 Cor 10:16), "participation in" the blood and body of Christ (RSV).

SIGNS AND WORKS John's Gospel contains seven signs: changing water to wine (2:1-11); healing the official's son (4:46-54); healing the infirm man (5:1-18); feeding the five thousand (6:1-15); walking on water (6:16-21); healing the blind man (ch. 9); and raising Lazarus (11:1-44). The term *sign(s)* occurs seventeen times in John. *Signs* are one of the seven points of sensitivity in interpreting John's Gospel (Motyer 1997: 62; cf. 2008: 36–73, discussing six other points of sensitivity). Why? Do signs *automatically* lead to faith, or are they necessary only to hold culpable those who refuse to believe, as the end of the Book of Signs (chs. 1–12) might suggest (12:36c-41)? The next verse says, *Nevertheless, many, even of the authorities, believed in him* (v. 42a). Commentators struggle with whether *signs* are positive or negative in John (cf. Mark 8:11-13, which regards signs negatively). Some verses in John may suggest that signs do not generate true faith that leads to discipleship: 2:23-25; 6:26; 11:47; 12:37. Bultmann (207) regards John's signs negatively. R. Brown regards *"signs-belief"* as only a preliminary step to salvation (1966: 528). But this flies in the face of the Gospel's purpose statement (20:30-31).

John intends that *signs* and *works* should lead people to faith. As Thompson (1991: 93–94) says, "A sign is a manifestation, through the person of Jesus, of God's work in the world." Jesus' signs are intended to lead people—Motyer says *Jews* specifically—to faith in Jesus as Messiah and Son of God. Yet it is possible for people to see the signs without believing. Why do signs lead some to faith and not others? When one sees in the signs God's self-manifestation "as life-giving and responds to Jesus as mediating that life," faith is born (Thompson 1991: 96). On the other hand, when people do not respond in faith, Jesus' signs and works condemn those who do not believe: *If I had not done among them the works that no one else did, they would not have sin* (15:24; see also 14:10-11; cf. Exod 34:10). Jesus' signs and works testify to Jesus' identity. They constitute evidence of the Father's partnering with the Son to lead people to faith (John 5:20, 36; see also 7:3; 9:3; 15:24). The works are the Father's witness to the Son's authority. In 20:30-31 signs are testimony; they prompt christological responses.

Johns and Miller (528–33) have examined four passages in John that have been used to bolster a negative view of signs in the Gospel: 2:23–3:2; 4:48; 6:26-27; 20:25, 29. Johns and Miller persuasively show that these texts actually support a positive view of signs. Overall, *signs* prompt belief; they play a positive role. In 2:23–3:2, *many believed* when they saw Jesus' *signs* (v. 23), but *Jesus on his part would not entrust himself to them, because he knew all people and needed no one to testify about anyone* (vv. 24-25). Does Jesus reject faith based on signs, implying that those who believe with a "signs faith" cannot be trusted? This section also introduces Nicodemus, who comes to Jesus and affirms that Jesus is *a teacher who has come from God; for no one can do these signs that you do apart from the presence of God* (3:2). Nicodemus, likely a *secret* believer (19:38-39), comes to Jesus because of the signs that God empowers (3:2c), but he lacks the understanding of the Spirit; he fails to confess Jesus openly.

In a second pertinent text, Jesus responds to the official's request to heal his son, saying, *Unless you see signs and wonders you will not believe* (4:48). This may be an implicit rebuke of a "signs faith": Jesus is saying that people should be able to believe without seeing signs. Yet Johns and Miller (526–27) point out that in John 5 Moses, who performed God's signs against Pharaoh, is portrayed positively (John 5:31-47). God's response to Moses's question, "Suppose they do not believe me or listen to me, but say, 'The Lord did not appear to you?'" (Exod 4:1) was to provide signs. Signs are God's attestation of Moses to Israel and to Pharaoh. Similarly, Jesus' signs testify to the people that the Father works in him (5:17). This claim, disclosing his identity, leads to *the Jews* charge: Jesus is *making himself equal to God* (5:18). Johns and Miller (531) paraphrase Jesus' response: *You must understand that unless you see signs and wonders, you will certainly not believe, so I will give you signs and wonders, so that you may believe.* *Signs* prompt belief: they play a positive role.

The third text, 6:26-27, comes after Jesus feeds the five thousand. Some people seek him out afterward, and Jesus responds, *You are looking for me, not because you saw signs, but because you ate your fill of the loaves. Do not work for food that perishes, but for food that endures for eternal life.* Here Jesus is not downplaying signs but challenging them to see and recognize the sign as a revelation of his true identity rather than simply to seek another meal. Jesus goes on to give them another sign—the sign of his own *flesh* (6:51). In Jesus' theology, signs are positive.

John 20:25 is the fourth text, where Thomas declares, *Unless I see, . . . I will not believe.* Jesus later replies, *Put your finger here and see my hands. Reach out your hand and put it in my side* (20:27). *Blessed are those who have not seen and yet have come to believe* (20:29). Thomas believes! (20:28). Jesus' rebuke is not because Thomas wants evidence but because he insists on a certain type of evidence. He insists on the evidence of his own eyes rather than accepting the evidence of those who have seen and testified to Jesus. Jesus is saying, *Blessed are those who are satisfied to rely on secondary evidence, the faithful testimony of others* (v. 29 AT). Johns and Miller observe that this was the situation of the Johannine believers. Faithful witnesses pass along to them the testimony of Jesus' identity. The conclusion that follows Thomas's confession is the Gospel's purpose statement: *These [signs] are written so that you may come to believe that Jesus is the Messiah, the Son of God, and that through believing you may have life in his name* (20:31). First John opens with "what we have heard, seen, gazed upon, and touched, that we declare to you" (1:1-5 AT). Here too, faithful witnesses pass along the testimony of Jesus. Thompson (1991: 92) rightly says, "What the signs make known, specifically, is the unity of the Son and the Father."

Another approach is to recognize somewhat diverse emphases regarding signs in John, as Carter (2006: 96–98) does in stating four views of how signs function. But this confuses more than it helps, since it leaves the impression that signs function differently in different instances and for different people. Although the signs present some ambiguity in their function, the Johns and Miller treatment resolves this. The ambiguity regarding the function of signs in John arises in that they both conceal and reveal, as described in John 9:39: the blind see, and those who see become blind. Signs may show the presence of the divine, but the disposition of those who see the signs determines the response (cf. Schneiders 2003: 67; Mark 4:12 and the Synoptic parables).

This does not annul the signs' positive intent, clearly stated in John 20:31. Schnelle stresses that in the *signs* the "Preexistent and Exalted One" *incarnate* and "the hour" of Jesus' final glorification blend to attest his true humanity (2005: 82–83). Jesus' death and resurrection are continuous with his signs and works (2006: 22).

SOPHIA **AND** *LOGOS* John's Gospel nowhere mentions *Sophia* (wisdom personified as in Proverbs 8 and Sir 1:1-10; 24:1-22), though Matthew (23:34; cf. 11:29; 12:42; 13:34) explicitly connects Jesus with *Sophia*. Luke does also when Jesus quotes the "Wisdom of God" (11:49) to describe impending judgment (Swartley 1994: 180–83). The Synoptics contain Jesus' parables, a genre that fits the *Sophia* tradition. In the Synoptic Gospels, Jesus' portrait is readily that of wisdom teacher (Borg: 97–124). But John has no parables and no explicit *Sophia* sayings.

As indicated in the Web material for the prologue, many commentators readily blend the traditions of Word/*Logos* and Wisdom/*Sophia*. Evans (1993a: 112n1) cites Ashton and Painter, who contend that John presents the Word (Jesus) as the incarnation of wisdom. Evans holds that Philo is the crucial link between the wisdom tradition and John's Gospel. The parallels are indeed impressive, as Carter shows (2006: 137, table). Carter presents a masterful summary of the Gospel's main themes with "Jesus/wisdom" as the subject (137–39). See the more extended consideration of scholarly views supporting the view that *Sophia* is significant to John's Gospel, as well as reasons why John avoids use of *Sophia*.[w1]

In a novel perspective on this matter, Jane Heath assesses John's relation to the wisdom tradition by focusing on John 7:12b, *Some were saying, "He is good"* (AT).[w2] Heath mines the overlooked christological import of John's use of *good* (*agathos*) in several texts: Nathanael's question (1:46), the *good* [*kalos*] *wine* (2:10), and Jesus as *the good shepherd* (ch. 10). She cites a wisdom parallel (Wis 7:26-27) where wisdom is described as "an image of [God's] goodness"—powerful for many things and entering "holy souls in each generation and making them friends of God and neighbors" (paraphrased). She observes this similarity to wisdom in John's portrayal of Jesus. But she notes striking differences as well: in John "Jesus is more personal, more concrete, and unlike wisdom is subject to a death without which his 'goodness' cannot be properly conveyed. John avoids the term *eikōn* [image] entirely; Jesus is not the *image* or likeness of God's goodness in John, but rather he *is* 'good'" (535). This sheds new christological light on John's other uses of *good* as well.[w3]

Should any doubt remain on whether or not John is intended to be understood as a *Sophia* Gospel, consider the OT sources of John's eighteen explicit quotations, as identified in Nestle-Aland's *Novum Testamentum Graece* (27th ed., Appendix IV): eight from the Psalms (none of which are Wisdom Pss), six from Isaiah, two from Exodus, and one or two from Zechariah—none from wisdom literature! (see Clark-Soles: 222). Nor is the wisdom literature trope "the fear of the Lord" (requisite for seeking wisdom) in John.

TEXTUAL VARIANTS A "textual variant" in the NT means that the text reads differently among the Greek manuscripts. The Gospel of John has several notable textual variants:

John 1:18. The manuscript evidence leans strongly toward *God* (*theos*): with support from p[66, 75] ℵ B C* D L W* 33 850 (sa) bo (Or) Cyr-Alex. The early manuscript evidence for *Son* (*huios*) is slight: A C Θ Ψ W *f*[1, 13] (sa) it sy[pal, c, h] arm Eus Cl Ir Tert and the mass of later, less reliable Byzantine manuscripts. The original, no longer extant, likely abbreviated the word, a common scribal practice for sacred names (*nomina sacra*). The two readings in this form look much alike. While external evidence supports *theos*, the internal evidence also points to *theos* as the more difficult reading, but it is characteristic of John to designate Jesus as Son (*huios*), as in 3:16, 18, and 1 John 4:9. Rhetorically, *Son* flows better.

Metzger's discussion of this variant considers also the matter of the inclusion or deletion of the definite article *ho*. He regards its omission as the original. It was added when *huios* supplanted *theos*. Tagged on to the Committee's opinion, represented above, is Allen Wikgren's dissenting position, which holds it doubtful that the original read *theos* (Metzger 1994: 169–70).

John 5:2. The RSV translation, *Bethzatha*, is supported by Codex Sinaiticus, the minuscule manuscript 33, Old Latin manuscripts, and Eusebius, who knew Jerusalem. Some other readings, *Bethsaida* and *Bethesda* ("House of Divine Mercy"), have significant textual support also, while *Belzetha* has weaker support. A related spelling, without manuscript support, *Bethseta*, has been proposed since it means "House of Sheep" (Burge 2000: 173).

John 7:37d. p[66] and other MSS omit *to me* (*pros eme*); p[75] and B include it.

John 7:53–8:11. This portion in John does not appear in Eastern manuscripts until the twelfth century. It appears in some Western manuscripts earlier: some old Latin and Codex Bezae (fifth century). A *similar* story appears in the *Gospel of the Hebrews* (Eusebius, *Hist. eccl.* 3.29.17), and a clearer narrative about this adulteress is in the third-century Syriac *Didascalia Apostolorum* (2.24.6). The account is not mentioned by Tertullian or Cyprian (both third century), but it is cited by the Western Fathers Ambrose and Augustine (fourth–fifth centuries). The earliest in the East to mention it is Euthymius Zigabenus (twelfth century; Metzger 1994: 188).

It is unclear where the passage belongs since manuscripts locate it at various places: after John 7:36 (MS 225), after 7:44 (several Georgian MSS), after 21:25 (a few minuscules), or several other places in chapter 8. Other manuscripts put it after Luke 21:38 (f^{13}) or at the end of Luke (MS 1333), thus locating the event in the temple. When placed after Luke 21:38, it occurs on Jesus' journey from the Mount of Olives to the temple, where he teaches. The story finally "settled" where it is now, in John 8. (See the above comments on the text; for fuller discussion, see Metzger 1994: 187–89).

John 9:38. While some reliable manuscripts (p[75] ℵ W) lack verse 38, most manuscripts, including early reliable ones, include it. The intrinsic evidence is divided. The shorter and more difficult reading favors omitting it. It is more difficult to explain its omission by scribes than its addition, since scribes were more likely to err by conforming readings to orthodox beliefs. Hence, it is easier to see how it was added than it is to see how it was omitted. However, readings that represent characteristic emphases of the author are more likely to be original. Because the fourth evangelist readily confesses Jesus' divine status, he would consider worship appropriate. Nevertheless, this is the only occurrence of a person *worshiping Jesus* (*proskyneō*) in John. After considering the pros and cons, Metzger says that "in view of the overwhelming preponderance of external attestation in favor of the longer text, it appears that the omission, if not accidental, is to be regarded as editorial, made in the interest of unifying Jesus' teaching in verses 37 and 39" (1994: 195).

John 18:5, 7. Nazōraion has the strongest textual support. It most likely denotes a Nazareth location (see Matt 2:23; 26:71). For other views, see R. Brown 1970: 810 (Heb. root *nzr* could denote a messianic remnant or root of Jesse). But the text is about personal identification. Pilate's inscription on the cross corroborates this point. It begins, *Jesus of Nazareth* (19:19).

John 18:5. The textual variants that add *Iēsous* either before or after *I AM* (*he*) have good support, at least if it stands before (if before, *Iēsous* goes with *he said* and specifies who *he* is; if *Iēsous* comes after, it would be a predicate noun with *I AM*), but the readings omitting it (p^{60} D etc.) are strong as well. The Nestle-Aland Greek text (27th ed., 1993) omits *Iēsous*, but both NRSV and NIV include it: *Jesus said* (NIV); *Jesus replied* (NRSV).

John 19:35b. This is a translation issue. The *he* (NRSV) preceding *knows* in Greek is *that one* (*ekeinos*), which likely refers to *that disciple* in 18:15b and to the disciple identified in 21:20 and 24, thus denoting the eyewitness bearer of the Johannine traditions about Jesus.

John 20:18. Considering the textual variants, the original is either *angellousa* or *apangellousa*. A third reading, *anangellousa*, does not have enough support to be considered. The evidence for *angellousa* is p^{66*} ℵ* A B 078. 0250 *pc*, and for *apangellousa* is p^{66c} ℵ² D L Θ $f^{1, 13}$ and the Majority text, which is not as strong. The Nestle-Aland text considers *angellousa* the stronger reading, so that *announce* would be the better translation. However, the mass of manuscripts through the ages read *apangellousa*. This witnesses to the church's high regard for Mary prior to the Reformation, emphasizing Mary's role as apostolic proclaimer.

John 20:31. The issue is whether the tense of the verb *believe* is present or past (aorist). Textual support for *pisteusēte* (aorist) is from all text types: ℵ² A C D L W Ψ $f^{1, 13}$ 33 565 700 et al. Syr$^{s, p, h, pal}$. Support for *pisteuēte* (present) is p^{66vid} ℵ* B Θ 892. The latter includes strong early manuscript witness, but the former has wide support, and some early strong support especially in the *f* family, 33, 565, and Syriac rescensions. The comments on 20:31 explain the resulting different nuances. Since the evidence is close to a "draw," I suggest that both meanings be part of the church's emphases in the use of the text.

UNSETTLED MATTERS See [w1]

WITNESS AND TESTIFY John's Gospel has been understood as a grand trial-*witness* scene, with Isaiah's lawsuit motif (*rib*) at the heart of the narrative plot (Lincoln 2000). Isaiah 43:10-13 declares,

> You are my *witnesses*, says the Lord, and my servant whom I have chosen, so that you may know and believe me and understand that *I am he*. Before me no god was formed, nor shall there be any after me. *I am the Lord*, and besides me there is no savior. I declared and saved and proclaimed, when there was no strange god among you; and you are my *witnesses*, says the Lord. I am God, and also henceforth *I am He*;

there is no one who can deliver from my hand; I work and who can hinder it? (emphasis added)

Witness and *I AM* [*he*] (*egō eimi*) intertwine. Isaiah 40–55 is the prophetic cradle of John's Jesus.

Witness as verb (*martyreō*) appears thirty-three times in John; the noun (*martyria*), fourteen times. This is over one-third of the NT uses (verb, 79x; noun, 37x). English translations may use *witness* or *testify* as a dynamic equivalent for the verb in John. We might also refer to John as John the Testifier to distinguish him from *martys*, which can mean "witness" or "martyr." The noun *martys* ("witness" or "martyr") occurs five times in Revelation and thirteen times in Acts, but nowhere in John. A witness may become a martyr; in Revelation, the author regularly expects this to be the case (Yeatts: 128–31, 137, 469, 458–61).

John appears as *witness/testifier* in the prologue, and Jesus' first disciples in John 1:37-50 *witness/testify* to Jesus' identity. In chapter 5, when Jesus is accused of making himself equal to God, he defends himself by citing numerous witnesses that certify his divine authority in both his speech and works. Bauckham (2008a: 123) identifies seven witnesses in the first "trial" phase of Jesus' ministry in John.[w1] These are "John the Baptist [Witness] (1:7, etc.), Jesus himself (3:11, etc.), the Samaritan woman (4:39), God the Father (5:32), Jesus' works or signs (5:36), the Scriptures (5:39), and the crowd who testify about Jesus' raising of Lazarus (12:17)." The two witnesses in the second phase, the disciples, including the beloved disciple, and the Paraclete, bear testimony in the future, from the time perspective of the narrative.

Thanks to the beloved disciple, the Gospel itself continues to testify to Jesus, using multiple witnesses. The christological confessions in the Gospel also certify Jesus' divine identity. Seven confessions occur before the resurrection and two afterward. The confessions begin with Andrew, Philip, and Nathanael (1:41-50). They continue with the Samaritan woman and her villagers (4:29, 42), Peter's confession representing that of the twelve (6:69), the blind man's testimony (9:17, 30-33, 35-38), and Martha (11:27). The confessions that follow the resurrection, culminating the orchestral voice, are those of Mary Magdalene (20:18) and Thomas (20:28) [*Christology, p. 507*]. These are important to the Gospel's testimony to Jesus' identity, the one sent from God. Bauckham's own *testimony* to the beloved disciple's gift of the written Gospel is pertinent:

The Beloved Disciple's written witness encompasses them all and enables them still to testify. To be sure, the Gospel also interprets the seven witnesses: what John the Baptist says, in the Gospel, is doubtless not a mere report of what even the Beloved Disciple heard him say at the time. But the Beloved Disciple's written witness can only interpret the seven witnesses if at the same time it does in some sense report them. Otherwise the temporal succession of the two phases of the trial immediately collapses and the seven witnesses become no more than forms of expression of the Beloved Disciple's own witness. The Gospel's own careful array of witnesses in this way does set some limits to the degree of creativity the Beloved Disciple (or the author) can be understood to have exercised if his own witness is not to contradict and refute itself. (Bauckham 2008a: 124)

The seven prepassion witnesses disclose Jesus' identity; the three postresurrection appearances in John 20 with a fourth in ch. 21 confirm that identity, looping back to the Gospel's beginning. They thus represent a climax in the Christology of the Gospel, preparing well for the Gospel's purpose statement in 20:31. Jesus' signs (20:30-31) are also testimony. The beloved disciple is the metawitness in the Gospel's narrative, certifying the credibility of all the other witnesses and presenting the entire story as a witness to and of Jesus [*Beloved Disciple, p. 505*].

WOMEN IN JOHN Women play important roles in John's Gospel, in 2:1-11; 4:4-42; 11:1-44; 12:1-8; 19:25-27; and 20:1-18. In the Synoptic Gospels women are mostly "seen but not heard," a phenomenon that Dewey (1997) has assessed critically. But in John's Gospel, women are vocal. They voice key confessions in the Gospel's unfolding drama of Jesus as God's revelation to humanity. R. Brown recognizes women's importance (1975: 688-99; 1979: 183-98). Bauckham's distinctive contribution (2002) analyzes *named* women in John and the named women in the Synoptics and other early noncanonical Gospels.

Two extensive contributions merit consideration. Conway undertakes a careful study of ten characters in John: five women and five men. These ten characters are the mother of Jesus, Nicodemus, the Samaritan woman, the man born blind, Martha and Mary of Bethany, Pilate, Simon Peter, the beloved disciple, and Mary Magdalene. Conway rightly critiques much of the earlier work on women in John that tries to prove that women are equal to men in narrative roles and importance. Conway says, "Gender analysis does not simply equal the study of women." Rather, "the term *gender* signifies, among other things, the relational aspect of the categories 'male' and 'female'" (48). Conway emphasizes "the network of meaning created in and between the presentation of characters" (126n170).

Conway regards Martha's confession most notable:

Nowhere else in the Gospel does an individual character's confession conclude a conversation the way that Martha's does. The confessions of Nathanael (1:49), Peter (6:69), and Thomas (20:28) are followed by some sort of reprimand by Jesus, and the profession of faith by the formerly blind man (9:38) is followed by a judgment from Jesus. In contrast, Martha's confession stands on its own. The only other place where this occurs is 4:42, where the Samaritan villagers declare Jesus "Savior of the World." (143)

Martha's confession extends that of the Samaritan woman's villagers. These blend with the later confession of Mary Magdalene in 20:18, *I have seen the Lord*. Each occurs in the concluding chapters of the Gospel's three main

structural divisions (chs. 1–4; 5:1–12:8 [Mary's anointing of Jesus complements Martha's confession]; and chs. 12:9–20:31). These women's confessions are crucial to Jesus' christological identity. The anointing of Jesus by
Mary of Bethany as devotion to him, along with Mary Magdalene's role in
20:1-18, bookend the third division. This structural pattern likely reflects
the prominence of women in leadership among the Johannine believers.

Conway's presentation and profile of the mother of Jesus excel, and so
does her portrait of the Samaritan woman, which concludes: "As the mother of Jesus is the co-worker of God the Father, so the Samaritan woman
becomes an 'indispensable co-worker' of Jesus" (125). Her treatment of all
ten characters is a rich feast in both the mimetic and functional aspects of
characterization. Puzzling, however, is why in her brief conclusion (201–5)
she does not correlate more explicitly and fully her contribution with key
Gospel emphases—especially Christology and the structure of the narrative, which she earlier affirmed in Baruch Hochman's work (Conway: 55–57;
Hochman: 41–42). She might have said more on the positive roles of the
women in relation to the structure of the Gospel, as noted above.

Conway concludes that all five women (see above) "are presented in
incomparably positive ways as persons who are closely linked to the self-
revelation of Jesus and to the coming of his hour" (203). In contrast to these
five women—whose identity as female is not coincidental—the men are
portrayed more negatively. Only two, the blind man and the beloved disciple, are presented positively. Conway considers whether female and male
characters are intentionally developed in comparison: "Nicodemus with
the Samaritan woman, Mary of Bethany with Judas, Mary Magdalene with
the beloved disciple, and perhaps Martha with Peter" (203). Had she
included chapter 21 in her analysis, Peter would be more positive, hardly a
contrast to Martha.

Beirne's study turns new ground also. In John's Gospel women and men
are treated as "a discipleship of equals." Beirne qualifies the term, however, with respect to her discussion of the meaning of *equality* when
applied to gender. In John's Gospel she sees six examples of "gender pairs"
of characters (cf. Luke's similar pairing feature). Each of the six pairs is
portrayed in a parallel or contrasting faith encounter with Jesus, when
assessed in relation to the Gospel's stated purpose (20:31). The contrasts
are Nicodemus (3:1-12) and the Samaritan woman (4:4-42); and Mary of
Bethany and Judas (12:1-8). The parallels are the mother of Jesus (2:1-11)
and the royal official (4:46-54); the man born blind (9:1-41) and Martha
(11:1-44); the mother of Jesus and the beloved disciple (19:25-27); and Mary
Magdalene (20:11-18) and Thomas (20:24-29).[w1]

Most important, women play key roles as characters that bring each of
John's three structural divisions to a climax: chapters 1–4; 5:1–12:8; and
12:9–20:31. The mother of Jesus, who bookends Jesus' ministry, is not compared readily with any other narrative character, unless perhaps the *Father*
who directs Jesus' ministry. With the prominence of women's roles in John,
as well as in Mark (Swartley 1997), the function of women in leadership
roles in early Christianity merits further study. In John, women *hear, see,
believe, confess, witness, and even proclaim* (Mary Magdalene) as *exemplars.*[w2]

WORLD Carter (2006: 91) sees both positive and negative connotations for the term *world*. *World* (*kosmos*) occurs 185 times in the NT; more than half appear in the Johannine literature (78x in the Gospel, 23x in 1 John, once in 2 John, and only 3x in Rev). Although the Anabaptist tradition has tended to use *world* with negative overtones, the NT usage is more complex and nuanced. In John 1–12, *world* is a *positive* descriptor of the realm of human activity by approximately a 2 to 1 ratio. Jesus' ministry is generally received, and the Gospel's aim is to communicate God's incarnational love to the world, to all humanity, even to *the Jews*. In John 13–19 a roughly four to one negative use occurs (approximately the same negative ratio in 1 John). Both portray heightened conflict between Jesus and his followers on one hand, and those who reject him and his disciples on the other hand (McDermond: 52–53, 74–75, 134–36).

World is used in different senses in John's Gospel, though Howard-Brook in response to an early draft of this work says *world* means *world*: it is the perspective from which it is viewed that differs. However, differing connotations do appear in the text. First, a *neutral* usage designates the *cosmos* that God created through the agency of the Word (the Son) (1:1-5, 18). The phrase *before the foundation of the world* in 17:24d uses *world* in this sense also. Second, *world* may designate the people who inhabit the cosmos, as in John 3:16. God loves all people, and thus God sends the Son to *give* himself for the salvation of the world—one might contend that the first and second are really one, since God's love extends to redemption of the cosmos, as Paul says in Romans 8. Third, *world* denotes the *hostility* of the religious leaders: the chief priests, Pharisees, and *the Jews*. The hostile Jewish authorities hand Jesus over to Pilate for crucifixion. This hostility is inspired by the ruler (*archōn*) of the world, whom Jesus *cast out* (12:31 RSV) and *condemned* (16:11) in his glorification and victory over the world (16:33).

A fourth usage combines the second and third (i.e., the people of the *world*), in contrast to those who believe in Jesus. Dominant in 17:9-19, this use denotes the people of the world who form a *sphere of unbelief and hostility*, though verse 13 seems to reflect the first use—Jesus' being in the world as a human being. In the farewell discourse, *the world* denotes those who hate Jesus and his followers (15:18-25). The world is judged to be wrong by the Holy Spirit (16:8-11). Jesus declares, *I have conquered the world* (16:33); he resists Satan's temptation to detour his ministry into militant messiahship (6:15; 11:45-48; 12:12-15; 18:11, 36). Instead, Jesus speaks peace to his disciples (14:27; 16:33; 20:19-26), breathing *into them . . . the Holy Spirit* (20:22 AT).

Although the world hates Jesus and the believers (15:18-25), Johannine believers are not instructed to hate the *world* (unbelievers), even in 1 John 2:15. Meeks (1993: 58–61) vacillates on whether the Johannine believers hate or love the world. Rensberger (138–52) correctly correlates John's "sectarianism" with the Gospel's strong mission emphasis.

Palestine in New Testament Times

+ Means city has uncertain location

Bibliography

Abbreviations: CBQ   *Catholic Biblical Quarterly*
                  JBL   *Journal of Biblical Literature*
                  SBL   Society of Biblical Literature

Alexander, Denis, and Robert S. White
    2006   *Science, Faith, and Ethics: Grid or Gridlock? A Christian Approach to Controversial Topics in Science.* Peabody, MA: Hendrickson.

Alexis-Baker, Andy
    2012   "Violence, Nonviolence and the Temple Incident in John 2:13-15." *Biblical Interpretation 20, nos. 1-2*: 73–96.

Anderson, Paul N.
    1996   *The Christology of the Fourth Gospel: Its Unity and Disunity in the Light of John 6.* WUNT, 2nd Series 78. Tübingin: J. C. B. Mohr.
    1999   "The Having-Sent-Me Father: Aspects of Agency, Encounter, and Irony in the Johannine Father-Son Relationship." In *God the Father in the Gospel of John*, edited by Adele Reinhartz, 33-58. Atlanta: SBL.
    2007   *The Fourth Gospel and the Quest for Jesus: Modern Foundations Reconsidered.* New York: T&T Clark.
    2011   *The Riddles of the Fourth Gospel.* Minneapolis: Fortress.

Anderson, Paul N., Felix Just, and Tom Thatcher, eds.
    2008   *Jesus, John, and History.* Vol. 1: *Critical Appraisals of Critical Views.* Atlanta: SBL.
    2009   *Jesus, John, and History.* Vol. 2: *Aspects of Historicity in the Fourth Gospel.* Atlanta: SBL.

Appold, Mark L.
    1976   *The Oneness Motif in the Fourth Gospel.* Tübingen: J. C. B. Mohr.

Arterbury, Andrew F.
    2010   "Breaking the Betrothal Bonds: Hospitality in John 4." *CBQ* 72: 63–83.

Ashton, John
    1985   "The Identity and Function of the 'Ioudaioi' in the Fourth Gospel." *Novum Testamentum* 27:40–75.

2007   *Understanding the Fourth Gospel.* Second edition. Oxford: University Press.

Ball, David Mark
1996   *"I AM" in John's Gospel: Literary Function, Background and Theological Implications.* Journal for the Study of the New Testament: Supplement Series 124. Sheffield Academic.

Bamford, Christopher, trans. and ed.
2000   *The Voice of the Eagle: The Heart of Celtic Christianity; John Scotus Eriugena's Homily on the Prologue to the Gospel of St. John.* Great Barrington, MA: Lindisfarne Books.

Barclay, William
1975   *The Gospel of John.* Vol. 2. Daily Study Bible Series. Rev. ed. Philadelphia: Westminster.

Barrett, C. K.
1972   "The Dialectical Theology of St. John." In *New Testament Essays*, 49–69. London: SPCK.
1978   *The Gospel According to St. John.* London: 2nd ed. London, SPCK. 1st ed., Philadelphia: Westminster, 1955.

Barth, Karl
1960   *The Doctrine of Creation.* Vol. III/2 of *Church Dogmatics.* Edinburgh: T&T Clark.

Barton, Stephen C.
2008   "Johannine Dualism and Contemporary Pluralism." In *The Gospel of John and Christian Theology*, edited by Richard Bauckham and Carl Mosser, 3–18. Grand Rapids: Eerdmans.

Bauckham, Richard
1998a   *God Crucified: Monotheism and Christology in the New Testament.* Grand Rapids: Eerdmans.
1998b   *The Gospels for All Christians.* Grand Rapids: Eerdmans.
2002   "The Women in John." In *Gospel Women: Studies of the Named Women in the Gospels*, 257–302. Grand Rapids: Eerdmans.
2006   *Jesus and the Eyewitnesses: The Gospels as Eyewitness Testimony.* Grand Rapids: Eerdmans.
2007   *The Testimony of the Beloved Disciple: Narrative, History, and Theology in the Gospel of John.* Grand Rapids: Eerdmans. The chapter "The 153 Fish and the Unity of the Fourth Gospel" (271–84) appears also in *Neotestamentica* 36 (2002): 77–88.
2008a   "The Fourth Gospel as the Testimony of the Beloved Disciple." In Bauckham and Mosser, *The Gospel of John and Christian Theology.* Grand Rapids: Eerdmans, 120–39.
2008b   "Historical Characteristics of the Gospel of John." *New Testament Studies* 53:17–36.

Bauckham, Richard, and Carl Mosser, eds.
2008   *The Gospel of John and Christian Theology.* Grand Rapids: Eerdmans.

Beasley-Murray, George R.
1991   *Gospel of Life: Theology in the Fourth Gospel.* Peabody, MA: Hendrickson.
1999   *John.* Word Biblical Commentary 36. 2nd ed. Nashville, TN: Thomas Nelson Publishers.

Beirne, Margaret M.
    2004   *Women and Men in the Fourth Gospel.* New York: T&T Clark.
Bieringer, Reimund, Didier Pollefeyt, and Frederique Vandecasteele-
            Vanneuville
    2001   *Anti-Judaism and the Fourth Gospel.* Louisville: Westminster John
            Knox.
Bird, Michael F.
    2007   *Jesus and the Origins of the Gentile Mission.* Library of New
            Testament Studies 331. New York: T&T Clark.
Bligh, John
    1962   "Jesus in Samaria." *Heythrop Journal* 3:329–46.
Blomberg, Craig L.
    2001   *The Historical Reliability of the Gospel of John.* Leicester: Inter-Varsity.
Blough, Neal
    1994   "The Holy Spirit and Discipleship in Pilgram Marpeck's Theology."
            133–45 in *Essays in Anabaptist Theology*, TR 5, edited by H. Wayne
            Pipkin, 133-45. Elkhart, IN: IMS.
Blue, Debbie
    2010   "Living by the Word" [on John 2:1-11]. *Christian Century* 127, no.
            1 (Jan. 12): 18.
Boccaccini, Gabriele
    2002   *Roots of Rabbinic Judaism: An Intellectual History, from Ezekiel to
            Daniel.* Grand Rapids: Eerdmans.
Boccaccini, Gabriele, ed.
    2007   *Enoch and the Messiah Son of Man: Revisiting the Book of Parables.*
            Grand Rapids: Eerdmans.
Boers, Arthur, et al.
    2010   *Take Our Moments and Our Days: An Anbaptist Prayer Book. Vol. 2:
            Christian Seasons: Advent through Pentecost.* Elkhart, IN: IMS;
            Scottdale, PA: Herald Press.
Boers, Hendrikus
    1988   *Neither on This Mountain nor in Jerusalem.* SBL Monograph Series
            35. Atlanta: Scholars Press.
Borchert, Gerald L.
    1966   *John 1-11.* New American Commentary 25A. N.p.: Broadman &
            Holman.
Borg, Marcus J.
    1987   *Jesus: A New Vision; Spirit, Culture, and the Life of Discipleship.* San
            Francisco: Harper & Row.
Borgen, Peder
    1965   *Bread from Heaven: An Exegetical Study of the Concept of Manna in
            the Gospel of John and the Writings of Philo.* Novum Testamentum
            Supplements 10. Leiden: E. J. Brill.
    1983   *Logos Was the True Light, and Other Essays on the Gospel of John.*
            Trondheim, Norway: Tapir.
Botha, J. Eugene
    1991   *Jesus and the Samaritan Woman: A Speech Act Reading of John 4:1-42.*
            Leiden: E. J. Brill.

Boyarin, Daniel
 1999 *Dying for God: Martyrdom and the Making of Christianity and Judaism.* Stanford, CA: Stanford University Press.
 2001 "The Gospel of the *Memra*: Jewish Binitarianism and the Prologue to John." *Harvard Theological Review* 94:243–84.
 2002 "The Ioudaioi in John and the Prehistory of Judaism." In *Pauline Conversations in Context: Essays in Honor of Calvin J. Roetzel*, edited by J.C. Anderson, et al., 216-39. Sheffield: Sheffield Academic Press.
 2007 "Judaism as a Free Church: Footnotes to John Howard Yoder's *The Jewish-Christian Schism Revisited.*" *Cross Currents* 56.4:6–21.

Braght, Thieleman J. van
 1950 *Martyrs Mirror* [MM]. Translated by Joseph F. Sohm from the 1660 Dutch ed. and published at Elkhart, IN, in 1886. Reprinted, Scottdale, PA: Herald Press.

Brant, Jo-Ann A.
 2004 *Dialogue and Drama: Elements of Greek Tragedy in the Fourth Gospel.* Peabody, MA: Hendrickson.

Bredin, Mark R.
 2003 "John's Account of Jesus' Demonstration in the Temple: Violent or Nonviolent?" *Biblical Theology Bulletin* 33, no. 2:44–50.

Brodie, Thomas L.
 1993 *The Gospel According to John: A Literary and Theological Commentary.* Oxford: University Press.

Brown, Jeannine K.
 2010 "Creation's Renewal in the Gospel of John." *CBQ* 72:275–90.

Brown, Raymond E.
 1966 *The Gospel According to John.* Vol. 1. Anchor Bible 29. Garden City, NY: Doubleday.
 1970 *The Gospel According to John.* Vol. 2. Anchor Bible 29A. Garden City, NY: Doubleday.
 1975 "Roles of Women in the Fourth Gospel." In *The Community of the Beloved Disciple*, 183–98. Ramsey, NJ: Paulist Press. Published earlier in *Theological Studies* 36 (1975): 688–99, with attention to the topic already in his 1966 commentary, 183–98.
 1979 *The Community of the Beloved Disciple.* Ramsey, NJ: Paulist Press.
 1984 *The Churches the Apostles Left Behind.* Ramsey, NJ: Paulist Press.
 1998 *A Retreat with John the Evangelist: That You May Have Life.* Cincinnati: St. Anthony Messenger Press.
 2003 *An Introduction to the Gospel of John.* Edited and revised by Francis J. Moloney. New York: Doubleday. Brown first published this in 1998, just before his death.

Bruce, F. F.
 1983 *The Gospel of John: Introduction, Exposition, and Notes.* Grand Rapids: Eerdmans.

Bruce, Patricia
 2005 "John 5:1-18. The Healing at the Pool: Some Narrative, Socio-Historical and Ethical Issues." *Neotestamentica* 39:39–56.

Bruner, Dale Frederick
   1970   *A Theology of the Holy Spirit: The Pentecostal Experience and the New Testament Witness.* Grand Rapids: Eerdmans.
Bryan, Steven M.
   2005   "The Eschatological Temple in John 14." *Bulletin for Biblical Research* 15, no. 2:187–98.
Bultmann, Rudolf
   1971   *The Gospel of John: A Commentary.* Translated by G. R. Beasley-Murray, R. W. N. Hoare, and J. K. Riches. Philadelphia: Westminster.
Burer, Michael H.
   2012   *Divine Sabbath Work.* Bulletin for Biblical Research Supp. 5. Winona Lake, IN: Eisenbrauns.
Burge, Gary M.
   1987   *The Anointed Community: The Holy Spirit in the Johannine Tradition.* Grand Rapids: Eerdmans.
   2000   *John.* The NIV Application Commentary. Grand Rapids: Zondervan.
   2009   "Revisiting the Johannine Water Motif: Jesus, Ritual Purification and the Pool of Siloam in John 9." Paper presented at the 2009 Meeting of the SBL.
Burroughs, Presian R.
   2006   "Stop Grumbling and Start Eating: Gospel Meal Meets Scriptural Spice in the Bread of Life Discourse." *Horizons in Biblical Theology* 28:73–94.
Busse, Ulrich
   1991   "Open Questions on John 10." In *The Shepherd Discourse of John 10 and Its Content: Studies,* edited by Johannes Beutler and Robert T. Fortna, 6–17. Society for New Testament Studies Monograph Series 67. Cambridge: Cambridge University Press.
Cahill, P. Joseph
   1982   "Narrative Art in John IV." *Religious Studies Bulletin* 2 (April): 41–48.
Card, Michael
   1995   *The Parable of Joy: Reflections on the Wisdom of the Book of John.* Nashville: Nelson.
Carmichael, Calum M.
   1980   "Marriage and the Samaritan Woman." *New Testament Studies* 26:332–46.
Carson, D. A.
   1991   *The Gospel According to John.* Grand Rapids: Eerdmans.
Carter, Warren
   2006   *John: Storyteller, Interpreter, Evangelist.* Peabody, MA: Hendrickson.
   2008   *John and Empire: Initial Explorations.* New York: T&T Clark.
Cassidy, Richard J.
   1992   *John's Gospel in New Perspective: Christology and the Realities of Roman Power.* Maryknoll, NY: Orbis Books.
Charlesworth, James H., ed.
   1983   *The Old Testament Pseudepigrapha.* Vol. 1. Garden City, NY: Doubleday.

1995   *The Beloved Disciple: Whose Witness Validates the Gospel of John?*
        Valley Forge, PA: Trinity Press International.
Chennattu, Rekha M.
    2006   *Johannine Discipleship as a Covenant Relationship.* Peabody, MA:
            Hendrickson.
Clark-Soles, Jaime
    2003   *Scripture Cannot Be Broken: The Social Function of the Use of Scripture
            in the Fourth Gospel.* Boston: Brill Academic Publ.
Coakley, J. F.
    1995   "Jesus' Messianic Entry into Jerusalem (John 12:12-19 Par.)."
            New Testament Studies 46:461–82.
Coats, George W.
    1968   *Rebellion in the Wilderness: The Murmuring Motif in the Wilderness
            Tradition of the Old Testament.* Nashville: Abingdon.
Collins, Adela Yarbro
    1982   "New Testament Perspectives: The Gospel of John." *Journal for
            the Study of the Old Testament* 22:47–53.
Collins, John J.
    1995   *The Scepter and the Star: The Messiahs of the Dead Sea Scrolls and
            Other Ancient Literature.* New York: Doubleday.
Collins, Matthew S.
    1995   "The Question of *Doxa*: A Socioliterary Reading of the Wedding
            at Cana." *Biblical Theology Bulletin* 25:100–9.
Collins, Raymond F.
    1990   *These Things Have Been Written: Studies on the Fourth Gospel.* Louvain
            Theological and Pastoral Monographs 2. Grand Rapids: Eerdmans.
Coloe, Mary L.
    2001   *God Dwells with Us: Temple Symbolism in the Fourth Gospel.*
            Collegeville, MN: Liturgical Press.
    2004   "Welcome into the Household of God: The Foot Washing in John
            13." *Catholic Biblical Quarterly* 66:400–15.
    2006   "Sources in the Shadows: John 13 and the Johannine Community."
            In *New Currents Through John: A Global Perspective*, edited by
            Francisco Lozanda Jr. and Tom Thatcher, 69–82. Atlanta: SBL.
    2007   *Dwelling in the Household of God: Johannine Ecclesiology and Spir-
            ituality.* Collegeville, MN: Liturgical Press.
Conway, Colleen M.
    1999   *Men and Women in the Fourth Gospel: Gender and Johannine
            Characterization.* SBL Dissertation Series 167. Atlanta: SBL.
Cook, Michael
    1987   "The Gospel of John and the Jews." *Review and Expositor* 84:259–71.
Cullmann, Oscar
    1953   *Early Christian Worship.* Studies in Biblical Theology 10. Chicago:
            Alec R. Allenson.
    1976   *The Johannine Circle.* Translated by John Bowden. Philadelphia:
            Westminster.
Culpepper, R. Alan
    1983   *The Anatomy of the Fourth Gospel.* Minneapolis: Fortress.

1991   "The Johannine *Hypodeigma*: A Reading of John 13." *Semeia* 53:133–52.

1996   "The Gospel of John as a Document of Faith in a Pluralistic Culture." In *Readers and Readings of the Fourth Gospel*, vol. 1 of *What Is John?* edited by Fernando Segovia, 107–27. Atlanta: Scholars Press.

1998   *The Gospel and the Letters of John.* Interpreting Biblical Texts. Nashville: Abingdon.

2000   Introduction to *The Johannine Literature*, by Barnabas Lindars, Ruth B. Edwards, and John M. Court, 9–39. Sheffield: Sheffield Academic Press.

2001   "Anti-Judaism in the Fourth Gospel as a Theological Problem for Christian Interpreters." In *Anti-Judaism and the Fourth Gospel*, edited by R. Bieringer, D. Pollefeyt, and F. Vandecasteele-Vanneuville, 61–82. Louisville: Westminster John Knox.

2002   "Inclusivism and Exclusivism in the Fourth Gospel." In *Word, Theology, and Community in John*, edited by John Painter, R. Alan Culpepper, and Fernando F. Segovia, 85–108. St. Louis: Chalice.

2009   "John 21:24-25: The Johannine *Sphragis*." In *John, Jesus, and History*, edited by Paul N. Anderson, Felix Just, and Tom Thatcher, 2:349–65. Early Christianity and Its Literature 2. Atlanta: SBL.

Culpepper, R. Alan, and C. Clifton Black, eds.

1996   *Exploring the Gospel of John: In Honor of D. Moody Smith.* Louisville: Westminster John Knox. Essays on many aspects of the Gospel.

Culpepper, R. Alan, and Fernando F. Segovia, eds.

1991   *The Fourth Gospel from a Literary Perspective. Semeia* [Journal] 53. Atlanta: SBL.

D'Angelo, Mary Rose

1992   "*ABBA* and 'Father': Imperial Theology and the Jesus Traditions." *JBL* 111:611–30.

Daise, Michael A.

2007   *Feasts in John: Jewish Festivals and Jesus' "Hour" in the Fourth Gospel.* Wissenschaftliche Monographien zum Alten und Neuen Testament 2.229. Tübingen: Mohr Siebeck.

Daube, David

1973   *The New Testament and Rabbinic Judaism.* New York: Arno.

Day, Janeth Norfleete

2002   *The Woman at The Well: Interpretation of John 4:1-42 in Retrospect and Prospect.* Leiden: E. J. Brill.

De Boer, Esther A.

2004   *The Gospel of Mary: Beyond a Gnostic and Biblical Mary Magdalene.* New York: T&T Clark.

de Wit, Hans and Louis Jonker, Marleen Kool, and Daniel Schipani, eds.

2004   *Through the Eyes of Another: Intercultural Reading of the Bible.* Elkhart, IN: IMS; Amsterdam: Vrije Universiteit.

Dennis, John

2006   *Jesus' Death and the Gathering of True Israel: The Johannine Appropriation of Restoration Theology in the Light of John 11.47-52.*

Wissenschaftliche Monographien zum Alten und Neuen Testament 2/217. Tübingen: Mohr Siebeck.

Dewey, Joanna
1997 "Women in the Synoptic Gospels: Seen but Not Heard?" *Biblical Theology Bulletin* 27 (1997): 53–60.

Dodd, C. H.
1952 *According to the Scriptures: The Substructure of New Testament Theology.* London: Nisbet & Co., Ltd.
1953 *The Interpretation of the Fourth Gospel.* Reprinted, 1968. Cambridge: Cambridge University Press.
1957 "The Prologue to the Fourth Gospel and Christian Worship." In *Studies in the Fourth Gospel,* edited by F. L. Cross, 9–22. London: A. R. Mowbray.
1962 "The Prophecy of Caiaphas (John xi 47-53)." In *Neotestamentica et patristica: Eine Freundesgabe, Herrn Professor Dr. Oscar Cullmann zu seinem 60. Geburtstag überreicht,* edited by Bo Reicke and Willy Rordorf, 134–43. Leiden: E. J. Brill.
1963 *Historical Tradition in the Fourth Gospel.* Cambridge: Cambridge University Press.

Donahue, John
1992 "Who Is My Enemy? The Parable of the Good Samaritan and the Love of Enemies." In *Love of Enemy and Nonretaliation in the New Testament,* edited by Willard M. Swartley, 137–56. Louisville: Westminster John Knox.

Draper, J. A.
1997 "Temple, Tabernacle and Mystical Experience in John." *Neotestamentica* 31:263-88.

Duke, Paul D.
1985 *Irony in the Fourth Gospel.* Atlanta: John Knox.

Dumm, Demetrius R.
2001 *A Mystical Portrait of Jesus: New Perspectives on John's Gospel.* Collegeville, MN: Liturgical Press.

Dunkerley, R.
1959 "Short Studies." *New Testament Studies* 5:321–27.

Dunn, James D. G.
1970 "The Washing of the Disciples' Feet in John 13:1-20." *Zeitschrift für die neutestamentliche Wissenschaft und die Kunde der älteren Kirche* 61:247–52.
1971 "John VI—A Eucharistic Discourse?" *New Testament Studies* 17:328–38.
1991 "Let John Be John: A Gospel for Its Time." In *The Gospel and the Gospels,* edited by Peter Stuhlmacher, 293–322. Grand Rapids: Eerdmans.
2005 *A New Perspective on Jesus: What the Quest for the Historical Jesus Missed.* Grand Rapids: Baker Academic.

Dyck, Cornelius J.
1984 "Hermeneutics and Discipleship." In *Essays on Biblical Interpretation: Anabaptist-Mennonite Perspectives,* edited by Willard M. Swartley,

29–44. Text Reader Series 1. Elkhart, IN: Institute of Mennonite Studies.

1995   *Spiritual Life in Anabaptism*. Translator and editor. Waterloo, ON/ Scottdale, PA: Herald Press.

Dyck, Cornelius J., William E. Keeney, and Alvin J. Beachy, trans. and eds.

1992   *The Writings of Dirk Philips, 1504-1568*. Classics of the Radical Reformation 6. Scottdale, PA: Herald Press.

Dyrness, William

1979   *Themes in Old Testament Theology*. Downers Grove, IL: InterVarsity.

Edwards, Mark

2004   *John*. Blackwell Bible Commentaries. Malden, MA: Blackwell.

Edwards, Ruth B.

1997   "Reading the Bible 4: The Gospel According to John." *Expository Times* 108, no. 4:101–5.

2003   *Discovering John*. London: SPCK.

Eichrodt, Walther

1984   "In the Beginning: A Contribution to the Interpretation of the First Word of the Bible." In *Creation in the Old Testament*, edited by Bernhard W. Anderson, 65–73. Issues in Religion and Theology 6. Philadelphia: Fortress. Reprint of essay in *Israel's Prophetic Heritage: Essays in Honor of James Muilenburg*, edited by Bernhard W. Anderson and Walter J. Harrelson, 1–10. New York: Harper & Brothers, 1962.

Elias, Jacob W.

2006   *Remember the Future: The Pastoral Theology of Paul the Apostle*. Scottdale, PA: Herald Press.

Ellis, Peter F.

1984   *The Genius of John: A Composition-Critical Commentary on the Fourth Gospel*. Collegeville, MN: Liturgical Press.

Ellul, Jacques

1985   *The Humiliation of the Word*. Translated by Joyce Main Hanks. Grand Rapids, Eerdmans.

Elowsky, Joel C., ed.

2004   *John 1-10*. Ancient Christian Commentary on Scripture: New Testament 4A. General Editor, Thomas C. Oden. Downers Grove, IL: InterVarsity.

Erdmann, Martin

1988   "Mission in John's Gospel and Letters." In *Mission in the New Testament: An Evangelical Approach*, edited by William F. Larkin Jr. and Joel F. Carpenter, 207–26. Maryknoll, NY: Orbis Books.

Esler, Philip R., and Ronald Piper

2006   *Lazarus, Mary and Martha: Social-Scientific Approaches to the Gospel of John*. Minneapolis: Fortress.

Eslinger, Lyle

1987   "The Wooing of the Woman at the Well: Jesus, the Reader and Reader-Response Criticism." *Literature and Theology* 1:167–83.

Eslinger, Richard

2008   "Blessed If You Do Them." In *Preaching John's Gospel: The World It Imagines*, edited by David Fleer and Dave Bland, 43–47. St. Louis: Chalice.

Eusebius
    1962   *Eusebius' Ecclesiastical History.* Grand Rapids: Baker.

Evans, Craig A.
    1990   Review of J. Kügler, *Der Jünger, den Jesus Liebte. Biblica* 71:266–69.
    1993a   *Word and Glory: On the Exegetical and Theological Background of John's Prologue.* Journal for the Study of the New Testament: Supplement Series 89. Sheffield Academic Press.
    1993b   "Faith and Polemic: The New Testament and First-Century Judaism." In *Anti-Semitism and Early Christianity: Issues of Polemic and Faith,* edited by Craig A. Evans and Donald A. Hagner, 1–20. Minneapolis: Fortress.
    2006   *Fabricating Jesus: How Modern Scholars Distort the Gospels.* Downers Grove, IL: InterVarsity.

Fee, Gordon
    1978   "Once More—John 7:37-39." *Expository Times* 88, no. 4:116–18.

Ferguson, Everett
    2001   "Catechesis and Initiation." In *The Origins of Christendom in the West,* edited by Alan Kreider, 229–68. New York: T&T Clark.

Ferguson, John
    1970   *The Politics of Love: The New Testament and Nonviolent Revolution.* Cambridge: James Clarke; Nyack, NY: Fellowship Publications; Greenwood, SC: Attic Press.

Filson, Floyd V.
    1963   *Saint John.* Laymans Bible Commentary. London: SCM.

Finger, Thomas N.
    2004   *A Contemporary Anabaptist Theology: Biblical, Historical, Constructive.* Downers Grove, IL: InterVarsity.

Fleer, David, and Dave Bland, eds.
    2008   *Preaching John's Gospel: The World It Imagines.* St. Louis: Chalice.

Ford, J. Massyngbaerde
    1995   "Jesus as Sovereign in the Passion According to John." *Biblical Theology Bulletin* 25:110–17.
    1997   *Redeemer—Friend and Mother: Salvation in Antiquity and in the Gospel of John.* Minneapolis: Augsburg Fortress.

Fortna, Robert T.
    1970   *The Gospel of Signs: A Reconstruction of the Narrative Source Underlying the Fourth Gospel.* Cambridge: Cambridge University Press.

Franck, Eskil
    1985   *Revelation Taught: The Paraclete in the Gospel of John.* Coniectanea Biblica: New Testament Series 14. Lund, Sweden: CWK Gleerup.

Freed, E. D.
    1965   *Old Testament Quotations in the Gospel of John.* Novum Testamentum Supplements 11. Leiden: E. J. Brill.
    1979   "*Egō eimi* in John 1:20 and 4:25 [26]." *Catholic Biblical Quarterly* 41:288–91.

Freyne, Seán
    1988   *Galilee, Jesus, and the Gospels: Literary Approaches and Historical Investigations.* Philadelphia: Fortress.

Frick, Peter
    2007   "Johannine Soteriology and Aristotelian Philosophy: A Herme-
            neutical Suggestion on Reading John 3:16 and 1 John 4:9." *Biblica*
            88, no. 3:415–21.
Friesen, Ivan D.
    2009   *Isaiah*. Believers Church Bible Commentary. Scottdale, PA:
            Herald Press.
Furnish, Victor Paul
    2010   *The Love Command in the New Testament*. Rev. ed. Nashville:
            Abingdon.
García Martínez, Florentino
    1996   *The Dead Sea Scrolls Translated*. 2nd ed. Grand Rapids: Eerdmans.
Gardner, Richard B.
    1991   *Matthew*. Believers Church Bible Commentary. Scottdale, PA:
            Herald Press.
Geddert, Timothy J.
    2001   *Mark*. Believers Church Bible Commentary. Scottdale, PA: Herald
            Press.
Gench, Frances Taylor
    2007   *Encounters with Jesus*. Louisville: Westminster John Knox.
Giblin, Charles H.
    1983   "The Miraculous Crossing of the Sea [John 6:16-21]." *New
            Testament Studies* 29:96–103.
Gibson, Shimon
    2005   "The Pool of Bethesda in Jerusalem and Jewish Purification
            Practices of the Second Temple Period." *Proche-orient chrétien*
            55:270–93.
    2009   *The Final Days of Jesus: The Archaeological Evidence*. New York:
            HarperOne.
Gingerich, Owen
    2006   *God's Universe*. Cambridge, MA: Belknap Press of Harvard
            University Press.
Girard, René
    1986   *The Scapegoat*. Translated by Yvonne Freccero. Baltimore, MD:
            The John Hopkins University Press.
Grant, Robert M.
    1942   "The Fourth Gospel and the Church." *Harvard Theological Review*
            35:95–116.
    1963   "Scripture and Tradition in St Ignatius of Antioch." *CBQ* 25:322–35.
Greenspoon, Leonard
    1981   "The Origin of the Idea of the Resurrection." In *Traditions in
            Transformation: Turning Points in Biblical Faith*, edited by Baruch
            Halpern and Jon D. Levenson, 247–321. Winona Lake, IN:
            Eisenbrauns.
Griffith, Terry
    2008   "'The Jews Who Had Believed in Him' (John 8:31) and the Motif
            of Apostasy in the Gospel of John." In *The Gospel of John and
            Christian Theology*, edited by Richard Bauckham and Carl Mosser,
            182–92. Grand Rapids: Eerdmans.

Guenther, Allen
    1998   *Hosea and Amos*. Believers Church Bible Commentary. Scottdale, PA: Herald Press.
Gundry, Robert H.
    1967   "In My Father's House Are Many Monai." *Zeitschrift für die neutestamentliche Wissenschaft und die Kunde der älteren Kirche* 58:68–72.
    2002   *Jesus the Word According to John the Sectarian: A Paleofundamentalist Manifesto for Contemporary Evangelicalism, Especially Its Elites, in North America*. Grand Rapids: Eerdmans.
Gundry-Volf, Judith
    1995   "Spirit, Mercy, and the Other." *Theology Today* 51:508–23.
Haitch, Russell
    2007   *From Exorcism to Ecstasy: Eight Views of Baptism*. Louisville: Westminster John Knox.
Hakola, Raimo
    2005   *Identity Matters: John, the Jews and Jewishness*. Novum Testamentum Supplements 118. Boston: E. J. Brill.
Hamilton, James M., Jr.
    2006   *God's Indwelling Presence: The Holy Spirit in the Old and New Testaments*. Nashville: B&H Publishing.
Hanson, Anthony Tyrell
    1991   *The Prophetic Gospel: A Study of John and the Old Testament*. Edinburgh: T&T Clark.
Harner, Philip B.
    1970   *The "I Am" of the Fourth Gospel: A Study in Johannine Usage and Thought*. Facet Books; Biblical Series 26. Philadelphia: Fortress.
    1988   *Grace and Law in Second Isaiah: "I Am the Lord."* Ancient Near Eastern Texts and Studies 2. Lewiston, NY: Edwin Mellen.
Harris, Elizabeth
    1994   *Prologue and Gospel: The Theology of the Fourth Evangelist*. Sheffield: Sheffield Academic Press.
Hatch, Edwin, and Henry A. Redpath
    1867   *A Concordance to the Septuagint and Other Greek Versions of the Old Testament (Including the Apocryphal Books)*. Reprint, Grand Rapids: Baker Book House, 1963.
Hays, Richard B.
    1996   *The Moral Vision of the New Testament*. San Francisco: Harper.
    2003   "Reading Scripture in Light of the Resurrection." In *The Art of Reading Scripture*, edited by Ellen F. Davis and Richard B. Hays, 216–38. Grand Rapids: Eerdmans.
    2008a   "The Materiality of John's Symbolic World." In *Preaching John's Gospel: The World It Imagines*, edited by David Fleer and Dave Bland, 5–12. St. Louis: Chalice.
    2008b   "Standing by the Fire." In *Preaching John's Gospel: The World It Imagines*, edited by David Fleer and Dave Bland, 13–16. St. Louis: Chalice.
Heath, Jane
    2010   "Some Were Saying, 'He Is Good.'" (John 7:12b): "'Good' Christology in John's Gospel?" *New Testament Studies* 56:513–35.

Hengel, Martin
    1989   *The Johannine Question*. Translated by John Bowden. Philadelphia:
            Trinity Press International.
    2008   "The Prologue of the Gospel of John as the Gateway to
            Christological Truth." In *The Gospel of John and Christian Theology*,
            edited by Richard Bauckham and Carl Mosser, 265–94. Grand
            Rapids: Eerdmans.
Heschel, Abraham J.
    1962   *The Prophets*. New York: Harper & Row.
Hiett Umble, Jeni
    1998   "Mutual Aid Among Augsburg Anabaptists, 1526–1528." In
            Building Communities of Compassion, edited by Donald B. Kraybill
            and Willard M. Swartley, 103–18. Scottdale, PA: Herald Press.
Hill, Charles E.
    2004   *The Johannine Corpus in the Early Church*. Oxford: University Press.
Hillerbrand, Hans J.
    1990   "Martin Luther and the Jews." In *Jews and Christians: Exploring the
            Past, Present, and Future*, edited by James H. Charlesworth, 127–
            50. New York: Crossroad.
Hillmer, Melvin R.
    1996   "'They Believed in Him': Discipleship in the Johannine
            Tradition." In *Patterns of Discipleship in the New Testament*, edited
            by Richard N. Longenecker, 77–97. Grand Rapids: Eerdmans.
Hochman, Baruch
    1985   *Character in Literature*. Ithaca, NY: Cornell University Press.
Hooker, Morna
    2008   "Seeing and Believing: John 20:1-18." In *The World It Imagines*,
            edited by David Fleer and Dave Bland, 139–43. St. Louis: Chalice.
Horst, Irvin B.
    1972   *The Radical Brethren: Anabaptism and the English Reformation to
            1558*. Supplementary Theses. Bibliotheca humanistica & refor-
            matorica 2. Nieuwkoop: De Graaf.
Hoskins, Paul M.
    2006   *Jesus as the Fulfillment of the Temple in the Gospel of John*. Paternoster
            Biblical Monographs. Waynesboro, GA: Paternoster.
Hoskyns, E. C.
    1947   *The Fourth Gospel*. Edited by Francis Noel Davey. London: Faber &
            Faber.
Howard-Brook, Wes
    1994   *Becoming Children of God: John's Gospel and Radical Discipleship*.
            Maryknoll, NY: Orbis Books.
    1997   *John's Gospel and the Renewal of the Church*. Maryknoll, NY: Orbis
            Books.
Hultgren, Arland J.
    1982   "The Johannine Footwashing (13:1-11) as Symbol of
            Eschatological Hospitality." *New Testament Studies* 28:539–46.
Hurtado, Larry W.
    2003   *Lord Jesus Christ: Devotion to Jesus in Earliest Christianity*. Grand
            Rapids: Eerdmans.

2005   *How on Earth Did Jesus Become a God? Historical Questions about Earliest Devotion to Jesus.* Grand Rapids: Eerdmans.

Hylen, Susan E.
2009   *Imperfect Believers: Ambiguous Characters in the Gospel of John.* Louisville: Westminster John Knox.

Hymnal: A Worship Book [*HWB*]
1992   Prepared by Churches in the Believers Church Tradition. Elgin, IL: Brethren Press.

Ito, Hisayosu
2000   "Johannine Irony Demonstrated in John 9." Parts 1–2. *Neo-testamentica* 34, no. 2:361–87.

Jacob, Edmund
1958   *Theology of the Old Testament.* New York/Evanston: Harper & Row.

Janzen, Waldemar
2000   *Exodus.* Believers Church Bible Commentary. Scottdale, PA: Herald Press.

Jaubert, Annie
1965   *The Date of the Last Supper.* Staten Island, NY: Alba House.
1990   "The Calendar of Qumran and the Passion Narrative in John." In *John and the Dead Sea Scrolls,* edited by James H. Charlesworth, 62–75. New York: Crossroad. Enlarged ed. of *John and Qumran.* London: Geoffrey Chapman, 1972.

Jeremias, Joachim
1969   *Jerusalem in the Time of Jesus.* Philadelphia: Fortress.

Johns, Loren L.
2003   *The Lamb Christology of the Book of Revelation: An Investigation into Its Origins and Rhetorical Force.* Wissenschaftliche Monographien zum Alten und Neuen Testament 2/167. Tübingen: Mohr.

Johns, Loren, and Douglas Miller
1994   "The Signs as Witnesses in the Fourth Gospel: Re-examining the Evidence." *CBQ* 56:519–35.

Johnson, Luke Timothy
1996   *The Real Jesus: The Misguided Quest for the Historical Jesus and the Truth of the Traditional Gospels.* San Francisco: Harper.
1999   *Living Jesus: Learning the Heart of the Gospel.* San Francisco: HarperCollins.

Johnston, George
1970   *The Spirit-Paraclete in the Gospel of John.* Cambridge: University Press.

Kanagaraj, Jey J.
2005   *The Gospel of John: A Commentary; With Elements of Comparison to Indian Religious Thoughts and Cultural Practices.* Secunderabad, India: OM Books.

Karris, Robert J.
1990   *Jesus and the Marginalized in John's Gospel.* Zacchaeus Studies. Wilmington, DE: Liturgical Press/M. Glazier.

Käsemann, Ernst
1968   *The Testament of Jesus: A Study of the Gospel of John in Light of John 17.* London: SCM.

Kasper, Walter (Cardinal)
   2005   "Ecumenical Situation—Ecumenical Problems—Ecumenical Perspectives." Section 2 in http://www.lehighchurches.org/doc/campbell/2005_Campbell_Lecture_1.pdf. See also his *Sacrament of Unity: The Eucharist and the Church*. New York: Herder & Herder, 2004.

Katongole, Emmanuel, and Chris Rice
   2008   *Reconciling All Things: A Christian Vision for Justice, Peace, and Healing*. Downers Grove, IL: InterVarsity.

Keener, Craig S.
   2003   *The Gospel of John*. 2 vols. Peabody, MA: Hendrickson.

Kelly, Anthony J., and Francis J. Moloney
   2003   *Experiencing God in the Gospel of John*. New York: Paulist Press.

Kenneson, Philip D.
   1999   *Life on the Vine: Cultivating the Fruit of the Spirit in Christian Community*. Downers Grove, IL: InterVarsity.

Kerr, Alan R.
   2002   *The Temple of Jesus' Body: The Temple Theme in the Gospel of John*. Journal for the Study of the New Testament: Supplement Series 220. Sheffield Academic Press.

Kierspel, Lars
   2008   "'Dematerializing Religion: Reading John 2–4 as a Chiasm." *Biblica* 89:526–54.

Kilpatrick, G. D.
   1960   "The Punctuation of John vii 37-38." *Journal of Theological Studies* 11:340–42.

Kinman, Brent
   2005   "Jesus' Royal Entry in Jerusalem." *Bulletin for Biblical Research* 15:223–60.

Klaassen, Walter
   2001   *Anabaptism: Neither Catholic nor Protestant*. 3rd ed. Kitchener, ON: Pandora Press; Scottdale, PA: Herald Press.

Klassen, William
   1984   "Anabaptist Hermeneutics: The Letter and the Spirit." In *Essays on Biblical Interpretation: Anabaptist-Mennonite Perspectives*, edited by Willard M. Swartley, 77–90. Text Reader Series 1. Elkhart, IN: Institute of Mennonite Studies.
   1996   *Judas: Betrayer or Friend of Jesus*. Minneapolis: Fortress.

Klassen, William, and Walter Klaassen, trans. and ed.
   1978   *The Writings of Pilgram Marpeck*. Kitchener, ON; Scottdale, PA: Herald Press.

Klink, Edward W., III
   2007   *The Sheep of the Fold: The Audience and Origin of the Gospel of John*. Society for New Testament Studies Monograph Series 141. Cambridge: Cambridge University Press.

Koester, Craig R.
   1990   "The Savior of the World (John 4:42)." *JBL* 109:665–80.
   2003   *Symbolism in the Fourth Gospel: Meaning, Mystery, Community*. 2nd ed. Minneapolis: Fortress. 1st ed., 1995.

2008   *The Word of Life: A Theology of John's Gospel.* Grand Rapids: Eerdmans.

Köstenberger, Andreas J.
1995   "The Challenge of a Systematized Biblical Theology of Mission: Missiological Insights from the Gospel of John." *Missiology: An International Review* 23:449.
1998   *The Missions of Jesus and His Disciples According to the Fourth Gospel: With Implications for the Fourth Gospel's Purpose and the Mission of the Contemporary Church.* Grand Rapids: Eerdmans.
2005   "The Destruction of the Second Temple and the Composition of the Fourth Gospel." *Trinity Journal* 26, no. 2:205–42.
2009   *A Theology of John's Gospel and Letters.* Grand Rapids: Zondervan.

Kovacs, Judith L.
1995   "'Now Shall the Ruler of This World Be Driven Out': Jesus' Death as Cosmic Battle in John 12:20-36." *JBL* 114:227–47.

Kragerud, Alv
1959   *Der Lieblingsjünger im Johannesevangelium.* Hamburg: Osloer Universitätsverlag.

Kraybill, Donald B.
2003   *The Upside-Down Kingdom.* 25th anniversary ed. Scottdale, PA: Herald Press.

Kreider, Alan
2006   *The Change of Conversion and the Origin of Christendom.* Eugene: OR: Wipf & Stock. Reprint of the original, Harrisburg, PA: Trinity Press International, 1999.

Kügler, Joachim
1988   *Der Jünger, den Jesus liebte.* Stuttgarter biblische Beiträge 16. Stuttgart: Katholisches Bibelwerk.

Kysar, Robert
1976   *John, the Maverick Gospel.* Atlanta: John Knox.
2005   *Voyages with John: Charting the Fourth Gospel.* Waco: Baylor University Press.

Lacomara, Alfred
1974   "Deuteronomy and the Farewell Discourse (Jn 13:31-16:33)." *CBQ* 36:65–84.

Lapp, John A.
2009   "Remember Who You Are: Four Trajectories of My Life." In *Continuing the Journey: The Geography of Our Faith; Mennonite Stories Integrating Faith and Life and the World of Thought,* edited by Nancy V. Lee, 50–71. Telford, PA: Cascadia Publishing House.

Larsson, Tord
2008   "Glory or Persecution: The God of the Gospel of John in the History of Interpretation." In *The Gospel of John and Christian Theology,* edited by Richard Bauckham and Carl Mosser, 82–88. Grand Rapids: Eerdmans.

Lee, Dorothy Ann
1993   "The Story of the Woman at the Well: A Symbolic Reading (John 4:1-42)." *Australian Biblical Review* 41:35–48.

1994   *The Symbolic Narratives of the Fourth Gospel: The Interplay of Form and Meaning.* Journal of the Study of the New Testamemt Supplements 95. Sheffield Academic Press.

1999   "The Symbol of Divine Fatherhood." 177–88 in *God the Father in the Gospel of John,* edited by Adele Reinhartz. Atlanta: SBL.

2002   *Flesh and Glory: Symbol, Gender, and Theology in the Gospel of John.* New York: Crossroad.

2010   "The Gospel of John and the Five Senses." *JBL* 129:115–27.

Léon-Dufour, Xavier
1981   "Towards a Symbolic Reading of the Fourth Gospel." *New Testament Studies* 27:439–56.

Levenson, Jon D.
2006   *Resurrection and the Restoration of Israel: The Ultimate Victory of the God of Life.* New Haven: Yale University Press.

Lieu, Judith
2008   "Anti-Judaism, the Jews, and the Worlds of the Fourth Gospel." In *The Gospel of John and Christian Theology,* edited by Richard Bauckham and Carl Mosser, 168–82. Grand Rapids: Eerdmans.

Lincoln, Andrew T.
2000   *Truth on Trial: The Lawsuit Motif in the Fourth Gospel.* Peabody, MA: Hendrickson.

2005   *The Gospel According to Saint John.* Black's New Testament Commentaries. Peabody, MA: Hendrickson.

Lind, Millard C.
1996   *Ezekiel.* Believers Church Bible Commentary. Scottdale, PA: Herald Press.

Lindars, Barnabas
1957   "The Fourth Gospel as an Act of Contemplation." In *Studies in the Fourth Gospel,* edited by Frank L. Cross, 23–35. London: A. R. Mowbray.

1972   *The Gospel of John.* New Century Bible Commentary. Grand Rapids: Eerdmans.

1981   "The Persecution of Christians in John 15:18–16:4a." In *Suffering and Martyrdom in the New Testament,* edited by William Horbury and Brian McNeil, 48–69. Cambridge: Cambridge University Press.

Loader, William
1997   *Jesus' Attitude Towards the Law: A Study of the Gospels.* Tübingen: Mohr Siebeck. Reprint, Grand Rapids: Eerdmans, 2002.

Lowe, Malcolm
1976   "Who Were the Judaioi?" *Novum Testamentum* 18:101–30.

Lozanda, Francisco Jr., and Tom Thatcher, eds.
2006   *New Currents Through John: A Global Perspective.* Atlanta: SBL.

Maccini, R.
1995   *Her Testimony Is True: Women as Witnesses According to John.* Journal for the Study of the New Testament: Supplement Series 125. Sheffield: Sheffield Academic Press.

Macgregor, George H. C.
1954   *The New Testament Basis of Pacifism.* Nyack, NY: Fellowship of Reconciliation.

1962   "The Eucharist in the Fourth Gospel." *New Testament Studies*
        9:111–19.

Malatesta, Edward

1978   *Interiority and Covenant.* Rome: Biblical Institute Press.

Manns, F.

1983   *Le symbole eau-espirit dans le Judaïsme ancien.* SBFA 19. Jerusalem:
        Franciscan Printing Press.

Mardaga, Hellen

2005   "Reflection on the Meaning of John 17:21 for Ecumenical
        Dialogue." *Ecumenical Trends*: 148–52.

Marpeck, Pilgram. *See* Klassen and Klaassen.

Marsh, John

1968   *The Gospel of Saint John.* Harmondsworth, UK: Penguin.

Marshall, Chris

2013   "'Making Every Effort': Peacemaking and Ecclesiology in Ephesians
        4:1-6." In *Struggles for Shalom*, edited by Laura Brenneman and
        Brad Schantz. Eugene: OR: Wipf & Stock. Forthcoming.

Marshall, I. Howard

1980   *Last Supper and Lord's Supper.* Grand Rapids: Eerdmans.

Martens, Elmer A.

1986   *Jeremiah.* Believers Church Bible Commentary. Scottdale, PA:
        Herald Press.

Martin, Ernest D.

1993   *Colossians, Philemon.* Believers Church Bible Commentary.
        Scottdale, PA: Herald Press.

Martyn, J. Louis

1978   *The Gospel of John in Christian History: Essays for Interpreters.*
        Ramsey, NJ: Paulist Press. Esp. ch. 3, "Glimpses into the History
        of the Johannine Community," © 1979.

2003   *History and Theology in the Fourth Gospel.* 3rd ed. Louisville:
        Westminster John Knox. Cf. earlier editions: 1st 1968 and 2nd
        1979, Nashville: Abingdon.

Mast, Gerald J.

2008   "Jesus' Flesh and the Faithful Church in the Theological Rhetoric
        of Menno Simons." In *The Work of Jesus Christ in Anabaptist
        Perspective: Essays in Honor of J. Denny Weaver*, edited by Alain Epp
        Weaver and Gerald J. Mast, 173–90. Telford, PA: Cascadia
        Publishing House; Scottdale, PA: Herald Press.

Matand Bulembat, Jean-Bosco

2007   "Head Waiter and Bridegroom of the Wedding at Cana: Structure
        and Meaning of John 2:1-12." *Journal for the Study of the New
        Testament* 30:55–73.

Matera, Frank J.

1988   "'On Behalf of Others,' 'Cleansing,' and 'Return': Johannine
        Images for Jesus' Death." *Louvain Studies* 13:161–88.

Matson, Mark A.

2001   *In Dialogue with Another Gospel? The Influence of the Fourth Gospel on
        the Passion Narrative of the Gospel of Luke.* SBL Dissertation Series
        178. Atlanta: SBL.

Matsunaga, Kikuo
    1981   "Is John's Gospel Anti-Sacramental? A New Solution in the Light of the Evangelist's Milieu." *New Testament Studies* 27:516–24.
Mbon, Friday
    1982   "Deliverance in the Complaint Psalms: Religious Claim or Religious Experience." *Studies in Biblical Theology* 12:3–15.
McCaffrey, James
    1988   *The House with Many Rooms: The Temple Theme of Jn. 14,2-3.* Analecta biblica 114. Rome: Pontifical Biblical Institute.
McDermond, J. E.
    2011   *1, 2, 3 John.* Believers Church Bible Commentary. Scottdale, PA: Herald Press.
McGrath, James F.
    1998   "A Rebellious Son? Hugo Odeberg and the Interpretation of John 5.18." *New Testament Studies* 44:470–73.
    2001   *John's Apologetic Christology: Legitimation and Development in Johannine Christology.* Society for New Testament Studies Monograph Series 111. Cambridge: Cambridge University Press.
McKelvey, Robert J.
    1969   *The New Temple: The Church in the New Testament.* London: Oxford University Press.
McWhirter, Jocelyn
    2004   *The Bridegroom Messiah and the People of God: Marriage in the Fourth Gospel.* Society for New Testament Studies Monograph Series 138. Cambridge: Cambridge University Press.
Mealand, David L.
    1978   "The Christology of the Fourth Gospel." *Scottish Journal of Theology* 31:449–67.
Meeks, Wayne A.
    1967   *The Prophet-King: Moses Traditions and the Johannine Christology.* Novum Testamentum Supplements 14. Leiden: E. J. Brill.
    1972   "The Man from Heaven in Johannine Sectarianism." *JBL* 91:44–72.
    1975   "'Am I a Jew?' Johannine Christianity and Judaism." In *Christianity, Judaism and Other Greco-Roman Cults: Studies for Morton Smith at Sixty*, edited by Jacob Neusner, Part 1:163–86. Leiden: E. J. Brill.
    1990   "Equal to God." In *The Conversation Continues: Studies in Paul and John: In Honor of J. Louis Martyn*, edited by Robert T. Fortna and Beverly R. Gaventa, 309–21. Nashville: Abingdon.
    1993   *The Origins of Christian Morality: The First Two Centuries.* New Haven: Yale University Press.
    1996   "The Ethics of the Fourth Evangelist." In *Exploring the Gospel of John: In Honor of D. Moody Smith*, edited by R. Alan Culpepper and C. Clifton Black, 317–26. Louisville: Westminster John Knox.
Meier, John P.
    1994   *Mentor, Message, and Miracles.* Vol. 2 of *A Marginal Jew: Rethinking the Historical Jesus.* New York: Doubleday.
    2001   *Companions and Competitors.* Vol. 3 of *A Marginal Jew: Rethinking the Historical Jesus.* New York: Doubleday.

Bibliography   559

Menno Simons
    1956   *The Complete Writings of Menno Simons.* Translated by Leonard
          Verduin. Edited by J. C. Wenger. Scottdale, PA: Herald Press.
Mennonite Church
    1977   The Holy Spirit in the Life of the Church: A Summary Statement
          Adopted by Mennonite General Assembly, June 18–24, 1977,
          Estes Park, Colorado. http://www.gameo.org/encyclopedia/
          contents/H6583.html.
    1995   *Confession of Faith in a Mennonite Perspective.* Published by
          arrangement with the General Board of the General Conference
          Mennonite Church and the Mennonite Church General Board.
          Scottdale, PA: Herald Press. http://www.mcusa-archives.org/
          library/resolutions/1995/index.html.
Metzger, Bruce M.
    1987   *The Canon of the New Testament: Its Origin, Development, and
          Significance.* Oxford: Oxford University Press.
    1992   *The Text of the New Testament: Its Transmission, Corruption, and
          Restoration.* 3rd ed. Oxford: Oxford University Press.
    1994   *A Textual Commentary on the Greek New Testament.* On behalf of and in
          cooperation with the Editorial Committee of the United Bible
          Societies' Greek New Testament. 2nd ed. Stuttgart: Deutsche
          Bibelgesellschaft. Cf. 1st ed., New York: United Bible Societies, 1971.
Meyer, Paul W.
    1996   "'The Father': The Presentation of God in the Fourth Gospel." In
          Exploring the Gospel of John: In Honor of D. Moody Smith, edited by R.
          Alan Culpepper and C. Clifton Black, 255–73. Louisville: West-
          minster John Knox.
Michaels, J. Ramsey
    2010   *The Gospel of John.* New International Commentary on the New
          Testament. Grand Rapids: Eerdmans.
Miller, Douglas B.
    2010   *Ecclesiastes.* Believers Church Bible Commentary. Scottdale, PA:
          Herald Press.
Miller, Ed L.
    1989   *Salvation History in the Prologue of John: The Significance of John
          1:3-4.* Leiden: E. J. Brill.
Minear, Paul S.
    1960   *Images of the Church in the New Testament.* Philadelphia:
          Westminster.
    1977   "The Beloved Disciple in the Gospel of John." *Novum Testamentum*
          19:105–23.
    1983   "The Original Function of John 21." *JBL* 102:85–98.
    1984   *John, the Martyr's Gospel.* New York: Pilgrim.
Miranda, José Porfirio
    1977   *Being and the Messiah: The Message of John.* Translated by John
          Eagleson. Maryknoll, NY: Orbis Books.
Miyazaki, Homare
    2004   "A Chiastic Reading of the Passover Narratives in the Fourth Gospel."
          MA thesis. Elkhart, IN: Associated Mennonite Biblical Seminary.

Moberly, Robert W. L.
   2003   "How Can We Know the Truth? A Study of John 7:14-18." In *The Art of Reading Scripture*, edited by Ellen F. Davis and Richard B. Hays, 239–57. Grand Rapids: Eerdmans.
Moessner, Donald P.
   1989   *Lord of the Banquet: The Literary and Theological Significance of the Lukan Travel Narrative*. Minneapolis: Fortress.
Moloney, Francis J.
   1976   "The Johannine Son of Man." *Biblical Theology Bulletin* 6:177–89. This summarizes his 1975 dissertation with the same title, published in the series Bibliotheca di scienze religiose 14. Rome: Libreria Ateneo Salesiano, 1976. Reprint of the 2nd ed., Eugene, OR: Wipf & Stock, 2007.
   1998   *The Gospel of John*. Sacra pagina 4. Collegeville, MN: Liturgical Press.
   2005   "The Gospel of John as Scripture." *CBQ* 67:454–68.
Moltmann, Jürgen
   1967   *Theology of Hope: On the Ground and the Implications of a Christian Eschatology*. New York: Harper & Row.
   1997   *The Source of Life: The Holy Spirit and the Theology of Life*. Minneapolis: Fortress.
   2012   *Ethics of Hope*. Trans. Margaret Kohl. Minneapolis, MN: Fortress Press.
Moore, Stephen D.
   1994   *Poststructuralism and the New Testament: Derrida and Foucault at the Foot of the Cross*. Minneapolis: Fortress.
Mor, Menachem
   1989   "The Persian, Hellenistic, and Hasmonean Period." In *The Samaritans*, edited by Alan D. Crown, 1–18. Tübingen: Mohr Siebeck.
Morris, Leon
   1995   *The Gospel According to John*. New International Commentary on the New Testament. Rev. ed. Grand Rapids: Eerdmans.
Motyer, Stephen
   1997   *Your Father the Devil? A New Approach to John and "the Jews."* Carlisle, UK: Paternoster.
   2001   "The Fourth Gospel and the Salvation of Israel: An Appeal for a New Start." In *Anti-Judaism and the Fourth Gospel*, edited by R. Bieringer, D. Pollefeyt, and F. Vandecasteele-Vanneuville, 83–100. Louisville: Westminster John Knox.
   2008   "Bridging the Gap: How Might the Fourth Gospel Help Us Cope with the Legacy of Christianity's Exclusive Claim over Against Judaism." In *The Gospel of John and Christian Theology*, edited by Richard Bauckham and Carl Mosser, 143–67. Grand Rapids: Eerdmans.
Mowery, Robert L.
   2002   "Son of God in Roman Imperial Titles and Matthew." *Biblica* 83:100–110.

Need, Stephen W.
:   2003 "Re-Reading the Prologue: Incarnation and Creation in John 1.1-18." *Theology* 106, issue 834 (Nov.–Dec.): 397–404.

Nes, Solrunn
:   2001 *The Uncreated Light: An Iconographical Study of the Transfiguration in the Eastern Church.* Fairfax, VA: Eastern Christian Publications. Reprint, Grand Rapids: Eerdmans: 2007.

Nestle-Aland
:   1993 *Greek-English New Testament.* Stuttgart: Deutsche Bibelgesellschaft.

Neville, David J.
:   2013 *A Peaceable Hope: Contesting Violent Eschatology in New Testament Narratives.* Grand Rapids: Baker Academic.

Newbigin, Lesslie
:   1982 *The Light Has Come: An Exposition of the Fourth Gospel.* Grand Rapids: Eerdmans.

Neyrey, Jerome
:   1994 "What's Wrong with This Picture? John 4, Cultural Stereotypes of Women, and Public and Private Space." *Biblical Theology Bulletin* 24:77–91.

:   2006 *The Gospel of John.* New Cambridge Bible Commentary. New York: Cambridge University Press.

Nickelsburg, George W. E.
:   1992 "Son of Man." *Anchor Bible Dictionary*, edited by D. N. Freedman, 6:137–50. New York: Doubleday.

Nielsen, Jesper Tang
:   2011 "The Narrative Structures of Glory and Glorification in the Fourth Gospel." *New Testament Studies* 56 (2011): 343–66.

O'Day, Gail R.
:   1986a "Narrative Mode and Theological Claim: A Study in the Fourth Gospel." *JBL* 105:657–68.

:   1986b *Revelation in the Fourth Gospel: Narrative Mode and Theological Claim.* Philadelphia: Fortress.

:   1991 "'I Have Overcome the World' (John 16:33): Narrative Time in John 13–17." *Semeia* 53:153–66.

:   1995 *The Gospel of John.* New Interpreter's Bible. Nashville: Abingdon.

:   1998 "John." In *The Women's Bible Commentary*, edited by Carol A. Newsom and Sharon H. Ringe, 381–93. Rev. ed. Louisville: Westminster John Knox.

:   2002 *The Word Disclosed: Preaching the Gospel of John.* Rev. and Expanded Edition. St. Louis: Chalice.

:   2008a "Jesus as Friend: Courage for the Present." A section in "Friendship as the Theological Center of the Gospel of John," in *Preaching John's Gospel: The World It Imagines*, edited by David Fleer and Dave Bland, 33–42. St. Louis: Chalice.

:   2008b "The Paraclete as Friend: Hope for the Future." In *Preaching John's Gospel: The World It Imagines*, edited by David Fleer and Dave Bland, 61–72. St. Louis: Chalice.

O'Day, Gail R., and Susan E. Hylen
    2006   *John.* Westminster Bible Companion. Louisville: Westminster John Knox.
O'Donovan, Oliver
    1986   *Resurrection and Moral Order: An Outline for Evangelical Ethics.* Grand Rapids: Eerdmans.
Okure, Teresa
    1988   *The Johannine Approach to Mission: A Contextual Study of John 4:1-42.* Wissenschaftliche Monographien zum Alten und Neuen Testament 2/31. Tübingen: Mohr Siebeck.
Ollenburger, Ben
    1984   "The Hermeneutics of Obedience." In *Essays on Biblical Interpretation: Anabaptist-Mennonite Perspectives*, edited by Willard M. Swartley, 45–61. Text Reader Series 1. Elkhart, IN: Institute of Mennonite Studies.
    2013   "Creation and Violence." In *Struggles for Shalom*, edited by Laura Brenneman and Brad Schantz. Eugene: OR: Wipf & Stock. Forthcoming.
O'Neill, James C.
    2003   "Son of Man, Stone of Blood (John 1:51)." *Novum Testamentum* 45:374–81.
Oyer, Linda
    1997   "Interpreting the New in Light of the Old: A Comparative Study of the Post-Resurrection Commissioning Stories in Matthew and John." ThD diss., Faculté de Théologie et de Sciences Religieuses, Institut Catholique de Paris.
Packull, Werner O.
    1977   *Mysticism and the Early South German-Austrian Movement 1525-1531.* Studies in Anabaptist and Mennonite History 19. Scottdale, PA and Kitchener, ON: Herald Press.
Pagels, Elaine H.
    1989   *The Johannine Gospel in Gnostic Exegesis: Heracleon's Commentary on John.* SBL Monograph Series 17. Atlanta: Scholars Press.
    2003   *Beyond Belief: The Secret Gospel of Thomas.* New York: Vintage Books.
Painter, John
    1986   "John 9 and the Interpretation of the Fourth Gospel." *Journal for the Study of the New Testament* 28:31–61.
    1994   "The Quotations of Scripture and Unbelief in John 12:36b-43. In *The Gospels and the Scriptures of Israel*, edited by Craig A. Evans and W. Richard Stegner, 429–58. Journal for the Study of the New Testament: Supplement Series 104. Sheffield: Sheffield Academic.
Pamment, Margaret
    1985   "The Son of Man in the Fourth Gospel." *Journal of Theological Studies* 36:56–66.
Pancaro, Severino A.
    1975   *The Law in the Fourth Gospel: The Torah and the Gospel, Moses and Jesus, Judaism and Christianity According to John.* Leiden: E. J. Brill.

Parsenios, George L.
  2005   *Departure and Consolation: The Johannine Farewell Discourse in Light of Greco-Roman Literature.* Boston: E. J. Brill.

Pazdan, Margaret
  1987   "Nicodemus and the Samaritan Woman: Contrasting Models of Discipleship." *Biblical Theology Bulletin* 17:145–48.
  1991   *The Son of Man: A Metaphor for Jesus in the Fourth Gospel.* Collegeville, MN: Liturgical Press.

Pelikan, Jaroslav
  1997   *The Illustrated Jesus Through the Centuries.* New Haven: Yale University Press.

Petersen, Norman R.
  1993   *The Gospel of Light and the Sociology of Light: Language and Characterization in the Fourth Gospel.* Valley Forge, PA: Trinity Press International.

Peterson, Eugene H.
  2010   *Practice Resurrection: A Conversation on Growing Up in Christ.* Grand Rapids: Eerdmans. Reviewed by M. Craig Barnes in *Christian Century* 127, no. 9 (May 4, 2010): 44–45.

Pfeiffer, Cara
  2012   "Healing and the Holy Spirit: A Component of the 'Already, but Not Yet,' Kingdom." *Vision: A Journal for Theology and Church* 13.1 (Spring issue on *The Holy Spirit and the Christian Life,* edited by Karl Koop): 48–55.

Philips, Dirk. *See* Dyck, Cornelius J., William E. Keeney, and Alvin J. Beachy.

Pilch, John J.
  2000   *Healing in the New Testament: Insights from Medical and Mediterranean Anthropology.* Minneapolis: Fortress.

Pipkin, Wayne, and John H. Yoder, trans. and eds.
  1989   *Balthasar Hubmaier: Theologian of Anabaptism.* Classics of the Radical Reformation 5. Scottdale, PA: Herald Press.

Poettcker, Henry
  1984   "Menno Simons' Encounter with the Bible." In *Essays on Biblical Interpretation: Anabaptist-Mennonite Perspectives,* edited by Willard M. Swartley, 62–76. Text Reader Series 1. Elkhart, IN: Institute of Mennonite Studies.

Porteous, Norman
  1962   "The Theology of the Old Testament." In *Peake's Commentary on the Bible,* edited by Matthew Black and H. H. Rowley, 151–59. London: Thomas Nelson & Sons.

Reich, Ronny, and Eli Shukron
  2005   "The Siloam Pool from the Second Temple Period in Jerusalem." *Qadmoniot* [Heb.] 38, no. 130: 91–96 (ET by G. Rivkin).

Reinhartz, Adele
  1998   "The Johannine Community and its Jewish Neighbors" A Reappraisal." In *Literary and Social Readings of the Fourth Gospel, "What Is John?"* edited by Fernando Segovia, Vol. 2, 111-38. Atlanta: Scholars Press.

2001a   *Befriending the Beloved Disciple: A Jewish Reading of the Gospel of John.* New York/London: Continuum.

2001b   "'Jews' and Jews in the Fourth Gospel." In *Anti-Judaism and the Fourth Gospel*, edited by Bieringer, et al., 213-27.

2003   "Women in the Johannine Community: An Exercise in Historical Imagination." In *A Feminist Companion to John*, edited by Amy-Jill Levine with Marianne Blickenstaff, 2:14-33. Sheffield: Sheffield Academic.

2009   "'Rewritten Gospel': The Case of Caiaphas the High Priest." *New Testament Studies* 55:166-78.

Reinhartz, Adele, ed.

1999   *God the Father in the Gospel of John. Semeia* [Journal] 85. Atlanta: SBL.

Rempel, John D.

1993   *The Lord's Supper in Anabaptism: A Study of the Christology of Balthasar Hubmaier, Pilgram Marpeck, and Dirk Philips.* Studies in Anabaptist and Mennonite History 33. Scottdale, PA: Herald Press.

Rensberger, David

1984   "The Politics of John: The Trial of Jesus in the Fourth Gospel." *JBL* 103: 395-411.

1988   *Johannine Faith and Liberating Community.* Philadelphia: Westminster.

Reynolds, Benjamin E.

2008   *The Apocalyptic Son of Man in the Gospel of John.* WUNT 249. Tübingen: Mohr Siebeck.

Ridderbos, Herman

1997   *The Gospel of John: A Theological Commentary.* Translated by John Vriend. Grand Rapids: Eerdmans.

Ringe, Sharon H.

1999   *Wisdom's Friends: Community and Christology in the Fourth Gospel.* Louisville: Westminster John Knox.

Robinson, John A. T.

1976   *Redating the New Testament.* Philadelphia: Westminster.

1985   *The Priority of John.* Edited by J. F. Coakley. Oak Park, IL: Meyer-Stone.

Root, Michael

2009   "In Tough Straights: Can the Ecumenical Logjam Be Broken?" *Christian Century* 126, no. 26 (Dec. 29): 10-11.

Rossé, Gérard

2009   *Community of Believers: A New Look at the Johannine Writings.* Translated by Matthew J. O'Connell. New York: New City Press. New ed. of *The Spirituality of Communion: A New Approach to the Johannine Writings.* 1998.

Ruprecht, Louis A., Jr.

2008   *This Tragic Gospel: How John Corrupted the Heart of Christianity.* San Francisco: John Wiley.

Sanders, Ed P.

1985   *Jesus and Judaism.* Philadelphia: Fortress.

Sanders, Joseph N. [, and B. A. Mastin]
    1968   *Commentary on the Gospel According to St. John.* Edited and completed by B. A. Mastin. Harper's New Testament Commentaries. New York: Harper & Row.

Sanford, John A.
    1993   *Mystical Christianity: A Psychological Commentary on the Gospel of John.* New York: Crossroad.

Sattler, Michael. *See* Yoder, John H.

Schertz, Mary
    2010   "Why Footwashing?: Biblical Teaching and Liturgical Practices." Bridgefolk speech.

Schnackenburg, Rudolf
    1980–82 *The Gospel According to St. John.* ET, 3 vols. New York: Seabury.

Schneiders, Sandra M.
    1999   *The Revelatory Text: Interpreting the New Testament as Sacred Scripture.* 2nd ed. Collegeville, MN: Liturgical Press. 1st ed., HarperSanFrancisco, 1991.
    2002   "To See or Not to See: John 9 as a Synthesis of the Theology and Spirituality of Discipleship." In *Word, Theology, and Community in John,* edited by John Painter, R. Alan Culpepper, and Fernando F. Segovia, 189–209. St. Louis: Chalice.
    2003   *Written That You Might Believe: Encountering Jesus in the Fourth Gospel.* Rev. and expanded ed. New York: Crossroad.

Schnelle, Udo
    2005   *The Anti-Docetism of the Gospel of John: An Investigation of the Place of the Fourth Gospel in the Johannine School.* Translated by Linda M. Maloney. Minneapolis: Fortress.
    2006   "Kreuz und Auferstehung im Johannesevangelium." Paper at Society for New Testament Studies, July 25–29, University of Aberdeen, 1–22.
    2009   *The Theology of the New Testament.* Translated by Eugene M. Boring. Grand Rapids: Baker Academic.

Schoneveld, Jacobus
    1990   "Torah in the Flesh: A New Reading of the Prologue of the Gospel of John as a Contribution to a Christology Without Anti-Judaism." In *The New Testament and Christian-Jewish Dialogue: Studies in Honor of David Flusser,* edited by Malcom F. Lowe, 77–93. Immanuel 24/25. Jerusalem: Ecumenical Theological Research Fraternity in Israel.

Schoon, Simon
    2001   "Escape Routes as Dead Ends: On Hatred Towards Jews and the New Testament, Especially in the Gospel of John." In *Anti-Judaism and the Fourth Gospel,* edited by R. Bieringer, D. Pollefeyt, and F. Vandecasteele-Vanneuville, 144–58. Louisville: Westminster John Knox.

Schottroff, Luise
    1998   "The Samaritan Woman and the Notion of Sexuality in the Fourth Gospel." In *Literary and Social Readings of the Fourth Gospel,* vol. 2 of *What Is John?* edited by Fernando Segovia, 157–81. Atlanta: Scholars Press.

Schrage, Wolfgang
    1988   *The Ethics of the New Testament.* Translated by David E. Green.
            Philadelphia: Fortress.
Schuchard, Bruce G.
    1992   *Scripture Within Scripture: The Interrelationship of Form and Function
            in the Explicit Old Testament Citations in the Gospel of John.* SBL
            Dissertation Series 133. Atlanta: Scholars Press.
Schweitzer, Albert
    1964   *The Quest of the Historical Jesus.* Translated by W. Montgomery.
            New York: Macmillan. Original, 1906.
Scobie, Charles H. H.
    1982   "Johannine Geography." *Studies in Religion / Sciences Religieuses*
            11:77–84.
Segovia, Fernando F.
    1981   "The Love and Hatred of Jesus and Johannine Sectarianism."
            Catholic Biblical Quarterly 43:258–72.
    1982   *Love Relationships in the Johannine Tradition:* Agapē/Agapan *in I
            John and the Fourth Gospel.* SBL Dissertation Series 58. Chico, CA:
            Scholars Press.
    1985   "'Peace I Leave with You; My Peace I Give to You': Discipleship
            in the Fourth Gospel." In *Discipleship in the New Testament,* edited
            by Fernando F. Segovia, 76–102. Philadelphia: Fortress.
    1991   "The Final Farewell of Jesus: A Reading of John 20:30–21:25."
            Semeia 53:167–90.
Shanks, Hershel
    2005   "The Siloam Man: Where Jesus Cured the Blind Man." *Biblical
            Archaeology Review* 31, no. 5:16–23.
Sheeley, Steven M.
    1995   "Lift Up Your Eyes: John 4:4-42." *Review and Expositor* 92:81–87.
Shellard, Barbara
    1995   "The Relationship of Luke and John: A Fresh Look at an Old
            Problem." *Journal of Theological Studies* 46:71–98.
Shenk, Sara Wenger
    2003   *Anabaptist Ways of Knowing: A Conversation About Tradition-Based
            Critical Education.* Telford, PA: Cascadia; Scottdale, PA: Herald Press.
    2007   "Formation Beyond Education: Interview." *Leader* (Summer): 13–15.
Shepherd, David
    2010   "'Do You Love Me?' A Narrative-Critical Reappraisal of ἀγαπάω
            and φιλέω in John 21:15-17." *JBL* 129:777–92.
Shillington, V. George
    2012   "The Spirit-Paraclete as Jesus' Alter Ego in the Fourth Gospel (John
            14–16)." *Vision: A Journal for Theology and Church* 13.1 (Spring issue on
            The Holy Spirit and the Christian Life, edited by Karl Koop): 31–39.
Shirbroun, G. Franklin
    1985   *The Giving of the Name of God to Jesus in John 17:11, 12.* PhD Thesis:
            Princeton Theological Seminary.
Sing the Journey
    2005   *Hymnal: A Worship Book—Supplement 1.* Scottdale, PA: Mennonite
            Publishing Network.

Sing the Story
    2007   *Hymnal: A Worship Book—Supplement 2.* Scottdale, PA: Mennonite Publishing Network.

Smalley, Stephen S.
    1998   *John: Evangelist and Interpreter.* 2nd ed. Downers Grove, IL: InterVarsity.

Smith, D. Moody, Jr.
    1995   *The Theology of the Gospel of John.* Cambridge: Cambridge University Press.
    1999   *John.* Abingdon New Testament Commentaries. Nashville: Abingdon.
    2001   "Johannine Studies Since Bultmann." *Word and World* 21:342–51.
    2002   "Ethics and the Interpretation of the Fourth Gospel." In *Word, Theology, and Community in John,* edited by John Painter, R. Alan Culpepper, and Fernando F. Segovia, 109–22. St. Louis: Chalice.
    2003   "The Contribution of J. Louis Martyn to the Understanding of the Gospel of John." In Martyn's *History and Theology in the Fourth Gospel,* 1–23. 3rd ed. Louisville: Westminster John Knox.
    2005   "Future Direction of Johannine Studies." In *Life in Abundance: Studies of John's Gospel in Tribute to Raymond E. Brown,* 52–62. Collegeville, Minn.: Liturgical Press.
    2008   *The Fourth Gospel in Four Dimensions: Judaism and Jesus, the Gospels and Scripture.* Columbia: University of South Carolina Press.

Smith, Jacob Brubaker
    1955   *Greek-English Concordance to the New Testament.* Scottdale, PA: Herald Press.

Snyder, C. Arnold, ed.
    2001   *Sources of South German/Austrian Anabaptism.* Translated by W. Klaassen, F. Friesen and W. Packull. Kitchener, ON: Pandora Press.

Snyder, C. Arnold
    2012   "Bread, Not Stone: Refocusing an Anabaptist Vision." *Vision: A Journal for Theology and Church* 13.1 (Spring issue on *The Holy Spirit and the Christian Life,* edited by Karl Koop): 64–73.

Snyder Belousek, Darrin W.
    2012   *Atonement, Peace, and Justice: The Message of the Cross and the Mission of the Church.* Grand Rapids: Eerdmans.

Staley, Jeffrey Lloyd
    1991   "Stumbling in the Dark, Reaching the Light: Reading Character in John 5 and 9." *Semeia* 53:55–80.

Stassen, Glen H., and David P. Gushee
    2003   *Kingdom Ethics: Following Jesus in Contemporary Context.* Downers Grove, IL: InterVarsity.

Stibbe, Mark W. G.
    1992   *John as Storyteller: Narrative Criticism and the Fourth Gospel.* Cambridge: Cambridge University Press.

Stott, John R. W.
    1975   *Christian Mission in the Modern World.* Downers Grove, IL: InterVarsity.

Suderman, Robert J.

1994   *The Replacement Pattern in the Fourth Gospel: A Persecuted Community Confronts Its Past.* Dissertation Series. Bogotá: Pontificia Universidad Javeriana.

Suggit, John

1993   *The Sign of Life: Studies in the Fourth Gospel and the Liturgy of the Church.* Pietermaritzburg: Cluster Publications.

Swartley, Willard M.

1973   "The *Imitatio Christi* in the Ignatian Letters." *Vigiliae Christianae* 27:81–103.

1981   *Mark: The Way for All Nations.* Scottdale, PA: Herald Press. Reprinted, Eugene, OR: Wipf & Stock, 1999.

1983   *Slavery, Sabbath, War, and Women: Case Issues in Biblical Interpretation.* Scottdale, PA: Herald Press.

1990   "God as Father: Patriarchy or Paternity." *Daughters of Sarah* 16 (November–December): 12–15.

1994   *Israel's Scripture Traditions and the Synoptic Gospels: Story Shaping Story.* Peabody, MA: Hendrickson.

1997   "The Role of Women in Mark's Gospel." *Biblical Theology Bulletin* 27:16–22.

1998   "Mutual Aid Based in Jesus and Early Christianity." In *Building Communities of Compassion,* edited by Donald B. Kraybill and Willard M. Swartley, 21–39. Scottdale, PA: Herald Press.

2006a   *Covenant of Peace: The Missing Peace in New Testament Theology and Ethics.* Grand Rapids: Eerdmans.

2006b   "Biblical Faith Confronts Evil Spiritual Realities," 24–40; "Reflections on Deliverance Ministry;" 108–13; "Appendix 2: Prayer for Protection," 177; "Bibliography for Deliverance Ministries," 183–200. In *Even the Demons are Subject: Continuing Jesus' Ministry of Deliverance,* edited by Loren L. Johns and James R. Krabill. Institute of Mennonite Studies and Herald Press.

2006c   "Jesus Christ: Victor over Evil," 96–112, and "Resistance and Nonresistance: When and How?" 129–42. In *Transforming the Powers: Peace, Justice, and the Domination System,* edited by Ray Gingerich and Ted Grimsrud. Minneapolis: Fortress Press.

2006d   "Jesus and Believers at Prayer." *Vision: A Journal for Theology and Church* 7.2 (Fall issue edited by Mary Schertz): 10–21.

2007   *Send Forth Your Light: A Vision for Peace, Mission, and Worship.* Scottdale, PA: Herald Press.

2009   "Jesus Triumphs Over Evil." In *Jesus Matters,* edited by James Krabill and David W. Shenk, 89–102. Scottdale, PA: Herald Press.

2012a   *Health, Healing and the Church's Mission: Biblical Perspectives and Moral Priorities.* Downers Grove, IL: InterVarsity.

2012b   Review of *The Gospel and Letters of John,* by Urban von Wahlde [Eerdmans Critical Commentary. Grand Rapids: Eerdmans, 2010], in *Ashland Theological Journal* 44:108–110.

2013   *Living Gift: John's Jesus in Meditation and Poetry, Art and Song.* Nappanee, IN: Evangel Press.

Swartley, Willard M., ed.
1992   *The Love of Enemy and Nonretaliation in the New Testament.*
       Louisville: Westminster John Knox.
2000   *Violence Renounced: René Girard, Biblical Studies, and Peacemaking.*
       Telford, PA: Pandora Press; Scottdale, PA: Herald Press.
Talbert, Charles H.
1992   *Reading John: A Literary and Theological Commentary on the Fourth
       Gospel and the Johannine Epistles.* New York: Crossroad.
Tan, Yak-hwee
2006   "The Johannine Community: Caught in Two Worlds." In *New
       Currents Through John: A Global Perspective*, edited by Francisco
       Lozanda Jr. and Tom Thatcher, 167–79. Atlanta: SBL.
Temple, William
1939   *Readings in St. John's Gospel: First Series, Chapters I-XII.* London:
       Macmillan.
1940   *Readings in St. John's Gospel: Second Series, Chapters XIII-XXI.*
       London: Macmillan.
Thatcher, Tom
2006   "The New Current Through John: The Old 'New Look' and the
       New Critical Orthodoxy." In *New Currents Through John: A Global
       Perspective*, edited by Francisco Lozanda Jr., and Tom Thatcher,
       1–26. Atlanta: SBL.
2009   *Greater than Caesar.* Minneapolis: Fortress Press.
Thomas, John Christopher
1987   "A Note on the Text of John 13:10." *Novum Testamentum* 29:46–52.
1991   *Footwashing in John 13 and the Johannine Community.* Journal for
       the Study of the New Testament: Supplement Series 61.
       Sheffield: JSOT Press.
Thompson, Marianne Meye
1988   *The Humanity of Jesus in the Fourth Gospel.* Philadelphia: Fortress.
       Reprinted as *The Incarnate Word: Perspectives on Jesus in the Fourth
       Gospel.* Peabody, MA: Hendrickson: 1993.
1991   "Signs and Faith in the Fourth Gospel." *Bulletin for Biblical
       Research* 1:89–108.
1999   "The Living Father." In *God the Father in the Gospel of John*, edited
       by Adele Reinhartz, 19–32. Atlanta: SBL
2000   *The Promise of the Father: Jesus and God in the New Testament.*
       Louisville: Westminster John Knox.
2001a *The God of the Gospel of John.* Grand Rapids: Eerdmans.
2001b "What Is the Gospel of John?" *Word and World* 21:333–42.
2003   "'His Own Received Him Not': Jesus Washes the Feet of His
       Disciples." In *The Art of Reading Scripture*, edited by Ellen F. Davis
       and Richard B. Hays, 258–73. Grand Rapids: Eerdmans.
2008a "The Raising of Lazarus in John 11: A Theological Reading." In
       The Gospel of John and Christian Theology, edited by Richard
       Bauckham and Carl Mosser, 233–44. Grand Rapids: Eerdmans.
2008b "Word of God, Messiah of Israel, Savior of the World: Learning
       the Identity of Jesus from the Gospel of John." In *Seeking the*

Identity of Jesus: A Pilgrimage, edited by Beverly Roberts Gaventa and Richard B. Hays, 166–79. Grand Rapids: Eerdmans.

Toews, John E.
2004   *Romans*. Believers Church Bible Commentary. Scottdale, PA: Herald Press.

Trudinger, Paul
1992   "Of Women, Weddings, Wells, Waterpots and Wine! Reflections on Johannine Themes (John 2:1-11 and 4:1-42)." *St. Mark's Review* 151 (Spring): 10–16.

Truex, Jerry Duane
2002   "The Problem of Blasphemy: The Fourth Gospel and Early Jewish Understandings." PhD diss., Durham University (UK).

Valentine, Simon Ross
1996   "The Johannine Prologue—A Microcosm of the Gospel." *Evangelical Quarterly* 68, no. 4 (Oct.): 291–304.

Van der Watt, Jan Gabriel
2006   "Ethics and Ethos in the Gospel of John." *Zeitschrift für die neutestamentliche Wissenschaft und die Kunde der älteren Kirche* 97:147–76.

Volf, Miroslav
1996   *Exclusion and Embrace: A Theological Explanation of Identity, Otherness, and Reconciliation*. Nashville: Abingdon.
2008   "Johannine Dualism and Contemporary Pluralism." In *The Gospel of John and Christian Theology*, edited by Richard Bauckham and Carl Mosser, 19–50. Grand Rapids: Eerdmans.

Von Speyr, Adrienne
1987   *The Farewell Discourses: Meditations on John 13-17*. Translated by E. A. Nelson. San Francisco: Ignatius Press.

Von Wahlde, Urban C.
1984   "Literary Structure and Theological Argument in Three Discourses with the Jews in the Fourth Gospel." *JBL* 103:575–84.
1990   *The Johannine Commandments: 1 John and the Struggle for the Johannine Tradition*. New York: Paulist Press.
2009   "The Pool of Siloam: The Importance of the New Discoveries for Our Understanding of Ritual Immersion in Late Second Temple Judaism and the Gospel of John." In *Jesus, John, and History*, Vol. 2: *Aspects of Historicity in the Fourth Gospel*. Anderson, Just, and Thatcher, eds., 155–74 Atlanta: SBL.
2010   *John*. 3 vols. Eerdmans Critical Commentaries. Grand Rapids: Eerdmans.

Wallace, Daniel B.
1990   "John 5:2 and the Date of the Fourth Gospel." *Biblica* 71, no. 2:177–205.

Waltner, Erland
1999   *1-2 Peter*. Believers Church Bible Commentary. Scottdale, PA: Herald Press.

Waltner, James H.
2006   *Psalms*. Believers Church Bible Commentary. Scottdale, PA: Herald Press.

Webber, Robert E.
    1986   *Celebrating Our Faith: Evangelism Through Worship*. San Francisco: Harper & Row.

Webster, Jane S.
    2003   *Ingesting Jesus: Eating and Drinking in the Gospel of John*. Atlanta: SBL.

Weiss, Herold
    1979   "Footwashing in the Johannine Community." *Novum Testamentum* 21:298–325.

Wengst, Klaus
    1987   *Pax Romana and the Peace of Jesus Christ*. Translated by John Bowden. Philadelphia: Fortress Press.

Wenham, David
    1998   "A Historical View of John's Gospel." *Themelios* 23, no. 2:5–20.

Whitacre, Rodney A.
    1999   *John*. The IVP New Testament Commentary Series. Downers Grove, IL: InterVarsity.

Williams, Rowan
    2002   *Writing in the Dust: After September 11*. Grand Rapids: Eerdmans.

Wilson, Jeffrey
    1981   "The Integrity of John 3:22-36." *Journal for the Study of the New Testament* 10:34–41.

Wink, Walter
    1994   "Abiding, Even Under the Knife." *Christian Century* 111, no. 13 (Apr. 20): 413.

Witherington, Ben, III
    1995   *John's Wisdom: A Commentary on the Fourth Gospel*. Louisville: Westminster John Knox.
    2006   "The Last Man Standing." *Biblical Archaeological Review*, March/April, 24, 76.

Wright, Nicholas Thomas
    1996   *Jesus and the Victory of God*. Minneapolis: Fortress.

Yeatts, John R.
    2003   *Revelation*. Believers Church Bible Commentary. Scottdale, PA: Herald Press.

Yee, Gale
    1989   *Jewish Feasts and the Gospel of John*. Wilmington, DE: M. Glazier.

Yoder, Eldon T., and Monroe D. Hochstetler
    1969   *Biblical References in Anabaptist Writings*. Aylmer, ON; Lagrange, IN: Pathway Publishers.

Yoder, John Howard
    1958   *The Ecumenical Movement and the Faithful Church*. Focal Pamphlet No. 3. Scottdale, PA: Mennonite Publishing House.
    1984   "The Hermeneutics of the Anabaptists." In *Essays on Biblical Interpretation: Anabaptist-Mennonite Perspectives*, edited by Willard M. Swartley, 11–28. Text Reader Series 1. Elkhart, IN: Institute of Mennonite Studies.
    1994   *Politics of Jesus*. 2nd ed. Grand Rapids: Eerdmans. 1st ed., 1972.

Yoder, John H., trans. and ed.
1973   *The Legacy of Michael Sattler*. Classics of the Radical Reformation 1. Scottdale, PA: Herald Press.

Yoder Neufeld, Thomas R.
2002   *Ephesians*. Believers Church Bible Commentary. Scottdale, PA: Herald Press.
2003   "'*For He Is Our Peace*': Ephesians 2:11-22." In *Beautiful Upon the Mountains*, edited by Mary H. Schertz and Ivan Friesen, 215–33. Elkhart, IN: Institute of Mennonite Studies; Scottdale, PA: Herald Press.

Yokota, Paul
2004   "Jesus the Messiah of Israel: A Study of Matthew's Narrative Christology with Reference to His Messianic Interpretation of Scripture." PhD diss., St. Andrews University (UK).

York, Tripp
2008   *The Purple Crown: The Politics of Martyrdom*. Scottdale, PA: Herald Press.

Zehr, Paul
2010   *1 and 2 Timothy, Titus*. Believers Church Bible Commentary. Scottdale, PA: Herald Press.

Zorrilla, Hugo
1985   "The Feast of Liberation of the Oppressed: A Rereading of John 7:1–10:21." *Mission Focus* 13, no. 2 (June): 21–24.

Online sources:
For Tabernacles Feast
       http://www.hebrew4christians.com/Holidays/Fall_Holidays/Sukkot/sukkot.html.

Selected Resources

Basic Orientation to John

Augsburger, Myron. *Discovering John.* Carmel, NJ: Guideposts Associates, 1986. This marvelous picturesque book is a delight to see and read. It initiates one into the world and text of John's Gospel. Each commentary section ends with "What This Scripture Means to Me," by Dorothy Shellenberger.

Barclay, William. *The Gospel of John.* Rev. ed. Philadelphia: Westminster, 1975. This is a long-standing favorite for scholarly information with a pastoral touch.

Kysar, Robert. *John's Story of Jesus.* Philadelphia: Fortress, 1984. A wonderful guide to John's Gospel as story. Written for laity and pastors, yet tuned to scholarly awareness.

Matson, Mark A. *John.* Interpretation Bible Studies. Louisville: Westminster John Knox, 2002. A useful overall introduction, with scholarly underpinning; easy read.

Smith, Dennis E., and Michael E. Williams. *John.* Vol. 10 of *The Storyteller's Companion to the Bible.* Nashville: Abingdon. Giving brief description of the background for each text and often imagining a contemporary scene, this book prepares one to tell John as story, in a meaningful manner.

Studies in More Depth

Anderson, Paul N. 2011. *The Riddles of the Fourth Gospel.* Minneapolis: Fortress. This compact, 296-page volume introduces current issues defining Johannine scholarship. It masterfully guides one through the Gospel's mind-stretching riddles.

Bauckham, Richard. 2007. *The Testimony of the Beloved Disciple: Narrative, History, and Theology in the Gospel of John.* Grand Rapids: Eerdmans. This book boldly cuts new ground in understanding the role and identity of the beloved disciple. A must for those trying to understand the Gospel's historical origins based in the testimony of an eyewitness (19:35; 21:24) and the beloved disciple's ideal role in the Gospel narrative.

Bauckham, Richard, and Carl Mosser, eds. 2008. *The Gospel of John and Christian Theology*. Grand Rapids: Eerdmans. What a treasure of extraordinary articles written for scholarly pursuit of understanding John! The book blends exegesis and theological interpretation, and it deals with some difficult hermeneutical issues.

Brant, Jo-Ann A. 2011. *John*. Paideia: Commentaries on the New Testament. Grand Rapids: Baker Academic. Informed by Greco-Roman rhetoric and sources, Brant's commentary excels in pedagogical clarity and attractive layout. It often presents concise information in sidebars: archaeology, maps, definitions of terms. Each unit is located within the larger Gospel. It is a commentary of choice, complementing this volume.

Brodie, Thomas L. 1993. *The Gospel According to John: A Literary and Theological Commentary*. Oxford: Oxford University Press. With distinctive perspectives, Brodie appeals to mind and heart. The commentary is wisely critical and spiritually refreshing.

Brown, Raymond E. 1966–70. *The Gospel According to John*. 2 vols. Anchor Bible 29–29A. Garden City, NY: Doubleday. This magnum opus is a major contribution of enduring value.

Bruner, Frederick Dale. 2011. *The Gospel of John: A Commentary*. Grand Rapids: Eerdmans. Though appearing too late for my work, it promises strength in its historical interpretation of John, fresh biblical insights, theological depth, and appealing pastoral appropriation.

Burge, Gary M. 2000. *John*. NIV Application Commentary. Grand Rapids: Zondervan. Burge's 618-page outstanding commentary has a format similar to the BCBC series. Its alternative to the TBC and TLC sections is "Bridging Contexts" and "Contemporary Significance." The footnotes contain helpful information.

Carter, Warren. 2006. *John: Storyteller, Interpreter, Evangelist*. Peabody, MA: Hendrickson. The three sections of the book are packed with rich insights. With many numbered or bulleted lists and diagrams, it illumines John's distinctive literary features and theology.

———. 2008. *John and Empire: Initial Explorations*. New York: T&T Clark. This is a must for understanding John within the political realities of the late first century.

Cassidy, Richard J. 1992. *John's Gospel in New Perspective: Christology and the Realities of Roman Power*. Maryknoll, NY: Orbis Books. Cassidy has turned new ground in understanding the political dimensions of John's Gospel. The book's value continues.

Chennattu, Rekha M. 2006. *Johannine Discipleship as a Covenant Relationship*. Peabody, MA: Hendrickson. This valuable contribution understands John through the dual lens of covenant and discipleship. The Roman Catholic author, based in India, offers many insights appropriate for the believers church.

Coloe, Mary L. 2001. *God Dwells with Us: Temple Symbolism in the Fourth Gospel*. Collegeville, MN: Liturgical Press. Coloe shows how foundational temple and dwelling emphases are in John, especially important for John 2–4 and 14–15.

Culpepper, R. Alan. 1983. *The Anatomy of the Fourth Gospel: A Study in Literary Design*. Minneapolis: Fortress. This classic volume excels for introducing readers to John's distinctive literary features.

———. 1998. *The Gospel and the Letters of John*. Interpreting Biblical Texts. Nashville: Abingdon. A master scholar of John's Gospel, Culpepper packs this accessible commentary with rich insights.

Fleer, David, and Dave Bland, eds. 2008. *Preaching John's Gospel: The World It Imagines*. St. Louis: Chalice. This is a valuable resource for anyone who preaches on John's Gospel. The numerous essays consist mostly of short, remarkably insightful sermons.

Howard-Brook, Wes. 1994. *Becoming Children of God: John's Gospel and Radical Discipleship*. Maryknoll, NY: Orbis Books. This probing study of John illumines multiple features of the text, often using chiastic structure. It enables readers to hear John's call to radical discipleship.

Koester, Craig. 2008. *The Word of Life: A Theology of John's Gospel*. Grand Rapids: Eerdmans. Koester engages John's Gospel by treating key topics that emerge from studying John, notably God, Jesus, the Spirit, and "Discipleship in Community and World," among others.

Kysar, Robert. 1976. *John, the Maverick Gospel*. Atlanta: John Knox. This compact, accessible volume presents key topics/issues that mark the distinctiveness of John's Gospel.

———. 2005. *Voyages with John: Charting the Fourth Gospel*. Waco: Baylor University Press. This book helps us understand Johannine scholarship over the last four decades.

Lincoln, Andrew T. 2000. *Truth on Trial: The Lawsuit Motif in the Fourth Gospel*. Peabody, MA: Hendrickson. A decade before this groundbreaking volume, a layperson suggested to me that John appears to be written as a trial narrative! Lincoln's in-depth analysis shows that this is the case. It provides a rich, distinctive angle into the Gospel.

Moloney, Francis J. 1998. *The Gospel of John*. Sacra pagina 4. Collegeville, MN: Liturgical Press. This volume draws upon and offers in integrated form the best insights of his three previous volumes, the last of which appeared also in 1998.

Newbigin, Lesslie. 1982. *The Light Has Come: An Exposition of the Fourth Gospel*. Grand Rapids: Eerdmans. A distinctive contribution in mission and ecumenicity perspectives.

Neyrey, Jerome. 2006. *The Gospel of John*. New Cambridge Bible Commentary. New York: Cambridge University Press. Valuable information from a social-science perspective.

O'Day, Gail R. 1995. *The Gospel of John*. New Interpreter's Bible. Nashville: Abingdon. O'Day is consistent in wise interpretation, and the "Reflection" sections of the series offer valued insights for pastors.

Rensberger, David. 1988. *Johannine Faith and Liberating Community*. Philadelphia: Westminster. This landmark study in John's Gospel focuses on selected topics that are of enduring significance in interpreting John. It works well for small-group study.

Schneiders, Sandra M. 2003. *Written That You Might Believe: Encountering Jesus in the Fourth Gospel*. Rev. and expanded ed. New York: Crossroad. In her usual and sometimes provocative style, Schneider unpacks the text in fresh ways. She regards her exegesis and interpretation as an endeavor in spirituality.

Sloyan, Gerald. 2006. *What Are They Saying About John?* New York: Paulist Press. This is a brief introduction to scholarly views on the main issues of the Gospel.

Smalley, Stephen S. 1998. *John: Evangelist and Interpreter*. 2nd ed. Downers Grove, IL: InterVarsity. With typical British terseness and clarity of insight, Smalley contributes a well-balanced interpretation of John's Gospel.

Smith, D. Moody, Jr. 1995. *The Theology of the Gospel of John*. Cambridge: Cambridge University Press. A good summative analysis of the leading theological themes of the Gospel.

———. 1999. *John*. Abingdon New Testament Commentaries. Nashville: Abingdon. Smith does not disappoint readers. Both scholars and pastors will find this commentary useful.

Talbert, Charles H. 1992. *Reading John: A Literary and Theological Commentary on the Fourth Gospel and the Johannine Epistles*. New York: Crossroad. Talbert has a unique gift of packing much into an accessible-length commentary. Rich insights.

Webster, Jane S. 2003. *Eating and Drinking in the Gospel of John*. Atlanta: SBL. With commentary on eight meals in John, Webster's angle into John's Gospel is insightful and rewarding.

Index of Ancient Sources

The Author

Willard Swartley is professor emeritus at Anabaptist Mennonite Biblical Seminary in Elkhart, Indiana. He joined the faculty at AMBS in 1978 and continued teaching until 2004. He served as academic dean at AMBS for seven years (1979–81; 1995–2001).

Willard was the youngest in a family of eight children growing up on a farm near the Delaware River on the rolling hills of Bucks County, Pennsylvania. He is a graduate of Eastern Mennonite University, Goshen Biblical Seminary, and Princeton Theological Seminary where he received a PhD in 1973.

While he was in seminary, Willard became pastor and was ordained at Locust Grove Mennonite Church in Elkhart. He has served the church in many capacities over the years, leading seminars at church-wide conventions, serving on special study committees, and teaching in congregational settings.

He has authored *Health, Healing and the Church's Mission* (InterVarsity, 2012); *Covenant of Peace* (Eerdmans, 2006); *Slavery, Sabbath, War, and Women* (Herald Press, 1983); and *Mark, the Way for All Nations* (Herald Press, 1983, Wipf & Stock, 1999). He has also edited over thirty books, including, with Perry B. Yoder, *The Meaning of Peace* (Institute of Mennonite Studies, 2001); *Love of Enemy and Nonretaliation in the New Testament* (W/JK, 1992; now available from editor Swartley); and with C, J. Dyck, *Annotated Bibliography of Mennonite Writings on War and Peace: 1930–1980* (Herald Press, 1987; now available from the Institute of Mennonite Studies).

Willard and his wife, Mary, are actively involved in the Belmont Mennonite Church and are the parents of Louisa Swartley Oyer and Kenton Swartley, and grandparents of John and Michael Oyer, and Kristen, Jeremy, Libby, and Michelle Swartley.